Professional Stage

Module F

Financial Strategy

ACCA Textbook

2311/J00

British Library Cataloguing-in-Publication Data

A catalogue record for this book is available from the British Library.

Published by Foulks Lynch Ltd
Number 4
The Griffin Centre
Staines Road
Feltham
Middlesex
TW14 0HS

ISBN 0 7483 4231 1

© Foulks Lynch Ltd, 2000

Acknowledgements

We are grateful to the Association of Chartered Certified Accountants, the Chartered Institute of Management Accountants and the Institute of Chartered Accountants in England and Wales for permission to reproduce past examination questions. The answers have been prepared by Foulks Lynch Ltd.

CONTENTS

PREFACE

This Textbook is the ACCA's official text for paper 14, Financial Strategy, and is part of the ACCA's official series produced for students taking the ACCA examinations. It has been produced with direct guidance from the examiner specifically for paper 14, and covers the syllabus and teaching guide in great detail giving appropriate weighting to the various topics.

This Textbook is, however, very different from a reference book or a more traditional style textbook. It is targeted very closely on the examinations and is written in a way that will help you assimilate the information easily and give you plenty of practice at the various techniques involved. Particular attention has been paid to producing an interactive text that will maintain your interest with a series of carefully designed features.

- **Introduction with learning objectives**. We put the chapter into context and set out clearly the learning objectives that will be achieved by the reader.

- **Definitions**. The text clearly defines key words or concepts. The purpose of including these definitions is **not** that you should learn them - rote learning is not required and is positively harmful. The definitions are included to focus your attention on the point being covered.

- **Brick-building style**. We build up techniques slowly, with simpler ideas leading to exam standard questions. This is a key feature and it is the natural way to learn.

- **Activities**. The text involves you in the learning process with a series of activities designed to arrest your attention and make you concentrate and respond.

- **Conclusions**. Where helpful, the text includes conclusions that summarise important points as you read through the chapter rather than leaving the conclusion to the chapter end. The purpose of this is to summarise concisely the key material that has just been covered so that you can constantly monitor your understanding of the material as you read it.

- **Self test questions**. At the end of each chapter there is a series of self test questions. The purpose of these is to help you revise some of the key elements of the chapter. The answer to each is a paragraph reference, encouraging you to go back and re-read and revise that point.

- **End of chapter questions**. At the end of each chapter we include examination style questions. These will give you a very good idea of the sort of thing the examiner will ask and will test your understanding of what has been covered.

Complementary Revision Series, Lynchpins and Audio Tapes

Revision Series - The ACCA Revision Series contains all the relevant current syllabus exam questions from June 1994 to December 1999 with the examiner's own official answers, all updated in January 2000.

What better way to revise for your exams than to read and study the examiner's own answers!

Lynchpins - The ACCA Lynchpins, pocket-sized revision aids which can be used throughout your course, contain revision notes of all main syllabus topics, all fully indexed, plus numerous examples and diagrams. They provide invaluable focus and assistance in keeping key topics in the front of your mind.

Audio Tapes - Our 'Tracks' audio tapes are fully integrated with our other publications. They provide clear explanations of key aspects of the syllabus, invaluable throughout your studies and at the revision stage.

FORMAT OF THE EXAMINATION

The examination will have the following format:

	Number of marks
Section A: 2 compulsory questions (both questions at least 30 marks)	70
Section B: 3 (out of 5) questions of 10 marks each	30
	100

Time allowed: 3 hours

Section A will consist of mini case studies/scenario type questions.

Present value table, annuity table and formula sheet will be provided in the exam.

SYLLABUS

Professional stage - Module F Paper 14: FINANCIAL STRATEGY

Chapter reference

(1)   CORPORATE GOVERNANCE   1 - 2

(a)   The aims and objectives of an organisation and the goals of the different interest groups involved, the significance of these for business planning.

(b)   The relationship between shareholders, bondholders, bankers and directors, the potential for conflicts of interest. The contribution of agency theory to the debate on governance.

(c)   The concept of goal congruence and how it may be achieved.

(d)   The role of executive share option schemes (ESOPs), non-executive directors, management buy-outs and buy-ins, administrators etc.

(2)   BUSINESS PLANNING   10 - 17

(a)   Proposing, evaluating and implementing ways to meet short and medium term financial objectives (eg, budgeting, monitoring and controlling cash flow, pricing, raising finance, repaying debt).

(b)   Advising on the purpose and benefits of setting short term objectives consistent with long term strategy.

(c)   Seeking, clarifying and confirming information relevant to the determination of business objectives (eg information on current business position and past performance by ratio and other analysis, planned changes, systems and processes used).

(d)   Developing and analysing business plans to meet agreed objectives, including risk assessment of plans and all aspects of the business that they will influence, analysis to include measures of value, profit, optimisation, and utility.

(e)   Long term financial planning including

(i)   the issues to be considered in the decision whether to expand through organic growth or through acquisition

(ii)   advising clients on the strategies a company might use in order to expand or maintain its current market position

(iii)   the techniques for valuing individual shares and other securities and for valuing a business, the application of these techniques in merger and acquisition situations

(iv)   the arguments for and against mergers and acquisitions

(v)   methods of financing an acquisition

(vi) advising clients on appropriate merger and acquisition strategies and tactics

(vii) tactics to follow when defending against a take-over bid

(viii) planning for post-merger success and post merger audit

(ix) identifying schemes for financial restructuring and the issues involved in the decision process; methods of restructuring; buyouts, buyins, going private, share repurchases, rescheduling debts, and joint ventures.

(3) FURTHER ISSUES RELATING TO LONG TERM INVESTMENTS   3 - 9

(a) The relationship of investment decisions to long term financial planning.

(b) Portfolio theory and its relevance to decision making and financial management practice.

(c) The capital asset pricing model and its uses in financial management.

(d) Calculating the cost of capital, the significance of the dividend-based model and the capital asset pricing model in such calculations. The cost of various forms of debt. The use of the weighted average cost of capital approach.

(e) The adjusted present value approach and its application in decision-making.

(f) The factors to take into account in deciding upon a dividend policy. Taxation and dividends. The impact of dividends on share prices. The concept of signalling.

(4) TREASURY MANAGEMENT   18 - 21

(a) Optimising the flow of financial assets for an organisation/individual.

(b) Risk management and cost saving within the organisation by use of

(i) options, including caps, floors and collars
(ii) futures
(iii) swaps
(iv) the scope and benefits of financial engineering.

(c) Foreign exchange markets and hedging against foreign exchange risk.

(5) **ECONOMIC INFLUENCES ON INTERNATIONAL FINANCIAL MANAGEMENT DECISIONS**   14

International factors affecting business developments

(a)   Trends in global competition with particular reference to the role of Japan and the USA.

(b)   The role of multi-national companies in the world economy.

(c)   The theory and practice of free trade and problems of protectionism.

(d)   Balance of payments and implications of policies to achieve equilibrium.

(e)   Trade agreements and areas GATT, EFTA etc.

(f)   Customs Unions/common markets.

(g)   Exchange rate determination and alternative exchange rate regimes including Exchange Rate Mechanism (ERM).

(h)   International institutions such as the World Bank and International Monetary Fund (IMF) and their role.

(i)   Economic relations between developed and developing countries: problems of debt and development.

(6) **INTERNATIONAL FINANCIAL MANAGEMENT DECISIONS**   22 - 24

(a)   Advising clients on the alternative methods of financing imports and exports.

(b)   The workings of the international money and capital markets and the opportunities that they offer to companies as a source of finance, and as a repository for the investment of funds.

(c)   The management of financial resources within a group of companies including

    (i)   payments between companies
    (ii)   cash management
    (iii)   transfer pricing
    (iv)   judging the performance of companies within a group
    (v)   the financial control of a group of companies.

(d)   The appraisal of international capital investments, applying the appropriate techniques, and the consideration of the major issues in the decision-making process including

    (i)   strategic objectives

    (ii)   the principle of home country versus host country returns

(iii)   the form of foreign investment, branch versus subsidiary, European Economic Interest Groups (EEIGs)

(iv)   the effect of taxation on the foreign investment decision (basic principles only)

(v)   discounted cash flows

(vi)   adjusted present value

(vii)   political risk analysis

(viii)   an analysis of the different methods of financing the investment.

THE OFFICIAL ACCA TEACHING GUIDE

Paper 14 - Financial Strategy

	Syllabus Reference	*Chapter Reference*

Session 1   *Financial Strategy: Its Nature and Scope*

- describe what is meant by financial strategy   1a   1
- identify the importance of financial strategy to the organisation
- discuss the relationship between financial strategy and overall corporate strategy

Corporate Governance
- identify the aims and objectives of organisations
- describe the goals of different interest groups
- understand the significance of changing share ownership patterns for the company
- define the meaning of corporate governance from a UK perspective and briefly contrast between UK practices and those of other countries especially the USA, Continental Europe and the Far East
- understand the debate regarding corporate governance, including the Cadbury Report
- identify the role of auditors, audit committees, non-executive directors etc, in corporate governance

Session 2   *Conflicts of Interest and their Resolution*

- identify directors' powers and behaviour, including the significance of   1b, c, d   2
creative accounting, off-balance sheet finance and the influence of the threat of takeover
- understand the principles of agency theory and their contribution to the debate on governance
- understand the potential for conflict between owners, directors, managers and other interest groups
- discuss the meaning of goal congruence, and understand how it might be achieved through the use of alternative reward systems including share option schemes and profit related pay
- discuss the role of non-executive directors, administrators etc, with respect to the organisation

Session 3   *Translating Market Disciplines*

- explain and quantify what is meant by adequate financial return,   2c   3
contrasting profit based measures with net present value of expected cash   3a
flows
- understand the benefits of using net present value, and how the use of net present value can serve as a unifying long term objective for the enterprise as a whole
- revise NPV analysis, including the identification of relevant cash flows and the impact of price level changes
- describe the efficient markets hypothesis including weak, semi-strong and strong form efficiency
- understand the meaning of market efficiency and its significance to financial decision-making based upon NPV
- explain the meaning of the term structure of interest rates, including the forms of the yield curve and the expectations, liquidity preference and market segmentation theories
- understand the significance of yield curves to financial managers

Session 4   ***The Valuation of Securities***

◆   understand models for the valuation of shares and bonds, dividend   2e   4
        growth models, earnings growth models and use such models to estimate
        value from given information
◆   be aware of the theoretical and practical limitations of such models
◆   discuss the relevance of accounting information to share valuation
◆   be aware of practical influences on share price, including reasons why
        shares prices differ from their theoretical values
◆   understand and apply models for the valuation of debt and other
        securities

Session 5   ***Portfolio Theory***

◆   understand the benefits of portfolio diversification   3b   5
◆   estimate the risk and return of portfolios
◆   understand the meaning of mean-variance efficiency for two asset
        portfolios and portfolios of many assets, efficient portfolios and the
        efficient frontier
◆   understand the concept of utility and its importance to portfolio selection
◆   explain portfolio selection when both risky and risk free assets are
        available
◆   discuss the nature and significance of the Capital Market Line
◆   discuss the relevance of portfolio theory to practical financial
        management
◆   discuss the limitations of portfolio theory

Session 6   ***The Capital Asset Pricing Model***

◆   understand the meaning and significance of systematic and unsystematic   3c   6
        risk
◆   discuss the Security Market Line
◆   understand what is meant by alpha and beta factors, their interpretation
        and how they are calculated
◆   discuss the problems of using historic data as the basis for future
        decision-making, and evidence of the stability of beta over time
◆   describe the assumptions of CAPM
◆   understand the uses of the model in financial management
◆   discuss the limitations of the model, including some of the instances
        when it does not perform as expected (eg, low beta investments, low PE
        investments, day of week effects etc)

Session 7   ***The Cost of Capital***

◆   estimate the cost of equity, using the CAPM and dividend valuation   3d   7
        models
◆   estimate the cost of debt, for both redeemable and irredeemable debt
◆   understand the weighted average cost of capital of a company, and how it
        is estimated
◆   discuss the theories of Modigliani and Miller including their
        assumptions, and the value and limitations of their theories and their
        implications for the capital structure decision
◆   estimate the cost of capital for individual investments and divisions,
        including use of the 'pure play' method with ungearing and regearing
        beta

◆   describe alternative strategies for long-term growth, organic growth versus external growth, and the key dimensions of strategy that need to be addressed if a business is considering organic growth

Session 12   *Mergers and Acquisitions*

◆   understand the arguments for and against mergers and acquisitions   2e   12
◆   contrast merger and acquisition activity in the UK and USA with activity in continental Europe and Japan, and discuss the implications of the differences that exist for corporate governance
◆   describe the alternative strategies and tactics of mergers and acquisitions
◆   discuss how possible acquisition targets may be identified using financial or other information
◆   estimate the value of potential target companies
◆   distinguish between the various methods of financing mergers and acquisitions - cash, debt equity and hybrids, and assess the attractiveness of different financing alternatives to vendors
◆   evaluate the various defences against takeovers, and be aware of any restrictions on their use as specified by the City Code
◆   identify key issues that influence the success of acquisitions, and recommend appropriate actions for a given situation
◆   understand the importance of post-audit and monitoring of post-acquisition success

Session 13   *Financial Restructuring Alternatives and Decisions*

◆   describe the nature of, and reasons for, divestments   2e   13
◆   describe 'unbundling' and 'de-merging' of quoted companies

Management Buy-outs
◆   discuss the advantages of buy-outs, and understand the issues that a management team should address when in the preparation of a buy-out proposal
◆   identify situations in which a management buy-out is likely to offer the best value for a disposer
◆   evaluate alternative sources of finance for buy-outs
◆   assess the viability of buy-outs from the viewpoint of both the buy-out team and the financial backers
◆   identify the advantages and disadvantages of management buy-ins

Capital Reconstruction Schemes
◆   identify and justify when a capital reconstruction may be required or appropriate
◆   be aware of the importance of taking into account the interests of the various suppliers of capital in a reconstruction situation
◆   formulate a feasible reconstruction from given information

Session 14   *Economic Influences on International Financial Management Decisions*

Multinational Companies and Trends in Global Competition
◆   understand the nature, size and significance of multinational companies   5a,b,c,   14
     in the world economy   d,e,f
◆   discuss the influence of exchange rates, international capital markets and changes in global competition patterns on the strategies of multinational companies, with particular reference to the EU, USA and Japan

International Trade and Protectionism
- ◆ understand the theory and practice of free trade, and the problems of protectionism, through tariff and non-tariff barriers
- ◆ describe the major trade agreements and customs unions (the European Union, North American Free Trade Area, EFTA etc)
- ◆ understand the nature and significance of the balance of payments and the possible effects of national balance of payments problems on the financial decisions of companies
- ◆ explain the objectives and function of GATT and the World Trade Organisation (WTO), and describe the major rounds of GATT and their achievements

Self study
- ◆ most of these items, especially where descriptions of the institutional framework is concerned, could be undertaken by self study

Session 15   *The International Financial System*

- ◆ understand the role of the major international financial institutions, including the IMF, The Bank for International Settlements and the International Bank for Reconstruction and Development (The World Bank)   5h, i   15
6b

International Banking
- ◆ understand the workings of international money markets
- ◆ outline the major factors affecting the development of international banking
- ◆ understand the role of international banks in international finance, including international bank lending through syndication and multi-option facilities and other means

International Capital Markets
- ◆ describe the nature and development of the Euromarkets, including the Eurocurrency, Eurobond and Euroequity markets
- ◆ explain the types of financing instruments that are available to corporate treasurers on the Euromarkets, for both borrowing and financial investment
- ◆ understand the role of domestic capital markets, especially stock exchanges, in the financing the activities of multinational companies

Self study
- ◆ understand the nature of the Global Debt problem and its effects on relations between developed and developing countries
- ◆ be aware of the role of international financial markets and institutions in the global debt problem, and the effect of the problem on multinational companies and international banks
- ◆ be aware of the methods that have been suggested for dealing with the problem

Session 16   *Foreign Trade*

- ◆ advise clients on the alternative methods of exporting and importing   6a   16
- ◆ understand the risks of foreign trade, currency, credit/commercial and political
- ◆ explain the advantages and disadvantages of using documentary letters of credit, bills of exchange, acceptances etc, in foreign trade

♦   describe the insurance that is available to protect against the risks of foreign trade

♦   describe and evaluate the sources of finance for foreign trade, including forfaiting and international factoring

♦   describe the main features of countertrade, and various alternatives that exist for foreign trade deals other than for monetary payments

Session 17   *Exchange Rate Systems*

♦   describe the major developments in exchange rate systems since Bretton Woods, including the European Monetary System, the ERM, EMU and the development of the Euro   4c   17
    5g

♦   explain the workings of the foreign exchange markets, types of quotation, spot and forward rates

The Determinants of Exchange Rates

♦   discuss the relationship between foreign exchange rates and interest rates in different countries

♦   explain the meaning and significance of the purchasing power parity theory

♦   discuss whether exchange rates may be successfully forecast using modelling or other techniques

Session 18   *Currency Risk*

♦   discuss and identify the types of currency risk - transaction, translation and economic exposure, and their importance to companies   4c   18

♦   evaluate alternative strategies that companies might adopt with respect to currency exposure

♦   discuss and evaluate traditional methods of currency risk management, including currency of invoice, leading and lagging, netting, matching, and internal asset and liability management

♦   evaluate hedging strategies using forward foreign exchange contracts

Session 19   *Risk Management*

♦   outline the recent volatility of interest rates and exchange rates   4b   19

♦   describe the main instruments that are available to help manage the volatility of such rates

Futures Markets and Contracts

♦   explain the nature of futures contracts

♦   discuss the use of margin requirements and the functions of futures Clearing Houses

♦   explain how price movements are recognised within futures markets

♦   described the major interest rate futures (short-term and long-term) and currency futures contracts

♦   evaluate hedging strategies with both interest rate and currency futures using given information

♦   contrast the use of currency futures with forward contracts

Session 20   *Options*

♦   describe the main features of options including puts and calls, the exercise price, American and European options, in and out of the money   4b   20

♦   differentiate between traded options and Over-the-Counter options

	Syllabus reference	Chapter reference

- discuss the determinants of option prices, including the Black-Scholes model and its limitations
- explain the advantages and disadvantages of options compared to futures
- describe the various types of interest rate options, including short-term options, caps, collars and floors, and the nature of currency options
- be aware of the nature and benefits of low cost or zero cost options
- evaluate alternative hedging scenarios using interest rate and currency options

Session 21   Swaps

• describe nature of interest rate and currency swaps	4b	20

- understand the value of swaps to the corporate treasurer
- understand the role of banks in swap activity
- describe the various types of risk that are associated with swaps
- describe hybrid forms of instruments such as swaptions, and the value of financial engineering
- evaluate hedging scenarios using swaps and swaptions

Session 22   Transfer Pricing

• explain the importance of transfer pricing to multinational companies	6c	21

- understand the legal regulations affecting transfer pricing, particularly with respect to the attitude of tax authorities
- discuss the use of tax havens to try to maximise the benefits of transfer pricing
- explain the potential adverse motivational effects of transfer pricing on individual subsidiaries or divisions

Performance Measurement
- describe the guidelines appropriate to the regular financial reports required from overseas operations
- evaluate the performance of all or part of an international group of companies using ratio and other forms of analysis

Session 23   The International Treasury Function

• discuss the merits of defining the treasury as a cost centre or profit centre	4a	22
• discuss the arguments for the centralisation versus decentralisation of international treasury activities	6c	

- describe the main forms of international cash transfer mechanisms
- describe the short term investment opportunities that exist in international money markets and in international marketable securities

Session 24   International Operations

• describe the forms of entity that are available for international operations, including the relative merits of branch, subsidiary, joint venture licensing and economic interest groups	6d	23

Foreign Direct Investment
- discuss the complexities of foreign direct investment, including the possible forms and implications of political risk and its importance to the investment decision process

◆ discuss the impact of blocked funds and restrictions on the remittance of funds to the parent company, and the use of royalties, management charges etc, to avoid restrictions on remittances

Session 25 International Capital Budgeting

◆ estimate the international cost of capital for an organisation, using the CAPM   24
◆ evaluate how APV might be used in international investment appraisal
◆ illustrate the effect of taxation on international investment, including the possibility of double taxation
◆ discuss the advantages and disadvantages of international portfolio diversification

Session 26 The International Capital Structure Decision

◆ discuss the factors that influence the type of finance used in international operations   6d   24
◆ describe the strategic implications of international financing, with respect both to the type of finance used, and the currency in which the financing is denominated
◆ undertake a detailed appraisal of an international capital investment proposal using given information - this could be either by organic growth or acquisition

Session 27/28 Question Practice

(NB As an alternative to a block of question practice at the end of the course, individual sessions could be used during the course. The emphasis during these sessions should be on detailed case scenarios questions of the format that are likely to appear in the examination)

Present value table

Present value of £1 ie, $\dfrac{1}{(1+r)^n}$ or $(1+r)^{-n}$

where   r   =   discount rate

          n   =   number of periods until payment

Discount rates (r)

Periods (n)	1%	2%	3%	4%	5%	6%	7%	8%	9%	10%	
1	0.990	0.980	0.971	0.962	0.952	0.943	0.935	0.926	0.917	0.909	1
2	0.980	0.961	0.943	0.925	0.907	0.890	0.873	0.857	0.842	0.826	2
3	0.971	0.942	0.915	0.889	0.864	0.840	0.816	0.794	0.772	0.751	3
4	0.961	0.924	0.888	0.855	0.823	0.792	0.763	0.735	0.708	0.683	4
5	0.951	0.906	0.863	0.822	0.784	0.747	0.713	0.681	0.650	0.621	5
6	0.942	0.888	0.837	0.790	0.746	0.705	0.666	0.630	0.596	0.564	6
7	0.933	0.871	0.813	0.760	0.711	0.665	0.623	0.583	0.547	0.513	7
8	0.923	0.853	0.789	0.731	0.677	0.627	0.582	0.540	0.502	0.467	8
9	0.914	0.837	0.766	0.703	0.645	0.592	0.544	0.500	0.460	0.424	9
10	0.905	0.820	0.744	0.676	0.614	0.558	0.508	0.463	0.422	0.386	10
11	0.896	0.804	0.722	0.650	0.585	0.527	0.475	0.429	0.388	0.350	11
12	0.887	0.788	0.701	0.625	0.557	0.497	0.444	0.397	0.356	0.319	12
13	0.879	0.773	0.681	0.601	0.530	0.469	0.415	0.368	0.326	0.290	13
14	0.870	0.758	0.661	0.577	0.505	0.442	0.388	0.340	0.299	0.263	14
15	0.861	0.743	0.642	0.555	0.481	0.417	0.362	0.315	0.275	0.239	15

	11%	12%	13%	14%	15%	16%	17%	18%	19%	20%	
1	0.901	0.893	0.885	0.877	0.870	0.862	0.855	0.847	0.840	0.833	1
2	0.812	0.797	0.783	0.769	0.756	0.743	0.731	0.718	0.706	0.694	2
3	0.731	0.712	0.693	0.675	0.658	0.641	0.624	0.609	0.593	0.579	3
4	0.659	0.636	0.613	0.592	0.572	0.552	0.534	0.516	0.499	0.482	4
5	0.593	0.567	0.543	0.519	0.497	0.476	0.456	0.437	0.419	0.402	5
6	0.535	0.507	0.480	0.456	0.432	0.410	0.390	0.370	0.352	0.335	6
7	0.482	0.452	0.425	0.400	0.376	0.354	0.333	0.314	0.296	0.279	7
8	0.434	0.404	0.376	0.351	0.327	0.305	0.285	0.266	0.249	0.233	8
9	0.391	0.361	0.333	0.308	0.284	0.263	0.243	0.225	0.209	0.194	9
10	0.352	0.322	0.295	0.270	0.247	0.227	0.208	0.191	0.176	0.162	10
11	0.317	0.287	0.261	0.237	0.215	0.195	0.178	0.162	0.148	0.135	11
12	0.286	0.257	0.231	0.208	0.187	0.168	0.152	0.137	0.124	0.112	12
13	0.258	0.229	0.204	0.182	0.163	0.145	0.130	0.116	0.104	0.093	13
14	0.232	0.205	0.181	0.160	0.141	0.125	0.111	0.099	0.088	0.078	14
15	0.209	0.183	0.160	0.140	0.123	0.108	0.095	0.084	0.074	0.065	15

Annuity Table

Present value of an annuity of 1 ie, $\dfrac{1-(1+r)^{-n}}{r}$

where   r   =   discount rate

             n   =   number of periods

Discount rates (r)

Periods (n)	1%	2%	3%	4%	5%	6%	7%	8%	9%	10%	
1	0.990	0.980	0.971	0.962	0.952	0.943	0.935	0.926	0.917	0.909	1
2	1.970	1.942	1.913	1.886	1.859	1.833	1.808	1.783	1.759	1.736	2
3	2.941	2.884	2.829	2.775	2.723	2.673	2.624	2.577	2.531	2.487	3
4	3.902	3.808	3.717	3.630	3.546	3.465	3.387	3.312	3.240	3.170	4
5	4.853	4.713	4.580	4.452	4.329	4.212	4.100	3.993	3.890	3.791	5
6	5.795	5.601	5.417	5.242	5.076	4.917	4.767	4.623	4.486	4.355	6
7	6.728	6.472	6.230	6.002	5.786	5.582	5.389	5.206	5.033	4.868	7
8	7.652	7.325	7.020	6.733	6.463	6.210	5.971	5.747	5.535	5.335	8
9	8.566	8.162	7.786	7.435	7.108	6.802	6.515	6.247	5.995	5.759	9
10	9.471	8.983	8.530	8.111	7.722	7.360	7.024	6.710	6.418	6.145	10
11	10.37	9.787	9.253	8.760	8.306	7.887	7.499	7.139	6.805	6.495	11
12	11.26	10.58	9.954	9.385	8.863	8.384	7.943	7.536	7.161	6.814	12
13	12.13	11.35	10.63	9.986	9.394	8.853	8.358	7.904	7.487	7.103	13
14	13.00	12.11	11.30	10.56	9.899	9.295	8.745	8.244	7.786	7.367	14
15	13.87	12.85	11.94	11.12	10.38	9.712	9.108	8.559	8.061	7.606	15

	11%	12%	13%	14%	15%	16%	17%	18%	19%	20%	
1	0.901	0.893	0.885	0.877	0.870	0.862	0.855	0.847	0.840	0.833	1
2	1.713	1.690	1.668	1.647	1.626	1.605	1.585	1.566	1.547	1.528	2
3	2.444	2.402	2.361	2.322	2.283	2.246	2.210	2.174	2.140	2.106	3
4	3.102	3.037	2.974	2.914	2.855	2.798	2.743	2.690	2.639	2.589	4
5	3.696	3.605	3.517	3.433	3.352	3.274	3.199	3.127	3.058	2.991	5
6	4.231	4.111	3.998	3.889	3.784	3.685	3.589	3.498	3.410	3.326	6
7	4.712	4.564	4.423	4.288	4.160	4.039	3.922	3.812	3.706	3.605	7
8	5.146	4.968	4.799	4.639	4.487	4.344	4.207	4.078	3.954	3.837	8
9	5.537	5.328	5.132	4.946	4.772	4.607	4.451	4.303	4.163	4.031	9
10	5.889	5.650	5.426	5.216	5.019	4.833	4.659	4.494	4.339	4.192	10
11	6.207	5.938	5.687	5.453	5.234	5.029	4.836	4.656	4.486	4.327	11
12	6.492	6.194	5.918	5.660	5.421	5.197	4.988	4.793	4.611	4.439	12
13	6.750	6.424	6.122	5.842	5.583	5.342	5.118	4.910	4.715	4.533	13
14	6.982	6.628	6.302	6.002	5.724	5.468	5.229	5.008	4.802	4.611	14
15	7.191	6.811	6.462	6.142	5.847	5.575	5.324	5.092	4.876	4.675	15

FORMULAE

Ke   (i) $E(r_j) = r_f + [E(r_m) - r_f]\beta_j$

          (ii) $\dfrac{D_1}{P_0} + g$

WACC $Ke_g \dfrac{E}{E+D} + Kd(1-t)\dfrac{D}{E+D}$

or $Ke_u \left(1 - \dfrac{Dt}{E+D}\right)$

2 asset portfolio $\sigma_p = \sqrt{\sigma_a^2 x^2 + \sigma_b^2(1-x)^2 + 2x(1-x)p_{ab}\sigma_a\sigma_b}$

Purchasing
power parity $\dfrac{i_f - i_{uk}}{1 + i_{uk}}$

Corporate beta $\beta a = \beta e \dfrac{E}{E+D(1-t)} + \beta d \dfrac{D(1-t)}{E+D(1-t)}$

1 CORPORATE GOVERNANCE

INTRODUCTION & LEARNING OBJECTIVES

This chapter begins by introducing the nature and scope of the financial strategy process. Financial strategy is seen to be that area of a company's overall strategy that falls within the scope of the financial managers.

The principles of good corporate governance are then examined. This is an area of financial strategy that has become particularly topical since the publication of the Cadbury, Greenbury and Hampel reports in recent years.

When you have studied this chapter you should be able to do the following:

- Understand the meaning of financial strategy
- Appreciate the importance of financial strategy to the organisation
- Discuss the aims and objectives of organisations and of the different interest groups within an organisation
- Define the meaning of corporate governance
- Explain how the publication of the Cadbury, Greenbury and Hampel reports have improved the environment for good corporate governance in the UK
- Discuss the impact of the Stock Exchange Combined Code on corporate governance.

1 THE NATURE AND SCOPE OF FINANCIAL STRATEGY

1.1 The meaning of financial strategy

Definition An organisation's strategy has been defined as 'a course of action, including the specification of resources required, to achieve a specific objective'.

This definition stresses the importance of identifying objectives before a strategy can be agreed, so this chapter includes a comprehensive discussion of the objectives of organisations.

Conclusion Financial strategy can therefore be understood as that area of an organisation's overall strategy that falls within the scope of the financial managers.

1.2 The importance of financial strategy to the organisation

An organisation's financial managers must plan their courses of action to achieve the organisation's financial objectives; decisions that they must take include:

- from which sources should funds be raised?

- should proposed investments be undertaken?

- how large a dividend should be paid?

- how should working capital be controlled eg, should discounts be offered to debtors for prompt payment?

- should hedging strategies be adopted to avoid currency or interest rate risk?

This text sets out to examine these questions and many more to enable the financial managers to carry out their work. Without a financial strategy, the financial managers' work would be impossible.

1.3   Financial strategy and overall corporate strategy

Each level of a business can have its own strategy. Three levels are commonly identified:

Corporate strategy concerns the decisions to be made by senior management such as the particular business that the company is in, and whether new markets should be entered or current markets withdrawn from. Such decisions can often have important financial implications. If, for example, a decision is taken to enter a new market, should an existing company in that market be bought, or should a new company be started from scratch? The questions of merger, acquisition and divestment is dealt with in some detail later in this text.

Business strategy concerns the decisions to be made by the separate strategic business units within the group. Each unit will try to maximise its competitive positions within its chosen market.

Operational strategy concerns how the different functional areas within a strategic business unit plan their operations to satisfy the corporate and business strategies being followed. We are of course most interested in the decisions facing the finance functions.

2   AIMS AND OBJECTIVES OF ORGANISATIONS

2.1   Introduction

With decision making subjects it is important to have a clear idea of ultimate objectives. Unfortunately there are no clear-cut answers to the question of appropriate company objectives. In the 1970s there were two major UK studies of corporate reporting objectives.

(a)   **The Corporate Report** - a study of company reporting under the auspices of the Accounting Standards Committee (now the Accounting Standards Board).

(b)   **The Sandilands Report** - a government study of inflation accounting.

Both of these reports examined company objectives because of their relevance to the conclusions of the Reports. Both produced a lengthy, and open-ended, list of groups with an interest in corporate performance. Neither came anywhere near defining a single all-embracing corporate objective.

In order to apply analytical techniques to the making of decisions, some more precise definitions of objectives are essential. These are considered under four heads:

(a)   the concepts of maximising and satisficing

(b)   the group whose returns are maximised

(c)   the measurement of return

(d)   the relationship between risk and return.

At the end, an objective that can be applied in subsequent analysis will be suggested.

2.2   Maximising and satisficing

[Definition]   **Maximising** or **optimising** involves the seeking of the best possible outcome. **Satisficing** involves finding a merely adequate outcome.

Thus, management could on the one hand, constantly seek the maximum level of profitability, even though this might involve exposure to risk and much higher management work-loads. On the other hand, management might decide to hold profits at a satisfactory level, avoiding risky ventures and reducing work-loads.

Within a company, management will seek to maximise the return to some groups (eg, shareholders) and satisfy the requirements of other groups (eg, employees). The discussion about objectives is really about which group's returns management is trying to maximise.

The issue is clouded by the fact that the management may itself be unclear about the difference between maximising and satisficing. Thus management may believe that it is, say, maximising shareholder returns, when in fact it has reduced effort and accepted a merely satisfactory level of shareholder return.

Nevertheless, the objectives, if not the applications of maximising as compared to satisficing should be clear.

3   GOALS OF DIFFERENT INTEREST GROUPS

3.1   Introduction

It is generally accepted that the strategic objective of an organisation is the long-term goal of the maximisation of the wealth of the shareholders. However an organisation has many other stakeholders with both long and short term goals:

(a)   **The community at large**

Laudable, but hardly practical as an objective for the management of a company. There are also problems of measurement - what are returns to the community at large? The goals of the community will be broad but will include such aspects as legal and social responsibilities, pollution control and employee welfare.

(b)   **Company employees**

Obviously, many trade unionists would like to see their members as the residual beneficiaries from any surplus the company creates. Certainly, there is no measurement problem: returns = wages or salaries. However, maximising the returns to employees does assume that risk finance can be raised purely on the basis of satisficing.

(c)   **Company managers/directors**

Such senior employees are in an ideal position to follow their own aims at the expense of other stakeholders. Their goals will be both long term (defending against takeovers, sales maximisation) and short term (profit margins leading to increased bonuses).

(d)   **Equity investors (ordinary shareholders)**

Within any economic system, the equity investors provide the risk finance. In the UK, it is usually ordinary shareholders, or sometimes the government. There is a very strong argument for maximising the wealth of equity investors. In order to attract funds, the company has to compete with other risk-free investment opportunities eg, government securities. The attraction is the accrual of any surplus to the equity investors. In effect, this is the risk premium which is essential for the allocation of resources to relatively risky investments in companies.

(e)   **Customers**

Satisfaction of customer needs will be achieved through the provision of value for money products and services.

(f)   **Suppliers**

Suppliers to the organisation will have short term goals such as prompt payment terms alongside long term requirements including contracts and regular business. The importance of the needs of suppliers will depend upon both their relative size and the number of suppliers.

(g)   **Finance providers**

Providers of finance (banks, loan creditors) will primarily be interested in the ability of the firm to repay the finance including interest. As a result it will be the firm's ability to generate cash both long and short term that will be the basis of the goals of these providers.

(h)   **The government**

The government will have political and financial interests in the firm. Politically they will wish to increase exports and decrease imports whilst monitoring companies via the Competition Commission. Financially they require long term profits to maximise taxation income.

$\boxed{\textbf{Conclusion}}$ The long term financial objective of a firm is to maximise the wealth of equity investors. However one of the major criticisms of the stock market is that it does not do this, but is mainly concerned with short term profit maximisation.

Whilst this is the overall long term objective, a firm has many other stakeholders with many conflicting long and short term interests.

3.2   Shareholders' wealth

Shareholders' wealth is affected by two main factors: the rate of return earned on the shares, and the risk attached to earning that return. For a quoted company, expectations about these two factors will play a major part in determining the market price of the shares.

Market price will not necessarily be increased by increasing the expected rate of return, if this is achieved by increasing the risk of the company's operations. Indeed many risk-averse shareholders may sell out, causing a drop in market value. There is therefore a trade-off between risk and return.

Firstly it is necessary to consider the problem of measuring the rate of return on ordinary shares. There are four possible candidates:

(a)   **Total profits available to equity**

The profit measure is familiar to accountants. The use of total profits, however, is misleading in that profits could be increased, for example, by an acquisition which so diluted the equity, that earnings per share actually declined.

Example 1

	A plc	B plc
Number of issued £1 ordinary shares	2m	1m
Earnings available to equity	£1m	£.2m
EPS	£.5	£.2

If A plc acquired the shares in B plc in a one-for-one share exchange, the new data for A plc would be:

	A plc (incorporating B plc)
Number of issued ordinary £1 shares	3m
Earnings available to equity	£1.2m
EPS	£.4

Thus, earnings per share for the former shareholders in A have declined as a result of dilution, although those of the former shareholders in B have increased.

(b)   **Earnings per share**

Definition

$$EPS = \frac{\text{Attributable equity profit for period}}{\text{Number of equity shares ranking in issue}}$$

The use of earnings per share overcomes the above criticisms, and is of course now widely used as a measure of return to equity.

The disadvantage of EPS is that it does not represent income of the shareholder. Rather, it represents that investor's share of the income generated by the company according to an accounting formula.

Whilst there is obviously a correlation between earnings and the wealth received by individual shareholders, they are not synonymous.

(c)   **Dividend yield**

Definition

$$\text{Dividend yield} = \frac{\text{Dividend per share}}{\text{Market price per share}} \times 100\%$$

The dividend yield provides a direct measure of the wealth received by a shareholder. It is however, incomplete in that it ignores the capital gain on the share which most investors would expect.

(d)   **Dividend yield and capital growth**

The addition of capital growth provides a more complete measure of return.

Example 2

One year ago the share price of C plc was 220p (ex div). A dividend of 40p has just been paid and the ex div price is now 242p. What return has been earned over the past year?

Solution

	p
Current market price, ex div	242
Current dividend	40
Total value of holding now	282
Value one year ago	220

$$\text{Rate of return} = \frac{282 - 220}{220} = 0.28, \text{ or } 28\%$$

Alternative

Dividend yield $\qquad \dfrac{40}{220} \qquad = \quad 18\%$

Capital growth $\qquad \dfrac{242 - 220}{220} \qquad = \quad 10\%$

Total rate of return $\qquad\qquad\qquad\quad 28\%$

Note: that any tax credits on the dividend have been ignored in this example. The dividend yields quoted in the *Financial Times* are net of any tax credit.

The actual return received will depend on the shareholder's marginal rate of income tax and capital gains tax suffered on the capital gain.

| Conclusion | The best measure of returns to equity investors is dividend yield plus capital growth. Obviously, in making decisions about the future it is the anticipated dividend yield and capital growth that becomes important.

3.3   Activity

AB plc's share price was 180p ex div on 1 January 19X0 and 200p ex div on 31 December 19X0. During the year dividends of 15p have been paid. Estimate the total rate of return enjoyed by a shareholder during 19X0.

3.4   Activity solution

$\qquad\qquad\qquad\qquad\qquad\qquad\qquad\qquad\qquad\qquad\quad$ %

Dividend yield $= \dfrac{15p}{180p}$ $\qquad\qquad\qquad\qquad\qquad\quad$ 8.3

Capital growth $= \dfrac{200p - 180p}{180p}$ $\qquad\qquad\qquad\quad$ 11.1

Total rate of return $\qquad\qquad\qquad\qquad\qquad\qquad\quad$ 19.4%

3.5   The relationship between risk and return

In considering return, the trade-off with risk is of fundamental importance. In this context risk refers not to the possibility of total loss, but rather to the likelihood of actual returns varying from those forecast.

Consider four investment opportunities: A, B, C, and D. These may be described on the following risk and return graph:

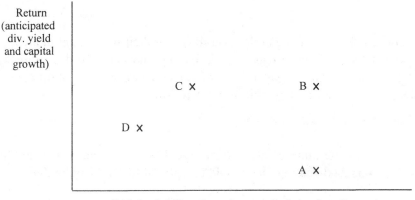

Note that: Risk A   =   Risk B
                     Return B =   Return C

In choosing between the investment opportunities:

      B is preferable to A – higher return, same risk

      C is preferable to B – same return, lower risk

The question is whether D is preferable to C - lower return, lower risk. This question can only be answered if the trade-off between risk and return is known. We shall return to this problem later.

3.6   Managerial objectives

We should not forget that the managers of the firm will have their own objectives which could conflict with those of the shareholders and other interested parties. For example, managers could be interested in maximising the sales revenue of the firm or the number of employees so as to increase their own prestige and improve their career prospects. Alternatively they could be interested in maximising their short-term financial return by increasing salaries or managerial 'perks'. It is also important to note that different groups of managers may be following differing objectives. Marketing management may be interested in maximising sales revenue, whilst production managers may be more interested in developing the technological side of the firm as far as possible.

Although the firm is owned by the shareholders the day to day control is in the hands of the managers (the **divorce of ownership and control**) and they are in an ideal position to follow their own objectives at the expense of other parties. Whilst in theory shareholders can replace the management of a company by voting out the directors at the AGM, in practice the fragmented nature of shareholdings makes this unlikely. Specific examples of the conflicts of interest that might occur between managers and shareholders include:

(a)   **Take-overs**

Target company managers often devote large amounts of time and money to 'defend' their companies against take-over. However, research has shown that shareholders in companies that are successfully taken over often earn large financial returns. On the other hand managers of companies that are taken over frequently lose their jobs. This is a common example of the conflict of interest between the two groups.

(b)   **Time horizon**

Managers know that their performance is usually judged on their short-term achievements; shareholder wealth on the other hand is affected by the long-term performance of the firm.

Managers can frequently be observed to be taking a short-term view of the firm which is in their own best interest but not in that of the shareholders.

(c)   Risk

Shareholders appraise risks by looking at the overall risk of their investment in a wide range of shares. They do not have 'all their eggs in one basket' and can afford a more aggressive attitude toward risk-taking than managers whose career prospects and short-term financial remuneration depend on the success of their individual firm.

(d)   Gearing

As managers are likely to be more cautious over risk than shareholders they might wish to adopt lower levels of financial gearing than would be optimal for the shareholders.

3.7   Non-financial objectives

The influence of the various parties with interests in the firm results in firms adopting many non-financial objectives, eg:

(a)   growth;
(b)   diversification;
(c)   survival;
(d)   maintaining a contented workforce;
(e)   becoming research and development leaders;
(f)   providing top quality service to customers;
(g)   maintaining respect for the environment.

Some of these objectives may be viewed as specific to individual parties (eg, engineering managers may stress research and development), whereas others may be seen as straight surrogates for profit, and thus shareholder wealth (eg, customer service). Finally areas such as respect for the environment may be societal constraints rather than objectives.

3.8   Conclusions on corporate objectives

In the real world organisations undoubtedly follow objectives other than the maximisation of shareholder wealth. The return to equity holders will be an important consideration in financial decisions but it is unlikely to be the only one.

It is important, however, not to overplay the above conflicts. Most managers know that if they let the shareholders down share prices will fall and this could result in difficulty in raising further finance, unwanted take-over bids and the end of managerial careers. Also the increasing concentration of shares in the hands of institutional investors such as insurance companies and pension funds means that the divorce of ownership and control is far from complete. Institutional investors, because of their large shareholdings, are considered to hold great potential power over company management. Actions of institutions, particularly in times of take-over bids, can determine the future of the firm and their objectives must be carefully considered by managers.

| Conclusion | A compromise view of corporate objectives would be that for a listed company shareholder wealth will be the paramount objective but it will be tempered by the influences and objectives of other parties.

4   SHARE OWNERSHIP PATTERNS IN THE UK

4.1   Recent trends in ownership

If it is agreed that the fundamental financial objective is to maximise the wealth of equity investors, it will be instructive to ascertain just who the shareholders of the company are. For example, are they mainly individuals or unit trusts, charities or pension funds? A predominance of one category of shareholder might influence the way in which returns should be paid, since dividends and capital gains could be treated differently for tax purposes.

The patterns of shareholdings of UK quoted companies over the last thirty years have seen two significant trends:

- an increase in institutional shareholders
- a decrease in private individual shareholders

These trends are illustrated in the following table:

Percentage holdings of UK listed equities held by different groups

	1963	1973	1983	1989	1994	1997
	%	%	%	%	%	%
Insurance companies	11	16	22	25	22	23
Pension funds	7	12	29	29	28	30
Investment trusts	9	10	6	3	2	2
Unit trusts	1	3	4	6	7	8
Total institutions	28	41	61	63	59	63
Persons	59	42	25	18	20	16
Others*	13	17	14	19	21	21
	100	100	100	100	100	100

*Others include charities, companies, overseas investors, etc.

4.2   Why have institutional shareholdings grown so much?

The main reasons for the growth in institutional shareholdings over the past thirty years are

(i)   tax advantages of institutional investment. For example payments into a pension fund are allowable against tax, they grow in the fund tax free, and a tax free lump sum can be taken on retirement. A private investor has to buy shares out of his post-tax income and pay income tax on dividends received and capital gains tax on capital gains realised.

(ii)   the growth in occupational pension schemes and personal pension plans. Government encouragement has led to a far higher proportion of the population saving for their retirements rather than relying on a basic state pension expected to decline in real terms.

(iii)   growth in unit trusts. Unit trusts offer the private investor the benefits of professional investment management and investment diversification at reasonable cost. If bought through a tax-free savings vehicle such as an ISA (previously a PEP), they can also be free of taxes.

(iv)   individuals have concentrated their savings in the purchase of their home rather than on buying shares.

(v)   firms of stockbrokers have marketed their services to institutions rather than on cultivating private investors.

In the 1990s the Conservative government's privatisation programme, the demutualisation of many building societies and the end of rocketing house prices have slowed down the rate of increase in institutional shareholdings, but the proportion of UK shares held by institutions is still expected to rise.

4.3   The significance of institutional dominance

There are both advantages and disadvantages in the dominance of institutional shareholders over other categories of investor.

Advantages

- larger amounts in pension funds should improve the standard of living of future pensioners and reduce their need for state benefits

- diversification of private wealth should reduce the risk of heavy losses from single events

Disadvantages

- the large institutions are now so big that their decisions can move markets by themselves. An efficient capital market relies on no investor being this big, so the efficiency of the market has been compromised

- the 'buy and hold' policy adopted by most institutions effectively removes a large proportion of each company's shares from the market, making it harder for other investors to buy shares at reasonable prices

5   CORPORATE GOVERNANCE

5.1   The meaning of corporate governance

 The Committee on the Financial Aspects of Corporate Governance (the Cadbury committee) defines corporate governance as 'the system by which companies are directed and controlled'.

In the late 1980s there was widespread belief that the traditional UK system enshrined in the Companies Acts, with the board of directors responsible for a company and the auditors appointed by the shareholders but remunerated by the directors, was insufficient to control modern companies.

Compare traditional UK practice with the practices of other countries:

USA practice

Although the basic structure of corporate governance is the same in the US as the UK, with a single board of directors and a firm of auditors appointed by the shareholders, many of the detailed regulations are stricter in the US than the UK. For example:

- the Securities and Exchange Commission (which has no equivalent counterpart in the UK) requires US listed companies to report their results quarterly

- all US listed companies are required to have audit committees composed entirely of independent directors

- Financial Accounting Standards set by the Financial Accounting Standards Board are often stricter than the equivalent UK accounting standard.

The UK tradition is for a regime of self-regulation with voluntary codes of best practice, as in the Financial Services Act, while the US has proceeded with tighter statutory controls. This in part has led to a more litigious atmosphere in the US where lawsuits against companies and auditors are common.

German practice

Since both Germany and the UK are members of the EC, their systems of corporate control are subject to European Community Directives on company law and have a common philosophy. However important differences do exist:

- large German companies often have a two-tier board with a senior supervisory board responsible for general policy and a separate junior board dealing with day-to-day management. Germans argue that the senior board can fulfil the company's responsibilities to all stakeholders more easily since they can take a detached view of the company's operations.

- German companies often have higher gearing ratios than would be common in the UK, with banks providing much of the additional borrowings. Representatives of these banks sit on the supervisory board.

- externally funded pension funds are far less developed in Germany than the UK. Thus the influence of institutional investors is less strong in Germany.

Japanese practice

Japanese corporate decision-making is characterised by principles of compromise and negotiated agreement rather than by managers issuing decrees. All the stakeholders in a Japanese company are expected to work together in the best long-term interests of the company as a whole, which compares to the priority given to ordinary shareholders in UK companies. Other differences include the following:

- traditionally companies wishing to do business with each other would buy shares in each other to symbolise their long-term relationship. Many companies were therefore sheltered from the attentions of external shareholders requiring dividends and interested in day-to-day matters. However the system of cross-holdings is now reducing.

- as in Germany, the gearing of Japanese companies is higher than would be thought normal in the UK. Effectively the Japanese banks are providing long-term finance as quasi-equity and they would expect to participate in the decision-making process.

6   THE DEBATE ON CORPORATE GOVERNANCE IN THE UK

6.1   Introduction

During the 1990s in the UK, there have been three separate committees set up to consider aspects of corporate governance. Each committee in turn issued a report with its recommendations:

- The Cadbury report in 1992 focused on the control functions of boards of directors, and on the role of auditors.

- The Greenbury report in 1995 focused on the setting and disclosure of directors' remuneration.

- The Hampel report in 1998 brought together all the previous recommendations and submitted a proposed Code to the Stock Exchange which listed companies should comply with.

The Stock Exchange published the final version of its 'Principles of good governance and code of best practice' (known as the Combined Code) in June 1998. Under an amendment to the Listing Rules, listed companies now have to disclose how they have applied the principles and complied with the Code's provisions in their annual report and accounts.

The Combined Code can be thought of as incorporating all the recommendations of the three reports which preceded it. We now look briefly at each of these reports.

6.2   The Cadbury Code of Best Practice

The Cadbury committee was set up to review those aspects of corporate governance specifically related to financial reporting and accountability. Although there were concerns about these aspects when the committee was set up, they were then heightened by BCCI, Maxwell and controversy over directors' pay rising despite reporting reduced profits.

At the heart of the Committee's recommendations is a Code of Best Practice (ie, voluntary code rather than a recommendation for legislation). This code is directed to the boards of directors of all UK listed companies (though other companies are also encouraged to comply).

Institutional shareholders were asked to use their influence to ensure that companies in which they have invested comply with the code.

The proposals aim to strengthen the unitary board system and increase its effectiveness, not to replace it, for example with a two-tier German style system.

The Cadbury code of best practice is reproduced here in full:

THE CODE OF BEST PRACTICE

1   The Board of Directors

1.1   The board should meet regularly, retain full and effective control over the company and monitor the executive management.

1.2   There should be a clearly accepted division of responsibilities at the head of a company, which will ensure a balance of power and authority, such that no one individual has unfettered powers of decision. Where the chairman is also the chief executive, it is essential that there should be a strong and independent element on the board, with a recognised senior member.

1.3   The board should include non-executive directors of sufficient calibre and number for their views to carry significant weight in the board's decisions.

1.4   The board should have a formal schedule of matters specifically reserved to it for decision to ensure that the direction and control of the company is firmly in its hands.

1.5   There should be an agreed procedure for directors in the furtherance of their duties to take independent professional advice if necessary, at the company's expense.

1.6   All directors should have access to the advice and services of the company secretary, who is responsible to the board for ensuring that board procedures are followed and that applicable rules and regulations are complied with. Any question of the removal of the company secretary should be a matter for the board as a whole.

2   Non-Executive Directors

2.1   Non-executive directors should bring an independent judgement to bear on issues of strategy, performance, resources, including key appointments, and standards of conduct.

2.2   The majority should be independent of management and free from any business or other relationship which could materially interfere with the exercise of their independent judgement, apart from their fees and shareholding. Their fees should reflect the time which they commit to the company.

2.3   Non-executive directors should be appointed for specified terms and reappointment should not be automatic.

2.4   Non-executive directors should be selected through a formal process and both this process and their appointment should be a matter for the board as a whole.

3   Executive Directors

3.1   Directors' service contracts should not exceed three years without shareholders' approval.

3.2   There should be full and clear disclosure of directors' total emoluments and those of the chairman and highest-paid UK director, including pension contributions and stock options.

Separate figures should be given for salary and performance-related elements and the basis on which performance is measured should be explained.

3.3   Executive directors' pay should be subject to the recommendations of a remuneration committee made up wholly or mainly of non-executive directors.

4   **Reporting and Controls**

4.1   It is the board's duty to present a balanced and understandable assessment of the company's position.

4.2   The board should ensure that an objective and professional relationship is maintained with the auditors.

4.3   The board should establish an audit committee of at least three non-executive directors with written terms of reference which deal clearly with its authority and duties.

4.4   The directors should explain their responsibility for preparing the accounts next to a statement by the auditors about their reporting responsibilities.

4.5   The directors should report on the effectiveness of the company's system of internal control.

4.6   The directors should report that the business is a going concern, with supporting assumptions or qualifications as necessary.

6.3   The role of auditors and others

Further recommendations in the Cadbury report include the following:

-       The auditors should examine interim statements (Auditing Practices Board to recommend how);

-       the perceived objectivity of the audit should be enhanced by:

    -       disclosing non-audit fees
    -       rotating audit partners;

-       auditors should report on the directors' statement on the effectiveness of their system of internal control;

-       auditors should be given statutory protection to report suspicion of fraud freely to the appropriate authorities;

-       interim financial statements should be expanded to include a balance sheet;

-       institutional investors should disclose their policies on the use of voting rights;

-       the accounting profession should continue its efforts to improve its standards and procedures so as to strengthen the standing and independence of auditors.

Elements of corporate governance relating to auditors, audit committees and accounting standards are further discussed in paper 10, 'Accounting and Audit Practice'.

6.4   The Greenbury report

The Greenbury report included its own code of best practice in determining and accounting for directors' remuneration. Each listed company was recommended to set up a remuneration committee of non-executive directors, to determine the company's policy on executive remuneration and specific packages for each of the executive directors. The board of directors itself should determine the remuneration of non-executive directors.

The remuneration committee should report each year to the shareholders, either as part of or annexed to, the company's annual report. In particular, any service contracts containing notice periods in excess of one year should be disclosed and the reasons for the longer notice periods explained.

6.5 The Hampel report

The Combined Code arising from the Hampel report replaces the Cadbury and Greenbury codes. Hampel's aim was to avoid a mechanical 'checklist' approach to corporate governance. Good corporate governance is not achieved by complying with detailed rules and ticking them off. The Combined Code requires explanation in the annual report of **how** (not just whether) the principles of good governance have been applied.

6.6 Future developments

Hampel should be the last of the ad hoc committees set up to consider aspects of corporate governance. In future, any necessary changes to the Combined Code should be implemented by the Stock Exchange.

7 CHAPTER SUMMARY

This chapter has introduced you to the process of determining an appropriate financial strategy. Financial strategy is defined as a course of action to achieve specific financial objectives. The primary financial objective of most organisations is assumed to be the maximisation of the wealth of the equity investors.

The chapter points out the increasing dominance of institutional shareholders over the past thirty years, a trend which offers both advantages and disadvantages to companies and to the market.

Good corporate governance is an important area which has bounced to the forefront of UK debate following publication of the Cadbury and other reports. Recent scandals indicate however that disputes between directors, shareholders and loan creditors are not always friendly arguments over "how the cake is divided". When directors decide to take the law into their own hands, using other people's money there is a tendency to make the external auditor a scapegoat. The debate over corporate governance is of great importance to the future of the accountancy profession.

8 SELF TEST QUESTIONS

8.1   What is meant by an organisation's financial strategy? (1.1)

8.2   Distinguish between maximising and satisficing. (2.2)

8.3   What is the generally assumed financial objective of a business? (3.1)

8.4   How is the return on an investment best measured? (3.2)

8.5   Why will an investor not necessarily choose investments with the highest expected returns? (3.5)

8.6   Why has there been such a growth in institutional investment in the UK in recent years? (4.2)

8.7   What is meant by corporate governance? (5.1)

8.8   Distinguish between the UK and German systems of corporate governance. (5.1)

8.9   What principles does the Cadbury Code of Best Practice contain for the selection of non-executive directors? (6.2)

8.10   Who does the Greenbury Code state should decide the level of executive directors' pay? (6.4)

9 EXAMINATION TYPE QUESTIONS

9.1 Private v public sector objectives

Assume that you are a financial manager in a state owned enterprise that is about to have its majority ownership transferred from the government to the private sector and to become a listed company on the Stock Exchange.

Discuss the differences in financial objectives that you are likely to face and the changes in emphasis that are likely to occur in your strategic and operational decisions as a finance manager.

(15 marks)

9.2 Acre plc

A recent board meeting of Acre plc discussed what financial objectives the company should have. Four different views were expressed:

(a)   The company should maximise profits.

(b)   The company should maximise turnover.

(c)   The company should maximise shareholder wealth.

(d)   The company should maximise benefits to employees and to the local community.

Comment upon the implications of the four views that have been expressed.   **(15 marks)**

10 ANSWERS TO EXAMINATION TYPE QUESTIONS

10.1 Private v public sector objectives

(Tutorial note

This is a fairly wide ranging question and you need to apply a general knowledge of business operations as well as specific knowledge of financial management. A wide variety of answers would be acceptable; the major points are covered in the following essay plan.*)*

(a)   **Financial objectives**

    (i)   State owned enterprise

        (1)   Overall objective is commonly to fulfil a social need.

        (2)   Because of problems of measuring attainment of social needs the government usually sets specific targets in accounting terms.

        (3)   Examples include target returns on capital employed, requirement to be self financing, cash or budget limits.

    (ii)   Private sector

        (1)   Firm has more freedom to determine its own objectives.

        (2)   Stock market quotation will mean that return to shareholders becomes an important objective.

        (3)   Traditionally financial management sees firms as attempting to maximise shareholder wealth. Note that other objectives may exist, eg, social responsibilities, and the concept of satisficing various parties is important.

(b)   **Strategic and operational decisions**

The major change in emphasis will be that decisions will now have to be made on a largely commercial basis. Profit and share price considerations will become paramount. Examples of where significant changes might occur include:

-    **Financing Decisions:** The firm will have to compete for a wide range of sources of finance. Choices between various types of finance will now have to be made, eg, debt versus equity.

-    **Dividend Decision:** The firm will now have to consider its policy on dividend payout to shareholders.

-    **Investment Decision:** Commercial rather than social considerations will become of major importance. Diversification into other products and markets will now be possible. Expansion by merger and takeover can also be considered.

-    **Threat of takeover:** If the government completely relinquishes its ownership it is possible that the firm could be subject to takeover bids.

-    **Other areas:** Pricing, marketing, staffing etc, will now be largely free of government constraints.

10.2   Acre plc

(a)   **Maximise profits**

These are a number of problems with the concept of profit maximisation.

(i)   It is not clear whether the objective is to maximise profit as an absolute figure, or to maximise profit as a % return on capital employed. If the former, then any investment which increased profits would be accepted, even if the necessary capital was extremely large. If the latter, then the tendency would be for the company to contract down in size to its single best investment in terms of ROCE.

(ii)   It is not possible to distinguish between short-term and long-term profits.

(iii)   Profit is calculated according to accounting principles. Different policies and techniques will result in different accounting profits being shown eg, depreciation and stock valuation. What is of economic importance is the long-term cash flows.

(b)   **Maximise turnover**

(i)   No account is taken as to whether the turnover produces either positive cash flows or profits.

(ii)   Increased turnover can often be achieved by reducing selling prices to a point where a loss is inevitable. Turnover should not be increased to a point where marginal costs are greater than marginal revenues.

(iii)   Excessive increases in profitable turnover can lead to overtrading and cash flow problems.

(c)   **Maximise shareholder wealth**

Most financial theory is based on the assumption that a company's primary financial objective is to maximise the wealth of its shareholders. Shareholder wealth includes both dividends and share prices, which are influenced by the company's investment and financing decisions. If shareholders perceive their wealth increasing, the raising of further finance will be much easier.

In practice, due to the separation of ownership and stewardship and other social pressures, decisions may be made which do not maximise shareholder wealth. 'Satisficing' has been suggested as a more common objective in the real world.

(d)   **Maximise benefits to employees and to the local community**

A company will have some responsibility to its employees and the local community.

Employees will appreciate such benefits as fair wages, social facilities, profit sharing etc, which should improve motivation and assist the company in meeting its main objectives.

Good relationships with the local community, through the provision of employment, pollution control etc, may also help in achieving other goals eg, obtaining planning permission for expansion.

However, this cannot be seen as the company's main objective, since if it is carried to the extreme it may lead to liquidation. Furthermore, it does not specify any financial criterion.

In conclusion, it may be that companies either set single objectives for limited time periods, changing the objective as circumstances change, or alternatively, set multiple objectives. This latter course however makes the monitoring of performance very difficult.

2 CONFLICTS OF INTEREST

INTRODUCTION & LEARNING OBJECTIVES

The previous chapter explained how a company may have several different interest groups participating in its operations: employees, directors, shareholders, creditors, etc. Each of these interest groups will try to steer the company in its own self-interest and it is possible that conflicts of interest will arise if the objectives of each group are not the same.

This chapter examines the possible conflicts of interest that might arise and looks at methods of trying to ensure that each of the groups is trying to steer the company in the same direction (the principle of goal congruence).

When you have studied this chapter you should be able to do the following:

- Understand the pressures on directors which may lead them to indulge in creative accounting, etc
- Discuss agency theory and its relevance to corporate governance
- Appreciate the conflicts of interest that may arise between an organisation's different interest groups
- Discuss how goal congruence may be achieved to minimise the risk of such conflicts of interest

1 DIRECTORS' POWERS AND BEHAVIOUR

1.1 Directors' powers and responsibilities

The powers of directors are given by the Companies Acts and by the company's articles of association. Public companies must also comply with the rules and regulations of the stock exchange. Shareholders entrust the day-to-day management of their company to the directors and the directors generally set their own agenda to run the business. Shareholders may vote in general meeting to add to or curtail these powers, but in practice the board is seldom constrained by shareholders. If shareholders are unhappy with directors' actions, they tend to simply sell their shares rather than confront the directors.

The Cadbury report gives the responsibilities of directors as including 'setting the company's strategic aims, providing the leadership to put them into effect, supervising the management of the business and reporting to shareholders on their stewardship'.

1.2 Directors' behaviour

In recent years, following the Maxwell scandal and others, the spotlight has fallen squarely on the activities of directors, and the allegation has been made that directors have been making corporate decisions in their own interests rather than for the company as a whole.

Specific allegations include

- excessive remuneration levels
- empire building
- creative accounting
- off balance sheet finance
- reaction to takeover bids
- unethical activities

1.3 Remuneration

The UK recession in the early 1990s led to many companies reporting sharply reduced profits and laying off staff or cutting levels of employee pay. At the same time many boards of directors voted themselves large increases in pay, citing comparative pay levels in the US and in other companies as justification, but the public was unconvinced. Similarly the public has failed to understand why senior executives in newly privatised utility companies should enjoy substantial pay rises after privatisation for doing essentially the same job.

1.4 Empire building

The high level of corporate takeover activity in the 1980s led to many chief executives believing that building as large a group as possible was a valid aim in itself, an objective described as empire building. Executives gained prestige from successful bids and from being in charge of large conglomerates, but the returns to shareholders were often disappointing.

1.5 Creative accounting

The directors are responsible for selecting the accounting policies to be used by their company, subject to UK accounting standards and the opinion of the auditors. Despite the constraints upon them, the directors are still free to use creative accounting techniques to flatter their published accounts and perhaps artificially boost the share price. Examples of such techniques are

- capitalising expenses on the balance sheet (eg, development expenditure, advertising expenditure)

- not depreciating fixed assets

- maximising the value of intangibles on the balance sheet (eg, putting a value to brands)

- recognising revenue on long-term contracts at the earliest possible time (eg, profits on leasing photocopiers)

The ASB's continuing work programme aims to cut out creative accounting practices as much as practically possible.

1.6 Off balance sheet finance

Definition Off balance sheet finance refers to ways of financing assets where the method of funding is not recorded on the balance sheet.

One example is the use of leased assets rather than purchased assets. Before SSAP 21 a lessee's obligation to the lessor was omitted from the lessee's balance sheet and he could therefore report a lower gearing ratio and raise new funds at lower interest rates. SSAP 21 now requires that assets acquired under finance leases must be capitalised on the lessee's balance sheet together with the corresponding obligation to the lessor. The ASB's FRS 5 aims to restrict off balance sheet finance still further, for example by requiring quasi subsidiaries to be consolidated into the group accounts.

1.7 Takeover bids

Boards of directors often spend considerable amounts of time and money attempting to defend their companies against takeover bids, even when it appears that the takeover would be in the best interests of the target company's shareholders. These directors are accused of trying to protect their own jobs, fearing that they will be retired if their company is taken over. Directors of public companies must comply with the City Code on Takeovers and Mergers during a bid period; this is dealt with in a later chapter.

1.8   Unethical activities

Unethical activities might not be prohibited by the Companies Acts or stock exchange regulations, but are believed by many to be undesirable to society as a whole. Examples are trading with countries ruled by dictatorships, testing products on animals, emitting pollution or carrying out espionage against competitors. The importance of good business ethics has been recognised in recent years and it is hoped that further progress has been made throughout the 1990s.

> **Conclusion**   Although directors are supposed to be acting in the interests of the shareholders of their company, they stand accused in recent years of having made decisions on the basis of their own self-interest.

2   AGENCY THEORY

2.1   The principles of agency theory

The relationships between the various interested parties in the firm are often described in terms of *agency theory*.

> **Definition**   Agency theory examines the duties and conflicts that occur between parties who have an agency relationship.

Agency relationships occur when one party, *the principal*, employs another party, *the agent*, to perform a task on their behalf. Agency theory can help to explain the actions of the various interest groups in the corporate governance debate.

For example, managers can be seen as the agents of shareholders, employees as the agents of managers, managers and shareholders as the agents of long- and short-term creditors, etc. In most of these principal-agent relationships conflicts of interest will exist. We have already noted conflicts between shareholders and managers and in a similar way the objectives of employees and managers may be in conflict (in crude terms employees might desire high wages for shorter hours whilst management might require reduced unit costs). Loan creditors might wish the maximum security for their funds whereas shareholders might wish to use them in more risky ventures.

Although the actions of all parties are united by one mutual objective of wishing the firm to survive, the various principals involved might make various arrangements to ensure their agents work closer to their own interests.

For example, shareholders might insist that part of management remuneration is in the form of a profit related bonus. Perhaps the most effective method is one of long-term share option schemes to ensure that shareholder and manager objectives coincide. Management audits can also be employed to monitor the actions of managers. Managers might use productivity bonus schemes to encourage employees to work in their interests. Creditors commonly write restrictive covenants into loan agreements to protect the safety of their funds. These arrangements all involve time and money both in initial set-up, and subsequent monitoring, these being referred to as *agency costs*.

Agency theory will be revisited later in the text when discussing the problems of companies which have borrowed heavily.

2.2   Example

Fill the gaps in the following table of agency relationships in a company:

Principal:	Shareholders	....	Loan creditors
Agent:	....	Employees	....
Agent's responsibility:	....	....	....

2.3   Solution

Principal:	Shareholders	Management	Loan creditors
Agent:	Management	Employees	Management
Agent's responsibility:	To run the company in the best interests of the shareholders	To work hard as instructed by management	To manage the funds lent without taking excessive risks

3   POTENTIAL FOR CONFLICTS OF INTEREST

3.1   Problems with the assumed objective of maximisation of shareholder wealth

Although most financial management theory is developed subject to the assumed objective of maximising shareholder wealth it is important to realise that in the real world companies may be working toward other objectives.

3.2   Objectives of other parties

We have already noted that other parties with interests in the organisation (eg, employees, the community at large, creditors, customers etc,) have objectives that differ to those of the shareholders. As the objectives of these other parties are likely to conflict with those of the shareholders it will be impossible to maximise shareholder wealth and satisfy the objectives of other parties *at the same time*. In this situation the firm will face *multiple, conflicting objectives*, and *satisficing* of interested parties' objectives becomes the only practical approach for management. If this strategy is adopted then the firm will seek to earn a satisfactory return for its shareholders while at the same time (for example) paying reasonable wages and being a "good citizen" of the community in which it operates.

4   GOAL CONGRUENCE

4.1   The meaning of goal congruence

We have already discussed in the previous couple of sections the fact that the objectives of shareholders and managers may not coincide and thus managers may engage in policies and practices which would not be consistent with those desired by shareholders. This is quite an important topic and examination questions have been set on this area of study.

> **Definition**   Goal congruence is the term which describes the situation when the goals of different interest groups coincide.

A way of helping to achieve goal congruence between shareholders and managers is by the introduction of carefully designed remuneration packages for managers which would motivate managers to take decisions which were consistent with the objectives of the shareholders.

Important factors to include in such schemes are

(a)   The schemes should be easy to monitor, clearly defined and impossible to manipulate by managers.

(b)   Management compensation should be linked to changes in shareholder wealth, if possible reflecting the managers' contribution to increased shareholder wealth.

(c)   The time horizon of managers should match that of shareholders. For example, if shareholders require long-term share price maximisation managers should be encouraged to take decisions in line with this objective and not decisions that maximise short-term profits.

(d)   Shareholders' and managers' attitudes to risk should be encouraged to be similar although this is extremely difficult since shareholders can diversify away part of their risk, but managers cannot easily do this.

4.2   Alternative reward systems

Types of remuneration schemes include:

(a)   **A bonus based upon a minimum level of pre-tax profit**

This scheme would be easy to set up and monitor.

Disadvantages are that the scheme may lead to managers taking decisions that would result in profits being earned in the short term at the expense of long term profitability. It could also lead to managers under achieving ie, relaxing as soon as the minimum is achieved. The scheme might also tempt managers to use creative accounting to boost the profit figure.

(b)   **A bonus based on turnover growth**

There are several disadvantages.

Turnover growth could be achieved at the expense of profitability eg, by reducing selling prices or by selecting high revenue product lines which may not necessarily be the most profitable. Maximising turnover is unlikely to maximise shareholder wealth.

(c)   **An executive share option scheme (ESOP)**

This scheme has the advantage that it will encourage managers to maximise the value of the shares of the company ie, the wealth of the shareholders. Such schemes are normally set up over a relatively long period thereby encouraging managers to make decisions to invest in positive NPV projects which should result in an increase in the price of the company shares. However, efficient managers may be penalised at times when share prices in general are falling.

(d)   **Profit related pay**

The UK government has acted in recent years to encourage companies to establish profit related pay schemes by permitting employees to receive a limited amount of tax-free pay related to profit performance. The amount of tax-free profit related pay cannot exceed 20% of an employee's total non-profit related pay, with an overriding maximum of £1,000 for profit periods beginning in the year to 31 December 1999. The scheme must be registered with the Revenue and amounts of tax-free pay must be certified by an independent accountant after each profit period.

This scheme, however, is being phased out and no further relief is available for profit periods beginning on or after 1 January 2000.

5   THE ROLE OF NON-EXECUTIVE DIRECTORS AND OTHERS

The role of non-executive directors was covered in the previous chapter. They bring an independent judgement to bear on issues of strategy, resources, including key appointments, and standards of conduct.

Where a company is in financial distress, an administrator or a receiver may be appointed. An administrator is appointed by the court at the request of the directors to reorganise a company's finances while it continues to trade. He has an equal duty to all creditors and tries to give the company a 'breathing space' from its creditors to get it back on its feet again.

A receiver is appointed by a secured creditor following default by a company. Typically the company may have failed to pay the interest due on a debenture or other loan stock. The receiver's duty is to the creditor to ensure that the loan is repaid according to the terms of the trust deed, by selling assets or parts of the business to third parties.

An alternative approach to dealing with a company is to launch a management buy-out or buy-in. In a management buy-out the existing management of a company join with financing institutions to buy the business from the current shareholders. A management buy-in is similar, although the management buying the company from the current shareholders comes from outside the existing business. Management buy-outs and buy-ins are dealt with in more detail in a later chapter.

6   CONCLUSIONS ON CORPORATE OBJECTIVES

6.1   Objectives of listed companies

For the purposes of studying financial strategy you are recommended to initially accept the 'classical' objective of the maximisation of shareholder wealth for the purpose of theory building but when it comes to the evaluation and criticism of the theories then to be prepared to relax this objective.

6.2   Objectives of small firms

Most of the above discussion of objectives has centred around large stock market listed companies. Unlisted companies will differ in two major ways:

(a)   Their owners will often be their managers and hence many of the agency problems referred to above will not apply

(b)   As they are not listed on the stock market the value of shareholder wealth is not directly observable by reference to share prices. It is not unreasonable to assume, however, that the objective of the owners would be the maximisation of owners' wealth (tempered perhaps by the desire to remain independent) and therefore the financial management techniques developed for use by listed companies should be largely applicable to small firms. The major problem will be appraising how successful past decisions have been.

6.3   Financial objectives in public corporations

This category of organisation includes such bodies as nationalised industries and local government organisations. They represent a significant part of the UK economy and sound financial management is essential if their affairs are to be conducted efficiently. The major problem here lies in obtaining a measurable objective.

For a stock market listed company we can take the maximisation of shareholder wealth as a working objective and know that the achievement of this objective can be monitored with reference to share price and dividend payments. For a public corporation the situation is more complex. The two questions to be answered are:

(a)   in whose interests are they run? and

(b)   what are the objectives of the interested parties?

Presumably such organisations are run in the interests of society as a whole and therefore we should seek to attain the position where the gap between the benefits they provide to society and the costs of their operations is the widest (in positive terms). The cost is relatively easily measured in accounting terms. However many of the benefits are intangible. On first sight the benefits of enterprises such as a nationalised coal company could be measured in terms of the sales value of coal produced, but this measure would not take account of possible hidden benefits such as cheap energy provided for the rest of industry if coal prices were being kept artificially low. The benefits of such bodies as the National Health Service or Local Education Authorities are almost impossible to quantify.

Because of the problem of quantifying the non-monetary objectives of such organisations most public bodies operate under government (and hence electorally) determined objectives such as obtaining a given accounting rate of return, cash limits, meeting budget, or breaking even in the long run.

Despite these differences in the objectives of public corporations many of the financial management theories developed in this text will be applicable in the public sector as they are concerned with the efficient management of resources. Financial managers in the public sector, however, are not usually concerned with raising outside finance but more with budgeting within the limitations of existing financial resources. As a consequence theories in the areas of capital structure and dividend policy will obviously not be relevant. Techniques for the management of current assets and investment appraisal will however be useful.

Finally a word of caution. Although we have suggested that certain financial management techniques are transferable from the private to the public sector, care must be taken in using their results. For example, it is unlikely that NHS hip replacement operations would show a good rate of return in accounting terms, but we must appreciate that the benefits of such operations are other than purely financial.

7   CHAPTER SUMMARY

This chapter has revised the possible objectives which private sector companies have and has also briefly discussed objectives of public sector organisations. It has concentrated on conflicts of interest between the various parties who are interested in the firm. Agency theory is one way of interpreting these conflicts, especially those between shareholders and directors or between loan creditors and the shareholder/director coalition. You should expect questions on this subject, as you should on remuneration schemes for directors.

8   SELF TEST QUESTIONS

8.1   How does the Cadbury report describe the responsibilities of directors? (1.1)

8.2   Give three examples of common creative accounting techniques. (1.5)

8.3   What is off balance sheet finance? (1.6)

8.4   Give three examples of corporate unethical behaviour which is legal but arguably undesirable. (1.8)

8.5   What is the relevance of agency theory to the current debate on corporate governance? (2.1)

8.6   Explain the meaning of goal congruence. (4.1)

8.7   Why might shareholders and managers appraise business risks differently? (4.1)

8.8   What is an executive share option scheme? (4.2)

8.9   What is profit related pay? (4.2)

8.10   Distinguish between an administrator and a receiver appointed to a company in financial distress. (5.2)

9   EXAMINATION TYPE QUESTION

9.1   Agency relationships

Explain the term 'agency relationships' and discuss the conflicts that might exist in the relationships between:

(a)   shareholders and managers;
(b)   shareholders and creditors.

What steps might be taken to overcome these conflicts?   **(13 marks)**

10   ANSWER TO EXAMINATION TYPE QUESTION

10.1   Agency relationships

Agency relationships exist when one or more persons, the principal(s), hire another person, the agent, to perform some task on his (or their) behalf. The principal will delegate some decision-making authority to the agent. The problems of agency relationships occur when there is a conflict of interest between the principal(s) and the agent.

(a)   Shareholders and managers

As the manager's share of total equity decreases (the divorce of ownership and control) the cost to him of decisions that are not optimal for other shareholders also decreases. Examples of possible conflict include:

(i)   Managers might not work industriously to maximise shareholder wealth if they feel that they will not fairly share in the benefits of their labours.

(ii)   There might be little incentive for managers to undertake significant creative activities, including looking for profitable new ventures or developing new technology.

(iii)   Managers might award themselves high salaries or 'perks'.

(iv)   Managers might take a more short-term view of the firm's performance than the shareholders would wish.

(b)   Shareholders and creditors

(i)   Creditors (including the lenders of loan finance) provide funds for a company on the basis of the company's assets, gearing levels and cash flow (both present and anticipated). If the managers take on more risky projects than expected by the creditors, the burden of the extra risk will fall largely upon the creditors. Conversely, if the risky investments were successful, the benefits would accrue to the shareholders.

(ii)   If gearing is increased, the providers of 'old debt' will face a greater risk of the company getting into financial distress or going into liquidation.

In order to try to ensure that managers act in the best interests of shareholders, the shareholders incur agency costs. Such costs include:

(1)   cost of monitoring management actions, eg, management audit;

(2)   cost of structuring corporate organisation to minimise undesirable management actions.

If the remuneration of management is partially a function of the success of the firm, then conflict of interest should be reduced. This might involve share option schemes, performance shares (eg, based on earnings per share) and profit based salaries or bonuses.

The threat of firing (including the board being 'deposed' by discontented shareholders), is suggested to be an incentive for efficient management, as is the possibility of job loss if a company's share price through management action is low and a takeover occurs.

It has been suggested that the nature of the managerial labour market negates much of the agency problem. A manager's wealth is made up of present wealth plus the present value of future income. The better the manager's performance the higher the company's share price, and the greater the salary, both now and in the future, the manager can obtain. The manager's desire for wealth maximisation will tend to cause him to act in the shareholders' interests.

The main way in which creditors might protect themselves against conflicts of interest with shareholders is to insist on restrictive covenants being incorporated into loan agreements. Such covenants might restrict the level of additional debt finance that might be raised, or prevent management (here acting on the shareholders' behalf) from disposing of major fixed assets without the agreement of the providers of debt, or restrict the level of dividends that can be paid. Additionally, if creditors perceive that they are being unfairly treated, they can either refuse to provide future credit, or only agree to provide further credit at higher than normal rates, both of which are likely to have adverse effects on shareholder wealth, and are deterrents to managers acting unfairly against the creditors' interests.

3 TRANSLATING MARKET DISCIPLINES

INTRODUCTION & LEARNING OBJECTIVES

This chapter develops the ideas of the first two chapters. If it is agreed that the fundamental objective is to increase shareholder wealth, it is important that possible investment projects can be appraised in the light of this objective. We see that the best measure to appraise an investment is the net present value of expected cash flows.

The subject of NPV analysis is revised, including the effects of inflation.

The efficient markets hypothesis (EMH) is introduced. If securities markets are believed to be strongly efficient, share prices will react immediately to the decision to proceed with investment projects, and share prices will fairly measure shareholder wealth in accordance with the fundamental objective.

Finally we examine the implications of the term structure of interest rates. Financial managers should be aware of the current shape of the yield curve when making decisions so that they are aware of likely future movements in levels of interest rates.

When you have studied this chapter you should be able to do the following:

- Explain why NPV is theoretically superior to profit based measures of determining an investment project's financial return
- Calculate NPVs, including the effects of inflation
- Distinguish between the weak, semi-strong and strong forms of the efficient markets hypothesis (EMH)
- Explain the relevance of EMH to financial decision-making
- Understand the term structure of interest rates and the various theories that explain possible shapes of the yield curve

1 FINANCIAL RETURNS

1.1 Adequate financial return

Businesses wish to earn an adequate financial return from their assets. Shareholders wish to make an adequate financial return from their investments. But what do we mean by an adequate financial return? Some possibilities in measuring the financial return from an asset are

- the accounting rate of return (ARR)
- the absolute level of profits earned
- discounted cash flow (DCF) methods

You will have met these methods in your earlier studies and should already be convinced that calculating the net present value (NPV) of a project's relevant cash flows is the best method.

1.2 Why cash flows rather than profits?

(a) *Cash is what ultimately counts* - profits are only a guide to cash availability: they cannot actually be spent.

(b) *Profit measurement is subjective* - there being the question of which time period income and expenses are recorded in, and so on.

(c) *Cash is used to pay dividends* - the ultimate method of transferring wealth to equity.

Students should note that, in practice, the cash flow effects of a project are likely to be similar to the project's effects on profits. Major differences in cash and profit flows will be linked to:

(a)   changes in working capital;
(b)   asset purchase and depreciation;
(c)   deferred taxation;
(d)   capitalisation of research and development expenditure.

1.3   Incremental cash flow approach

Projects will be appraised by '*discounting relevant cash flows*'.

The relevant cash flows are the incremental cash flows of the organisation as a whole as a result of accepting projects. Those cash flows which would have arisen anyway, irrespective of whether or not the project was undertaken, can be ignored.

1.4   Problems in establishing which cash flows are relevant

(a)   *Considering all alternatives* - questions will often ask for either project A or project B to be accepted. In these cases one or the other will generally be preferred. However, there are often other, still better, options available - sometimes simply doing nothing. These options should also be considered.

(b)   *'Sunk costs'* - money already spent or committed is irrelevant to the decision. We are concerned only with future cash flows.

(c)   *Opportunity costs* - cash flows should be included at their economic or opportunity cost, ie, the cost incurred as a result of diverting the resource from its next best available use to the project under review eg, if a project occupies premises which could otherwise be let at £1,000 pa, then that £1,000 could be regarded as a relevant cash outflow (in fact it is a cash inflow forgone).

(d)   *Interest payments* - since the analysis is based on discounting, it would be double counting to include the interest payments on the finance used to fund the project in the cash flows. Interest payments arise because money has a time value and it is precisely this time value which discounting and compounding is designed to account for. The only exception is when appraising leasing or hire-purchase agreements, dealt with later. Tax relief on interest payments should also be ignored.

(e)   *Dividend payments* - representing appropriation of the benefits of project acceptance rather than a relevant element in its appraisal. Incremental dividend cash flows should thus be ignored.

(f)   *Taxation payments* - these are a cash outflow when they are paid; capital allowances or tax losses may be treated as cash receipts at the point in time when they reduce a tax payment.

(g)   *Scrap or terminal proceeds* - where any equipment used in a project is scrapped, then the proceeds are a cash inflow.

(h)   Accounting treatment of costs is often irrelevant (eg, depreciation, stock valuation, methods of allocating overheads) because it has no bearing on cash flows, except to the extent that it may affect taxation payable. Overheads attributed to projects should, in the examination, be taken as absorbed figures unless specified otherwise. It should be assumed there is no change to actual overhead paid, and thus no relevant cash flow.

1.5   More on opportunity costs in project appraisal

If there are scarcities of resources to be used on projects (eg, labour, materials, machines), then consideration must be given to revenues which could have been earned from alternative uses of the resources.

For example, the skilled labour which is needed on the new project might have to be withdrawn from normal production causing a loss in contribution. This is obviously relevant to the project appraisal. The cash flows of a single department or division cannot be looked at in isolation. It is always the effects on cash flows of the whole organisation which must be considered.

There are several ways of defining opportunity cost.

[Definition]   For our purposes, the opportunity cost of a resource may be defined as *the revenue forgone if a unit of resource is used on the project instead of in the best alternative way.*

Example 1

A new contract requires the use of 50 tons of metal ZX 81. This metal is used regularly on all the firm's projects. There are 100 tons of ZX 81 in stock at the moment, which were bought for £200 per ton. The current purchase price is £210 per ton, and the metal could be disposed of for net scrap proceeds of £150 per ton. With what cost should the new contract be charged for the ZX 81?

Solution

The use of the material in stock for the new contract means that more ZX 81 must be bought for normal workings. The cost to the organisation is therefore the money spent on purchase, no matter whether existing stock or new stock is used on the contract. Assuming that the additional purchases are made in the near future, the relevant cost to the organisation is current purchase price, ie,

  50 tons × £210   =   £10,500

Example 2

Suppose the organisation has no use for the ZX 81 in stock. What is the relevant cost of using it on the new contract?

Solution

Now the only alternative use for the material is to sell it for scrap. To use 50 tons on the contract is to give up the opportunity of selling it for

  50 × £150   =   £7,500

The contract should therefore be charged with this amount.

Example 3

A mining operation uses skilled labour costing £4 per hour, which generates a contribution, after deducting these labour costs, of £3 per hour.

A new project is now being considered which requires 5,000 hours of skilled labour. There is a shortage of the required labour. Any used on the new project must be transferred from normal working. What is the relevant cost of using the skilled labour on the project?

Solution

What contribution cash flow is lost if the labour is transferred from normal working?

	£
Contribution per hour lost from normal working	3
Add back Labour cost per hour which is not saved	4
Cash lost per labour hour as a result of the labour transfer	7

The contract should be charged with 5,000 × £7	£35,000

Example 4

Suppose the facts are as in Example 4, but there is a surplus of skilled labour already employed (and paid) by the business and sufficient to cope with the new project. The presently idle men are being paid full wages.

Solution

What contribution cash flow is lost if the labour is transferred to the project from doing nothing? Nothing.

The relevant cost is zero.

1.6   Relevant costs and the decision to abandon

During our initial consideration of project appraisals, it was noted that past costs were irrelevant to any decision regarding the future of a project. This remains true for those occasions when the company has already started a project and wishes to establish whether it should continue with it, or whether it should abandon the project part-way through its life. The only relevant costs are future costs: these will be compared with future revenues to decide the viability of abandonment. Management is often reluctant to take a decision to abandon a project half-way through, as it is often considered to reflect a poor past decision; however true this may be, it would be even worse to compound the error by making another poor decision. Projects must, therefore, be kept constantly under review.

2   THE BENEFITS OF USING NPV

2.1   Investors' required returns

It is assumed throughout this syllabus that investors seek to maximise their wealth. We will see in the next chapter that the true value of any security to an investor is the net present value of the expected cash flows deriving from owning that security. The investor will take account of the risk of the security by varying the discount rate that he uses in his NPV calculation.

> **Conclusion**   The percentage return required by an investor is the discount rate that he applies to the expected cash flows from owning the asset.

If the NPV of the expected cash flows discounted at this return is less than the security's current price, the security should be sold. If the NPV exceeds the current price, the security should be bought.

2.2   NPV as a unifying long-term objective

We assume that, in theory at least, shareholders appraise their investment in a company by carrying out NPV analysis on the amounts expected to be paid out (eg, as dividends) by the company. The company must itself earn the same required return on its investments, otherwise it will not be able to satisfy its shareholders' expectations.

> **Conclusion**   The discount rate used by a company to appraise possible new projects should be the minimum rate of return required by the company's shareholders on their own investments.

NPV therefore acts as a unifying long-term objective between the interests of the shareholders and the management of a company. Management can select an appropriate discount rate to appraise new projects by examining the returns required by shareholders.

In practice, this approach is not so easy. The new project may be more or less risky than the company's existing activities, so shareholders may need a higher or lower return to accept the new project before they are satisfied. Additionally the company may be financed by loans or preference shares as well as by equity shares. Should the appropriate discount rate be an average of all the sources of funds or just the rate demanded by the equity shareholders? These and other problems are covered in later chapters.

3   REVISION OF NPV ANALYSIS

3.1   The time value of money

A simple method of comparing two investment projects would be to compare the amount of cash generated from each – presumably, the project which generates the greater net cash inflow (taking into account all revenues and expenses) is to be preferred. However, such a simple method would fail to take into account the **time value of money**, the effect of which may be stated as the general rule below:

> 'There is a time preference for receiving the same sum of money sooner rather than later. Conversely, there is a time preference for paying the same sum of money later rather than sooner.'

3.2   Reasons for time preference

The reasons for time preference are threefold:

(a)   **Consumption preference** – money received now can be spent on consumption.

(b)   **Risk preference** – risk disappears once money is received.

(c)   **Investment preference** – money received can be invested in the business, or invested externally.

If consideration is given to these factors it can be seen that inflation affects time preference but is not its only determinant. Higher inflation for instance, will produce greater consumption preference and thus greater time preference, all else being equal.

The discounting analysis is based on (c), and in particular the ability to invest or borrow and receive or pay interest. The reason for this approach is that even where funds are not actually used and borrowed in this way, interest rates do provide the market measure of time preference.

The analysis, therefore, proceeds in terms of the way interest payments and receipts behave.

3.3   Discounting

We know that an amount of £500 receivable now is to be preferred to the same amount receivable in one year's time because if the amount were received immediately it could be invested to earn interest. We now wish to know how great is this preference.

We can answer this by considering how much we would need now in order to give £500 in one year's time, given the rate of interest, r.

The amount needed is $\frac{500}{1+r}$ since we know that an initial investment of £P will be equal to £P $(1 + r)$ after one year. Thus, if r = 20%, or 0.2 as a proportion, the initial investment equals:

$$\frac{500}{1+r} \quad = \quad \frac{500}{1.2} \quad = \quad \underline{£416.67}$$

Proof

	£
Initial investment	416.67
Interest at 20%	83.33
Closing balance	500.00

Thus, if we can invest at 20%, we would be indifferent between £500 in 1 year and £416.67 now - they have the same time value.

£416.67 is known as the present value of £500 arising in 1 year's time (at 20%).

Similarly, what amount is needed today in order to give us £500 in two years' time?

$$\frac{£500}{1.2^2} = £347.22$$

Proof

	£
Initial investment	347.22
Interest earned – year 1	69.45
Closing balance – year 1	416.67
Interest earned – year 2	83.33
Closing balance	500.00

£347.22 is the present value of £500 arising in 2 years' time, at 20%.

[Definition] The present value of an amount S receivable n years hence is that sum of money which, invested at the current annual rate of interest, r, will amount after compounding to S after the expiry of n years.

We know that if P is invested for n years at a rate r, it gives:

$$S = P(1 + r)^n \qquad \text{(terminal value)}$$

Hence, by rearranging it can be seen that:

$$P = S(1 + r)^{-n} \qquad \text{(present value)}$$

Example

What is the present value of:

(a)   £400 in 2 years, r = 15%; and
(b)   £600 in 4 years, r = 20%.

Solution

(a) $$P = \frac{£400}{(1 + 0.15)^2}$$

$$= \frac{£400}{1.3225}$$

$$= £302$$

(b) $P = \dfrac{£600}{(1+0.2)^4}$

$= \dfrac{£600}{2.0736}$

$= £289$

3.4   Present value tables

At the front of this text you will find a copy of the present value tables which are provided in the examination.

The tables provide a value for $(1 + r)^{-n}$ for different values of r and n. r (the interest or discount rate) values are reflected in the column headings; n (time period) values are reflected as row headings.

The procedure for using present value tables to determine the present value of a particular future cash flow may be summarised as follows:

Step 1   Select the appropriate column for the appraisal discount rate.

Step 2   Select the row for the year at which the cash flow occurs.

Step 3   Read off the value at the intersection of the row and column selected in steps 2 and 1, respectively – this is the 'present value factor'.

Step 4   Multiply the present value factor by the actual cash flow for which present value is to be determined to find its present value.

Notes:

(a)   Inspection of the table reveals that discount factors become smaller as either the discount rate or the number of years is increased. This is consistent since the present value factor is that part of £1 which would need to be invested now to accumulate to £1 in n years at r% pa. The larger either n or r becomes, the smaller the amount which needs to be invested now.

(b)   Usually, it is the present value which is unknown. The tables, however, may be used to solve problems where any one factor, P, S, r or n, is unknown.

(c)   Choice of the base year is not critical. Provided the same year is used consistently, it does not matter which year is in fact 'year 0'. If cash flows occur before year 0 they are compounded forwards.

Note: 'year 0' is in fact the *point in time* defined as the start of the project - ie, the beginning of the first year of the project.

3.5   Activity

An investment opportunity is available which requires a single cash outlay of £850. Cash inflows of £388 will then arise at twelve month intervals for three years commencing in one year's time.

Bank overdraft finance is available at 8% pa.

(a)   Show the movement on the firm's bank account assuming that all cash flows associated with the project are paid into or out of the overdraft account.

(b)   Compute the net terminal value of the project.

(c)   Compute the net present value of the project.

(d)   Show the relationship between the numerical solutions derived in (a), (b) and (c).

3.6   Activity solution

(a)

Beginning of year	Opening balance of overdraft £	Interest @ 8% £	Less repayments £	Closing balance £	End of year
1	850	68	388	(530)	1
2	530	42	388	(184)	2
3	184	15	388	189	3

(Overdrawn closing balances are shown in brackets.)

Closing balance is a credit of £189.

(b)   **Net terminal value**

The net terminal value of a project is equal to the net amount of all the cash flows associated with the project compounded forward to the end of the project's life.

Year	Cash flow £	Compounding factor		Terminal value £
0 **	(850)	1.08^3 =	1.26	(1,071)
1	388	1.08^2 =	1.17	453
2	388	1.08^1 =	1.08	419
3	388	1.08^0 =	1.0	388

Net terminal value   189

** For convenience, in almost all investment appraisal methods cash flows are assumed to arise at twelve monthly intervals at the **end** of the relevant year. By convention, 'now' is denoted as year 0, twelve months' time as the end of year 1, and so on. Cash flows that arise part way through a year, or accrue over a year, are assumed by convention to occur at the end of that year.   Thus, for example, revenues earned gradually over the second year following commencement of a project would be included in the cash flow tabulation 'at year 2'.

(c)   **Net present value**

The net present value of a project is the net amount of all the cash flows associated with the project discounted back to the beginning of the project.

Year	Cashflow £	Present value factor at 8%	Present value £
0	(850)		(850)
1	388	$1/(1 + 0.08)$ = 0.926	359
2	388	$1/(1 + 0.08)^2$ = 0.857	333
3	388	$1/(1 + 0.08)^3$ = 0.794	308

Net present value   150

Note that discount (or present value) factors can be found either from the formula or the present value tables.

(d)   As can be seen from (a) and (b), the net terminal value of the project is also equivalent to the net amount which would be in the bank if all cash flows associated with the project were paid into and out of a single bank account.

The net present value (NPV) of £150 is related to the net terminal value (NTV) of £189 by:

$$£150 \quad = \quad \frac{£189}{(1.08)^3}$$

ie, $\quad$ NPV $\quad = \quad \dfrac{\text{NTV}}{(1+r)^n} \qquad$ where n is the total number of years of investment.

$\qquad\qquad\qquad = \quad$ the present value of the net terminal value

3.7   Annuities

In the activity above, there was an equal annual cash flow (£388) occurring over a number of years (1-3). Instead of discounting each of these flows individually using the 'simple' discount factor $1/(1 + r)^n$, then adding the results together, it is generally quicker to use an 'annuity' or 'cumulative' discount factor. This is the sum of all the simple discount factors from Time 1 to Time n.

Using the above example:

Present value (PV) of £388 per annum for 3 years at 8%:

$$= \quad £388 \times \frac{1}{1.08} + £388 \times \frac{1}{(1.08)^2} + £388 \times \frac{1}{(1.08)^3}$$

$$= \quad £388 \left(\frac{1}{1.08} + \frac{1}{(1.08)^2} + \frac{1}{(1.08)^3}\right) = £388 \,(0.926 + 0.857 + 0.794)$$

$$= \quad £388 \times 2.577$$

$$= \quad £1,000$$

2.577 is the 'annuity' or 'cumulative' discount factor for 3(n) years' worth of equal annual cash flows, **starting at Time 1**, at 8(r)%. These cumulative factors can also be found in tables at the beginning of the text or computed from the following formula $\dfrac{1}{r}\left(1 - \dfrac{1}{(1+r)^n}\right)$ and is sometimes denoted by $A\,\overline{n}\,r$

3.8   Perpetuities

Where an equal annual cash flow is expected to continue indefinitely (to perpetuity, $n \rightarrow \infty$,) the above formula can be shown to simplify to $\dfrac{1}{r}$.

Thus if the £388 had been in perpetuity, its PV at 8% = $£388 \times \dfrac{1}{0.08} = \dfrac{388}{0.08} = £4,850$.

3.9   Internal rate of return

For so-called conventional projects, that is those where a single cash outflow is followed by subsequent cash inflows, it is often useful to compute the internal rate of return (IRR) of the project.

[Definition]   The internal rate of return is that discount rate which gives a net present value of zero.

It is sometimes known as the yield, or DCF yield, or internal yield, but these terms are confusing and their use is not recommended.

In practice, it is generally necessary to compute the IRR by trial and error, that is to compute NPVs at various discount rates until the discount rate is found which gives an NPV of zero. This can be done very quickly on a computer; in the examination, however, you will only be expected to use two rates.

Example

Find the IRR of the project in the previous activity.

Solution

The NPV was computed at 8% and found to be £150. Our next estimate of the discount rate must be greater than 8% since the larger the discount rate, the lower the present value of future cash receipts. Try 20% (£150 being a relatively high NPV in relation to the cash flows).

Year	Cash flow £	PV factor @ 20%	Present value £
0	(850)	1.000	(850)
1 - 3	388	2.106*	817
Net present value			(33)

* this is the cumulative factor for three years at 20%.

As this gives a negative result, the IRR lies between 8% and 20%. A closer estimate can be found by linear interpolation:

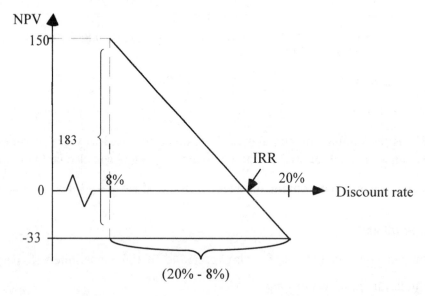

This graphical profile is typical for a conventional project. As the discount rate increases, NPV falls. The relationship is often close to linear.

From the graph, and by similar triangles, it can be seen that:

$$\frac{IRR - 8\%}{150 - 0} = \frac{20\% - 8\%}{150 - (-33)}$$

Thus, the   IRR   = $8\% + \left(12\% \times \dfrac{150}{183}\right)$

                 =   17.8%

or approx.   17% (conservatively rounded down)

3.10   Activity

Estimate the IRR of a project which has an NPV of £250 when discounted at 8% and - £120 when discounted at 11%.

3.11   Activity solution

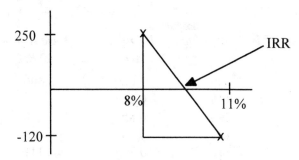

By similar triangles, $\dfrac{IRR - 8\%}{250} = \dfrac{11\% - 8\%}{250 - (-120)}$

$$IRR = 8\% + \left(\frac{250}{370} \times 3\%\right)$$

$$= 10\% \text{ approx.}$$

The IRR is estimated to be 10%.

3.12   Applying discounting in investment decisions

It is now possible to develop criteria for accepting or rejecting investment opportunities. Consider the situation where management can acquire funds at a known rate of interest and are considering whether to **accept or reject an investment project**. There are two possible approaches:

(a)   **Internal rate of return approach** – is the IRR on the project greater than the borrowing rate? – if so, accept.

(b)   **Net present value (NPV) approach** – using an appropriate discount rate, is the present value of cash inflows less initial cash outflows (ie, the net present value) positive? – if so, accept.

In the type of decisions described above ie, for conventional projects or investments, both methods will lead to identical conclusions.

Example

An initial investment of £2,000 in a project yields cash inflows of £500, £500, £600, £600 and £440 at twelve month intervals. There is no scrap value. Funds are available to finance the project at 12%.

You are required to decide whether the project is worthwhile, using:

(a)   Net present value approach.
(b)   Internal rate of return approach.

Solution

It is useful to set out the cash flows diagrammatically:

Years	0	1	2	3	4	5
	– £2,000	+ £500	+ £500	+ £600	+ £600	+ £440

Note that year 0 is, in fact, the beginning of year 1 and thereafter cash receipts are assumed to occur in 'lumps' at the end of each year. This is a working approximation to a continuous flow of cash over the year, which has only a small effect on the accuracy of the results.

for (b)

(a)   **Net present value approach**

Year	Cash flow £	PV factor @ 12%	Present value £	PV factor @ 8%	Present value @ 8%
0	− 2,000	1.000	− 2,000	1.000	-2,000
1	+ 500	0.893	+ 446	0.926	+463
2	+ 500	0.797	+ 398	0.857	+428
3	+ 600	0.712	+ 427	0.794	+476
4	+ 600	0.636	+ 382	0.735	+441
5	+ 440	0.567	+ 249	0.681	+300
Net present value			− 98		+108

Since the net present value is negative, the project should be rejected.

(b)   **Internal rate of return approach**

Calculating IRR requires a trial and error approach. Since we have already calculated in (a) that NPV at 12% is negative, we must decrease the discount rate to bring the NPV towards zero – try 8%. See above - NPV is + £108.

Thus, the IRR lies between 8% and 12%. We may estimate it by interpolation, as before.

$$\frac{IRR - 8\%}{108 - 0} = \frac{12\% - 8\%}{108 - (-98)}$$

Thus, the IRR $= 8\% + (4\% \times \frac{108}{206})$

$= 10.1\%$

or approx.   10%

Conclusion

The project should be rejected because the IRR is less than the cost of borrowing, which is 12% ie, the same conclusion as in (a) above.

Note that, for examination purposes, it is permissible to use **any** two 'reasonable' discount rates for NPV calculations towards determination of the IRR, unless rates are actually specified by the examiner. They do not have to give NPV's that are either side of zero.

3.13   Definition of inflation

[Definition]   For the purpose of this subject, inflation may be defined as **a general increase in prices**, or **a general decline in the real value of money**.

3.14   Inflation and project evaluation

Inflation generally increases the cash flows in projects. In addition, in a period of increasing inflation lenders will require an increasing return. Interest rates typically comprise two components, a **real** underlying interest rate, and an allowance for inflation.

Example

An investor lends £100 now, for repayment in one year of the principal, plus interest. During the intervening year he expects a rate of inflation of 5%. What rate of interest must he earn in order to increase his purchasing power by 10%?

Solution

The investor has £100 now. In order to simply **maintain** the purchasing power of his money he will need £100 + 5% in one year ie, £105.

To **increase** his purchasing power by 10%, he will need £105 × 1.1 = £115.50. He must therefore earn £15.50 interest on £100, representing a 15.5% rate.

The situation can be summarised as follows - note the terminology:

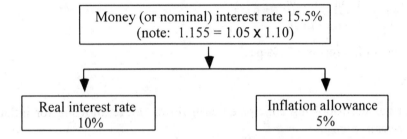

From this example you should note two key concepts. Firstly that:

Money interest rates and cash flows **include** the effect of inflation.
Real interest rates and cash flows **exclude** the effect of inflation.

Secondly, that analysis can take place in either money or real terms, as long as the two are not muddled.

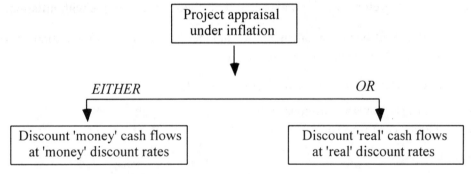

It is further worthy of note that you may obtain real rates of return using:

$$(1 + r) \quad = \quad \frac{(1+m)}{(1+i)};$$

where r, m, and i are the real, money, and inflation rates, respectively. In the last example:

$$(1 + r) \quad = \quad \frac{(1+0.155)}{(1+0.05)} \quad = \quad 1.1, \quad \text{giving the real rate of return as 10\%.}$$

Tutorial note: these two approaches are only equivalent if the general rate of inflation that has been incorporated into the money discount rate is the same as that expected to apply to all cash flows in the project.

3.15   Activity

Consider the level of interest rates current at the time that you are reading this. How much of the money interest rate is the real interest rate and how much the effects of inflation?

3.16   Activity solution

For example, when this paragraph was written, the gross yield on long gilts was 5.96% (on 2½ % Consols) while inflation was 2.6% pa.

$$m = \text{money rate of interest} = 5.96\%$$
$$i = \text{inflation rate} = 2.6\%$$

∴ real rate of interest, r, is given by

$$1 + r = \frac{1+m}{1+i} = \frac{1.0596}{1.026} = 1.0327$$

The real rate of interest is 3.27% pa.

3.17   Example

A project has the following anticipated cash flows before allowing for inflation (in current terms/in today's prices):

Year	Cash flow £
0	(750)
1	330
2	242
3	532

These are not, therefore, the flows expected if all figures grow in line with inflation.

The cost of capital has been calculated to include an allowance for inflation at 15.5%. The rate of inflation is expected to remain constant at 5%.

You are required to evaluate the project in terms of:

(a)   real cash flows and discount rates;
(b)   money cash flows and discount rates.

Solution

(a)   **Real discount rates and cash flows**

Discount rate as per the question of 15.5% includes investor's/lender's inflation expectation of 5%.

Hence 'real' discount rate, r, is given by

$$1 + r = \frac{1+m}{1+i}$$

where   m   =   money interest rate
        i   =   rate of inflation

Substituting

$$1 + r = \frac{1+0.155}{1+0.05} = 1.10$$

and   r is once again 0.10 or 10%

Discounting the cash flows as per the question:

Year	Cash flow £	PV factor @ 10%	Present value £
0	(750)	1.000	(750)
1	330	0.909	300
2	242	0.826	200
3	532	0.751	400
Net present value			150

(b)   Money discount rates and cash flows

The discount rate as per the question of 15.5% is the money discount rate.   Cash flows, however, need to be increased by 5% compound each year from year 0, to allow for inflation.

Year (i)	Real cash flow (ii) £	Inflation factor (iii)	Money* cash flow (iv) = (ii) × (iii) £	Discount factor @ 15.5%	Present value £
0	(750)	1	(750)	1.000	(750)
1	330	$1 + 0.05$	346	0.866	300
2	242	$(1 + 0.05)^2$	267	0.750	200
3	532	$(1 + 0.05)^3$	616	0.649	400
Net present value					150

Conclusion

It is concluded that, **provided** a constant rate of inflation applies to all factors, either approach yields identical conclusions (allowing for rounding).   When appraising a project, either discount actual (money) cash flows using actual (money) discount rates, or real cash flows using real discount rates.   If a constant rate of inflation does not apply to all factors, the best approach is to use money cash flows and money discount rates.

* ie, ACTUAL cash flows.

3.18   Conclusions on NPV analysis

Projects should be appraised by discounting the relevant cash flows at the company's cost of capital. Inflation is, and will continue to be, a major factor in project appraisal.   It may be dealt with either; by discounting at, and expressing cash flows in, money terms, or alternatively; by discounting at, and expressing cash flows in, real terms.

Either approach will give the same results.   Where there are varying rates of inflation, the money terms approach is simpler to work.

4   THE EFFICIENT MARKETS HYPOTHESIS

4.1   The efficiency of financial markets

The efficiency to which this hypothesis relates is that relating to information processing - the extent to which information regarding the future prospects of a security is reflected in its current market price.

A high level of such efficiency is of great importance to financial management as it means that the results of management decisions should be quickly and accurately reflected in share prices.   For example, if a firm undertakes an investment project which will generate a large surplus then in an efficient market it should see the value of its equity rise. Accordingly there have been many tests of the so-called Efficient Markets Hypothesis (EMH) for the USA and the UK stock markets.

> **Definition**   The Efficient Markets Hypothesis argues that stock markets are efficient, in that information is reflected in share prices accurately and rapidly.

For the purposes of testing, the EMH is usually broken down into three categories, as follows:

(a)   the weak form;

(b)   the semi-strong form; and

(c)   the strong form.

These are examined in the following sections. Each concerns the **type** of information which is reflected in share prices.

4.2   Efficient markets hypothesis - weak form

> **Definition**   The weak form of the hypothesis states that share prices fully reflect information included in **historic share price movements and patterns**.

If this hypothesis is correct, then it should be impossible to predict future share price movements from historic patterns. For example, if a company's share price had increased steadily over the last few months to a current price of £2.50, this price will already fully reflect the information about growth. The next change in share price could be either upwards or downwards, with equal probability. If this is the case, technical analysis or 'chartism' will not enable investors to choose undervalued shares and consistently make above average returns. Chartism involves the tracking of share price movements, possibly graphically.

Because of this randomness in share price movements, this is frequently referred to as the **random walk hypothesis**. This means that the movements of share prices over time approximate to a random walk. It also follows that because the current share price fully reflects past information about price changes it is the best estimate of the share's value. Thus it makes no sense to talk about a share being 'below' its normal value just because its present price is less than the former. There is no evidence to suggest that the price will climb to its so called 'normal' level rather than fall still further.

There is strong evidence to support the random walk view, and hence the weak form of the efficient markets hypothesis.

4.3   Efficient markets hypothesis - semi-strong form

> **Definition**   The semi-strong form of the hypothesis states that current share prices reflect not only historic share price information but also **current publicly available information** about the company.

This hypothesis can be tested by examining the way in which the market reacts to new information about a company, eg, share splits (see later), interim results, and so on. If the market is semi-strong form efficient, fundamental analysis will not enable investors to earn consistently above average returns. Fundamental analysis usually involves the study of the company accounts and other publicly available information to find a 'true' value for the company, in the hope of finding undervalued shares.

The evidence also tends to confirm the semi-strong form of the hypothesis.

4.4   Efficient markets hypothesis - strong form

> **Definition**   The strong form of the hypothesis states that current share prices reflect not only historic share price patterns and current public knowledge, but also **all possible (ie, including inside) information** about the company.

This hypothesis can be tested by analysing market response to the release of previously confidential information about the company. If the hypothesis is correct then the mere publication of the information should have no impact on the share price, consequently it should not be possible to make profits by dealing in response to 'inside' information. (This would be insider dealing and is illegal in both the UK and the USA.)

The evidence is that the market does react when information is published. Profits could therefore be made by insider dealing, and thus it would appear that the strong form of the Efficient Markets Hypothesis is not supported.

4.5 Implications of the EMH for financial decision-makers

The above tests demonstrate that although the stock market is not completely efficient it is largely so. This has significant implications for financial decision making.

(a)   **Timing of financial policy**

Some financial managers argue that there is a right and a wrong time to issue new securities. New share issues should only be made when the market is at a high rather than a low. However, if the market is efficient how are financial managers to know if tomorrow's prices are going to be higher or lower than today's? Today's 'low' could turn out to be the highest the market will stand for the next five years. All current information is already reflected in share prices and unless the financial manager knows something the rest of the market does not then it is impossible to say in which direction the market will turn.

(b)   **Project evaluation based upon NPV**

When evaluating new projects financial managers usually use required rates of return drawn from securities traded on the capital market. For example, the rate of return required on a particular project may be determined by observing the rate of return required by shareholders of firms investing in projects of similar risks. (This idea will be explained in more detail later.) This assumes that securities are fairly priced for the risk they carry - in other words that the stock market is efficient. If this is not the case then financial managers could be appraising projects on the wrong basis and therefore making bad investment decisions, since their estimates of the projects' NPVs would be unreliable.

(c)   **Creative accounting**

In an efficient stock market share prices are based upon the expected future cash flows offered by securities and their level of risk. (Again, this will be discussed in more detail in a later chapter.) In turn these expectations reflect all current information. There is little point in firms attempting to distort current information to their advantage as investors will quickly see through any such attempts.

One American test of the semi-strong form of the hypothesis by Kaplan and Roll examined the impact on share prices of companies moving from accelerated to straight-line depreciation. This change only increased reported accounting earnings: actual cash flows remained unaltered as tax allowable depreciation remained unchanged.   Initially share prices rose, possibly because the investors were not immediately informed of the changes, but within three months share prices fell as investors concluded that the cosmetic alterations to earnings were a sign of weakness rather than strength.

Other studies support this conclusion and it seems unlikely that investors can be 'fooled' by the manipulation of accounting profit figures or changes in capital structure resulting from capitalisation issues. Eventually (and usually sooner rather than later) investors will realise the cash-flow consequences and alter share prices appropriately.

(d)   **Mergers and takeovers**

If shares are correctly priced this means that the purchase of a share is a zero NPV transaction. In other words the expected returns when discounted to present value will equal the current price of the security. This does not mean that the share is a bad investment but merely that it is fairly priced - its price is commensurate with its risk and return.

If this is true the rationale behind many mergers and takeovers may be questioned. If companies are acquired at their current equity valuation then the purchasers are effectively breaking even. If they are to make a significant gain on the acquisition then they must rely upon operating economies or rationalisation to provide the savings. If the acquirer pays current equity value plus a premium of 50% (which is not uncommon) these savings would have to be considerable to make the takeover attractive.

(e)   **Validity of current market price**

If the market is efficient, statements such as 'XYZ shares are under-priced' are meaningless. The market reflects all known information in existing share prices and investors therefore know that if they purchase a security at current market price they are receiving a fair risk and return combination for their money. Financial managers should also know that if they sell new equities at current market prices they are raising funds at a fair cost.

Therefore there should be no need for substantial discounts on new issues: if the current price is fair investors will need no great extra incentive to purchase the securities as in an efficient capital market they are unlikely to find better buys elsewhere.

5   THE TERM STRUCTURE OF INTEREST RATES

5.1   The meaning of term structure

[Definition]   The term structure of interest rates refers to the way in which the yield of a debt security or bond varies according to the term of the security ie, to the length of time before the borrowing will be repaid.

Analysis of term structure is normally carried out by examining risk-free securities such as UK government stocks, also called gilts. Newspapers such as the **Financial Times** show the gross redemption yield (ie, interest yield plus capital gain/loss to maturity) and time to maturity of each gilt on a daily basis.

For example, the yields on three gilts may be shown as follows

Name of gilt	*Gross redemption yield (%)*
Treasury 13% 2000	7.75
Treasury 8% 2009	7.81
Treasury 8¾% 2017	7.84

These three exhibit the typical situation, with yields rising as the term to maturity increases. A graph can be drawn of the yield for each gilt against the number of years to maturity; the best curve through this set of points is called the yield curve.

A typical yield curve looks as follows.

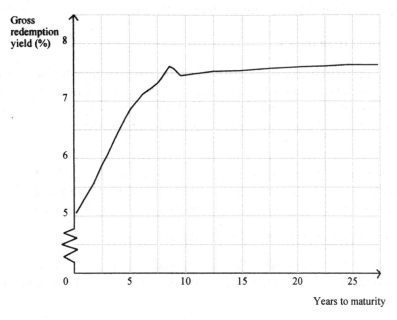

Years to maturity

The redemption yield on shorts is less than the redemption yield of mediums and longs, and there is a 'wiggle' on the curve between 5 and 10 years.

However, it should be noted that, at the time of writing, the yields on gilts were **falling** with increasing maturity terms, due to expectations of falling interest rates - see below.

5.2   Explanations for the shape of the yield curve

The shape of the yield curve at any particular point in time is generally believed to be a combination of three theories acting together:

- expectations theory
- liquidity preference theory
- market segmentation theory

Expectations theory

This theory states that the shape of the yield curve varies according to investors' expectations of future interest rates. A curve that rises steeply from left to right indicates that rates of interest are expected to rise in future. There is more demand for short-term securities than long-term securities since investors' expectation is that they will be able to secure higher interest rates in the future so there is no point in buying long-term assets now. The price of short-term assets will be bid up, the price of long-term assets will fall, so the yields on short-term and long-term assets will consequently fall and rise.

A falling yield curve (also called an inverted curve, since it represents the opposite of the usual situation) implies that interest rates are expected to fall. For much of the period of sterling's membership of the ERM, high short-term rates were maintained to support sterling and the yield curve was often inverted since the market believed that the long-term trend in interest rates should be lower than the high short-term rates.

A flat yield curve indicates expectations that interest rates are not expected to change materially in the future.

Liquidity preference theory

Investors have a natural preference for holding cash rather than other investments, even low risk ones such as government securities. They therefore need to be compensated with a higher yield for being deprived of their cash for a longer period of time. The normal shape of the curve as being upwards sloping can be explained by liquidity preference theory.

Market segmentation theory

This theory states that there are different categories of investor who are interested in different segments of the curve. Typically, banks and building societies invest at the short end of the market while pension funds and insurance companies buy and sell long-term gilts. The two ends of the curve therefore have 'lives of their own', since they might react differently to the same set of new economic statistics.

Market segmentation theory explains the 'wiggle' seen in the middle of the curve where the short end of the curve meets the long end - it is a natural disturbance where two different curves are joining and the influence of both the short-term factors and the long-term factors are weakest.

5.3   Significance of yield curves to financial managers

Financial managers should inspect the current shape of the yield curve when deciding on the term of borrowings or deposits, since the curve encapsulates the market's expectations of future movements in interest rates.

For example, a yield curve sloping steeply upwards suggests that interest rates will rise in the future. The manager may therefore wish to avoid borrowing long-term on variable rates, since the interest charge may increase considerably over the term of the loan. Short-term variable rate borrowing or long-term fixed rate borrowing may instead be more appropriate.

6   CHAPTER SUMMARY

The chapter began by revising Net Present Value as a means of investment appraisal and explained how the concept of NPV can unify shareholders and management in a common long-term objective.

The efficient markets hypothesis attempts to assess whether securities are priced fairly in a market such as the UK stock market. If the market is efficient, then investment profits from buying shares which are 'underrated' are impossible; every share will be valued correctly.

The term structure of interest rates examines how the yield available on interest bearing securities varies with the term to maturity. The analysis is normally carried out on risk-free securities such as UK gilts and the results explained by the theories of expectations, liquidity preference and market segmentation.

7   SELF TEST QUESTIONS

7.1   Why should investment projects be appraised on the basis of their expected cash flows rather than their profits? (1.2)

7.2   How should sunk costs be dealt with in an NPV analysis? (1.4)

7.3   How does NPV analysis unite the managers and shareholders of a company in a common objective? (2.2)

7.4   What information is given in present value tables? (3.4, 3.7)

7.5   What is the IRR of a project? (3.9)

7.6   Explain the importance of the information processing efficiency of a financial market. (4.1)

7.7   What is the weak form of the EMH? (4.2)

7.8   What are the implications of the EMH for project evaluation by financial managers? (4.5)

7.9   What is meant by the term structure of interest rates? (5.1)

7.10   Explain the expectations theory of interest rates. (5.2)

8   EXAMINATION TYPE QUESTIONS

8.1   Breckall plc

Assume that you have been appointed finance director of Breckall plc. The company is considering investing in the production of an electronic security device, with an expected market life of five years.

The previous finance director has undertaken an analysis of the proposed project; the main features of his analysis are shown below.

He has recommended that the project should not be undertaken because the estimated annual accounting rate of return is only 12.3%.

Proposed Electronic Security Device Project

	Year 0 £'000	Year 1 £'000	Year 2 £'000	Year 3 £'000	Year 4 £'000	Year 5 £'000
Investment in depreciable fixed assets	4,500					
Cumulative investment in working capital	300	400	500	600	700	700
Sales		3,500	4,900	5,320	5,740	5,320
Materials		535	750	900	1,050	900
Labour		1,070	1,500	1,800	2,100	1,800
Overhead		50	100	100	100	100
Interest		576	576	576	576	576
Depreciation		900	900	900	900	900
		3,131	3,826	4,276	4,276	4,276
Taxable profit		396	1,074	1,044	1,014	1,044
Taxation		129	376	365	355	365
Profit after tax		240	698	679	659	679

Total initial investment is £4,800,000
Average annual after tax profit is £591,000

All of the above cash flow and profit estimates have been prepared in terms of present day costs and prices as the previous finance director assumed that the sales price could be increased to compensate for any increase in costs.

You have available the following additional information:

(a)   Selling prices, working capital requirements and overhead expenses are expected to increase by 5% per year.

(b)   Material costs and labour costs are expected to increase by 10% per year.

(c)   Capital allowances (tax depreciation) are allowable for taxation purposes against profits at 25% per year on a reducing balance basis.

(d)   Taxation of profits is at a rate of 35% payable one year in arrears.

(e)   The fixed assets have no expected salvage value at the end of five years.

(f)   The company's real after-tax discount rate (or weighted average cost of capital) is estimated to be 8% per year, and nominal after-tax discount rate 15% per year.

Assume that all receipts and payments arise at the end of the year to which they relate except those in year 0 which occur immediately.

You are required to:

(a)   Estimate the net present value of the proposed project. State clearly any assumptions that you make.   **(16 marks)**

(b)   Calculate by how much the discount rate would have to change to result in a net present value of approximately zero.   **(4 marks)**

(Total: 20 marks)

8.2   Functions of the capital market

(a)   Briefly outline the major functions performed by the capital market and explain the importance of each function for corporate financial management. How does the existence of a well functioning capital market assist the financial management function?

(8 marks)

(b)   Describe the efficient markets hypothesis and explain the differences between the three forms of the hypothesis which have been distinguished.   **(6 marks)**

(Total: 14 marks)

9   ANSWERS TO EXAMINATION TYPE QUESTIONS

9.1   Breckall plc

(Tutorial notes

(1)   As different items are inflating at different rates the only realistic approach is to discount money cash flows at the nominal (money) discount rate. This is particularly true as taxation is involved and the amount of tax payable will be based upon a taxable profit figure which in turn is determined by items subject to various rates of inflation.

(2)   The general procedure will be:

(a)   Determine the corporation tax liability.
(b)   Determine other relevant cash flows (in money terms).
(c)   Discount these cash flows to present value at the nominal WACC.*)

(a)   **Calculation of corporation tax liability**

	1 £	2 £	3 £	4 £	5 £	
Sales (5% rise p.a.)	3,675	5,402	6,159	6,977	6,790	
Materials (10% rise p.a.)	588	907	1,198	1,537	1,449	
Labour (10% rise p.a.)	1,177	1,815	2,396	3,075	2,899	
Overheads (5% rise p.a.)	52	110	116	122	128	Note 2
Capital allowances	1,125	844	633	475	1,423	Note 1
Taxable	733	1,726	1,816	1,768	891	
Tax (35%)	256	604	636	619	312	

Notes

1. **Capital allowances**

	Opening balance £	Capital allowance £
Year 1	4,500	1,125
Year 2	3,375	844
Year 3	2,531	633
Year 4	1,898	475
Year 5	1,423	1,423 (balancing allowance)

This assumes that the capital expenditure takes place at year 0 so that the first capital allowance is available in the first year and that the balancing allowance is taken in year 5. Note that capital allowances are based upon original cost of assets.

2. Depreciation is replaced by the capital allowance.

Interest is not deducted in calculating the tax liability. The tax deductibility of interest will have been allowed for in the calculation of the weighted average cost of capital $(kd' = kd(1 - t))$.

Discount relevant cash flows to present value

Cash flow estimates (£'000)

Year	0	1	2	3	4	5	6
Inflows							
Sales	–	3,675	5,402	6,159	6,977	6,790	–
Outflows							
Materials	–	588	907	1,198	1,537	1,449	–
Labour	–	1,177	1,815	2,396	3,075	2,899	–
Overheads (note 3)	–	52	110	116	122	128	–
Fixed assets	4,500						
Working capital (note 4)	300	120	131	144	156	(851)	–
Taxation (note 5)			256	604	636	619	312
Net cash flows	(4,800)	1,738	2,183	1,701	1,451	2,546	(312)
Discount factors at 15%		0.870	0.756	0.658	0.572	0.497	0.432
Present values	(4,800)	1,512	1,650	1,119	830	1,265	(135)

NPV = £1,441,000 and on this basis the project should be accepted.

3. Once again interest is not included. The cost of interest is taken care of in the discounting process. If we were to charge interest against cash flow and include it in the WACC we would be double counting. This is a *very* common examination trap and should be avoided.

4. We require the incremental investment in working capital each year. Adjusting for inflation this is

Year 0	300		
Year 1	$(400 \times 1.05) - 300$	=	120
Year 2	$(500 \times 1.05^2) - (400 \times 1.05)$	=	131
Year 3	$(500 \times 1.05^3) - (500 \times 1.05^2)$	=	144
Year 4	$(700 \times 1.05^4) - (600 \times 1.05^3)$	=	156
Year 5	$(700 \times 1.05^5) - (700 \times 1.05^4)$	=	42

Year 5   refund of working capital assumed
(700 × 1.05^5)   = 893
Net   (851)

5.   Tax payment lagged by one year.

(b)   *(Tutorial note*

This is a roundabout way of asking what is the IRR of the project.*)*

By normal linear interpolation (or trial and error) procedures this may be determined as follows:

Year	Cashflow	20% discount	PV	27% Discount	PV
0	(4,800)		(4,800)		(4,800)
1	1,738	0.833	1,488	0.787	1,368
2	2,183	0.694	1,515	0.620	1,353
3	1,701	0.579	985	0.488	830
4	1,451	0.482	699	0.384	557
5	2,546	0.402	1,023	0.303	771
6	(312)	0.335	(105)	0.238	(74)
			765		5

The discount rate would have to change from 15% to approximately 27% to produce a net present value of zero. This is a change of approximately 80%.

9.2   Functions of the capital market

(*Tutorial note:* an analysis into the primary and secondary market functions is the best framework for such questions.)

(a)   The two major functions of the capital market are described below.

The primary market

This gives firms the facility to raise new funds. Its importance for financial management includes the following points.

(1)   It brings surplus and deficit units together in an organised meeting place. It also allows firms to invest any surplus funds.

(2)   It facilitates the growth of institutions who transform the small short term investments of individual investors into large long term 'parcels' of funds which are more attractive to industry.

(3)   It minimises transaction costs (if working efficiently).

(4)   It provides a variety of securities in various risk return combinations and for various maturities. It therefore attracts a wide clientele of investors.

The secondary market

This permits investors in existing securities to sell those securities. This does not raise any new finance for the firm but has a significant impact upon financial management in the following ways.

(1)   It encourages investors to use the primary markets as they know they will easily be able to realise their investments.

(2)   It allows investors to buy other securities and therefore spread their risks by diversifying their holdings.

(3)   If efficient, its prices will accurately reflect the performance of the firm.

(b)   An efficient market is one where share prices always fully reflect all information available to participants in the market.

Three forms of the hypothesis have been distinguished - very largely as a by-product of the empirical testing of the hypothesis. The description of an efficient market given above would be virtually impossible to test unless the terms relating to 'information available to participants in the market' and 'relevant information' etc, were more precisely defined. The three forms differ according to the extent of the information sets deemed available to market participants - broadly, the three forms are as follows.

Weak

The information available is restricted to information concerning past share prices, returns and trading volumes.

Semi-strong

The information set is restricted to publicly available information. Therefore the semi-strong form of the hypothesis implies that all publicly available information is speedily reflected in share prices.

Strong

The information set is all information whether publicly available or not.

4 THE VALUATION OF SECURITIES

INTRODUCTION & LEARNING OBJECTIVES

The concepts in the chapter are based on one of the most important ideas in financial management, the dividend valuation model. This says that the price which shareholders are willing to pay for a security equals the future cash receipts expected to be generated by the security, discounted at the shareholders' required rate of return.

When you have studied this chapter you should be able to do the following:

- State the dividend valuation model and discuss the assumptions it makes.
- Carry out calculations of share price or cost of equity using the dividend valuation model, both with and without tax.
- Estimate future dividend growth rates using the historic growth pattern and the earnings growth model.
- Calculate the cost of irredeemable securities, with and without corporation tax.
- Calculate the cost of securities which are redeemable at the current market price, with and without corporation tax.
- Calculate the cost of securities which are redeemable at other than the current market price, with and without corporation tax.
- Evaluate whether a company should redeem its debt.
- Calculate the cost of convertible debentures and discuss their use as a source of finance.
- Discuss the use of warrants in raising finance.
- Define and calculate the formula values of convertible debt and warrants, and discuss their connection with market prices.

1 MODELS FOR THE VALUATION OF SHARES

1.1 The concept of a cost of equity

Definition   The cost of equity is the cost to the company of providing equity holders with the return they require on their investment.

In an earlier chapter we defined return to shareholders as being dividend yield (dividend/market price) plus capital growth, both of which are based upon current market price.

In an efficient market, shareholders (both existing and prospective) are assumed to have the same perception of risk of the investment, and thus the same level of required return. They will use available information about the future plans of the company to formulate their expectations about future dividends and capital growth. If this does not give them their required return, there will be a move to sell the shares, and the market price will fall, thereby increasing the relative return until it meets the target (conversely, if the returns expected are above the required level, demand for the shares will rise, and market prices will follow to again bring the return in line with requirements).

Conclusion   The cost of equity equals the rate of return which investors expect to achieve on their equity holdings, determined principally by the relative level of risk involved. The market price of equity shares will settle at a level that provides this return.

In order to determine the equity shareholders' required return, and thus their cost of equity, a company's management must therefore ascertain

- the current equilibrium market price

- the expectations of future dividends (and thus future growth - see later)

- the model used by equity to convert their expectations into the current price, via the required rate of return. It is this aspect that we address next.

1.2   The equilibrium share valuation model

We shall now look at the development of a model that a prospective purchaser of equity shares of a company may use to decide the right price to pay in order to achieve at least his anticipated (required) rate of return.

The anticipated rate of return on a share acquired in the market consists of two components:

Component 1 - Dividends paid until share sold
Component 2 - Price when sold

Applying the concept of compound interest, in making a purchase decision it is assumed that the investor discounts future receipts at a personal discount rate. For the illustration below define this rate as 'i'.

In order to make a purchase decision, the shareholder must believe the price is at or below the value of the receipts, ie,

$$\text{Current price, } P_0 \leq \frac{\text{Dividends to sale} + \text{Sale price}}{\text{Discounted at rate } i}$$

Algebraically, if the share is held for n years
then sold at a price P_n
and annual dividends to year n are $D_1, D_2, D_3, \dots D_n$

Then

$$P_0 \leq \frac{D_1}{1+i} + \frac{D_2}{(1+i)^2} + \frac{D_3}{(1+i)^3} + \dots + \frac{D_n + P_n}{(1+i)^n}$$

By similar logic, the seller of the share must believe that

$$P_0 \cdot \frac{D_1}{1+i} + \frac{D_2}{(1+i)^2} + \frac{D_3}{(1+i)^3} + \dots + \frac{D_n + P_n}{(1+i)^n}$$

These different views may occur in practice for two reasons.

(a)   Different forecasts for D_1, D_2, etc and for P_n by the different investors.
(b)   Different discount rates being applied by different investors.

However, it is assumed that the major institutional players in the market - pension funds, life assurance companies etc - will have similar expectations concerning returns and risks of the investments, and will cause an equilibrium price to be set at:

$$P_0 = \frac{D_1}{1+i} + \frac{D_2}{(1+i)^2} + \frac{D_3}{(1+i)^3} + \dots + \frac{D_n + P_n}{(1+i)^n} \qquad \text{---------- (1)}$$

1.3   Limitations of the above valuation model

It is important to appreciate that there are a number of problems and specific assumptions in this model.

(a)   **Anticipated values for dividends and prices** - all of the dividends and prices used in the model are the investor's estimates of the future.

(b)   **Assumption of investor rationality** - the model assumes investors act rationally and make their decisions about share transactions on the basis of financial evaluation.

(c)   **Application of discounting** - it assumes that the conventional present value approach equates cash flows at different points in time.

(d)   **Share prices are ex div** - (see later).

(e)   **Dividends are paid annually** with the next dividend payable in one year.

1.4   The dividend valuation model

The dividend valuation model is a development of the share valuation model described above.

The important feature of the dividend valuation model is the recognition of the fact that shares are in themselves perpetuities. Individual investors may buy or sell them, but only very exceptionally are they actually redeemed.

Thus, when in the model above the share is sold in year n at price P_n, suppose at that point in time the market is in equilibrium and anticipated subsequent dividends are:

$$D_{n+1}, D_{n+2}, D_{n+3}, \ldots D_{n+z}$$

and the share is to be sold z years after year n at a price P_{n+z}.

Then the value at time n,

$$P_n = \frac{D_{n+1}}{1+i} + \frac{D_{n+2}}{(1+i)^2} + \frac{D_{n+3}}{(1+i)^3} + \ldots + \frac{D_{n+z} + P_{n+z}}{(1+i)^z} \qquad \text{---------- (2)}$$

Substituting for P_n in equation (1):

$$P_0 = \frac{D_1}{1+i} + \frac{D_2}{(1+i)^2} + \frac{D_3}{(1+i)^3} + \ldots + \frac{D_n}{(1+i)^n} + \frac{D_{n+1}}{(1+i)^{n+1}} + \frac{D_{n+2}}{(1+i)^{n+2}}$$

$$+ \frac{D_{n+3}}{(1+i)^{n+3}} \ldots + \frac{D_{n+z} + P_{n+z}}{(1+i)^{n+z}}$$

Because time (n + z) is further into the future, the value of P_{n+z} will be less significant than the value P_n in equation (1).

Ultimately, if the time-scale is extended to time j, where j is a very large number, then the price in year j can be ignored as immaterial, ie.

$$P_0 = \frac{D_1}{1+i} + \frac{D_2}{(1+i)^2} + \frac{D_3}{(1+i)^3} + \ldots + \frac{D_j + P_j}{(1+i)^j}$$

Or ignoring, P_j as immaterial:

$$P_0 = \frac{D_1}{1+i} + \frac{D_2}{(.1+i)^2} + \frac{D_3}{(1+i)^3} + \ldots \text{ to perpetuity} \qquad \text{---------- (3)}$$

Expression (3) is a statement of the dividend valuation model. It may be expressed verbally as:

[Definition]   The dividend valuation model states that the current share price is totally determined by the anticipated future dividends, discounted at the investors' discount rate.

For examination purposes, it is important to note that the dividend valuation model technically includes the assumptions of perpetual dividend payments (thus $d_j = d_\infty$) and thus an infinite business. Both are unrealistic, but nevertheless the most workable assumptions that can be made.

Conclusion   The dividend valuation model states that the value of a security equals the future expected returns from that security, discounted at the security holders' required rate of return.

Note: that shareholders' required rate of return (i) equals the cost of equity, (denoted by K_e in the formulae sheet; we shall use this latter notation from now on).

1.5   The pattern of future dividends

In the basic model developed above, each year's dividend must be forecast separately. This is both cumbersome and probably unrealistic as a representation of the investors' value forecasts.

The most convenient assumptions are that dividends either remain constant, or grow at some constant annual rate, g.

Under both of these assumptions, the model becomes a 'geometric progression', where each term in the sum is a constant multiple of the previous one. There are formulae for the sums of such series in perpetuity, which allow the model to be expressed quite simply as follows:

(a)   If dividends per share remain at current level:

$$P_0 = \frac{D}{K_e} \qquad \text{or} \qquad K_e = \frac{D}{P_0}$$

or

(b)   If dividends per share grow at constant annual rate, g:

$$P_0 = \frac{D_0(1+g)}{K_e - g} = \frac{D_1}{K_e - g} \qquad \text{or} \qquad K_e = \frac{D_0(1+g)}{P_0} + g = \frac{D_1}{P_0} + g$$

Where P_0 is the price of shares ex div
　　　D_0 is the dividend just paid (per share)
　　　K_e is the equity investors' anticipated rate of return (also the cost of equity)
　　　D_1 is the dividend to be paid next year (per share).

In this model it is assumed that dividends are paid at annual intervals.

These models, if accepted, will therefore allow a company to easily deduce its cost of equity from the market price.

However, there are obvious flaws in such simple models of anticipated dividend behaviour. In particular note:

(a)   g must be less than K_e.

If g equals K_e, the share price becomes infinitely high, a nonsense result. But note that a growth rate this high **to perpetuity** is impossible. It implies a company which would very soon swallow up the entire world.

(b)   In practice companies are likely to experience periods of varying growth rates. More sophisticated models have been developed to cope with such forecasts, but they do not need to be considered computationally.

The pattern of future dividends is usually referred to as the **dividend stream**.

1.6   Activity

Use the formulae above to answer the following questions:

(a)   A company's shares are quoted at £2.50 excluding the value of the dividend just paid of £0.50. No growth in dividends is expected. What rate of return, K_e, do the investors anticipate?

(b)   As (a), but with an anticipated growth rate in dividends of 10% pa.

(c)   Investors in a company are known to require a rate of return of 15%. Current dividends are 30p per share, just paid. No increase is anticipated. Estimate the share price, P_0.

(d)   As in (c), but dividends are expected to growth at 5% pa.

1.7   Activity solution

(a) K_e $= \dfrac{D}{P_0}$

$= \dfrac{£0.50}{£2.50}$

$= 0.2$ or 20%.

(b) K_e $= \dfrac{D(1+g)}{P_0}+g$

$= \dfrac{£0.50(1.1)}{£2.50}+0.1$

$= 0.32$ or 32%

(c) P_0 $= \dfrac{D}{K_e}$

$= \dfrac{£0.3}{0.15}$

$= £2$

(d) P_0 $= \dfrac{D(1+g)}{K_e-g}$

$= \dfrac{£0.3(1.05)}{0.15-0.05}$

$= £3.15$

1.8   Cum div and ex div share prices

Definition   If a dividend is just about to be paid on a share, an investor buying the share cum div is entitled to the dividend. An investor buying the share ex div is **not** entitled to the dividend. The seller of the share receives the dividend.

Dividends are paid periodically on shares. During the period prior to the payment of dividends, the price rises in anticipation of the payment. At this stage the price is **cum div**.

Some time after the dividend is declared the share becomes **ex div**, and the price drops. This may be expressed diagrammatically:

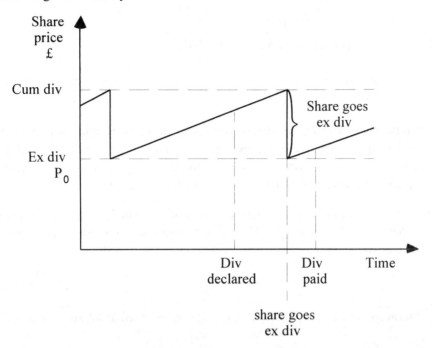

share goes
ex div

This share price profile is easily proved. Consider example (c) above with, for simplicity, a shareholder rate of time preference that does not change with time (ie, which remains at 15%).

$$\text{Share price (\textbf{ex div}) now} = \frac{£0.3}{0.15} = £2$$

$$\text{Expected share price (\textbf{ex div}) a year from now} = \frac{£0.30}{0.15} \quad \text{(expected returns pa from year 2 as a perpetuity)}$$

$$= £2$$

Thus, expected share price, **cum div** = £2.30 (value of the share **ex div** plus the dividend a purchaser would get at year 1 if **cum div**)

Similarly, **cum div** prices just before dividend payments could be expected to be £2.30 every year, with £2 as the price as the share goes **ex div**. Hence the share price profile in the diagram.

Conclusion Ex div share price + dividend just about to be paid = cum div share price.

Notice, however, that if dividends with growth are expected the general position is slightly different. Consider the detail in example (d) above. We would have:

	At year 0 £	At year 1 £	At year 2 £
Share price **ex div**	3.15	3.31	3.47
Dividend	0.30	0.32	0.33 ... and so forth
Logical share price **cum div**	3.45	3.63	3.80

The process of calculation is as before. Check the figures yourself. As examples:

$$\text{Share price (just \textbf{ex div}) at year 1} = \frac{£0.30(1.05)^2}{0.15 - 0.05} \text{ (expected dividend at year 2)} = £3.31$$

$$Dividend\ at\ year\ 1\ =\ £0.30 \times 1.05$$
$$=\ £0.315$$
$$=\ £0.32$$

Logical share price **cum div** = £3.63 (£3.31 + £0.32)

Conclusion   The share price grows year on year at a rate consistent with the dividend growth rate of 5%.

It will be noted that the share goes **ex div** shortly before the dividend is paid. Any person acquiring the share after this point in time will not receive the dividend, which will be paid to the original shareholder. The reason is that the time it takes for the company to amend its register of members requires a cut-off point somewhat before the dividend is paid.

Thus, when a share is quoted **cum div**, the price includes both the underlying **ex div** value of the share (P_0), and the dividend due shortly (D_0). Use of the dividend valuation model and the formulae developed thus far requires an **ex div** share price to determine the P_0 value.

1.9   Activity

A share is quoted **cum div** at £4.50. The dividend has been declared at £0.50. What is the probable **ex div** price?

1.10   Activity solution

The problem may be viewed diagrammatically:

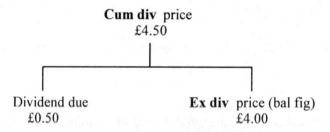

Hence the forecast **ex div** price is £4.00. After all, a person buying the share **ex div** would expect to receive all the value that would be obtained from a **cum div** purchase **except** the present year dividend.

2   DIVIDEND GROWTH MODELS

2.1   Estimating growth rates - historic pattern

The anticipated growth rate, g, is an unknown, representing a subjective estimate made by individual investors. It cannot be calculated precisely, but an important factor in the investor's estimate will be the historical pattern of growth in dividends and earnings.

Definition   A growth rate may be estimated from historic data:

$$D_{-n}\,(1+g)^{n} = D_0$$

Where D_{-n} is a dividend n years in the past and D_0 is the current dividend.

Example

A company currently pays a dividend of 32p; five years ago the dividend was 20p.

Estimate the annual growth rate in dividends.

Solution

$$20p \times (1 + g)^5 = 32p$$

or $$(1 + g)^5 = \frac{32}{20}$$

$$= 1.60$$

$$\therefore 1 + g = 1.6^{1/5} \approx 1.1, \text{ so } g = 0.1 \text{ or } 10\%.$$

If you do not have a calculator which can take a fifth root, you may use compounding tables.

From compounding tables, we can find that £1 accumulated at 10% for five years amounts to £1.61 ie, g is 10% approximately.

Note: If four years' growth is being considered, the fourth root can be found by taking the square root twice. For the examination, however, ensure you have a calculator that works roots to various powers.

Earnings may be used instead of (or as well as) dividends to estimate growth from historic trends.

Conclusion   The future average growth rate, g, can be estimated from past dividends using the following formula.

$$1 + g = \left(\frac{D_0}{D_{-n}}\right)^{1/n}, \text{ where } D_0 \text{ is the most recent dividend and } D_{-n} \text{ is the dividend paid}$$

n years ago.

2.2   Activity

A company is just about to pay a dividend of 40p. Four years ago its dividend was 28p. What was the average annual growth rate over the four years?

2.3   Activity solution

Step 1   The most recent dividend , D_0, is 40p.

Step 2   The historic dividend, D_{-4}, is 28p.

Step 3   Applying the formula:

$$1 + g = \left(\frac{40}{28}\right)^{1/4} \approx (1.43)^{1/4} \approx 1.09$$

$$\therefore g = 0.09 \text{ or } 9\%$$

2.4   Alternative growth model (the earnings retention model)

Definition   A growth rate·for equity-financed companies may be estimated as rb, where r is the current accounting rate of return and b is the proportion of profits retained for reinvestment.

The model is based on the premise that the higher the company's level of retentions, the greater is the potential growth rate. Although students will appreciate that this reliance on accounting profits is dubious, the model is not totally unreasonable. It follows from looking at the rate of growth of retained profits (for a wholly equity financed company). If all measures are constant, then it may be shown that 'g' the rate of growth of dividends is equal to the rate of growth of profits is equal to the rate of growth of share prices and so on.

This model is sometimes called the Gordon growth model. Given sufficient data, an examination candidate may be required to estimate a growth rate based on the above model, as illustrated below.

Example

Consider the following summarised financial statement for XYZ plc

Balance sheet as at 31 December 19X1

	£		£
Assets	200	Ordinary shares	100
		Reserves	100
	200		200

Profits after tax for the year ended 31 December 19X2	£20
Dividend (a 40% payout)	£8

Balance sheet as at 31 December 19X2

	£		£
Assets	212	Ordinary shares	100
		Reserves 100 + (20 – 8)	112
	212		212

If the company's accounting rate of return and earnings retention rate remain the same what will be the growth in dividends in the next year?

Solution

Profit after tax as a % of capital employed will be $\dfrac{20}{200}$ = 10%.

10% × asset value at 31 December 19X2 = 10% × £212 = £21.20.

Dividends will therefore be 40% × £21.20 = £8.48.

This represents a growth of 6% on the year.

Normally this is more directly calculated by the following equation:

$$\begin{aligned}
g &= \text{r (accounting rate of return)} \times \text{b (the earnings retention rate)} \\
&= 10\% \times 60\% \\
&= 6\%.
\end{aligned}$$

Note: that the accounting rate of return is calculated with reference to opening balance sheet values.

Conclusion	Using the earnings retention/Gordon growth model, the annual growth in dividends, g, is estimated as g = rb, where r is the accounting rate of return and b is the proportion of funds retained by the company each year.

As stated above, the major problem with this model is its reliance on accounting profits and the assumption that r and b will be constant. Inflation can substantially distort the accounting rate of return if assets are valued on an historic cost basis.

3   DISCUSSION OF DIVIDEND VALUATION MODEL

3.1   Value of the dividend valuation model

Few would argue with the basic premise of the model that the value of a share is the present value of all its future dividends. Its major weakness stems from limitations in the input data.

Current market price

P_0 - this can be subject to other short term influences, such as rumoured takeover bids, and thus considerably distort the estimate of the cost of equity.

Future dividends

For simplicity we usually assume no growth or constant growth. These are unlikely growth patterns. Further, growth estimates based on the past are not always useful; market trends, economic conditions, inflation, etc need to be considered. In exam questions future dividends are often estimated rather mechanically but it is important to think about influences on future dividends other than past dividends.

3.2   Relevance of earnings in the dividend valuation model

Earnings do not feature as such in the dividend valuation model. However, earnings should be an indicator of the company's long-term ability to pay dividends and therefore in estimating the rate of growth of future dividends, the rate of growth of the underlying profits must also be considered. For example, if dividends grow at 10% whilst earnings grow at 5%, before long the firm will run out of funds with which to pay dividends. Similarly, if dividends grow at 5% and profits at 10%, the firm will soon accumulate excess funds.

3.3   Taxation and the dividend valuation model

It can be shown that, under the present imputation system, as long as shareholders are basic rate taxpayers, tax does not affect the cost of equity calculations already described. The dividend used in the formula is the (net) dividend paid by the company. Unless told otherwise, assume that shareholders are basic rate taxpayers.

4   THE VALUATION OF BONDS, DEBT AND OTHER SECURITIES

4.1   Cost of debt finance

Traditionally, most debt finance was subject to fixed interest rates and was raised on the stock market by the sale of securities. We will deal with this type of finance initially and then consider other variants of debt. As with equity, the basis for the calculations will be the dividend valuation model (with interest payments replacing dividends).

Note that debt finance will be taken to include preference shares.

4.2   The two computational problems

Purely from a computational point of view, there are two different aspects to the problem:

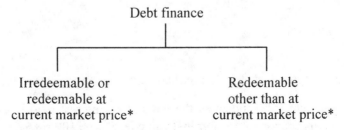

* Or issue price if the debt being considered is currently under issue.

The computational problems differ, and are dealt with below. In either case, the following points should be borne in mind.

(a)   The object is to find the cost in annual interest rate terms.

(b)   The object is to estimate the cost of raising new finance in the same category.

5   IRREDEEMABLE SECURITIES

5.1   Introduction

If securities are irredeemable the company does not intend to repay the principal but simply to pay interest for ever. The most common example is an irredeemable preference share.

In this case the equivalent formula to the 'constant dividends' equity model may be used:

$$P_0 = \frac{I}{K}$$

Where P_0 =   present market price

I =   annual interest (starting in one year's time)

K =   required return/cost

5.2   Example

A preference share is issued at its nominal value of 25p. The dividend is 5p per annum.

We know that $25p = \dfrac{5p}{K}$

$\therefore\ K = \dfrac{5p}{25p}$

$= 20\%$

By buying preference shares at 25p investors have accepted a return of 20%. The cost of preference shares is therefore 20%.

$\boxed{\text{Conclusion}}$ In general terms the cost of irredeemable loans is:

$$\text{Cost} = \frac{\text{Annual interest}}{\text{Current market price}}$$

$$= \frac{I}{P_0}$$

5.3   Example

An irredeemable government security is quoted at £40 per £100 stock. The nominal interest rate (coupon rate) is 5%.

The return on this investment $= \dfrac{£5}{£40}$

$= 0.125$ or 12.5%.

Notes:

(1)   The term '£40' means that £100 nominal value can be purchased for £40.

(2)   The coupon rate (5%) indicates the amount of interest paid annually on the security. The interest equals coupon rate × nominal value ie, 5% × £100 = £5.

(3)   By only paying £40 for the security, investors have forced the return up to 12.5%. They presumably would not pay £100 for it as interest per £100 of nominal stock would yield £5 and this would give them a return of only

$$\frac{£5}{£100} = 5\%$$

(4)   £40 is the current market value of the government security. If the loan stock had originally been issued at £100 then its historic cost (ie, the cost to the government of issuing the stock in the first place) would be 5%. More importantly, if the government came to raise new debt now it would cost 12.5%.

5.4   Activity

A 4% irredeemable debenture is quoted at £106. What is the debenture holders' required rate of return?

5.5   Activity solution

As with equity, the cost of the debenture equals the debenture holders' required rate of return (although corporation tax changes this result - see later).

Using the above formula, the debenture holders' required rate of return is therefore $\frac{4\% \times £100}{£106} \approx 0.038$ or 3.8%.

Note that the 4% in the question was the debt's **coupon rate**, not the required return. It allows you to calculate the **absolute** amount of interest paid on the debt each year (= coupon rate × nominal value). Also note that debt is referred to in quantities of £100 nominal value, unless you are told otherwise.

5.6   Redeemable at current market price

If in the preference share example above the 25p preference share had been redeemable in 1 year's time at 25p, would this have offered any extra (or less) return to investors?

Instead of enjoying the receipt of 5p per year from year 2 to infinity they would receive 25p repayment principal at year 1. The present value of 5p per year from year 2 to infinity, in year 1 terms, is:

$$\frac{5p}{0.2} = 25p \text{ ie, the same as the redemption amount.}$$

Therefore, the rate of return is the same.

Similarly, if in the second example the government stock were to be redeemed at £40 in three years' time there would be no change in investors' returns.

[Conclusion]   Where the security is irredeemable or the current market price equals redemption price, then:

$$\text{Cost to company} = \text{Return to investor} = \frac{\text{Annual interest payment}}{\text{Market price (no taxation)}}$$

(Tutorial note: this cost is sometimes called the 'interest yield' on a security.)

6   REDEEMABLE AT OTHER THAN CURRENT MARKET PRICE

6.1   Introduction

Where there is a difference between current market price and redemption price, then there are two potential elements to the cost of that security as reflected by the returns required by a new investor. These are as follows.

(a)   Interest payments; and

(b)   Capital value at redemption.

6.2   Example

Suppose a debenture has a current market price of £74. Interest is 10% on the nominal value (ie, coupon rate is 10%), paid annually, and has just been paid. Redemption is at par in four years' time, together with the final interest payment.

The objective is to find a way of expressing this situation in terms of an annual rate of return. This problem is, of course, common in dealing in such securities. The total return is referred to as the **gross redemption yield** (or 'yield to maturity'). In practice bond yield tables would be used, but you are required to be able to calculate the gross yield from first principles.

Definition   Gross redemption yield is the rate of return on a security, taking into account interest payments and the redemption premium, but ignoring income tax.

The approach is best explained by an analogy: if the £74 which the debentures cost were invested in a bank deposit account, what rate of interest (compounded annually) would that deposit account have to pay to match the £10 pa interest payments and the £100 redemption proceeds?

The answer is in fact 20%, and is demonstrated as follows:

Year	Balance at start of year	Interest for year @ 20%	Payment	Balance at end of year
1	74.00	14.80	(10)	78.80
2	78.80	15.76	(10)	84.56
3	84.56	16.91	(10)	91.47
4	91.47	18.29	(110)	Nil (rounding difference)

In practical terms, this suggests that a current investment of £74 that generates subsequent returns of £10 per annum for four years (payable annually in arrears) plus a capital repayment of £100 after four years gives an average return of 20% pa.

This can be further proved since the £74 currently paid would equal the total present value of the subsequent returns assessed at a discount rate of 20%:

$$£74 = \text{(PV of £10 for 4 years @ 20\%)} + \text{(PV of £100 in 4 years @ 20\%)}$$

$$= (2.589 \times £10) + (0.482 \times £100) \text{ (using present value factor tables)}$$

$$= £74.09 \text{ (difference arises due to rounding).}$$

Thus, the yield to maturity is that discount rate which equates the two sides.

Conclusion   For redeemable debt the cost of finance (or debt holders' required rate of return) is that value of discount rate, K_d which equates the present value of interest payments, I, and redemption price, R, to the current market price, P_0.

In answering problems where the value of k is required, you must use trial and error.

Note that this is the method we adopt to determine IRRs.

6.3   Practical hints on finding k

From the above, you should see that the cost of debt, K_d, is the IRR of the following project:

Time		Cashflow
0	P_0	Market price
1 - n	(I)	Interest payments
n	(R)	Redemption payment

You can therefore estimate the cost by using the IRR approximation method revised earlier, using two different rates and interpolating/extrapolating. As a guide for picking the first rate, if the debt was irredeemable, the rate would be I/P_0 - in this case 10/74 = 13.5%. Start with a rate around this (higher is better - as redemption is above current price, this will add to the cost) - say 15%.

6.4   Activity

Debenture stock is quoted at £65.75. Interest is 9% pa, just paid. Redemption is in 15 years at par. Estimate the debenture holders' required rate of return, using the procedure above.

6.5   Activity solution

Time		Cashflow	15% PV factor (see below)	PV
0	65.75	Market price	1	65.75
1-15	(9)	Interest payments	5.847	(52.62)
15	(100)	Redemption payment	0.123	(12.30)
				0.83

Irredeemable cost = 9/65.75 = 13.7%, so start with, say, 15%.

The result at 15% is very close to zero, and it is reasonable to conclude that the cost is just below this (note that as the later flows are outflows, we need to have them *less* discounted to negate the small positive result). If the result had been larger, and still positive, you could have repeated the NPV calculation at a *lower* rate and used the IRR interpolation formula.

6.6   Redemption opportunities

Where companies have redeemable debentures in issue on the market, they are legally entitled to buy their debentures and redeem them at any point in time. Management should, therefore, constantly appraise the cost against other sources of finance and redeem them if it is to the benefit of the firm.

Redemption will be worthwhile if other sources of finance have a lower cost than the redeemable debentures.

6.7   Activity

A company's debentures have a market value of £48.30. They are redeemable at par in 15 years and the interest rate is 5% per annum. Other funds are available at a cost of 12%. Should the debentures be redeemed? Ignore issue and redemption costs and taxation.

6.8   Activity solution

It can be estimated, using the above method, that the debentures have a cost of 13% (see workings). It is, therefore, marginally beneficial to redeem them and replace them with finance costing 12%.

WORKINGS

Time	Cashflow £	13% PV factor	PV £
0	48.30	1	48.30
1-15	(5)	6.462	(32.31)
15	(100)	0.160	(16)
			(0.01)

7   TAX AND THE COST OF DEBT

7.1   Introduction

An important aspect in evaluating the cost of finance is the effect of taxation. Loan interest is an allowable charge for corporation tax, which effectively reduces the cost of loan finance to the company.

7.2   Example - irredeemable debt

Consider two companies, A Ltd and B Ltd. Both have identical operating profits on which they pay corporation tax at (say) 30%. However, B Ltd has in issue £50,000 of debentures on which it is paying 20% interest. The debentures are valued at par in the market, giving a return on debt of 20%.

	A Ltd £	B Ltd £	Difference (A-B) £
Operating profit	100,000	100,000	
Interest	-	10,000	(10,000)
Profit before tax	100,000	90,000	
Tax @ 30%	30,000	27,000	3,000
Earnings available for equity	70,000	63,000	(7,000)

Thus, the effective interest cost to the company is £7,000, or $\dfrac{£7,000}{£50,000}$ = 14%. This may be expressed in a general form where K is the pre-tax cost, and t the corporate tax rate:

Net of tax cost of debt, $K' = K(1 - t)$

In this example $K' = 20\% (1 - 0.3) = 14\%$ (as above).

This adjustment is only valid for irredeemable loan stocks or those redeemable at current market price (or issue price if currently being issued).

Conclusion	For irredeemable loan stock, or stock redeemable at current market price, the **cost** of debt to the company equals $K(1 - t)$, where K is the debt holders' required rate of return and t is the corporation tax rate. Note that the cost of debt and the required rate of return on the debt are no longer equal.

7.3   Taxation and premium on redemption

Where there is a premium on redemption, the tax position is more complex because there is only relief on the interest payment element, not the redemption premium. Thus, the correct procedure is to reduce only the interest element by the corporation tax rate. Thus, the net of tax cost is the value K' which is the IRR of the following flows:

Time	Cashflow
0	P_0
1 - n	$I(1-t)$
n	R

Example

In a previous example, the rate of return on a 10% debenture, redeemable at par in four years' time and quoted at £74, was calculated as 20%. If the corporation tax rate is 30%, K' is the value which is the IRR of:

Time	Cashflow
0	74
1-4	(10 (1-0.3))
4	(100)

which works out at approximately 15%, the effective cost of debt to the company.

7.4   Activity

An 8% debenture, redeemable in five years' time at £105, is currently quoted at £95.42. What is the required return of the debenture holders? If the corporation tax rate is 30%, what is the cost of the debt to the company?

7.5   Activity solution

(a)   **Required return of the debenture holders**

This is the value of K which is the IRR of:

Time	Cashflow
0	(95.42)
1-5	8
5	105

Note (i) that corporation tax is not relevant to the debenture holders, (ii) the inflows/outflows are reversed from those from the company's viewpoint.

By applying the trial and error procedure, you will find that the required return is 10%:

$$(£95.42) + (3.79 \times £8) + (0.62 \times £105) = 0$$

(b)   **Cost of debt to the company**

As the debt is redeemable, it is not correct to apply the formula $K' = K(1 - t) = 10\%(1 - 0.30) = 7\%$. The IRR approximation method must be repeated, adjusting interest payments for tax relief.

K' is therefore found as the IRR of

Time	Cashflow
0	95.42
1-5	(8 (1 − 0.3))
5	(105)

You should find that K' is between 7 and 8%.

(Remember that with the approximation method slightly different answers will be produced depending on the rates used for the initial calculations. Don't expect to produce exact answers.)

8   OTHER TYPES OF DEBT

8.1   Deep discounted bonds and zero coupon bonds

> **Definition**   Deep discounted bonds are those where the coupon rate being offered is below the market rate at the time of issue. There might even be no annual interest payment, these being referred to as zero coupon bonds.

The attractions of these bonds to the company are as follows.

(a)   The initial financing cash outflows are small.

(b)   The discount element of the bond is amortised and allowed annually against corporation tax.

From the investors' viewpoint, there are two other advantages.

(a)   There is little chance of the bond being called early, as this would prove very expensive to the firm.

(b)   Although the Revenue amortise the discount element for tax purposes, the tax on this element of return to the investor is not normally payable until redemption.

8.2   Long-term bank loans and variable rate loans

Many firms nowadays raise much of their long-term debt finance from the banks. If this is in the form of fixed rate loans the cost of debt is simply the interest rate quoted by the bank, subject to the normal adjustment for tax relief, ie:

$$\text{Interest rate} \times (1 - t)$$

In practice, however, many bank loans are now offered at variable interest rates. For example, an interest rate of LIBOR + 4% may be quoted. LIBOR is the London inter-bank offered rate (an average of major bank deposit rates) and can vary from day to day. The borrower will pay interest on the loan at 4% above this rate.

From a cost of capital viewpoint it is very difficult to calculate the cost of a source of finance where the interest rate varies periodically. The usual approach is either to take the current cost or to substitute in the cost of a similar but fixed rate loan.

9   CONVERTIBLE DEBENTURES AND WARRANTS

9.1   Introduction

Convertible debentures are a hybrid of debt and equity and it is convenient to deal with them at this stage. Warrants have many similarities to convertibles and will also be considered.

> **Definition**   **Warrant** - an option to buy shares in a company at a stated price, usually within a stated period.

> **Definition**   **Convertible debenture** - a debenture which at the option of the holder may be converted into shares in a company, under specific conditions.

Thus, whereas a warrant is merely an option, a convertible debenture combines an option with a debenture ie, a warrant is not linked to an underlying security.

Warrants are commonly issued as 'sweeteners' with an issue of loan stock.

Note that in both cases there is no compulsion on the holder to exercise his right. However, if he chooses to do so the firm must oblige.

9.2   Example

(1)   Raybeck plc issues 8% unsecured loan stock 19X1/X5 as part of the consideration for the acquisition of companies. With the loan stock are subscription rights (warrants) on the basis that holders of £100 loan stock could subscribe for up to 30 ordinary shares in Raybeck at a price of £8.75 per share. The option could be exercised any time between 19X2 and 19X5.

(2)   Associated Engineering plc issues 7% convertible loan stock 19X8/X9. The conversion option is 80 ordinary shares for each £100 loan stock, and is exercisable between 19X1 and 19X5. If the option is not exercised, the debentures are redeemable at par between 19X8 and 19X9.

Comment

Note the difference between these two issues. In the Raybeck case, the option is separate from the loan stock, which continues to exist whether or not the option is exercised. Also, the exercise of the option costs money. On the other hand, conversion of Associated Engineering loan stock is an actual replacement of the loan stock by shares, with no cash effect.

It should be noted that there are a number of variations on the theme of conversion rights, including, for example, convertible preference shares. There is no need for you to memorise all the possibilities.

9.3   Attractions of convertibles as a source of finance

Convertibles offer a number of advantages to the company as follows:

Advantage	*Comment*
Immediate finance at low cost	Because of the conversion option, the loans can be raised at below normal interest rates.
Attractive, if share prices are depressed	Where companies wish to raise equity finance, but share prices are currently depressed, convertibles offer a 'back-door' share issue method.
Self-liquidating	Where loans are converted into shares, the problem of repayment disappears.
Exercise of warrants related to need for finance	Options would normally only be exercised where the share price has increased. If the options involve the payment of extra cash to the company, this creates extra funds when they are needed for expansion.

9.4   The decision to exercise

Investors will exercise their rights to convert if it is profitable to do so.

If firstly we examine the warrants issued by Raybeck plc we can see that they would be worth exercising if the share price of Raybeck were above £8.75. For example if the share price rose to £10 on the exercise date then the value of the warrant would be:

Current market price − Exercise price = £10 − £8.75 = £1.25

If share prices fell below £8.75 the warrant would be worthless. The above calculation is referred to as the formula value of the warrant. It should be noted that the warrant will also have some 'time value' in addition to the 'formula value' if the price differential being considered is in advance of the exercise date.

| Conclusion | The formula value of a warrant = current market price of share less exercise price of warrant (where current market price exceeds exercise price); or zero otherwise. |

If we now consider the convertible we can see that the conversion option is worth exercising if the share price rises above:

$$\frac{\text{Value of £100 loan stock}}{80 \text{ shares}}$$

Above this price, shareholders would receive equity of greater value than the £100 loan stock. Unlike a warrant, however, below this share price the value of the convertible does not fall to zero, but would settle at the market value of the security as a straight debenture.

Example

Rexel plc has in issue a convertible debenture with a coupon rate of 12%. Each £100 unit may be converted into 20 ordinary shares at any time until the date of expiry and any remaining debentures will be redeemed at £100. The debenture has five years left to run. Investors would normally require a rate of return of 8% per annum on a five year debt security.

Should investors convert if the current share price is:

(a)   £4.00;
(b)   £5.00;
(c)   £6.00.

Solution

Value as debt

If the security is not converted it will have the following value to the investor:

	PVF @ 8%	PV £
Interest £12/year for 5 years	3.993	47.916
Redemption £100 in 5 years	0.681	68.100
		116.016

Note the present value is calculated at 8% - the required rate of return on a straight debt security.

Value as equity

Market price £	Value as equity
4.00	£80 (ie, 20 × £4)
5.00	£100
6.00	£120

If the market price of equity rises to £6.00 the security should be converted, otherwise it is worth more as debt. The 'break-even' conversion price is £5.80 per share (£116/20 shares).

The value of a convertible is the higher of its value as debt and its converted value. This is also known as its formula value. Again, a convertible will have 'time value' in addition to this formula value if the maturity date has not yet arrived.

| Conclusion | The formula value of a convertible is the higher of its value as debt and its converted value. |

9.5 Activity

A company has a 7% redeemable debenture in issue, quoted at £140. It is redeemable in six years' time at £140. It also has a 10% convertible debenture, which has six years to run. The terms of conversion are 30 shares per £100 debenture. If the debenture is not converted, it will be redeemed at £106. At what current share price would a debenture holder be indifferent between converting the debenture now, or holding on to it?

9.6 Activity solution

Step 1 Calculate debenture holders' required rate of return, using the figures relating to the 7% debenture.

Since the market price equals the redemption price, the irredeemable debenture formula can be used.

$$\text{Required return} = \frac{7\% \times £100}{£140} = 5\%$$

Step 2 Calculate the value of the convertible debenture if it is not converted.

The value equals the future flows discounted at 5%:

$$= \text{PV} (£10 \text{ for 6 years at } 5\%) + \text{PV} (£106 \text{ in 6 years at } 5\%)$$

$$= (£10 \times 5.076) + (£106 \times 0.746) = £129.84$$

Step 3 Calculate the equivalent current share price

Each debenture could be converted into 30 shares. For the investor to be indifferent, the shares must be worth $\dfrac{£129.84}{30} = £4.33$ each.

9.7 Formula values and market values

In practice convertibles often trade at considerably above their formula value. This excess is known as the **conversion premium**.

| Definition | The conversion premium of a convertible debenture is the difference between the debenture's formula value and its market value. |

9.8 The cost of a convertible debenture

It is quite easy to evaluate the cost of convertibles given certain information. The problem is directly analogous to valuing redeemable debentures, but the conversion value of the shares replaces the redemption price.

(a) Example without tax

Current debenture price is £50. Interest is £5 per annum. The debenture stock is expected to be converted in 5 years. Conversion ratio is 50 shares per £100 stock. Share price is expected to be £1.50 in 5 years' time. The cost of the convertibles is the IRR of

Time	Cashflow	
0	50	Price
1-5	(5)	Interest
5	(50 × 1.50)	Conversion value

which approximates to 17%.

It is concluded that the return on the convertible is 17%.

(b)   **Example with tax**

From the point of view of the company, the cost is reduced by the tax relief on the interest payments. If the corporation tax rate is 30%, the cost is the IRR of the flows shown above, with annual interest now being $5 \times (1-0.3) = 3.5$.

You should be able to show this is approximately 14%.
The major problem here is the input data. Specifically, the following questions may be asked.

(a)   How do we know what the share price will be in the future?

(b)   When will investors convert - normally several conversion dates are possible?

(c)   Will the firm 'call' the debenture? Early redemption on the part of the firm is normally possible, as with a straight debenture.

10   THE RELEVANCE OF ACCOUNTING INFORMATION TO SHARE VALUATION

10.1   Application of financial accounts

Financial accounting information is traditionally prepared under the historical cost convention, so it is recording past events. The value of a share theoretically equals the present value of future cash inflows, whose size is unknown since they will only be paid in the future. So the principal use of financial accounts will be as a basis to forecast the future.

Some specific uses have already been seen:

- the past growth in annual dividend payments can be calculated and used to estimate the future growth in dividends.

- the historical accounting rate of return can be used in the earnings growth model $g = rb$ to estimate the future growth in dividends.

There are other methods for valuing shares which are based on the figures in published financial accounts.

- net assets basis
- earnings basis

10.2   Net assets basis

One valuation basis for shares is to equate the value of a share with the net asset backing per share, so that

$$\text{Value per share} = \frac{\text{Net realisable value of assets - liabilities}}{\text{Number of shares}}$$

Such a basis is relevant if the company is about to be wound up, but it is inappropriate for a going concern.

10.3 Earnings basis

A valuation method can be applied using price earnings ratios of similar companies.

$$\text{PE ratio} = \frac{\text{Price per share}}{\text{Earnings per share}}$$

So we can use the equation:

Price per share = Earnings per share × PE ratio

For example, if the latest set of accounts for a food retailing company show earnings per share of 20p, and quoted food retailing companies are showing a prospective PE ratio of 15 at the time of valuation, the price per share would be estimated at 20p × 15 = £3.

11 PRACTICAL INFLUENCES ON SHARE PRICES

Share valuation is not an exact science. The above methods of valuing shares can all be applied to estimate the fair value of a particular share, but it is possible that the actual share price is different from all these theoretical values. Such a difference arises from a number of reasons

- different investors will apply different required rates of return to their NPV calculations, for example because of different tax positions

- technical factors. There is always likely to be an imbalance of buyers and sellers in the market for a particular share, a temporary surplus of buyers driving up the price while a temporary surplus of sellers would depress the share price

- arrival of new information. In an efficient stock market the share price will continually react to the publishing of new information relevant to the share.

| Conclusion | Share prices will not stay constant as predicted by valuation techniques, but will vary randomly about the fair values calculated by these models.

12 CHAPTER SUMMARY

Using the dividend valuation model, the formula for the price of a share was developed:

$$P_0 = \frac{D_0(1+g)}{K_e - g} = \frac{D_1}{K_e - g},$$
where P_0 is the ex div share price,

D_0 is the dividend just paid; D_1 is next year's dividend
K_e is the shareholders' required rate of return
(the cost of equity); and
g is the expected future growth rate of dividends.

The formula can be adapted to a share paying constant future dividends by putting g equal to zero; or rearranged to work out:

$$K_e = \frac{D_0(1+g)}{P_0} + g = \frac{D_1}{P_0} + g$$

g can be worked out by extending the past pattern of dividends, or by using the earnings growth model, g = rb, where r = the accounting rate of return and b = the proportion of earnings retained.

Since dividends are paid net of basic rate tax, as long as shareholders are basic rate taxpayers (the standard assumption), no adjustments need be made to account for tax.

The dividend valuation model principle can be applied to work out the cost of debt. There are different approaches for the three possible situations:

(i)   irredeemable debentures;

(ii)   redeemable debentures with market price = redemption price;

(iii)   redeemable debentures with market price ≠ redemption price;

Remember that when corporation tax is included, the return achieved by the debt holders (K) does not equal the cost of debt to the company (K').

Convertible debt and warrants are common alternatives to straight debt. The cost of a convertible debenture is calculated as if it were a redeemable debenture, with the conversion value replacing the redemption proceeds.

13   SELF TEST QUESTIONS

13.1   What is the cost of equity? (1.1)

13.2   What is a cum div share price? (1.8)

13.3   Describe the Gordon growth model. (2.4)

13.4   How are earnings treated in the dividend valuation model? (3.2)

13.5   How does tax affect the cost of equity in the dividend valuation model? (3.3)

13.6   Of which flows is the cost of redeemable debt ignoring corporation tax the IRR? (6.2)

13.7   How does corporation tax affect the cost of debt? (7.1)

13.8   What is a deep discounted bond? (8.1)

13.9   What is a convertible debenture? (9.1)

13.10   How is the cost of convertible debt calculated? (9.8)

14   EXAMINATION TYPE QUESTIONS

14.1   Investors' discount rate

(a)   An investor buys a share today at a cost of £1.50, ex div. He expects to hold it for five years, receiving a constant dividend each year of 10p, and sell it at the end of the period for £1.81, ex div.

What is the investor's required rate of return?   **(5 marks)**

(b)   Given the following information about shares, compute their current market price.

    (i)   X Ltd has 100,000 £1 ordinary shares, current dividends 10p each, expected to remain constant.

    (ii)   Y Ltd has 10,000 £1 ordinary shares, current dividend £500, expected to remain constant.

    (iii)   Z Ltd has 100,000 £1 ordinary shares. The dividend just paid was 5p, and this is expected to grow at 5% per annum.

Assume investors' required rate of return is 10%.   **(3 marks)**

(c)   Given the information that shares in M Ltd are currently quoted at 150p each ex div and the dividend just paid was 15p, what is the investors' required rate of return if:

    (i)   no growth in dividends is expected?

    (ii)   growth of 5% pa in dividends is expected?   **(2 marks)**

(Total: 10 marks)

14.2   Trendy and Jumbo

You are given the following information about two companies, which are both financed entirely by equity capital:

	Trendy Ltd	Jumbo Ltd
Number of ordinary shares of £1 ('000)	150,000	500,000
Market value per share, ex div (£)	3.42	0.65
Current earnings (Total) (£'000)	62,858	63,952
Current dividend (Total) (£'000)	6,158	48,130
Balance sheet value of capital employed (£'000)	315,000	293,000
Dividend five years ago (Total) (£'000)	2,473	37,600

Both companies are in the same line of business and sell similar products.

(a)   Estimate the cost of capital for both companies, using growth models.   **(5 marks)**

(b)   Describe, giving your reasons, any additional evidence to which you would refer in order to increase your confidence in the estimates of the cost of capital in practice.   **(5 marks)**

(Total: 10 marks)

14.3   Options, warrants and convertibles

(a)   Your company wishes to raise new debt capital on the stock market. Your managing director has heard of warrants and traded options and suggests that an issue of debt, accompanied by either attached warrants or traded options might be attractive to investors and have benefits for your company.

You are required to discuss whether you consider your managing director's suggestion to be useful.   **(5 marks)**

(b)   Several years ago Nopen plc issued 15% 15 year loan stock with warrants attached. The warrants may be exercised at any time during the next four years and each warrant allows the purchase of one ordinary share at a price of 400 pence.

The company has also issued a 9% convertible debenture which is due for redemption at the par value of £100 in five years' time. Conversion rights, which are available at any time up to the redemption date, allow the conversion of one debenture into 25 ordinary shares. The current market yield on straight debentures for a company of Nopen's risk class is 12% per year.

You are required: to estimate the minimum market price of a warrant and of a £100 convertible debenture if the current share price of Nopen is:

(i)   300 pence;
(ii)   420 pence;
(iii)   500 pence.

Explain why the market price of a warrant or convertible debenture is likely to be more than the price that you have estimated. Taxation may be ignored.   **(13 marks)**

(Total: 18 marks)

15   ANSWERS TO EXAMINATION TYPE QUESTIONS

15.1   Investors' discount rate

(a)   *(**Tutorial note:** this is **not** a constant dividend situation as there is a capital gain on the sale of the share. The following approach must therefore be used.)*

$$P_0 = \frac{D}{1+K_e} + \frac{D}{(1+K_e)^2} + \frac{D}{(1+K_e)^3} + \frac{D}{(1+K_e)^4} + \frac{D}{(1+K_e)^5}$$

where D = annual dividend or other inflow
                    K_e = investor's required return.

Substituting

$$150p = \frac{10p}{1+i} + \frac{10p}{(1+i)^2} + \frac{10p}{(1+i)^3} + \frac{10p}{(1+i)^4} + \frac{10p}{(1+i)^5} + \frac{181p}{(1+i)^5}$$

By trial and error this equation is satisfied when $K_e = 10\%$

Using factors from the tables

$$\begin{aligned} P_0 \quad &= \quad (3.791 \times 10)p + (0.621 \times 181)p \\ &= \quad 37.91 + 112.40 \\ &= \quad 150.31p \\ &\approx \quad 150p \text{ (the current price)} \end{aligned}$$

(b) $P_0 = \dfrac{D_0\,(1+g)}{K_e - g}$

Where P_0 =   current market price
            K_e =   investors' required rate of return
            D_0 =   annual dividend
            g =   annual growth rate.

Substituting

(i) $P_0 \quad = \quad \dfrac{£0.10}{0.1} \quad = £1.00$

(ii) $P_0 \quad = \quad \dfrac{£500}{10,000} \times \dfrac{1}{0.1} \quad = £0.50$

(iii) $P_0 \quad = \quad \dfrac{0.05(1+0.05)}{(0.1-.05)} = £1.05$

(c)   From equation in (b), $K_e = \dfrac{D_0\,(1+g)}{P_0} + g$

Substituting

(i) $K_e \quad = \quad \dfrac{£0.15}{£1.50} \quad = 0.10 \text{ or } 10\%$

(ii) $K_e \quad = \quad \dfrac{£0.15(1+0.05)}{£1.50} + 0.05 = 0.155 \text{ or } 15.5\%$

15.2   Trendy and Jumbo

(Tutorial note: dividend growth is an important variable in this question. In general terms try to use both the approaches we have developed if the data is available.*)*

(a)   The cost of equity can be estimated using the dividend valuation model involving predicted growth in dividends.

$$P_0 = \frac{D_0(1+g)}{K_e - g}$$

Where P_0 = market value per share at present, ex dividend
D_0 = dividend per share just paid
g = predicted constant growth rate in dividends
K_e = shareholders' required rate of return (cost of equity).

Rearranging

$$K_e = \frac{D_0(1+g)}{P_0} + g$$

The first step involves estimating the shareholders' prediction of the future growth rate. This might be taken from the past rate of growth, or by using accounting information and the Gordon growth model.

Estimates of g

(i)   **Past growth rate**

	Trendy Ltd	Jumbo Ltd
$\dfrac{\text{Current dividend}}{\text{Dividend five years ago}}$	$\dfrac{6{,}158}{2{,}473} = 2.49$	$\dfrac{48{,}130}{37{,}600} = 1.28$
Growth rate $(1+g)^5$ from compounding tables	20%	5%

(ii)   **Gordon growth model**

$g = rb$

where r = average rate of return on funds reinvested
b = proportion of profits reinvested.

According to Gordon, r might be estimated by shareholders as the return on capital employed from the published accounts.

	Trendy Ltd	Jumbo Ltd
$r = \dfrac{\text{Current earnings}}{\text{Capital employed}}$	$\dfrac{62{,}858}{315{,}000} = 0.1995$	$\dfrac{63{,}952}{293{,}000} = 0.2183$
$b = \dfrac{\text{Current earnings less current dividend}}{\text{Current earnings}}$	$\dfrac{62{,}858 - 6{,}158}{62{,}858}$	$\dfrac{63{,}952 - 48{,}130}{63{,}952}$
	$= 0.902$	$= 0.2474$
$g = rb$	0.18 or **18%**	0.054 or **5.4%**

Cost of equity shares

	Trendy Ltd	*Jumbo Ltd*

$$K_e = \frac{D_0(1+g)}{P_0} + g$$

g from past growth rate $\quad \dfrac{6{,}158 \times 1.2}{150{,}000 \times 3.42} + 0.2 \qquad \dfrac{48{,}130 \times 1.05}{500{,}000 \times 0.65} + 0.05$

$$= \textbf{21.44\%} \qquad\qquad = \textbf{20.55\%}$$

g from Gordon model $\quad \dfrac{6{,}158 \times 1.18}{150{,}000 \times 3.42} + 0.18 \qquad \dfrac{48{,}130 \times 1.054}{500{,}000 \times 0.65} + 0.054$

$$= \textbf{19.42\%} \qquad\qquad = \textbf{21.01\%}$$

Despite the difference in dividend policies and growth rates between the two companies it can be seen that their cost of capital is roughly equal. If the companies are in the same type of business and have the same level of risk, these results are in line with the prediction of the dividend valuation model.

(b)   **Additional evidence which might increase confidence in the estimates**

    (i)   The structure of interest rates at present - in order to see whether the figures are of a reasonable order of magnitude. The cost of equity shares should be equal to the 'risk-free' rate of interest (estimated from short-dated government stocks) plus a 'risk premium' which depends on the risk of the company.

    (ii)   Movements of market value of the shares over the last five years. It is assumed that the current market value is an equilibrium value which has resulted from steady growth over the period. If market values are abnormally high or low at the moment (eg, because a takeover bid is expected) the calculations will be invalid.

    (iii)   Dividends for each of the last five years for more confidence in the past growth rate. Similar figures for earnings and market value should give roughly the same growth rate.

    (iv)   Details of any published plans for the companies which might alter shareholders' expectations.

15.3   Options, warrants and convertibles

(Tutorial note: the managing director is in fact in error. Companies do not issue traded options.)

(a)   Warrants allow the holders at their option to buy a predetermined number of shares at a given price at a given time. They usually have an expiry date and if by this time the market price of the underlying share has not risen above the warrant exercise price then holders will choose not to exercise them. Alternatively if share prices have risen above this level they allow holders to buy equity at less than market price. A loan stock with warrants can be used by the company for two main reasons:

    (i)   A 'sweetener' for the debt issue. The possibility of buying equity at a discount price means that the interest rate on the loan stock can be set at a lower level than straight debt.

    (ii)   A way of providing new equity capital in the future if warrants are exercised.

Traded options are **not** issued by companies. They are options arranged through a broker to buy (call) or sell (put) shares in a number of major companies. They are for periods of three to nine months and allow the holders to buy or sell shares at a predetermined price and time.

Issuing debt with warrants could be a useful tactic for the company but the suggestion of using traded options is of no value as firms do not issue traded options.

(b)   **Warrant**

Minimum value of warrant is the higher of zero (the warrant is not exercised) or its underlying equity value

Share price (pence)	Minimum value of 400p warrant
300	0
420	20p (420 – 400)
500	100p (500 – 400)

Convertible debenture

Minimum value of a convertible loan stock is the higher of its value as debt (ie, as a straight loan stock) or its value when converted into equity.

Value as debt: =   PV [£9 for 5 years at 12%] + PV [£100 in 5 years at 12%]

(Discount rate employed is that for a straight loan stock)

$$= \quad (3.605 \times £9) + (100 \times 0.567)$$

$$= \quad £89.145$$

Share price pence	Value as debt £	Value as equity £	Minimum market price £
300	89.145	75 (300p × 25)	89.145
420	89.145	105 (420p × 25)	105
500	89.145	125 (500p × 25)	125

These figures represent minimum values. If investors believe there is further potential for growth in equity prices then significant premiums could be paid. This premium is usually most apparent when current conversion is only just worthwhile as at this point the investment can easily rise in price but it cannot fall ie, there is little downside risk.

5 PORTFOLIO THEORY

INTRODUCTION & LEARNING OBJECTIVES

The straightforward calculations of the cost of capital of the various financial instruments were covered fully in the previous chapter. In this chapter, we examine how risk can affect considerations of the cost of capital.

This chapter combines aspects of your earlier studies dealing with indifference curves and with statistical measures. You are shown how the risk and return characteristics of a portfolio can be calculated from the risks and returns of the individual investments that make up the portfolio. This area of investment analysis is called portfolio theory.

Don't worry if the mathematics in this chapter looks complicated when you first see it. Try to pick up the basic conclusions first, and the mathematical proofs can follow later.

When you have studied this chapter you should be able to do the following:

- Understand how combining investments can reduce overall risk without reducing expected returns.
- Appreciate that the degree of risk reduction possible depends on the correlation between the underlying investments.
- Calculate correlation coefficients between two investments.
- Explain the trade-off between risk and return when combining a risky security with a risk-free security.
- Understand the conclusion that any investor's optimal portfolio is a weighting between risk-free securities and the market portfolio, depending on his personal indifference curves.
- Explain the equation of the capital market line.

---

1 INTRODUCTION TO PORTFOLIO THEORY

1.1 Uncertainty in returns

One approach for dealing with uncertainty in project returns is to increase the required rate of return on risky projects.

Such an approach is commonly taken by investors. For example, if we were comparing a Building Society investment with one in equities we would normally require a higher return from equities to compensate us for their extra risk. In a similar way if we were appraising equity investments in a food retailing company against a similar investment in a computer electronics firm we would usually demand higher returns from the electronics investment to reflect its higher risk.

Clearly use of a 'risk adjusted discount rate' can be employed in almost any situation involving risk. The practical problem is how much return should we demand for a given level of risk. To solve this problem we can turn to the Stock Exchange – a place where risk and return combinations (securities) are bought and sold every day. If, for example, we can better the return earned by investors on the stock market by investing in a physical asset offering the same level of risk, we can increase investor wealth and the investment should be adopted.

Unfortunately the required approach is not as simple as this. Investors seldom hold securities in isolation. They usually attempt to reduce their risks by 'not putting all their eggs into one basket' and therefore hold portfolios of securities. Before we can deduce a risk-adjusted discount rate from stock exchange returns we need to identify the risks taken by investors in their diversified investment portfolios.

1.2   The benefits of portfolio diversification

A portfolio is simply a combination of investments. If an investor puts half of his funds into an engineering company and half into a retail shops firm then it is possible that any misfortunes in the engineering company (eg, a strike) may be to some extent offset by the performance of the retail investment. It would be unlikely that both would suffer a strike in the same period.

This effect can be demonstrated more formally in the following graphs. Assume we have two companies, A and B, whose fortunes are inversely correlated (ie, when A does well B does badly and vice versa).

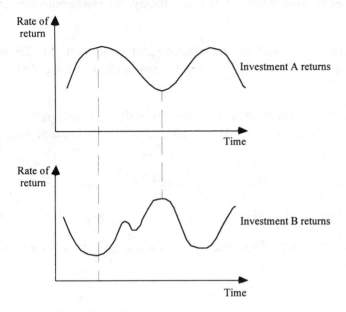

Both investment A and investment B show fluctuating returns over time. They both have roughly the same amount of variability. When A does well, B does badly, and vice versa.

If both investments are held, the resulting portfolio will generate a greater average (absolute) return than with either one alone but a greatly reduced risk, because the 'ups' of A cancel with the 'downs' of B and vice versa.

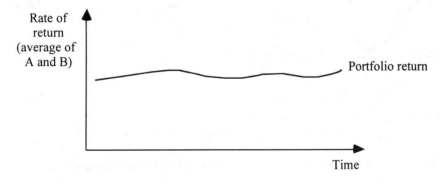

The same effect can be illustrated by a simple computational example.

Example 1

Mr Mario sells ice cream from a stall on the seafront at Brighton during the tourist season. His sales are affected by the British weather which is rather unpredictable. There are two possible states of the weather: sun and rain. In Brighton, when it is sunny, it is sunny all day, but when it rains, it rains all day. Mr Mario has noticed that during the tourist season half the days are sunny and half are rainy. When the sun is out he makes a daily contribution of £200, but when it rains he only makes £20.

A few yards down the road Mr Hashimoto also operates a stall, from which he sells cheap throw-away Japanese umbrellas which always seem to last one day before the spokes break. These are very popular with tourists who are caught out by the rain. When it rains, Mr Hashimoto makes a daily contribution of £200, but when the sun shines, he only makes £20.

State	Sun	Rain	Average	Risk
Probability	0.5	0.5		
Contribution: ice creams	200	20	110	High
Contribution: umbrellas	20	200	110	High

Although both businesses are profitable, the traders are a bit unhappy about riding the roller-coaster of risk. Also, they never talk to each other because when Mr Mario is happy, Mr Hashimoto is miserable and vice versa.

As it happens, one bank holiday Monday, a well known management consultant, Mr Drizzle, is spending the day on Brighton beach. He succeeds in persuading the two traders to swap their secrets and pool their resources.

Now both Mr Mario and Mr Hashimoto hold half their stock as umbrellas and half as ice creams. When it is sunny they both make $(1/2 \times 200) + (1/2 \times 20) = £110$, and when it rains they both make $(1/2 \times 20) + (1/2 \times 200) = £110$.

State	Sun	Rain	Average	Risk
Probability	0.5	0.5		
Contribution	110	110	110	Zero

Now both men are reasonably happy all the time. They each have as much money as before, but it is earned risk-free. They even talk to each other.

1.3   Correlation

Correlation is a statistical measure of how strong the connection is between two variables. In portfolio theory the two variables are the returns of two investments. **High positive correlation** means that both investments tend to show increases (or decreases) in return at the same time:

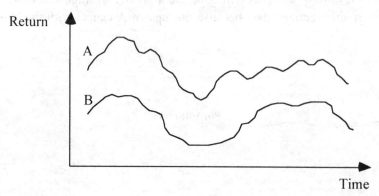

High negative correlation means that as returns on A increase, returns on B decrease:

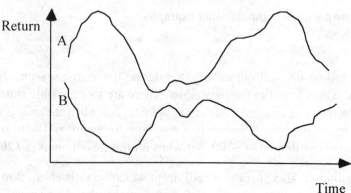

The degree of risk reduction possible by combining the investments depends on the correlation between them.

The coefficient of correlation is measured on a scale from −1 (perfect negative correlation) to +1 (perfect positive correlation).

Perfect negative correlation can, but will not always, completely eliminate risk (see Example 1).

A correlation coefficient *less than +1* can reduce risk. The further the correlation coefficient is from +1 the greater the potential risk reduction.

1.4   Activity

State why it is that combining two investments with perfect negative correlation might not completely eliminate risk.

1.5   Activity solution

The investments might have returns which, although they are perfectly negatively correlated, are of different absolute sizes.

Consider, for example, Mr Mario earning £400 when it is sunny and £40 when it rains, while Mr Hashimoto earns £20 when it is sunny and £200 when it rains.

Once more the investments have perfect negative correlation but their combination offers £420 when it is sunny and £240 when it rains ie, some risk remains.

1.6   The risk and return of portfolios

A formal analysis of the combination of two investments is now presented. Because portfolio theory has its roots in the management of stock exchange investments, this is referred to as the **two-security portfolio**. The theory starts by identifying measures of risk and return for an investment.

The analysis is usually presented in terms of **rates of return** over a single time period.

|Definition| The rate of return (IRR) over a single time period is simply:

$$\frac{(\text{End of period value} - \text{start of period value}) + \text{Dividend paid}}{\text{Start of period value}}$$

For example, if an investment is predicted to rise from a value now of £8,000 to a value in one year of £9,000, and a dividend of £1,000 will be paid in the period, it has a predicted rate of return of

$$\frac{£(9,000 - 8,000) + £1,000}{£8,000} = 25\%$$

This is just as we have defined return to investors previously - dividend yield plus capital growth.

We also need a measure of the risk of a particular security.

|Definition| The **risk** of an investment can be measured by the **Standard deviation** of its expected returns.

Remember that, if possible returns are R_1, R_2,........R_n, with associated probabilities P_1, P_2,........P_n, then the standard deviation is calculated as

$$\sigma = \sqrt{\Sigma\left(R_i - \bar{R}\right)^2 P_i} \quad \text{where } \bar{R} \text{ is the average return, } \Sigma R_i P_i$$

Example 2

Suppose we are trying to forecast the possible rates of return of two investments over the next year.

We make predictions as follows:

Economic climate	Probability of economic climate	Returns from A %	Returns from B %
Recession	0.2	10	6
Stable	0.5	14	15
Expansion	0.3	20	11
	1.0		

Firstly, calculate the expected return and standard deviation of each investment. This tells us the risk and return of each security if held in isolation.

Investment A

Economic climate	Probability P	Return R_A%	$P \times R_A$	$R_A - \bar{R}_A$	$P(R_A - \bar{R}_A)^2$
R	0.2	10	2	-5	5.0
S	0.5	14	7	-1	0.5
E	0.3	20	6	+5	7.5
			$\bar{R}_A = 15\%$	Variance of return A =	13.0
				SD, σ_A	$=**\sqrt{13.0}$
					$=$ 3.6%

** recall that standard deviation $= \sqrt{variance}$

Investment B

Economic climate	Probability P	Return R_B%	$P \times R_B$	$R_B - \bar{R}_B$	$P(R_B - \bar{R}_B)^2$
R	0.2	6	1.2	−6	7.2
S	0.5	15	7.5	+3	4.5
E	0.3	11	3.3	−1	0.3
			$\bar{R}_B = 12\%$	Variance of return B =	12.0
				SD, σ_B =	$\sqrt{12.0}$
					= 3.46%

Summary

Investment	A	B
Expected return	15%	12%
Risk, σ	3.60%	3.46%

Consider now constructing a portfolio consisting of one-half of the total amount invested in investment A and one-half in investment B.

Under each economic climate the return of the portfolio would be the average of A and B. Compute the expected value and standard deviation of this portfolio:

Portfolio $\frac{1}{2}$A and $\frac{1}{2}$B

Economic climate	Probability P	Return R%	PR	$R - \bar{R}$	$P(R-\bar{R})^2$
R	0.2	$\frac{(10+6)}{2} = 8$	1.60	−5.5	6.05
S	0.5	$\frac{(14+15)}{2} = 14.5$	7.25	+1.0	0.50
E	0.3	$\frac{(20+11)}{2} = 15.5$	4.65	+2.0	1.20

$$\bar{R} = 13.50\%$$

Variance of return B = 7.75

SD, σ = $\sqrt{7.75}$ = 2.78%

The portfolio has an expected return which is equal to the weighted average of the two investment returns, but its risk, as measured by standard deviation, is lower than either of the two original investments. (This can also be seen by looking at the low **spread** of possible returns of the portfolio: 8% to 15.5%.)

1.7 Indifference curves

Consider the three possible portfolios constructed so far.

	100% A	100% B	50% A and 50% B
Return	15%	12%	13.5%
Risk	3.60%	3.46%	2.78%

Which of these portfolios is preferable? It all depends on the investor's attitude to risk against return, which may be depicted diagrammatically as 'indifference curves'. The following diagram shows three possible investments (R, S and T), their positions on the graph being determined by their return/risk combination. The investor who is trying to decide between them has indifference curves as shown.

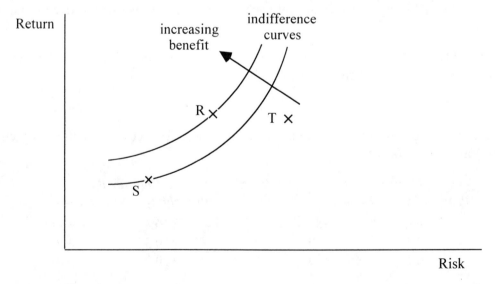

The indifference curves represent alternative combinations of risk and return between which the investor is indifferent. Obviously each investor will have different indifference curves, but they will tend to be of the slope indicated above. This is because most investors are averse to risk, and will demand a higher return to compensate.

Thus, the indifference curves represent the trade-off between risk and return for an individual investor.

In this example, the investor would prefer R to S as it is on a higher indifference curve – the lower level of risk for S does not adequately compensate for the lower level of return.

Question:

Would the investor prefer T to R on the above diagram?

Solution:

No - R is on a higher indifference curve than T.

Note that another investor with a more risk-averse attitude may have much steeper indifference curves (requiring a much greater compensation in return for the same change in risk) which could mean they have a different order of preference:

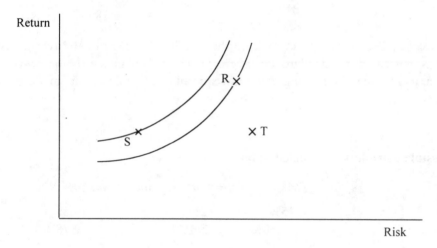

Here, the investor would prefer S to R.

1.8   The concept of utility

One way of drawing up an investor's indifference curves is to examine the concept of utility. The technique involves establishing utility values for each of the possible cash flows which might result from the investment.

In this context, utility simply measures the satisfaction felt at receiving or losing a sum of money and it is conveniently measured on a scale from 0 to 100.

Example

Mr Hayser, the Managing Director of Kite Ltd, is offered a choice between two contracts which have the following possible cash flows:

	Contract A			*Contract B*	
Probability	*NPV in £'000*			*Probability*	*NPV in £'000*
0.6	+80			0.5	+50
0.1	+10			0.3	+30
0.3	−30			0.2	−10
Expected monetary NPV	40				32

By computing the expected monetary NPV it appears that Contract A is preferable. However, a closer look at the possible results shows that A is more risky than B. The company may not be prepared to take the risk of losing £30,000. In general,

the more widely dispersed the possible results are, the more risky the investment is seen to be.

To take account of this problem, we decide to establish the decision maker's attitude to gaining or losing sums from + £80,000 to − £30,000.

To start with we arbitrarily assign a utility value of 100 to + £80,000 and a value of 0 to - £30,000.

To establish the utility values for the other sums we must ask Mr Hayser a number of questions. These take the form of preference tests. For example, to establish the utility of £50,000 we may ask: which would you prefer:
(a)   £50,000 for certain; or
(b)   a 75% chance of gaining £80,000 and a 25% chance of losing £30,000?

Disregarding expected values, Mr Hayser may say 'I prefer £50,000 with certainty'. We therefore increase the odds of gaining and try again. Suppose Mr Hayser is just about indifferent between:

(a)   gaining £50,000 for certain; and
(b)   a 90% chance of gaining £80,000 and a 10% chance of losing £30,000.

We then calculate his utility value for £50,000 as follows:

$$U (£50,000) = 0.9 \times U (£80,000) + 0.1 \times U (- £30,000)$$
$$= 0.9 \times 100 + 0.1 \times 0$$
$$= 90$$

We then establish utility for all the other possible outcomes in the same manner.

Assuming Mr Hayser is a typically risk averse investor, the utility values would be something like this:

Money £'000	Utility
80	100
50	90
30	80
10	50
0	30
− 10	20
− 30	0

The expected utility value of each contract, which takes into account Mr Hayser's attitude to risk, is:

Contract A: $(0.6 \times 100) + (0.1 \times 50) + (0.3 \times 0)$ =   65

Contract B: $(0.5 \times 90) + (0.3 \times 80) + (0.2 \times 20)$ =   73

The expected utility value of doing nothing is 30.

It can be seen that contract B is preferred by Mr Hayser, indicating that he is risk averse when confronted with sums of money of this magnitude.

1.9   The shape of the utility function

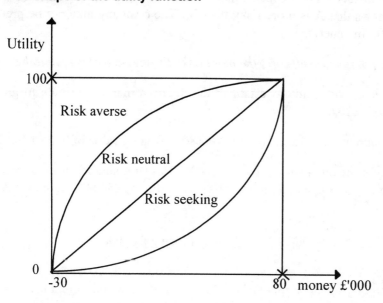

A risk neutral decision maker assigns utility proportionately to the money value.

For a risk averse individual, increasing money shows a decreasing rate of increase in utility. For a risk seeker, who tends to ignore possible losses, but derives great pleasure from contemplating possible gains, the curve shows an increasing slope.

Information derived from the formulation of an investor's utility function can be used to construct his/her indifference curves for comparison at investments with different risk/return combinations.

1.10   Activity

Plot a graph of utility against money value for Mr Hayser in the last example, and convince yourself that he is indeed risk averse.

1.11   Practical problems of utility

Utility is often described as an elegant but unpractical solution to the treatment of risk. In theory, it can overcome the obvious problems of expected value but in practice it is very difficult to derive the utility functions of decision-makers.

The above question and answer approach has been used to determine individual utility functions (try it yourself) but problems arise on its application to groups. Decisions are commonly made by groups of managers and it is likely that their utility functions will differ considerably.

Further, if managers are acting as representatives of shareholders, decisions should be made accordingly to investor utility functions. However, the chances of compiling a utility function that represents the attitudes of all shareholders would seem slim.

1.12   Graphical illustration

Ignoring the practical problems in deriving utility functions, we can plot a series of indifference curves for a particular investor to decide whether he would prefer the original choice of investments: A, B or a portfolio of half A and half B

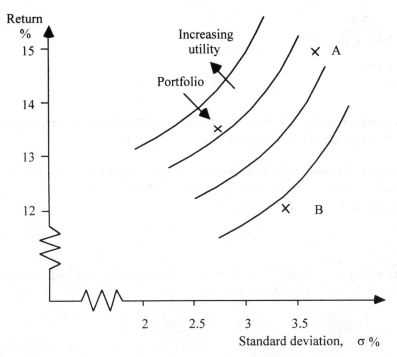

The investor whose indifference curves are illustrated prefers the portfolio to either of investments A or B in isolation.

1.13   Covariance and correlation

The risk reduction in the last example was made possible by low correlation between the investments. Just looking at the possible returns of A and B shows that there is no consistent positive or negative relationship between them. The correlation coefficient will probably be just higher than zero.

One way of computing the correlation coefficient is to first compute the covariance, which is defined as:

$$\text{Cov}_{x,\,y} = \Sigma\, p\, (x - \overline{x})\, (y - \overline{y})$$

where x, y are corresponding returns from investments X and Y arising with probability p

The covariance will be positive for positive correlation and negative for negative correlation, but its size depends on the size of the figures in the original data and is difficult to interpret.

The correlation coefficient is the ratio of the covariance to the product of the two standard deviations and will vary between – 1 and +1.

$$\text{Correlation},\ \rho_{x,y}\quad = \quad \frac{\text{Cov}_{x,\,y}}{\sigma_x \sigma_y}$$

(The Greek letter ρ (rho) is normally used for correlation in portfolio theory, because the usual symbol R would be confused with return.)

Applying these formulae to the two investments in the example:

Covariance (A, B)

Economic climate	Probability P	$R_A - \overline{R}_A$	$R_B - \overline{R}_B$	$P(R_A - \overline{R}_A)(R_B - \overline{R}_B)$
R	0.2	–5	–6	+6.0
S	0.5	–1	+3	–1.5
E	0.3	+5	–1	–1.5
			Cov (A, B)	+3.0

$$\text{Correlation, } \rho_{A,\,B} \quad = \quad \frac{+3.0}{3.6 \times 3.46}$$

$$= \quad +0.24$$

Conclusion The positive covariance tells us there is a positive relationship between returns on A and B but the strength of the relationship is not quantified.

The correlation coefficient indicates that the positive correlation is quite weak. Significant risk reduction is therefore possible. *Note* once again that negative correlation is not necessary for risk reduction.

1.14 Activity

Without carrying out any calculations, estimate the correlation coefficient between investments A and B, between B and C, and between A and C from the data below.

Economic climate	Probability	Expected investment returns		
		A %	B %	C %
Recession	0.3	5	10	10
Stable	0.5	10	8	12
Expansion	0.2	15	4	15

1.15 Activity solution

A and B have strong negative correlation, approximately –0.95

B and C have strong negative correlation, approximately –0.95

A and C have strong positive correlation, approximately +0.95

1.16 Formulae for the two-security portfolio

In general, the risk of a two-security portfolio will depend on:

(a)   the risk of the constituent investments in isolation;
(b)   the correlation between them; and
(c)   the proportion in which the investments are mixed.

General formulae for the return and risk of the two-security portfolios have been developed. These are now stated:

If $\bar{r}_A$ =   expected return of investment A (as a percentage)

$\bar{r}_B$ =   expected return of investment B (as a percentage)

x_A =   proportion of investment A in the portfolio

$(1-x_A)$ =   proportion of investment B, then:

Expected return of the portfolio, $\bar{r}_p = x_A \bar{r}_A + (1 - x_A)\bar{r}_B$

Conclusion The expected return on a portfolio equals the weighted average of the expected returns of its constituent investments.

Note: proportions are measured as amounts invested in each of A and B compared to total amount invested.

If Var_A =   variance of investment A

        Var_B =   variance of investment B

        $Cov_{A, B}$ =   Covariance between them, then:

Variance of the portfolio, $Var_p = x_A{}^2 Var_A + (1-x_A)^2 Var_B + 2x_A(1-x_A) Cov_{A, B}$

The standard deviation can then be found by taking the square root.

You could be required to know these equations in the examination.

These formulae will now be applied to the example where A and B were mixed half and half.

	A	B
Investment:	A	B
Expected return:	15%	12%
Variance:	13	12

Covariance:	3
x_A:	0.5

Expected return of portfolio, $\overline{r_p}$ = $(0.5 \times 15\%) + (0.5 \times 12\%)$

                                                    =   13.5%

Variance of portfolio, Var_p = $(0.5^2 \times 13) + (0.5^2 \times 12) + (2 \times 0.5 \times 0.5 \times 3)$

                                          =   3.25 + 3 + 1.5

                                          =   7.75

Portfolio standard deviation   = $\sqrt{7.75}$

                                            =   2.78%

Note: that this is less than the weighted average of the standard deviations of the constituent securities. This will be the case unless we are dealing with perfect positive correlation.

These results are in accordance with those produced from first principles in the previous paragraphs.

The advantage of the formulae is that they provide a way of quickly assessing portfolio return and risk if the investments are combined in different proportions.

Example 3

Compute the return and risk of portfolios of investments A and B when the proportions of total amount invested are as follows:

		A	B
Investment:		A	B
(a)	Proportion:	0.2	0.8
(b)	Proportion:	0.7	0.3

Solution

(a) $x_A = 0.2$

      r_p = $(0.2 \times 15\%) + (0.8 \times 12\%)$

              =   12.6%

      Var_p = $(0.2^2 \times 13) + (0.8^2 \times 12) + (2 \times 0.2 \times 0.8 \times 3)$

              =   9.16

$$\sigma_p = \sqrt{9.16}$$
$$= 3.03\%$$

(b) $x_A = 0.7$

$$r_p = (0.7 \times 15\%) + (0.3 \times 12\%)$$
$$= 14.1\%$$

$$\text{Var}_p = (0.7^2 \times 13) + (0.3^2 \times 12) + (2 \times 0.7 \times 0.3 \times 3)$$
$$= 8.71$$

$$\sigma_p = \sqrt{8.71}$$
$$= 2.95\%$$

These results can be presented on the usual graph of return and risk:

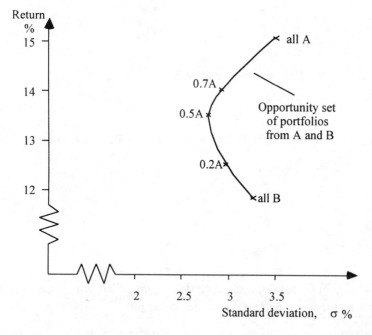

The graph now shows the 'opportunity set' of all possible portfolios which can be constructed from investments A and B by varying the proportions of each investment.

The optimal combination of A and B would be found by superimposing the indifference curves for a particular investor on the graph:

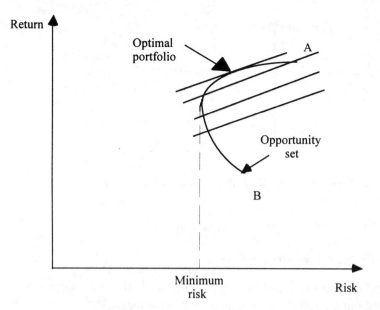

The rationale is as for all indifference curve theory you have encountered in earlier studies. The optimal portfolio is the point where an indifference curve is a tangent to (just touches) the opportunity set.

1.17 Two-security portfolios – Effect of the correlation coefficient

Maximum risk reduction is possible with a correlation of –1. In this case, risk can be (but is not always) reduced to zero. If correlation is +1, the portfolio risk is simply a weighted average of the investment risks.

In both these cases, the opportunity set of possible portfolios will lie along straight lines on the graph, as shown below.

For a correlation less than +1 but greater than –1, the opportunity set will lie along a curve as in the previous example.

The effect is conveniently illustrated on a set of graphs:

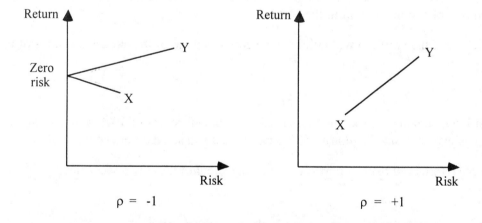

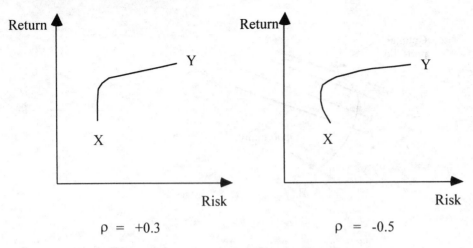

$$\rho = +0.3 \qquad\qquad\qquad \rho = -0.5$$

1.18   Portfolio selection with both risky and risk-free assets

There is a special case of the two-security portfolio which is particularly important for our later studies. This is the case of combining a risk-free security with a risky security.

A 'risk-free' security is one which shows no variability in its predicted returns. In other words its return is known with certainty. In practice it can be approximated by an investment in government stocks or bank deposit accounts at fixed interest (although varying rates of inflation would mean the real return on these investments becomes uncertain).

A risk-free security has a zero variance, and a zero covariance with any other security (check that this must be so by examining the formulae for variance and covariance).

The formula for the variance of the two-security portfolio therefore reduces as follows:

$$Var_p = x_A^2 \, Var_A + 0 + 0$$

where Var_A = variance of risky investment A.

Taking square roots: $\sigma_p = x_A \, \sigma_A$

In other words, the portfolio standard deviation is simply the standard deviation of the risky investment times the proportion of that investment in the portfolio.

The expected return of the portfolio will still be a weighted average of the expected returns of the two investments.

Example 4

You can invest in Government stock, showing a risk-free annual return of 10%, and also in shares in BP plc, which you expect to show a return of 25% pa, subject to a standard deviation of 10%.

Show the possible returns and risks of portfolios constructed out of these two securities.

Solution

Let x_A be the proportional amount of investment in shares in the portfolio.

x_A	Portfolio expected return	Portfolio risk $x_A\sigma_A$
1	25%	10%
0.8	$(0.8 \times 25\%) + (0.2 \times 10\%) = 22\%$	$0.8 \times 10\% = 8\%$
0.5	$(0.5 \times 25\%) + (0.5 \times 10\%) = 17.5\%$	$0.5 \times 10\% = 5\%$
0	10%	0

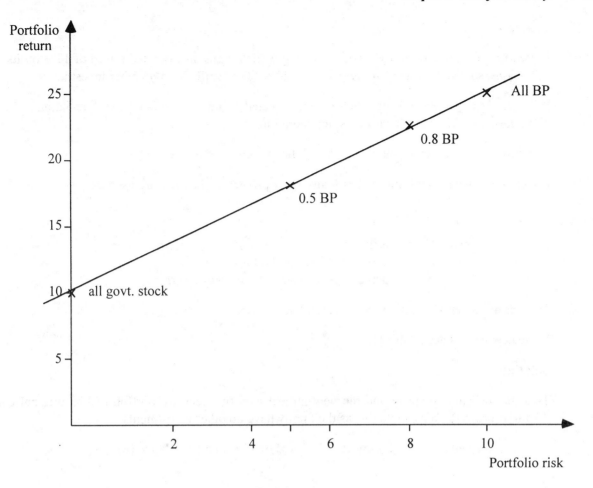

> | Conclusion | When combining a risk-free security with a risky security, there is a **straight line** trade-off between return and risk.

1.19   Activity

What sort of risk-free return is currently available at the time that you read this? You can obtain estimates from looking up the returns available from deposit accounts at banks and building societies, or from government stocks.

1.20   Activity solution

When this paragraph was written, building society 90-day notice deposit accounts were offering about 7.6% gross pa, while short-term gilts were offering about 6.9% gross pa as gross redemption yield.

1.21   Portfolio theory and project appraisal

We are now in a position to apply the principles of portfolio theory to project appraisal by a firm. We cannot yet develop a risk-adjusted discount rate but in considering risk the following fundamental point should be clear.

The relevant risk of a security (or any investment) is not its own risk but its effect on the risk of the portfolio to which it is added.

(To demonstrate: In section 1.6 above it would be unwise only to independently evaluate the risk of security A and B by considering their individual standard deviations, as when combined together their risk is greatly reduced.)

Example 5

Haven Ltd is a private family owned company which earns an expected return of 12% on its existing operations, subject to a standard deviation of 20%. The family hold no other investments.

It is considering a new project which has an expected return of 16%, a standard deviation of 32% and a correlation of 0.25 with Haven's existing operations.

The new project would account for 25% of Haven's operations if accepted.

Haven uses a measure of utility to appraise risky projects. The measure used is:

$$U = 100r - \sigma^2$$

where U = utility

r = percentage expected return

σ = percentage standard deviation of return.

Projects are acceptable if they increase total utility.

Is the new project acceptable?

Solution

Treat the original company and the new project as a two-security portfolio (0.75 original company: 0.25 new project). We can do this as the family have no other investments.

Expected return with project	=	$(0.75 \times 12\%) + (0.25 \times 16\%)$
	=	13%
Variance of original company	=	20^2
	=	400
Variance of project	=	32^2
	=	1,024
Covariance	=	$\rho\, \sigma_A \sigma_B$
	=	$0.25 \times 20 \times 32$
	=	160
∴ Variance of company with project	=	$x_A^2\, Var_A + (1-x_A)^2\, Var_B + 2x_A\,(1-x_A)\, Cov_{A,B}$
	=	$(0.75^2 \times 400) + (0.25^2 \times 1,024) + (2 \times 0.75 \times 0.25 \times 160)$
	=	349
∴ Standard deviation with project	=	$\sqrt{349}$
	=	18.68%

Summary

	Without project	With project
Expected return, r	12%	13%
Standard deviation, σ	20%	18.68%
Utility, $100r - \sigma^2$	800	951

The project is clearly worthwhile. It is expected to increase return and lower overall risk, and also increase shareholders' utility.

| **Conclusion** | The above technique is interesting, but clearly unworkable in practice. Its real purpose is to show what factors **should** be considered in project appraisal and hence to show up the weaknesses of applying simple project appraisal techniques which ignore risk. |

If portfolio theory went no further than this it would be a very minor part of decision making theory. However, the principles of portfolio theory can be developed into a workable model for investment appraisal. This will be explored in the following sections.

2   THE DIVERSIFIED SHAREHOLDER AND THE CAPITAL MARKET

2.1   Mixing many risky securities

Portfolio theory has its roots in the management of investors' portfolios of stock exchange investments and fixed interest stocks. The following sections show how the attempt to identify an optimal portfolio for investors has led to a comprehensive but simple theory of how the capital market relates risk and return. This, in turn, will assist us in our attempt to adjust discount rates to allow for risk.

The previous section considered portfolios of two securities. It is easy to extend this theory to cover portfolios of many securities, noting that where returns are assessed in percentage terms:

(a)   The expected return of a portfolio is equal to the weighted average of the returns of the individual securities in the portfolio.

(b)   The risk of the portfolio depends on:

    (i)   the risk of each security in isolation;
    (ii)   the proportions in which the securities are mixed;
    (iii)   the correlations between every pair of securities in the portfolio.

When two securities were mixed, the possible portfolios lie on a curve linking the two securities (see above).

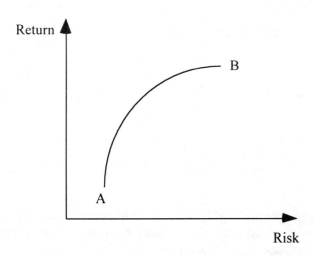

When three securities are mixed, the possible portfolios lie across an area on the graph like this:

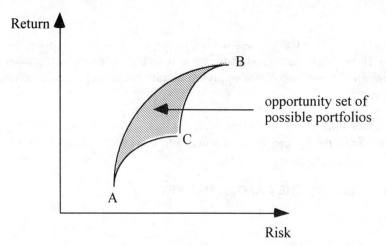

When many securities are mixed, the opportunity set is bigger:

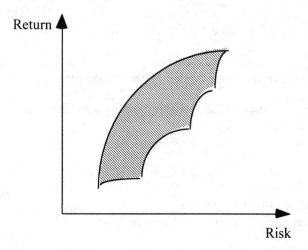

The shaded area shows the return and risk of all the possible portfolios constructed from the securities by mixing them in all possible proportions. In the 1950s, H M Markowitz developed this theory and showed how 'efficient portfolios' can be identified.

2.2   Efficient portfolios, mean-variance efficiency and the efficient frontier

It is possible to identify which of these portfolios are really worth holding.

A rational risk-averse investor would define an **efficient portfolio** as one that has:

(a)   a higher return than any other portfolio with the same risk; and

(b)   a lower risk than any other with the same return.

This simple approach is known as the **mean-variance efficiency rule** (return = mean or expected return; risk = variance or standard deviation).

So, out of all the possible portfolios which an investor could make out of his chosen securities, which are mean variance efficient? (Put another way, which portfolios would the investor select from, given logical assessment of the mean returns and variances of all those available?)

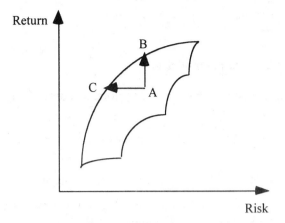

If we started with any portfolio A, in the middle of the opportunity set, then a better portfolio could be identified by moving upwards (higher return, same risk) or to the left (lower risk, same return).

Thinking in this way leads us to the conclusion that the efficient portfolios must lie along the top left hand edge of the opportunity set. This is called the **efficient frontier**.

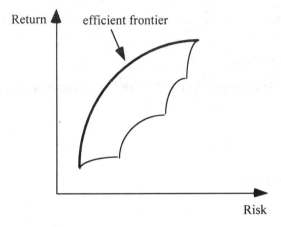

All other portfolios can now be ignored. Only the efficient ones need be considered. Logical investors would eliminate all others.

Notice the shape of this efficient frontier. As we attempt to increase return, risk begins to grow at an increasing rate.

An optimal portfolio could be identified for any investor by superimposing indifference curves on the efficient frontier.

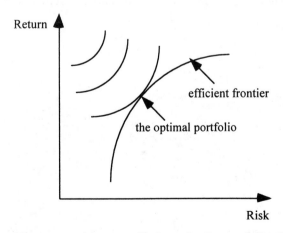

However, this so-called optimal portfolio has ignored the existence of fixed interest risk-free securities. These now need to be introduced. At this stage, it is convenient to build a simplified model of investor behaviour.

2.3   The market portfolio

The assumptions

A few assumptions are now made, in order to build a simple model:

(a)   Investors base their portfolio investment decisions on expected returns, standard deviation and correlations between all pairs of investments.

(b)   All investors have the same expectations about future outcomes over a one-period time horizon.

(c)   Investors may lend and borrow without limit at the (same) risk-free rate of interest.

(d)   There are no market imperfections: investments are infinitely divisible, information is costless, there are no taxes, transaction costs or interest rate charges, and no inflation.

Some of these assumptions are obviously unrealistic, but they greatly simplify the model-building process. Furthermore, even if the assumptions are relaxed, the theory will still hold approximately.

Building the model

(a)   Firstly, consider all the portfolios which could be constructed out of risky securities quoted on the stock market.

(b)   Then identify the efficient portfolios from these.

(c)   Then consider mixing any one of these efficient portfolios, A, with a risk-free investment, R_F:

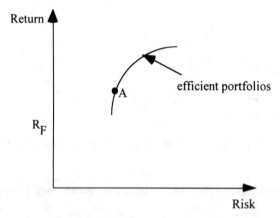

If all the investor's funds were put into the risk-free investment, he would earn the risk-free rate of interest and have no risk. If all his funds were put into portfolio A, he would have the return and risk of portfolio A. Referring back to paragraph 1.17, if he split his investment between R_F and A, the return and risk he would get would lie anywhere up a line joining R_F and A, depending on the proportions in which the funds were split.

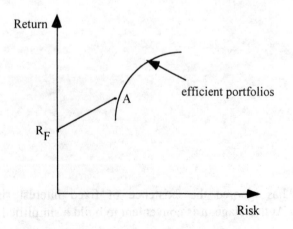

The section of the efficient frontier below A now becomes redundant because those portfolios are not so attractive as a combination of A with risk-free investments (the latter have a lower risk for the same return).

Portfolio A was chosen at random. If we chose one higher up the efficient frontier, the effect would be better:

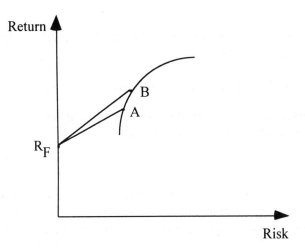

Any combination of R_F with portfolio B is better than ('dominates') a combination of R_F with portfolio A (higher return for the same risk).

Proceeding in this way, the best portfolio is M in the following diagram, where a line drawn from R_F just touches the efficient frontier at a tangent:

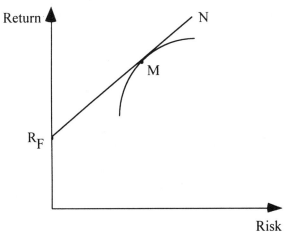

The surprising conclusion is that:

Conclusion	'Out of all the possible portfolios that could be constructed from risky investments, only one portfolio is worth considering – portfolio M.'

A combination of R_F and M produces portfolios which are better than any others in terms of the return which is offered for any given level of risk.

However, given the existence of risk-free investment, investors would choose from those on the revised efficient frontier represented by line R_FM.

Portfolios on the line R_F M are achieved by mixing portfolio M with risk-free investments. Portfolios on the line M N are achieved by borrowing at the risk-free rate (remember we have assumed that the risk-free rate applies to borrowing as well as lending) and investing our own funds plus borrowed funds in portfolio M.

What is portfolio M?

Because we have assumed that all investors have the same expectations about the future outcomes of investments, it follows that:

All investors will come to the conclusion that portfolio M is the best portfolio consisting solely of risky investments to hold.

Now, if any quoted share was not in portfolio M, then nobody would wish to hold it. It would therefore have no value. We must therefore conclude that:

Portfolio M includes every risky security which is quoted on the market.

Portfolio M is in fact simply a slice of the whole stock market; the proportions of shares held in it are the same as the total market capitalisations of the shares on the stock market:

Portfolio M is called the market portfolio.

All rational risk-averse investors will hold the market portfolio, according to the model we have just constructed. *Note* that it is not necessary for every investor to hold every share on the stock market. Close replicas of portfolio M may be generated by holding as few as fifteen shares. Investment in unit trusts will also achieve the same result.

However, all investors do not have the same attitude to risk. By using the market portfolio, and by either lending or borrowing suitably at the risk-free rate, the investor can choose any level of risk he likes and can predict the return which the market will give him. This return will be the best that he could possibly get for the risk taken.

By adding the investor indifference curves, we have:

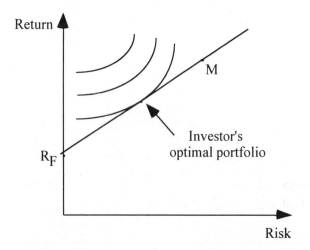

The trade-off between return and risk which is offered by this sensible use of the capital market is called the **capital market line**. This is effectively, as previously mentioned, our new efficient frontier.

2.4   Nature of the capital market line

We have already seen that combinations of risk-free and risky investments give a straight line trade-off between risk and return.

To draw the capital market line we therefore need only two observations:

(a) R_f – the risk-free rate of interest, which can be approximated by the return on government stock;

(b) R_M and σ_M – the risk and return of the market portfolio. As the market portfolio should contain all risky investments, this can be estimated by using the risk and return on a stock market index such as the Financial Times All Share Index.

Example 6

An investor has £100 to invest. The following information is available:

$$R_M \quad = \quad 15\%(\text{Return on portfolio M})$$
$$\sigma_M \quad = \quad 10\%(\text{Risk of portfolio M})$$
$$R_f \quad = \quad 6\%(\text{Risk-free rate of return}).$$

You are required to plot the capital market line and show that a lending portfolio (of £50 invested at the risk-free rate and £50 invested in portfolio M) and a borrowing portfolio (of £50 borrowed at risk-free rate and £150 invested in portfolio M) lie on this line.

Solution

To calculate portfolio returns we can treat the two investment opportunities as a two-asset portfolio, hence:

$$R_p \quad = \quad X_a \times \overline{R_a} + (1 - X_a) \times \overline{R_b}$$

$$\sigma_p \quad = \quad \sqrt{X_a^2 \times \text{Var}_a + (1 - X_a)^2 \text{Var}_b + 2X_a(1 - X_a)\text{Covar}_{a,b}}$$

Lending portfolio

$$R_p \quad = \quad 0.5 \times 15\% + 0.5 \times 6\%$$

$$\quad = \quad 10.5\%$$

$$\sigma_p \quad = \quad \sqrt{(0.5^2 \times 10^2) + (0.5^2 \times 0) + (2 \times 0.5 \times 0.5 \times 0)}$$

$$\quad = \quad \sqrt{0.5^2 \times 10^2}$$

$$\quad = \quad 5\%$$

Borrowing portfolio

Note: 150% of original stake is invested in M, 50% is borrowed.

$$R_p \quad = \quad (1.5 \times 15\%) - (0.5 \times 6\%)$$
$$\quad = \quad 19.5\%$$

$$\sigma_p \quad = \quad \sqrt{1.5^2 \times 10^2}$$
$$\quad = \quad 15\%$$

(This shows that gearing up equity portfolios is a profitable but risky business.)

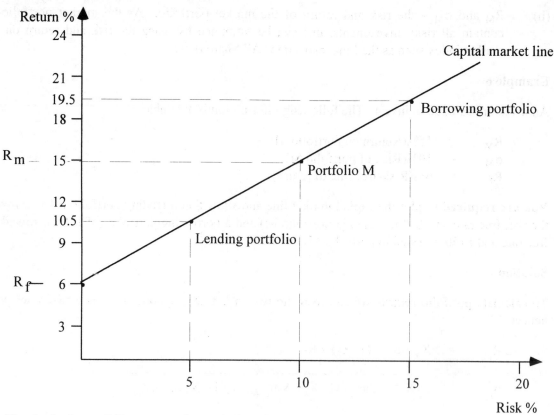

Clearly, both portfolios rest on the capital market line (CML).

2.5   Significance of the capital market line

The capital market line tells us for a given level of risk the return an investor should expect on the stock exchange. It is often referred to as giving the market price of risk. That is if we choose to take a given level of risk on the stock exchange then we can expect a given level of return.

The equation of the capital market line is given below:

If R_f =   risk-free rate

        R_M =   expected return on the market portfolio

        σ_M =   standard deviation of returns on the market portfolio

        σ_p =   the risk of the investment we are considering

then $\overline{R_p}$, the return we could expect for the level of risk σ_p

$$=   R_f + \frac{\sigma p}{\sigma m}\left(\overline{R}_m - R_f\right)$$

In words, this says that the expected compensation for facing a proportion $\frac{\sigma p}{\sigma m}$ of market risk will be that same proportion of the 'market premium' $\left(\overline{R}_m - R_f\right)$ above the risk-free rate.

Assume we were evaluating a project which had a risk measured by a standard deviation of returns equal to 12%. Using the same data as in Example 6 for a level of risk of $\sigma = 12\%$ we could expect a stock market investment with similar risk to have a return of:

$$6\% + \frac{12\%}{10\%} \times (15\%\text{-}6\%) = 16.8\%$$

(The project carries $\dfrac{12}{10} = 1.2$ times the risk of the market. It should therefore attract 1.2 times the market premium (9%) on top of risk free).

If this is less than that offered by the project, it is tempting to say that the project should be accepted. However, there is a flaw in this logic.

The problem with this analysis is not in determining the capital market line but in determining the risk of an individual investment.

If we were appraising an investment project which demonstrated a standard deviation of returns of 12% we could not simply say that its required rate of return was at least 16.8% as a similar risk investment (portfolio) on the stock exchange would yield 16.8%.

The 12% standard deviation measures **total risk** of the investment. Much of this risk can be diversified away when it is added to a well-diversified portfolio. If we persisted in judging this investment in terms of a 12% risk we would be making the same mistake as evaluating security A (Example 2) based on its own standard deviation, rather than on its risk once added to a well-diversified portfolio.

As a final step we need to know how much of the total risk can be removed by diversification. We can then judge investments on their remaining or undiversifiable risk. This final step is provided by the Capital Asset Pricing Model (CAPM), developed in the next chapter.

3   PRACTICAL ASPECTS OF PORTFOLIO THEORY

3.1   The relevance of portfolio theory to practical financial management

Our analysis of portfolio theory started by looking at two-security portfolios and was then developed to deal with portfolios combining many securities with a risk-free security. It would theoretically be possible for financial managers to assess whether to accept a proposed project by applying the two-security portfolio theory.

Security A   =   the company's existing operations
Security B   =   the proposed project

On a risk-return graph both 'security A' and 'security A plus security B' should be plotted. When shareholders' indifference curves are superimposed on the graph it should be possible to decide whether the addition of security B increases the shareholders' utility, ie, whether it should be accepted.

However such an analysis would prove very difficult in practice for the following reasons

- the risks and returns of the existing operations and of the proposed project will be impossible to estimate accurately

- different shareholders will have different attitudes to risk; the concept of a single set of shareholder indifference curves is unrealistic

- the theory examines risks and returns over a single time period only; in practice managers are responsible over a series of successive time periods.

| Conclusion | Portfolio theory is not a practical method of project appraisal for financial managers. However, it usefully introduces managers to the concept of risk reduction through diversification, and it leads on to the Capital Asset Pricing Model which is more useful in practice. Perhaps portfolio theory is most valuable for the proportion of each shareholder's wealth. |

3.2   The limitations of portfolio theory

Several limitations have already been touched on:

- risk is assessed in terms of the total risk of individual investments, but in practice much of this risk will be diversified away when the investment is added to an already well diversified portfolio.

- it is a single period model.

- plotting indifference curves is a theoretical exercise which is impossible to carry out accurately in practice.

- forecasting returns and the correlations between returns will be hazardous in practice.

It should also be noted that measuring risk as the standard deviation of expected returns is not the only component of risk. There are other costs (eg, the risk of bankruptcy) associated with high risk investment strategies.

4   SELF TEST QUESTIONS

4.1   What is meant by saying that two investments show high negative correlation? (1.3)

4.2   What is the correlation coefficient between two investments with perfect positive correlation? (1.3)

4.3   How is the risk of an investment measured? (1.6)

4.4   What is the formula for the covariance between two investments? (1.13)

4.5   What is the formula for the variance of a two-security portfolio? (1.16)

4.6   What is meant by the opportunity set of possible portfolios from given investments? (2.1)

4.7   What is an efficient portfolio? (2.2)

4.8   What is the meaning of the capital market line? (2.4)

4.9   State the equation of the capital market line. (2.5)

4.10   What are the main limitations of portfolio theory analysis? (3.2)

5   EXAMINATION TYPE QUESTION

5.1   Two-security portfolios

You have identified two quoted shares which you believe will exhibit negative correlation in their possible returns over the next year, as follows:

		Predicted rate of return	
State	Probability	Hi-tech plc ords	Reddibank plc ords
A	0.30	25%	14%
B	0.45	22%	18%
C	0.25	12%	20%
	————		
	1.00		

(a)   Calculate the expected return, variance and standard deviation of each security.

(5 marks)

(b) Calculate the covariance between the two securities and the correlation coefficient, ρ, using the formula

$$\rho_{(x,y)} = \frac{Cov_{(x,y)}}{\sigma_x \sigma_y}$$ **(5 marks)**

(c) You construct a portfolio consisting of 70% by value of Hi-tech shares and 30% Reddibank shares. What are the returns of this portfolio for each of the possible states, A, B and C?

Calculate the expected return, variance and standard deviation of the portfolio from these figures. **(5 marks)**

(d) The general formulae for the mean return and variance of a two-security portfolio are as follows:

Mean return, $\bar{r}_p = a \; \bar{r}_x + (1-a) \; \bar{r}_y$

Variance, $Var_p = a^2 Var_x + (1-a)^2 \, Var_y + 2a\,(1-a)\,Cov_{x,y}$

Where p = portfolio, x and y are the two securities
and a = proportion of security x in the portfolio.

Using these formulae calculate the mean return, variance and standard deviation when the portfolio contains 0.7 Hi-tech and 0.3 Reddibank by value. **(4 marks)**

(e) Calculate the expected returns and standard deviations for portfolios of the two shares where a is 0.1, 0.3 and 0.5.

Plot all your results on a graph of portfolio return (y axis) against portfolio standard deviation (x axis). You have six points to plot including the all Hi-tech and all Reddibank portfolios. **(8 marks)**

(f) Indicate how the graph would have looked if the correlation coefficient had been
+ 1, +0.5 or − 1.0. **(3 marks)**
 (Total: 30 marks)

6 ANSWER TO EXAMINATION TYPE QUESTION

6.1 Two-security portfolios

Note: this question is included to check your grasp of the statistical aspects of portfolio theory. You will be expected to know the relevant equations in the exam as they may not be given.

(a) **Expected returns**

Probability p	Returns of Hi-tech, r_x	pr_x	Returns of Reddibank r_y	pr_y
0.30	25%	7.5	14%	4.2
0.45	22%	9.9	18%	8.1
0.25	12%	3.0	20%	5.0
———		———		———
1.00		$\bar{r}_x = 20.4\%$		$\bar{r}_y = 17.3\%$

Variances and standard deviations

p	$r_x - \bar{r}_x$	$p\left(r_x - \bar{r}_x\right)^2$	$r_y - \bar{r}_y$	$p\left(r_y - \bar{r}_y\right)^2$
0.30	4.6	6.348	−3.3	3.267
0.45	1.6	1.152	0.7	0.221
0.25	−8.4	17.640	2.7	1.823
———		———		———
1.00		$Var_x = 25.140$		$Var_y = 5.310$

$$\sigma_x = 5.014 \qquad\qquad \sigma_y = 2.304 \ (\sigma = \sqrt{\text{Var}})$$

(b)   **Covariance**

p	$r_x - \bar{r}_x$	$r_y - \bar{r}_y$	$p(r_x - \bar{r}_x)(r_y - \bar{r}_y)$
0.30	4.6	−3.3	−4.554
0.45	1.6	0.7	+0.504
0.25	−8.4	2.7	−5.670
1.00			Cov_{xy}: −9.720

$$\rho_{x,y} = \frac{\text{Cov}_{x,y}}{\sigma_x \sigma_y} = \frac{-9.720}{5.014 \times 2.304}$$

$$= -0.84$$

The two securities are almost perfectly negatively correlated.

(c)   The possible returns are given by the weighted average of the returns of each security for the state.

State	p	Portfolio return, r	pr
A	0.30	$0.7 \times 25\% + 0.3 \times 14\% = 21.7\%$	6.51
B	0.45	$0.7 \times 22\% + 0.3 \times 18\% = 20.8\%$	9.36
C	0.25	$0.7 \times 12\% + 0.3 \times 20\% = 14.4\%$	3.60
	1.00		$\bar{r} = 19.47\%$

Portfolio variance and standard deviation

p	$r - \bar{r}$	$p(r - \bar{r})^2$
0.3	2.23	1.492
0.45	1.33	0.796
0.25	−5.07	6.426
1.00		Var = 8.714

$$\sigma = 2.95$$

(d)   Using the formulae.

$$\bar{r}_p = (0.7 \times 20.4)\% + (0.3 \times 17.3)\% = 19.47\%$$

$$\text{Var}_p = (0.7^2 \times 25.14) + (0.3^2 \times 5.31) + (2 \times 0.7 \times 0.3 \times -9.72)$$

$$= 8.714$$

$$\sigma_p = \sqrt{\text{Var}_p} = 2.95$$

(e)   Varying the proportions in the portfolio

If a = 0.1

$$\bar{r}_p = (0.1 \times 20.4\%) + (0.9 \times 17.3\%) = 17.61\%$$

$$\text{Var}_p = (0.1^2 \times 25.14) + (0.9^2 \times 5.31) + (2 \times 0.1 \times 0.9 \times -9.72) = 2.80$$

$$\sigma_p = \sqrt{2.80} = 1.67$$

If a $= 0.3$, $\bar{r}_p = (0.3 \times 20.4\%) + (0.7 \times 17.3\%) = 18.23\%$

$$\text{Var} = (0.3^2 \times 25.14) + (0.7^2 \times 5.31) + (2 \times 0.7 \times 0.3 \times -9.72)$$

$$= 0.782$$

$$\sigma_p = \sqrt{0.782} = 0.88$$

If a $= 0.5$, $\bar{r}_p = (0.5 \times 20.4\%) + (0.5 \times 17.3\%) = 18.85\%$

$$\text{Var}_p = (0.5^2 \times 25.14) + (0.5^2 \times 5.31) + (2 \times 0.5 \times 0.5 \times -9.72)$$

$$= 2.75$$

$$\sigma_p = \sqrt{2.75} = 1.66\%$$

Graphical representation of possible portfolios

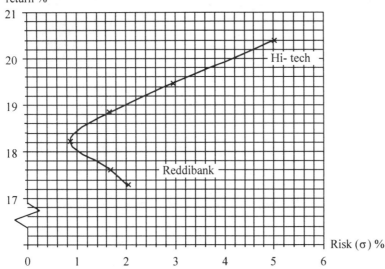

(f)   Varying the correlation coefficient produces graphs as follows (not accurately drawn):

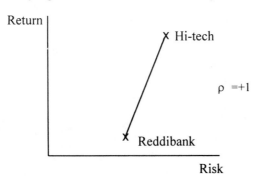

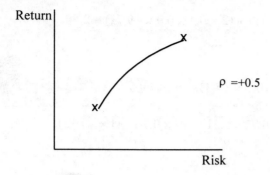

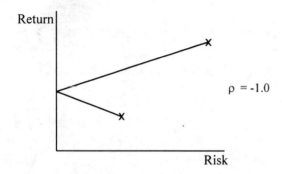

6 THE CAPITAL ASSET PRICING MODEL

INTRODUCTION & LEARNING OBJECTIVES

The Capital Asset Pricing Model (CAPM) is a favourite exam topic. In the previous chapter portfolio theory considered the relationship between the risk and reward of a portfolio, where risk was measured as the standard deviation of returns. CAPM recognises that total risk (as considered in portfolio theory) comprises two elements: systematic risk and unsystematic risk. An investor who already holds a well-diversified portfolio is able to diversify away any unsystematic risk, so he only looks to be rewarded for a share's systematic risk.

CAPM uses the β value of a share to measure its systematic risk. The higher an investment's β, the higher a return an investor will require to compensate him for the risk.

The chapter goes on to explain how CAPM theory can be applied to general project appraisal exercises. Based on the perceived risk of a project, CAPM can calculate a required rate of return that the project must be expected to earn if the project is to be accepted.

Finally the chapter examines an alternative to CAPM called Arbitrage Pricing Theory.

When you have studied this chapter you should be able to do the following:

- Understand the split of total risk between systematic risk and unsystematic risk.
- Argue that an investor with an existing portfolio need only be rewarded for a share's systematic risk.
- Define the beta value and alpha value of an investment.
- Draw a security market line.
- Calculate the beta value of an investment.
- Explain how CAPM can be applied in practice to calculate required rates of return for proposed projects.
- Discuss Arbitrage Pricing Theory as an alternative to CAPM.

1 THE CAPITAL ASSET PRICING MODEL

1.1 Introduction

We have already stated that the relevant risk of a security is not its total risk but the impact it has on the risk of the portfolio to which it is added. CAPM simply allows us to split the total risk of a security into the proportion that may be diversified away, and the proportion that will remain after the diversification process. This remaining risk is the relevant risk for appraising investments.

1.2 Systematic and unsystematic risk

If we start constructing a portfolio with one share and gradually add other shares to it we will tend to find that the total risk of the portfolio reduces as follows:

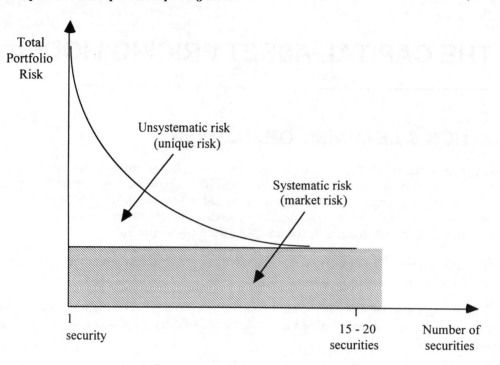

Initially substantial reductions in total risk are possible; however, as the portfolio becomes more and more diversified, risk reduction slows down and eventually stops.

Definition   The risk that can be eliminated by diversification is referred to as unsystematic or unique risk.

This risk is related to factors that affect the returns of individual investments in unique ways (eg, the risk that a particular firm's labour force might go on strike).

Definition   The risk that cannot be eliminated by diversification is referred to as systematic or market risk.

To some extent the fortunes of all companies move together with the economy. Changes in macro-economic variables such as interest rates, exchange rates, taxation, inflation, etc, affect all companies to a greater or lesser extent and cannot be avoided by diversification. That is, they apply systematically right across the market.

The relevant risk of an individual security is its systematic risk and it is on this basis that we should judge investments. Non-systematic risk can be eliminated and is of no consequence to the well-diversified investor. *Note* that it is not necessary to hold the market portfolio to diversify away non-systematic risk – a portfolio of 15-20 randomly selected securities will eliminate the vast majority of it.

1.3   The Security Market Line

As non-systematic risk can be diversified away, investors need only concern themselves with (and will only earn returns for taking) systematic risk. The next problem is how to measure the systematic risk of investments.

The method adopted by CAPM to measure systematic risk is an index, normally referred to as beta (β). As with any index we need to establish some base points and then other observations will be calibrated around these points. The two base points are as follows:

(a)   **The risk-free security**

This carries no risk and therefore no systematic risk. The risk-free security hence has a beta of zero.

(b)   **The market portfolio**

This represents the ultimate in diversification and therefore contains only systematic risk. We will set beta to 1.00 for the market portfolio and this will represent the average systematic risk for the market.

These two points may be represented on the following graph:

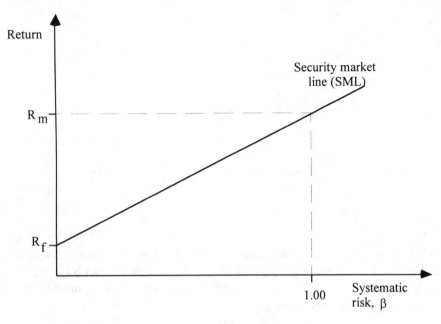

The Security Market Line gives the relationship between systematic risk and return. (This is not to be confused with our earlier graph of the Capital Market Line, which had standard deviation as the x axis, rather than β.) From the graph it can be seen that the higher the systematic risk the higher the required rate of return. The SML is often referred to in the form of an equation,

$$R_j = R_f + \beta_j (R_m - R_f)$$

where R_j =   required rate of return on investment j

R_f =   risk-free rate of interest

R_m =   return on the market portfolio

β_j =   index of systematic risk for security j

1.4   Establishing beta factors for individual securities

In theory we need to determine future β factors for the individual company (in order to appraise future investments). In practical terms we will content ourselves with establishing past βs and use these to appraise required returns on fresh investment projects, assuming such fresh projects do not affect overall company risk as viewed by investors.

The normal way of measuring βs is to use regression analysis to examine the relationship between percentage returns on the securities of particular companies and returns on the market portfolio (ie, on an average market investment). The following diagram gives the graphical representation of this analysis.

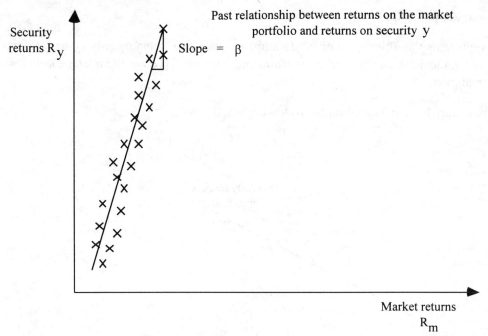

Comments on the graph

(a)   It can be seen that small changes in market returns in the past have been accompanied by much larger changes in the return on this particular security. From this we can infer that security y carries more systematic risk than the market portfolio - ie, it reacts to a greater than market average extent to changes in the economy etc.

(b)   The exact amount of systematic risk can be determined by establishing the slope of the line of best fit (the security characteristic line). The slope of the line in fact equals the security's β factor. In this case the line is very steep and its slope (and therefore its β factor) will be greater than 1.00. This confirms our observation in (a).

(c)   The spread of observations around the line is of no great concern to us. This generally represents the non-systematic risk and will be diversified away by well-diversified investors.

If we performed similar analysis for another security we might obtain the following results:

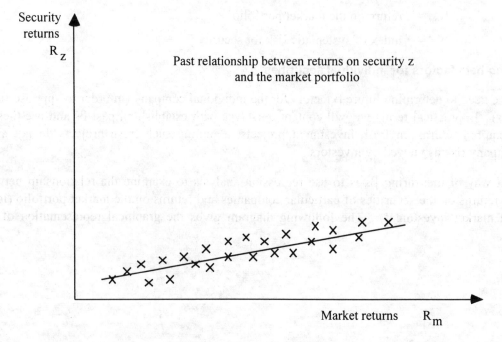

In this case security z is of a low degree of systematic risk as it is far less volatile than the market portfolio. Its beta factor will be less than 1.00.

1.5   Activity

Put the following investments in a list of ascending beta value:

Ordinary shares in Glaxo plc
Units in an international unit trust
Short-dated government stocks
Ordinary shares in a small electronics company

1.6   Activity solution

Low beta: short-dated gilts
$\beta \approx 1$:   units in an international unit trust
$\beta > 1$:   ordinary shares in Glaxo plc
High β: ordinary shares in a small electronics company

1.7   Computing beta

The slope of the regression line, beta, represents the relationship between the systematic risk of the individual investment and the overall market risk. It is therefore measured as follows:

$$\beta_{securityj} = \frac{systematic\ risk_{security}}{market\ risk}$$

Systematic risk is the proportion of the total risk that is directly related to market movements (and thus cannot be diversified away). This proportion is measured by the correlation coefficient between the security and the market ($\rho_{j,m}$). Thus beta can be calculated as

$$\beta_{securityj} = \frac{systematic\ risk_{security}}{market\ risk} = \frac{\rho_{j,m}\sigma_j}{\sigma_m}$$

Note that you may come across other formulae for beta, eg, involving covariance instead of correlation, but they will all be equivalent, as such measures are closely and easily related (see question at the end of the chapter).

Example

Larch wishes to estimate its equity beta and has recorded the following information.

Month	Return on the market portfolio = Rm	Return on Larch's equity = Rj
1	2	3
2	−1	−2
3	3	4
4	0	1
5	2	2.5

The following have been calculated for this data:

Standard deviations

Market σ_m = $\sqrt{2.16}$

Larch σ_L = $\sqrt{4.36}$

Correlation coefficient $\rho_{m,L}$ =   +0.96

Solution

To estimate β we need to use

$$\beta = \frac{Covar_{L,m}}{Var_m} = \frac{\rho_{m,L} \times \sigma_L}{\sigma_m}$$

$$= \frac{0.96 \times \sqrt{4.36}}{\sqrt{2.16}}$$

$$= \frac{2.00}{1.47} = 1.36$$

(*Note:* in practice βs would be calculated from far more observations, normally at least 60.)

If the risk-free rate of interest for some future period was anticipated to be 10% pa and the return on the market portfolio for the same period was expected to be 14%, then the required rate of return on Larch's shares, according to CAPM, for the same period would be:

$$R_L \quad = \quad R_f + \beta\,(R_m - R_f)$$

$$= \quad 10\% + 1.36\,(14\% - 10\%)$$

$$= \quad 15.44\%$$

This situation could also be represented by drawing the security market line:

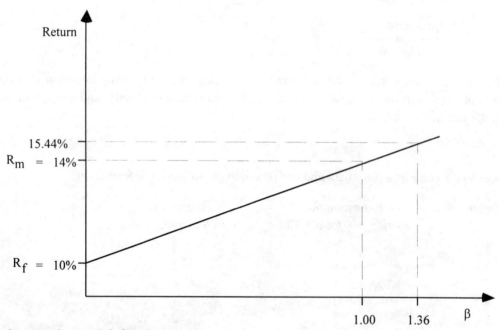

1.8   Aggressive and defensive shares

The expected return on the market portfolio will change in relation to changed economic expectations. This, in turn, will cause a change in the expected return of shares which depends on their beta factors.

Example

The risk-free rate is 10%. The expected return on the market index has been revised upwards from 16% to 17% as a result of favourable tax legislation just announced.

How will this affect the expected return of a share with a beta factor of (a) 1.4, (b) 0.7?

Solution

(a)   **Share with beta of 1.4**

Original expected return was $10\% + (16\%-10\%)1.4 = 18.4\%$

New expected return is $10\% + (17\%-10\%)1.4 = 19.8\%$

Thus, a 1% increase in the expected return of the market will cause a 1.4% increase in the share's expected return.

Similarly, a 1% decrease in the expected market return would cause a 1.4% decrease in the share's expected return.

(b)   **Share with beta of 0.7**

Prove for yourself that a 1% change in $\overline{R_m}$ would cause only a 0.7% change in the share's expected return.

Thus, beta is a measure of the responsiveness of the expected share returns to changes in the returns of the market. Shares with high betas are termed **aggressive** (bearing high risk) and those with betas less than one are termed **defensive**.

As far as stock market investment tactics are concerned, an investor should buy high beta shares if the market is expected to rise because they can be expected to rise faster than the market. If the market is expected to fall, low beta shares are more attractive.

The only problem with this strategy is the need to forecast general market movements in advance, otherwise you might end up holding an aggressive share in a falling (bear) market. Your study of the efficient market hypothesis should have convinced you that it is not easy to forecast future market movements.

1.9   Activity

Regent plc is expected to show a rate of return of 22% over the next year, compared with an expected return of 16% on the stock market index and a 10% return on short-dated Government stocks.

The share is, however, quite volatile. The standard deviation of its returns is estimated to be 40% compared with a standard deviation of 8% for the market index.

Much of Regent's risk is due to specific, as opposed to general, economic factors. Its correlation with the market index has been 0.4 in the past and is expected to continue at this figure.

What is Regent's beta factor, and is its expected return in line with the prediction of the CAPM?

1.10   Activity solution

Overall risk of Regent (σ_y) =   40%

Systematic risk of Regent $(\rho_{y,m} \cdot \sigma_y)$ = $0.4 \times 40\%$

      =   16%

ie, 0.6 of the overall risk is removed by holding Regent as a share in the market portfolio.

Beta factor of Regent $= \dfrac{\text{Systematic risk}}{\text{Market risk}}$

      $= \dfrac{16\%}{8\%} = 2$

Hence from the CAPM the required return of Regent's shares is:

$R_f + (R_m - R_f)\beta$ $=$ $10\% + (16\% - 10\%)2$
                                                $=$ 22%

The share's expected return is therefore in line with the predictions of the CAPM.

1.11   Activity

Determine the required return of Hilton plc from the following data:

R_f $=$ 10%
R_m $=$ $16\%, \sigma_m = 8\%$

Hilton's standard deviation is 25% and its correlation with the market is 0.8.

1.12   Activity solution

Hilton's overall risk is 25%. Its systematic risk is $0.8 \times 25\% = 20\%$.

Its Beta factor is therefore $\dfrac{20\%}{8\%} = 2.5$

Its required return from the CAPM is:

$10\% + (16\% - 10\%)2.5 = 25\%$

Thus Hilton has to show a higher return than Regent even though its overall risk is lower. This is because most of its risk is caused by general economic factors and cannot be removed by diversification (high systematic risk).

1.13   Activity

Ordinary shares in X plc have shown a beta of 1.4 over the past 5 years. Short-dated gilts yield 6% and the FT All Share Index has returned 16% over the past year. Shares in X are expected to return 25% over the coming year; are they an attractive buy?

1.14   Activity solution

Return suggested by CAPM is

R_s $=$ $R_f + \beta (R_m - R_f)$
             $=$ $6 + 1.4 (16 - 6)$
             $=$ 20%

Since the expected return of 25% exceeds the fair return suggested by CAPM, the shares are an attractive buy.

1.15   Alpha factors

The shares in X plc in the activity above have an expected return of 25% while CAPM suggests that a fair return is only 20%. The 5% excess return, or abnormal return, is called the alpha factor for the share. Alpha can be determined algebraically by the equation.

$R_s = R_f + \beta(R_m - R_f) + \alpha$

The expected value of α is zero according the CAPM, although the actual value of α for any particular period is likely to be non-zero.

1.16   Problems in calculating beta factors

Beta factors for a company are calculated statistically from past observed returns; for example the London Business School 'Risk Measurement Service' is published quarterly, using monthly returns from the previous five years to calculate each quoted share's beta. Such an analysis begs two questions:

- is it reasonable to use a beta factor, calculated from the past, as the basis of decision-making about the future?

- are beta values observed to be stable over time?

If beta values were not observed to be almost stationary over time, the whole theory would collapse. Luckily the evidence is that both US and UK shares do exhibit stable betas, the stability being stronger for highly diversified shares such as investment trusts than for more focused companies. Naturally beta will only be stable if the company's systematic risk remains the same ie, the company carries on the same areas of business in the long term.

Since betas are calculated statistically, the calculated beta value will be more reliable the more separate data went into its calculation. Therefore the longer the period underlying the calculations the better. However if the beta will be used to estimate a required rate of return for a future project, it is important that the company's risk class in future will be more or less unchanged by accepting the project. Many businesses deal with this apparent paradox by using a sector average beta rather than using their own calculated beta.

2   FURTHER DISCUSSION OF CAPM

2.1   Assumptions of CAPM

The CAPM shows how the minimum required return on a quoted security depends on its risk. For simplicity, various assumptions are made:

(a)   a perfect capital market;
(b)   unrestricted borrowing or lending at the risk-free rate of interest;
(c)   uniformity of investor expectations;
(d)   all forecasts are made in the context of one time period only.

From this it is deduced that all investors will hold a well-diversified portfolio of shares, known as the market portfolio, which is really a 'slice' of the whole stock market. Although the market portfolio is not really held by investors, in practice even a limited diversification will produce a portfolio which approximates its behaviour, so it is a workable assumption.

The attractiveness of any individual security is therefore judged in relation to its effect when combined with the market portfolio.

A security whose returns are highly correlated with fluctuations in the market is said to have a high level of systematic risk. It does not have much risk-reducing potential on the investor's portfolio and therefore a high return is expected of it. On the other hand, a security which has a low correlation with the market (low systematic risk) is valuable as a risk reducer and hence its required return will be lower. The measure of the systematic risk of a security relative to that of the market portfolio is referred to as its beta factor.

The CAPM shows the linear relationship between the risk premium of the security and the risk premium of the market portfolio.

Risk premium of share = market risk premium $\times \beta$

ie,   Required return of share = risk-free rate + market risk premium $\times \beta$

or $\overline{R_y} = R_f + (\overline{R_m} - R_f)\beta$

The same formula can be applied to computing the minimum required return of a capital investment project carried out by a company, because the company is just a vehicle for the shareholders who will view the project as an addition to the market portfolio.

In practice many of the assumptions underlying the development of CAPM are violated. However, rather than 'nit-pick' it is more sensible to ask 'does the theory work?' ie, does it explain the returns on securities in the real world?

Fortunately, the answer is yes. Practical empirical tests, whilst showing that betas are not perfect predictors of rates of returns on investments, do show a strong correspondence between systematic risk and rate of return. Certainly CAPM outperforms other models in this area, and in particular it gives a far better explanation of the rate of return on a security than is obtained by looking at its total risk.

2.2   Advantages of the CAPM

(a)   It provides a market based relationship between risk and return, and assessment of security risk and rates of return given that risk.

(b)   It shows why only systematic risk is important in this relationship.

(c)   It is one of the best methods of estimating a quoted company's cost of equity capital.

(d)   It provides a basis for establishing risk-adjusted discount rates for capital investment projects.

2.3   Limitations of the CAPM

(a)   By concentrating only on systematic risk, other aspects of risk are excluded; these unsystematic elements of risk will be of major importance to those shareholders who do not hold well-diversified portfolios, as well as being of importance to managers and employees. Hence it takes an investor-orientated view of risk.

(b)   The model considers only the **level** of return as being important to investors and not the way in which that return is received. Hence, dividends and capital gains are deemed equally desirable. With differential tax rates the 'packaging' of return between dividends and capital gain may be important.

(c)   It is strictly a one-period model and should be used with caution, if at all, in the appraisal of multi-period projects.

(d)   Some of the required data inputs are extremely difficult to obtain or estimate, for example:

(i) R_f – **risk free interest rate.** Can be obtained from quoted rates. From the wide range of quoted interest rates a relevant rate must be decided on. Ideally, the rate ought to relate to a security with the same duration as the project being appraised.

(ii)   **Beta – the measure of systematic risk.** Here an estimate is usually required. Such estimates may be derived from subjective judgement, sensitivity analysis or, in some cases, by analysing (and, where necessary, adjusting) the beta coefficient of quoted firms which are thought to display the same risk characteristics as the project being appraised. Use of regression analysis is subject to statistical error, the presence of unsystematic risk, and the effects of not having a perfect investment market – security prices not always simply reflecting underlying risk.

(iii) $\overline{R_m}$ – **expected return on the market portfolio**. Extremely difficult to determine as the market is volatile and the expected return is likely to vary with changes in the risk-free rate. Hence, users often attempt to estimate $(\bar{R}_m - R_f)$, the excess return on the market. Historically in the UK this excess return has averaged about 6% to 9% and this figure may be used if:

(1)   it is felt that historic data is likely to be a good estimate of the future; and

(2)   the expected excess return is thought to be a constant arithmetic amount above the risk-free rate.

(e)   In practice there are certain instances when it is found that the CAPM does not perform as expected, for example investments with low betas, investments with low PE ratios, investments with a strong seasonality.

Generally the basic CAPM is seen to overstate the required return for higher beta securities and understate the required return for low beta securities. However this problem mostly disappears when the effects of taxation are introduced to develop the basic model.

Similarly, CAPM does not seem to generate accurate forecasts for returns for companies with low price earnings ratios and is unable to account for seasonal factors observed in the UK stock market over the years. January appears nearly always to be an outstandingly successful month for investing in UK shares, but no-one can explain why this is the case.

2.4   Activity

Estimate the excess return on the UK stock market for the year ending on the date that you are reading this.

2.5   Activity solution

In the year ending when this paragraph was written:

	%
Capital growth on FT-A All Share Index	9
Dividend yield on FT-A All Share Index	4
	13

Short-dated gilts have a gross redemption yield of 6.5%.

∴ the excess return $R_m - R_f$ is currently $13 - 6.5 = 6.5\%$

3   APPLICATION OF THE CAPM TO PROJECT APPRAISAL

3.1   Uses of CAPM in financial management

The capital asset pricing model was originally developed to explain how the returns earned on shares are dependent on their risk characteristics. However, its greatest potential use in the financial management of a company is in the setting of minimum required returns (ie, risk adjusted discount rates) for new capital investment projects.

The great advantage of using the CAPM for project appraisal is that it clearly shows that **the discount rate used should be related to the project's risk**. It is not good enough to assume that the firm's present cost of capital can be used if the new project has different risk characteristics from the firm's existing operations. After all, the cost of capital is simply a return which investors require on their money given the company's present level of risk, and this will go up if risk increases.

Also, in making a distinction between systematic and unsystematic risk, it shows how a highly speculative project such as mineral prospecting may have a lower than average required return simply because its risk is highly specific and associated with the luck of making a strike, rather than with the ups and downs of the market (ie, it has a high overall risk but a low systematic risk).

It is important to follow the logic behind the use of the CAPM in this way:

(a)   The company's assumed objective is to maximise the wealth of its ordinary shareholders.

(b)   It is assumed that these shareholders all hold the market portfolio (or a proxy of it).

(c)   The new project is viewed by shareholders, and therefore by the company, as an additional investment to be added to the market portfolio.

(d)   Therefore, its minimum required rate of return can be set using the capital asset pricing model formula: $r_y = r_f + (\overline{r_m} - r_f)\beta$ where β is the beta factor of the new project.

(e)   Surprisingly, the effect of the project on the company which appraises it is irrelevant. All that matters is the effect of the project on the market portfolio. The company's shareholders have many other shares in their portfolios. They will be content if the anticipated project returns simply compensate for its systematic risk. Any unsystematic or unique risk the project bears will be negated ('diversified away') by other investments in their well diversified portfolios.

In practice, it is found that large listed companies are typically highly diversified anyway and it is likely that any unsystematic risk will be negated by other investments of the company that accepts it, thus meaning that investors will not require compensation for its unsystematic risk.

Before proceeding to some examples it is important to note that there are two major weaknesses with the assumptions.

(a)   The company's shareholders may not be diversified. Particularly in smaller companies they may have invested most of their assets in this one company. In this case the CAPM will not apply. Using the CAPM for project appraisal only really applies to quoted companies with well diversified shareholders.

(b)   Even in the case of such a large quoted company, the shareholders are not the only participants in the firm. It is difficult to persuade directors and employees that the effect of a project on the fortunes of their company is irrelevant. After all, they cannot diversify their job.

In addition to these weaknesses there is the problem that the CAPM is a single period model and that it depends on market perfections. There is also the obvious practical difficulty of estimating the beta of a new investment project.

Despite the weaknesses we will now proceed to some computational examples on the use of the CAPM for project appraisal.

3.2   Examples of project appraisal

Example

Tussac plc is an all equity company with a cost of capital of 15% pa.

It wishes to invest in a project with an estimated beta of 1.2. If $r_f = 10\%$ and $\overline{r_m} = 18\%$, what is the minimum required return of the project?

Solution

The firm's cost of capital is probably irrelevant because the new project almost certainly has risk characteristics different from the firm's existing operations.

Using the project beta, its minimum required return is $10\% + (8\% \times 1.2)$ $=$ $\underline{19.6\%}$

Example

Comhampton plc is an all equity company with a beta of 0.8. It is appraising a one year project which requires an outlay now of £1,000 and will generate cash in one year with an expected value of £1,250. The project has a beta of 1.3. r_f = 10%, r_m = 18%.

(a)   What is the firm's current cost of equity capital?

(b)   What is the minimum required return of the project?

(c)   Is the project worthwhile?

Solution

(a)   Cost of capital = 10% + (8% × 0.8) = 16.4%

(b)   Project required return = 10% + (8% × 1.3) = 20.4%

(c)   Expected project return = $\dfrac{1,250 - 1,000}{1,000}$ = 25%

Thus the project is **worthwhile** because its expected rate of return is higher than its minimum required return. This again assumes investors will not want any returns to compensate for the unsystematic risk on the new project, for reasons already developed.

Alternatively, the NPV of the project at its minimum required return is:

$$£(-1,000 + \frac{1,250}{1.204}) \quad = \quad £38.20$$

The NPV shows the gain made by the shareholders if the project is accepted.

The 20.4% minimum required return is often referred to as the project's **hurdle rate**, or alternatively its **risk-adjusted discount rate**.

3.3   Activity

The risk-free rate is 8% and the expected return on an average market portfolio is 15%.

Kingswick plc is an all equity financed company with a cost of capital of 18.5%. It is considering the following capital investment projects:

Project	Outlay now £	Expected receipt in one year £	Beta factor
A	1,000	1,095	0.3
B	1,000	1,130	0.5
C	1,500	1,780	1.0
D	2,000	2,385	1.5
E	2,000	2,400	2.0

(a)   Calculate Kingswick's beta factor.

(b)   Calculate the CAPM required return for each project.

(c)   Calculate the expected rate of return of each project.

(d)   Plot the project expected returns over a graph of the security market line to illustrate which projects are acceptable.

(e)   Show which projects would be accepted and rejected if they were discounted at the firm's cost of capital, and highlight those projects where an incorrect decision would be made.

3.4 Activity solution

(a) $\overline{R}_y = R_f + (\overline{R}_m - R_f)\beta$ (assuming the current cost of capital properly reflects the beta factor ie, it is in equilibrium with the marked)

Therefore $\beta = \dfrac{\overline{R}_y - R_f}{\overline{R}_m - R_f}$

Kingswick's beta factor for its equity securities $= \dfrac{18.5\% - 8\%}{15\% - 8\%} = \underline{1.5}$

(b) & (c)

Project	CAPM required return		Expected return		
A	$8\% + (7\% \times 0.3) =$	10.1%	$\dfrac{95}{1,000} =$	9.5%	Reject
B	$8\% + (7\% \times 0.5) =$	11.5%	$\dfrac{130}{1,000} =$	13%	Accept
C	$8\% + (7\% \times 1) =$	15%	$\dfrac{280}{1,500} =$	18.7%	Accept
D	$8\% + (7\% \times 1.5) =$	18.5%	$\dfrac{385}{2,000} =$	19.3%	Accept
E	$8\% + (7\% \times 2) =$	22%	$\dfrac{400}{2,000} =$	20%	Reject

(d) & (e)

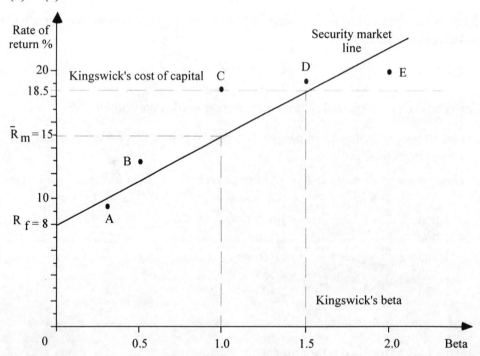

Using the CAPM, the acceptable projects are those above and to the left of the security market line.

Projects B, C and D are accepted. A and E are rejected.

If the projects were discounted at the company's cost of capital, 18.5%, then only those above the cost of capital line (ie, those with yield $\geq$ 18.5%) would be accepted ie, the company would accept C, D and E reject A and B.

Using the firm's cost of capital is clearly wrong because it does not allow for the different risks of the projects. It is simply a required rate of return given company risk at the time capital cost is evaluated. The projects where an incorrect decision would be made by using the firm's cost of capital are:

Project B   =   a valuable low risk project is incorrectly rejected.

Project E   =   this would be accepted despite the fact that its return is not high enough to compensate for its high systematic risk.

4   ARBITRAGE PRICING THEORY

Arbitrage pricing theory (APT) is an alternative pricing model to CAPM, developed by Ross in 1976.

CAPM is a single index model in that the expected return from a security is a function of only one factor, its beta value.

$$R_s = R_f + \beta(R_m - R_f)$$

However APT is a multi-index model in that the expected return from a security is a linear function of several independent factors.

$$R_s = a + b_1 f_1 + b_2 f_2 + \ldots$$

where R_s = the expected return from a security

$a, b_1, b_2, \ldots$ are constants

$f_1, f_2, \ldots$ are the various factors which influence security returns

For example f_1 could be the return on the market (as in CAPM), f_2 could be an industry index specific to the sector in which the company operates, f_3 could be an interest rate index, etc.

Ross showed that, if shares are assumed to form an efficient market, an equilibrium is reached when

$$R_s = R_f + \beta_1(R_1 - R_f) + \beta_2 (R_2 - R_f) + \ldots$$

where R_s =   the expected return from a security

R_f =   the risk free rate

β_i =   constants expressing the security's sensitivity to each factor

R_i =   the expected return on a portfolio with unit sensitivity to factor i and zero sensitivity to any other factor

Equilibrium is reached at this point since no arbitrage profits are then available, ie, no better return is available from a different portfolio at the same level of risk.

APT has gained in popularity as empirical tests of CAPM in practice have raised significant doubts as to CAPM's validity. However it is fair to say that empirical testing of APT has to date been only limited, so its effectiveness remains to be proved. CAPM is certainly simpler than APT, being a single index rather than a multi-index model, so CAPM will remain popular for some time.

Further work is necessary on APT to identify further:

- the factors affecting specific security prices.
- methods of estimating R_f and the β_i in the model.

5   SELF TEST QUESTIONS

5.1   What is the difference between systematic risk and unsystematic risk? (1.2)

5.2   Roughly how many investments need to be held in a portfolio for nearly all the unsystematic risk to be diversified away? (1.2) *15 – 20*

5.3   What is the beta value of a risk-free security? (1.3)

5.4   What is the equation of the Securities Market Line? (1.3)

5.5   State a formula for β. (1.7)

5.6   If you expect the stock market to rise, should you buy high beta or low beta shares for your portfolio? (1.8)

5.7   Do empirical tests show that CAPM works in practice? (2.1)

5.8   What sort of figure has the excess return from the stock market generally been historically? (2.3)

5.9   How can CAPM be used to set minimum required returns for new capital projects? (3.1)

5.10   State two major weaknesses in the theory of using CAPM in this way. (3.1)

6   EXAMINATION TYPE QUESTIONS

6.1   Bewcast plc

A division of Bewcast plc has been allocated a fixed capital sum by the main board of directors for its capital investment during the next year.   The division's management has identified three capital investment projects, each potentially successful, each of similar size, but has only been allocated enough funds to undertake two projects.   Projects are not divisible and cannot be postponed until a later date.

The division's management proposes to use portfolio theory to determine which two projects should be undertaken, based upon an analysis of the projects' risk and return.   The success of the projects will depend upon the growth rate of the economy.   Estimates of project returns at different levels of economic growth are shown below.

Economic growth	*Probability of*	*Estimated return (%)*		
(annual average)	*occurrence*	*Project 1*	*Project 2*	*Project 3*
Zero	0.2	2	5	6
2 per cent	0.3	8	9	10
4 per cent	0.3	16	12	11
6 per cent	0.2	25	15	11

You are required

(a)   to use the above information to evaluate and discuss which two projects the division is likely to undertake. All relevant calculations must be shown.   **(14 marks)**

(b)   to state the weakness of the evaluation technique used in (a) above. What further information might be useful in the evaluation of these projects?   **(4 marks)**

(c)   to suggest why portfolio theory is not widely used in practice as a capital investment evaluation technique.   **(3 marks)**

(d)   to recommend, and briefly describe, an alternative investment evaluation technique that might be applied by the division.   **(4 marks)**

(Total: 25 marks)

6.2   Pastel Ltd

Pastel Ltd is considering whether to accept one of two major new investment opportunities, project 1 and project 2. Each project would require an immediate outlay of £10,000, and Pastel Ltd expects to have available enough resources to undertake only one of them.

The directors of Pastel Ltd believe that returns from existing activities and from the new projects will depend on which of three economic environments prevails during the coming year.   They estimate returns for the coming year (that is cash flows to be received at the end of the year plus project value at that time), and the probabilities of the three possible environments, as follows:

	Environment		
	A	*B*	*C*
Probability of environment	0.3	0.4	0.3
	£	£	£
Returns from project 1	12,500	12,500	9,500
Returns from project 2	10,000	11,750	13,000
Aggregate returns from existing portfolio of projects	90,000	120,000	130,000

The company has a current market value of £100,000. The directors of Pastel Ltd believe that the risk and returns per £ of market value of their existing activities are similar to those for the stock market as a whole, including their dependence on whichever economic environment prevails. The current rate of interest on short-dated government securities and on bank deposit accounts is 10% per annum.

You are required:

(a)   to use the capital asset pricing model to prepare calculations for the directors of Pastel Ltd showing which, if either, of the two proposed projects should be accepted.   **(15 marks)**

(b)   to write a brief report to the directors of Pastel Ltd explaining the principles you have used in arriving at your recommendation.   **(10 marks)**
        (Total: 25 marks)

Ignore inflation and taxation.

7   ANSWERS TO EXAMINATION TYPE QUESTIONS

7.1   Bewcast plc

Note: as there are only three projects to be considered (and only two of these can be adopted) the simplest solution is to calculate the standard deviations and mean returns of the two asset portfolios directly.

Portfolio (50% Project 1 : 50% Project 2)

Probability	Return		Return Deviations*	*(Return deviations)²* × Probability
0.2	$(2 \times 0.5) + (5 \times 0.5)$	= 3.5	(7.95)	12.64
0.3	$(8 \times 0.5) + (9 \times 0.5)$	= 8.5	(2.95)	2.61
0.3	$(16 \times 0.5) + (12 \times 0.5)$	=14.0	2.55	1.95
0.2	$(25 \times 0.5) + (15 \times 0.5)$	=20.0	8.55	14.62
1.0	Expected value	11.45	Variance	31.82

(* Estimated return – Expected value)

Standard deviation $= \sqrt{31.82} = 5.64$

Portfolio (50% Project 1 : 50% Project 3)

Probability	Return		Return Deviations	(Return deviations)^2 × Probability
0.2	$(2 \times 0.5) + (6 \times 0.5)$	= 4.00	(7.15)	10.22
0.3	$(8 \times 0.5) + (10 \times 0.5)$	= 9.00	(2.15)	1.39
0.3	$(16 \times 0.5) + (11 \times 0.5)$	=13.50	2.35	1.66
0.2	$(25 \times 0.5) + (11 \times 0.5)$	=18.00	6.85	9.38
1.0	Expected value	11.15	Variance	22.65

Standard deviation = $\sqrt{22.65}$ = 4.76

Portfolio (50% Project 2 : 50% Project 3)

Probability	Return		Return Deviations	(Return deviations)^2 × Probability
0.2	$(5 \times 0.5) + (6 \times 0.5)$	= 5.50	(4.50)	4.05
0.3	$(9 \times 0.5) + (10 \times 0.5)$	= 9.50	(0.50)	0.08
0.3	$(12 \times 0.5) + (11 \times 0.5)$	=11.50	1.50	0.68
0.2	$(15 \times 0.5) + (11 \times 0.5)$	=13.00	3.00	1.80
1.0	Expected value	10.00	Variance	6.60

Standard deviation = $\sqrt{6.60}$ = 2.57

Summary

Projects	Return	Risk (Standard deviation)
1 and 2	11.45	5.64
1 and 3	11.15	4.76
2 and 3	10.00	2.57

No portfolio is absolutely dominant in mean variance efficiency terms, ie, higher return is always accompanied by higher risk. Much will depend upon the investors utility functions for risk but portfolio (2 and 3) seems to offer a fair return for a very low risk.

Note: an alternative approach using covariances is given below:

Calculation of expected return and risk

(a)   **Project 1**

Return %	Probability		Return Deviations	(Return deviations)^2 × Probability
2	0.2	0.4	(10.6)	22.47
8	0.3	2.4	(4.6)	6.35
16	0.3	4.8	3.4	3.47
25	0.2	5.0	12.4	30.75
	Expected return	=12.6		Variance =63.04

Project 2

Return %	Probability		Return Deviations	*(Return deviations)²* *× Probability*
5	0.2	1.0	(5.3)	5.62
9	0.3	2.7	(1.3)	0.51
12	0.3	3.6	1.7	0.87
15	0.2	3.0	4.7	4.42
	Expected return	= 10.3		Variance = 11.42

Project 3

Return %	Probability		Return Deviations	*(Return deviations)²* *× Probability*
6	0.2	1.2	(3.7)	2.74
10	0.3	3.0	0.3	0.03
11	0.3	3.3	1.3	0.51
11	0.2	2.2	1.3	0.34
	Expected return	= 9.7		Variance = 3.62

Projects 1 and 2

Expected return is $\dfrac{12.6 + 10.3}{2} = 11.45\%$

Portfolio risk, using

$$\sigma_p = \sqrt{\sigma_A^2 X^2 + \sigma_B^2 (1 - X)^2 + 2(X)(1 - X)\ \text{covariance}_{AB}}\ \text{ where}$$

A and B are projects in a two project portfolio

σ_p is portfolio risk

σ_A is $\sqrt{\text{variance of project A}}$

σ_B is $\sqrt{\text{variance of project B}}$

X is the proportion of the total investment that is invested in project A.

Covariance between Projects 1 and 2 is

(Return deviation 1)	×	(Return deviation 2)	×	(Probability)		
(10.6)		(5.3)		0.2	=	11.24
(4.6)		(1.3)		0.3	=	1.79
3.4		1.7		0.3	=	1.73
12.4		4.7		0.2	=	11.66
				Covariance	=	26.42

$$\sigma_p = \sqrt{63.04(0.5)^2 + 11.42(0.5)^2 + 2(0.5)(0.5)26.42}$$

$$= \sqrt{15.76 + 2.86 + 13.21} = 5.64$$

Projects 1 and 3

Expected return is $\dfrac{12.6+9.7}{2}=11.15\%$

Covariance between Projects 1 and 3 is

(Return deviation 1)	×	(Return deviation 2)	×	(Probability)		
(10.6)		(3.7)		0.2	=	7.84
(4.6)		0.3		0.3	=	(0.41)
3.4		1.3		0.3	=	1.33
12.4		1.3		0.2	=	3.22
				Covariance	=	11.98

$$\sigma_p = \sqrt{63.04\ (0.5)^2\ +\ 3.62(0.5)^2 + 2(0.5)(0.5)11.98}$$

$$= \sqrt{15.76+0.91+5.99}$$

$$= 4.76$$

Projects 2 and 3

Expected return is $\dfrac{10.3+9.7}{2}=10\%$

Covariance between Projects 2 and 3 is

(Return deviation 1)	×	(Return deviation 2)	×	(Probability)		
(5.3)		(3.7)		0.2	=	3.92
(1.3)		0.3		0.3	=	(0.12)
1.7		1.3		0.3	=	0.66
4.7		1.3		0.2	=	1.22
				Covariance	=	5.68

$$\sigma_p = \sqrt{11.42(0.5)^2 + 3.62(0.5)^2 + 2(0.5)(0.5)\ 5.68}$$

$$= \sqrt{2.86+0.91+2.84}$$

$$= 2.57$$

(b)   Weaknesses of the evaluation technique used in (a).

(i)   It only considers the diversification effects of a two asset portfolio. The impact of the new projects on all Bewcast's existing projects would be much more important.

(ii)   Accurate data on returns and probabilities is required.

Other information:

(i)   Are the projects of different lives?

(ii)   How have the returns been measured?

(iii)   Can further cash be raised if all the projects can be demonstrated to have positive NPV's?

(c)   Reasons for the lack of use of portfolio theory.

(i)   If we wished to analyse the impact of the new project on all of Bewcast's existing projects the number of calculations would be enormous.

(ii)   Accurate forecasts of returns are required.

These two problems would make the practical application of portfolio theory a time consuming and costly business.

(d)   One such alternative technique is the capital asset pricing model. Given certain assumptions (including perfect capital markets and homogenous investor expectations) the capital asset pricing model states that the required rate of return on an investment is the risk free rate plus the market risk premium weighted by a premium for systematic (undiversifiable) risk. Systematic risk is measured by beta which relates the covariance between the expected return on the investment and expected return on the market portfolio to the variance of the market portfolio. The model may be used in the determination of an appropriate weighted average cost of capital to use as a discount rate in a capital investment, a rate which takes into account the specific systematic risk of the project concerned. The model is, however, subject to criticism with respect to its theoretical assumptions and practical application.

Other suggestions include:

Simulation
Sensitivity analysis
Certainty equivalents
Capital rationing techniques.

7.2   Pastel Ltd

(a)   *Note:* the procedure is to use the CAPM to determine the ß's (and hence the required rates of return) on each project. This information can then be used to judge the benefit of each project.

When computing β from scratch, it is easier to use a slightly different version of the formula:

$$\beta = \frac{\rho_{j,m}\sigma_j}{\sigma_m} = \frac{\text{Covar}_{j,m}}{\sigma_j\sigma_m} \times \frac{\sigma_j}{\sigma_m} = \frac{\text{Covar}_{j,m}}{\sigma_m^2}$$

using the relationship between correlation and covariance.
This eliminates the need to compute σ_j separately.

As a first step we must calculate the rate of return on each project and then estimate the variance of the market return and the covariance of individual project returns with the market return.

(i)   **Expected rates of return from Project 1, Project 2 and the company's existing portfolio**

For single period forecasts the rate of return is calculated as:

$$\frac{\text{Value at end of year - Value at beginning of year}}{\text{Value at beginning of year}}$$

Environment	Probability p	Rate of return, r		
		Project 1	Project 2	Existing portfolio
A	0.3	0.25	0	−0.1
B	0.4	0.25	0.175	0.2
C	0.3	−0.5	0.3	0.3
Expected return $\sum pr = \bar{r}$		0.16	0.16	0.14

(ii)   Variance of the market

This can be estimated as the variance of the company's existing portfolio

Environment	Probability, p	$r_m - \bar{r}_m$	$p(r_m - \bar{r}_m)^2$
A	0.3	−0.24	0.01728
B	0.4	0.06	0.00144
C	0.3	0.16	0.00768
Variance $\sum p(r_m - \bar{r}_m)^2$			0.02640

(iii)   Covariance of project returns with the market

Environment	Probability, p	$(r_1 - \bar{r}_1)$ Project 1	$p(r_1 - \bar{r}_1)(r_m - \bar{r}_m)$	$(r_2 - \bar{r}_2)$ Project 2	$p(r_2 - \bar{r}_2)(r_m - \bar{r}_m)$
A	0.3	0.09	−0.00648	−0.16	0.01152
B	0.4	0.09	0.00216	0.015	0.00036
C	0.3	−0.21	−0.01008	−0.14	0.00672
$\text{Cov}(r_j, r_m) = \sum p(r_j - \bar{r}_j)(r_m - \bar{r}_m)$			−0.01440		0.01860

(iv)   ß's of projects 1 and 2.

$$\text{ß Project 1} = \frac{\text{Covar (project 1 and market)}}{\text{Variance market}}$$

$$= \frac{-0.01440}{0.02640} = -0.545$$

Note: this is a negative ß, Project 1 is inversely related to the rest of the market.

$$\text{ß Project 2} = \frac{\text{Covar (Project 2 and market)}}{\text{Variance market}}$$

$$= \frac{+0.01860}{0.02640} = +0.7045$$

(v)   Required rates of return on each project.

$$\text{for Project 1} \quad = \quad Rf + \beta_1(Rm - Rf)$$

$$= \quad 10\% - 0.545\,(14\%^{\text{note 1}} - 10\%)$$

$$= \quad 7.82\%$$

$$\text{for Project 2} \quad = \quad Rf + \beta_2(Rm - Rf)$$

$$= \quad 10\% + 0.7045\,(14\% - 10\%)$$

$$= \quad 12.82\%$$

(vi)   **Evaluation of projects**

Two approaches are possible:

Internal rate of return

This would not normally be the recommended approach for mutually exclusive projects. However, since they both require the same initial investment and last for only one period we can say that since Project 1 shows the greatest excess of expected return (16% from step 1) over required return (7.82% step 5) then it should be accepted.

Net present value

The more usual approach in the case of mutually exclusive projects would be to discount expected future cash flows to present value at the project's required rate of return.

$$\text{Project 1} \quad \text{NPV} \quad = \quad -10,000 + \frac{11,600^{\text{note 2}}}{1.0782} = \text{£}758.6$$

$$\text{Project 2} \quad \text{NPV} \quad = \quad -10,000 + \frac{11,600^{\text{note 3}}}{1.1282} = \text{£}281.8$$

Hence once again we would select project 1.

Note 1 $=$ Expected return on market ($=$ existing portfolio step 1)

Note 2 $=$ $(12,500 \times 0.3) + (12,500 + 0.4) + (9,500 \times 0.3)$

Note 3 $=$ $(10,000 \times 0.3) + (11,750 \times 0.4) + (13,000 \times 0.3)$

(b)

REPORT

To: Directors of Pastel Ltd

From: The management accountant

Date: X-X-19XX

Subject: **Principles involved in the investment recommendation**

The recommendation that Project 1 should be undertaken is made after taking into consideration the risk and the expected return of the two projects, and how this relates to the company's (and the stock market's) existing risk and expected return relationship. It is based on the principles and conclusions of portfolio theory.

This theory, under a set of restrictive assumptions, shows that when risky investments (ie, investments whose outcomes are uncertain) are combined (into a portfolio), the expected return that results is a simple weighted average of the expected returns of the individual investments. However, the risk of the resulting combination (measured by the standard deviation or variance of the possible returns), may be less than, or equal to the weighted average of the risk of the individual investments. The actual outcome depends upon the sign and the magnitude of the correlation coefficients of possible returns of the combined investments.

Therefore, when considering the addition of a new investment to an existing collection of investments (as Pastel is now considering), the effect of the action on the company's overall risk level is the point of importance in determining the expected return required from the new investment. As a result, the required expected returns from the two investment projects under consideration are determined not by their own overall risk levels (ie, their standard deviations of possible returns) but by the effect each would have (if accepted) on the overall risk level of the company.

One way of utilising this result is to divide an investment project's overall risk level into two components: systematic and unsystematic risk. Systematic risk is, in effect, that part of an investment's total risk which actually affects the existing risk level of the company. Unsystematic risk is the residual part which can effectively be ignored as it does not affect the company's existing risk (it is in fact eliminated through the combining process).

Therefore, to choose between the two projects, their respective levels of systematic risk have to be found and used to estimate their **required** expected returns. These are then judged against their **actual** expected returns. This procedure was carried out for the two investment projects under consideration and it appears that both produce an expected return above the level required by the systematic risk of each. However, the greatest excess of expected return is likely to be provided by Project 1 and thus this is held to be the preferred alternative. (This excess return should translate itself into an increased market price of the company's equity and enhance the shareholders' wealth.)

Two further points of importance need to be made to present a more correct picture of the principles used when arriving at the recommendation. First, although the reasoning has been couched in terms of the relationship between project risk and the risk of the company, in truth the relationship of importance is between project risk and general stock market risk. However, it is correct for Pastel to view the relationship in terms of the project and the company because the company's risk and return is thought to reflect the risk and return of the market as a whole.

The second point is that portfolio theory is constructed under a number of strict assumptions which may not hold in the real world. However, its general conclusions are logically sound and probably form useful guidelines for investment decision-making in practice. Of particular importance is the idea that an investment project's return should not be viewed in terms of its own overall risk level, but in terms of the effect of combining it with other investments on the **overall** risk of that combination.

SIGNATURE

7 THE COST OF CAPITAL

INTRODUCTION & LEARNING OBJECTIVES

This chapter brings together the different costs of capital to calculate an overall, weighted average cost for all the funds used by a firm.

It then goes on to look at the effect of financial structure on the cost of capital. There are two opposing views, the 'traditional' and the 'Modigliani and Miller' models. The two theories have conflicting results, which cannot be reconciled; neither has been proved right or wrong. The dispute is fundamental to the study of financial strategy, so ensure that you understand the ideas thoroughly. They may need to be re-read a number of times, as they are complicated.

When you have studied this chapter you should be able to do the following:

- Calculate a weighted average cost of capital and discuss when it can be used in project appraisal.
- Define and calculate financial and operating gearing and risk measures.
- Discuss factors affecting a firm's choice of capital structure.
- Explain the meaning of personal gearing.
- Explain the traditional view of the effect of gearing on the weighted average cost of capital (WACC), and draw the graphs demonstrating this view.
- Explain the Modigliani and Miller view of the effect of gearing on the WACC with and without tax, draw the graphs demonstrating this view, and discuss its reasonableness.
- Reproduce calculations demonstrating the arbitrage process.
- Reproduce and use the Modigliani and Miller formulae.

1 THE COST OF EQUITY, THE COST OF DEBT AND THE WEIGHTED AVERAGE COST OF CAPITAL

1.1 The concept of a weighted average cost of capital

In previous chapters you have already seen a variety of methods of estimating a company's cost of equity and cost of debt. You should already be familiar with the following equations:

Cost of equity

Using CAPM, $k_e = r_f + \beta_{equity} (r_m - r_f)$ ⎞ these should, in theory, give the same
⎟ result if the assumptions of
Using the dividend valuation model, ⎟ the CAPM hold
⎠

$$k_e = \frac{D_o (1+g)}{P_o} + g$$

Cost of debt

Irredeemable $\quad k = \dfrac{\text{Annual interest}}{\text{Current market price}}$

Redeemable $\quad$ k is the IRR of the related flows: initial market value, annual interest, final redemption

Go back and revise the earlier chapter on 'The valuation of securities' if you have forgotten these equations. In this chapter we recognise that a company is likely to have a variety of sources of finance, each with its own cost. These costs must be averaged together to obtain the company's overall average cost of finance.

Definition   The weighted average cost of capital is the average cost of the company's finance (equity, debentures, bank loans) weighted according to the proportion each element bears to the total pool of capital.

In the analysis so far carried out, each source of finance has been examined in isolation. However, the practical business situation is that there is a continuous raising of funds from various sources. These funds are used, partly in existing operations and partly to finance new projects. There is not normally any separation between funds from different sources and their application to specific projects:

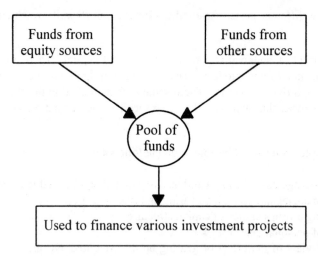

In order to provide a measure for evaluating these projects, the cost of the pool of funds is required. This is variously referred to as the combined or weighted average cost of capital (WACC).

The general approach is to calculate the cost of each source of finance, then to weight these according to their importance in the financing mix.

1.2   Market or book weights

If we use the current proportions in which funds are raised their weights may be measured by reference to book values or market values.

Example

The accounts of Apollo plc reveal the following capital structure.

	£
£1 ordinary shares	2,000,000
Reserves	3,000,000
10% debentures	1,000,000
	6,000,000

Market values of the above are as follows:

Ordinary shares	£3.75 each ex div
Debenture stock	£80.

The cost of equity is estimated to be 20%, the cost of debt is 7.5% (after tax).

What is the weighted average cost of capital using book weights?

Solution

	£
Equity (ordinary shares + reserves) £2,000,000 + £3,000,000	5,000,000
Debt	1,000,000
Total	6,000,000

Proportions $\quad\frac{5}{6}$ Equity $\qquad\frac{1}{6}$ Debt

Combined cost of capital $\quad\left(\frac{5}{6}\times 20\%\right)\quad+\quad\left(\frac{1}{6}\times 7.5\%\right)\quad=\quad 17.92\%$

1.3   Activity

What is the WACC using market values as weights?

1.4   Activity solution

		£
Equity	2,000,000 shares × £3.75/share	7,500,000 (see note below)
Debt	$1,000,000 \times \dfrac{80}{100}$	800,000
Total		8,300,000

Proportions $\quad\dfrac{7,500,000}{8,300,000}$ Equity $\qquad\dfrac{800,000}{8,300,000}$ Debt

Combined cost of capital:

$$\left(\frac{7,500,000}{8,300,000}\times 20\%\right)+\left(\frac{800,000}{8,300,000}\times 7.5\%\right)=18.79\%$$

Note: when using market values, reserves are ignored. They are in effect incorporated in the value of equity.

Book weights give a lower cost as the proportion of equity is much smaller. Market weights are far more meaningful. Remember, the costs themselves are based on market values. Book weights depend upon the historic accident of when the security was issued. Note however that for non-quoted companies only book values exist.

Conclusion The weightings used in the WACC calculation should be based on market values whenever possible.

1.5   Procedure for calculating the combined cost of capital

The calculation involves a series of steps.

Step 1   Calculate weights for each source of capital.

Step 2   Estimate cost of each source of capital.

Step 3   Multiply proportion of total of each source of capital by cost of that source of capital.

Step 4   Sum the results of step 3 to give the weighted average cost of capital.

Example

Bacchante plc has a capital structure as follows:

	Cost of capital %	Book value £m	Market value £m
Bank loans	9	5	5
Debenture loans	12	8	6
Ordinary shares	15	18	39

The company's current operations are carried out from two locations. The Oxford factory shows a cash surplus of £1,750,000 on capital employed of £27.5m, while Cambridge produces a cash surplus of £640,000 on its capital of £3.5m.

It is proposed to invest a further £1.5m in facilities at Cambridge which will increase cash flow by £150,000 to perpetuity.

You are required:

(a)   to calculate Bacchante's combined cost of capital.

(b)   to comment on the proposed expansion.

Ignore taxation.

Solution (S = Step)

(a)   Combined cost of capital is as follows:

Source	Market value £m	Proportions (S1)	Cost of capital (S2) %	Weighted cost (S3) %
Bank loans	5	0.10	× 9 =	0.90
Debenture loans	6	0.12	× 12 =	1.44
Ordinary shares	39	0.78	× 15 =	11.70
	50	1.00		14.04 (S4)

(b)   Rate of return on current operations is as follows:

	Capital employed £m	Cash flow £'000	Return %
Oxford	27.5	1,750	6.4
Cambridge	3.5	640	18.3
Total	31.0	2,390	7.7

The return on the additional facilities at Cambridge is estimated to be:

$$\frac{£150,000}{£1,500,000} = 10\%$$

Conclusion	(1)	The proposal's return is below current WACC and should be rejected.
	(2)	Note that current facilities at Oxford appear to yield a very low return, though without more data (eg, is capital employed at current valuation?) the significance of this fact is difficult to evaluate.

1.6   Activity

Butch Fashions plc has £1m debenture stock in issue, quoted at £50 per £100 of nominal stock; £625,000 preference shares of £1 each quoted at 40p; and 5m ordinary £1 shares standing at 25p. The cost of capital of these securities is 9%, 12% and 18% respectively. This capital structure is to be maintained.

Calculate the combined cost of capital.

1.7   Activity solution

(S = Step)

Security	Market value		Cost of capital (S2)	Weighted cost (S3)
	£'000	Proportions (S1)	%	%
Debentures	500	0.250	× 9.0 =	2.25
Preference shares	250	0.125	× 12.0 =	1.50
Ordinary shares	1,250	0.625	× 18.0 =	11.25
	2,000	1.000		15.00 (S4)

The combined cost of capital is therefore 15%. This figure represents an approximate cut-off rate of return on new investments.

1.8   When to use the weighted average cost of capital

The weighted average cost of capital calculated in the above example is based on the firm's current costs of equity and debt. In using it to appraise projects we are implicitly making the following assumptions.

(a)   **The historic proportions of debt and equity are not to be changed**

The cost of equity and debt based on current market information reflects the firm's current gearing ratio. If the firm substantially changes the long run proportions in which funds are raised then the cost of equity and debt are likely to change with a resultant change in the combined cost of capital. We will explore this problem further later.

(b)   **The operating risk of the firm will not be changed**

Definition	A firm's operating (or business) risk is the risk resulting from the nature of the firm's operations.

The firm's current cost of equity and debt also reflect its current area of operations. For example high risk electronics companies are likely to have higher costs of funds than, say, low risk food manufactures. If a food manufacturing company were to diversify into electronics its costs of finance would change. Current estimates of the cost of capital are therefore only suitable for appraising investments of similar operating risk. This problem is further investigated later.

(c)   **The finance is not project specific**

In some circumstances it is unwise to use the average cost of a pool of funds. Suppose a government offered a multinational company an interest free loan to encourage it to invest in a particular country. In this situation it would be unwise to put the cheap loan into the pool of funds and spread its benefit over all projects as it is associated with only one specific project. In these circumstances we would need to credit the benefits of the cheap finance to the project.

Other problems with the weighted average cost of capital

(a)   **Which sources of finance to include**

The above examples have concentrated on the cost of long-term finance. Firms also raise finance from short-term sources eg, overdrafts, short-term loans, trade credit etc. It is possible to calculate a cost for short-term finance and we need to decide whether it should be included in our calculations.

The usual argument is that the weighted average cost of capital is a tool for appraising long-term investments and as these should only be financed by long-term funds then the costs of short-term funds should be excluded.

However, if it is clear that short-term finance is being used to fund long-term projects then it should be included.

(b)   **Loans without market values**

Bank loans do not have market values in the same way as debentures. All we can do in this case is to take the book value of loans as an approximation of market value.

1.9   The cost of capital for unlisted companies and public sector organisations

There are particular problems in trying to calculate the cost of capital for unlisted companies and public sector organisations.

For unlisted companies no external share price exists, so no cost of equity or beta can be directly calculated. A further problem arises in that the level of dividend each year is likely to be manipulated depending on the shareholders' personal tax positions, so the annual growth in dividends may be erratic. The best method of estimating the cost of capital of an unlisted company is probably to take the cost of a similar listed company and add a risk premium.

The lack of an external share price presents similar difficulties when trying to estimate the cost of capital of a public sector organisation. Often the government will set a discount rate in real terms against which all large public sector projects should be appraised. However there are significant non-financial costs and benefits from most public sector projects which should also be taken into account. This is usually done as part of a formal cost benefit analysis exercise.

1.10   The margin of error involved in cost of capital estimates

All the above discussion has shown the very real practical problems involved in estimating appropriate WACC and discount rates. A company's WACC can only be used directly to appraise new projects if acceptance will not alter the company's gearing ratio or operating risk. Where this is not the case, either the WACC should be used as an approximate indication only of the discount rate, or more sophisticated techniques can be used which are described later.

2   FINANCIAL GEARING AND EFFECT OF ALTERNATIVE FINANCIAL STRUCTURES

2.1   Introduction

Definition   Financial gearing (known in the US as leverage) is the proportionate relationship between borrowings and total capital.

Gearing is expressed as a percentage and may be calculated by reference to either of the following:

(a)   Book or market capital values ie, $\dfrac{\text{Debt}}{\text{Debt} + \text{Total equity finance}}$ or

(b)   Income ie, $\dfrac{\text{Debt interest}}{\text{Operating profits before debt interest and tax}}$

Note that we use the term 'capital' quite loosely to include debentures (borrowed capital) and all the finance of the firm attributable to shareholders ie, including retained profits. Note also that preference shares should be treated as debt.

We wish to study the effect that financing gearing has on the value of a firm, comparing traditional ideas with the theories of two economists, Modigliani and Miller. Before embarking on this, however, you must be sure that you can calculate the gearing ratios for particular companies.

2.2   Example

Enceladus plc has a capital structure as follows:

Capital	*Book value* £'000	*Market value* £'000
8% Debenture stock	2,000	1,500
Ordinary shareholders' capital (including reserves)	3,500	5,000
	5,500	6,500

Calculations of gearing:

(a)   **Capital gearing**

(i)   Book value: $\dfrac{2m}{5.5m}$ =   36.36%

(ii)   Market value: $\dfrac{1.5m}{6.5m}$ =   23.08%

(b)   **Income gearing** $\dfrac{160,000\,(= 8\% \times £2m)}{(400,000 \div 50\%) + 160,000}$ =   16.67%

This illustration proves yet again how important it is for the student to ensure that like is being compared with like. If given figures of gearing for two companies, ensure that both figures are calculated on the same basis before drawing conclusions.

2.3   Definitions of terms

Capital structure	-	the relationship of long-term capital
Financial structure	-	the relationship of all financing, short, long and medium-term
EBIT	-	earnings before interest and tax (ie, operating profit).
Business (or operating) risk	-	the variability in EBIT as a result of the operations the firm is engaged in.
Financial risk	-	the additional risk introduced by the use of gearing.

2.4   Illustration of alternative financing policies

Plato plc manufactures only one product, a sophisticated machine tool. This sells at a unit price of £200,000. Because of the nature of the machine tool business, demand is very variable, but is expected to grow.

The company has to raise £4m in order to increase productive capacity. This can be done either by issuing debentures at par with an interest yield of 10%, or by issuing shares at their market price of £2 each. Current financing consists of 5m ordinary shares and £5m 10% loan stock.

The following sales and EBIT forecasts and their related probabilities are available, given the extra production capacity.

Plato plc - profit calculations at various sales levels

Unit sales	30	50	100
Probability	0.4	0.5	0.1
	£'000	£'000	£'000
Sales	6,000	10,000	20,000
Costs:			
Fixed	(2,000)	(2,000)	(2,000)
Variable (40% sales)	(2,400)	(4,000)	(8,000)
EBIT	1,600	4,000	10,000

If corporation tax is payable at 30%, the EPS under each financing option is calculated as follows:

Debenture financing	£'000	£'000	£'000
EBIT	1,600	4,000	10,000
Interest costs (10% × £9m)	(900)	(900)	(900)
Earnings before tax	700	3,100	9,100
Corporation tax @ 30%	(210)	(930)	(2,730)
Net earnings	490	2,170	6,370
EPS on 5m shares	£0.098	£0.434	£1.274

Expected EPS = 0.4 × 0.098 + 0.5 × 0.434 + 0.1 × 1.274 = £0.384

Equity financing	£'000	£'000	£'000
EBIT	1,600	4,000	10,000
Interest costs (10% × £5m)	500	500	500
Earnings before tax	1,100	3,500	9,500
Corporation tax @ 30%	(330)	(1,050)	(2,850)
Net earnings	770	2,450	6,650
EPS on 7m shares	£0.110	£0.350	£0.950

Expected EPS = 0.4 × 0.11 + 0.5 × 0.35 + 0.1 × 0.95 = £0.314

Note that the solution assumes the tax losses are either carried forward, or set off against the profits of other operations, and can therefore be treated as reducing the loss.

Thus the mean (or expected) EPS under the two policies are as follows.

(a)   Debenture finance - £0.384
(b)   Equity finance - £0.314.

The mean (or expected) sales is the same under both policies ie, $(6m \times 0.4) + (10m \times 0.3) + (20m \times 0.2) = £9.4m$.

This favours debenture finance. However, looking at the expected values of the two policies is inadequate. Comparing the sets of figures, it is apparent that although the expected EPS of the debenture finance is higher, so is the degree of variability: crudely, the debenture financing EPS ranging from £0.098 to £1.274 in comparison to the narrower equity finance range of £0.110 to £0.950.

The higher expected return of the debenture financing is paid for in a greater degree of uncertainty.

| Conclusion | Although debt finance is cheaper than equity finance, it increases the variability of net returns to equity ie, it increases the risk of those returns.

2.5   Other factors influencing financial structures

(a)   **Growth and stability of sales**

Where growth rates are high, equity is likely to be relatively cheap because of the attractiveness of the company. On the other hand, the cost of debt finance can easily be sustained, and the gearing effect will maximise the gain for equity.

If growth is stable, the ability to sustain high gearing levels increases.

(b)   **Competitive structure of the industry**

Sales are only one factor in determining profits. Another is the degree of competition and the profit margins in the industry.

(c)   **Asset structure**

Where the firm's asset structure largely consists of fixed assets, then there will be a tendency to use long-term finance. If there is an emphasis on short-term assets eg, retailing, then short-term finance will be used.

(d)   **Management attitudes - in particular, towards control and risk**

For quoted companies, sale of shares is attractive, with access to capital markets, less risk, and control being irrelevant.

For unquoted smaller companies, the issue of shares is often avoided so as to preserve control, and avoid dilution of equity.

(e)   **Lender attitudes**

The attitudes of lenders to the company and its financial structure dictate how much, and at what cost, the company can borrow.

3   OPERATING GEARING

3.1   Introduction

> **Definition**   Operating gearing is the relationship between fixed and variable costs. It can be measured as the percentage change in earnings before interest and tax for a percentage change in sales; or as the ratio of fixed to variable costs.

Operating gearing (also called operational gearing) measures the cost structure (fixed and variable) of the firm. Firms with high levels of fixed costs are usually described as having high operating gearing.

Firms with high operating gearing are risky as fixed cost payments must be made no matter the level of contribution.

3.2   Example

Consider two firms:

	Firm A £m	Firm B £m
Sales	5	5
Variable costs	3	1
Fixed costs	1	3
EBIT (Earnings before interest and tax)	1	1

What would be the impact of a 10% increase in sales volume on the EBIT of each firm?

Firm A New EBIT = (5m − 3m) × 1.1 − 1 = £1.2m   ie, a 20% increase.

Firm B New EBIT = (5m − 1m) × 1.1 − 3 = £1.4m   ie, a 40% increase.

Operating gearing

	Firm A	Firm B
$\dfrac{\% \text{ change in EBIT}}{\% \text{ change in sales}}$	$\dfrac{20\%}{10\%} = 2$	$\dfrac{40\%}{10\%} = 4$

Alternatively:

	Firm A	Firm B
$\dfrac{\text{Fixed costs}}{\text{Variable costs}}$	$\dfrac{1}{3} = 0.33$	$\dfrac{3}{1} = 3$

B carries a higher operating gearing because it has higher fixed costs. Its operating earnings are more volume sensitive.

3.3   Relationship between financial and operating gearing

The above illustrates that the company with the higher operating gearing will have greater variability in sales. This variability in EBIT can then be further increased before we reach earnings available to equity by the presence of financial gearing.

> **Conclusion**   It is apparent that there is a trade-off between operating and financial gearing. If a firm has a high degree of operating gearing, then unless sales were very stable it would prefer to avoid financial gearing, and vice versa.

4   PERSONAL AND CORPORATE GEARING

4.1   Introduction

The discussion so far has been concerned with corporate gearing ie, the way in which a company combines debt with equity to give a beneficial financing mix. It is, however, perfectly possible for an individual to borrow money to use in conjunction with the funds he already has available; in other words, he is said to adopt a level of **personal gearing**. This is a very important concept as it underlies the theories of Modigliani and Miller that we are coming on to. To illustrate it, an example is probably most useful.

4.2   Example

Mr X has £1m available, which he can invest in either Company G or U. Both companies have a total market value of capital of £5m, but while U is totally equity-financed, G has £2m debt finance. Show that Mr X can achieve exactly the same income by either investing in company G and taking advantage of its corporate gearing, or by adopting personal gearing to the same level as company G and investing in company U. Both Mr X and company G will have to pay interest at 10% on borrowings.

Ignore taxation.

Solution

Step 1   Analyse the capital structure of the firms.

	Company G £m	Company U £m
Equity-market value	3	5
Debt @ 10%	2	-
	5	5
Corporate gearing	2/5	Nil

Step 2   Analyse Mr X's purchase options.

Own money available	1.0	1.0
Borrowings (to create personal debt: equity of 2 : 3, when investing in U)	-	0.67
Total funds available	1.0	1.67
Personal gearing	Nil	2/5
Proportion of equity which Mr X can purchase	1/3	1/3

Step 3   Analyse Mr X's income from each company at various different profit levels.

For example, assume the following profit levels for both companies G & U:

Year 1:   £1,000,000
Year 2:   £2,000,000
Year 3:   £500,000

	Profits before interest £'000	10% interest £'000	Profit after interest £'000	Mr X's share ($\frac{1}{3}$) £'000	Interest 10% £'000	Net receipts £'000
G Ltd						
Year 1	1,000	200	800	266	-	266
Year 2	2,000	200	1,800	600	-	600
Year 3	500	200	300	100	-	100
U Ltd						
Year 1	1,000	-	1,000	333	67	266
Year 2	2,000	-	2,000	667	67	600
Year 3	500	-	500	167	67	100

The figures in the end column show that investment in G Ltd with corporate gearing is indeed equivalent to investment in U Ltd with equal personal gearing.

Conclusion   The implications of the above argument are that an investor will be indifferent as between personal and corporate gearing.

However, empirical evidence suggests that in fact investors prefer gearing to be undertaken by companies rather than by themselves. The reasons for this are discussed later.

5   GEARING AND THE COMBINED COST OF CAPITAL

5.1   Introduction

We have already established that debt finance is normally cheaper than equity. If firms are attempting to minimise their cost of financing it would seem on first sight that they should go for as high a gearing as possible. This approach, however, ignores the effect of gearing on equity holders. We have seen that as gearing increases earnings available to equity holders become increasingly variable (risky). To compensate themselves for this risk equity holders will ask for higher returns. This increase in the cost of equity could well cancel the benefit of cheaper debt. This balance between the cost of debt, equity and the weighted average cost of capital has been the subject of much academic investigation and will be examined in the remainder of this chapter.

5.2   The concept of financial risk

When investing in a business an investor faces two types of risk.

(a)   **Business (or operating) risk**

The variability in earnings before interest and tax associated with the industrial sector in which the firm operates. For example an oil prospecting venture would carry more business risk than a property company.

(b)   **Financial risk**

The additional risk introduced by the use of gearing.

In this chapter we are primarily concerned with financial risk.

5.3   Alternative views

Several views are taken on the effect of gearing on the weighted average cost of capital. The two main positions are set out below.

(a)   **Traditional view** (or net income view)

Judicious use of debt finance can lower the weighted average cost of capital until an optimum level is reached. Gearing beyond that level will push the cost of capital up again.

(b)   **Modigliani and Miller view** (or net operating income view) - which initially ignores taxation

The cost of capital will be unaffected by gearing.

We will examine each view in turn.

5.4   Traditional view of gearing

As an organisation introduces debt into its capital structure the weighted average cost of capital will fall because initially the benefit of cheap debt finance more than outweighs any increases in the cost of equity required to compensate equity holders for higher financial risk.

As gearing continues to increase the equity holders will ask for increasingly higher returns and eventually this increase will start to outweigh the benefit of cheap debt finance, and the weighted average cost of capital will rise. At extreme levels of gearing the cost of debt will also start to rise (as debt holders become worried about the security of their loans) and this will also contribute to an increasing weighted average cost of capital.

The diagram below demonstrates this position in which

k_e is the cost of equity;
k_d is the cost of debt; and
k_o is the overall or weighted average cost of capital.

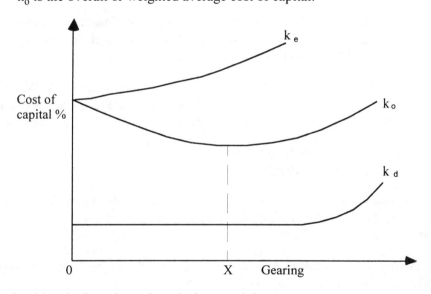

X = optimal level of gearing, where k_o is at a minimum.

The traditional view therefore claims that there is an optimal capital structure where weighted average cost of capital is at a minimum. This is represented by point X on the above diagram.

At point X the overall return required by investors (debt and equity) is minimised. It follows that at this point the combined market value of the firm's debt and equity securities will also be maximised. (If investors are offered the same £ return but the % return they require has fallen market pressures will make the value of the securities rise.)

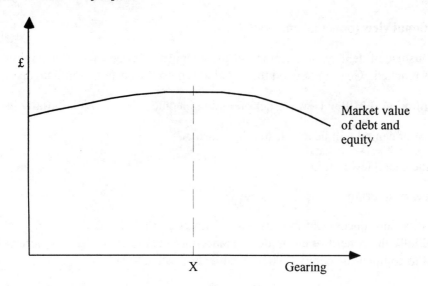

(Tutorial note: examination questions concerning the capital structure that minimises the weighted average cost of capital, or maximise the value of the firm are basically asking the same question. Maximising market value and minimising weighted average cost of capital are identical concepts.*)*

The main support for the traditional view is that it simply accords with 'common sense' and until 1958 it was not questioned.

5.5 Problems arising out of the traditional view

The use of a weighted average cost of capital to appraise the cash flows of investment projects has been justified in situations where the gearing ratio is not expected to change in the long run.

A difficult situation is encountered if a large investment project is financed by a major issue of funds which moves the company to a new level of gearing. Can the project then be appraised simply by discounting at a WACC, and if so which WACC should be used?

If financial risk was ignored by investors there would be no problem because the WACC would be the same at all levels of gearing. However, it is probably not the case and the shareholders are likely to make a gain or loss made up of two elements as follows.

(a)   A gain or loss caused by accepting the project.

(b)   A gain or loss caused by the changed gearing.

Following the traditional view, if the company moves towards the optimal level of gearing, the shareholders will make a gain under heading (b), whereas if it moves away from the optimal level, they will make a loss.

As the traditional view does not follow any prescribed model, it will be difficult to assess the overall impact of a project and its finance on shareholders.

6 THE THEORIES OF MODIGLIANI AND MILLER

6.1 Modigliani and Miller view (excluding the effect of taxation)

In 1958, two American economists, Professors Modigliani and Miller, challenged the traditional view of capital structure.

The Modigliani and Miller (M & M) view is that

> companies which operate in the same type of business and which have similar operating risks must have the same total value, irrespective of their capital structures.

Their view is based on the belief that the value of a company depends upon the future operating income generated by its assets. The way in which this income is split between returns to debt holders and returns to equity should make no difference to the total value of the firm (equity plus debt). Thus, the total value of the firm will not change with gearing, and therefore neither will its weighted average cost of capital.

Their view is represented in the following diagrams.

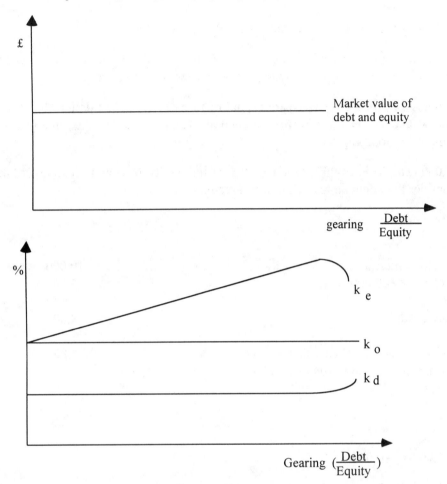

If the weighted average cost of capital is to remain constant at all levels of gearing it follows that any benefit from the use of cheaper debt finance must be exactly offset by the increase in the cost of equity.

The essential point made by M & M is that a firm should be indifferent between all possible capital structures. This is at odds with the beliefs of the traditionalists.

M & M support their case by demonstrating that market pressures (arbitrage) will ensure that two companies identical in every aspect apart from their gearing level will have the same overall market value.

6.2   The arbitrage process

This is best demonstrated by example:

Example

Two firms, U and G, both have the same level of business risk and both generate £10,000 annual earnings before interest, which are not expected to change. All available earnings are paid out as dividends.

Firm U is entirely equity-financed. The equity has a total market capitalisation of £100,000. Thus, the rate of return to investors (the cost of equity) is:

$$\frac{£10,000}{£100,000} \times 100 = 10\% \text{ (no growth model)}$$

Firm G has some debt financing, with a market value of £40,000 and a rate of interest on the market value of 5%. Now, under the 'traditional' view, G might be expected to have a lower combined cost of capital and hence a higher total market capitalisation (ie, market value of debt + equity). By way of example, assume the total market capitalisation of G is £120,000.

Hence, value of equity = £120,000 – £40,000 = £80,000.

M & M claim that this situation could not continue. G is overvalued with respect to U and investors could exploit this misvaluation. The arbitrage process will work as follows.

Assume Mr X holds 10% of the equity share capital of firm G. He sells this for £8,000 cash (10% of the market value as above). He then borrows £4,000 at 5% so that he has the same gearing as firm G (debt being one-third of total capital).

From this £12,000 (£8,000 + £4,000) he buys 10% of the equity in firm U costing £10,000 (10% of £100,000). Consider the effect on his net dividend receipts.

Solution

	£	£
Earnings of G before interest		10,000
Less: Interest of 5% × £40,000		2,000
		——
Available for dividends		8,000
		——
Proportion received by Mr X (when a shareholder) – 10%		800
Dividends from new holding in U 10% × £10,000	1,000	
Less: Interest on borrowings 5% × £4,000	(200)	
	——	
Net receipts		800
		——

Spare funds £12,000 – £10,000 = £2,000.

Clearly Mr X has gained by switching from letting firm G provide the gearing to providing it for himself. Note that the actual level of gearing is the same in both situations as is the return. However, when investing in U he has £2,000 spare with which he can earn returns elsewhere and increase his wealth. Other investors in G will recognise this fact and follow his example. This will lead to the following market pressures.

> Investors sell shares in G – ∴ its equity value falls.
> Investors buy shares in U – ∴ its equity value rises.

This process will continue until the total value of the two companies is the same and no further arbitrage profits are possible (see 6.5).

(Tutorial note: some students ask 'why doesn't Mr X borrow even more at 5% and make an even greater gain?' The answer is that he could do so but only at the cost of increasing his risk. The example shows he can make a gain with no increase in risk by substituting personal gearing for corporate gearing exactly.)

The arbitrage process could also work in the opposite direction ie, by an investor without personal gearing taking advantage of favourable corporate gearing.

6.3   Activity

Data as in the previous example, except that the market value of equity for G is £50,000 ie, total market value is £50,000 + £40,000 = £90,000. In this case M & M would see the ungeared company as being overvalued.

Ms Y holds 10% of the equity in U and she wishes to profit by arbitrage. To do so she must sell her stake in U and invest in G's equity. The equity in G carries financial risk as G is geared. Her original position in U was ungeared and to obtain an ungeared position in G she must invest in a proportionate amount of G's debentures to cancel the gearing risk.

Show the effect on Ms Y of selling her shareholding in U and buying 10% of each of G's debt and equity.

6.4   Activity solution

Ms Y's earnings from U	10% × £10,000	=	£1,000
Proceeds from sale of shares	£100,000 × 10%	=	£10,000
Cost of purchase of 10% of G's equity	10% × £50,000	=	£5,000
Cost of purchase of 10% of G's debt	10% × £40,000**	=	£4,000

** The gearing risk of G's equity caused by having to support debt finance is cancelled by investing in the debt finance itself.

Ms Y's earnings from G:

		£
Equity	£8,000 × 10% (as before)	800
Debt	£4,000 × 5%	200
		1,000

Spare funds: £10,000 – (5,000 + 4,000) = £1,000

These spare funds can be invested elsewhere to increase her return above that earned from U and her risk position is unchanged. In this case market pressures would lead to a fall in U's share price and a rise in that of G until no spare funds resulted from the transactions and therefore no arbitrage profits were available.

| Conclusion | The examples demonstrate how market pressures will cause two companies which are identical, except for their capital structure, to have the same market value. |

6.5   The equilibrium position under the arbitrage process

We have demonstrated that any misvaluations of companies will be subject to arbitrage; we now need to consider how long this process will continue. Consider once again the first arbitrage example where company U is valued at £100,000 and company G at £120,000. We have noted that profits can be earned by selling shares in G and buying shares in U.

If we assume that all the price changes are concentrated on G's equity value we can identify the point at which profits from arbitrage will cease.

Mr X's gain is due to his having the same income from U as from G, but with £2,000 spare. If £2,000 were not spare then arbitrage would not be attractive. To lose this advantage he would have had to sell his shares in G for £2,000 less ie, £6,000 only. Therefore the total value of all G's equity would have to be £60,000 for arbitrage to stop and the market to be in equilibrium.

At this point the market value of the two companies would be:

U = All equity £100,000
G = Equity £60,000 + Debt £40,000 = £100,000.

6.6   Cost of capital at the equilibrium position

Consider the cost of capital of G in the revised situation:

Source	Cost	Proportion	WACC
Equity	$\dfrac{8,000}{60,000}$ = 0.133 or 13.3%	0.6	8
Debt	5%	0.4	2
		1.0	10

Graphically:

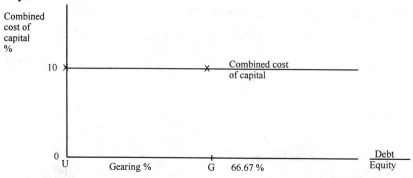

This coincides with the constant cost of capital of M & M's net operating income approach.

The example could be extended by taking a number of companies with the same business risk as U and G, but different levels of gearing. In every case, the equilibrium position would fall on the above line.

6.7   Conclusion reached from the arbitrage process

The above numerical examples provide the basis for the net operating income argument.

> The combined cost of capital is unaffected by the level of gearing and remains constant at the cost of equity of an ungeared company of that business risk class.

It will be noted that if M & M are correct WACC does not change with gearing, the only determinant of WACC being the firm's level of business risk.

There can be no doubt that the model described above is valid given the assumptions on which it rests. Dispute about its validity therefore rests on criticisms of these assumptions.

6.8   Criticisms of the assumptions in the 1958 M & M model

(a)   Market inefficiencies hamper the arbitrage process

The examples above assumed no dealing costs; they require informed investors. Though the security markets are efficient in a technical economist's sense, they are not perfect. Dealing costs do exist and will hamper the arbitrage process.

However, if the arbitrage process is viewed as a long-term trend, rather than an immediate response, the market imperfections become less important.

(b)   **Personal borrowing is not a perfect substitute for corporate borrowing**

This really breaks down to three distinct points.

(i)   Companies can often borrow on better terms than individual investors.

(ii)   Corporate borrowing does not expose the investor to personal liability in the way that personal borrowing does.

(iii)   Some institutional investors are prohibited from indulging in 'home-made' gearing.

All of these points have some validity. What is not apparent is whether they are significant enough to invalidate the M & M view, especially since some investors are themselves limited liability companies which can, therefore, borrow on equivalent terms to the investee.

(c)   **The cost of equity declines at extreme leverage**

The model assumes that the cost of equity capital actually declines at extreme leverage. This assumption is necessary to maintain a constant overall cost if it is accepted that the cost of debt rises at extreme leverage.

The concept of this decline in the cost of equity is extremely improbable, and no evidence has been produced to support such a view. However, the problem is largely theoretical as companies in the UK do not normally operate at very high gearing levels.

(d)   **The model ignores taxation**

This is the case and the effects are sufficiently important to warrant incorporation separately.

7   THE EFFECT OF TAXATION ON THE MODIGLIANI AND MILLER MODEL

7.1   Introduction

In their original model M & M ignored taxation. In 1963 they amended their model to include corporation tax. This alteration changes the implication of their analysis significantly.

Previously they argued that companies that differ only in their capital structure should have the same total value of debt plus equity. This was because it was the size of a firm's operating earning stream that determines its value, not the way in which it was split between returns to debt and equity holders. However, the corporation tax system carries a distortion under which returns to debt holders (interest) are tax deductible to the firm, whereas returns to equity holders are not. M & M, therefore, conclude that

geared companies have an advantage over ungeared companies ie, they pay less tax and will, therefore, have a greater market value and a lower weighted average cost of capital.

The arbitrage process once again supports their position.

7.2   Example of tax and arbitrage

Take the situation in the first arbitrage example above, but assume that corporation tax is payable at 30%.

For convenience, the figures will be restated.

Market capitalisations:

	U £	G £
Equity shares	100,000	80,000
Debt (cost 5% × MV)	-	40,000
	100,000	120,000
Annual expected earnings before interest and tax EBIT	10,000	10,000
Less: Interest 5% × £40,000	-	2,000
Earnings before tax	10,000	8,000
Corporation tax @ 30%	3,000	2,400
Earnings available to equity	7,000	5,600

$$\left(\text{Cost of equity} \qquad \frac{7,000}{100,000} = 7\% \qquad \frac{5,600}{80,000} = 7\%\right)$$

Consider what happens if Mr X adopts the arbitrage process. He owns 10% of the shares in G, which he now wishes to sell. His dividends from G are made more risky by the annual debt interest which the company has to pay. G's total annual interest payment is £2,000, but net of corporation tax it amounts to £2,000 $(1 - 0.3) = £1,400$. Mr X's 'share' of this is £140. When he exchanges corporate for personal gearing **and keeps risk constant** he therefore wishes to suffer the same annual debt interest of £140 pa. Since debt interest is not allowable against personal tax, he should borrow only £2,800 personally, at the market interest rate of 5% pa $(£2,800 \times 5\% = £140)$. His borrowings are therefore not £4,000 as before, but £4,000 $(1 - 0.3) = £2,800$.

	£	£
Income from G (10% × £5,600)		560
Sale proceeds from G	8,000	
Personal borrowings @ 5%	2,800	
Funds available	10,800	
Invested in U's shares	10,000	
Income from U 10% × £7,000	700	
Less: Personal interest = £2,800 × 5%	140	
Net income		560
Spare funds £10,800 – £10,000 =	800	

Once again he is taking the same level of risk but his total returns will be higher due to the £800 spare funds. Note, however, that under a corporation tax regime the amount of spare funds is less (it was £2,000 with no corporation tax). This reflects the fact that companies can borrow more efficiently than individuals because of the corporation tax shield on debt interest.

7.3   Equilibrium position with corporation tax

Once again shareholders will move from company G to company U forcing down the price of G's shares. Again assume the price of U's shares remains constant.

The equilibrium position will occur when Mr X's income is the same and he has no spare funds available. For this to occur the proceeds from the sale of 10% of G's shares will have to decline by £800, and the value of G's total equity by £8,000.

Thus, in equilibrium G's total value will be:

	£
Debt	40,000
Equity	72,000 (ie, £80,000 – £8,000)
	112,000

This is £12,000 higher than the ungeared firm, due to the corporation tax benefits of corporate borrowing. With no corporation tax their values were the same.

The annual advantage of corporate borrowing may be calculated as follows:

Amount borrowed (D) × interest rate (i) × tax rate (t)

If this borrowing is permanent (ie, every year to perpetuity) then the present value of the tax savings =

$$\frac{D \times i \times t}{i}$$

(Remembering that the present value of a perpetuity equals $\frac{\text{Annual cash flow}}{\text{Interest rate}}$).

This simplifies to Dt = £40,000 × 0.3 = £12,000.

Conclusion	The relationship between the total market value of two firms identical in every aspect apart from gearing may be expressed as:

$$V_g = V_u + Dt$$

where V_g = market capitalisation of the geared firm (debt + equity)

V_u = market capitalisation of the ungeared firm

D = market capitalisation of the geared firm's debt

t = corporate tax rate.

Hence at equilibrium:

V_g = Firm G = £112,000

V_u = Firm U = £100,000

D = G's debt = £40,000

t = 30%

with £112,000 = £100,000 + (£40,000 × 0.3) at equilibrium.

Note: the 'Dt' term above is often called the 'tax shield' of the debt.

7.4 Activity

Calculate the WACC of G in equilibrium, with tax at 30%.

7.5   Activity solution

As the geared firm now has a higher value its WACC will be lower than that of the ungeared firm.

	MV £	*Proportion*	*Net of tax cost*	*Proportion × cost* %
Equity	72,000	0.643	$\dfrac{5,600}{72,000} = 7.78\%$	5.00
Debt	40,000	0.357	$5\% \, (1 - 0.3) = 3.5\%$	1.25
	112,000	1.000	WACC	6.25

Alternatively, for perpetuities when tax relief is considered,

$$\text{WACC} \;=\; \frac{\text{Equity dividend + Net of tax debt interest}}{\text{Total market capitalisation}}$$

$$=\; \frac{5,600 + 2,000(1 - 0.3)}{112,000}$$

$$=\; 6.25\%$$

$$\text{WACC ungeared firm} = \text{cost of equity} = \frac{7,000}{100,000} \times 100 = 7\%$$

7.6   Graph of M & M model with tax

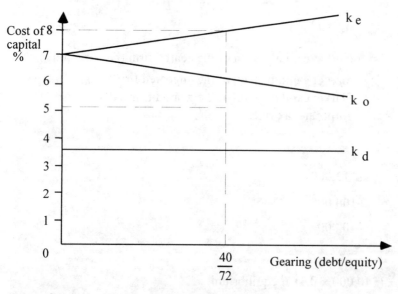

As gearing increases, the WACC steadily decreases.

Conclusion   If the other implications of the M & M view are accepted, the introduction of taxation suggests that the higher the level of taxation, the lower the combined cost of capital. More importantly for financial strategy, the higher the level of the company's gearing, the greater the value of the company. The logical conclusion is that companies should choose a 99.9% gearing level.

8   MODIGLIANI AND MILLER FORMULAE

8.1   The formulae

M & M developed the following formulae which can be applied to finding the value, cost of equity or WACC of firms which have a given level of business risk, but varying financial risk.

	Without tax	*With tax*
Value of firm	$V_g = V_u$	$V_g = V_u + Dt$
Cost of equity	$k_{eg} = k_{eu} + \dfrac{D}{E}(k_{eu} - k_d)$	$k_{eg} = k_{eu} + (1-t)\dfrac{D}{E}(k_{eu} - k_d)$
WACC	$WACC_g = WACC_u$	$WACC_g = WACC_u\left(1 - \dfrac{Dt}{D+E}\right)$

Where V = Value of firm (V_g = value of geared firm, V_u = value of ungeared firm).

k_e = Cost of equity (k_{eg} = cost of equity in geared firm, k_{eu} = cost of equity in ungeared firm).

k_d = Cost of debt (**must be gross of tax**)

D = MV of debt

E = MV of geared firm's equity.

t = Corporation tax rate.

$WACC$ = weighted average cost of capital (suffices as above).

It may be seen that the without tax formulae are simply a special case of the with tax formulae, with $t = 0$.

8.2   Activity

Apply these formulae to the equilibrium positions in the sections above to ensure you are happy with their workings.

8.3   Activity solution

	Without tax	*With tax*
Value of firm	$V_g = V_u$ £100,000 = £100,000	$V_g = V_u + Dt$ £112,000 = £100,000 + (£40,000 × 0.3)
Cost of equity	$k_{eg} = k_{eu} + \dfrac{D}{E}(k_{eu} - k_d)$ $13.33\% = 10\% + \dfrac{40}{60}(10\% - 5\%)$	$k_{eg} = k_{eu} + (1-t)\dfrac{D}{E}(k_{eu} - k_d)$ $7.78\% = 7\% + (1 - 0.3)$ $\dfrac{40}{72}(7\% - 5\%)$
WACC	$WACC_g = WACC_u$ 10% = 10%	$WACC_g = WACC_u\left(1 - \dfrac{Dt}{D+E}\right)$ $6.25\% = 7\%\left(1 - \dfrac{40 \times 0.3}{112}\right)$

9   CHAPTER SUMMARY

The chapter started by bringing together the costs of different types of capital to derive the overall cost of all capital provided to a business. This weighted average cost of capital reflects the pool of funds used to finance investment projects and, as long as risk is not affected by a new project or the finance method used, can be used to appraise the potential project.

However, the WACC is affected by, amongst other things, financial gearing ie, the firm's capital structure. Although the cost of equity is higher than the cost of debt (as the existence of debt increases risk by making returns fluctuate more), a firm cannot necessarily reduce its WACC by issuing more debt. This is because the more debt there is, the higher the cost of equity, which reflects the increased financial risk.

The overall effect on WACC of gearing up depends on which view one takes. The traditional view is that at fairly low levels of debt, bringing in more debt will not significantly affect the cost of equity, with the net result that the WACC will fall. However, after a certain point, the cost of equity will start rising more rapidly as more debt is brought in, as will the WACC. The result is that there is an optimal gearing level at which a firm's WACC is minimised and its market value is therefore maximised.

The Modigliani and Miller view is that when tax is ignored, the value of a firm (and its WACC) depends only on its operating profits, not on how those profits are distributed ie, it is independent of the capital structure of the firm. They prove this using the arbitrage process.

However, when corporation tax is considered, the tax deductibility of debt interest confers an advantage on debt, so the more debt a company has, the higher its market value (and the lower its WACC).

Ensure that you can explain, discuss and draw the diagrams demonstrating the two views. You must also be able to reproduce and use the M & M formulae given in the text, and demonstrate arbitrage techniques.

The meaning and impact of operating gearing was also briefly discussed.

10   SELF TEST QUESTIONS

10.1   How is the weighted average cost of capital defined? (1.1)

10.2   What assumptions are made when using a firm's WACC to appraise projects? (1.8)

10.3   How does debt financing affect the net returns to equity? (2.4)

10.4   Name four factors, other than cost, which influence firms' financial structures. (2.5)

10.5   How is personal gearing created? (4.1)

10.6   What is business risk? (5.2)

10.7   What is the shape of the weighted average cost of capital curve in the traditional view of gearing? (5.4)

10.8   What is the effect of arbitrage on the value of firms? (6.2 - 6.5)

10.9   What are the main criticisms of the Modigliani and Miller 1958 model of capital structure? (6.8)

10.10   Give the formula for the cost of equity in the M & M model with tax. (8.1)

11   EXAMINATION TYPE QUESTIONS

11.1   Arditti plc, Beranek plc and Crockett plc

(a)   Arditti plc is an all-equity company with 15 million £1 ordinary shares in issue. Its ordinary shares currently stand at £2.75 (19X5). The dividend for this year has just been paid.

Financial data	*EPS*	*Dividend/share*
	p	p
19X1	14	10
19X2	28	12
19X3	34	15
19X4	45	18
19X5	58	22

Book value of equity/share was £3.87 in 19X5.

You are required to estimate the cost of equity capital using:

(i)   dividend growth model;

(ii)   earnings retention model.   **(3 marks)**

(b)   Beranek plc has the following debt in its capital structure as at 31 December 19X1. All interest has just been paid.

Type	*Book value* £'000	*Market value*	*Redemption value*	*Redemption date*
7% irredeemable	10,000	£70 per cent	-	-
5% redeemable	5,000	£80 per cent	par	31.12.X9
8% redeemable	6,000	£82 per cent	£104 per cent	30.06.X6

Interest payments - 7% and   5% - annually in arrears
                               8% - semi-annually in arrears

You are required to estimate the annual cost of each type of debt. Ignore taxation.

(5 marks)

(c)   The following figures are taken from the current balance sheet of Crockett plc.

	£'000
Ordinary share capital	
Authorised: 20,000,000 of £1	20,000
Issued: 18,000,000 of £1	18,000
Share premium	6,000
Reserves	10,000
	34,000
6% irredeemable debentures	10,000
	44,000

The ordinary shares are standing at £2.58 with a dividend of 18p to be paid shortly. Dividends have grown at 7% per annum for the last six years and this growth is expected to continue. The interest is also due to be paid on the debt which has a market value of £74.

You are required to estimate the weighted average cost of capital of Crockett plc.   **(2 marks)**
                                                                              (Total: 10 marks)

11.2   Westerly plc

(a)   What should the ultimate financial aims of a company be and what role should the finance function play in their achievement? In particular, which of the related responsibilities of the finance department involve a direct interface with line management?   **(10 marks)**

(b)   Under what circumstances would a company, deciding that it needed more share capital, opt for preference rather than ordinary shares? What are the disadvantages from the company's and the shareholders' point of view?   **(10 marks)**

(c)   Westerly plc decides that it needs approximately £1m more in shareholders' funds. Its £5m issued (par value 25p) shares are currently selling at 115p, and its merchant bankers say that a five-for-one rights issue at 100p could be achieved. However, another merchant bank is proposing that the £1m should be raised by means of a convertible loan with a coupon of 9% pa against a market rate of 11% pa, with conversion possible after two years at eighty shares for every £100 of stock held.

The board is attracted to the idea of a cheaper interest rate and avoiding the need to sell shares at a discount, particularly as it is reasonably certain, given trading prospects, that the share price will be over 140p within two years. It turns to the finance director for her advice.

What should she say?   **(10 marks)**
    (Total: 30 marks)

11.3   Karim plc and Roshan plc

Karim plc and Roshan plc are quoted companies. The following figures are from their current balance sheets.

	Karim plc *£'000*	*Roshan plc* *£'000*
Ordinary share capital		
Authorised: 2,000,000 shares of 50p	1,000	1,000
Issued: 1,000,000 shares of 50p	500	500
Reserves	1,750	150
Shareholders' funds	2,250	650
6% irredeemable debentures	-	2,500

Both companies earn an annual profit, before charging debenture interest, of £500,000 which is expected to remain constant for the indefinite future. The profits of both companies, before charging debenture interest, are generally regarded as being subject to identical levels of risk. It is the policy of both companies to distribute all available profits as dividends at the end of each year.

The current market value of Karim plc's ordinary shares is £3.00 per share cum div. An annual dividend is due to be paid in the very near future.

Roshan plc has just made annual dividend and interest payments both on its ordinary shares and on its debentures. The current market value of the ordinary shares is £1.40 per share and of the debentures £50.00 per cent.

Mr Hashim owns 50,000 ordinary shares in Roshan plc. He is wondering whether he could increase his annual income, without incurring any extra risk, by selling his shares in Roshan plc and buying some of the ordinary shares of Karim plc. Mr Hashim is able to borrow money at an annual compound rate of interest of 12%.

You are required to do the following:

(a)   Estimate the cost of ordinary share capital and the weighted average cost of capital of Karim plc and Roshan plc.   **(4 marks)**

(b)   Explain briefly why both the cost of ordinary share capital and weighted average cost of capital of Karim plc differ from those of Roshan plc.   **(3 marks)**

(c)   Prepare calculations to demonstrate to Mr Hashim how he might improve his position in the way he has suggested, stating clearly any reservations you have about the scheme.

(10 marks)

(d)   Discuss the implications of your answers to (a), (b) and (c) above for the determination of a company's optimal financial structure in practice.   **(8 marks)**

(Total: 25 marks)

Ignore taxation for (a), (b) and (c) but not for (d).

12   ANSWERS TO EXAMINATION TYPE QUESTIONS

12.1   Arditti plc, Beranek plc and Crockett plc

Definitions

k	=	Weighted average cost of capital
k_s	=	Cost of equity capital
k_b	=	Cost of debt capital
S	=	Ex-div market value of equity
B	=	Ex-int market value of debt
d_t	=	Dividend at time t
g	=	Annual growth rate

(a)   **Arditti plc**

(i)   Dividend growth model

Assuming a constant underlying growth rate over the relevant period:

$$22p \quad = \quad 10p\,(1 + g)^4$$

$$\therefore (1 + g)^4 \quad = \quad \frac{22}{10} = 2.2$$

$$(1 + g) \quad = \quad \sqrt[4]{2.2} = 1.218$$

$$g \quad \approx \quad 22\%$$

$$k_s \quad = \quad \frac{d_0(1+g)}{S} + g$$

$$= \quad \frac{22 \times (1 + 0.22)}{275} + 0.22 = 0.3176 \text{ (say 32\%)}$$

(ii)   Retention rate

$$b \quad = \quad \frac{EPS - DPS}{EPS}$$

$$= \quad \frac{58 - 22}{58} = 62\%$$

ROCE

$$r \quad = \quad \frac{EPS}{\text{Book value of capital employed/ share}}$$

$$= \quad \frac{58}{387} = 15\%$$

$$\therefore \text{growth rate} \quad g = br$$

$$= 0.62 \times 0.15 = 9.3\%$$

$$\text{hence } k_s = \frac{d_o(1+g)}{S} + g$$

$$= \frac{22 \times (1+0.093)}{275} + 0.093$$

$$= 0.18044 \text{ (say 18\%)}$$

(b)   **Beranek plc**

Interest is paid at the coupon rate based upon the £100 nominal value.

7% irredeemable debt

$$\text{Using} \qquad k_b = \frac{\text{Interest}}{B}$$

$$k_b = \frac{7}{70} = 0.10 \text{ (or 10\%)}$$

5% redeemable debt

k_b is the discount rate which equates future income and redemption value with B.

Try $k_b = 10\%$

				£
Present value of interest	=	£5 × 5.335	=	26.68
Present value of redemption	=	£100 × 0.467	=	46.70
				73.28
Market value	=			(80.00)
				£(6.62)

Try $k_b = 5\%$

				£
Present value of interest	=	£5 × 6.463	=	32.32
Present value of redemption	=	£100 × 0.677	=	67.70
				100.02
Market value	=			(80.00)
				£20.02

Using linear interpolation

$$k_b \approx 5\% + \frac{20.02}{20.02 + 6.62}(10-5)\% = 8.8\%$$

8% redeemable debt

Interest is paid semi-annually ie, £4 every 6 months.

There will be nine more interest payments.

The cost of debt is the discount rate which equates the future payments (interest and redemption) with the current market value.

Try 5%

				£
Present value of interest	=	£4 × 7.108	=	28.43
Present value of redemption	=	£104 × 0.645	=	67.08
				95.51
Market value				(82.00)
				£13.51

Try 10%

				£
Present value of interest	=	£4 × 5.759	=	23.04
Present value of redemption	=	£104 × 0.424	=	44.10
				67.14
Market value	=			(82.00)
				£(14.86)

Using linear interpolation

$$k_b \approx 5\% + \frac{13.51}{13.51 + 14.86}(10 - 5\%) = 7.381\% \text{ per 6 months}$$

$\therefore$ Annual $k_b \approx (1 + 0.07381)^2 - 1 = 15\%$

(c)   **Crockett plc**

(Tutorial note: since the dividend and the interest are about to be paid, the shares and the debentures must be cum div and cum int respectively.)

$$k_s \quad = \quad \frac{18 \times (1 + 0.07)}{258 - 18} + 0.07 \approx 15\%$$

$$k_b \quad = \quad \frac{6}{74 - 6} = 0.0882 \text{ (say 8.8\%)}$$

$$S \quad = \quad 18m \times £2.40 = £43.2m$$

$$B \quad = \quad £10m \times 0.68 = £6.8m$$

$$k \quad = \quad \left(k_s \times \frac{S}{S + B}\right) + \left(k_b \times \frac{B}{S + B}\right) = \frac{k_s S + k_b B}{S + B}$$

$$\quad = \quad \frac{(0.15 \times 43.2) + (0.088 \times 6.8)}{43.2 + 6.8}$$

$$\quad = \quad 0.1416$$

Thus $k \approx 14\%$

12.2   Westerly plc

(a)   Every limited company has shareholders, who are the owners of the company, and for whose ultimate financial benefit, subject to the welfare of the employees and social responsibilities, the business is run. This financial benefit is also called shareholders' wealth, and the ultimate financial goal of limited companies is therefore generally expressed as 'the maximisation of shareholders' wealth'. So far as the company is concerned, shareholders' wealth is made available in two ways: the cash dividends received from the company, and the capital value of the shareholders' investment ie, the cash which would be raised were the shares to be sold. The combination of these two represent the shareholders' wealth so far as the company is concerned, and the company's financial objective must be so to balance dividends and the capital value of shares so that the maximum value is achieved for shareholders.

The finance function has three main areas of responsibility: its role in the development of business strategy, the development of its own functional strategy, and, within the latter, the day-to-day responsibilities. The main impact on the maximisation of the shareholders' funds lies in the area of business strategy, but with clear relevance to its own functional strategic and day-to-day responsibilities, as follows.

(i)   The provision of finance to enable the business to attain its strategic objectives. The latter would be primarily commercial aims, and in many businesses the finance function would have a co-ordinating hand in their development.

Within this, the finance function would be involved in the identification of debt capacity and debt levels which would in effect set a target relationship between debt and equity. So far as the debt element was concerned, the function would determine appropriate maturity structures, as well as achieving an appropriate balance between fixed and floating rate debt.

Furthermore, since finance can be sourced from both lenders and shareholders' funds, it becomes a functional responsibility to ensure that the level of the latter is consonant with target levels, and, where it is too low or likely to fall to an unsatisfactory level, to determine how the position can be rectified and, where appropriate, to raise the necessary equity.

The provision of finance tends to be a largely functional responsibility but some interface with line management occurs in regard to the ultimate constraints which availability of finance places on strategic development, and in the coordination of the latter.

(ii)   The financial measurement of commercial success. Commercial management's objectives must ultimately be translated into financial terms, and clearly, working directly with commercial management, certain strategic targets will be identified such as growth in the pre-interest trading profits, return on trading capital employed, or real increase in earnings per share.

(iii)   The allocation of resources within a group. No group has unlimited resources, but it is necessary on a regular basis to determine, usually by joint action between line and financial management at the top level, how cash resources should be allocated. In particular, the finance function would have an important role in determining the criteria by which such allocation decisions might be made, and the pre-eminent consideration would be the attainment of financial objectives consonant with shareholders' wealth maximisation.

(iv)   Reviewing acquisitions and divestments. Groups grow and contract organically, but more dramatically and radically through acquisitions and divestments, presumably in striving towards the attainment of group strategic objectives. Line management and finance will work closely in developing such projects, and the financial role will be particularly important in respect of appraising them financially and in the resources allocation questions they raise.

(v)   Dividend policy.   Whilst groups cannot have direct control over one aspect of shareholder wealth maximisation - share price - they have direct control over the other - the payment of cash dividends, always subject of course to final shareholders' approval.   The development of dividend policy and recommendations for individual dividend dealings is a direct responsibility of the finance function alone, although the discussion of and final recommendation for such a dividend will always remain with the board of directors.

(b)   If a company is presented with a choice between ordinary and preference shares its decision is likely to be influenced by three factors - cost, flexibility and performance.   The name 'preference' indicates that preference shareholders have certain advantages over ordinary shareholders, relating basically to preference in respect of dividends, and in liquidation.   It follows that in general terms the risk for preference shareholders is less than for ordinary shareholders, and accordingly the return on investment expectation (the preference dividend) is lower than the ordinary shareholders' (cash dividend plus capital appreciation), which equally becomes the cost to the company.   The preference dividends have an advantage to the company in that they are a cheaper source of capital.

They are also, unless convertible at the shareholders' option, a more flexible form of capital since they are often redeemable, and ordinary share repurchase is, under most tax and legal regimes, a complicated procedure.

However, this very flexibility can be a disadvantage for the company if permanence is required.   In addition, ordinary shares can be subscribed on a partly paid basis, which, whilst it does not get over the problem, if redemption of shareholders' funds is required, does enable the capital fall to take place in tranches over a period, rather than in one amount.

The shareholder in deciding between preference and ordinary shares should, in theory at least, be indifferent; each has different risk and reward characteristics, and his choice will depend very much on his investment objectives.   However, in broad terms, he must trade off the potentially lower return on a preference share issue, and their lack of control and voting rights (which do accrue to ordinary shareholders) for the fixed, preferential dividend, and the preference in liquidation.

(c)   The decision which the board faces should be seen in the context of the financial effect of the proposals on the shareholders themselves.

The rights issue is of a pre-emptive nature, and thus has no dilution effect on the existing shareholders.   Those shareholders who do not care to take up their rights can sell them in the market, the value they receive being the difference between the share price before the rights issue and after the rights issue.   Existing shareholders will suffer no financial disadvantages.

However, the picture is rather different with the convertible loan issue: the shareholders will benefit to the tune of (11-9) − 2% pa on the full amount of the issue, being the difference between market rate interest and the coupon on the issue.   Against this, the current outlook shows that Westerly could issue straight debt and refinance in two years' time via an equity issue at the then market rate, which is forecast to be 140p per share.   However the striking price of the conversion option is $\dfrac{100}{80}$ = 125p per share, and the loss to the shareholders generated by the convertible is therefore 140 − 125 = 15p per share.

The financial cost to the existing shareholders, ignoring tax and assuming all the loanstock holders convert after two years, is therefore:

		£
Loss (as above) £0.15 × 80 × $\dfrac{1,000,000}{100}$	=	120,000
Less interest benefit ($\dfrac{2}{100}$ × 1,000,000)	=	(20,000)
Net financial cost to existing shareholders	=	100,000

Even allowing for tax, the convertible loan is clearly financially disadvantageous to existing shareholders. The rights issue has no disadvantages, and the finance director should advise her board to accept that alternative, despite its cosmetic disadvantages.

12.3   Karim plc and Roshan plc

(Tutorial note: this question requires a demonstration of the arbitrage process. In part (d) a brief overview of the weakness of the M and M no tax position must be given.)

(a)   **Cost of capital**

Karim plc

Since the profits and hence dividends are expected to remain constant, the formula $Vo = \dfrac{d}{i}$ is applicable.

where   Vo = ex div share price
$\quad$ d = dividend per share
$\quad$ i = cost of ordinary share capital

Annual profit = £500,000.

∴ Dividend per share $\dfrac{£500,000}{1,000,000}$ = 50p per share

Market price = £3 per share cum div, ∴ £2.50 per share ex div.

Applying above formula, $2.50 = \dfrac{0.50}{i}$

$i = \dfrac{0.50}{2.50} = 0.2$ or 20%. This is also the WACC, as Karim is all-equity financed.

Roshan plc

Ordinary share capital

	£
Annual profit	500,000
Less: Debenture interest	150,000
Available for dividends	350,000
∴ Dividend per share	0.35

Applying above formula, $1.40 = \dfrac{0.35}{i}$

$i = \dfrac{0.35}{1.40} = 0.25$ or 25%

Debentures

Applying the irredeemable debt formula (as the formula for cost of equity with constant dividends).

$$i = \frac{6\% \times £100}{£50} = 12\%$$

Roshan plc: weighted average cost of capital

Source	Market value		Cost of capital	WACC
	£'000	Proportion	%	%
Equity	1,400	0.528	25	13.20
Debentures	1,250	0.472	12	5.66
	2,650	1.000		18.86

Summary of results

	Cost of ordinary share capital	Weighted average cost of capital
	%	%
Karim plc	20	20
Roshan plc	25	18.86

(b)   **Explanation of differences in cost of ordinary share capital and weighted average cost of capital**

From the data given the difference in the cost of ordinary share capital must be entirely explained in terms of the different gearing of the two companies. The effect of the higher gearing of Roshan plc is to increase the level of financial risk and, therefore, decrease the relative attractiveness of the ordinary shares.

This may be explained in terms of the objectives with which investors acquire and hold ordinary shares. In the first place investors will seek to maximise their return. However, at the same time investors are in general averse to risk and, therefore, will seek to minimise the uncertainty inherent in those returns. Uncertainties may be explained in terms of the variance of the returns about their expected values.

In any business investment there must be an element of business risk. The effect of a company using borrowing to increase its financial gearing is to magnify the effect of such business risk. This is because of the fixed nature of interest charges, which must be borne irrespective of the level of profitability and which, therefore, leaves a smaller margin of equity investment to carry the same absolute levels of variation in return.

Because, as indicated above, investors are averse to such uncertainty, they will demand a higher rate of return to compensate them for the higher level of uncertainty. This clearly explains why the cost of equity of Roshan plc, (25%) is higher than that of Karim plc, (20%).

However, two American writers, Modigliani and Miller have taken this a stage further and used a quantitative analysis to suggest that the relationship between the increasing costs of equity and the benefits of introducing cheaper debt finance must exactly cancel each other out (in the absence of taxation). The mechanism by which this takes place is known as the arbitrage process and is, indeed, described in the example below. This being so, the difference in the weighted average cost of capital of the two companies must be explained in one of the three terms.

(i)   The situation is an unstable one which will be rectified by investors carrying out arbitrage operations so as to take advantage of the gains which are available to them.

(ii)   The data given does not coincide with investors' evaluations of the two companies and they are not, in fact, seen as identical (for example their respective earnings are subject to differing degrees of business risk).

(iii)   The basic assumptions in the Modigliani-Miller hypothesis are not valid, and the data reflects their invalidity.

Any one of these three would provide an explanation. Despite a number of studies, the difficulty of evaluating data means there is as yet no conclusive evidence on the validity of the Modigliani-Miller hypothesis.

(c)   **Mr Hashim**

Present annual income 50,000 × £0.35 = £17,500
Market value of holding 50,000 × £1.40 = £70,000

Amount to be borrowed

Mr Hashim's level of risk will be unchanged if he employs personal gearing to the same extent as Roshan plc ie, so that debt is 47.2% of total capital or so that debt and own funds are in the ratio 1,250 : 1,400 or 625 : 700. Amount to be borrowed is therefore $\dfrac{625}{700} \times 70,000 = £62,500$.

Number of shares to be purchased

Total capital available = £132,500 (= £70,000 +£62,500)

Number of shares in Karim plc which can be purchased (ex div)

$$\frac{132,500}{2.5} = 53,000$$

Annual income following the scheme

	£
Dividend receipts 53,000 @ 50p	26,500
Less: Interest @ 12% on £62,500	7,500
Net income	19,000

Mr Hashim's annual income would therefore increase by £1,500 or 8.6% as a result of the scheme.

Reservations

(1)   The level of gearing in Roshan plc is high. By adopting a similarly high personal level of gearing Mr Hashim is accepting a high risk from which he has no limited liability.

(2)   Mr Hashim may find it difficult to borrow such a large sum unless he provides additional security. The cost may well be greater than the company's borrowing rate.

(3)   Other investors may see the possibility of providing additional income by the same process thus increasing the share price of Karim. Mr Hashim may therefore be required to pay the higher price thus reducing his anticipated increase.

(4)   Transaction costs have been ignored.

(d)   **Implications for the determination of the company's optimum financial structure**

In the absence of taxation the Modigliani-Miller thesis suggests that the company should be indifferent as between differing capital structures.

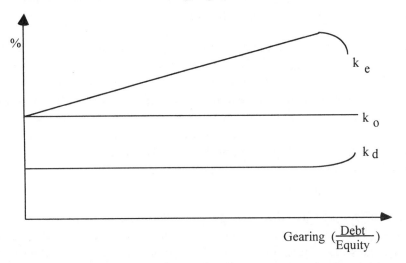

This view changes dramatically if we introduce the effects of taxation. If the Modigliani-Miller view is still accepted, then the cost of capital will decline at a gradient which is equal to the marginal rate of tax saving on the debt finance being introduced.

The Modigliani-Miller view conflicts with the more traditional view, which suggested that the judicious use of debt finance could, in fact, lower the weighted average cost of capital so that a company could achieve an optimal financing structure, even without considering the effects of taxation.

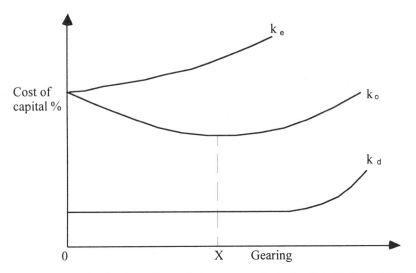

There is no doubt that given their assumptions the Modigliani-Miller analysis is correct. The question, therefore, lies in terms of the assumptions. These may be summarised as follows.

(i)   Company shares are traded in an efficient market. This means that if an opportunity arises for investors to improve their position without increasing their risk, they will recognise and take such opportunities. The level of transaction costs is so low as to be immaterial.

        In practice, there is considerable doubt as to whether the securities market is a sufficient approximation to an efficient market for such a process to work with any degree of reliability.

(ii)   The thesis also presumes that investors can borrow and lend at the same interest rates as companies. This is unlikely for private investors who must operate at a disadvantage as against major corporate investors. This is emphasised within the UK by the legal structure and the difficulty of providing security on individual borrowings. On the other hand, in practice a significant proportion of investors are themselves institutional in nature and for these investors borrowing rates are likely to be similar to those of the companies in which they invest.

(iii)   At high levels of gearing the cost of borrowed funds for the company is itself likely to start rising as the level of risk for lenders becomes significant. In order to maintain the hypothesis of a constant weighted average cost of capital, Modigliani-Miller introduced the idea of 'risk-seeking' investors who would be attracted by the high levels of financial leverage, and would enter the market to buy shares in highly geared companies, thereby lowering the cost of equity. There is no evidence to support this view, which seems highly improbable. However, it is not of great practical significance as most companies do not operate at the high levels of gearing where this would become important.

(iv)   The analysis also assumes that personal taxes have no distorting impact upon net returns to an investor. In practice many investors find that debt income is taxed at higher rates than equity income and this could make them reluctant to allow firms to take high levels of gearing. In this situation we would need to contrast the corporation tax saving to the firm with the personal tax losses to its investors.

As indicated above the evidence on the validity of the Modigliani-Miller view is inconclusive. However, under either view in the presence of taxation there must be substantial advantages for companies introducing some element of debt financing. The only question is the extent to which debt finance should be used. This is clearly much higher if the Modigliani-Miller view, rather than the traditional view, is accepted. However, in practice the parameters are likely to be set by other factors, in particular, the attitude of the business managers to the uncertainty of running a highly geared company, and putting their own jobs at risk. Therefore, although a theoretical conclusion may be elusive, a practical conclusion is at hand. This is that companies should borrow a significant proportion of their financing requirements, and that the limitation is likely to be set by the attitude to risk of the managers, rather than the investors of whose behalf they are purportedly acting.

8 FURTHER ASPECTS OF THE COST OF CAPITAL

INTRODUCTION & LEARNING OBJECTIVES

This chapter starts by looking more closely at the Modigliani and Miller theories. It starts by investigating why companies do not have extremely high debt levels, as the model presented in the previous chapter would predict. It then explains the work done by Miller to adjust the original models for the effect of personal tax, in an attempt to explain the steady 'medium' gearing levels seen in practice.

Next, the capital asset pricing model is linked to the M&M theories in an analysis of how to quantify the effect of financial gearing on cost of capital. Do not be surprised if you find this section difficult - it may need to be re-read a number of times, as the concepts it covers are complex.

Finally, the adjusted present value technique of investment appraisal is discussed. This is an alternative to conventional NPV analysis of operating cash flows.

When you have studied this chapter you should be able to do the following:

- Discuss the effects of bankruptcy costs, agency costs and tax exhaustion on the value of a firm.
- Analyse in outline the effect of personal taxes on the capital structure decision.
- Show how the M&M models can be used in conjunction with the CAPM to calculate a risk adjusted discount rate for project appraisal.
- Calculate and discuss the APV technique of investment appraisal.

1 CAPITAL STRUCTURE AND HIGH GEARING

1.1 Problems associated with high levels of gearing

The M & M 1963 position implies that companies should take gearing to a maximum to obtain the largest tax shield on debt possible and therefore maximise the wealth of their investors. A brief examination of company balance sheets would reveal that this does not happen in reality. Other problems dissuade companies from taking on high levels of gearing. These problems are usually categorised as follows:

(a) Bankruptcy costs;
(b) Agency costs;
(c) Tax exhaustion; and
(d) Personal taxes.

1.2 Bankruptcy costs

As firms take on high levels of gearing the chances of default on repayments, and hence bankruptcy, increase. Investors will be concerned over this possibility and this concern will result in a fall in the value of the company's securities, with a corresponding increase in the firm's cost of funds. To optimise capital structure financial managers must therefore not increase gearing beyond the point where the cost of investor worries over bankruptcy outweigh the benefits gained from the increased tax shield on debt. We can therefore rewrite our basic M & M with tax equation:

  Market value of the firm = Value if all equity financed + Value of the tax shield

to be: Market value of the firm = Value if all equity financed + Value of the tax shield –
  Expected present value of bankruptcy costs

Tutorial note: it is not bankruptcy in itself that is the problem but the costs that accompany it. These costs may be categorised as follows:

(a)   **Direct costs of bankruptcy**

If a firm is liquidated it is well known that its assets are usually sold at less than their going concern value. Liquidation costs, redundancy costs and distress prices for assets due to thin markets can all lead to assets realising less than their economic value. These costs mean that at any point the company's going-concern value will be greater than its wind-up value. This loss in value will often be borne by the debt holders in the event of bankruptcy. To compensate for this investors will ask for high rates of return from highly-geared companies and thus drive down the prices of their securities.

(b)   **Indirect costs of bankruptcy**

These costs can be suffered by companies that eventually go bankrupt or by those that hover close to bankruptcy for many years. They relate to the problems of operating a company under severe financial distress.

In highly-geared firms managers might find that the bulk of their time and attention is spent on keeping creditors happy rather than on seeking the best course of action for the future prosperity of the firm.

Additionally the firm may find that key employees leave rather than stay and risk being tainted by association with the bankrupt firm. Suppliers may refuse to supply trading stock and customers may refuse to buy if they perceive a risk that the after sales service will not be there. These operating problems will reduce the future cash flows of the business and hence its value.

1.3   Agency costs

In a situation of high gearing, shareholder and creditor interests are often at odds regarding the acceptability of investment projects.

Shareholders may be tempted to gamble on high-risk projects as if things work out well they take all the 'winnings' whereas if things turn out badly the debenture holders will stand part of the losses, the shareholders only being liable up to their equity stake.

There are further ways in which managers (appointed by shareholders) can act in the interests of the shareholders rather than the debt holders:

(a)   *Dividends* - We have seen how shareholders may be reluctant to put money into an ailing company. On the other hand they are usually happy to take money out. Large cash dividends will secure part of the company's value for the shareholders at the expense of the creditors.

(b)   *Playing for time* - In general, because of the increasing effect of the indirect costs of bankruptcy, if a firm is going to fail, it is better that this happens sooner rather than later from the creditors' point of view. However, managers may try to hide the extent of the problem by cutting back on research, maintenance, etc, and thus make 'this year's' results better at the expense of 'next year's'.

(c)   *Changing risks* - The company may change the risk of the business without informing the lender. For example, management may negotiate a loan for a relatively safe investment project offering good security and therefore carrying only modest interest charges and then use the funds to finance a far riskier investment. Alternatively management may arrange further loans which increase the risks of the initial creditors by undercutting their asset backing. These actions will once again be to the advantage of the shareholders and to the cost of the creditors.

It is because of the risk that managers might act in this way that most loan agreements contain restrictive covenants for protection of the lender, the costs of these covenants to the firms in terms of constraints upon managers' freedom of action often being referred to as *agency costs* (mentioned earlier).

Covenants used by suppliers of debt finance may place restrictions on:

- **issuing new debt** - with a superior claim on assets

- **dividends** - growth to be linked to earnings

- **merger activity** - to ensure post-merger asset backing of loans is maintained at a minimum prescribed level.

- **investment policy**

Contravention of these agreements will usually result in the loan becoming immediately repayable, thus allowing the debenture holders to restrict the size of any losses.

1.4   Tax exhaustion

Definition   Tax exhaustion occurs when a company has insufficient taxable profits to make use of all the tax reliefs available to it.

A further disincentive to high gearing is that the firm must be in a taxpaying position to obtain the tax shields on debt. At a certain level of gearing companies will discover that they have no taxable income left against which to offset interest charges. After this point firms will experience all the problems of gearing but none of the advantages. The level of investment can also affect the point at which tax exhaustion occurs. This is because capital allowances granted on capital investments will reduce taxable profits.

1.5   Impact of personal taxes

The 1963 M & M position includes the effect of corporate taxes on the capital structure decision, but not the impact of personal taxes. In 1977 one of the M's, Miller, corrected this omission in his now famous article *Debt and Taxes,* which was prompted by the fact that companies do not, in practice, follow a policy of high or even moderate gearing as proposed by their 1963 theory.

To explain this Miller explains that personal taxes must also be considered. You only need to be aware of the basic arguments and conclusions of this theory.

If we first of all imagine a world with no taxes and no market imperfections we know that firms would be indifferent between issuing debt or equity. We now need to introduce taxes to this world. Let us assume for the moment that personal taxes on equity income are at a zero rate. This is not totally outrageous if we specify that all equity income is in the form of capital gains and these gains are never realised. On the other hand we will assume that income received on debt investments (mainly the interest payments) is subject to income tax at normal rates. Corporation tax is assumed to operate in the normal way.

With the introduction of corporation tax firms would begin to replace equity finance with debt finance to take advantage of the tax shield. To do this they would need to persuade some equity holders to become debt holders so as to purchase the new debt issues that were replacing equity. Some investors would have no qualms about such a switch providing the interest rates on the debt were commensurate with the risks they were taking. These would be the investors who were not subject to income taxes (the best example being pension funds) as they would simply be switching from a tax-free equity income to a tax-free debt income. Consider, however, the position of taxpaying investors. They would have to switch from a tax-free equity income to a taxable debt income. To persuade these people to switch, firms would have to increase the interest rates on debt to make it worth their while. Firms could afford to do this by using some of the gains they were making from the tax shield on debt. As more and more debt were issued investors in higher and higher income tax brackets would have to be persuaded to switch from equity to debt and the costs of persuading them to switch would rise correspondingly. Firms could only afford to continue upping the interest rates to persuade these investors to switch until the gain made on the tax shield exactly equalled the personal tax loss suffered by investors.

After this point the attractions of issuing further debt would disappear as the tax shield gain would be eaten up by the enlarged interest payments required on debt and firms would therefore issue no more debt. In the context of the overall financial system an equilibrium ratio of debt to equity would have been reached.

1.6   Implications of Miller's analysis

(a)   There is an equilibrium level of debt for the overall economy that depends upon the rate of corporation tax, the rate of personal tax on debt and equity income, and the amount of funds available to investors in each of the tax brackets.

(b)   *For the individual firm all capital structures are optimal.* Imagine the position of a firm issuing new capital once this overall equilibrium had been achieved. The only advantage of issuing debt is the corporation tax shield on debt and this will only be attractive if it can be issued to low-rate taxpayers. Unfortunately low-rate taxpayers will have been persuaded to hold debt long ago. The only potential debt investors left would be those in higher tax brackets, and to persuade these to switch the 'bribe' in the way of increased interest rates would exactly cancel out the benefit of the tax shield. It therefore becomes a matter of indifference to firms if they issue debt or equity, and therefore all capital structures are optimal.

(c)   Miller's analysis also explains the relatively stable debt ratios experienced in the UK and the USA despite the significant changes in corporation tax rates. The key lies in the fact that as corporation tax rates have changed so have personal tax rates. As the benefits of gearing have changed so have the costs and the equilibrium level of debt has remained largely unchanged.

(d)   Note also that Miller's analysis does not rely on the tax rate on equity income being zero. As long as personal tax rates on debt income are significantly higher than those on equity income, and this differential outweighs the benefit of the corporation tax shield, at some point there will be an overall equilibrium level of debt in the economy and the conclusion that all capital structures are optimal will stand.

(e)   Finally Miller's analysis thus implies that:

	WACC of a geared firm	=	WACC of an ungeared firm
and	Valued of a geared firm	=	Value of an ungeared firm

These are exactly the same conclusions as M & M 1958 but for different reasons.

1.7   A UK perspective on Miller's analysis

The validity of Miller's argument is doubtful when applied to the UK. With our system for taxing dividends and progressive capital gains tax rates the personal tax costs of gearing would only rarely outweigh the corporation tax benefits. Consequently it is unlikely that Miller's equilibrium position for the overall economy would ever be achieved. In the UK context his argument is best viewed as reducing, rather than eliminating, the net tax benefit of gearing. Note however that examiners do not always restrict themselves to real world tax systems!

2   CONCLUSIONS ON CAPITAL STRUCTURE

2.1   Summary of views

The various opinions of the impact of capital structure on the firm's cost of capital may be summarised in the following graphs:

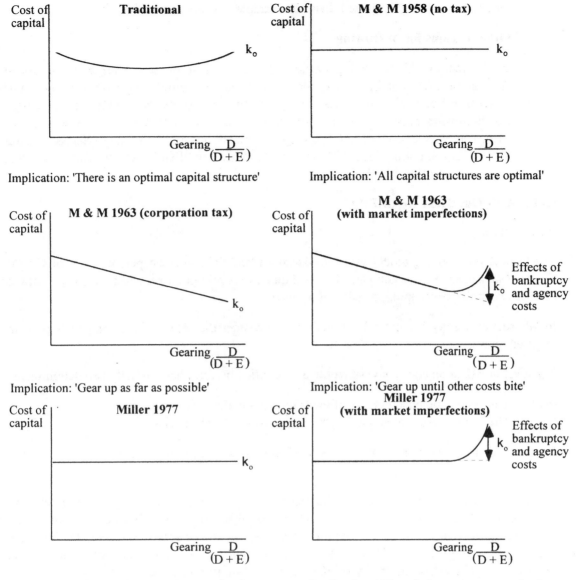

2.2   Practical aspects

Perhaps it is sensible to close this section with some practical guidelines on capital structure.

(a)   **Tax position**

Before borrowing a company must consider its tax position. If it is unlikely to be paying tax in the future it will not obtain the major benefit of debt finance (the corporation tax shield) but it will suffer the personal tax costs and possibly agency and bankruptcy costs. In this situation debt financing would not be attractive.

(b)   **Business risk**

Bankruptcy and agency costs are likely to be higher for firms with high business risk. It is not sensible to compound high business risk by taking on high financial risk. Note that in practice high-risk investments tend to be funded mainly by equity.

(c)   **Asset quality**

Bankruptcy costs and agency costs are likely to be higher for companies with a high proportion of intangible assets. Creditors know that it is easier to get their money back on land and buildings than it is on trademarks. In practice companies with large investments in property tend to be more highly geared than, for example, service companies.

(d)   Other reasons for borrowing

In the real world borrowing carries advantages that often outweigh the potential costs. Arrangement costs on bank loans (the current source of much corporate debt) are significantly lower than flotation costs on new equity. Many small firms are unable to raise equity finance and borrowing becomes the only alternative if they wish to see their business grow. Other firms may wish to engage in borrowing overseas to hedge off foreign exchange exposure or to protect against political risk. These considerations can often be as important as the theoretical arguments put forward above.

3   CAPM AND THE COST OF CAPITAL

3.1   Introduction

The capital asset pricing model was introduced earlier. The greatest potential use of CAPM in the financial management of a company is the ability to set minimum required returns (ie, risk adjusted discount rates) for new capital investment projects.

In this section we need to extend the analysis to consider the effect of the company's gearing on the required return.

The level of risk of an equity investment to a diversified investor has basically two determinants:

(a)   The systematic business risk of the company's underlying assets; and

(b)   The level of gearing adopted by the company (its financial risk).

We have already seen that different business sectors carry differing degrees of systematic business risk.

We now need to turn our attention to the second factor and examine how gearing affects risk. To a large extent we have covered this ground already. By this stage of your studies it should be clear that an ordinary share in an all equity chemical company would be safer than a similar investment in a chemical company carrying 90% gearing. Accordingly the required rate of return on the latter investment would be higher, and by similar logic so would its equity beta.

For purposes of analysis this effect needs to be quantified. The relationship between the level of gearing and equity betas has in fact little to do with CAPM but rather is firmly based upon the theories of Modigliani and Miller including the effects of corporation tax but not personal taxes. These theories have been examined already and we simply need to express them in terms of the impact of gearing upon betas rather than on required rates of return. As betas give a measure of required rates of return it will be appreciated that this is only a small step.

3.2   Activity

Given the following information, estimate the company's cost of equity and cost of debt, using both the dividend valuation model and the CAPM.

Market value of shares	£1.50 per share
Dividend just paid	30 pence per share
Expected future dividend growth rate	5% per annum
Market value of 8% irredeemable debentures	£80 per £100 nominal value
Corporation tax	Nil
Risk-free rate	10% per annum
Market rate	18% per annum
Beta of company's dividends	2

3.3   Activity solution

(a)   Dividend valuation model (DVM)

Cost of equity, $k_e = \dfrac{D_0\,(1 + g)}{MV} + g$.   The market value given in the question is ex dividend, as the dividend has just been paid. D_0 is £0.3 and g is 0.05. Applying the formula to these figures:

$$k_e = \frac{0.3 \times 1.05}{1.5} + 0.05 = 0.26 \text{ or } 26\%$$

Cost of debt, k_d, which here is the same as the return to the debt-holders, as there is no corporation tax, equals $\dfrac{I}{MV}$. I is £8 (the coupon rate is 8%). Applying the formula to these figures:

$$k_d = \frac{8}{80} = 0.1 \text{ or } 10\%$$

(b)   Capital asset pricing model (CAPM)

The cost of equity is given by $k_e = R_f + \beta\,(R_m - R_f)$. R_f is 10%, R_m is 18% and the beta of the company's dividends is 2. Therefore, the cost of equity is:
$10 + 2 \times (18 - 10) = 26\%$, as with the dividend valuation model.

The cost of debt is the risk-free rate, which is 10%, as with the dividend valuation model.

This equality between the required return indicated by the current market value (as derived via the DVM) and that predicted by the CAPM indicates that the investor and market assumptions of the CAPM hold and the markets is in equilibrium. This will not always be the case.

3.4   Modigliani and Miller 1958

Recall that M & M demonstrate that in a no tax world:

k_0 ungeared firm $= k_0$ geared firm.

ie k_0 ungeared firm $= (k_e$ geared firm $\times \dfrac{E}{E + D}) + (k_d$ geared firm $\times \dfrac{D}{E + D})$

where k_0 = overall cost of capital (= WACC)
   k_e = cost of equity
   k_d = cost of debt
   E = market value of equity
   D = market value of debt

(Tutorial note: k_0 ungeared firm equals its cost of equity (it must do, as equity is its only source of finance).)

The above equation can easily be restated as:

$$\beta \text{ equity ungeared firm} = (\beta \text{ equity geared firm} \times \frac{E}{E + D}) + (\beta \text{ debt geared firm} \times \frac{D}{E + D})$$

(Tutorial note: β equity of ungeared firm is often referred to as β asset. This is because it has no financial risk (gearing) and therefore reflects only the systematic business risk of the firm's underlying assets.)

If we assume that β debt equals zero ie, that corporate debt is risk free, then the second term of the last equation drops out and we are left with:

$$\beta \text{ equity ungeared firm} = (\beta \text{ equity geared firm} \times \frac{E}{E + D}) + (0 \times \frac{D}{E + D})$$

Conclusion

$$\beta \text{ equity ungeared firm} = \beta \text{ equity geared firm} \times \frac{E}{E + D}$$

('ungeared β')   ('geared β')

This equation then quantifies the theoretical relationship between gearing and the cost of equity in a no tax world. You need to memorise it for exam purposes.

Do not worry too much about the assumption that corporate debt is risk free. Investment in the debt securities of large firms is in fact virtually as safe as investing in the government and hence would carry a β of zero.

3.5   Example

Brocade plc has an equity β (geared β) of 1.5 and is financed by 60% equity and 40% debt (at market values). Its debt securities are considered virtually risk free.

$R_m = 25\%$, $R_f = 10\%$, corporation tax rate = 0%, (where R_m is the rate of return on the market and R_f is the risk free rate of return).

Required:

(a)   What is the company's:

    (i)   current cost of equity;

    (ii)   current cost of debt; and

    (iii)   current WACC?

(b)   What would its cost of equity be (and hence its WACC) if it were an all equity firm?

3.6   Solution

(a)   (i)   Cost of equity (using CAPM equation)

$$k_e = R_f + \beta (R_m - R_f)$$
$$= 10\% + 1.5 (25\% - 10\%)$$
$$= 32.5\%$$

    (ii)   Cost of debt $= R_f = 10\%$

    (iii)   WACC

$$= (k_e \times \frac{E}{E + D}) + (k_d \times \frac{D}{E + D})$$
$$= (32.5\% \times 0.6) + (10\% \times 0.4)$$
$$= 23.5\%$$

(b) Cost of equity if ungeared (= WACC):

$$\beta \text{ equity ungeared} = \beta \text{ equity geared} \times \frac{E}{E + D}$$

$$= 1.5 \times \frac{0.6}{1.00}$$

$$= 0.9$$

Its cost of equity and hence WACC would therefore be

$$k_e = R_f + \beta (R_m - R_f)$$

$$= 10\% + 0.9 (25\% - 10\%)$$

$$= 23.5\%$$

(Tutorial note: the answer here is exactly the same as the WACC for the geared firm. This should not be a surprise in a 1958 M & M world. Students should also note that exam questions will much more commonly focus on a world with tax. See 3.7 below.*)*

3.7 Modigliani and Miller 1963

In a world with corporation tax the benefit to the general company of the tax shield on debt interest must be included in our analysis. Thus:

$$\beta \text{ equity ungeared} = \beta \text{ equity geared} \times \frac{E}{E + D (1 - t)} + \beta \text{ debt} \times \frac{D(1 - t)}{E + D(1 - t)}$$

This equation is provided in the formulae sheet in the exam.

Assuming debt is risk free and that β debt is therefore zero:

$$\beta \text{ equity ungeared} = \beta \text{ equity geared} \times \frac{E}{E + D (1 - t)}$$

It will be noted that this is almost identical to the last equation apart from the adjustment for tax.

3.8 Activity

Requirements as in the previous example, but use with-tax formulae and a corporation tax rate of 30%.

3.9 Activity solution

(a) Current cost of equity capital

(i) $$k_e = R_f + \beta (R_m - R_f)$$

$$= 10\% + 1.5 (25\% - 10\%)$$

$$= 32.5\%$$

(Tutorial note: the β given in the question is the geared β and is not affected by the introduction of corporation tax.*)*

(ii)   Cost of debt:

$$k_d \quad = \quad 10\% \, (1-t)$$

$$= \quad 10\% \, (1-0.30)$$

$$= \quad 7\%$$

(iii)   WACC:

$$(k_e \times \frac{E}{E+D}) + (k_d \times \frac{D}{E+D}) \quad = \quad (32.5\% \times 0.6) + (7\% \times 0.4)$$

$$= \quad 22.3\%$$

(b)   Cost of equity if ungeared (= WACC)

$$\beta \text{ equity ungeared} \quad = \quad \beta \text{ equity geared} \times \frac{E}{E + D(1-t)}$$

$$= \quad 1.5 \times \frac{0.6}{0.6 + 0.4(1-0.30)}$$

$$= \quad 1.023$$

$$k_e \quad = \quad R_f + \beta \, (R_m - R_f)$$

$$= \quad 10\% + 1.023 \, (25\% - 10\%)$$

$$= \quad 25.345\%$$

3.10   Comments on activity

Note that the result here shows the geared firm having a weighted average cost of capital substantially lower than the ungeared firm. Keen students of M & M 1963 should not be surprised by this result.

Even keener students will have already memorised the following M & M equation and will hence be able to demonstrate that this result simply reflects what we already know.

Recall:

$$k_o \text{ geared firm} \quad = \quad k_o \text{ ungeared firm} \times (1 - \frac{Dt}{E+D}) \text{ (ref Chapter 7, 8.1)}$$

$$= \quad 25.345\% \times (1 - \frac{0.4 \times 0.30}{0.6 + 0.4})$$

$$= \quad 22.3\%$$

4   PROJECT-RELATED DISCOUNT RATES AND GEARING

4.1   The 'pure play' method of ungearing and regearing beta values

Discount rates for capital investment appraisal should be related to the systematic risk of the project in question. In a similar way it could also be argued that they ought also to be related to the gearing level of the project.

4.2   Example

Hubbard, an all equity food manufacturing firm, is about to embark upon a major diversification in the consumer electronics industry. Its current equity beta is 1.2, whilst the average equity β of electronics firms is 1.6. Gearing in the electronics industry averages 30% debt, 70% equity. Corporate debt is considered to be risk free.

R_m = 25%, R_f = 10%, corporation tax rate = 30% (notation as before).

Required:

What would be a suitable discount rate for the new investment if Hubbard were to finance the new project in each of the following ways.

(a)   Entirely by equity;
(b)   By 30% debt and 70% equity;
(c)   By 40% debt and 60% equity?

4.3   Solution

In all three situations the best approach is to treat the project as a 'mini-firm' and tailor the discount rate to reflect its level of systematic business risk and financial risk.

(a)   **Project financed entirely by equity**

To reflect the business risk of the new venture we should start with the equity β of the electronics industry ie, 1.6.

As our project is to be ungeared we should then remove the financial risk element.

$$\beta \text{ equity ungeared} \quad = \quad \beta \text{ equity geared} \times \frac{E}{E + D (1 - t)}$$

$$= \quad 1.6 \times \frac{0.7}{0.7 + 0.3(1 - 0.30)}$$

$$= \quad 1.23$$

The pure cost of equity (and hence WACC in the all equity case) would then be:

$$k_e \quad = \quad R_f + \beta (R_m - R_f)$$

$$= \quad 10\% + 1.23(25\% - 10\%)$$

$$= \quad 28.45\%$$

The project should be evaluated at a rate of 28.45%.

(b)   **Project financed by 30% debt, 70% equity**

In this case the observed equity beta of the electronics industry would reflect the level of business risk and financial risk of the project. No adjustments are therefore required.

To obtain a suitable discount rate we must simply weight the cost of equity and the cost of debt, hence:

$$(k_e \times \frac{E}{E + D}) + (k_d \times \frac{D}{E + D})$$

$$k_e \quad = \quad R_f + \beta (R_m - R_f)$$

$$= \quad 10\% + 1.6(25\% - 10\%) = 34\%$$

$$k_d = R_f(1-t)$$
$$= 10\%\,(1-0.30) = 7\%$$

Suitable discount rate for project $\quad = \quad (34\% \times 0.7) + (7\% \times 0.3)$
$$= \quad 25.9\%$$

(Tutorial note: it is the WACC which is needed as the discount rate, not just the cost of equity.

(c)   **Project financed by 40% debt and 60% equity**

In this case the equity beta of the electronics industry reflects a lower level of gearing than that for the proposed project. The simplest procedure is to take a two step approach to the gearing adjustment.

Step 1   Calculate the equity beta for an ungeared electronics company, (as in (a)).

β equity ungeared $\quad = \quad 1.23$

This is a measure of the pure systematic risk of electronics companies. We now adjust this pure beta in the light of the given financial gearing ratio.

Step 2   Work out the equation 'backwards' to calculate the cost of equity for an electronics company with 60% equity and 40% debt.

$$\beta \text{ equity ungeared} \quad = \quad \beta \text{ equity geared} \times \frac{E}{E + D(1-t)}$$

$$1.23 \quad = \quad \beta \text{ equity geared} \times \frac{0.6}{0.6 + 0.4(1-0.30)}$$

$$\frac{1.23}{0.6818} \quad = \quad \beta \text{ equity geared}$$

$$= \quad 1.80$$

The cost of equity for such a firm would then be:

$$k_e \quad = \quad R_f + \beta\,(R_m - R_f)$$
$$= \quad 10\% + 1.80\,(25\% - 10\%)$$
$$= \quad 37.0\%$$

The cost of debt would be as before.

$$k_d \quad = \quad R_f(1-t)$$
$$= \quad 10\%\,(1-0.30)$$
$$= \quad 7\%$$

and a suitable discount rate for the project would be:

$$\left(k_e \times \frac{E}{E+D}\right) + \left(k_d \times \frac{D}{E+D}\right) \quad = \quad (37\% \times 0.6) + (7\% \times 0.4)$$

$$= \quad 25\%$$

4.4   Conclusion

[Conclusion]   Suitable discount rates for the project should reflect both its systematic business risk and its level of gearing. As we are operating under an M & M 1963 world the higher the level of gearing the lower the discount rate.

4.5   Activity

A company is considering a project, which will probably yield a return of 22% per annum before tax. The beta of the company's dividends is 1.3. The project is expected to be financed two-thirds by equity and one-third by debt (the proportions given are in terms of market values). The beta associated with the project's dividends is 0.9. The risk free rate is 10% and the market is expect to yield a return of 19%. Should the project be taken on? Corporation tax is charged at 30%.

4.6   Activity solution

[Step 1]   Work out the WACC of the project [ie, the **required** return for its systematic and financial risk]

The beta of its dividends will give the cost of equity; note that the company's beta, 1.3, is not relevant.

$k_e = R_f + \beta (R_m - R_f) = 10 + 0.9 \times (19 - 10) = 18.1\%$.

The cost of debt is the risk-free rate adjusted for tax relief:

$k_d = 10 \times 0.7 = 70\%$

The WACC is the combination of the costs of equity and of debt, in proportion to their market values:

$$\text{WACC} = (18.1\% \times \frac{2}{3}) + (70\% \times \frac{1}{3}) = 14.4\%$$

[Step 2]   Appraise the project

The WACC can be compared with the project's **expected** returns **after** tax $22\% \times 0.7 = 15.4\%$. The project is just worth doing, as satisfying the requirements of the providers of capital will cost 14.4%.

Note that this is the IRR approach to investment appraisal; it compares the IRR of the project, 15.4%, with the discount rate, which is the WACC. The alternative would be to discount the project's future flows at 14.4% and work out their net present value. This method cannot be used here, as we are not given the project cash flows.

4.7   Conclusions on adjusting betas for gearing

Several versions of the formula for adjusting betas for gearing are commonly used, and students could well encounter alternatives. They are all basically the same and do the same job. You only need to know one for exam purposes and it is suggested that the one used in earlier examples is the easiest one to remember.

More importantly, you must consider the limitations of the above analysis. The approach employed is based on the theories of Modigliani and Miller, and therefore is subject to the limitations of their theory (bankruptcy costs, agency costs, tax exhaustion and personal taxes) which have already been examined. It appeared from the last example that the firm could continually reduce the discount rate for the project by simply increasing gearing. With your knowledge of the limitations of M & M's theory you should be able to debunk this argument.

Finally, in using M & M's equations to adjust discount rates note that they make two important assumptions, as follows:

(a)   Debt is risk free.

(b)   Debt is permanent (ie, irredeemable).

Commonly these assumptions are violated and the analysis applied in this section is then invalid.

5   THE ADJUSTED PRESENT VALUE TECHNIQUE

5.1   The APV technique of investment appraisal

Traditionally financial management has appraised new investments by discounting their after-tax operating cash flows to present value at the firm's weighted average cost of capital and with the use of the WACC have seen that adjustments are commonly needed to tailor the discount rate to the systematic business risk and the financial risk of the project under consideration.

M & M based adjustments to the cost of capital are one approach to this problem. Here we examine another (Adjusted Present Value (APV)), which offers significant advantages. Consider the following example.

Example

Blades plc is considering diversifying its operations away from its main area of business (food manufacturing) into the plastics business. It wishes to evaluate an investment project which involves the purchase of a moulding machine which costs £450,000. The project is expected to produce net annual operating cash flows of £220,000 for each of the three years of its life. At the end of this time its scrap value will be zero.

The assets of the project will support debt finance of 40% of its initial cost (including issue costs). The loan is to be repaid in three equal annual instalments. The balance of finance will be provided by a placing of new equity. Issue costs will be 5% of funds raised for the equity placing and 2% for the loan. Issue costs are allowable for corporation tax.

The plastics industry has an average equity beta of 1.368 and an average debt:equity ratio of 1:5 at market values. Blade's current equity beta is 1.8 and 20% of its long-term capital is represented by debt which is generally regarded to be risk-free.

The risk-free rate is 10% pa, and the expected return on an average market portfolio is 15%. Corporation tax is at a rate of 30%, payable one year in arrears. The machine will attract a 70% initial capital allowance and the balance is to be written off over the three years and is allowable against tax. The firm is certain that it will earn sufficient profits against which to offset these allowances.

Evaluation of the project

Three approaches will be considered:

(a)   Using the current WACC.

(b)   Using a WACC adjusted for business and financial risk.

(c)   Adjusted present value.

(a)   **Using the current WACC**

   The firm's current WACC would be:

   $K_e \times 0.8 + K_d \times 0.2$ = $(10\% + 1.8 (15\% - 10\%)) \times 0.8 + (10\% (1 - 0.30)) \times 0.2$

   =   16.6%

However, if this figure were used to discount the operating cash flows of the project we would be making several errors.

(i)   The current WACC is based upon Blades' existing business risk (ie, that of the food manufacturing industry). The plastics project involves considerably different business risk and should therefore be evaluated at a discount rate appropriate to its own business risk.

(ii)   The plastics project seems able to support far more debt than Blades' existing operations. From our knowledge of capital structure we know that firms should gear up to gain the advantages of the tax shield on interest payments until bankruptcy and other costs of high gearing start to bite. In this situation it appears that the investment in plastics will allow the firm to increase its gearing ratio. Normally this would be the case if creditors felt that the bankruptcy costs associated with the project were much lower than with the firm's existing assets (it could be, for example, that a good second-hand market existed for this type of moulding machine). As this project allows the firm to take on a higher than normal level of gearing, the WACC based on existing gearing is not appropriate.

(iii)   The existing WACC ignores issue costs.

(b)   **Adjusting the WACC for the business and financial risk of the project**

To adjust for the business risk of the project we should use the cost of equity of a firm engaged in a similar line of business to the new project. In this case we will employ the equity beta of the plastics industry.

However, as the plastics industry is at a different level of gearing to the project we should adjust for financial risk also.

$$\beta \text{ equity ungeared} \quad = \quad \beta \text{ equity geared} \times \frac{E}{E + D(1 - t)}$$

$$= \quad 1.368 \times \frac{5}{5 + 1(1 - 0.30)}$$

$$= \quad 1.2$$

Equity beta for an ungeared firm in the plastics business = 1.2

(Note that we have adjusted to a geared β with debt ratio 5 equity to 1 debt to align with Blades' existing financial risk.)

As Blades' plastics operation will be 40% debt : 60% equity we must 'regear' using the same equation:

$$1.2 \quad = \quad \beta \text{ equity geared} \times \frac{0.6}{0.6 + 0.4(1 - 0.30)}$$

$$\beta \text{ equity geared} \quad = \quad 1.76$$

Equity beta for the Blades' plastic project at 40% debt : 60% equity = 1.76

This would give a cost of equity of 10% + 1.76 (15% − 10%) = 18.8% and a WACC for the plastics project of:

$$\frac{E}{E + D} \times 18.8\% + \frac{D}{E + D} \times 10\%(1 - t) \quad = \quad \frac{60}{100} \times 18.8\% + \frac{40}{100} \times 7\%$$

$$= \quad 14.08\%$$

Note that these weights are based on the mix of funds for the project.

Therefore an appropriate discount rate for the plastics project would appear to be approximately 14%

However, before using this rate we should note some problems:

(i)   The degearing and regearing procedure we have used is a product of the M & M 1963 position. To use these equations debt must be perpetual and risk-free. In our example the debt might be risk-free but it is certainly not perpetual. Therefore we will have overvalued the tax shield on debt.

(ii)   The value E + D used in the above equation should represent market values of debt and equity after the project has been adopted (ie, the equity value should include the NPV of the project). By using a ratio of 60% equity : 40% debt we have assumed that the project has a zero NPV - this is unlikely to be the case. If the project has a positive NPV this calculation will assume that borrowing is proportional to the present value of future cash flows rather than the initial value of the asset. This is not the situation for Blades.

(iii)   We have still not included issue costs on equity.

(c)   **Adjusted present value approach**

APV is often described as a 'divide and conquer approach'. To do this the project will first be evaluated as if it were being undertaken by an all-equity company, 'side effects' like the tax shield on debt and the issue costs being ignored. This first stage will give us the so-called base case NPV. The second stage is to calculate the present value of the side effects (in this case the issue costs and the tax shield on the loan interest) and to add this to the base case NPV. The result is the APV which shows the net effect on shareholder wealth of adopting the project.

> **Conclusion**   The APV method therefore sees the value of the project to shareholders as being:

Project value if all equity financed (the base case NPV)   +   Present value of tax shields on the loan   +   Present value of other side effects

> **Step 1**   **Base case net present value**

First compute the ungeared beta for this project type (based on the equity beta for the plastics industry) - as in (b):

$$\beta \text{ equity ungeared} = \beta \text{ equity geared} \times \frac{E}{E + D(1-t)}$$

$$= 1.368 \times \frac{5}{5 + 1(1 - 0.30)}$$

$$= 1.2$$

$$\text{Required return of project} = 10\% + (15\% - 10\%)\,1.2$$

$$= 16\% \text{ pa}$$

Then discount the project cash flows at 16%

Year	0	1	2	3	4
	£'000	£'000	£'000	£'000	£'000
Equipment	(450)				
Capital allowances (W1)		94.5	13.5	13.5	13.5
Operating cash flows		220.00	220.00	220.00	
Tax on operating cash			(66.00)	(66.00)	(66.00)
	(450)	314.5	167.5	167.5	(52.5)
16% factors	1	0.862	0.743	0.641	0.552
PV	(450)	271.10	124.45	107.37	(28.98)

Base case NPV = £23,940

Workings - Capital allowances

		Tax @ 30%
	£	£
Cost of machine	450,000	
First year allowances (70%)	315,000	94,500
	135,000	
Writing down allowances (straight line) (for each of next three years)	45,000	13,500

Note: It is assumed that the company as a whole is making profits so that the project's first year allowances can be offset against tax on profits made in other areas of the company in year 1.

Step 2   **Adjusted present value (the side effects)**

Issue costs

	£
Capital requirements:	
Equity (60%)	270,000
Debt (40%)	180,000
	450,000

		£
Issue costs:		
Equity	5/95 × £270,000	14,210
Debt	2/98 × £180,000	3,673
		17,883

Net of tax costs (best discounted at risk free rate)

$$= £17,883 - \frac{30\% \times £17,883}{1.1}$$

$$= £13,006$$

Tax relief on loan interest

Gross value of loan   =   £180,000 + £3,673 (issue costs)

       =   £183,673

Annual repayments $= \dfrac{\pounds183,673}{\text{3 year annuity factor at 10\%}}$

       $= \dfrac{\pounds183,673}{2.487}$

       =   £73,853

Loan schedule

Year	Opening balance £	Interest £	Repayment £	Closing balance £
1	183,673	18,367	73,853	128,187
2	128,187	12,819	73,853	67,153
3	67,153	6,715	73,853	15
				(difference due to rounding)

Tax relief at 30% on interest (one year's delay):

Year	Cash £	10% factor	PV £
2	5,510	0.826	4,551
3	3,846	0.751	2,888
4	2,015	0.683	1,376
			8,815

Adjusted present value

	£
Base case NPV	23,940
Issue costs	(13,006)
Tax shield	8,815
The project APV is	19,749

The project will increase shareholder wealth by £19,749 and is therefore acceptable.

5.2   Practical problems of the APV approach

The APV technique has the following limitations and practical problems.

(a)   The process of degearing the industry beta to obtain a beta for an all-equity firm still relied upon M & M's 1963 case. For the equation used to be valid the debt of the plastics industry must be risk-free and perpetual. In practice this may not be the case. It also relies on the M & M theory being correct. As discussed earlier in the text, when market imperfections such as bankruptcy costs are introduced, it is unlikely that M & M's 1963 position is valid.

(b)   The discount rates used to evaluate the various side effects can be difficult to determine. In our example we have used the risk-free rate to evaluate the corporation tax savings on the loan interest and issue costs. This is valid as the firm is certain that it will be earning sufficient profits to take immediate advantage of the tax relief. If the firm were not certain then the situations is more risky and a higher discount rate should be used. The problem is how much higher? This would largely be a matter of educated guesswork.

(c)   In complex investment decisions the calculations can be extremely long.

5.3   Advantages of the APV approach

To appreciate the advantages of APV it must be contrasted with the more traditional approach of altering the weighted average cost of capital and discounting net of tax operating cash flows to present value to arrive at an NPV.

(a)   To adjust the WACC we would also have to use M & M's 1963 equations and once again the assumptions of perpetual risk-free debt would be problematic. Furthermore, the normal WACC treatment of debt assumes that the amount of debt supported by the project is proportional to the present value of the project (so that the gearing ratio doesn't change). This would be unusual as most creditors lend in relation to the initial cost of the investment rather than its future cash flows. APV can incorporate the tax shield on any size of loan, for any duration and with any type of repayment structure.

(b)   M & M's 1963 equations also assume that the tax relief on debt interest is risk-free. Again this might not be the case.

(c)   APV can easily handle problems of changing capital structure, by including the value of any additional tax shield gained by financing existing assets (as well as the project) by additional debt.

(d)   APV is useful for valuing any type of financial advantage. Assume for example that the plastics project was to be located in an area of high unemployment, and that to encourage our firm to invest the government offered to loan the funds to Blades at an interest rate of 5% pa rather than the normal 10% from commercial sources. The value of the loan subsidy can be obtained by calculating the present value of the interest and principal repayments using the company's normal market borrowing rate as the discount rate and subtracting the initial funds advanced.

Gross value of the loan   =   £183,673

Annual repayment schedule at 5% pa   = $\dfrac{£183,673}{3 \text{ year annuity factor at } 5\%}$

  = $\dfrac{£183,673}{2.723}$

  =   £67,452

Loan schedule:

Year	Opening balance £	Interest £	Repayment £	Closing balance £
1	183,673	9,184	67,452	125,405
2	125,405	6,270	67,452	64,223
3	64,223	3,211	67,452	(18)
				(difference due to rounding)

Value of the subsidised loan is therefore:

183,673 − (67,452 × 3 year annuity factor at 10%) = 183,673 − (67,452 × 2.487) = 15,920

However, the tax relief on interest (at 30%) will now only be:

Year	Cash	10% factor	PV
	£		£
2	2,755	0.826	2,276
3	1,881	0.751	1,413
4	963	0.683	658
			4,347
Value of tax shield on 10% loan (5.1(c))			8,815
Loss of tax savings			4,468

Overall value of subsidy = Value of subsidy before tax – Reduced tax shield

= £(15,920 - 4,468) = £11,452

(This assumes the same issue costs will still be paid.)

This allows management to identify precisely the value of the subsidised loan.   This information would not be available using a WACC/NPV approach.

(e)   Adjusting the WACC for various side effects can become a very complex (if not impossible) operation.   The process is simplified by using the APV 'divide and conquer' approach. Although APV might appear a very long-winded approach its step by step procedure leads to a clearer understanding of all the elements of the decision. This is perhaps its greatest virtue.

In conclusion APV offers an alternative approach to project evaluation which is likely to gain increasing popularity in the future.

6   **CHAPTER SUMMARY**

The original M & M analysis implied that firms should gear up as much as they possibly could. As this does not happen in the real world, there has been much discussion about the reasons for the failure of the analysis to capture the essential elements of debt finance.

The four main reasons are bankruptcy costs, agency costs, tax exhaustion and the effect of personal taxes, which were explored by Miller in 1977.

Use the summary of views on capital structure presented in the text to help you sort out the different opinions. Also be aware of the practical factors affecting capital structure choice.

The measurement of debt capacity is an extension of the practical side of raising debt, which moves away from the more rarified world of pure theory.

Ensure that you can combine M & M and the capital asset pricing model. The latter says that the firm's cost of equity is measured by $k_e = R_f + \beta (R_m - R_f)$. If the firm is ungeared, its β is ungeared. If the firm is geared, then the geared β which reflects the firm's gearing level should be used. The β s of two companies which are identical, except that one is geared and the other is not, are linked by the equation:

$$\beta \text{ ungeared} = \beta \text{ geared} \times \frac{E}{E + D (1 - t)}$$

This can be converted to the no tax case by putting t = 0.

The discount rate suitable for appraising projects is the weighted average of the cost of equity applicable to their risk, and the cost of debt.

Finally the APV technique of investment appraisal was described, separating the base case NPV from the financing side effects of an investment.

7   SELF TEST QUESTIONS

7.1   What are the direct costs of bankruptcy? (1.2)

7.2   What types of covenant may be used by suppliers of debt finance? (1.3)

7.3   What is tax exhaustion? (1.4)

7.4   According to Miller (1977), on what does the equilibrium level of debt for the whole economy depend? (1.6)

7.5   What is the practical effect of asset quality on optimum capital structure? (2.2)

7.6   How does gearing affect risk? (3.1)

7.7   Give the equation linking geared and ungeared betas, taking account of corporation tax. (3.7)

7.8   What are the limitations of the theory which produces this equation linking geared and ungeared betas? (4.7)

7.9   What is the base case NPV? (5.1)

7.10   What are the limitations of the APV technique? (5.2)

8   EXAMINATION TYPE QUESTIONS

8.1   Corporate and personal taxation

It has been suggested that in a world with only corporate taxation the value of a firm = the value if all equity financed + the present value of the tax shield on debt finance.

(a)   If the above equation applied, what would be the most appropriate capital structure for a company?

How far do existing capital structures of companies compare with the most appropriate structure according to the equation?   **(3 marks)**

(b)   Discuss how and why the existence of personal taxation might alter the choice of capital structure suggested in part (a) above.   **(7 marks)**

(c)   If a financial manager agrees with the implications for the choice of capital structure that you have suggested in part (b) above, what problems might arise in applying them within his company?   **(3 marks)**

(d)   (i)   Give examples of possible costs associated with a high level of gearing.   **(7 marks)**

   (ii)   Discuss how such costs might influence the capital structure of the following.

      (1)   A medium sized electronics company entering the home computer market; and

      (2)   An established company owning and managing a chain of hotels.

   (5 marks)
   (Total: 25 marks)

8.2   Rickery plc

The board of directors of Rickery plc is discussing whether to alter the company's capital structure. Corporate legislation permits Rickery plc to repurchase its own shares and it is proposed to issue £5 million of new debentures at par, and to use the funds to repurchase ordinary shares.

A summary of Rickery's current balance sheet as at 31 December 19X7:

	£'000
Fixed assets (net)	24,500
Current assets	12,300
Current liabilities	(8,600)
	28,200

	£'000
Financed by	
25p ordinary shares	4,500
Reserves	14,325
	18,825
5% debentures redeemable at par in ten years' time	9,375
	28,200

The company's current ordinary share price is 167p, and its debenture price is £80. Rickery's finance director does not expect the market price of the existing ordinary shares or debentures to change as a result of the proposed issue of new debentures.

Debenture interest is payable at the end of each year. Issue costs and transactions costs may be assumed to be zero.

Rickery's cost of equity is estimated by a leading firm of stockbrokers to be 17%.

Required:

(a)   Evaluate the likely effect on the weighted average cost of capital of Rickery plc if the company restructures its capital

     (i)   If the company pays tax at the rate of 35%.
     (ii)   If the company does not expect to pay corporate taxes for the foreseeable future.

All the relevant calculations must be shown. State clearly any assumptions that you make.

(15 marks)

(b)   Rickery's finance director believes that the market price of the company's existing ordinary shares and debentures will not change. Explain why he might be wrong in his belief and suggest what changes might occur. **(10 marks)**

(Total: 25 marks)

Ignore personal taxes.

8.3   Bigoyte Inc

(a)   Explain why the adjusted present value technique (APV) is sometimes advocated as being a more appropriate way of evaluating a project than net present value. **(4 marks)**

(b)   Bigoyte Inc is developing a new personal computer with an expected life of three years. The investment has a total initial cost of $283 million, of which $106 million will be provided from internally generated funds, $90 million from a rights issue and the remainder from a fixed rate term loan at 12% per year. The proportion represented by the term loan reflects the optimum debt capacity of the company.

Issue costs are estimated at 3.5% for the rights issue and 1% for the term loan. Corporate taxes are payable at a rate of 40% on net operating cash flows in the year that the cash flows occur. The Treasury Bill yield is 9%, market return 14%, and an appropriate asset beta for the investment is believed to be 1.5.

Project net operating cash flows (after tax)

Year	*1*	*2*	*3*
	$89 million	$198 million	$59 million

Additionally, a residual value of $28 million (after all taxes) is expected at the end of year three.

Required:

Estimate the adjusted present value of the investment and recommend whether the investment should be undertaken. **(9 marks)**

(Total: 13 marks)

9 ANSWERS TO EXAMINATION TYPE QUESTIONS

9.1 Corporate and personal taxation

*(**Tutorial note:** this question concentrates on the weaknesses of the 1963 Modigliani and Miller theory. In part (d) you are required to discuss the practical impact of these weaknesses.)*

(a) The implication of the equation is that as long as a firm is paying mainstream corporation tax it can continually increase its total market value (and therefore decrease its cost of capital) by increasing its gearing ratio. Therefore the most appropriate capital structure would be virtually 100% debt remembering that some equity must be present in order that the firm may remain a company.

Average gearing in the UK (debt/equity) is approximately 55% and although this varies between industrial sectors no companies approach 100% gearing.

(b) If personal taxes are levied on different types of personal income at different rates then it could well be worth breaking the above 'rule'. For example if personal taxes on debt interest were much higher than taxes on equity income (dividend and capital gains) then firms might not gear up to the levels indicated above. Gearing up would save on the corporation tax bill but it would have a cost to investors in personal tax terms.

In 1977 Miller developed this argument to demonstrate that once personal taxes are brought into the capital structure argument then once again all capital structures could be considered optimal. If we accept that for many investors taxes on equity income are less than taxes on debt income then firms will only gear up until the corporation tax saving (Dt) is equal to the personal tax losses (the extra personal tax to be paid due to receiving returns as debt income rather than equity income). Once this position is reached the benefit of any further gearing would be immediately and exactly offset by personal tax losses. Miller claims that in a competitive capital market this position would have been reached long ago, so there is an optimal gearing ratio for the overall economy. At this equilibrium point the individual firm would find no advantage (or disadvantage) in issuing debt and hence all capital structures are optimal ie, they will all result in the same total market value and the same cost of capital.

Miller's argument is unproven but it could explain the large variation in gearing ratios than can be observed between firms. Even if Miller's case is not accepted it is still clear that personal taxes should be considered in the capital structure debate.

(c)   If the financial manager accepts Miller's argument then one capital structure would be considered as good as another and there should be no problem in applying them in a particular company.

If on the other hand the manager rejects the equilibrium argument then it would be necessary to consider the individual tax position of all investors in deciding upon the optimal capital structure. Two substantial problems would then be encountered.

(i)   Determining the tax position of all the firm's investors. For the typical listed company considerable variation between different groups of investors should be expected.

(ii)   Reconciling the conflicting requirements of the different groups. For example groups paying high rates of income tax might not wish to receive returns as debt income. It would be almost impossible to please all investors at the same time.

(d)   (i)   Several costs can be associated with high levels of gearing.

(1)   **Bankruptcy costs**

The higher the firm's gearing the more likely it is to experience the administrative, legal and accounting costs of liquidation. Even if a firm does not go into liquidation there are significant management costs of operating at high gearing levels.

(2)   **Agency costs**

The objectives of the agents of the company (the management) may not be identical to those of the providers of finance. For example, when gearing is high, management might take sup-optimal decisions to prevent the possible loss of their jobs.

There may also be conflicts of interest between providers of equity and loan finance. For example a loan could be raised to finance a low-risk project, but the funds then used to finance a high-risk project. The providers of debt will not then receive the appropriate return for the risk they are taking. The shareholders would be content to see a risky project financed by 'cheap' debt. Restrictive covenants in the loan agreement may eliminate the above possibility, but even these will involve additional legal and monitoring costs, which are ultimately borne by the shareholders.

(3)   **Tax exhaustion**

At extreme levels of gearing it is unlikely that the firm will have sufficient profits against which to offset its large interest bill. If this occurs the corporation tax advantage of debt finance is lost.

(4)   **Personal taxes**

Personal tax costs of high gearing as discussed in (b) are also important.

(ii)   A medium sized computer company entering a new market is likely to have relatively high business risk and poor asset marketability in the event of failure. This could lead to relatively high bankruptcy and agency costs. Also, if large amounts of new investment have been made, capital allowances may reduce taxable profit and lead to tax exhaustion.

An established company in the hotel business is likely to have low business risk and high quality assets. Its bankruptcy and agency costs are likely to be much lower and one would expect it to take a much higher level of gearing than the computer firm.

9.2   Rickery plc

(a)   **Cost of debt**

Pre-tax. As there is a premium on redemption the IRR approach must be used.

We need to find the approximate IRR of the following flows:

Time		Cashflow
0	80	Market value
1-10	(5)	Interest pre-tax
10	(100)	Redemption

PV at (say) 10%   =   £10.72
PV at 5%   =   £(20.00)

$$IRR \approx 5 + \frac{(20)}{(20) - 10.72} (10 - 5)$$

$$\approx 8.26$$

The pre-tax cost of debt ≈ 8%

Post tax

Follow the same procedure but reduce all interest payments by $(1 - t)$ ie, find the IRR of

Time	Cashflow
0	80
1-10	$(5) \times 0.65$
10	(100)

PV at 5% ≈ £(6.49)
PV at 7% ≈ £6.34

The IRR must therefore be approximately half way between these two.

Post tax cost of debt = 6%

Cost of capital calculations

Current situation

No tax

	Market value £'000	Proportion	Cost %	Weighted cost %
Equity	30,060	0.80	17	13.6
Debt	7,500	0.20	8	1.6
WACC				15.2

With tax

	Market value £'000	Proportion	Cost %	Weighted cost %
Equity	30,060	0.8	17	13.6
Debt	7,500	0.2	6	1.2
WACC				14.8

New situation - assuming equity is bought back at current market price

No tax

	Market value £'000	Proportion	Cost %	Weighted cost %
Equity	25,060	0.67	17	11.4
Debt	12,500	0.33	8	2.6
WACC				14.0

With tax

	Market value £'000	Proportion	Cost %	Weighted cost %
Equity	25,060	0.67	17	11.4
Debt	12,500	0.33	6	2.0
WACC				13.4

On the basis of these calculations the restructuring should take place as no matter what the tax position of the firm it leads to a fall in the weighted average cost of capital.

(b)   *(Tutorial note:* you are instructed to ignore the impact of personal taxes.)

If Rickery's finance director believes that the price of the firm's securities will not change he is inferring that no matter the level of gearing the cost of debt and equity will remain the same. This would imply that by continually gearing up, and substituting cheap debt capital for expensive equity capital, a continual decrease in the WACC may be obtained. This situation seems unlikely to say the least. All the major theories of capital structure recognise that the cost of equity finance will increase (with a resultant change in equity value) as financial risk is increased. The main subject for debate is the size of the change.

In a world without taxation Modigliani and Miller argue that as gearing increases the cost of equity rises, the cost of debt remains constant (except at extreme levels of gearing) and the overall cost of capital remains constant. The overall value of the company remains unchanged but the value of equity will fall.

In a world with corporate taxes Modigliani and Miller argue that the cost of equity will rise, the cost of debt will remain constant, but the overall cost of capital will fall due to the benefit of the tax shield on debt interest payments. Once again, the market value of equity will fall.

The traditional theory argues that both the cost of equity and debt will rise as gearing increase, which results in either a reduction or increase in the overall cost of capital (depending on the current level of gearing of the company), and a change in the value of both equity and debt. For example the use of more debt will increase the risk to shareholders and lead to a fall in share price. The overall effect could be either a rise or fall in share price.

When bankruptcy costs, agency costs and other costs of high gearing are also considered the likelihood of a change in the value of equity becomes even greater as gearing increases.

The finance director is therefore likely to be wrong in his belief that the market price of the company's existing shares and debentures will not change. The value of existing equity could either increase or decrease; the value of existing debt is likely to decrease if new debt, at a higher price, is issued by the company.

9.3   Bigoyte Inc

(Tutorial note: the question is quite vague on the repayment structure of the loan and the timelag in tax payments. Given the choice the simplest alternatives have been selected.)

(a)   Traditionally in financial management it is assumed that the financing decision and the investment should be handled separately. However, in practice the two decisions are often dependent. For example the level of gearing a firm can adopt is often influenced by the type of assets in which it invests. In this situation the APV technique offers some advantages over NPV:

(i)   If the level of gearing is influenced by the type of project adopted the weighted average cost of capital would need to be adjusted before calculating the NPV of the project. These adjustments usually involve using Modigliani and Miller's 1963 hypothesis on capital structure and their underlying assumptions (permanent and risk free debt) are questionable.

(ii)   APV takes a divide and conquer approach, firstly determining a base case NPV for an all equity company and then adding on the present value of financing side effects. If therefore avoids the complexities of adjusting the WACC for gearing.

(iii) APV can be used to evaluate almost any financial side effect, including such items as the value of subsidised loans. Because it evaluates projects in a piecemeal manner it is often simpler to employ than NPV.

(b)   APV = Base case NPV + Present value of financing side effects.

Base case NPV

This is the NPV that would be obtained if an all equity firm financed the project.

The cost of funds for an all equity firm

$$= \quad Rf + (Rm - Rf)\, \beta u$$
$$= \quad 9\% + (14\% - 9\%)\, 1.5 = 16.5\%$$

$$\text{Net present value (\$m)} = \quad (283) + \frac{89}{(1.165)} + \frac{198}{(1.165)^2} + \frac{87}{(1.165)^3}$$
$$= \quad \$(5.7)m$$

Financing side effects

To cover the shortfall sufficient funds must be raised to fund \$87m of the project and to cover the issue costs. In total then

$$\frac{\$87m}{0.99} \quad = \quad \$87.879m$$

Tax shield on loan

No detail is given on the repayment structure of the loan but the simplest assumption is that all principal is repayable in three years time.

$\therefore$ Annual interest   =   \$87.879m × 0.12   =   \$10.55m
       Annual tax saving =   \$10.55m × 0.4   =   \$4.22m

Assuming no lag in tax payments this has a present value of:

        \$4.22m × 3 year annuity factor at 12%
$$= \quad \$4.22m \times 2.402 \quad\quad\quad = \quad \$10.136m$$

	Issue costs	*$m*
		Funds required
Rights issue	90	$90 \times \dfrac{3.5}{96.5} = 3.264$
Debt	87	$87 \times \dfrac{1}{99} = 0.879$
		4.143m

(We will assume that issue costs are not tax allowable.)

Adjusted present value

	$m
Base case NPV	(5.7)
Tax shield on interest	10.136
Issue costs	(4.143)
APV	+0.293

The project is therefore marginally acceptable.

9 CORPORATE DIVIDEND POLICY

INTRODUCTION & LEARNING OBJECTIVES

Every year, every company has to decide the level of dividend to pay to its shareholders. Should it follow a specific policy of maintaining the level of dividends, or a steady rate of growth, from one year to the next, regardless of its actual cash position? Or should it decide how much it needs to retain to fund future investment, repay loans etc, and simply pay out what (if any) is left (the so-called 'residual approach')? This may result in an erratic pattern of dividends - how might this be perceived by the shareholders, and thus how might it impact on the market value of the shares?

This chapter looks at the practical influences on dividend policy, balanced against the theoretical argument of Modigliani and Miller (yes, they're here again!) which is that the pattern of dividends is irrelevant - it has no impact on shareholders' wealth.

When you have studied this chapter you should be able to do the following:

- Explain the legal position in relation to dividend payments.
- Discuss alternative dividend policies that can be employed in practice.
- Demonstrate the theoretical argument of dividend irrelevance.
- Argue that in practice the size of dividend payments is relevant.
- Discuss practical influences on dividend policy.

1 PRACTICAL INFLUENCES ON DIVIDEND POLICY

1.1 Legal position in relation to dividends

The *Companies Act 1980* (now embodied in the *Companies Act 1985*) imposed restrictions on the distribution of profits by companies. The provisions may be summarised as follows.

(a) **General rule**

A company may only pay dividends out of profits available for dividends: *S263 CA 1985*.

(b) **Profits available for dividend**

... accumulated, realised profits, so far as not previously utilised (by distribution or capitalisation) less its accumulated, realised losses, so far as not previously written off ... *S263(3) CA 1985*.

(i) **Accumulated** - the net of reserves less losses from previous years.

(ii) **Realised** - excluding, for example, unrealised profits on fixed assets created by revaluation.

(iii) **Capital profits** - it should be noted that the new definition does permit the distribution of a capital profit ie, a **realised** profit on the sale of a fixed asset.

(c) **Undistributable reserves (relevant only to public companies)**

These are made up of the following.

(i) Share premium account;

(ii) Capital redemption reserve;

(iii)   Unrealised profits (less unrealised losses unless previously written off); and

(iv)   Any other reserve which the company is prohibited from distributing by any statute or by its memorandum or articles: *S264(3) CA 1985.*

(d)   **Restrictions on distribution**

A public company (excluding certain investment companies), in addition to complying with *S263 CA 1985*, must not make a distribution of dividend if to do so would reduce its net assets below the aggregate of its called-up share capital and undistributable reserves: *S264 CA 1985.*

In addition, governments have operated policies of dividend restraint over various periods. However, no such restraints currently exist or are proposed.

1.2   Other aspects

(a)   **Profitability**

Profit is obviously an essential requirement for dividends. All other things being equal, the more stable the profit the greater the proportion that can be safely paid out as dividends. If profits are volatile it is unwise to commit the firm to a higher dividend payout ratio.

(b)   **Inflation**

In periods of inflation paying out dividends based on historic cost profits can lead to an erosion of the operating capacity of the business if dividend payment is higher than current cost profit. This could jeopardise the firm's survival, particularly when assets come to be replaced.

(c)   **Growth**

Rapidly growing companies commonly pay very low dividends, the bulk of earnings being retained to finance expansion.

(d)   **Other sources of finance**

If a firm has limited access to other sources of funds, retained earnings become a very important source of finance. Dividends will therefore tend to be small. This situation is commonly experienced by unquoted companies which have very limited access to external finance.

(e)   **Control**

The use of internally generated funds does not alter ownership or control. This can be advantageous particularly in family owned firms.

(f)   **Liquidity**

Sufficient liquid funds need to be available to pay the dividend.

(g)   **Tax**

Personal tax implications are discussed below. The corporation tax implications of paying dividends are very much simpler now that ACT has been abolished.

1.3   Alternative dividend policies

There are three major categories of dividend policy that a firm can employ.

(a)   **Stable dividend policy**

Paying out a fixed dividend per share each year. This could be fixed in either real or money terms.

(b)   **Constant payout ratio**

The company pays out a constant proportion of its earnings available for equity as dividends. This dividend will fluctuate from year to year in line with earnings.

(c)   **Residual approach to dividends**

Retained earnings are used to fund all profitable projects. Remaining funds (if any) are paid out as dividends.

Probably the most common policy adopted by listed firms is a variant on (a). Most main market companies go for a stable, but rising, dividend per share. This is best demonstrated in the following graph.

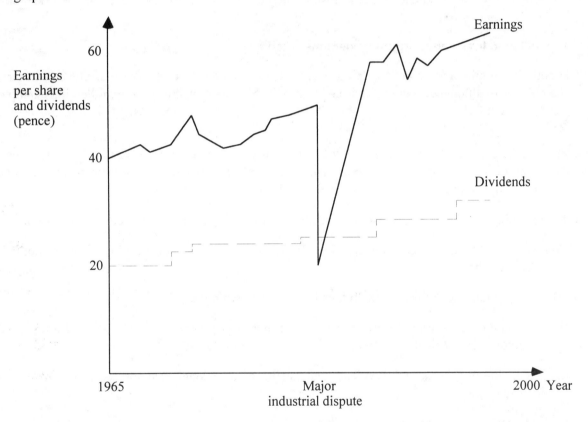

Note that the dividends lag behind earnings, but are maintained even when earnings fall below the dividend level, as happens when production is lost for several months during a major industrial dispute. This is often referred to as a 'ratchet' pattern of dividends.

This policy has the advantage of not signalling 'bad news' to investors. Also if the increases in dividend per share are not too large it should not seriously upset the firm's clientele of investors by disturbing their tax position.

A policy of a constant payout ratio is seldom used by listed companies because of the tremendous fluctuations in dividend per share which it could bring. Many firms, however, might work towards a long-run target payout percentage smoothing out the peaks and troughs each year. If sufficiently smoothed the pattern would be not unlike the ratchet pattern demonstrated above.

The residual approach to dividends contains a lot of financial commonsense. If positive NPV projects are available, they should be adopted, otherwise funds should be returned to shareholders. This avoids the unnecessary transaction costs involved in paying shareholders a dividend and then asking for funds from the same shareholders (via a rights issue) to fund a new project.

The major problem with the residual approach to dividends is that it can lead to large fluctuations in dividends, which could signal 'bad news' to investors.

2   DIVIDEND IRRELEVANCE

2.1   The classic view of the irrelevance of the source of equity finance

This view was developed by Modigliani and Miller, whose work on capital structure you have already studied. Their views were only published in 1961, but may now be regarded as the classic position.

Their argument is that the source of equity finance is in itself irrelevant. Since ultimately it represents a sacrifice of consumption (or other investment opportunities) by the investor at identical risk levels, it makes no difference whether dividends are paid to the investor, or equity is raised as new issues, or profits are simply retained.

The only differences would arise due to institutional frictional factors, such as issue costs, taxation and so on.

2.2   The dividend irrelevance argument demonstrated

If both new equity and retained earnings have the same cost then it should be irrelevant, in terms of shareholder wealth, where equity funds come from. This is demonstrated in the following example.

Example

Zeus plc has in issue 5,000,000 shares of £1 nominal value. These are currently quoted at £5 each **ex div**. The dividend proposed for the current year is 50p per share. No increase in this dividend is anticipated unless new projects are accepted. There is no long-term debt.

The company can invest cash surpluses at 10% pa at the same level of risk as current operations.

Compute the effect on shareholders' wealth (cash and capital) of the following options being considered by the company:

(a)   continuing with the current dividend and investment policy

(b)   retaining an extra (i)£1m or (ii) £2.5m, in both cases investing it at 10% and paying out the returns as additional dividends

(c)   paying out the normal dividend, and raising an additional £1m for investment at 10% by a rights issue

Ignore taxation and issue costs

Solution

We need to assess the impact of each option on the shareholders' cash position and market value of their shares. The cash will be affected by the level of current dividends received and cash contributions made; the capital position will be affected by the level of future dividends expected, and their required return.

As any new investment is not expected to change the risk, then it should have the same required return as prevails at the moment:

$$K_e = \frac{D}{P_0} = \frac{£0.50}{£5} = 10\%$$

			Market value £'000	*Cash* £'000	*Total wealth* £'000

(a)   Continuing current policies

       MV = 5m × £5 =   25,000
       Divi = 5m × £0.50 =   2,500   27,500

(b)   (i)   Retaining £1m and investing at 10%

              New future dividend = current divi + investment returns
                                   = 2,500 + 10%(1,000)
                                   = 2,600
              New market value = $\dfrac{\text{new D}}{K_e} = \dfrac{2,600}{0.1} =$ 26,000

              Current divi = normal divi - retention =   1,500   27,500

       (ii)   Retaining £2.5m and investing at 10%

              New future dividend = current divi + investment returns
                                   = 2,500 + 10% (2,500) =2,750
              New market value = $\dfrac{\text{new D}}{K_e} = \dfrac{2,750}{0.1} =$ 27,500
              Current divi = normal divi - retention =   -   27,500

(c)   New future divi = as (b) (i)   26,000
       Divi = as (a)   2,500
       Subscribed for shares   (1,000)   27,500

[Conclusion]   The shareholders' wealth is the same in each case. This illustrates two points:

- provided any cash retained is invested at the shareholders' required return, a cut in dividend of any size should not adversely affect the investor - the cash lost now is exactly compensated by an increase in the value of their shares. If the funds were actually invested at higher than the expected return for the level of risk, this would in fact increase shareholders' wealth

- it theoretically makes no difference whether the new investment is funded by retention of dividend or new equity raised.

3   ARGUMENTS FOR THE RELEVANCE OF DIVIDEND POLICY

3.1   Practical influences on dividend policy

It was shown above that in theory the level of dividend is irrelevant.

In a perfect capital market it is difficult to challenge the dividend irrelevance position. However, once these assumptions are relaxed, certain practical influences emerge and the arguments need further review.

3.2   Dividend signalling

In reality, investors do not have perfect information concerning the future prospects of the company. Many authorities claim, therefore, that the pattern of dividend payments is a key consideration on the part of investors when estimating future performance.

For example, an increase in dividends would signal greater confidence in the future by managers and would lead investors to increase their estimate of future earnings and cause a rise in share prices. A sudden dividend cut on the other hand could have a serious impact upon equity value.

This argument implies that dividend policy is relevant. Firms should attempt to adopt a stable (and rising) dividend payout to maintain investors' confidence.

Modigliani and Miller accept that dividends might be used as a short-run guide to future earnings, but explain that that is all they are - a guide. Investors are really interested in the size of future earnings (not dividends themselves) and will use any information they can to estimate this figure. If dividends turn out to be a bad long-run guide to future earnings investors will simply ignore them. Whilst this counter argument has validity in the long run it still means that short-run changes in dividends can be significant.

3.3   Preference for current income

Many investors require cash dividends to finance current consumption. This does not only apply to individual investors needing cash to live on but also to institutional investors, such as pension funds and insurance companies, who require regular cash outflows to meet day to day outgoings such as pension payments and insurance claims. This implies that many shareholders will prefer companies who pay regular cash dividends and will therefore value their shares more highly.

Modigliani and Miller once again challenge this argument and claim that investors requiring cash can generate 'home made dividends' by selling shares. This argument has some attractions but it does ignore transaction costs. The sale of shares involves brokerage costs and can therefore be unattractive to many investors. Some investors are not able to spend capital, only income may be used for consumption.

3.4   Resolution of uncertainty

One argument often put forward for high dividend payout is that income in the form of dividend is more secure than income in the form of capital gain. This, therefore, leads investors to place more value on high payout shares (sometimes referred to as the 'Bird in the Hand' theory).

This argument is, however, fallacious. Future dividends are just as uncertain as future capital gains. Dividends are only 'safe' when they are in the bank. A dividend in ten years' time is just as risky as a capital gain in ten years' time. Rational investors should not prefer one to the other.

3.5   Taxation

In many situations income in the form of dividend is taxed in a different way from income in the form of capital gains. This distortion in the personal tax system can have an impact on investors' preferences.

In the UK (up to the 1988 Budget) dividends were taxed at marginal income tax rates (27% – 60%), whereas capital gains were taxed at a marginal rate of 30%. For investors paying higher rate income tax it was far more beneficial to receive returns in the form of capital gains rather than dividends. On the other hand lower rate tax payers might prefer dividend income, and tax exempt institutions (pension funds) could be indifferent between the two. The preferences would very much depend upon the tax position of the individual investor.

The situation is now less clear-cut. Capital gains in the UK are now added to the income tax calculation and taxed as a further slice of income, so investors may be indifferent between dividends and capital gains. The 1998 budget has further complicated matters with tapered rates according to the length of time the asset is held. However, capital gains are only taxed when realised, and the annual exemption for capital gains exceeds the personal allowance for income tax, so there is still more scope for sheltering capital gains from tax than dividend income. Sophisticated investors therefore generally prefer low dividends and high capital appreciation from their shares.

From the corporate point of view this further complicates the dividend decision as different groups of shareholders are likely to prefer different payout patterns.

One suggestion is that companies are likely to attract a clientele of investors who favour their dividend policy (for tax and other reasons). In this case companies should be very cautious in making significant changes to dividend policy as it could upset their investors. Research in the USA tends to confirm this clientele effect with high dividend payout firms attracting low income tax bracket investors and low dividend payout firms attracting high income tax bracket investors.

3.6   Conclusions on dividend irrelevance arguments

Once market imperfections are introduced dividend policy does appear to have an impact upon shareholder wealth. If the clientele theory is taken into account three major points should be noted.

(a)   Reductions in dividend can convey 'bad news' to shareholders (dividend signalling). Serious consideration should be given to other forms of finance before cutting dividends.

(b)   Changes in dividend policy, particularly reductions, may conflict with investor liquidity requirements.

(c)   Changes in dividend policy may upset investor tax planning.

3.7   Activity

Read the Companies and Markets section of the **Financial Times** regularly, with particular regard to reported reactions of the markets to dividend announcements. Make a note of evidence of the dividend signalling hypothesis (eg, when a cut in dividends results in a fall in share price).

4   CHAPTER SUMMARY

When raising finance, one option which must be considered is reducing dividends, rather than making new issues. The theory put forward by Modigliani and Miller is that a firm's dividend policy should not affect the wealth of its shareholders. Funds which are retained, rather than being paid out as dividends, will increase the value of the shares, which can be sold for a capital gain by those shareholders who need income. An identical situation will result from raising additional equity capital instead of cutting a dividend.

In practice, it probably **is** important whether funds are raised by cutting a dividend or in other ways. There are a number of factors to consider when choosing between methods of issuing new equity and between cutting a dividend or raising new funds. As far as new issues are concerned, a rights issue is probably the best method, followed by a placing, with an offer for sale to the public coming last. As far as dividends are concerned, although retaining profits is cheaper than raising new funds, cutting a dividend may send adverse signals to the market about the company's health, and may upset the company's 'clientele' of investors who have chosen the company partly for its dividend policy. Note that there are other matters affecting the level of dividend paid, such as profitability and liquidity.

5   SELF TEST QUESTIONS

5.1   How do the Companies Acts define profits available for dividend? (1.1)

5.2   Does the *CA 1985* permit the distribution of capital profits? (1.1)

5.3   What is the effect of inflation on a company's payout ratio? (1.2)

5.4   What is the dividend policy adopted by most listed companies? (1.3)

5.5   What is the disadvantage of a residual approach to dividends? (1.3)

5.6   Who developed the argument of dividend irrelevance? (2.1)

5.7   What is the dividend irrelevance argument? (2.2)

5.8　　What is dividend signalling? (3.2)

5.9　　Does the UK tax system lead investors to prefer dividends or capital gains? (3.5)

5.10　　What is the clientele theory of dividend policy? (3.5)

6　　EXAMINATION TYPE QUESTION

6.1　　Feret plc

Feret plc an all equity company has ten million shares in issue and has been paying dividends of 10p per share for a number of years and with its existing business is expected to be able to continue to earn sufficient profits to enable it to pay such a dividend for the foreseeable future. The company has been offered a new contract which would take two years to complete and would involve an investment outlay of £500,000 in each of the next two years. The board plans to finance the investment by a reduction of dividend.

If the project is undertaken, when it is completed it will increase the earnings of the company above their expected level by £350,000 per annum for the foreseeable future.

The current market price of an equity share of Feret plc is £0.90. The management of Feret believes that the market value of shares in the company is based on dividends. Taxation can be ignored in (a) and (b) but not (c).

You are required to answer the following questions.

(a)　　Would an announcement of a decision to reduce dividends with an explanation of why this was being done and with details of the proposed investment, lead to an increase or decrease in the current share price? Show calculations to justify your conclusion.

(8 marks)

(b)　　Is it possible for an investor owning 100 shares in Feret plc who is dependent on the annual income from investments to increase his spending power during the next two years while still being able to maintain his spending potential in subsequent years? Illustrate your answer with appropriate figures.　　**(6 marks)**

(c)　　What are the implications of your analysis for dividend decision making? On what assumptions does your answer depend, and how might these deviate from what in fact happens in practice?　　**(6 marks)**

(Total: 20 marks)

7　　ANSWER TO EXAMINATION TYPE QUESTION

7.1　　Feret plc

(a)　　*(Tutorial note:* the procedure is to determine the shareholders' required rate of return and use this to discount the future dividend stream to obtain the market value of the firm's equity.*)*

Shareholders' required rate of return

Constant dividend situation, and assuming share price is ex div.

$$K_e = \frac{D}{Vo} = \frac{£0.10}{£0.90} \approx 11\%$$

Future dividend stream

	Y1	Y2	Y3	Y4	----	Y_∞
DPS	0.05 (W1)	0.05	0.135 (W2)	0.135		0.135

There are many ways of obtaining the present value of the above stream. One of the simplest is to say the above is equivalent to

a perpetuity @ 11% of 13.5p **less** a 2 year annuity of 8.5p (ie, 13.5p – 5p) at 11%

$$= \frac{13.5p}{0.11} - 8.5p \times 1.713 = 108p$$

Share price will **rise** to £1.08.

WORKINGS

(W1)   Dividend - year 1 and 2

Current dividend per share	10p
Reduction in dividend	
$\dfrac{£500,000}{10 \text{ million}} \times 100$	5p
	5p

(W2)   Dividend - year 3 onwards

Current dividend per share	10.0p
Additional earnings	
$\dfrac{£350,000}{10 \text{ million}} \times 100$	3.5p
	13.5p

(b)   The investor's original spending power is

100 shares × 10p = £10 pa.

For each of the next two years his annual dividend will fall to £0.05 per share, giving a total income of £5 pa. However, he will be able to more than make up for this shortfall in spending power by selling five shares in each of the next two years. In year one his total annual income will then rise to £5 + (5 × £1.08) = £10.40.

In year two it will be (95 × £0.05) + (5 × £1.14*) = £10.45

* note, share price in year 2 will be $(\frac{13.5p}{0.11} - 8.5p)$ = 114p

Thereafter his shareholding will have been reduced to 90 shares. However, with the increased dividend of £0.135, his annual income will rise to £12.15.

Thus, the investor will be able to increase his spending power during the next two years and more than maintain his spending potential in subsequent years.

(c)   In a perfect capital market with no taxation investors should not object to the proposed cut in dividend as the funds are profitably used and should lead to a capital gain that outweighs the dividend reduction. However, several reservations have to be made.

(i)   This assumes that the market is informed of the project and believes the information. Research on the informational content of dividends shows that dividend reductions are often seen as signals of bad news and lead to reductions in share price. Most listed companies try to avoid cuts in dividend.

(ii)   It assumes investors are happy to manufacture 'home-made dividends' by realising capital gains. Transaction costs may frustrate this process.

(iii)   The tax position of investors can also have a substantial effect on the decision. If investors are paying low rates of income tax they may prefer to receive returns in the form of dividend rather than capital gain. Research indicates that firms attract a clientele of investors whose personal tax position is suited to their dividend policy.

(iv)   The analysis assumes that the project should be evaluated at the company's existing cost of equity. However, if it is of substantially different risk this discount rate might not be appropriate.

In theory investors should not object to reductions in dividend provided that funds are profitably employed. However, in practice the above factors mean that a firm should exercise great care in tampering with dividend policy as it could have detrimental effects on equity value.

10 BUSINESS PLANNING

INTRODUCTION & LEARNING OBJECTIVES

This chapter and the three that follow it deal with section 2 of the syllabus Business planning. Businesses must plan and control their operations so that decisions can be taken in line with the company's objectives. You will see that plans are usually classified into strategic plans, tactical plans and operational plans depending on the level of management and the time scale involved.

This chapter then concentrates on short-term financial planning, in particular how cash flows should be managed to meet short-term financial objectives. Much of this material will be familiar to you from your previous studies.

When you have studied this chapter you should be able to do the following:

- Distinguish between the three levels of control: strategic, tactical and operational.
- Understand the contents of a short-term or medium-term financial plan.
- Explain the cash operating cycle within a business.
- Discuss the role of the cash budget in financial planning.
- Analyse financial performance through ratio analysis.
- Present comparisons of actual and expected financial performance.

1 INTRODUCTION TO PLANNING

1.1 The nature of financial control

 'Planning' has been defined as 'the establishment of objectives, and the formulation, evaluation and selection of the policies, strategies, tactics and action required to achieve them. Planning comprises long-term/strategic planning, and short-term operational planning. The latter is usually for a period of one year.'

In line with this definition, routine business planning is dealt with in two chapters in this text. This chapter covers short-term operational planning while the next chapter covers long-term planning.

The processes of planning and control are inter-related. Although it is possible to define each separately eg, planning as the setting of standards and control as the appraisal of actuals against standards, often it is the same people who carry out both activities and so it is best to consider both together.

In the context of business decisions, many business writers have sought to classify the planning and control process. The usual classification is as follows:

Strategic plans

Strategic plans are concerned mainly with external problems, and in particular with deciding which products or services to produce for which market.

Tactical plans

Tactical plans are concerned with ensuring that the company's resources are adequate for carrying out the strategic plans in order to reach the desired objective.

Operational plans

Operational plans are concerned with the way in which the company is to be run from day to day in order to optimise performance.

Corresponding with these classifications are the related terms of strategic control, tactical control and operational control. It is the financial aspects of these controls which are the subjects of this and the following chapter.

1.2 Information requirements for financial control

Since financial control contains strategic, tactical and operational aspects, it is necessary for the financial control process to contain information covering all three. For example, strategic control requires the monitoring of specific strategic decisions. These may be obtained from sources internal to the company, but are more likely to arise from external data about the state of the economy, new technology, data about competitors, etc.

Often objectives are stated in terms of ratios, eg, a strategic objective to maintain a certain return on capital employed over a ten year period. We will look closely at the use of ratios in both short-term and long-term planning over the next sections.

2 FINANCIAL PLANNING AND STRATEGIC PLANNING

2.1 Financial planning

The management function of planning requires the development, definition and evaluation of

(a)   the organisation's objectives; and

(b)   alternative strategies for achievement of these objectives.

The objectives of business activity are invariably concerned with money - as the universal measure of the ability to command resources. Thus, financial awareness permeates all business activities.

Nevertheless, finance cannot be managed in isolation from other functions of the business and, therefore, financial planning will be undertaken within the framework of a plan for the whole organisation, ie, a corporate plan.

2.2 The strategic planning approach to developing a business plan

Strategic planning is a systematic approach to decisions about the basic directions and purposes of a business and the development of plans to achieve those purposes. It may involve interpretation of policy, applying strategies, establishing corporate objectives and generally ensuring that a company develops in a planned, rather than haphazard fashion.

The period to be covered by a strategic plan will vary between different types of business. In general terms, the minimum period for a long-term plan will be that necessary for the implementation of decisions on such matters as

(a)   Development of new facilities (buildings, plant or equipment and the materials and manpower necessary to utilise them).

(b)   Development of new products or services.

(c)   Entry into a new field of marketing for existing products.

For control purposes, a strategic business plan may be broken down into the shorter term plans normally represented by annual budgets.

Strategic planning thus falls into six main steps

Step	Action
1	Business review and assessment (including appraisal of corporate strengths and weaknesses)
2	Establishment of objectives

3   Choice of strategies and their evaluation

4   Detailed evaluation of the strategic plan (sometimes then referred to as a *strategic budget*)

5   Establishment of annual or other short-term budgets

6   Implementing the plan and monitoring results

These steps are examined in more detail below.

Step 1   **Business review and assessment**

(a)   **Functional approach.** Each functional executive (eg, sales manager, production manager) reviews the strengths and weaknesses of the operations under his control, both in actual terms and in relation to major competitors. The object of the appraisal is to determine which strengths may be best exploited in planning for the long-term.

This analysis will be more useful if it is linked with method (b).

(b)   **Basic (or total entity) approach.** An attempt is made to re-analyse and express in simple terms the essential nature of the company's activity. Typical questions that might be asked in making such a survey are

(i)   What basic needs do the company's products satisfy? For example, a bus service is only one means of satisfying the basic need for transportation.

(ii)   To what markets could the company's products or skills be relevant? For example, greengrocery retailing could be developed either into a supermarket activity covering all domestic food consumption or into a specialised service for the catering industry.

The analysis of trends carried out in the course of the business review will enable a forecast to be made of future changes in sales, profitability and capital employed. The forecast thus made will be compared with the desired results emerging from a restatement of the corporate objectives; and any shortfall, ie, the profit or growth *gap*, must be made good by developing new strategies.

Step 2   **Establishment of objectives**

The concept of corporate objectives has been discussed at some length earlier. It is important at this stage that the objectives should be stated in a way which is both precise and measurable, eg,

(a)   a defined rate of growth expressed in quantitative terms such as sales value or market value of assets employed.

(b)   a defined rate of growth in earnings per share.

(c)   a defined rate of return on capital employed.

Step 3   **Choice of strategies**

The strategies for achieving the corporate objectives during the period of the plan may be based on products similar to those already in existence (*intensive* development) or on product diversification (*extensive* development).

Intensive development may be achieved by

(a)   Increased penetration of existing markets.

(b)   Introduction of the product range into new markets.

(c)   Product improvement, giving rise to increased demand.

The various product marketing strategies will be linked with strategic decisions of facilities and finance, for example, fixed asset additions and additional capital required.

Extensive development may be achieved in various ways, for example

(a)   Combining the company with others in related lines of business. This is known as *integration* and is one of two types

   (i)   *vertical integration*, whereby the firms merge with those above and below it in the production chain, eg, a wholesaler may merge with a producer or a retailer

   (ii)   *horizontal integration*, whereby firms at the same point in the production chain, but in slightly different markets, may combine.

(b)   Conglomerate diversification

   The further a company plans to develop away from its traditional type of business, the greater the risk involved; and the higher the rewards that should be expected.

Step 4   Detailed evaluation of the strategic plan

Whatever strategy is investigated, three questions have to be asked

(a)   Will the business be better off after the change than it was before?

(b)   What will be the effect of the proposal on the declared profits year by year?

(c)   Will there be sufficient money available to meet any cash outlays under the proposal?

In all but the simplest of evaluations, a degree of uncertainty will exist in the figures used, and where the uncertainty is significant, it is highly desirable that an evaluation should be made of the risk involved.

The techniques used for such analysis are described later.

Step 5   Establishment of annual or other short-term budgets

A preliminary strategic plan, or possibly alternative plans, will be developed by amending the basic forecast to reflect the results of evaluating various strategic possibilities so that the adjusted totals appear to satisfy the corporate financial objectives.

When this stage is reached then the validity of the plan must be confirmed, and it must be expressed in a form which will define management responsibilities for its achievement.

This is done by preparing detailed sales, resource utilisation and cost budgets for each year

The end result will be a series of annual plans with full supporting schedules analysed by responsibility. These together are sometimes referred to as the strategic or long-term budget.

Step 6   **Implementing the plan and monitoring results**

The overall corporate plan will consist of strategic plans, tactical plans and operational plans as described earlier. Once these plans are implemented, actual results can be compared with targets with the resulting information reinput back into the planning process to enable the targets and plans to be changed if required.

It has already been stressed that management should carry out three levels of control, corresponding to the three levels of planning identified above. An important tool to use in the control process is the use of ratios, for example the trend in return on capital employed over a number of years as a strategic control.

Planning is a continuous management function. The first year of the strategic budget should, therefore, be capable of conversion into the forthcoming annual budget for the business, against which control will be exercised.

The strategic budget should be reviewed regularly; as the first year's figures are extracted for current operational control, so the strategic budget should be extended a further year into the future with such modifications as may be necessary as new information becomes available.

3   SHORT TERM FINANCIAL PLANNING

3.1   Introduction

Most of this examination text is concerned with long term financial decisions, which involve long term assets and liabilities and decisions which cannot easily be reversed, committing the firm to a given course of action for a number of years.

Short term financial decisions involve short lived assets and liabilities and are usually fairly easy to reverse. However this does not mean that they are any less important. A firm which has carefully planned its long term capital investments, found its ideal debt/equity ratio and agreed on its dividend policy, may yet run into trouble because it manages its short term cash position badly. Hence the need for short term planning.

In the following sections we will review the major components of working capital, show how short term plans are drawn up, and illustrate how long term financing decisions can affect the firm's short term financial planning problem.

3.2   The information needs of short-term financial planning

Short-term financial planning can be assumed to relate to the forthcoming one year period. The plan would normally consist of

- projected profit and loss account

- projected cash flow statement

- projected balance sheet at the end of the period

- statement of relevant assumptions, eg, inflation rate, interest rates, exchange rates, growth in markets

- statement of contingency plans, to allow for events which may occur differently than in the projected accounting statements. Examples would be setting lower prices if projected sales volumes were not being achieved, or using financial futures to hedge exchange risks if exchange rates were not as anticipated

- financing implications of the plan, in particular how cash surpluses and deficits are to be dealt with. This aspect is examined later in a separate section

- methods of controlling the plan, eg, regular production of key ratios to be monitored by senior management. This aspect is also examined in more detail later.

3.3   The financing of working capital

Traditionally current assets were seen as fluctuating, originally with a seasonal agricultural pattern. Current assets would then be financed out of short-term credit, which could be paid off when not required, whilst fixed assets would be financed by long-term funds (debt or equity).

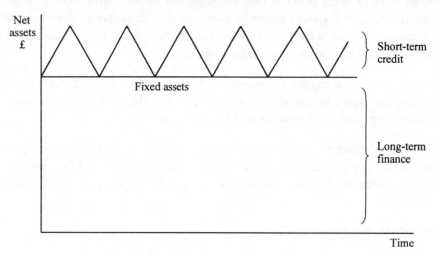

This analysis is rather simplistic. In most businesses a proportion of the current assets are fixed over time being thus expressed as 'permanent'. For example, certain base levels of stock are always carried, or a certain level of trade credit is always extended. If growth is added to this situation a more realistic business picture would be as follows:

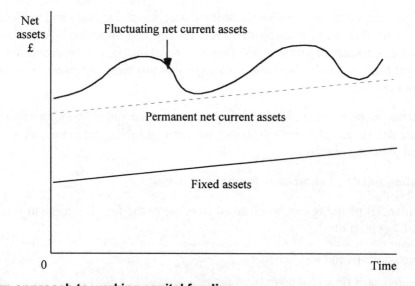

3.4   The modern approach to working capital funding

Given the permanent nature of a large proportion of current assets, it is generally felt prudent to fund a proportion of net current assets with long-term finance. The question is generally one of the extent to which such funding occurs. The possibilities include:

- some permanent current net assets financed by short-term credit
- all permanent and some fluctuating current net assets financed by long-term credit
- all current net assets and some fixed assets financed by short-term credit
- all current and fixed assets financed by long term credit

The choice is a matter for managerial judgement but the following trade-off must be considered:

The relative cheapness of short-term debt v The risks of short-term debt

3.5   The cost of short-term finance

Short-term finance is usually cheaper than long-term finance. This is largely due to the risks taken by creditors. For example, if a bank were considering two loan applications, one for one year and the other for twenty years, all other things being equal it would demand a higher interest rate on the twenty year loan. This is because it feels more exposed to risk on long-term loans as more could go wrong with the borrower over a period of twenty years than a period of one year (although it should be noted that occasionally this situation is reversed, with rates of return being higher on short-term finance as discussed in an earlier chapter).

Short-term finance also tends to be more flexible. For example, if funds are raised on overdraft and used to finance a fluctuating investment in current assets they can be paid off when not required and interest saved. On the other hand, if funds were borrowed long-term early repayment may not be possible, or, if allowed, early repayment penalties may be experienced. The flexibility of short-term finance may, therefore, reduce its overall cost.

Short-term finance includes items such as trade creditors, which are normally regarded as low cost funds, whereas long-term finance will include debt and equity. Equity finance is particularly expensive, its required returns being high, and non tax deductible.

3.6   Sources of short and medium-term finance

No hard and fast definitions hold in this area and authorities disagree on what constitutes 'short-term' and 'medium-term'. As a rough guide up to three years can be seen as short-term, and three to ten years as medium-term, but many firms would apply different definitions.

The most widely-used sources of short and medium-term funds are:

(a)   bank overdrafts and loans;
(b)   private loans;
(c)   trade and expense credit;
(d)   leasing and instalment credit; and
(e)   various forms of debtor related finance, including factoring of debts and invoice discounting.

3.7   The risks of short-term finance

Short-term financing has already been established as generally 'the cheaper option'. However, the price paid for reduced cost is increased risk for the borrower. There may be:

(a)   **Renewal problems** - short-term finance may need to be continually renegotiated as various facilities expire and renewal may not always be guaranteed.

(b)   **Stability of interest rates** - if the company is constantly having to renew its funding arrangements it will be at the mercy of fluctuations in short-term interest rates.

3.8   Conclusions on long term versus short term finance

No ideal financing package can be recommended. Much will depend upon the risk-return trade-off for individual companies,. The 'textbook' rule of thumb is that 'long-term assets should be financed by long-term funds and short-term assets by short-term funds'. This approach matches up the maturity of the finance with the duration of the investment and hence avoids many of the renewal problems. However, many companies choose to break this rule, often with great success.

3.9   Investment in working capital

Management of the investment in working capital can be considered at the individual current asset or liability level or in terms of total working capital requirement. For now, the total investment in working capital will be considered. Management of individual current asset and liability elements (ie, stocks, debtors, cash and creditors) will be considered in later sections.

Overall investment in working capital largely concerns trade-off. Here, the firm must consider the cost of investing in working capital (largely the financing cost) against the benefits it brings. With no investment in working capital there would be no stocks and no debtors, which would probably result in few sales and, therefore, little profit.

Cash flow is the lifeblood of the thriving business. Effectual (effective and efficient) management of the working capital investment is essential to maintaining control of business cash flow. Management must have full awareness of the profitability versus liquidity trade-off. Healthy trading growth typically produces:

(a)   increased profitability; and

(b)   requirement for increased investment in:

-    fixed assets and
-    working capital.

There is a trade-off under which trading growth and increased profitability squeezes cash. Ultimately, if not properly managed, increased trading can carry with it the spectre of overtrading and inability to pay the business creditors.

4   THE CASH CYCLE

4.1   The cash operating cycle

The investment made in working capital is largely a function of sales and, therefore, it is useful to consider the problem in terms of the firm's cash operating cycle (otherwise referred to as the working capital cycle).

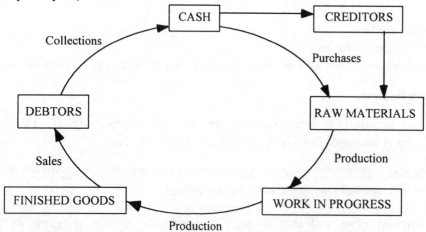

The cash operating cycle (or working capital cycle) reflects the firm's investments in working capital as it moves through the production process towards sales. The investment in working capital gradually increases firstly being only in raw materials, but then in labour and overhead as production progresses. This investment must be maintained throughout the production process, the finished goods holding period and up to the final collection of cash from trade debtors. Note that the net investment can be reduced by taking trade credit from suppliers.

The faster a firm can 'push' items around the operating cycle the lower its investment in working capital will be. However, too little investment in working capital can lose sales since customers will generally prefer to buy from suppliers who are prepared to extend trade credit, and if items are not held in stock when required by customers, sales may be lost.

With some fairly basic financial information it is possible to measure the length of the working capital cycle for a given firm.   The measurement is of the (average) time period that elapses between payment of cash to trade creditors and receipt of cash from sales. The idea is one of minimising the time period, thus minimising the cash tied up in working capital investment.

The cash cycle can be further illustrated as follows:

The length of the cash cycle equals:

Raw material stock period	*less*	Creditor payment period	*plus*	Production period	*plus*	Finished goods stock period	*plus*	Debtor payment period

If the components of the cycle are considered carefully, notice can be taken of the fact that improvements can be made ie, the cycle can be reduced in time by either:

(a)   improving production efficiency ('WIP stock-holding period');

(b)   improving finished goods and/or raw material stock turnover; and

(c)   improving debtor and creditor payment periods - ie, minimisation of the former (subject to not adversely affecting trading levels) and maximising the latter (subject to obtaining appropriate supplies).

The following activity considers a firm's investment in working capital and its budgeted level for the coming year.

4.2   Activity

Analyse the following information from the viewpoint of its implications for working capital policy:

	Position as of now	Budget position one year from now
Sales	250,000	288,000
Cost of goods sold	210,000	248,000
Purchases	140,000	170,000
Debtors	31,250	36,000
Creditors	21,000	30,000
Raw materials stock	35,000	60,000
Work-in-progress	17,500	30,000
Finished goods stock	40,000	43,000

Assume all sales and purchases are on credit terms.

4.3   Activity solution

Analysis of the figures (which are detailed below) shows that working capital investment is being increased. Debtor balances are moving pro-rata with sales, the current and budgeted collection period both being forty six days. However, some additional finance will be taken from creditors as a result of the payment period being increased from fifty five days to sixty four days. This increase represents about 16% and is not particularly significant unless creditors demand payment within sixty days, or offer discounts for payment within that time (which will be lost).

A significant change in the turnover of stock levels is anticipated. Raw materials stocks turnover will be decreased by 41% and work-in-progress by 47%, while finished goods stock turnover will increase by 10%. The implication is that production will increase while sales will fall; in the period following the budget, stocks will be very high. The overall impression is that unnecessarily high investment in raw materials and work-in-progress is being undertaken. A reappraisal of the situation should be made to see if these stocks can be reduced, thereby releasing funds for other uses. It may also be possible to reduce debtors to their current levels.

Workings

		Current	Budget
(1)	**Creditors**		

Average payment collection period

$$= \left(365 \times \frac{Creditors}{Purchases} \right) \qquad 365 \times \frac{21}{140} = \quad (55\ days) \quad 365 \times \frac{30}{170} = \quad (64\ days)$$

(2) **Debtors**

Average collection period

$$= \left(365 \times \frac{Debtors}{Sales} \right) \qquad 365 \times \frac{31.25}{250} = \quad 46\ days \quad 365 \times \frac{36}{288} = \quad 46\ days$$

(3) **Finished stock holding period**

$$= \left(365 \times \frac{Finished\ goods\ stock}{Cost\ of\ goods\ sold} \right) \qquad 365 \times \frac{40}{210} = 70\ days \qquad 365 \times \frac{43}{248} = 63\ days$$

(4) **Raw materials stock holding period**

$$= \left(365 \times \frac{Raw\ materials\ stock}{Purchases} \right) \qquad 365 \times \frac{35}{140} = 91\ days \qquad 365 \times \frac{60}{170} = 129\ days$$

(5) **Work-in-progress holding period**

$$= \left(365 \times \frac{Work\text{-}in\text{-}progress\ stock}{Cost\ of\ goods\ sold} \right) \quad 365 \times \frac{17.5}{210} = 30\ days \qquad 365 \times \frac{30}{248} = 44\ days$$

Length of cash operating cycle	182 days	218 days

Note: Calculation of work-in-progress period assumes no change in finished goods stock.

4.4 Influences on the cash operating cycle

The length of a firm's cash operating cycle and, therefore, its investment in working capital will be a function of several variables. The efficiency of control procedures and methods for determining budgeted investment in current assets will be examined in later sections. For now three other influences will be considered.

(a) **Industry influence**

In some industries the working capital cycle is very short (eg, food retailing) whilst in others (eg, construction) it is by necessity much longer. Hence, the length of the production process and the nature of the industry must be considered when examining working capital requirements.

(b) **Growth**

Rapid growth in sales will mean a rapidly increasing investment in working capital. This can cause particular problems as the extra investment in working capital will not be balanced by increased sales revenues until the extra sales have worked their way right through the cycle. Care must be taken in this situation as an increase in investment in current assets that is not supported by new funds can lead to 'overtrading'. This is a potentially dangerous situation where fixed assets might have to be sold to repay liabilities.

(c)   **Inflation**

Increases in the prices of raw materials and other factors of production can cause similar problems to growth in sales and mean that the firm has to finance an increased investment in working capital for the length of the cash operating cycle.

The lessons of the cash operating cycle are those of maximising all stock turnover, (including work in progress, thus maximising production efficiency), maximising supplier credit, and minimising that given to clients (subject to not adversely affecting business trading).

4.5   Short-term financial ratios

Analysis will be crucially concerned with the ability of the firm to settle its debts in the short-term and to operate profitability in the long-term. The majority of the ratios employed will be quite familiar from basic ratio analysis.

(a)   **The current ratio**

$$\frac{\text{Current assets}}{\text{Current liabilities}}$$

This is usually considered the major indicator of the firm's ability to meet its short-term debts. Although the 'textbook' norm is 2:1 considerable variation exists between industries. Sectors such as food retailing (with cash sales, minimal debtor levels, and good supplier credit) have operated successfully on ratios of 1.5 : 1 or less for many years. As stated earlier, the current ratio can be used as a measure of the current asset financing policy adopted by firms.

(b)   **The quick asset ratio or acid test ratio**

$$\frac{\text{Current assets - Stock}}{\text{Current liabilities}}$$

This is very similar to the current ratio but stock is omitted from the numerator as most companies would experience difficulties in quickly realising stock to meet a pressing short-term debt. The 'textbook' norm for this ratio is 1 : 1, but again considerable variation exists in practice.

(c)   **Cash flow ratios**

A firm's daily cash flow can be very crudely approximated by the following calculation:

$$\frac{\text{Net profit} + \text{Depreciation per period}}{\text{Number of trading days per period}}$$

This figure can then give an indication of the firm's ability to meet its commitments from operating cash flows. For example, if no other funds were available it could reveal how long a firm would need to pay off its trade creditors.

(d)   **Ratios for individual current assets and liabilities**

These are as computed for in activity solution 4.3:

*   Raw material holding period
*   Work-in-progress holding period

- Finished goods holding period
- Average debtor collection period
- Average creditor payment period

Strictly all of the numerators in these ratios should be average figures for the year but commonly year end figures are taken as an approximation. Note also that some of the figures will not be available from published accounts. These ratios can be monitored to reveal the level of investment in each area of working capital.

Care must be taken in the interpretation of these ratios. For example, an increase in the average debtor collection period could imply a deterioration in credit control but on the other hand might reflect a planned increase in credit granted to boost sales. In a similar way a decrease in a finished goods stock could mean more efficient stock control or it could be a result of production difficulties and be a cause of lost sales.

The normal methods of interpretation are to compare ratios with past performances so as to monitor trends, or to make comparisons with companies in a similar line of business. Again care must be exercised in using both these approaches to allow for changing conditions over time and differences in the positions or accounting policies of the companies used for comparisons.

5   BUDGETING, MONITORING AND CONTROLLING CASH FLOWS

5.1   The need for cash management

Policies followed for the individual components of the operating cycle will ultimately determine the level of cash available at any time - but how much should be kept as cash, and how much should be invested, if only short-term? As with all elements of working capital, the management of cash involves a trade off between

- liquidity - having enough cash available to meet everyday demands; and

- profitability/cost - holding high balances of cash is costly in terms of lost investment interest; whilst unexpected deficits can be expensive if emergency funding is required.

In practice, a carefully monitored cash budget will generally provide the basis for cash management; there are, however, two theoretical models of which you should be aware, as now discussed.

5.2   Uncertainty in cash flows - Miller-Orr model

It is considered unlikely that a calculation question would ever be set on this model but a knowledge of its workings could be required.

The model takes into account uncertainty in both receipts and payments of cash. It is best explained with reference to the following diagram:

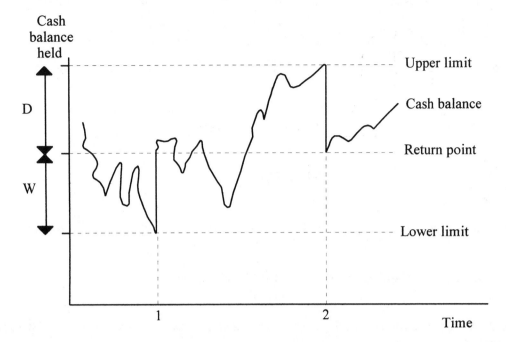

All cash receipts and payments are met from the cash balance and, as can be seen from the diagram, the cash balance of the firm is allowed to wander freely between two limits. The lower limit has to be specified by the firm and the upper limit is calculated by the model. If the cash balance on any day goes outside these limits action must be taken.

At point 1 the cash balance reaches the lower limit and must be replenished in some way, eg, by the sale of marketable securities or withdrawal from a deposit account. The size of this withdrawal is indicated on the diagram (W), and it is the distance between the return point (calculated by the model) and the lower limit.

At point 2 the cash balance reaches the upper limit and an amount (D) must be invested in marketable securities or placed in a deposit account. Again, this is calculated by the model as the distance between the upper limit and the return point.

The minimum cost return point and upper limit are calculated by reference to brokerage costs, holding costs and the variance of cash flows. The model has some fairly restrictive assumptions, eg, normally distributed cash flows but, in tests, Miller and Orr found it fairly robust and claim significant potential cost savings for companies.

In practical terms, the model closely follows stochastic models for inventory control.

5.3   Probability based models

Probability distributions of daily net cash inflows can be helpful in determining the minimum cash balance to hold.

Example

On the basis of past observations a firm discovers that its daily net cash outflow has a mean of zero with a standard deviation of £20,000 and is normally distributed.

Assuming that it is only prepared to accept a one-in-a-hundred chance of running out of cash, what is the minimum cash balance it must hold at the start of the day?

Solution

The probability distribution of net cash flows may be represented as follows:

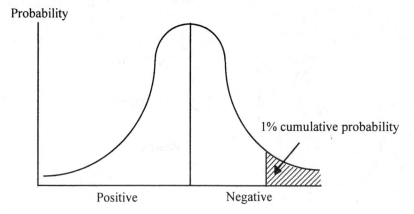

From normal distribution tables we know that there is only a 1% chance that the net cash outflow will exceed:

$$\text{Mean} + (2.326 \times \text{Standard deviation}) = £0 + (2.326 \times £20,000)$$
$$= £46,520$$

Therefore, if at the start of each day the firm has a cash balance of £46,520, there is only a 1% chance that it will run out of cash.

It is, of course, possible to have successive daily net cash outflows but it is assumed that the cash balance is brought back to this level, £46,520, daily.

5.4   Cash budgets

Once the firm has determined the cash balance it wishes to carry it needs to take action to ensure this balance will be maintained. The usual method adopted to control investment in cash is the cash budget. The following section will deal with the construction of short-term cash budgets together with other approaches that are used for predicting the medium-term cash position of the firm.

Objectives

(a)   To integrate and appraise the effect of operating budgets on the company's cash resources.
(b)   To anticipate cash shortages and surpluses, and allow time to plan how to deal with them.
(c)   To provide a basis for comparison with actual, to identify unplanned occurrences.

5.5   Relationship of forecast to budget

The cash budget is an integral part of the master budget of the business. It reflects the impact on cash resources of budgeted sales, costs and changes in assets structure, and is also confirmation that the plans are financially viable. It is important to distinguish between a budget and a forecast. A cash forecast is an estimate of cash receipts and payments for a future period under existing conditions before taking account of possible actions to modify cash flows, raise new capital, or invest surplus funds.

A cash budget is a commitment to a plan for cash receipts and payments for a future period after taking any action necessary to bring the preliminary cash forecast into conformity with the overall plan of the business. Cash forecasts and cash budgets can both be prepared in any of the ways described.

5.6   Scope

The period covered by the budget and the frequency with which it is revised will depend on the purpose for which it is made.

A cash budget may be *long-term* or *short-term*. A long-term cash budget will be made in connection with the long-term corporate plan, typically covering a period of three to five years. In some companies, however, the time horizon of budgeting may be less than a year, while in others (particularly those concerned with the exploitation of natural resources) budget periods in excess of five years may be necessary. A short-term cash budget relates to current operations. In a business which by choice or necessity gives very detailed attention to cash management, the shortest-term budget may be prepared daily or weekly and may cover perhaps one week or one month or more ahead.

5.7   Receipts and payments budgets/forecasts

(a)   **Method of preparation**

    (i)   Forecast sales.

    (ii)   Forecast time-lag on converting debtors to cash and hence forecast cash receipts.

    (iii)   Determine stock levels, and hence purchase requirements.

    (iv)   Forecast time-lag on paying suppliers, and thus cash payments.

    (v)   Incorporate other cash payments and receipts, including such items as capital expenditure and tax payments.

    (vi)   Collate this information so as to find the net cash flows.

(b)   **Layout**

A tabular layout should be used, with:

    (i)   Columns for months.
    (ii)   Rows for receipts and payments.

You should be quite familiar with the techniques required in cash forecast preparation from earlier studies. You will find a practice question at the end of this chapter.

5.8   Investment of short-term cash surpluses

Cash budgets and forecasts are used to identify shortages and surpluses of funds in advance.

Shortages of funds can be remedied by recourse to the short-term sources of finance discussed earlier, or by reducing investment in working capital.

Surplus funds can fall into two categories:

(a)   long-term surpluses which are normally used to repay liabilities, returned to shareholders via dividend payments, or used as fresh capital; or

(b)   short-term surpluses which need to be invested temporarily (perhaps in short-term securities or deposit accounts) until they are required.

5.9   Factors to be considered when investing short-term funds

Several considerations need to be made when formulating short-term investment policy:

(a)   **Liquidity**

How quickly the investment can be converted back to cash is of major importance. Factors such as how good a market exists for the chosen investment and the settlement period on any transaction should be considered.

(b)   **Risk**

The degree of risk attached to the investment in terms of variability of return and potential loss of principal.

(c)   **Return**

The income and capital gain from the chosen security.

These factors must be considered in the light of the firm's individual circumstances, in particular, the amount of funds available for investment and the duration of the surplus. For example, many investment opportunities are only available to large sums of cash. On the other hand, too much money concentrated on one security would impair its liquidity (it would be difficult to sell even 10% of the equity of a company in one day without affecting market price). Funds available for long periods of time can be safely tied up in longer term investment opportunities, whereas funds which may be needed at short notice should be placed in highly liquid investments.

In general, the lower the liquidity of an investment, and the higher its risk, the higher its expected return will be. Most treasurers will be concerned with preserving the value of their investment and having access to funds at short notice, and will usually not look to maximise returns.

5.10   Short-term investment opportunities

A wide (and expanding) number of short-term investment opportunities are available offering various degrees of liquidity, risk and return. A selection is listed below:

(a)   **Deposits**

These are available for various maturity dates and offer varying returns. Interest rates are normally variable. They include:

(i)   *Money market deposits* for periods of overnight upwards to six months or, occasionally, a year. Usually a minimum of £10,000 is required.

(ii)   *Bank deposits* which are similar to personal deposit accounts, with seven days' notice required for withdrawal. Interest penalties are usually levied for faster withdrawal.

(iii)   *Local authority deposits* with various maturities available; often the stocks are negotiable.

(iv)   *Sterling certificates of deposit* which are certificates issued by a bank when funds are deposited. The certificates may be sold to a third party, being fully negotiable instruments, and this makes the deposits highly marketable.

(b)   **Loan stocks and equities**

(i)   *Loan stocks* which are issued by governments (UK and foreign) and companies. Maturities, risks and returns vary.

(ii)   *Equities* which are probably the riskiest short-term investment opportunities and are, therefore, not popular with most corporate treasurers. If chosen, they are best used in the context of a well diversified portfolio.

6   ANALYSIS OF AN ORGANISATION'S PERFORMANCE

6.1   Ratio analysis

This section is concerned with evaluating the performance of a firm as a whole by means of ratios derived from its published accounts.

A single ratio on its own is not very useful: it only becomes meaningful if some yardstick is available against which to set this figure. There are three possible yardsticks, any or all of which may be used

(a)   comparison with the ratio of the same company in previous periods
(b)   comparison with ratios for other companies in the same industry; and
(c)   comparison with an *ideal* or *target* ratio

6.2   Stages of ratio analysis

Typically, students are presented with a seemingly endless list of important ratios which they proceed to memorise. This approach to ratio analysis is fundamentally wrong; calculating ratios is part of the systematic analysis of accounts and, as such, ratio analysis is an exercise in logic rather than memory. As an aid to logic, the following steps should be followed in the analysis.

Step 1   Identify the reasons for which the analysis is being made.

Consider the three most important purposes, ie,

(i)   to provide information for a potential purchase of shares (Stock Exchange ratios)
(ii)   to provide information for a potential creditor (solvency ratios); and
(iii)   to provide management information on operating efficiency (operating ratios).

Step 2   Identify the information relevant to those decisions.

Step 3   Identify the ratios which will assist in providing that information.

Step 4   Carry out the calculations, consider the results and carry out any further ratio analysis suggested.

Step 5   On the basis of the information and analysis, reach a decision.

Students should note that actually calculating ratios forms a relatively minor part of this sequence, and the most difficult part is deciding which ratios to calculate. This is the emphasis which should also be given in the examination room.

These concepts can now be put into practice in relation to the three situations indicated under Step 1. However, it is not possible to proceed to Step 5, because there is no yardstick against which to evaluate the results.

6.3   Illustration of calculation

Throughout the rest of this chapter, the following example will be used to illustrate the calculation of the various ratios.

Example

Cathcart plc - Summarised balance sheet at 31 December 19X4

	£'000	£'000		£'000	£'000
Share capital			Fixed assets		
Ordinary shares			Cost *less* depreciation		2,200
(£1 each)		1,000			
Preference shares					
(10%) (£1 each)		200			
Reserves			Current assets		
Revenue		800	Stock	400	
			Debtors	500	
Debentures			Cash	100	
10% Secured		600		———	1,000

Current liabilities

Creditors	400	
Corporation tax	100	
Dividends	100	
	——	
	600	
	3,200	3,200

Summarised profit and loss account for the year ended 31 December 19X4

	£'000	£'000
Turnover		3,000
Profit before interest and tax		400
Interest		60
		——
Profit before tax		340
Corporation tax		180
		——
Profit after tax		160
Dividends		
Ordinary - proposed and paid	125	
Preference	20	
	——	
		145
		——
Transferred to revenue reserves		15
		——
Current quoted price of £1 ordinary shares in Cathcart plc		£1.40

6.4   Stock exchange ratios

These are regarded as being significant in the context of reaching decisions about whether to buy or sell shares. Investors are concerned with the amount of cash, discounted to its present value, which they will receive from their investment in shares. This cash is the result of

(a)   dividends received; and

(b)   proceeds when the shares are ultimately sold.

Which ratios provide information about these cash flows? The simple answer is that no ratios directly provide the information, if for no other reasons than that ratios are based on historic accounting information whereas the required cash flows occur in the future. However, several ratios are regarded as being useful pointers.

(a)   dividend yield

(b)   earnings per share; and

(c)   price earnings ratio.

The calculation and significance of each of these ratios is examined below.

6.5   Dividend yield

This is the annual dividend per share expressed as an annual rate of return on the share price.

$$\text{Dividend yield} = \frac{\text{Total annual dividend}}{\text{Share price}} \times 100\%$$

6.6   Activity

What is the dividend yield of the ordinary shares of Cathcart plc in the example above?

6.7   Activity solution

$$\text{Dividend yield} = \frac{12.5}{140} \times 100\% = 8.93\%$$

Although this represents the actual cash return on ordinary shares, it is dependent on management decisions about the amount of dividend. However, the presumption is that profits retained in the business (ie, not paid out in dividends) will be reinvested to earn a higher return and, thence, eventually higher dividends. Thus, the yield is only a partial measure of the return to ordinary shareholders.

6.8   Earnings per share

It is more appropriate, in many circumstances, to base the calculations on earnings rather than dividends. The principles of calculating earnings per share (EPS) are simple

$$\text{EPS} = \frac{\text{Earnings}}{\text{Shares in issue}}$$

However, the definitions of both *earnings* and *shares in issue* present difficulties. You should be familiar with this from your earlier studies, in particular how FRS 14 now requires earnings to be calculated **including** the effects of extraordinary items.

6.9   Price earnings (P/E) ratio

This ratio is now widely regarded as a key statistic with which to evaluate a company's share price. Specific industries have typical P/E ratios and any major departure from them indicated by the price of shares of an individual company in that industry indicates that there are special factors, eg, expectations of higher future earnings.

Having defined EPS, the P/E ratio is simple to define

$$\text{P/E ratio} = \frac{\text{Share price}}{\text{EPS}}$$

6.10   Activity

What is the P/E ratio currently for Cathcart plc in the example above?

6.11   Activity solution

$$\text{In the example, P/E} = \frac{140p}{14p} = 10$$

However, there is no need to restrict oneself to historic data. One may talk about

(a)   Historic P/E - based on the last audited accounts.
(b)   Current P/E - based on estimated results for the year in progress.
(c)   Forecast P/E - refers to forecast earnings for some future year.
(d)   Exit P/E - that forecast when a share is sold at some future point in time.

Such predictive P/Es are the stock-in-trade of the investment advisor. The P/E ratio is important because

(a)   it relates EPS to the share price, either now or in the future; and

(b)   investors believe it to be important - this in itself enhances its significance.

7   SOLVENCY RATIOS

7.1   Objective

The objective of this group of ratios is to provide information to an actual or potential creditor or bank. Such a person is concerned with a company's ability to meet its obligations to him. These obligations will be met out of cash to be generated by the company in the future, but an examination of the (historic) accounts will provide three useful items of information:

(a)   The relationship of current assets and liabilities - an indication of the adequacy or otherwise of past cash flows.

(b)   Gearing - the relationship of debt and equity financing, and indication of the relative risk.

(c)   The relationship of the size of debt to past cash flows.

Students will note that in studying these areas below only five ratios are specified. These are fundamental and must be known, but other ratios may be devised to suit specific circumstances.

7.2   Relationship of current assets and current liabilities

The classic ratio is simply a comparison of current assets with current liabilities.

In Example

$$\text{Current ratio} \quad = \quad \frac{£1,000,000}{£600,000} = 1.67$$

Traditionally, an ideal current ratio has been regarded as 2. However, the use of such *ideal* ratios should be treated with extreme caution. Supermarkets, for example, normally sell their goods for cash long before they pay their suppliers for them. They are therefore, using creditors as a normal source of finance and have current ratios well below 2. The problem with the current ratio is that, in practice, one of the current assets, stock, may not be rapidly realisable and so the comparison may be meaningless. An alternative is therefore to exclude stock. This ratio is generally known as the acid test or quick ratio.

In Example

$$\text{Acid test} \quad = \quad \frac{£1,000,000 - £400,000}{£600,000} = 1.0$$

It is generally regarded as desirable that this ratio should be 1 (ie, debtors + cash = current liabilities). However, the same reservations as above may be applied to such a generalisation.

7.3   Gearing

Gearing is an expression of the relationship between the amount of finance provided by equity shareholders and the amount provided by lenders. For this purpose, since preference shareholders receive a fixed return they are treated in the same way as lenders (although, in theory, preference shareholders are only entitled to their dividends out of profits, in practice, companies which do not pay preference dividends are in difficult circumstances).

Gearing affects

(a)   the riskiness of the company; and

(b)   the potential return to ordinary shareholders.

In practice, limits are imposed on how highly geared a company can become by the willingness of lenders to provide finance. Generally, the more highly geared a company becomes, the less willing lenders become and, therefore, the higher the interest rate charged.

There are a number of different ways of measuring gearing, but one commonly used is

$$\text{Gearing} = \frac{\text{Borrowing} + \text{Liabilities} + \text{Preference shares}}{\text{Ordinary shares} + \text{Reserves}}$$

In Example

$$\text{Gearing} = \frac{£600,000 + £600,000 + £200,000}{£1,000,000 + £800,000} = 0.78$$

Students may like to note that alternative definitions of gearing include

$$\text{Gearing} = \frac{\text{Long-term finance} + \text{Preference shares}}{\text{Ordinary shares} + \text{Reserves}}$$

In Example $= \dfrac{£600,000 + £200,000}{£1,800,000} = 0.44$

or, approaching the problem from the profit and loss account

$$\text{Gearing} = \frac{\text{Interest charges and preference dividends}}{\text{Profit before interest, tax and dividends}}$$

In Example $= \dfrac{£80,000}{£400,000} = 0.20$

8   OPERATING RATIOS AND ROCE

8.1   Objective

The objective is to provide management with a set of ratios which are significant in the context of operating efficiency.   As we are now looking at ratios as a tool for evaluating and interpreting company accounting reports, we will not dwell on these ratios here.   However, *return on capital employed* is generally regarded as being an important ratio, since it gives a measure of how efficiently a business is using the funds available.   It is generally used as the key ratio in a set of management ratios.

8.2   Return on capital employed (ROCE)

As indicated in the previous point, this is treated as the key ratio.   Since operating efficiency is the key factor, operating profit is related to operating assets.

For this purpose, profit before interest and tax is compared with gross assets (ie, before deducting liabilities).   Thus

$$\text{ROCE} = \frac{\text{Operating profit}}{\text{Operating assets}} \times 100\%$$

In Example

$$\text{ROCE} = \frac{£400,000}{£3,200,000} \times 100\% = 12.5\%$$

8.3   Factors affecting ROCE

There are two factors affecting ROCE

(a)   profitability of sales: and
(b)   rate of asset utilisation

Note that the product of these two gives ROCE

$$\frac{\text{Operating profit}}{\text{Sales}} \times \frac{\text{Sales}}{\text{Operating assets}} = \frac{\text{Operating profit}}{\text{Operating assets}} = \text{ROCE}$$

In Example

$$\frac{\text{Operating profit}}{\text{Sales}} = \frac{£400,000}{£3,000,000} = 0.13$$

$$\frac{\text{Sales}}{\text{Operating assets}} = \frac{£3,000,000}{£3,200,000} = 0.94$$

(**Note**: $0.94 \times 0.13 \times 100 = 12.22\%$ ie, ROCE subject to a rounding difference).

These may be subdivided into their component elements.

8.4   Factors affecting operating profit : sales

Operating profit is of course affected by the various elements of cost, and

$$\frac{\text{Operating profit}}{\text{Sales}} = 1 - \frac{\text{Cost elements}}{\text{Sales}}$$

Cost elements may include production, marketing, distribution, administration, etc.   The ratio $\frac{\text{Cost elements}}{\text{sales}}$ may be subdivided as far as detail in the profit and loss account permits.

It may also be useful to examine $\frac{\text{Contribution}}{\text{sales}}$

8.5   Factors affecting operating assets: sales

In the first instance, operating assets may be subdivided into fixed and current assets, since

$$\frac{\text{Operating assets}}{\text{Sales}} = \frac{\text{Fixed assets}}{\text{Sales}} + \frac{\text{Current assets}}{\text{Sales}}$$

(Note: it is easier to handle this ratio if sales is made the denominator.)

Each of these may be appropriately subdivided, eg,

Fixed assets = Plant and machinery + Freehold, etc,
Current assets = Stock + Debtors + Cash, etc,

The ratio $\frac{\text{debtors}}{\text{sales}} \times 12$ gives the number of months' debtors carried.

In the case of stock, the ratio $\frac{\text{Stock}}{\text{cost of sales}} \times 12$ is more appropriate and gives the number of months' stock carried.   Alternatively, $\frac{\text{cost of sales}}{\text{stock}}$ is the stock turnover rate in number of times pa.

9   COMPARING ACTUAL AND EXPECTED PERFORMANCE

9.1   Introduction

The ratio analysis that we have just examined illustrates one way in which the actual performance of a company can be compared with an expected performance.   The expected performance could be the corresponding ratio from a prior year, from other firms in the same industry or an agreed ideal ratio. There are other common sense methods of presenting such comparisons - these are discussed below.

Horizontal analysis

Horizontal analysis is a line-by-line comparison of the current year's accounts with those of the previous year, with a '% change' column to highlight significant movements.

Vertical analysis

'Common size' balance sheets or profit and loss accounts can be prepared. Each balance sheet item is expressed as a percentage of the balance sheet total and each profit and loss account item as a percentage of sales (or earnings).

The great value of the above analyses is that they focus the eye onto figures that are unexpected in size, highlighting them as areas for possible further investigation.

Trend analysis

Extending the horizontal analysis over a number of years provides **trends**. To see more clearly the trend, the figure in the first year of the series is given a value of 100. Subsequent years figures are related to this base.

Example

Trend analysis: Mack plc

	19X0	*19X1*	*19X2*	*19X3*	*19X4*
Turnover (£m)	629.8	688.0	770.5	951.9	1,156.5
Index (19X0 base = 100)	100.0	109.2	122.3	151.1	183.6
Trading profit (£m)	44.8	48.0	55.9	73.4	93.8
Index (19X0 base = 100)	100.0	107.1	124.7	163.8	209.4

If inflation is taken account of, the figures or the indices could be restated. If in the above example the average RPI for each of the years was:

	19X0	*19X1*	*19X2*	*19X3*	*19X4*
RPI	130	136	146	140	160

The figures could be converted into 19X4 £m.

	19X0	*19X1*	*19X2*	*19X3*	*19X4*
Turnover (19X4 £m)	775.1	809.4	844.4	1,087.9	1,156.5
Trading profit (19X4 £m)	55.1	56.5	61.3	83.9	93.8

The working is:

$$\text{Figure} \times \frac{\text{RPI } 19X4}{\text{RPI for year figure taken from}}$$

Or the index could be adjusted.

	19X0	*19X1*	*19X2*	*19X3*	*19X4*
Turnover index	100.0	109.2	122.3	151.1	183.6
Adjusted for inflation	100.0	104.4	108.9	140.3	149.2

The working is:

$$\text{Index for the year} \times \frac{\text{RPI for base year}}{\text{RPI for the year}}$$

10 THE USE OF FREE CASH FLOW IN FINANCIAL PLANNING AND STRATEGY

Cash which is not retained and reinvested in a business is called free cash flow.

Free cash flow = Revenue − Costs − Investment

Figures calculated for free cash flow can be used in determining a company's cash flow ratios. For example:

$$\text{Dividend cover in cash terms} = \frac{\text{Free cash flow}}{\text{Dividends paid}}$$

It is argued that this measure of dividend cover is better than the conventional ratio of earnings divided by dividends paid, since dividends are paid in cash, and with no cash there can be no dividends.

Companies with large positive free cash flows are called cash cows and are attractive takeover targets. Financial management theory suggests that companies with more cash than positive-NPV investment opportunities should return the excess cash to their shareholders, say by paying a large special dividend, but in practice boards of directors are unwilling to do this and instead they undertake questionable capital investments. When these go sour, an acquisitive company can move in and buy the struggling company at a favourable price.

The trend of the last 20 years has been to pay increasing emphasis to a company's cash flows rather than its reported profit. The publication of cash flow statements required by FRS 1 has provided readers of accounts with additional information that they were seeking in this area.

11 CHAPTER SUMMARY

This chapter began by explaining the hierarchical classification of planning and control decisions into strategic, tactical and operational. You must be able to explain why such a classification is useful; decision-makers should only make plans or control activities within their sphere of authority in the business.

Most businesses fail because they run out of cash; it is therefore particularly important that cash resources are planned and controlled effectively. A cash budget will be central to this plan.

Ratio analysis is the traditional method of analysing the financial performance of organisations, but in an exam context your interpretation of ratios is much more important that the number of different ratios that you manage to calculate.

12 SELF TEST QUESTIONS

12.1   Distinguish between each of strategic plans, tactical plans and operational plans. (1.1)

12.2   List the six steps involved in a strategic planning exercise. (2.2)

12.3   Distinguish between vertical integration and horizontal integration. (2.2)

12.4   What is the traditional approach to financing fixed assets and current assets? (3.3)

12.5   List five common sources of short and medium-term funds. (3.6)

12.6   How do you calculate the length of a company's cash cycle? (4.1)

12.7   How do you estimate a company's daily cash flow? (4.5)

12.8   State three uses of a cash budget. (5.4)

12.9   Define three ratios which are relevant to investors when deciding whether to buy or sell a particular company's shares. (6.4)

12.10   What is meant by horizontal analysis of a company's accounts? (9.1)

13 EXAMINATION TYPE QUESTIONS

13.1 Noifa Leisure plc

Extracts from the annual report of Noifa Leisure plc are shown below:

Chairman's report

"The group's financial position has never been stronger. Turnover has risen 209% and the share price has almost doubled during the last four years. Since the end of the financial year the company has acquired Beddall Hotels for £100 million, financed at only 9% per year by a floating rate loan denominated in Euros which has little risk. Our objective is to become the largest hotel group in the United Kingdom within five years."

Profit and loss account summaries for the years ending 31 December

	19X6 £m	19X7 £m	19X8 £m	19X9 £m
Turnover	325	370	490	680
Operating profit	49	60	75	92
Investment income	18	10	3	1
	67	70	78	93
Interest payable	14	16	24	36
Profit before tax	53	54	54	57
Taxation	20	19	19	20
Profit after taxation	33	35	35	37
One-off items net of tax[1]	(3)	-	-	4
Profit attributable to shareholders	30	35	35	41
Dividends	12	12	12	12
Retained earnings	18	23	23	29

[1]Loss/gain on disposal of fixed assets

Balance sheet summaries as at 31 December

	19X6 £m	19X7 £m	19X8 £m	19X9 £m
Fixed assets				
Tangible assets	165	260	424	696
Investments	120	68	20	4
	285	328	444	700
Current assets				
Stock	40	45	70	110
Debtors	56	52	75	94
Cash	2	3	4	5
	98	100	149	209

Less: Current liabilities

Trade creditors	82	94	130	176
Taxation	18	19	19	20
Overdraft	-	-	42	68
Other	15	24	28	42
	115	137	219	306

Total assets less current liabilities	268	291	374	603

Financed by:

Ordinary shares				
(10 pence nominal value)	50	50	50	50
Share premium	22	22	22	22
Revaluation reserve	-	-	-	100
Revenue reserves	74	97	120	149
Shareholders' funds	146	169	192	321
Bank loans	42	42	102	102
13% debenture 2006 - 8	80	80	80	180
	268	291	374	603

Analysis by type of activity

	19X6		19X7		19X8		19X9	
	Turnover	Profit[1]	Turnover	Profit	Turnover	Profit	Turnover	Profit
	£m	£m	£m	£m	£m	£m	£m	£m
Hotels	196	36	227	41	314	37	471	45
Theme park	15	(3)	18	(2)	24	3	34	5
Bus company	24	6	28	8	38	14	46	18
Car hire	43	7	45	8	52	12	62	15
Zoo[2]	5	(1)	6	(1)	9	0	10	(1)
Waxworks	10	1	11	3	13	4	14	5
Publications	32	3	35	3	40	5	4	5
	325	49	370	60	490	75	680	92

[1]Operating profit before taxation.
[2]The zoo was sold during 19X9.

	19X6	19X7	19X8	19X9
Noifa plc average share price (pence)	82	104	120	159
FT 100 Share Index	1,500	1,750	1,800	2,300
Leisure industry share index	178	246	344	394
Leisure industry PE ratio	10:1	12:1	19:1	25:1

You are required

In his report the chairman stated that 'the group's financial position has never been stronger.' From the viewpoint of an external consultant appraise whether you agree with the chairman. Discussion of the group's financing policies and strategic objective, with suggestions as to how these might be altered, should form part of your appraisal. Relevant calculations must be shown.   **(30 marks)**

13.2   A wholesale company

A wholesale company ends its financial year on 30 June. You have been requested, in early July 19X5, to assist in the preparation of a cash forecast. The following information is available, regarding the company's operations:

(a)   Management believes the 19X4/X5 sales level and pattern is a reasonable estimate of 19X5/X6 sales. Sales in 19X4/X5 were as follows:

	£'000
July 19X4	360
August 19X4	420
September 19X4	600
October 19X4	540
November 19X4	480
December 19X4	400
January 19X5	350
February 19X5	550
March 19X5	500
April 19X5	400
May 19X5	600
June 19X5	800
Total	6,000

(b)   The accounts receivable at 30 June 19X5 total £380,000. Sales collections are generally made as follows:

	%
During the month of sale	60
In the first subsequent month	30
In second subsequent month	9
Uncollectable	1

(c)   The purchase cost of goods averages 60 per cent of selling price. The cost of the stock in hand at 30 June 19X5 is £840,000, of which £30,000 is obsolete. Arrangements have been made to sell the obsolete stock in July at half the normal selling price on a *cash on delivery* basis. The company wishes to maintain the stock, as of the first of each month, at a level of three months' sales as determined by the sales forecast for the next three months. All purchases are paid for on the tenth of the following month. Accounts payable for purchases at 30 June 19X5 total £370,000.

(d)   Payments in respect of fixed and variable expenses are forecast for the first three months of 19X5/X6 as follows:

July	£160,620
August	£118,800
September	£158,400

(e)   It is anticipated that cash dividends of £40,000 will be paid each half-year, on the fifteenth day of September and March.

(f)   During the year unusual advertising costs will be incurred that will require cash payments of £10,000 in August and £15,000 in September. The advertising costs are in addition to the expenses in item (d) above.

(g)   Equipment replacements are made at a rate which requires a cash outlay of £3,000 per month. The equipment has an average estimated life of six years.

(h)   A £60,000 payment of corporation tax is to be made on 15 September 19X5.

(i)   At 30 June 19X5 the company had a bank loan with an unpaid balance of £280,000. The entire balance is due on 30 September 19X5 together with accumulated interest from 1 July 19X5 at the rate of 12% per annum.

(j)   The cash balance at 30 June 19X5 is £100,000.

You are required to prepare a cash forecast statement by months for the first three months of the 19X5/X6 financial year. The statement should show the amount of cash on hand (or deficiency of cash) at the end of each month. All computations and supporting schedules should be presented in clear and readable form.

14   ANSWERS TO EXAMINATION TYPE QUESTIONS

14.1   Noifa Leisure plc

The chairman states in his report that turnover has risen dramatically (by 209%) and that the share price has almost doubled during the last four years. These comments are both accurate. However, he also states that the company's objective is to become the largest hotel group in the United Kingdom. This might suggest that a greater emphasis is being given to sales revenue maximisation rather than profit maximisation. Such a policy may result in a financial position which is not particularly strong. A more detailed analysis is performed below.

(1)   Profitability

	19X6	*19X7*	*19X8*	*19X9*
Return on turnover (Profit before tax and interest ÷ turnover)	21%	19%	16%	14%
Return on capital employed (Profit before tax and interest ÷ shareholders' funds and debt)	25%	24%	21%	15%
Return on total assets (Profit before tax and interest ÷ fixed assets and current assets)	17%	10%	13%	10%

Each of the profitability ratios calculated above shows a marked decline over the four-year period, indicating that levels of profitability have not kept pace with the rapid expansion.

(2)   Working capital and liquidity

	19X6	*19X7*	*19X8*	*19X9*
Stock turnover (Turnover ÷ stock)	8.1×	8.2×	7.0×	6.2×
Debtor days (Debtors ÷ average daily sales)	63	51	56	50
Current ratio (Current assets ÷ current liabilities)	0.85	0.73	0.68	0.68
Acid test ratio (Current assets less stock ÷ current liabilities)	0.50	0.40	0.36	0.32

The general trend in the company's collection period from debtors shows an improvement. However, the stock turnover has decreased over the period, perhaps due to less efficient management as expansion has occurred.

The liquidity ratios, on the other hand, are of greater concern since they show a steady deterioration, with the result of an overdraft being necessary for financing working capital from 19X7.

(3)   Gearing

	19X6	19X7	19X8	19X9
Total debt (including the overdraft) ÷ shareholders funds	83%	72%	117%	109%
Total debt ÷ total assets	62%	61%	68%	65%
Interest cover (Profit before tax and interest ÷ interest)	4.8×	4.4×	3.3×	2.6×

Gearing has increased substantially in 19X8 and then reduced slightly in 19X9. However, since 19X9 the company has acquired Beddall Hotels which involves an additional £100 million of debt, thus increasing the total debt: shareholders' funds to

$$\frac{102 + 180 + 68 + 100}{321} = 140\%$$

taking the 19X9 figures.

The interest cover has declined dramatically, partly as a response to the increased gearing, but also due to the lower profitability of the company.

(4)   Market factors

	19X6	19X7	19X8	19X9
Earnings per share (pence) (Profit after tax and one-off item ÷ 500 million shares)	6.0	7.0	7.0	8.2
Price earnings ratio (Share price ÷ earnings per share)	13.7	14.9	17.1	19.4

Both the earnings per share and price earnings ratio have increased over the few years. Given that there have been no new share issues, the earnings per share figures simply represent the modest increase in total profit which has not kept pace with the substantial increase in turnover.

The price earnings ratio appears to show a strong position until it is compared with the equivalent ratio for the leisure industry. In 19X6 Noifa has a P/E ratio in excess of that for the industry (13.7 against 10), but by 19X9 that position has been reversed with Noifa's P/E ratio being 19.4 and that of the industry 25. Similarly the increase in Noifa's share price (to which the chairman makes mention) is not particularly impressive when compared to the share index of the leisure industry. The latter shows an increase over the period of 121% ((394 − 178)/178) whereas the increase in Noifa's share price is only 94% ((159 − 82)/82).

(5)   Analysis by activity

In order to perform a meaningful analysis, it is necessary to convert the turnover and profit figures into percentage terms.

	19X6		19X7		19X8		19X9	
	Turnover	*Profit*	*Turnover*	*Profit*	*Turnover*	*Profit*	*Turnover*	*Profit*
Hotels	60.4	73.5	61.3	68.4	64.0	49.3	69.3	49.0
Theme park	4.6	(6.1)	4.9	(3.3)	4.9	4.0	5.0	5.4
Bus company	7.4	12.2	7.6	13.3	7.8	18.7	6.8	19.6
Car hire	13.2	14.3	12.2	13.3	10.6	16.0	9.1	16.3
Zoo	1.5	(2.0)	1.6	(1.7)	1.8	0	1.5	(1.1)
Waxworks	3.1	2.0	3.0	5.0	2.7	5.3	2.1	5.4
Publications	9.8	6.1	9.4	5.0	8.2	6.7	6.3	5.4
	100.0	100.0	100.0	100.0	100.0	100.0	100.0	100.0

Whereas there has been growth in most of the company's activities the most substantial expansion has been in the hotel business with turnover increasing from 60.4% of the total in 19X6 to 69.3% in 19X9. However, despite the increase in the proportion of turnover, the profit contributed has fallen dramatically from 73.5% of the total in 19X6 to 49.0% in 19X9. Therefore it is clearly the hotel expansion which has resulted in the overall decline in relative profitability.

(6)   Conclusion and recommendation

The analysis of the different segments of the business above would indicate that it may be preferable for the company to turn its attention away from hotel expansion to a more profitable area, such as the theme park (which has become profitable) or the bus company or the waxworks. This would involve a change in the stated objective of becoming the largest hotel group in the UK, but would probably benefit the shareholders in terms of the wealth maximising criterion.

Alternatively having increased the turnover to nearly 70% of the total it may be wise to concentrate on returning the relative profits to their former status. The implications of such a strategy would be to increase the future profit margins of the existing hotels. No indication is given in the question as to the 'star' ratings of the company's hotels. In order to raise the profit margins it may be necessary to increase these ratings hence attracting higher prices. The operating costs do not need to rise at the same rate as the prices. Ratings in the UK can be raised through the provision of a higher quality range of services such as 24-hour cleaning facilities. Such low cost services should be introduced allowing the hotels to charge higher prices to reflect their increased 'star' ratings. Such a strategy will maintain and indeed increase turnover whilst returning profit levels to their former position.

A second consideration is concerned with the financing and gearing ratio of the company. It has been shown above that the gearing level has increased dramatically over the four-year period and that it has subsequently risen still further as a result of the Euro loan to finance the acquisition of Beddall Hotels. Although the company has a large asset base to support the debt (£696 million of tangible fixed assets which will comprise hotel buildings with a high market value) the interest cover is deteriorating. Therefore if the hotel expansion does not become more profitable, the company could have difficulties in meeting its obligations.

An alternative means of financing future acquisitions, including that of Beddall Hotels, would therefore be desirable. Although the Euro loan is low risk, it has increased the gearing further and will also introduce foreign currency risk. Therefore an alternative of equity finance via a new issue of shares should be considered to reduce both the financial risk introduced through gearing and the currency risk.

14.2   A wholesale company

Cash forecast for first three months of 19X5/X6

Receipts	Workings	July £	August £	September £	Total £
Receipts from debtors	1	510,000	432,000	518,400	1,460,400
Obsolete stock	2	25,000	-	-	25,000
		535,000	432,000	518,400	1,485,400

Payments					
Payments to creditors	3	370,000	342,000	288,000	1,000,000
Expenses		160,620	118,800	158,400	437,820
Dividends		-	-	40,000	40,000
Advertising		-	10,000	15,000	25,000
Capital expenditure		3,000	3,000	3,000	9,000
Corporation tax		-	-	60,000	60,000
Bank loan		-	-	288,400	288,400
		533,620	473,800	852,800	1,860,220
Net cash inflow/(outflow)		1,380	(41,800)	(334,400)	(374,820)
Balance b/f		100,000	101,380	59,580	100,000
Balance /deficiency at month end		101,380	59,580	(274,820)	(274,820)

Workings

			July £	August £	September £
(1)	**Sales**	£			
	May	600,000	54,000	-	-
	June	800,000	240,000	72,000	-
	July	360,000	216,000	108,000	32,400
	August	420,000	-	252,000	126,000
	September	600,000	-	-	360,000
			510,000	432,000	518,400

(2)	**Obsolete stock, at cost**		30,000
	Normal sales price	$\frac{100}{60} \times £30,000$	50,000
	Realised	$\frac{1}{2} \times £50,000$	25,000

(3)   Payment to trade creditors

(i)	July 10 - balance b/f				370,000

(ii)   August 10

Sales in July		360,000	
Cost of goods sold (60%)		216,000	
Less: Opening stock	840,000		
Less: Obsolete	30,000		
	810,000		
Add: Closing stock 60% (£420,000 + £600,000 + £540,000)	936,000		
		126,000	
			342,000

(iii)   September 10

Sales in August		420,000	
Cost of goods sold (60%)		252,000	
Less: Opening stock	936,000		
Add: Closing stock (60%) (£600,000 + £540,000 + £480,000)	972,000		
		36,000	
			288,000

11 LONG-TERM PLANNING

INTRODUCTION & LEARNING OBJECTIVES

This chapter takes up the discussion of strategic planning by considering the issues in the decision of whether to expand or not, and if so, whether through organic growth or through acquisition.

We consider possible survival strategies including corrective strategies and risk reducing contingency strategies, and follow this with an analysis of different possible growth strategies. The reasons for acquisitions and mergers are discussed and will be further examined in the next chapter.

When you have studied this chapter you should be able to do the following:

- Explain the relationship between short-term and long-term planning.
- Discuss the potential conflicts between short-term and long-term objectives.
- Distinguish between top down and bottom up planning systems.
- Discuss various strategies for survival and growth.
- Classify synergy into various types.
- Explain the different forms of diversification strategy.

1 SHORT-TERM AND LONG-TERM PLANNING

1.1 The relationship between short-term and long-term financial planning

Financial planning must begin at the strategic level, where corporate strengths and weaknesses are reviewed and long-term objectives identified as discussed in the previous chapter. We saw that the business review should enable a forecast to be made of future changes in sales, profitability and capital employed. When this forecast is compared with the results desired by the corporate objectives, a gap may be identified which must be made good by developing new strategies.

Senior management must negotiate with middle management until a single strategic plan for the whole company is agreed. From this strategic plan, tactical plans must be drawn up (eg, pricing policies, personnel requirements, production methods) and a medium-term plan established. This medium-term plan can be broken down into a series of short-term financial plans as described in the previous chapter.

1.2 Potential conflicts between short-term and long-term objectives

Companies are often accused in the UK of favouring short-term profitability at the expense of long-term prosperity. For example an investment in the latest technology in production machinery might be postponed because of fear of increasing the depreciation charge, although longer-term profitability will be improved by the investment. A lot of academic research has been carried out in this area, to try to discover why businesses behave in this way.

1.3 Activity

Why do you think that managers of UK businesses might concentrate on short-term profitability at the expense of the long-term prosperity of their business?

1.4   Activity solution

Among the reasons that have been put forward are the following:

- managers' reward systems might encourage short-term results, for example if they are based on each year's reported earnings per share.

- fear of disappointing the markets and perhaps exposing the company to the threat of takeover, endangering the managers' jobs.

- managers are simply too busy dealing with short-term crises to think of the longer-term.

- managers are too complacent with satisfactory results to bother thinking about the future.

1.5   Top down versus bottom up planning systems

At this point it is helpful to define two possible types of planning system. In a **top down** system the senior management announce instructions which filter their way down through the organisation structure. In a **bottom up** system information is gathered from the lower levels of the business, which is consolidated until a summary is produced for the board.

An ideal planning system contains elements of both systems, with decisions passing up and down the organisation structure. Certainly all managers must be involved in the planning of their own sphere of activities, or else they will feel no responsibility to meet the targets given to them. Equally certainly, long-term strategic decisions are ultimately the responsibility of the senior management.

Successful conglomerate companies delegate as much responsibility as possible to their operating subsidiaries, while the main board ensures that the group remains focused on a particular sense of direction. The balance between control and autonomy of a conglomerate's subsidiaries is another rich area for academic research in recent years.

1.6   The use of budgets to influence the success of financial planning

The establishment of short-term budgets as part of the strategic planning process was explained in the previous chapter. It is possible for budgets to be drawn up for a longer term period, in which case budgets become part of the long-term planning exercise. The principles involved are fully explained in the section on strategic planning in the previous chapter.

1.7   Types of long-term strategy

In the remainder of this chapter we consider the different types of strategy that a company may adopt. These are examined under the following general headings

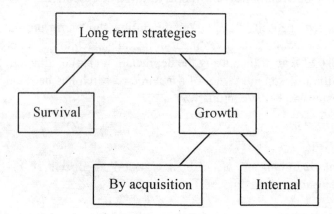

2   SURVIVAL STRATEGIES

2.1   Non-growth strategies

A non-growth strategy means no growth in *earnings*. This does not necessarily mean no growth in *turnover* - if margins are falling, turnover will need to increase to maintain the same level of earnings. Capital equipment will have to be kept up-to-date, but there will be no net increase in investment - all the earnings can therefore be paid out as dividends to the shareholders.

A company might pursue a non-growth strategy if it saw its non-economic objectives as more important that its economic objectives (given a certain minimum level of profit), although as we shall see a non-growth strategy does not imply a lack of attention to economic objectives.

Reasons for a non-growth strategy may include:

- anti-monopoly legislation
- public opinion pressure - where, for example, a planned modernisation/mechanisation would cause a significant loss of jobs in the area
- to maintain an acceptable quality of life
- lack of enough additional staff with sufficient expertise and loyalty
- to enable the owner-manager to retain personal control over operations
- dis-economies of scale of the particular production set-up.

Or there could even be negative growth, by paying out dividends larger than current earnings, so that shareholders are effectively receiving a refund of their capital investment, and there is a net fall in assets employed. A negative growth strategy can be adopted in pursuit of an objective to increase the percentage return to the shareholders - if the company pulls out of the least profitable areas of its operations first, it will increase its overall return on investment, although the total investment will be less.

This is not the same as simply allowing the company to run down. The negative growth strategy consists of an orderly, planned withdrawal from less profitable areas, and while the shareholder's dividend may eventually decline, his return can rise since the capital invested also falls. If the company simply runs down, his return will also fall.

2.2   Corrective strategies

A non-growth strategy certainly does not mean that the company can afford to be complacent (although the pressures on management and the risks they have to take will be less than with other strategies). A considerable amount of management time should be devoted to consider the actions needed to *correct* its overall strategic structure to achieve the optimum. This involves seeking a balance between different areas of operations and also seeking the optimum organisation structure for efficient operation.

Thus although there is no overall growth (or negative growth occurs) the company will shift its product-market position, it will employ its resources in different fields and it will continue to search for new opportunities. In particular it will aim to correct any weaknesses which it has discovered during its appraisal. For this reason the term *corrective strategy* is also used.

A non-growth strategy is bound to be a corrective strategy, but a corrective strategy can also be used in conjunction with, or as one component of, a growth strategy.

2.3   Risk-reducing contingency strategies

A company faces risk because of its lack of knowledge of the future. When it evaluates a project, it will at best be able to forecast that 'if event A happens we shall have such and such a return, but if event B happens we shall lose £xm'. The extent of the risk it faces can be revealed by the use of performance-risk gap analysis, where forecasts of the outcome in *n* years' time take into account not only the likely return but also the risk - ie, the probability of achieving various returns less than the likely level.

Using the terminology above - event A being favourable to the firm and event B unfavourable - there are four basic ways in which a company can reduce risk.

(a)   It can attempt to influence events so that event A happens and event B does not. For instance if the company thought that a Conservative government was likely to be more favourable to it than a Labour government it could give money to the Conservative party to back their campaign.

(b)   If it seemed fairly likely that event B was going to happen, the company could attempt to mitigate the effect that this would have.

       For example, if event B was 'a decline in demand at home' a possible strategy to mitigate the effect of that threat would be to expand its export activity.

       If event B was 'a general downturn in the world economy' a possible strategy would be to stockpile cash to see it through the crisis until the next upswing.

(c)   If event B seemed a fairly remote possibility, but its happening would have serious consequences for the firm, contingency plans should be prepared. For instance, there might be plans to cope with such events as the sudden death of the Managing Director; the merger of two competitors into one large unit; a breakthrough in technology.

(d)   Whatever the firm does to prepare for particular unfavourable events it must be recognised that the whole future is uncertain and it must put itself in a position where it can take advantage of new (unforeseen) opportunities and avoid unforeseen threats. Contingency plans can only be prepared against events which have been predicted, even though they may be unlikely to happen. To avoid being taken totally by surprise, a company must have a constant 'ear to the ground' to catch hints of potentially threatening or promising developments at an early stage. (It is equally bad to miss an opportunity as to fail to forecast a threat - an opportunity rapidly becomes a threat if we fail to take advantage of it but our competitors are quicker off the mark!)

While on the subject of risk, it should be remembered that although it is desirable to reduce risk, some risk is inevitably involved in any business. In fact there are different ways of looking at risk.

(a)   Risk which is **inevitable** in the nature of the business; this risk should be minimised as outlined above.

(b)   Risk which an organisation **can afford to take**. In general, high returns involve higher risk, and a company which is in a strong position might be prepared to take a higher risk in the hope of achieving a high return.

(c)   Risk which an organisation **cannot afford to take**. A company cannot afford to commit its last penny (and perhaps an overdraft as well) to a risky project. In the event of failure it would be left in an extremely vulnerable position and could even face winding up.

(d)   Risk which an organisation **cannot afford not to take**. Sometimes a company is forced to take a risk because it knows that its competitors are going to act and if it does not follow suit it could be left seriously behind.

3   STRATEGIES FOR LONG-TERM

3.1   Search for opportunities

Growth in the size of an organisation can be measured in many ways; profit, turnover, earnings per share, manpower etc, but the real aim of a growth strategy is growth in *profits*. The pursuit of size of increased turnover is not an end in itself but is only worthwhile if it leads to higher profits. If an organisation has decided that it does need growth in order to achieve its economic objectives, its search for new opportunities must be particularly active (although it would still need new opportunities even if pursuing a non growth strategy).

3.2   Closing the gap

During the initial stage of business review and assessment, management are likely to encounter a *profit or growth gap* between estimated future performance and the firm's desired position. Identification of the causes of the gap, and thus areas for strategic consideration, is known as gap analysis.

Different strategies for *closing the gap* may be summarised by the following grid.

	Existing products	*New products*
Existing markets	Internal efficiency Market penetration	Product development
New markets	Market development	Diversification

Improvements in internal efficiency are not something about which strategic decisions are taken. They should be constantly sought as part of the day-to-day running of the firm and so are covered in the operations plan (which is one of the sub-plans which elaborate the strategy).

Divestment - pulling out of less profitable areas - may be part of a non-growth strategy as already discussed, or of a growth strategy: when more profitable opportunities present themselves but resources are limited it may be necessary to drop some lines in order to concentrate on others.

Market penetration, product development and market development cover the expansion of a firm within its own industry. Diversification is concerned with moves into new product-market areas. The main strategic decisions to be taken are

(a)   Shall we attempt increased market penetration?

(b)   Can our objectives be achieved solely by increased market penetration or shall we need to expand the product range or market base or diversify as well or instead?

(c)   Shall we expand and if so in what general direction?

(d)   What resources are available or can be made available for expansion?

(e)   Shall we diversify, and if so into what general area(s)?

(f)   What resources are available or can be made available for diversification?

There will then follow the formulation of a detailed product-market plan within the overall strategy.

Questions (a) to (c) above are answered by considering the firm's position within its own industry; (e) is answered by considering the total industry sales potential compared with available capacity.

A firm will probably find that, no matter how well it does on market share, it cannot for long pursue a growth strategy without diversification if the total market for the industry's products is declining. The exception is where there is such an exodus from the declining industry that capacity falls below that needed to support the declining market, with the result that the few remaining firms can do very well.

3.3   The relationship of investment decisions to long-term planning

You should appreciate from the above that investment decisions are an important part of the long-term planning process, covering internal investment decisions (committing funds to new projects within the existing business and withdrawing from such projects if they turn out to be unsatisfactory), external investment decisions (merging with or acquiring new companies) and divestment decisions (selling part of the business, such a company no longer producing satisfactory profits).

The following sections consider the rationale behind these types of decision.

4   ORGANIC GROWTH VERSUS EXTERNAL GROWTH

4.1   Introduction

Companies make mergers or acquisitions as one means of achieving growth; to put up more effective barriers to the entry of new firms by acquisition in their own industry; in order to diversify; to cut costs by economies of scale; to obtain skills; to obtain liquid resources (the acquiring company can defray the purchase price by the issue of additional equity capital, particularly where the price-earnings ratio is high) etc. A company might wish to be acquired because the owner wants to retire or to obtain additional cash; in order to use the larger company's R&D facilities to assist its expansion; to provide more extensive career opportunities for the owner/directors, etc.

Among factors to be considered when deciding whether to grow internally (organic growth) or make an acquisition (external growth) are

(a)   **Timing** - If analysis of the proposed product-market area shows that time is of the essence, acquisition of a company already in the field is indicated as this can generally be achieved very much more quickly (except in the case of the relatively small number of industries where the lead time for product development is of the order of weeks or a few months rather than years, or where start-up synergy is large enough to allow a quick start).

(b)   **Start-up cost** - If the cost of entering a new area will be high it might be better to acquire.

(c)   **Synergy** (see 4.2) - If the new area has relatively little synergy with the old, acquisition might be better.

(d)   **Structure of the new industry** - If the competitive structure of the new industry would not readily admit another member, or if barriers to entry are high, acquisition is the only way. If there are no attractive acquisition opportunities in the area, internal growth is the only way.

(e)   **Relative cost and risk** - Acquisition is often more costly than internal development because one has to pay the owners of the acquired company for the risks they have already taken. On the other hand, if the company decides on internal growth it has to bear such risk itself, so that there is a trade-off between cost and risk.

(f)   **Relative price-earning ratio** - If the price-earnings ratio is significantly higher in the new industry than the present one, acquisition may not be possible because it would cause too great a dilution in earnings per share to the existing shareholders. On the other hand, if the present company has a high price-earnings ratio it can boost earnings per share by issuing its own equity in settlement of the purchase price.

(g)   **Asset valuation** - If the acquiring company believes that the potential acquisition's assets are under-valued it might acquire in order to undertake an *asset stripping* operation ie, selling off or using the company's assets rather than operating it as a going concern.

4.2 Synergy

[Definition] Synergy can be defined as the advantage to a firm gained by having existing resources which are compatible with new products or markets that the company is developing.

The process of developing new products or markets is often referred to as *product-market entries*.

Synergy has been described as the $2 + 2 = 5$ effect, where a firm looks for combined results that reflect a better rate of return than would be achieved by the same resources used independently as separate operations. The combined performance, therefore, is greater than the sum of its parts.

4.3 Categories of synergy

To assist in the quantification of the effects of synergy, it is useful to classify the types of synergy which may exist.

(a) **Sales synergy**

This is obtained through use of common marketing facilities such as distribution channels, sales staff and administration, and warehousing. Supplying a range of complementary products increases the productivity of the sales force. Shared advertising, sales promotion and corporate image can generate a much higher return for the same unit of outlay.

Televisions and video recorders are complementary goods which would be advertised jointly.

When Barclaycard acquired a travel agency in 1988, it advertised the travel agency's services by offering discounts if Barclaycard was used for the purchase of a holiday.

(b) **Operating synergy**

This arises from the better use of operational facilities and personnel, bulk purchasing, and producing more items with little or no increase in fixed costs. The cost savings associated with *learning curves* may be capable of being transferred from one product to another.

(c) **Investment synergy**

This results from the joint use of plant, common raw material stocks, transfer of research and development from one product to another. There is a wider use of a common investment in fixed assets, working capital or research.

(d) **Management synergy**

This is the advantage to be gained where management skills concerning current operations are easily transferred to new operations because of the similarity of problems in the two industries.

However the opposite may be true. There might be negative synergy at a top management level in situations where the problems inherent in new ventures are unrelated to current operations and attempts to solve them in the familiar way lead to incorrect decisions.

4.4 Activity

Consider a business merger or acquisition that you are familiar with, perhaps from your work experience, or perhaps in the news. Were any of the above types of synergy created, or was the combination a disappointment from this viewpoint?

5   GROWTH BY ACQUISITION: DIVERSIFICATION

5.1   Why and how firms diversify

Diversification means a change of both products and markets from the company's present base. Because of the extent of the change there is clearly more risk involved than in expansion, so we must consider the reasons why firms nevertheless diversify. Ansoff suggests three main reasons

(a)   **Objectives can no longer be met without diversification**. This would be identified by the status-quo forecast and the gap analysis. The reason for the dissatisfaction with the present industry might be either due to poor return caused by product decline, with little chance of technological innovation in the same field, or due to a lack of flexibility eg, unavoidable dependence on a single customer or a single product line.

(b)   **The firm has more cash than it needs for expansion**. Whether it prefers to invest this outside the business or to seek opportunities for diversification will depend on the relative rates of return obtainable (in general the return from operations exceeds the return from outside investments, but of course more risk is involved) and management preference (management have to balance the internal flexibility achieved by keeping reserves in liquid form with external flexibility offered by diversification).

(c)   Firms may diversify even if their objectives are being or could be met within their industry, if **diversification promises to be more profitable than expansion**.

If a firm is unable to reach a decision about the relative merits of expansion and diversification due to lack of quantifiable information, it might continue to search for diversification opportunities short of actually committing resources. In other words it delays the decision until better information is available, as has already been advocated.

A firm may diversify by itself developing a new product-market area, or by acquiring or merging with a firm already operational in the proposed new field. The former implies an active research department initiative. The latter can lead to quicker entry into the new area (time is often of the essence) and to *start-up* economies, but is not without its own difficulties.

5.2   External analysis

Synergy was introduced as the '2+2=5 effect'. You will no doubt already have deduced that by its very nature diversification will give less opportunity for the exploitation of synergistic effects than will expansion. However, there are some opportunities and if these are used, the risk inherent in a diversification might be lessened. Therefore, to complement the *internal* appraisal of itself and its industry, a firm contemplating diversification should undertake an *external* appraisal (ie, external to the industry) to identify the potential of different fields and to explore the possibility of synergy. As well as potential synergy, this appraisal should cover the following areas

(a)   Past and projected performance for the industry under consideration in relation to the general economy, in order to see what contribution would be made towards the company's objective

(b)   Nature of demand for the products (eg, is it cyclical)

(c)   Structure of the industry - how competitive is it? what barriers to entry exist? what sort of rate of investment is necessary? what factors appear to lead to success in the industry?

5.3 Diversification strategies

Ansoff lists four types of diversification which he illustrates by the following matrix

	New products	
Customers	*Related technology*	*Unrelated technology*
Same type	Horizontal diversification	
From its own business	Vertical diversification	
Similar type	Marketing & technology related concentric diversification	Marketing related concentric diversification
New type	Technology related concentric diversification	Conglomerate diversification

Synergy is highest in the case of *horizontal diversification*, especially if the technology is related - but the disadvantage is that little additional flexibility is provided. The majority of diversifications are however, of this type. (Example: a record manufacturer making hi-fi equipment).

Vertical diversification (or vertical integration) may be of two types - *backward* or *forward.*

In the former type the firm becomes the supplier to its existing processes (eg, a car manufacturer making tyres). This provides no additional flexibility since the end product is unchanged. Also the firm may find that its competitors in its existing business will not buy from it if it manufactures supplies in excess of its own requirement; while if it supplies too little for its own requirements, it might find its relationships with other suppliers not as good as when it was a larger customer.

In forward integration the firm becomes the customer for its existing products (example: an aluminium foundry which diversifies into aluminium windows or tools). The trouble here is that the firm is competing with its own customers.

In *concentric diversification*, also known as composite diversification, the 'common thread' with the firm's existing business is less strong but still present - and therefore there is still some potential for synergy.

The characteristic of *conglomerate diversification* is that there is no common thread, and the only synergy lies with the management skills (outstanding management seems to be the key to success as a conglomerate, and in the case of large conglomerates they are indeed able, because of their size and diversity, to attract high calibre managers with wide experience).

A firm may adopt a concentric strategy in order to build on a particular strength or to counteract a specific weakness. An example of a market-related concentric diversification would be that of an ice-cream seller who sold Christmas trees in winter to counteract the cyclical nature of his sales.

Ansoff distinguishes between a firm pursuing a conglomerate strategy as the result of a conscious decision, and another with no strategy at all which is, as he puts it, 'marching in all directions'. He gives three reasons for a conscious decision to adopt a conglomerate strategy

(a)   The existing firm is so highly specialised that there would be no synergy with any other industry.

(b)   The existing firm has such little depth of skill that there would be no synergy.

(c)   Management preference.

5.4   Conglomerates - advantages and disadvantages

Ansoff and Argenti set out the advantages and limitations of becoming a conglomerate

Advantages	*Disadvantages*
Increased flexibility.	Conglomerate acquisitions give no additional benefit to the shareholders - since there is no synergy the individual investor will do no better investing in a subsidiary company through a holding company than he would have done if he invested in the subsidiary directly.
Increased profitability by selecting the most profitable industries.	
Ability to grow quickly by making acquisitions in diverse fields.	
Better access to capital markets.	Since there is no synergy there is no operating advantage over several smaller firms (this is, however, often counteracted by the high calibre of the management found in conglomerates).
Avoidance of the disadvantages of other types of diversification - eg, anti-monopoly legislation.	
	Earnings of conglomerates and the price earnings ratios of their shares seem to be particularly badly affected by economic recession (and this may mean that during a recession they are unable to continue with acquisitions).

6   CHAPTER SUMMARY

This chapter has provided a brief summary of long term strategy alternatives to business organisations. It is very much a 'scene-setter' for the next chapter which concentrates on mergers and acquisitions. Whereas the subject matter of this chapter is unlikely to provide material for a complete question, it is important background information for discussion parts of some case study questions.

7   SELF TEST QUESTIONS

7.1   List four potential conflicts between short-term and long-term corporate objectives. (1.2)

7.2   Distinguish between top down and bottom up planning systems. (1.6)

7.3   What is gap analysis? (3.2)

7.4   Give three strategies that can help to close a profit gap. (3.2)

7.5   State three types of investment decision involved in the long-term planning exercise. (3.3)

7.6   What is meant by organic growth? (4.1)

7.7   What is the definition of synergy? (4.2)

7.8   Name four different types of synergy. (4.3)

7.9   Name four categories of diversification. (5.3)

7.10   State two advantages and two disadvantages of becoming a conglomerate. (5.4)

8   EXAMINATION TYPE QUESTION

8.1   Classes of strategy

It is recognised in most industrial, commercial and institutional organisations that there are three principal classes of strategy:

(i)   growth;

(ii)   corrective; and

(iii)   contingency.

Required

(a)   Explain and compare the three classes.   **(5 marks)**

(b)   What methods may be used to secure the objectives of a growth strategy?   **(10 marks)**

(Total: 15 marks)

9   ANSWER TO EXAMINATION TYPE QUESTION

9.1   Classes of strategy

(a)   (i)   A company pursuing a growth strategy is aiming to expand earnings, probably through an increase in turnover and increased investment in the company. Variables which may be used to measure growth include return on capital employed, profit, sales, earnings per share, manpower.

(ii)   A corrective strategy aims at correcting the balance of the company's operations so as to reduce risk and 'correcting' the organisation structure of the company in order to produce the most efficient operation.

(iii)   A contingency strategy is designed to ensure that action can be taken quickly if an unexpected event occurs. It consists of saying 'if event E happens we shall take action A'. For instance, a company might have a contingency strategy which it could put into effect in the event that its demand forecasts turn out to be 20% wrong.

Selecting a growth strategy primarily concerns decisions about the firm's product-market posture. A corrective strategy also involves decisions about organisation and resources.

(b)   Growth may be achieved by market penetration, product or market development, or diversification. The first of these involves improvements to existing products and or intensified marketing in order to sell more in the same markets; the other options involve developing new products or new markets or both. The firm pursuing a growth strategy should not, however, forget the importance of dropping some of its least profitable lines as well as developing new ones, especially if resources are scarce. Turnover might fall as a result of such divestment but earnings or return on capital employed can rise.

The same appreciation of the importance of growth in profits rather than in turnover must guide the use of pricing policy as a means of pursuing a growth strategy. Cutting prices to increase sales might not be the right method.

A growth strategy will probably necessitate an active research department to develop new products, new markets, and new applications for existing products. It is possible, however, to buy know-how or to manufacture under licence in order to achieve internal growth. As an alternative to internal growth an acquisition or merger might be sought - either to strengthen the company's position in its own industry or to achieve diversification.

Firms which decide to diversify can often achieve rapid growth by taking advantage of the most profitable opportunities, although the risks increase the further away the firm moves from its original business.

A growing company can often take advantage of economies of scale or synergy to achieve higher return on capital.

12 MERGERS AND ACQUISITIONS

INTRODUCTION & LEARNING OBJECTIVES

When two businesses combine their activities, the combination may take the form of an acquisition (also called a takeover) or a merger (also called an amalgamation). The primary purpose of any combination should be to increase shareholder wealth, such an increase normally coming from the effects of synergy.

It must be recognised that in practice the synergistic gains anticipated from a combination are often disappointing. This may be because managers generally prefer to grow their businesses through acquisition rather than organically.

Acquisitions of quoted companies are governed in the UK by the City Code on Takeovers and Mergers. This aims to ensure that all shareholders are treated equally and fairly during a bid for their shares, so that for instance a bidder cannot bid for only 51% of his target's shares.

When you have studied this chapter you should be able to do the following:

- Discuss further the meaning of synergy and explain the various explanations for synergistic gains.
- Explain why many business combinations do not in fact realise the gains that were hoped from them.
- Discuss the blend of assets comprising the consideration on an acquisition.
- Identify relevant rules from the City Code which impact on any given situation.

1 ARGUMENTS FOR AND AGAINST MERGERS AND ACQUISITIONS

1.1 Methods of mergers and acquisitions

Though the terms are used loosely to describe a variety of activities, in every case the end result is that two companies become a single enterprise, in fact if not in name.

Whether by acquisition or by merger, the end result may be achieved by:

(a)   transfer of assets; or
(b)   transfer of shares

The two methods are summarised below.

	Transfer of assets	*Transfer of shares*
Acquisition (B takes over A)	B acquires trade and assets from A for cash. A is then liquidated, and the proceeds received by the old shareholders of A.	B acquires shares in A from A's shareholders in exchange for cash. A, as a subsidiary of B, may subsequently transfer its trade and assets to its new parent company (B).
Merger (X and Y merge to form Z)	Z acquires trade and assets from both X and Y in return for shares in Z. X and Y are then liquidated and the shares in Z distributed in specie to the shareholders of X and Y.	Z acquires shares in X and Y in return for its own shares. X and Y as subsidiaries of Z may subsequently transfer their trade and assets to their new parent company (Z).

Other names that are used are Takeover (Acquisition) or Amalgamation (Merger).

Note: the term 'combination' will be used in the text where it is equally relevant to acquisitions or mergers.

1.2   Rationale for growth by combination

As in other areas of the syllabus the ultimate justification of any policy is that it leads to an increase in value, ie, it increases shareholder wealth. As in capital budgeting where projects should be accepted if they have a positive NPV, in a similar way combinations should be pursued if they increase the wealth of shareholders.

Suppose firm A has a market value of £2m and it combines with firm B, market value £2m, with considerations at current market prices.

If the resultant new firm AB has a market value in excess of £4m then the combination can be counted as a success, if less it will be a failure.

Essentially, for a successful combination we should be looking for a situation where:

$$\text{Market value of combined companies (AB)} > \text{Market value of A} + \text{Market value of B}$$

If this situation occurs we have experienced synergy, that is, the whole is worth more than the sum of the parts. This is often expressed as:

$$2 + 2 = 5$$

It is important to note that synergy is not automatic. In an efficient stock market A and B will be correctly valued before the combination and we need to ask how synergy will be achieved, ie, why any increase in value should occur.

1.3   Sources of synergy

Some sources of synergy were identified in the previous chapter. These break down into:

(a)   operating economies;
(b)   market power;
(c)   financial gains; and
(d)   others.

We will examine each in turn in the context of combinations.

1.4   Synergy from operating economies

(a)   **Economies of scale**

Horizontal combinations (of companies in a similar line of business) are often claimed to reduce costs and therefore increase profits due to economies of scale. These can occur in the production, marketing or finance areas. Note that these gains are not automatic and diseconomies of scale may also be experienced. These benefits are sometimes also claimed for conglomerate combinations (of companies in unrelated areas of business) in financial and marketing costs.

(b)   **Economies of vertical integration**

Some acquisitions involve buying out other companies in the same production chain, eg, a manufacturer buying out a raw material supplier or a retailer. This can increase profits by 'cutting out the middle man'.

(c)   **Complementary resources**

It is sometimes argued that by combining the strengths of two companies a synergistic result can be obtained. For example, combining a company specialising in research and development with a company strong in the marketing area could lead to gains.

(d)   **Elimination of inefficiency**

If the victim company in a takeover is badly managed its performance and hence its value can be improved by the elimination of inefficiencies. Improvements could be obtained in the areas of production, marketing and finance.

1.5   Financial synergy

Several financial arguments are proposed in this area.

(a)   **Diversification**

The argument goes that diversification normally reduces risk. If the earnings of the combined companies simply stay the same (ie, no operating economies are obtained) there could still be an increase in value of the company due to the lower risk. This argument can be developed by an example.

Example 1

The following data are available for two companies:

		Company A	*Company B*
(i)	Market value	£2m	£2m
(ii)	Earnings to perpetuity	£0.2m	£0.4m
(iii)	Rate of return $\frac{(ii)}{(i)}$	10%	20%
(iv)	Standard deviation of return	8%	18%

Correlation coefficient between returns of A and B = 0.3

The risk and return of the combined company may be calculated in a similar way to the analysis of a two asset portfolio (in portfolio theory).

$$\textbf{Return} \text{ (assuming no operating economies)} = \text{£0.2 + £0.4m}$$
$$= \text{£0.6m}$$

$$\textbf{Risk} \quad s_p = \sqrt{x_a^2 \text{var a} + (1 - x_a)^2 \text{var b} + 2x_a(1 - x_a)\rho\sigma_a\sigma_b}$$
$$= \sqrt{(0.5^2 \times 8^2) + (0.5^2 \times 18^2) + (2 \times 0.5 \times 0.5 \times 8 \times 18 \times 0.3)}$$
$$= 10.89\%$$

The same total earnings are available but the risk is considerably less than the weighted average of the risk of the two individual companies $(\frac{18 + 8}{2}) = 13\%$

Therefore the value of the combined company should be in excess of £4m and synergistic gains will have been obtained.

The major fallacy in this argument is that it is based on total risk. Well-diversified shareholders evaluate companies on the basis of systematic risk, which, in one of the conclusions of CAPM, cannot be eliminated by diversification.

Assume, for example, that the following additional data were available:

$$\beta A = 1.00$$
$$\beta B = 3.00$$
$$Rm = 10\%$$
$$Rf = 5\%$$

The systematic risk of the combined company would simply be given by the weighted average of the two β factors:

$$(0.5 \times 1.00) + (0.5 \times 3.00) = 2.00$$

This gives an implied required rate of return of:

$$Rf + \beta(Rm - Rf) \quad = \quad 5\% + 2.00\,(10\% - 5\%)$$
$$= \quad 15\%$$

On total earnings to perpetuity of £0.6m this would give a combined company value of:

$$\frac{£0.6m}{0.15} = £4m$$

No increase in value has occurred because no risk reduction has been obtained. The systematic risk of the combined company is simply the weighted average of the individual systematic risks.

From a shareholder's point of view, in the absence of any operating economies, there appears to be no gain from the merger.

Note, however, that managers often concentrate on total risk, as total risk affects their job security and the diversification argument can make sense from a managerial viewpoint if not a shareholder's.

(b)   **Diversification and financing**

If the future cash flow streams of the two companies are not perfectly positively correlated then by combining the two companies the variability of their operating cash flow may be reduced. A more stable cash flow is more attractive to creditors and this could lead to cheaper financing.

(c)   **The 'boot strap' or PE game**

It is often argued that companies with high PE ratios are in a good position to acquire other companies as they can impose their high PE ratio on the victim firm and increase its value.

The question we need to ask is 'In an efficient market why should this occur?'

The lower PE ratio given to the victim firm presumably reflected its higher risk or poorer growth prospects. Why should the market change its mind simply because ownership has changed?

It might do so because of likely future operating economies, but not simply because the predator has a high PE ratio. The moral is clear – a high PE ratio in the acquiring company in itself is not the cause of any increase in value. In an efficient market increases in value will be caused by other benefits. If no other benefits are forthcoming the new PE ratio will simply be the weighted average of the individual PE ratios and no gain would accrue.

(d)   **Other financial benefits**

These largely revolve around the elimination of inefficient financial management practices. Examples include:

(i)   Buying low geared companies with good asset backing in order that they may be geared up to obtain the benefit of the corporation tax shield on debt.

(ii)   Buying companies with accumulated tax losses in order that they may be offset against profits of the acquiring company.

1.6   Other synergistic effects

(a)   **Surplus managerial talent**

Companies with highly skilled managers can make use of this resource only if they have problems to solve. The acquisition of inefficient companies is sometimes the only way of fully utilising skilled managers.

(b)   **Surplus cash**

Companies with large amounts of surplus cash may see the acquisition of other companies as the only possible application for these funds. Of course, increased dividends could cure the problem of surplus cash, but this may be rejected for reasons of tax or dividend stability.

(c)   **Market power**

Horizontal mergers may enable the firm to obtain a degree of monopoly power which could increase its profitability.

(d)   **Speed**

Acquisition may be far faster than organic growth in obtaining a presence in a new and growing market.

1.7   Why a company may want to be acquired

Many combinations are by mutual agreement, so small companies being acquired may welcome such a move. There are a number of possible reasons:

(a)   **Personal** – eg, to retire, for security, because of the problem of inheritance tax.

(b)   **Business** – an expanding small company may find that it reaches a size where it is impossible to restrain growth, but funds or management expertise are lacking.

(c)   **Technical** – increasing sophistication presents a problem for the small company, eg:

(i)   cost of research and development may be prohibitive;

(ii)   inability to employ specialised expertise;

(iii)   inability to offer a complete range of services or products to customers.

Such factors can apply to companies that are quite large by most standards, eg, Rolls-Royce Ltd was too small to absorb the research costs on one new engine.

1.8   Gains from combinations

Acquisition or merger is a popular route to growth and we have noted several arguments to justify expansion based on these routes. We have also seen that many of these arguments are suspect.

Research in this area has two major conclusions:

(a)   Value or synergistic gains are in practice quite small.

(b)   Bidding companies usually pay a substantial premium over the market value of the victim company prior to the bid.

The implications of these findings are quite significant and may be demonstrated by considering the acquisition of company B by company A, both companies having a market value of £2m each in isolation.

Let us assume that when these are combined a small amount of synergy is obtained and their combined value rises to £4.5m.

Let us further assume that to acquire B's shares A has had to pay a premium of £1m, ie, total cost of B is £3m.

The benefit/(cost) of the takeover to A's shareholders is as follows:

	£
Market value of AB	4.5m
Original value of A	(2.0m)
Price paid for B	(3.0m)
Loss	(0.5m)

This loss will be to the cost of the acquiring company shareholders but to the benefit of the victim company shareholders (as they received the £1m premium).

This in fact reflects the overall conclusion of research in this area: the consistent winners in mergers and takeovers are victim company shareholders; the consistent losers are acquiring company shareholders.

1.9   Causes of failure

Reasons advanced for the high failure rate of combinations are:

(a)   Over-optimistic assessment of economies of scale. Such economies can be achieved at a relatively small size; expansion beyond the optimum results in disproportionate cost disadvantages.

(b)   Inadequate preliminary investigation combined with an inability to implement the amalgamation efficiently.

(c)   Insufficient appreciation of the personnel problems which will arise.

(d)   Dominance of subjective factors such as the status of the respective boards of directors.

(e)   Difficulty of valuation. In the Decca/Racal/GEC case of some while ago, Racal's original £65 million bid for Decca was approved by the Decca chairman and by 30% of the voting shares. After the intervention of GEC, Racal eventually took control with a bid in excess of £100 million. Such a large gap between the original and final valuation indicates the kind of variation in measures of value which can exist.

Perhaps the fact that combination is often favoured as an alternative to expansion by other means implies a tendency towards laziness in management. It is probably considered easier to acquire an existing business rather than to subject oneself to the discipline of seeking and justifying more difficult investment projects. Furthermore, the high level of redundancies evidenced in larger groups indicates that mergers and acquisitions create a situation where rationalisation (which would otherwise be shirked) may be carried out more acceptably.

1.10   Conclusions on growth by combination

(a)   Not all combinations are failures; some in fact are very successful. On average, however, research shows that expansion based on merger and acquisition seems to bring few value gains to acquiring company shareholders.

(b)   Combinations, however, are often in the interests of managers. They view success in a different light from shareholders and are often more concerned with the job security and career prospects brought by sheer size.

(c)   There are alternatives to growth by combination. It is sometimes argued that as markets become more global mergers are required to allow companies to be large enough to compete. For example, telecommunications companies need to be very large to support the required research and development overhead. Other industries have, however, found ways round this problem. Joint ventures in the car industry between Honda/BL and Ford/Mazda are examples of alternatives to combination.

1.11   Merger and acquisition activity in different countries

Merger and acquisition activity is much more common in the UK and USA than in Germany or Japan. This is principally because banks dominate the financial systems of Germany and Japan, and develop long-term relationships with the companies they serve, taking significant equity stakes and perhaps having board representation. These banks would not sell their stakes to a predator, whatever price is offered.

In the UK and USA most shares are held by institutional investors (pension funds, unit trusts, insurance companies, etc,). Their traditional tendency has been to sell their shares if they are dissatisfied with the company's performance or if offered a significant premium to market price.

Some commentators have also argued that lax accounting standards in the UK have encouraged takeover activity in the past. Mergers were generously defined in SSAP 23 so that many acquisitions could be structured to fall within the SSAP 23 definition of a merger and so be accounted for using merger accounting. Additionally SSAP 22 allowed purchased goodwill to be eliminated directly against reserves on acquisition, which was more generous than the international standard requiring capitalisation and amortisation. The ASB have considered both of these problems as part of their work programme and hope that FRS 6 and FRS 10 will prove more effective than SSAP 23 and 22 respectively.

The implications of high takeover activity in the UK and USA are not clear cut. One view is that this contributes to the efficiency of the market, with resources being directed towards good managements. The opposing view is that most anticipated synergy gains are not realised in practice and that high takeover activity simply leads to short-term investment horizons by managers. This is an interesting area of the current debate on corporate governance in the UK.

2   STRATEGIES AND TACTICS OF MERGERS AND ACQUISITIONS

The previous chapter identified both organic growth and external growth as possible long-term growth strategies. No external growth should be considered unless the organic alternative has been dismissed as inferior. Assuming then that external growth has been decided upon, the remainder of this chapter considers the steps to be taken. A possible sequence of steps is as follows (in the context of acquisitions, although much will apply to mergers as well):

Strategic steps

Step 1   Appraise possible acquisitions

Step 2   Select the best acquisition target

Step 3   Decide on the financial strategy ie, the amount and the structure of the consideration

Tactical steps

Step 1   Launch a dawn raid subject to the City Code

Step 2   Make a public offer for the shares not held

Step 3   Success will be achieved if more than 50% of the target company's shares are acquired

3   IDENTIFYING POSSIBLE ACQUISITION TARGETS

3.1   Information required for appraisal of acquisitions

Once a company has decided to expand by acquisition, it must seek out prospective targets in the business sectors it is interested in.

For each company examined, clearly the first objective is to examine the prospect closely from both a commercial and financial viewpoint. In general businesses are acquired as going concerns rather than the purchase of specific assets, and thus this section summarises the variety of areas which require special examination:

(a)   **Organisation**

Special requirements in examples

(i)   Organisation chart, key management and quality.
(ii)   Employee analysis, terms and conditions.
(iii)   Unionisation and industrial relations.
(iv)   Pension arrangements.

Clearly, businesses are about people, and their quality and organisation requires examination. Further, comparison needs to be made with existing group remuneration levels and pensions, to determine the financial impact of their adoption, where appropriate, on the acquisition.

(b)   **Sales and marketing**

Special requirements - examples:

(i)   Historic and future sales volumes by product group and geographical location
(ii)   Market position, including customers and competition for major product groups.
(iii)   Normal trading terms.
(iv)   Historic sales and promotions expenditure by product group.

This additional information should provide a detailed assessment of the market and customer base to be acquired.

(c)   **Production, supply and distribution**

Special requirements - examples:

(i)   Total capacity and current usage levels.

(ii)   Need for future capital investment to replace existing assets, or meet expanded volume requirements.

This would provide an assessment of the overhead burden due to undercapacity production and of the potential future capital requirements to maintain the required productive capacity of the business.

(d)   **Technology**

Special requirements - examples:

(i)   Details of particular technical skills inherent in the acquisition.
(ii)   Research and development organisation and historic expenditure.

Thus, an analysis would be made of the technical assets acquired, and their past and potential future maintenance costs.

(e)   **Accounting information**

Special requirements - examples:

(i)   Company searches for all companies.

(ii)   Historic consolidated and individual company accounts.

(iii)   Detailed explanation of accounting policies.

(iv)   Explanation of major fluctuations in sales, gross margins, overheads and capital employed.

These provide the background for basic financial analysis.

(f)   **Treasury information**

Special requirements:

(i)   Amounts, terms and security of bank facilities and all other external loans and leasing facilities (including capitalised value, if not capitalised).

(ii)   Details of restrictive covenants and trust deeds for such facilities.

(iii)   Details of forward foreign exchange contracts, and exchange management policies.

All this information will be useful in planning the financial absorption of the business into the acquiring group, and will in particular reveal any 'hidden assets' (eg, low coupon loans) and 'hidden liabilities' (guarantees liable to be called, or hedged foreign exchange positions).

(g)   **Tax information**

Special requirements - examples:

(i)   Historic tax computations, agreed, submitted and unsubmitted by company.

(ii)   Significant disputes with Revenue.

(iii)   Trading losses brought forward.

(iv)   Potential tax liabilities, including deferred tax, VAT and PAYE.

(v)   Understanding of tax position of vendors, especially with respect to capital gains tax liability as a result of sale.

This can identify any potential tax assets (eg, utilisable losses) and liabilities (eg, likely payments of tax not provided), and assist in pricing and structuring the transaction having regard to the vendor's tax position.

(h)   **Other commercial/financial information**

Special requirements - examples:

(i)   Details of ordinary and preference shareholders, with amounts held by each class, and voting restrictions if appropriate, together with share options held and partly paid shares.

(ii)   Contingent liabilities, including litigation, forward purchase or sales contracts, including capital commitments and loss-making contracts not otherwise provided for.

(iii)   Actuarial assessment of current pension funding, with assumptions.

This relates primarily to a better understanding of the capital structure and shareholdings to be acquired, and any potential financial liabilities overhanging the acquired company, of which the most significant may well be underfunded pension schemes.

4   ACQUISITION CONSIDERATION AND STRUCTURE

4.1   Introduction

In general a purchaser and a vendor will need to agree on three basic issues in regard to an acquisition:

(a)   Whether shares or assets are to be purchased.

(b)   Type of consideration.

(c)   Financial value.

Although determination of value is likely to take place prior to the decision on the type of consideration, they are considered here in reverse order as the complexity of valuation necessitates its own section.

4.2   Share or asset purchase

The 'shares or asset' issue does not generally arise when public companies are acquired, but with the purchase of private companies it will usually turn on the following points:

(a)   An asset purchase will enable the purchaser to claim tax allowances on certain assets acquired, principally fixed assets other than land. The vendor, on the other hand, will probably have certain tax 'claw-backs' or 'balancing charges' to pay arising from tax allowances he has taken earlier, again principally on fixed assets other than land. The consequence is that, at least so far as tax efficiency is concerned, vendors do not generally favour this route, whilst acquirers seek it wherever possible.

(b)   A share purchase is much more complicated, principally because of all the actual and contingent liabilities attaching to a company, as opposed to the underlying assets in the business, which can be sold separately from such liabilities. The documentation is much more lengthy and the cost of professional advisors far greater. In addition, stamp duty may be payable on the entire share transfer (as opposed to only on the property element of an asset sale). Where the vendor can be persuaded that his tax position is not prejudiced, therefore, this argues for an asset purchase.

A technique commonly used to mitigate the disadvantages of a share purchase is the **hivedown**. This is generally applied to a company only part of whose business is wanted by the purchaser. The part required is transferred to a clean 'off the shelf' or new company owned by the vendor; such a transfer can be accomplished without adverse tax consequences. The clean company, containing the business, is then sold without the documentary negotiation and complications which normally accompany the sale of a company which has been in existence for some time.

4.3   Type of consideration

The means of transferring the financial value of the shares or assets of the business, the consideration, can be satisfied in a combination of several alternatives:

(a)   Cash.

(b)   Debt.

(c)   Preference shares.

(d)   Ordinary shares.

In addition, debt and preference share consideration can be convertible into ordinary shares.

The value of ordinary shares issued is, generally speaking, based on their market value at the time of issue. In principle, too, the issue of shares is no more expensive to the purchaser than cash or debt consideration, despite the implicit difference in the cost of equity and debt. The reason for this is that, in general, projects, whether internal or external (ie, acquisitions) should be considered to be financed from a 'pool' of financial resources based on the optimum relationship between debt and equity, and basing the appropriate hurdle on the 'blended' cost of such a pool. If equity is issued as consideration for a project, the change in the debt/equity ratio resulting is usually considered to be temporary, and the group will subsequently make appropriate adjustments in the level of debt in order to optimise the ratio. Adjustments would equally have to be made where debt rather than equity is issued.

There are, however, certain complicating factors which require to be borne in mind and may go against the use of such shares:

(a)   **Temporary depression of share price**

The acquirer may feel the then current share price might rise in the future, either because the share market as a whole is depressed, or because the value of the acquiring company's shares are temporarily depressed. Thus, the vendor may be getting the shares 'cheap'.

(b)   **Dilution of existing shareholders' interests**

This will be a problem where the acquirer has a limited number of major shareholders who may not, for control or other reasons, wish to see their interests diluted.

(c)   **Difficulty in valuing shares**

Unquoted companies may have difficulty in establishing an appropriate price.

(d)   **Maintenance of debt/equity ratio**

If the change in the equity base is large in relation to the pre-acquisition level of equity, it may be difficult to get back to an optimum debt/equity ratio. Under these circumstances, the ordinary shares issue may indeed have a higher cost, closer to the cost of equity rather than to the 'blended cost of capital'.

The type, cost and term/redemption arrangement of debt or preference shares to be issued is a matter for negotiation. However, the vendor's capital gains tax may be deferred by the issue of either debt or shares of any type, the deferral being until repayment date/redemption date/date of sale of ordinary shares.

Where debt or preference shares are concerned, there is often a **quid pro quo** exacted by the acquirer in the form of a lower interest and dividend rate than the going market, in return for the tax advantage conveyed.

5   VALUATION OF SHARES

5.1   Introduction

Once a suitable takeover target has been identified the next decision is how much to pay. Share valuations are also needed for several other purposes and it is also convenient to handle the valuations of holdings below 100% in this section.

5.2   Reasons for valuation

Share valuations in both public and private companies are needed for several purposes by investors including:

(a)   to establish terms of takeovers and mergers, etc;

(b)   to be able to make buy and hold decisions in general;

(c)   to value companies entering the stock market;

(d)   to establish values of shares held by retiring directors, which the articles of a company specify must be sold;

(e)   for fiscal purposes (capital gains tax, inheritance tax);

(f)   divorce settlements, etc.

The various methods of valuation will often give widely differing results and depending on the need for the valuation it will be in the interests of the investor to argue that either a 'high' or 'low' value is appropriate. In view of the uncertainty attached to the valuations the final figure will be a matter for negotiation between the interested parties. In some cases the circumstances giving rise to the valuation may call for 'a value as would be agreed between a willing buyer and a willing seller' and may often be subject to independent arbitration.

In examination questions several methods of valuation are usually possible. It makes senses to attempt as many valuations as possible before providing reasoned arguments for your ultimate selection.

5.3   Quoted shares

Only a small percentage of companies are quoted on a stock exchange, and even then the price quoted is not necessarily an appropriate measure to use to value a shareholding in that particular company.

We have shown in earlier chapters that the shares should be traded until the present value of the future dividend payments (discounted at a rate appropriate to the level of risk, both operating and financial) is equal to the current share price. This, then, is what is meant by the 'value' of a share. But, given that in fact the market is not perfect, especially with respect to the availability of information to investors, the price quoted (on the Stock Exchange Daily List or Financial Times, etc) is normally a measure of the price at which the last recorded bargain was struck. Accordingly if the shares are relatively inactive, as is the case for a great number of the smaller UK quoted companies, the price may be 'out of date'.

More importantly it is a measure of the price at which stock market dealers are prepared to deal in relatively small parcels of shares. Where large parcels are to be bought or sold, the price is invariably affected commensurately, and thus the quoted price does not reflect the price at which a deal would be struck.

Nevertheless, in an efficient stock market share prices should reflect all publicly available information and if available are normally considered to be the best guide for valuation. In practice in an acquisition it is unlikely that the bidding company would succeed by offering less then current market price, and usually substantial premiums over market price are paid.

5.4   Unquoted shares

The valuation of shares in unquoted companies may be something which an accountant is required to do fairly regularly. In particular for fiscal purposes the accountant will need to negotiate figures with the Capital Taxes office of the Inland Revenue, and frequently the Articles of Association of private companies may call upon the auditor to value shares which are to be transferred between members, failing them reaching their own agreement.

The method of share valuation of shares in a private company essentially involve comparison of its activities with those of a similar quoted company and will be considered in the next section.

Note that the valuation methods for unquoted shares are often applied to quoted companies to check the 'reasonableness' of market values.

5.5   Bases of valuation

Shareholdings may be valued in two essentially different ways - either asset based value or income based value. Each of these may be further subdivided:

Income based   -   Present value
                -    Dividend valuation
                -    P/E ratio

Asset based   -   Book value
                -    Replacement cost/deprival value
                -    Break up value

Additionally methods based on a mixture of 'assets' and 'income' may be used.

Although from a theoretical point of view, the only sustainable valuation model is that based on the net present value of future earnings, this model is generally impossible to apply because of the practical difficulties associated with estimating future earnings streams, choosing an appropriate discount rate, etc. Accordingly in practice the other methods are more widely used, and may in any event be considered as surrogates for the one theoretically sound method.

Nevertheless we will begin by considering a present value approach.

5.6   Present value approach

In theory the value of any asset is the value of its future earnings discounted at a rate which reflects the systematic risk of these earnings.

Let us assume that A plc was considering the acquisition of B plc:

The value of B would then be determined as follows:

Present value of the future earnings of A and B combined at a discount rate reflecting the systematic risk of the combined company

Less

Present value of A's current earnings at a discount rate reflecting its level of systematic risk (in an efficient market this should be the market value of A)

= Maximum value of B

Note that this might well be different from the current market value of B as synergy could occur.

Alternatively this figure could be arrived at by:

Present value of B's earnings at a discount rate reflecting its level of systematic risk
Plus or minus
Present value of the gains and costs of the takeover

From our point of view the approach taken will depend upon the question set. Most questions in this area resemble capital budgeting questions - the major task being the identification of relevant cash flows.

An example follows.

5.7   Example 1 - present value approach

Your client, Egbert plc, has been negotiating with Beornwulf Ltd for the purchase of one of its manufacturing divisions. The divisions profit and loss account for the year just ended and the current balance sheet are summarised as follows:

Profit and loss account

	£'000	£'000
Sales - All to external customers		376
Less: Materials and components - external	52	
Materials and components - internal	43	
Manufacturing labour	124	
Depreciation of plant and equipment	15	
Other manufacturing overheads incurred in division	64	
Administrative overheads incurred in division	38	
Share of head office costs	24	
		(360)
Net profit		16

Balance sheet

	£'000
Plant and equipment - Cost less depreciation	34
Stock at cost	
Finished goods	72
Raw materials	26
Trade debtors	54
	186
Less: Trade creditors	(32)
Head office capital employed	154

You are given the following additional information.

(1) 'Materials and components - internal' represents items transferred from another division. Under Beornwulf's transfer pricing policy, these items are priced at variable cost plus 30% to cover fixed overheads. Egbert would manufacture the items concerned itself under similar conditions to Beornwulf as regards costs

(2) Egbert would take over all the assets of the division and discharge the creditors. However, the plant and equipment is believed to be obsolete. It would be sold for scrap at £10,000 and replaced by equipment leased on an annual contract for an initial rental of £25,000 per annum.

(3) Egbert believes that stocks of finished goods could be reduced to one-half of their present level. The reduction would be effected by a special sale immediately following the acquisition to realise £40,000.

(4) 'Share of head office costs' represents an allocation of administrative costs on the basis of divisional sales. The acquisition would cause Egbert's costs of general management to increase by £8,000 in the first year.

(5) It is expected that all items of cost and revenue for the division and all working capital items would increase at 15% per annum, in step with the Retail Price Index for the indefinite future. Egbert believes that a rate of return of 21% per annum, in money terms, reflects the systematic risk of the investment.

You may assume that all receipts and payments arise at annual intervals.

You are required to prepare a calculation to guide Egbert in deciding on the maximum sum it should pay for the division of Beornwulf.

Ignore taxation.

(*Tutorial note:* in this example we calculate the cash flows of the victim after acquisition and then take a present value to determine its worth.)

Calculation of maximum purchase price

Impact of acquisition on annual cash flow

	Notes	£'000	£'000
Sales			376
Less: Materials and components (external)		52	
Materials and components (internal)	1	33	
Manufacturing labour		124	
Other manufacturing overheads incurred in division	2	64	
Administrative overheads incurred in division	2	38	
Increase in cost of general management	3	8	
Leasing plant and equipment	4	25	
			344
Adjusted annual profit from acquisition			32

Cash flow from operations - Year 1

Profit for year 1 = £32,000 × 1.15

= £36,800

Now, profit for the year = Increase in working capital (including cash)

Opening working capital (beginning of year 1)

		£'000
Stock: Finished goods (on new basis ½ × 72)		36
Raw material		26
Debtors		54
		116
Less: Creditors		32
		84

Increase in these items during the year = 15% × £84,000

= £12,600

Cash surplus at end of year 1   = £(36,800 – 12,600)

= £24,200

Similarly, cash surplus at end of year 2 = £24,200 × 1.15

= £27,830 etc, growing by 15% pa

Present value at end of year 0 of future cash flows from operations $= \dfrac{£24,200}{0.21-0.15}$

= £403,333

Relevant cash flows for acquisition of business

	Year 0 £'000	Year 1 to perpetuity PV £'000
Receipts: Scrap	10	403.33
Stock	40	
Payment: Rent	(25)	
	25	

Maximum amount payable for business   =   £(403,333 + 25,000)
  =   £428,000

Notes

(1)   It is assumed that internally manufactured materials and components can be produced by Egbert Ltd without incurring any additional fixed costs. The validity of this assumption in the long term is doubtful. However, on this basis cash costs for Egbert become:

$$\frac{100}{100+30} \times £43,000 = £33,077, \text{ say } £33,000$$

(2)   It is assumed that overheads incurred in the division do not change with the acquisition.

(3)   The allocation of Beornwulf Ltd (Beornwulf) head office costs is irrelevant; however, the increase in general management costs are a cash outflow of the project. It is assumed that the £8,000 estimate is in real terms.

(4)   The depreciation charge (which is not a cash flow) is replaced by the leasing cost (which is a cash flow). Presumably the rental is payable annually in advance, so there is a cash flow now, as well as in subsequent years.

(5)   It is assumed that cash surpluses generated by the division are paid over to the acquiring company at the end of each year.

5.8   Conclusions on present value approach

The major problem is in determining the post merger cash flows, and makes this a method of little practical value. It is, however, sometimes asked in examinations. Clearly it is only really applicable for a controlling interest, as only with control could synergistic effects be obtained.

5.9   Dividend valuation

The dividend valuation model has already been looked at. In this application we can derive a value for a company by applying at cost of equity to a future stream of dividends, ie:

$$P_0 \quad = \quad \frac{D_0}{k_e} \qquad \text{(no growth situation)}$$

$$\text{or} \quad P_0 \quad = \quad \frac{D_1}{k_e - g} \qquad \text{(constant growth situation)}$$

where P_0 =   price of shares *ex-div*
    D_0 =   dividend at time 0, etc
    k_e =   cost of equity ie, the shareholders' required rate of return
    g =   growth in dividends

Note that more complex versions of the model involving non-constant growth are also possible.

To use the model to value a non-quoted company we need to establish:

(a)   the future dividend stream of the firm;
(b)   the shareholders' required rate of return.

The dividend stream is usually estimated by considering past patterns in dividends. Shareholders' required rate of return (k_e) is normally estimated by taking the cost of equity of a similar quoted company or may be obtained by using the capital asset pricing model. Comparability is important here and we must ensure that the quoted company is of a similar size and involved in the same line of business (ie, it carries the same level of systematic risk). Even if this is the case adjustments are usually made to reflect the non-marketability of unquoted shares (shareholders would normally accept a lower rate of return from quoted companies because their shares may be easily disposed of). Other specific problems of comparability to watch out for include:

(a)   Quoted companies are often more diversified in their activities than private companies. Consequently it may be difficult to find a quoted company with a similar range of activities.

(b)   Quoted companies are often bigger than private companies. Because of the generally accepted benefits which size brings, a higher dividend yield should be sought from a smaller, but otherwise comparable company.

(c)   Levels of gearing may differ between companies and hence affect the dividend yield.

(d)   If a small shareholding is being valued it may hold particular importance to either or both parties (eg, a 2% shareholding being acquired by a 49% shareholder). In such cases the purchaser may be prepared to pay far more than would be indicated by a valuation based on dividend yield.

5.10   Example 2 - dividend valuation

You are required to place a value on a 2% holding of shares in Claygrow Ltd, a small private company manufacturing flowerpots.

The following data are available:

Current dividend	18.5p per share
Past growth in dividends	5% per annum
Cost of equity of quoted flowerpot manufacturers	18%

If we assume constant growth and increase the cost of equity by (say) 25% to reflect the additional risk of a private company, then

$$P_0 \quad = \quad \frac{D_1}{k_e - g} \quad = \quad \frac{18.5(1.05)}{0.225 - 0.05} \quad = \quad 111p$$

This figure might well form a reasonable basis for valuing a small holding of shares, where the owner has little or no influence over the affairs of the company, and is or will be simply the passive recipient of dividends.

5.11   Dividend yield

A dividend yield approach is sometimes employed as a simplified version of the dividend valuation model.

The dividend yield is defined as:

$$\frac{\text{Total annual dividend}}{\text{Share price}} \times 100\%$$

Thus, for unquoted companies the formula is turned around to give:

$$\text{Share value} = \frac{\text{Total annual dividend}}{\text{Suitable dividend yield}}$$

There are then two elements to determine the total annual dividend to be paid by the private company and what is a 'suitable dividend yield'.

It is essential to compare like with like and consequently it is the current annual dividend which is taken into account irrespective of any growth prospects, etc.

5.12   Example 3 - dividend yield approach

You are required to place a value on a 2% holding of shares in Exco Ltd, a privately owned company. You establish the following additional information:

Issued share capital	100,000 £1 ordinary shares
Current dividend	3.5p per share

Quoted companies in Exco's industry generally have a dividend yield of 4%.

$$\text{Basic value} = \frac{\text{Dividend}}{\text{Dividend yield}}$$

			£
	$= \dfrac{3.5\text{p}}{4\%}$	$=$	0.88
Less: Discount for non-marketability - say 25%			(0.22)
Value per share			0.66

The dividend yield approach is usually considered inferior to the dividend valuation model as it ignores growth. However, if growth rates in the unquoted company are likely to be similar to those in quoted companies (the source of the dividend yield %) then it is an acceptable alternative.

5.13   Conclusions on dividend approaches

As with all valuation models the major problem is in obtaining the input data to the model. Dividend approaches are normally only considered suitable for small holdings of shares. If a controlling interest is attained the purchaser will have the power to influence future dividends and the valuation process becomes rather circular.

5.14   Earnings yield or P/E ratio

The P/E ratio is another figure which is published in the Financial Times and elsewhere and is widely regarded as an important measure. It is defined as:

$$\text{P/E ratio} = \frac{\text{Price per share}}{\text{Earnings per share in latest published accounts (EPS)}}$$

As with 'dividend yield' this formula is then turned around to value shares in unquoted companies.

$$\text{Value per share} = \text{EPS} \times \text{suitable P/E ratio}$$

Again any value thence computed is then normally reduced to take into account the non-marketability of the shares.

The basic choice for a suitable P/E ratio will be that of a quoted company of comparable size in the same industry; and the same difficulties apply as when a suitable dividend yield is sought.

In particular there is a tendency for dividends to be more stable than earnings, consequently since share prices are broadly based on expected future earnings a P/E ratio - based on a single year's reported earnings - may be very different for companies in the same sector, carrying the same systematic risk.

For example a high P/E ratio may indicate:

(a)   *Growth stock* - the share price is high because continuous high rates of growth of earnings are expected from the stock.

(b)   *No growth stock* - the P/E ratio is based on the last reported earnings, which perhaps were exceptionally low yet the share price is based on future earnings which are expected to revert to a 'normal' relatively stable level.

(c)   *Take-over bid* - the share price has risen pending a takeover bid.

(d)   *High security share* - shares in property companies typically have low income yields but the shares are still worth buying because of the prospects of capital growth and level of security.

Similarly a low P/E ratio may indicate:

(a)   *Losses expected* - future profits are expected to fall from their most recent levels eg, shares of certain banks in the early 1990s reflected possible future bad debt losses during the recession.

(b)   *Share price low* - as noted previously, share prices may be extremely volatile - special factors, such as a strike at a manufacturing plant of a particular company, may depress the share price and hence the P/E ratio.

Consequently the main difficulty in trying to apply the model is finding a similar company, with similar growth prospects.

A further difficulty is that the reported earnings are based on historical cost accounts, which in general makes a nonsense of trying to compare two companies. Also it is important to ensure that the earnings in the victim company reflect future earnings prospects. It would be unwise to value a company on freakishly high earnings.

In spite of these serious shortcomings the P/E ratio is regarded as an important measure by investment analysts etc, and cannot therefore be disregarded. As a broad brush measure, and as long as exceptional items are identified and treated as such, it may be used to value shares. It is generally considered to be appropriate where the size of the shareholding is sufficient to influence dividend policy - and therefore the shareholder is more concerned with the underlying level of earnings, rather than just dividends.

5.15   Example 4 - PE ratio approach

You are given the following information regarding Accrington Ltd, an unquoted company:

(a)   Issued ordinary share capital is 400,000 25p shares.

(b)   Extract from profit and loss account for the year ended 31 July 19X4

	£	£
Profit before taxation	260,000	
Less: Corporation tax	120,000	
Profit after taxation		140,000
Less: Preference dividend	20,000	
Ordinary dividend	36,000	
		(56,000)
Retained profit for the year		84,000

(c)   The P/E ratio applicable to a similar type of business (suitable for an unquoted company) is 12.5.

You are required to value 200,000 shares in Accrington Ltd on an earnings yield basis.

$$\text{Valuation of 200,000 shares} = 200{,}000 \times \text{P/E ratio} \times \text{EPS}$$

$$= 200{,}000 \times 12.5 \times \frac{(140{,}000 - 20{,}000)}{400{,}000}$$

$$= £750{,}000$$

5.16   Asset based measures

Asset based measures are generally considered appropriate when shareholdings greater than 50% are being valued. Such shareholdings give the holder the right to control the acquisition and disposal of the underlying assets.   Therefore, if there are assets not needed for generation of income, the controlling shareholder may cause these to be realised to generate cash.

As described above there are several possible asset-based measures which could be used.

(a)   *Book value* - this will normally be a meaningless figure as it will be based on historical costs.

(b)   *Replacement cost and deprival value* - this should provide a measure of the maximum amount that any purchaser should pay for the whole business, since it represents the total cost of forming the business from scratch. However, a major element of any business as a going concern is likely to be the 'goodwill'. Since this can only be defined as 'income based value of business - tangible assets' it may be seen that there is no real way of applying a pure 'asset based value' to a business - it is always necessary to consider an 'income based value' as well.

(c)   *Break up value* - the break up value of the assets in the business will often be considerably lower than any other computed value. It normally represents the minimum price which should be accepted for the sale of a business as a going concern, since if the income based valuations give figures lower than the break up value it is apparent that the owner would be better off by ceasing to trade and selling off all the assets piecemeal.

However, when a break up is considered in this way it must be remembered to include such items as redundancy costs, liquidator's expenses, etc, which may have significant effect on the final position.

In spite of these difficulties an asset value per share, based on deprival value, perhaps excluding goodwill, often provides a useful comparison with valuations based on capitalisation of income streams.

It is also important that you use your common sense when applying asset values. They might be very useful in valuing property companies, but the asset value of service businesses will normally bear no relationship to their income value as most of their value is represented by their workforce rather than their physical assets.

5.17   Example 5 - asset based approach

The following is an abridged version of the balance sheet of Grasmere Contractors Ltd, as at 30 April year 4:

	£
Fixed assets (net book value)	450,000
Net current assets	100,000
	550,000
Represented by	
£1 ordinary shares	200,000
Reserves	250,000
6% debentures year 19 (repayable at 102)	100,000
	550,000

You ascertain that:

(a)   market value of goodwill (not recorded in the books) is £50,000;
(b)   current market value of freehold property exceeds book value by £30,000;
(c)   all assets, other than property, are estimated to be realisable at their book value.

You are required to value an 80% holding of ordinary shares on an assets basis.

Calculation of value of 200,000 shares on an assets basis, as at 30 April year 4

	£	£
Fixed assets per balance sheet		450,000
Add: Unrecorded goodwill	50,000	
Undervalued freehold property	30,000	
		80,000
Adjusted value of fixed assets		530,000
Net current assets		100,000
Net assets		630,000
Less: Payable to debenture holders on redemption		102,000
		528,000

$$\text{Valuation of 80\% holding} = \frac{80}{100} \times 528,000 \qquad 422,400$$

Note: the debentures have been taken at redemption cost in year 19. Since this is some years distant, a fairer valuation might be produced by calculating the net present value, based on market rates of interest, of the future interest payments and redemption cost.

5.18   Other methods of valuation

(a)   *Berliner method*

This attempts to take into account both the asset value of a company and its earnings potential. Two values of the company are obtained:

(i)   based on capitalising expected future profits at an acceptable rate of return;
(ii)   based on the going concern value of the company's net tangible assets.

The value placed on the company is then calculated as $\frac{(i)+(ii)}{2}$ ie, the mean.

This is a compromise which has no particular theoretical support but it may produce an acceptable purchase figure.

(b)   *Dual capitalisation method*

This is similar to the Berliner method, but it recognises the two different types of asset - tangible and intangible; the latter, such as goodwill, are often risky investments.

The method used is to determine acceptable yields for both types of asset. Tangible assets are then valued and application of the yield determined for such assets gives a figure representing return on tangible assets. This is deducted from the profits figure to arrive at profit attributable to intangible assets, which is capitalised at the appropriate rate and added to the tangible assets value previously calculated to produce an overall company value.

5.19 Maximum and minimum values

Normally it is possible to apply most of the above methods in valuing a company. Usually the results will differ substantially and examination questions commonly ask students to specify:

(a)   the maximum amount the bidder should pay;

(b)   the minimum amount the seller will accept.

The maximum amount to be paid by the bidder is the present value of the victim company's earnings plus or minus any synergistic effects. Any more than this would result in the acquisition being a negative NPV investment. In practice, however, these figures are difficult to calculate. Another approach to this problem is to ask 'How much would a similar company cost?' This can sometimes be estimated by taking the replacement cost of assets plus an allowance for goodwill.

The minimum amount acceptable by the seller depends upon what can be obtained for the company elsewhere. This could involve estimates of net realisable value, the proceeds of an AIM quotation, or the present value of the owners' future dividends if they retired from the company and appointed managers to run it in their place.

5.20 Conclusions on valuation

It is important to appreciate that valuation is not an exact science. In a merger and takeover situation the final price paid will often depend on how badly the owners wish to sell and the bidders wish to buy.

Most of the above methods can be applied to other valuation problems, eg, valuing shares for a public offer for sale, but once again their limitations should be noted. In a public offer for sale, for example, small interests are usually held and dividend or earnings based approaches would be more appropriate. In this case firms would often offer a discount on valuation to encourage new shareholders to purchase (eg, government privatisation issues).

6   CASE STUDY OF A VALUATION PROBLEM

6.1   Example

You are asked to value a 60% and a 5% holding in Shade Ltd for the purposes of share transfer. The company manufacturers high quality children's toys, and is well known in this field.

The management of the company is regarded as satisfactory, having passed from the hands of the original founding family (a senior member of which is selling his shares) into the hands of professional management. The continuity of management is, at present, well organised.

Profit and dividend record (approximate figures)

Year to 31 January	Turnover £'000	Pre-tax profit £'000	%	Dividend £
19X4	900	150	5	7,500
19X5	1,000	165	10	15,000
19X6	1,200	210	12	18,000

Net asset position, per balance sheet at 31 January 19X6

	£'000	£'000	£'000
Fixed assets			
Freehold land and buildings at cost			430
Plant and machinery, at cost less depreciation			60
			490

Current assets

Stock		200
Debtors		350
		550

Current liabilities

Creditors	165	
Taxation	80	
Dividends	18	
Overdraft	20	
		283
		267
		757

8% debenture 19X9	50
	707

(1)   A note to the accounts indicates that the freeholds have this year been revalued, on an existing use basis, at £600,000.

(2)   Share capital at 31 January 19X6 consists of 150,000 £1 ordinary shares.

(3)   Assume corporation tax on income at 30% and on chargeable gains at 35%.

You ascertain the following data from the *Financial Times*:

	Dividend yield	P/E ratio
500 share index	6.2	9.7
Consumer goods (non-durable)	6.7	10.0
Toys and games	8.1	6.6

Indicate how you would value:

(a)   a 60% holding;
(b)   a 5% holding.

Do not ignore taxation.

6.2   Solution

Note: since there can never be a perfect solution, what follow are the suggested steps that would be worked through.

(a)   **60% holding**

(i)   The normal bases of valuing a holding of this size are by reference to assets and to earnings. Assuming the purchaser wished to continue the business of the company, the earnings basis is more relevant.

(ii)   The assets basis should include the revaluation of the property, less, arguably, taxation. Being prudent, the full liability of 35% on a chargeable gain should be allowed for.

	£'000	£'000
Net assets, per balance sheet		707.0
Revaluation of freeholds £(600 – 430)	170.0	
Less: 35% thereof	59.5	
		110.5
		817.5

Value per share $\dfrac{£817,500}{150,000}$ = £5.45 per share

(iii) The earnings basis requires the P/E, which would have applied to the shares had they been quoted, to be determined and applied to the likely future earnings per share. The P/E for a similar quoted company is 5.5; a similar unquoted company would operate on a lower P/E of, say, 4.5. (Remember, however, that P/E ratios of companies quoted on the Stock Exchange relate to dealings in relatively small parcels of shares, so a higher P/E than 4.5 may be more appropriate.)

Earnings per share must be calculated from past figures. There seems little point in averaging past years, since they reveal an increasing trend. The figure of EPS required is that for future years - the past is merely a guide to the future. In the circumstances, the results of the most recent year (to 31 January 19X6) appear to be the best to use as a guide to the future.

	£'000
Pre-tax profit	210,000
Less: Corporation tax	63,000
Earnings	147,000

Earnings per share $\dfrac{£147,000}{150,000}$ = 98 pence

Value per share 4.5 × 98 pence = £4.41 per share

(iv) Other factors which can be extracted from the information given:

Current ratio: $\dfrac{550}{283}$ = 1.94   :   Satisfactory

Liquid ratio: $\dfrac{350}{283}$ = 1.24   :   Satisfactory (if debtors are all recoverable, and overdraft limit not yet reached)

(v) The range of prices indicated for this majority holding is £4.41 to £5.45 per share. The higher end of the range reflects the high asset backing, and perhaps a continuation of the profit trend upwards. The assets, however, are unlikely to be realised, so that a more prudent valuation would be towards the lower end of the scale, say, in the region of £4.30 - £4.80.

(b)   **5% holding**

(i) The normal basis of valuing a holding of this size is by reference to dividends.

(ii) High asset backing, favourable ratios and trend of profits, all discussed above, are factors which would again influence the valuation.

(iii) The yield obtainable on similar quoted securities is 8.1%. It is normal to uplift this by 25% to 40% to compensate for the unmarketability of unquoted securities. One must also allow, at this stage, for the impressive factors referred to above - dividend cover, profits trend and asset backing. Accordingly, the lower uplift (25% × 8.1%) may be appropriate, producing a yield of 10%.

(iv)   The dividend yield valuation would thus be:

$$\frac{100}{10} \times 12 \text{ pence} = 120 \text{ pence per share}$$

This is considerably lower than the value per share of the majority holding.

(v)   It would be interesting to apply a dividend valuation approach, ie, including growth, but cost of equity figures are not given. (Note that dividend yield is not the cost of equity as it does not include the growth factor.)

7   OTHER FACTORS RELEVANT TO VALUATION

7.1   Introduction

As well as the above financial data other aspects of the victim company may need to be considered when assessing an acquisition. These are discussed below.

7.2   Background of market and industry

This may well be an important factor to a prospective shareholder. The type of information required includes:

(a)   Nature of the industry in which the company operates. Is it seasonal or volatile or prone to cyclical fluctuations?

(b)   Who are the main competitors? What are their respective market shares?

(c)   Are there possibilities of take-over of this company by other firms, or other firms by this company?

(d)   Who are the key sales customers and suppliers of the company? Are any of them crucial to the company's future success?

(e)   Are there any plans for diversification of activities in the future? Does the company possess any vital technological know-how? Are new ideas and projects protected by patents and trademarks?

7.3   Information regarding shares

The following must be considered.

(a)   *Size of shareholding to be acquired* - which will determine the level of control or influence gained

(b)   *Details of other shareholders* - how the remaining shares in the company are spread and the relationship between the other members (they may all belong to the same family) - this may mean that they can always be relied on to agree on major matters (or, in some families, to disagree).

(c)   *Rights attaching to the shares* - rights as regards voting, dividends and return of capital on liquidation.

(d)   *Possible restrictions on transfer* - the Articles of Association frequently contain an overriding clause, which states, in effect, that the directors have an absolute power to refuse to register a particular transfer of shares. This will have the effect of lowering the value of the shares.

7.4   Financial information

Investigation will involve close examination of both current and past financial statements, as well as future profit forecasts. Financial information will be examined under the headings of:

(a)   **Balance sheets**

    (i)   *Tangible assets*

        Essential concern is with market values of assets, on a going concern basis, as opposed to book values. The difference between market values and book values of freehold property might well be significant.

    (ii)   *Intangible assets*

        This includes items such as goodwill, patents and trademarks. In an established and expanding business, goodwill may well be a valuable asset even if it does not feature in the balance sheet. Patents and trademarks may be valuable too.

    (iii)   *Surplus funds*

        The business may possess surplus funds, that is funds not vital in the day-to-day operations of the business, which may be employed and invested more profitably outside the business.

    (iv)   *Capital gearing*

        Ordinary shareholders will be concerned with the extent of prior charges, ie, debentures and preference share capital.

    (v)   *Liquidity*

        Does the company possess sufficient working capital to finance future trading? Are there any unused overdraft facilities?

    (vi)   *Long-term borrowing power*

        Is there potential for raising long-term finance on assets such as freehold property, which are not at present the subject of a charge?

    (vii)   *Relevance of net asset backing*

        Net asset backing is essentially the value of net assets attributable to each ordinary share. The calculations are derived from balance sheet figures, and, therefore, in times of inflation may be on the conservative side.

        Frequently, however, adjustment is made for increases in property values where the directors have stated revaluations by way of note in the accounts.

(b)   **Profit and loss accounts**

Profit results of past periods are examined in order to help forecast future results. The value of shares now depends on rights and benefits expected to be received in the future. The following points are important:

    (i)   Adjust past profit results to allow for the effect of non-recurring items.

    (ii)   Examine the level of tax charges, particularly where deferred taxation policy has not been consistent.

(iii) Make allowances for excessive directors' remuneration, as these may distort comparisons and trends.

(vi) Apply ratio analysis wherever possible. Erratic trends of gross profit percentages, for example, may indicate that the company is operating in a speculative industry.

(v) Assess the reliability of the budgetary and forecasting system. Compare forecast results of previous periods with actual results attained. This may provide a clue as to the reliance to be placed on future forecasts.

(vi) If averaging past profits, use a weighted, not a simple, average.

(vii) Pay attention to the trend of profits and dividends. This is often most significant.

(viii) Bear in mind the effect inflation is likely to have had on the comparability of figures from year to year.

7.5   Directors, management and other key personnel

How successful have management been in the past? Does future prosperity of the company depend on certain key personnel? Obtain details of service contracts of key personnel. Do plans exist for effective management succession?

8   ACQUISITION PROCEDURES

8.1   The regulation of takeovers

The acquisition of quoted companies is circumscribed by the City Code on Takeovers and Mergers ('the City Code'), which is the responsibility of the Panel on Takeovers and Mergers. This code does not have the force of law, but it is enforced by the various City regulatory authorities, including the Stock Exchange, and specifically by the Panel on Takeovers and Mergers (the 'Takeover Panel'). Its basic principle is that of equity between one shareholder and another, and it sets out rules for the conduct of such acquisitions.

The Stock Exchange **Yellow Book** also has certain points to make in these circumstances:

(a) Details of documents to be issued during bids for quoted companies.
(b) Such documents to be cleared by the Stock Exchange.
(c) Timely announcement of all price sensitive information.

The Office of Fair Trading (OFT) regulates the monopoly aspects of bids. Many bids, because of their size, will require review by the OFT, and a limited number will subsequently be referred to the Competition Commission. In addition, if the offer gives rises to a **concentration** (ie, a potential monopoly) within the EC, the European Commission may initiate proceedings. This can result in considerable delay, and constitutes grounds for abandoning a bid.

8.2   Procedure for public bid - overview

The following steps will be followed in the takeover of a quoted company:

(a) Appointment of advisors - merchant bank, lawyers, accountants, stockbrokers

(b) Decision as to whether to approach target company before bid (in the hope of gaining preliminary support) or whether to launch a 'hostile' or 'predatory' bid

(c) Possible acquisition of shares in the market in combination with bid - regulated by the City Code:

3%   A stake over 3% must be disclosed to the target company.

15% – 30%	Limits are placed on the amount of additional shares that can be acquired within any seven day period.

The significance of this rule is that it limits to 15% of the total available the number of shares that can be bought in a 'dawn raid' – a quick, organised share-buying operation, usually over in a few minutes, which is often a prelude to a full bid. Such raids are considered by many to be inequitable to non-institutional shareholders who will not hear of the operation until it is over; but in any event, they are much rarer than in the past, since institutional shareholders have found in general that they obtain more for their shares by waiting for a full bid.

30% +	A bid must be made for the remaining shares.
50% +	Is the minimum amount the bidder must end up with as a result of a bid ie, the bidder cannot force acceptance if he is then left with say 40%.
90%	The normal percentage stipulated by the bidder below which he may still withdraw from the bid.

(d) Stages of the offer itself - deadlines and rules specified by City Code:

- **Offer document** - must be posted within twenty-eight days of the announcement of a bid, and is subject to the provisions of the **Yellow Book**. It will also generally contain a profit forecast (with merchant banker's and accountant's reports), and often a property revaluation.

- **Closing date** - an offer must generally stay open for twenty-one days after posting. If revised, it must stay open for a further fourteen days.

- **Withdrawal of acceptances** - a shareholder may withdraw his acceptance forty-two days after the offer document has been posted, if the offer has not gone 'unconditional'.

- **Revision** - no offer may be revised longer than forty-six days after posting.

- **Lapsing** - an offer must go unconditional, or will lapse sixty days after posting. An extension may, however, be granted if another bidder has made an offer.

(e) Offers may be for cash or, in principle, for any of the alternative forms of consideration set out above. If for cash, the bidder may use its existing cash or borrowing facilities, or, where shares are available as an alternative, such shares may be underwritten, so that acceptors can accept cash if they desire.

8.3   Acquisition of private companies

The acquisition of private companies can be undertaken without public scrutiny and, therefore, with the following particular characteristics:

(a) Detailed commercial and financial information will be available in advance of an agreement.

(b) There will be an agreed price structure and consideration to suit both parties.

(c) There will be detailed legal documentation, usually consisting of a contract between the two parties, including the following elements

- Structure and consideration for the transaction.

- Warranties given by the vendor in respect of the business covering accuracy of information supplied, asset valuations and trading results at/to a specified date after the latest accounts, realisability of current assets, contingent liabilities etc.

- Tax indemnity covering past, current, and often future tax liabilities resulting from trading up to the date of acquisition.

- How vendor's liability in relation to warranties and tax indemnity might be satisfied.

Completion is then accomplished when consideration passes in exchange for shares. However, an important event at either or both contract or completion is the tabling of a disclosure letter, as described above. This provides the vendor with a last chance to declare any facts which might form the basis for subsequent claims, and the purchaser to repudiate the contract.

Issues of desirable information, price structure and consideration have been discussed earlier. There are often one or more **intermediaries** involved who have been instrumental in bringing the two parties together. They may be **merchant/investment banks**, or they may be specialist **acquisition brokers**, usually small operations and often single traders. The scale of remuneration to the intermediaries is normally a function of the final amount of consideration paid. The fees will be charged either to the acquiring or to the acquired company, depending on for whom the intermediary is acting.

An important early stage in a transaction, usually after an initial expression of interest by a would-be acquirer, is the signing of a **confidentiality letter** by the latter. This would normally bind the would-be acquirer legally not to disclose any confidential information received by it to evaluate the possible acquisition to third parties, unless such information were already in its possession or in the public domain. It would also require, in the event of the transaction not going ahead, any confidential papers in its possession to be returned.

9   DEFENCE AGAINST TAKEOVERS

9.1   Management attitude to a bid

Every group is potentially subject to takeover, and clearly, as with any asset, there will be a price at which the owners (shareholders) may be induced to sell their shares.

A problem arises, however, where a publicly quoted group, with a widely spread shareholding, receives an unwelcome ('predatory') bid, with the clear objective of buying the group at a price below the value that **management** put on it. It is important to emphasise that this is a management, as opposed to shareholders', view, since presumably the latter, if they are induced to sell, will be happy with the transaction, on the 'willing buyer, willing seller' assumption.

It is also important to determine management's motives in defending a bid strongly, ie, whether its intention is genuinely to obtain the best price for the shares, and prevent them being sold below their intrinsic value, or merely to maintain the group's independence at any price – which may not be the best solution for shareholders.

9.2   Non-financial considerations

Two further reasons for strong resistance arise from time to time, regardless of the financial benefits to shareholders:

(a)   Monopoly. This is generally defined by reference to laws regulating market shares but can also involve any transaction above a defined size.

(b)   Employee interest. It is occasionally argued that employment will be more secure if the group remains independent than it would be under a new employer whose objectives may be major rationalisation/divestment, which may include reductions in the workforce.

The emphasis of current political attitudes to corporate law is increasingly on the rights of employees as well as shareholders, and so employment consideration may well become increasingly important in the future.

9.3   Reasons for predatory bids

The circumstances under which a predator may seek to buy a group at less than full value are usually as follows:

(a)   The share price is depressed. This can usually be identified by:

(i)   the group's market value being below the net value of its shareholders' funds; or

(ii)   the group's price/earnings ratio being below, or its yield being above that for its sector.

In this case, however, the predator may believe that under its management the group can recover and perform much better financially than under existing management.

(b)   The group's prospects are better than the share price would indicate. A period of fluctuating profits may be about to be followed by a good recovery. A predator might recognise this before it became apparent to the stock market as a whole, and seek to capitalise on the opportunity.

(c)   The group occupies a strong position in one or more markets. The predator may see the acquisition of the group as a unique opportunity to purchase a major market share, and wish to do so without paying the market premium which should, in theory, attach to such a one-off situation.

The purpose of corporate defence is, therefore, either to obtain a full and satisfactory price from an unwelcome bidder, or to ward off the bid, and remain independent. It would also seek to ward off the bid if it felt that national economic interest, as defined by law, or employees' interests might be seriously threatened.

9.4   Strategic defence

The principal aim of strategic defence is to try to eliminate, as far as possible, the attractions of the group to a would-be predator.

(a)   **Share price maximisation**

It is clear from above that a depressed share price, either from fundamental business difficulties, or where a recovery may be shortly forthcoming which has not yet been recognised by the market, is a major attraction for predators.

The fundamental causes of a depressed share price are poor or patchy profitability, however measured, and/or uncertainties about the future of the group.

Clearly a vital management objective is to maximise return on investment in whichever way this is defined. It is often possible to enhance this return by identifying assets or business units which do not conform to certain minimum profitability criteria. Elimination of such low returns can enhance the share price level substantially, and should receive priority from a management seeking a strong defensive position.

The elimination of business uncertainties is also important.   These uncertainties will principally concern any area of the group's trading – market, production, etc – where there are doubts affecting profitability. It is first of all necessary to identify the uncertainties, and then to seek to allay them, either by management action or, where the doubts are unjustified, by convincing the public that the uncertainties do not exist.

(b)   **The importance of group strategy**

A great strength in this regard is the existence of an agreed and well-understood group strategy, complemented by divisional strategies further down the line. Provided the strategy is communicated effectively externally and is well understood, and provided group action and results can be judged in the light of its existence, it will reassure shareholders and tend to maintain the share price. Furthermore, it should nominate specifically the approach to any major ongoing uncertainties.

(c)   **Communication**

In addition, a group may be vulnerable when recovery may be about to take place after a period of low profitability or losses. It should, therefore, work hard to communicate this potential recovery whilst being careful to give accurate information and assessments. Damage will be caused to the group if performance does not match the results which the outside world have been led to expect. The allaying of shareholders' fears regarding uncertainties, and the external communication of group strategy, both point to the importance of effective financial public relations in seeking to maximise share price. These can be cultivated in the following ways:

(i)   Use of a good external financial public relations adviser. Such a role should not in any way substitute for management's direct communication with the media, but should complement it, where appropriate, through extending the range of contacts, advising on the style and method of communication, and keeping an ear close to the ground.

(ii)   Development of a close relationship with the group's stockbrokers. The latter are usually seen as being a source of good quality information about the group, and they should therefore be provided with all publicly available material, and have a good grasp of the strategy and current trading.

(iii)   Development of a close relationship with the stock market research community and financial press. Most research analysts have a detailed knowledge of the markets they follow, and an understanding of a group's activities and sympathy with its objectives, together with personal relationships of trust and respect – all of which can be very helpful in external communications. In addition, many journalists use research analyst contact for background material for articles.

(iv)   Use of press and brokers' results conferences. Many groups use these occasions (which usually take place on the day that the preliminary announcement of interim or final results takes place) formally to restate their aims and objectives and to measure them against their actual trading results. They provide an opportunity to disseminate corporate financial messages to a wide media audience.

(v)   Enhancement of the quality of presentation, and depth of information, of the annual report. In particular, close attention should be paid to the clarity and content of the chairman's statements in the annual and interim reports, and at the annual general meeting. These are usually scrutinised and analysed in considerable detail.

(vi)   Development of direct shareholder relationships. Direct communication with as many shareholders as possible should be sought, through meetings and visits to the group's facilities. Institutional shareholders, who tend to hold the majority of shares, often take a very passive role but have become increasingly active in recent years.

(d)   **Dividend policy**

The level of cash dividend is often held to influence share price. Accordingly, it is argued that an increase in dividend should cause a rise in share price. However, Chapter 4 has argued that the level of dividend, and thus dividend policy, should be based fundamentally on the cash flow generation, debt policy and returns on assets generated by the group. Thus, a change in dividend without regard to these fundamentals, or changes in them, can only be a short-term expedient towards share price maximisation.

Furthermore, a high dividend payout narrows the scope for large increases in dividend in the event of a bid. Such a policy, if continued, may actually have the effect of weakening the group's defence following a bid.

Achievement of the correct level of dividend, having regard to the fundamentals, will, however, have the most beneficial effect on share price over time, and this, in contrast to short-term changes, is of vital significance.

(e)   **Strategic shareholdings**

Another strategic mechanism which is often used is the taking of a large strategic share stake by a friendly party, or of a cross-shareholding with that party. This has the advantage that it does, initially at least, deny any predator a major portion of the equity of the target company.

It does, however, have several disadvantages:

(i)   The attitude of an initially friendly shareholder may change, and a predator may make great efforts to dislodge his shareholding. It may be more expensive to acquire, but it may prove easier for a bidder to win over than a lot of small shareholdings.

(ii)   Such a shareholding or cross-shareholding may be interpreted as a sign of weakness and may actually attract predators.

(iii)   It is arguable whether such a shareholding, if its object is to prevent any bid, is in the best interests of shareholders. Furthermore, a cross-shareholding is often criticised, in that it ties up significant amounts of capital in both companies.

(f)   **Maximisation of total price payable**

It is also argued that, since most predators' resources are limited, it is worth maximising the total price payable, either by a rights issue, or by the acquisitions of assets for shares or loan stock.

In the case of a rights issue, the value of the equity will be increased, since the proceeds will initially go to reduce the company's borrowings in an equal and opposite amount. However, the defender's position may be weaker, in that, if a predator bids on a share-for-share basis, the total borrowings involved (in this case the internal debt of the target company) would be less. Under-gearing may in this case prove a substantial weakness since it would make the target company more attractive.

In the case of an increase in gearing, eg, buying assets in exchange for loan stock, two negative points apply. First, cash acquisitions causing an increase in gearing should be consonant with the group strategy: if not, they will become a waste of financial resource, and may lead to financial weakness which may even accelerate a bid. Second, if safe gearing limits are thereby breached, the group creates a further financial risk for itself.

However, high gearing, if within safe limits, may constitute some form of defence, in that, in contrast to the above, it will actually increase the total cash consideration for a share-for-share bidder with limited resources.

(g)   **Acquisitions by the target company**

Finally, acquisitions by the target company may themselves be a wise strategic defence, though again only if in accordance with group strategy. If for cash or debt they may increase group gearing, but they may also broaden the base of the group beyond areas of interest to the predator. If for shares, they may take the combined market capitalisation of the company target beyond a potential predator's reach. Further, where limited business areas of risk or uncertainty are present in group trading, they may reduce the impact of such risks/uncertainties by lowering the percentage of overall profits on which they impact.

9.5   Good housekeeping

There are four elements of good housekeeping which should be observed at all times.

(a)   A group should keep a close watch on its share register and share trading, in order to identify any sinister shareholding buildup at an early stage.

(b)   A group should also make sure its forecasting techniques are effective and understood throughout its business units. An accurate forecast for at least the current year's trading is a vital part of a defence document, and would normally have to be independently corroborated by a firm of accountants, so that it should stand up to rigid scrutiny.

(c)   Since a takeover offer may quickly follow the acquisition of an initial share stake as part of a predator's tactics, it is essential to be able to draft promptly a document in response, expressing the reasons why, in the opinion of the board and its advisors, the price which might be offered in the event of a predatory bid is inadequate.

This document would, **inter alia**, contain the following:

- Comparison of offer price with recent market price of the group, comments on premium offered, and comparison with net assets. Also, comment on the disadvantages to remaining shareholders of a sizeable share stake.

- Details of any asset revaluation which might be appropriate.

- Comments on current trading, emphasising recovery and growth situation in the light of group strategy.

- Profit and dividend forecast.

- Rebuttal of commercial logic of bid, taking each point put forward by offeror. Also reference, if appropriate, to regulatory environment and national interest.

(d)   An eye should be kept on all likely predators with a view to anticipating their actions. Clearly, considerations of size (has the relevant candidate the financial resource to acquire the group?) and industrial synergies will best determine such a list.

9.6   Executive action following a bid

Naturally, a key element of defence is to achieve the maximum advance preparation, but it is also necessary to examine the likely course of a bid, and what needs to be done to give the strongest possible position during that time.

This will vary from country to country, but as an example, the following sets out the possible course of a UK bid, which has not been agreed by the two parties, illustrating the large number of actions and responses which take place.

Day 1   Chairman of group receives letter from chairman of X informing him of X's intention to make an offer for group. (It is probable that X's merchant bankers will advise group's merchant bankers simultaneously).

Secretary of group will receive formal letter requesting a copy of the register of shareholders, together with a set of addressed envelopes.

Day 1/2   Board of group meets with their merchant bankers and, assuming it is agreed the offer is unacceptable and should be contested, issues press release to this effect. Merchant bankers will speak direct to certain City editors to ensure maximum publicity.

Merchant bankers and auditors should commence work on preparing and verifying any profit forecast which the board of the group considers it appropriate to make. This forecast has to be reported on, both by the auditors and by the group's merchant bankers (confirmatory letters from both parties must appear in any defence documents), and work on this should be completed by about Day 14.

Prior to day 28   X to post offer document.

Unless consent of the Takeover Panel is received to the contrary, X must have posted offer document to group's shareholders by Day 28. In practice, in a contested offer, it is unlikely that X will be in a position to post its document by Day 14, but the work on it should be substantially completed by then.

(Assuming posting is Day 14)

Days 15 – 35   This is the first twenty-one day period during which X's offer remains open for acceptance.

By Day 28   (ie, 14 days after the offer document has been dispatched) Group's first defence document posted. This will include financial and commercial reasons for rejecting the offer. Group's board will need to consider these in detail with merchant bankers.

By Day 33   X will probably respond to group's defence.

Depending on the timing, group may or may not have time to make a further response before Day 35. A response by press advertisement will often occur.

Day 35   In a contested offer, it is unlikely that X will have sufficient acceptances by the first closing date to go unconditional, and therefore the offer will probably be extended for a further period.

Day 40   Group's second defence document should be posted by this date.

Day 42   If offer is not unconditional as to acceptances, shareholders have right of withdrawal (twenty-one days after first closing date).

Day 60   X's final opportunity to declare offer unconditional as to acceptances. If it is not unconditional by this time the offer must lapse.

In this example the procedure lasts 60 days, but with pauses between events. It is very important that the time available be used to its best advantage, as over-hasty reactions can be as unhelpful as over-slow ones.

9.7   The reaction of the target company

A 'dawn raid', ie, a sudden entry into the stockmarket by the predator at a price above the previous market level, with a view to acquiring a major stake in a short space of time, in that it may lead to a further takeover offer a few days later, requires a quick reaction, for which the draft document set out in 9.5 above will be very helpful.

There are a number of key issues to consider at the outset of a bid. First, board authorities should be obtained swiftly, and many groups set up a small sub-committee of the board to deal with urgent matters during the course of a bid, which cannot be referred in time to the full board. Its authority should, however, be closely circumscribed by the board. It is usually essential for one senior executive only to be designated for press contacts.

All bids involve considerable numbers of public statements. Very little, apart from an outline, can be agreed in advance, although vital holding statements relating to dawn raids or outright bids can be prepared. The next moves will depend on circumstances, and in particular on the identity and stated intentions of the predator.

A particular tactic during an unfriendly/undesired bid is to find a 'white knight', a friendly party who would act in the interests of the defender. Such a friend might already have taken a share stake as suggested above. However, as also suggested, this could be a high risk strategy.

A 'white knight' might also, during the course of a bid, make a full counter-bid, as a more desirable acquirer than the initial predator, or might acquire shares which can be used in support of the board.

It may be desirable to have drawn up a short list of 'white knights' in advance of a bid, but a board which is confident of its ability to resist a bid may not wish to compromise its independence by involving other companies.

It is vital to ascertain, as early as possible, but preferably immediately a predator appears (eg, on the same day), what its intentions are. It may be difficult to draw these out in any detail, but the aim should be to obtain its plans for the group, how it intends to manage it, fund it and develop it. It is also important to analyse the predator's financial and commercial record, as well as its stated strategy, and the course both before and after acquisition of previous successful takeovers.

9.8   Anti-takeover mechanisms

Many companies, in a effort to remain independent or to win time to analyse effectively a takeover bid, have implemented anti-takeover mechanisms.

Examples are:

(a)   **Poison pill**

The most commonly used and seemingly most effective takeover defence is the so-called poison pill. Examples are:

(i)   **Flip-in pills** involve the granting of rights to shareholders, other than the potential acquirer, to purchase shares of the target company at a deep discount. This type of plan will dilute the ownership interest of the potential acquirer.

(ii)   **Back-end rights** are usually in the form of a cash dividend allowing shareholders other than the potential acquirer to exchange their shares for cash or senior debt securities at a price determined by the Board of Directors. The price set by the Board is usually well in excess of the market price or the price likely to be offered by a potential acquirer. Because the price that the target shareholder would receive is likely to be higher than that offered by the potential acquirer, shares will not be tendered.

(b)   **Pac Man**

Like the video game, the Pac Man defence occurs when a target company turns around and tries to swallow its pursuer, by use of a counter-tender offer. Pac Man, while colourful in name, has seldom been used successfully.

(c)   **Disposal of the Crown Jewels/Scorched Earth**

In a 'disposal of the Crown Jewels' defence, the target sells the assets which are of greatest interest to the raider. A more extreme variant of 'Crown Jewels' is the 'Scorched Earth' defence. In practical terms, this means that the target company liquidates all or substantially all of its assets. leaving nothing to the raider, thereby eliminating the raider's motive for acquiring the target.

(d)   **Fatman**

The other side of the 'Crown Jewels' and 'Scorched Earth' strategies is the 'Fatman' defence: the target company acquires a large and/or underperforming company in order to decrease its attractiveness to the raider.

(e)   **Golden parachutes**

One tactic that has often been mis-labelled as a takeover defence is the use of golden parachutes which are, quite simply, severance arrangements for senior officers of the firm should there be a change in the control. Although a golden parachute for one Chief Executive Officer involved in a takeover battle in the USA was reportedly US$35m, they usually are a low multiple of the most recent year's salary.

Set out below is a summary of the defence mechanisms available to the target company indicating whether they are more likely to be used pre or post offer.

Summary of defences against takeover bids

	Pre offer	*Post offer*
Maximise share price	✓	✓
Clear strategy	✓	✓
Communication	✓	✓
Strategic shareholdings	✓	✓
Strategic acquisitions	✓	✓
Defence document	-	✓
Press contact	-	✓
White knight defence	-	✓
Poison pill	-	✓
Pac man	-	✓
Crown jewels	-	✓
Golden parachutes	-	✓

9.9   Activity

Follow the developments of bids in progress every day by reading a good financial newspaper. Can you see examples of where the above anti-takeover mechanisms have been used successfully?

Set out below is a 'diary' of the events from the recent hostile takeover of Wellcome by Glaxo.

'Diary' of Glaxo hostile takeover of Wellcome (1995)

21 January	City speculation that Glaxo has obtained 4% shareholding in Wellcome.
24 January	Glaxo offers £9 billion. Wellcome Trust accepts offer for its 40% shareholding. Stock Exchange announces investigation into earlier leaks.
	Glaxo raises £6½ billion corporate loan to finance bid.
25 January	Wellcome board appoints Morgan Stanley and Barings to advise.
27 January	Wellcome board rejects 'inadequate offer' and starts search for white knight. Chief executive travelling to Germany, US.
28 January	Wellcome Trust signs irrevocable undertaking to accept bid if no higher offer is made.
30 January	Wellcome Board as part of defence makes early announcement of 'new drug' Valtrex - replacement for one of its major earners, Zovirax, about to come out of patent. Also makes early announcement of results.

7 February	Wellcome board announces details of another new drug, Lamiatal.
8 February	Glaxo issues former offer document.
15 February	Wellcome board launches formal defence document. Claims company is worth considerably in excess of £9 billion. Stresses favourable sales forecasts for Retrovir (Aids drug) and Valtrex.
18 February	Court rules that Wellcome Trust can sell. Extends deadline before commitment becomes irrevocable.
1 March	Glaxo bid wins anti-trust clearance from European Commission. Wellcome board still searching for white knight. Rumours that Zeneca is interested.
6 March	Shareholders in Glaxo approve bid and agree proposed name of Glaxo-Wellcome.
8 March	Wellcome board acknowledges failure to find a white knight that can better the offer. Recommends Glaxo's offer to its shareholders. Board is bitter about trust's perceived disloyalty.
24 March	Wellcome's chief executive resigns. New management structure announced.

9.10 Defence document

A vital part of a defence document, which will obviously be prepared with the group's merchant bankers, will be the section dealing with the reasons for preferring the group's continued independence. This is a topic which, when it comes to be debated, can prove very controversial and take considerable time and effort to resolve and draft internally. Accordingly, it seems sensible to prepare this element of the defence circulars in draft form as soon as possible, having reached a reasonable consensus.

The section can take the form of a review of the past few years, comparing strategy and objectives against achievement; and then projecting the continuing strategy forward. The arguments would then be based on the requirement for independence to achieve projected strategic objectives.

In particular, the document would examine closely the predator's intentions, as previously determined, against the group's projected strategy and objectives; and of course it would discuss its ability, real desire and likelihood of carrying them out.

Such an examination would be the crucial basis for a successful defence. It should be appreciated that the less a predator has been prepared to say, the more ammunition he might provide for a victim's defence against his predatory bid.

At an appropriate time during the course of the bid, but not necessarily in the first defence document, a forecast, duly corroborated by an independent firm of chartered accountants, would normally be presented, for at least the current year's trading. This has already been discussed above.

9.11 Acceptable offers

Any board recognises that there is a point at which an offer becomes irresistible, although it would normally be appropriate to offer strong and logical resistance right up to this point. This is based primarily on price, but with important considerations being the interests of employees and customers.

Of course, directors recommending acceptance of a bid clearly have a duty to make sure that the price is the best available in the circumstances, and that independence is still not a better course, bearing in mind longer term considerations. A board can legitimately believe that shareholders may be financially better off by retaining their shares for a further period, instead of accepting a takeover offer, however attractive.

10   ISSUES INFLUENCING THE SUCCESS OF ACQUISITIONS

10.1   Pre-offer issues

Many acquisitions do not bring the benefits anticipated at the time that the acquisition was planned. Prospective acquirers should ask themselves the following questions:

- has the alternative of organic growth been fully considered?

- have alternative target companies been researched?

- are we paying too much? If involved in a contested bid with several prospective purchasers, it is better to withdraw unsuccessfully from the contest than overpay

- will the key managers in both the acquiring and acquired company remain motivated after the takeover?

- will the target company's future resource needs be satisfied under its new owners?

10.2   Post-audit and monitoring of post-acquisition success

All too often a management's attention turns after an acquisition to planning the next acquisition rather than ensuring that the newly acquired company settles in to its new group comfortably.

However lessons can be learned by carrying out a post-audit of the acquisition some years after the date of the takeover to examine its progress and compare this with the plan. There are three reasons for undertaking these analyses:

(a)   To discourage managers from spending money on doubtful projects, because they may be called to account at a later date.

(b)   It may be possible over a period of years to discern a trend of reliability in the estimates of various managers.

(c)   A similar project may be undertaken in the future, and then the recently completed project will provide a useful basis for estimation.

The management writer Drucker has suggested five golden rules for the process of post-acquisition integration.

Rule 1   Both acquirer and acquiree should share a 'common core of unity' including shared technology and markets, not just financial links.

Rule 2   The acquirer should ask 'What can we offer them?' as well as 'What's in it for us?'

Rule 3   The acquirer should treat the products, customers etc, of the acquired company with respect, not disparagingly

Rule 4   The acquiror should provide top management with relevant skills for the acquired company within a year

Rule 5   Cross-company promotions of staff should happen within one year

11   CHAPTER SUMMARY

All topics in this chapter are highly examinable. Computational examples would usually be centred around the valuation of companies for acquisition or the predicted effects on share prices when mergers take place. There have in the past been many discussion elements of questions on all parts of this chapter however, and this is unlikely to change in the future.

12   SELF TEST QUESTIONS

12.1   Name four examples of synergy gained from operating economies. (1.4)

12.2   Why might a company want to be acquired? (1.7)

12.3   Why do most combinations fail to produce the anticipated benefits? (1.9)

12.4   Is merger and takeover activity more common in the UK or Germany? (1.11)

12.5   How did accounting standards used to encourage UK takeover activity? (1.11)

12.6   What is a dawn raid? (8.2)

12.7   What limits does the City Code place on dawn raids? (8.2)

12.8   What sequence of deadline dates does the City Code impose on offers? (8.2)

12.9   What is a golden parachute? (9.8)

13   EXAMINATION TYPE QUESTIONS

13.1   Defences against takeover

Your company is subject to an unexpected takeover bid by a rival company. Your board of directors proposes to reject the bid, but believes that increased bids might follow.

Discuss the policies that your company might adopt to defend itself against the takeover bid(s), and comment upon the significance of the **City Code** on takeovers and mergers in this process.

(13 marks)

13.2   Downcrest plc

Downcrest plc is a UK medium-sized company quoted on the Stock Exchange, whose 1m shares in issue are currently traded at 18p each. Its shareholders' funds are £250,000, and its post-tax earnings are 3.25p per share. It has maintained steady earnings, and has been able to reduce its debt to £50,000; market interest rates are approximately 12% pa.

Rawhide plc, also quoted on the Stock Exchange, has quietly built up a 2.9% stake in Downcrest and makes a market raid at 25p per share, acquiring 14.9% as a result. Rawhide has been a persistent predator, although it is basically in the same markets as Downcrest, and it has 10m shares in issue currently trading at 80p. Shareholders' funds are £8m. Its latest earnings are 11.7p per share and its acquisition activities have driven up its debt to £7m. Both companies are paying tax at 35%.

(a)   What is the likely course of events following the raid?

(b)   What defences could Downcrest mount against a full bid?

(c)   How might Downcrest have avoided the raid in the first instance?

(20 marks)

13.3   Sonhan Trust plc

Sonhan Trust plc is a large Anglo-French conglomerate. For some time the chairman has wanted the company to expand into the health-care industry and a number of companies have been examined as potential take-over targets. However so far, no suitable company has been identified.

Sonhan's auditors have recently brought to the chairman's attention a small US unquoted health-care company, Happy Health Inc and have provided the following financial information:

Latest balance sheet: Happy Health Inc

	$'000	$'000	$'000
Issued Common Stock			100
Reserves			810
			910
Financing:			
Production equipment (net)			1,305
Raw material stocks	250		
Finished product stocks	782		
Trade receivables	1,490		
Bank balances	316		
		2,838	
Less:			
Trade payables	1,507		
Short term bank loan	1,726		
		3,233	
			(395)
			910

Historical income statement record

($'000s)	Current year (est)	One year ago	Two years ago	Three years ago	Four years ago
Net income	106	96	100	138	62
Extraordinary items	10	(20)	-	(5)	-
	116	76	100	133	62
Dividend	50	50	50	45	41
Retained income	66	26	50	88	21

Sonhan Trust's corporate policy analysts have undertaken some further enquiries about Happy Health Inc and have estimated that the company's production equipment would have a replacement value of around $1.5 million and a sale value of $1 million. Similarly raw material and finished goods stocks would have a replacement cost value of around $1.2 million and a sale value of $1.1 million. The industry-standard level of bad debts is 1.9% of sale value.

Sonhan's corporate policy analysts have estimated that the average asset beta of quoted US health-care companies is 0.90 and the average price-earnings ratio is 10. The current return on US Treasury Bonds is 7.5% and the excess market return on the New York Stock Exchange is 5%. Sonhan Trust estimates that its own weighted average cost of capital is 17% and a price-earnings ratio of 15.

Ignore tax.

Required

(a)   Estimate the $ value of Happy Health Inc's equity capital on the basis of:

    (i)   balance sheet value;

       (ii)   asset replacement cost;

       (iii)   break-up value;

       (iv)   dividend valuation model;

       (v)   earnings.   **(10 marks)**

(b)   Discuss the usefulness and limitations of the various valuation approaches used to place a value on the US company.   **(10 marks)**

(c)   Recommend what value you would place on Happy Health Inc.   **(3 marks)**

(d)   Briefly suggest how Sonhan Trust may best finance its purchase of Happy Health Inc.

                    (2 marks)
                    (Total: 25 marks)

14   ANSWERS TO EXAMINATION TYPE QUESTIONS

14.1   Defences against takeover

(Tutorial note:

This is a largely factual question. Note that it is not necessary to reproduce the whole of the City Code but simply to draw attention to areas relevant to this situation.)

Possible defences include

(a)   Try to convince your shareholders that the terms of the offer are unacceptable. Two approaches are commonly adopted in this situation:

       (i)   Attempt to show that the current share price of your firm is unrealistically low relative to your future potential. Asset revaluations, new profit forecasts and promises of rationalisation are commonly employed here.

       (ii)   If the offeror is proposing a share for share exchange the 'victim' company can attempt to convince shareholders that the offeror's equity is currently overvalued. The suitability of the bidding company to run the merged business can also be questioned. Lack of experience, absence of logic in the link up, hostility of the workforce are all commonly used arguments in this situation.

(b)   A 'reverse takeover', ie, make a counter-offer for the other company. It is helpful in this situation if the bidding company is of a similar size to the 'victim'. However, with the advent of the levered takeover this may still be possible, even with a mismatch in size.

(c)   The so-called 'white knight' defence, ie, to try to find a more acceptable counter-bidder for your company. In this case all bidders must be supplied with the same information.

(d)   Attempt to have the bid referred to the Competition Commission. This will at least delay the takeover, and may prevent it completely.

The City Code has no legal authority but it is an attempt by the City to regulate the process of acquisitions and mergers. The major features of relevance to the above situation are:

       (i)   Directors of the offeree company must not sell their shares without consent of the Panel and when considering an offer they must act in the interests of the shareholders as a whole.

       (ii)   As soon as a firm offer is made shareholders must be informed by press notice.

       (iii)   Formal offers, supporting documents, press advertisements, recommendations of acceptance and rejection of an offer must be prepared with the same standard of care as a prospectus within the meaning of the *1985 Companies Act.*

(iv)   Shareholders must be put in possession of all the facts necessary for the formation of an informed judgement.

(v)   No new shares may be issued except where a formal contract already exists.

14.2   Downcrest plc

(a)   From Rawhide's past track record, it seems reasonably clear that the initial build-up of shares followed by the raid are a prelude to a full bid.

This bid could either follow the raid immediately, or Rawhide might choose the alternative route of buying further shares, in accordance with the Takeover Code, until it had achieved a 29.9% stake: 30% or over would require it to make a full bid.

Whenever the bid comes, it will be at least for 25p, which is the price paid in the market during the previous year. From Rawhide's point of view the procedure would be as follows:

(i)   Bid announced.

(ii)   Offer document posted (within twenty-eight days of announcement of bid) containing offer, which would be subject to at least two conditions:

(1)   No reference to the Competition Commission.

(2)   Acceptances in excess of 50%, and at Rawhide's option, not less than 90% of the share capital being received.

(iii)   Offer closes twenty-one days or later after the offer document posted, or offer revised and must, if revised, stay open for at least a further fourteen days, but it cannot be revised more than forty-six days after posting.

(iv)   Offer must go unconditional, or expire sixty days after posting, unless another bidder has made an offer.

From the Downcrest shareholders' point of view, acceptance of the first or any increased offer can take place at any time after the relevant document has been posted. In addition, if the offer has not gone unconditional within forty-two days (strictly twenty-one days after first closing date) the shareholder may withdraw.

From Downcrest's point of view, the objective must be either to resist an unattractive offer, or to obtain the very best price possible for the shares, having satisfied itself that the offer is in the interests of shareholders and taking into account the interests of employees and creditors.

The prime weapon which would be used by Downcrest would be its defence documents: in the event of a dawn raid followed by a build-up of a 29.9% shareholding prior to a full bid, these would probably take the form of a short interim document to Downcrest's shareholders, issued within days of the raid, followed by a full defence document about ten days after the offer document is posted.

Since Rawhide will almost certainly respond in detail to rebut the arguments in the first full defence document, a second document might be sent about fourteen days later.

(b)   Downcrest's defence is likely to have three prongs:

(i)   In view of Rawhide's position in the same market, it would certainly seem, **prima facie**, as if the Office of Fair Trading should be consulted to see whether they would consider making a recommendation to the Secretary of State for onward reference to the Competition Commission. This would certainly be relevant if either Downcrest or Rawhide held more than 25% of an appropriate national or regional market, and the consultation would normally take place very shortly after the bid was announced, and before the offer document was sent out.

(ii)   Downcrest would also argue that the price of 25p proposed was too cheap, being exactly equal to its book shareholders' funds and with no regard for its business prospects. It would in the first instance revalue its property assets, if appropriate, and emphasise its future earnings and cash generation capacity, with forecasts as appropriate, including a dividend forecast.

(iii)   Downcrest would argue that Rawhide's actual performance in the same industry was in reality worse than its own, as follows:

		Downcrest £'000	Rawhide £'000
1.	Debt	50	7,000
2.	Shareholders' funds	250	8,000
3.	Total value (1 + 2)	300	15,000
4.	Post-tax profit	32.5	1,170
5.	Pre-tax profit	50	1,800
6.	Interest paid	6	840
7.	Trading profit (5 + 6)	56	2,640
8.	Return on capital (7 ÷ 3)	18.7%	17.6%

It would therefore argue that it, Downcrest, was a better custodian of its assets by making a higher return on its capital; that it therefore had a higher quality management, and Rawhide certainly could not expect to improve on management performance, given its track record; and that there was therefore no commercial logic in the bid – Downcrest's shareholders, if they accepted Rawhide's shares as consideration, would become investors in a lower quality group.

(c)   Downcrest's defences probably needed strengthening as follows:

(i)   It allowed Rawhide to buy nearly 3% without noting the build-up in shares. This could have been avoided by watching the level of new shareholdings, and any unaccounted-for nominee accumulations in the shareholders' register.

(ii)   The fact that it was, before the raid, selling at a sizeable $\left(\dfrac{25-8}{25}\right)$ = 28% discount to net asset value, despite a better underlying trading performance than Rawhide, indicated that its financial communication programme could be much improved.

(iii)   It appeared to have given no thought to a possible 'white knight' in the event of an unfriendly bid. Given Rawhide's low level of attraction such an alternative bidder should at least bring some enhanced commercial value to Downcrest.

(iv)   It should give thought to increasing its gearing through good quality investment and acquisition in order to increase the return on shareholders' funds.

14.3   Sonhan Trust plc

(a)   (i)

	$'000
Unadjusted balance sheet value	910
Less: Estimated bad debts	(28)
Balance sheet value of company	882

(ii)

Balance sheet value of company	882
Plus increased worth of production equipment	195
Plus increased worth of stock	168
Replacement cost value of company	1,245

(iii)

Balance sheet value of company	882
Less reduced worth of production equipment	(305)
Plus increased worth of stocks	68
Break-up value of company	645

(iv)   On the basis that $g = r \times b$, where

$$r = \frac{106}{910} = 0.116$$

$$b = \frac{116 - 50}{116} = 0.569$$

$$g = 0.116 \times 0.569 = 0.066 \text{ or } 6.6\%$$

$$K_e = 7.5\% + (5\% \times 0.90) = 12\%$$

$$\text{Value of company} = \frac{\$50,000 \ (1.066)}{0.12 \ - \ 0.066} = \$987,000$$

In this calculation there is some scope to exercise judgement. Hence the profit before extraordinary items was used in the calculation of r, the company's return on capital employed. However, profit after extraordinary items was taken in the calculation of b, the rate of earnings retention. Finally, although the rate of discount used (12%) was the result of Sonhan's corporate policy analyst's estimate, this appeared to be more suitable to use than Sonhan's cost of capital which need bear no relationship to the required return from the health-care company.

Alternatively, on the basis of estimating 'g' from the past rate of dividend growth:

$$\$41,000 \ (1 + g)^4 = \$50,000$$

$$g = \left(\frac{50,000}{41,000}\right)^{1/4} - 1 = 0.051$$

Therefore the value of the company is

$$\frac{\$50,000 \ (1 + 0.051)}{0.12 - 0.051} = \$762,000$$

(v)   There is again scope to exercise judgement with this valuation. Valuing the company on the basis of the P/E multiple of similar companies, and again using the profit figure before extraordinary items produces a value of: $\$106,000 \times 10 = \$1.06$ million.

However, it is often recommended as a rule of thumb that when valuing an unquoted company a suitable reduction is made in the P/E of a similar but quoted company to allow for the lower liquidity of an investment in an unquoted company. Hence, an alternative value might be:

$$\$106,000 \times 8 = \$848,000$$

(b)   Each of the five valuation bases will be examined in turn. The balance sheet value of the company - especially when it is in historical cost terms as it appears to be in the case of the question - has severe limitations to its usefulness in the valuation process. The main limitation is that the asset values are based on historical costs, adjusted where necessary by relatively arbitrary accounting conventions (eg, depreciation and stock valuation methods). To be useful these values should be based on opportunity cost concepts. It is difficult to justify any role in the valuation process for this particular approach.

The replacement cost valuation of the company provides a useful figure as it could be interpreted as indicating to the prospective buyer the likely cost of gathering together - on a piecemeal basis - a collection of assets similar to that held by the company. In circumstances where the agreed purchase price is greater than this value, the difference would indicate the value placed on the company's intangible assets - for example, its management team and expertise and the management information systems which bind the assets together. One limitation of this valuation base is that it is only likely to be of interest in the valuation of a manufacturing company - as opposed to a service company - because of its focus on the tangible assets of the business. The other main limitation is caused by the difficulty in identifying replacement values, especially where the assets are specialised and/or subject to rapid technological change.

The break-up value of the company's assets provides a useful 'bottom line' valuation figure. It is referred to as the 'break-up' value of the business as it reflects what the existing owner of the business could expect to obtain if he were to sell off the assets of the business on a piecemeal basis, rather than as a going concern. It therefore represents the very minimum acceptable value of the company to the existing owner.

The drawbacks with the approach are similar to those encountered with replacement cost valuation. The approach is only of real interest when valuing an asset-intensive business and there may also be difficulties in obtaining reliable realisable values - especially where good second-hand markets in the company's assets do not exist.

The dividend valuation model approach is likely to provide the most valid valuation of the five approaches. It operates on the basis that the company's value is determined by the future cash flow stream generated by the company for its owners (ie, the dividends), discounted to present value. Thus this approach could be said to be valuing the company on an economic basis. The main limitations of the approach concern the reliability of the estimate of the future dividend stream that the investment will generate for its new owner and the identification of a discount rate that would correctly reflect the company's systematic risk.

The final valuation approach - using a P/E multiple - is very widely used and it is likely to provide an important valuation figure in practice. The limitation of the approach is the limitation of the P/E multiple itself. The P/E multiple is supposed to be a function of two characteristics of the company: its prospects for future earnings growth and the degree of uncertainty surrounding these future earnings (their so-called 'quality'). The problem is that there is no set of guide-lines as to how these two elements combine within a single P/E multiple.

Therefore although the question gives the average P/E multiple of health-care companies, whether Happy Health Inc is genuinely similar to the industry average - in both respects - is open to some doubt.

(c)   On the basis of the calculations carried out in part (a) of the answer, and in the light of the comments made above in part (b), it is possible to estimate the likely range of values around which negotiations between Sonhan Trust and Happy Health might take place.

The minimum value is likely to be provided by the break-up value of $645,000; whilst the maximum value might be given by that based on the P/E approach using a multiple of 10% $1.06 million. The final agreed value may well be around the $800,000 – $900,000 area suggested by the dividend valuation model and the P/E approach where the reduced multiple of 8 is used.

(d)   Sonhan Trust would be exposed to both transaction and translation foreign exchange risk through the purchase of Happy Health Inc. This exposure could be greatly reduced by financing the purchase with a matching $ loan raised either on the US capital market or the international (Euro-$) capital market.

13 FINANCIAL RESTRUCTURING

INTRODUCTION & LEARNING OBJECTIVES

This chapter examines the financial restructuring possibilities open to UK companies. It begins by looking at divestments, where a company withdraws its investment in all or part of a business that it operates.

The specific topic of management buyouts and buy-ins is examined next. MBOs became increasingly popular throughout the 1980s as a means of companies shedding non-core businesses without attracting the negative publicity accompanying closure.

Finally more general schemes of reconstruction are introduced. You must be able to propose a workable scheme given a specific scenario in the exam.

When you have studied this chapter you should be able to do the following:

- Explain why a company would carry out a divestment policy.
- Define MBOs and their possible variants.
- Explain why parent companies might wish to sell a company through an MBO.
- Discuss possible sources of financing MBOs.
- Explain buy-ins and their particular advantages and disadvantages.
- Understand reconstruction schemes under s.135 and s.425 *CA 1985*.

1 THE NATURE OF DIVESTMENT

1.1 Introduction

 Definition Divestment is the withdrawal of investment in a business. This can be achieved either by selling the whole business to a third party or by selling the business assets piecemeal.

The cash released by a divestment can either be returned to the investors, or invested elsewhere in another opportunity. It should be appreciated that divestment is just as common as investment as for every buyer there must be a seller.

1.2 Reasons for divestments

The principal motives for divestments will be if they either do not conform to group or business unit strategy; or if they fail **prima facie** to meet group financial hurdle rate criteria. They are often a cheaper and cleaner alternative than closure of the business. It is comparatively easy to identify divestment candidates against these two tests.

It is, however, also important to measure the financial impact of divestment before any final decision is taken on divestment candidates which fail the two tests suggested above. This evaluation would generally take the form of a comparison of the potential price available for the relevant business unit and the financial impact on the remainder of the group, against the financial returns (or losses) available from the business unit if it were retained. The divestment decision should, in principle, only be taken if the returns of the business unit as retained as compared with the 'disinvestment opportunity cost' – ie, the price obtainable for the business unit do not exceed the group hurdle rates. If the hurdle rates are exceeded, a further critical examination ought to be made as to whether or not the business unit should be kept, regardless of its strategic significance. Practically speaking, there are never many businesses which exceed the hurdles in this test; and those that do should not be hastily discarded.

As an example, a business unit is forecast to earn 120, or a 12% return on its capital employed of 1,000 in a group which has set a 20% ROCE hurdle target. It falls outside the group strategy, and could be sold for 800. Comparing return (120) with disinvestment opportunity cost (800) the implied ROCE is still only 15%, well under the group hurdle of 20%.

However, if the business unit could only be sold for 500, the comparison of return (120) with divestment opportunity cost (500) the implied ROCE rises to 24%. It may therefore be worth keeping the business unit after all, despite its strategic misfit. It should be noted that, in reverse, it could be purchased to yield 24%.

1.3   Information for divestments

In preparing for disinvestment, the information required of the vendor is generally sought in two stages. The first stage will involve the assessment of certain preliminary information, on which a would-be acquirer can base an initial expression of firm interest:

(a)   Historic financial information.

(b)   General description of marketing, production and distribution environment and facilities.

(c)   General description of management and employee resources.

The second stage will involve the would-be acquirer seeking further relevant detailed information in order to make a final decision. Thus, the vendor should be in a position to provide most or all of this information, at the outset of the divestment procedure.

1.4   Unbundling of quoted companies

After a period of acquisition activity, a company may find that it has bought several large groups of businesses, some related to its chosen core activities but some connected with non-core activities.

[Definition]   Unbundling is the process of selling off incidental non-core businesses to release funds, reduce gearing and allow management to concentrate on their chosen core businesses.

The 1980s were a period of intense takeover activity in the UK, with many companies buying a variety of different groups and becoming over-geared in the process. High interest rates in the late 1980s started a process of unbundling. Holding companies were forced to focus their activities clearly on a few core activities and reduce their gearing by selling their other non-core investments.

Perhaps the whole cycle will now start again with the low interest rate levels of the mid and late 1990s.

[Definition]   A demerger is the opposite of a merger. A group is split into two or more separate parts of roughly comparable size which are large enough to carry on independently after the split.

An example is the split of British Gas into BG and Centrica in the late 1990s. A demerger is appropriate if the sum of the values of the two companies after the split is greater than the value of the single company before the split.

2   MANAGEMENT BUYOUTS

2.1   Definitions

Management buyouts (MBOs) may be seen as another aspect of the merger and takeover area. In this case, however, the purchaser of the victim company is not another company, but the victim's existing management. Several variants of an MBO may be identified and are listed below.

(a)   **Management buyout**

Strictly these occur where the executive managers of a business join with financing institutions to buy the business from the entity which currently owns it. The managers may put up the bulk of the finance required for the purchase.

(b)   **Leveraged buyout**

These occur where the purchase price is beyond the financial resources of the managers and the bulk of the acquisition is financed by loan capital provided by other investors.

(c)   **Employee buyout**

This is similar to the above categories but all employees are offered a stake in the new business.

(d)   **Management buy-in**

This is where a group of managers from outside the business make the acquisition.

(e)   **Spin-out**

Similar to a buyout but the parent company maintains a stake in the business.

Overall the distinguishing feature of an MBO is that a group of managers acquires effective control and substantial ownership and forms an independent business.

2.2   Reasons for buyouts

Opportunities for MBOs may arise for several reasons:

(a)   The existing parent company of the 'victim' firm may wish to dispose of it. For example, the parent may be in financial difficulties and therefore require cash. Alternatively the subsidiary might not 'fit' with the parent's overall strategy, or might be too small to warrant the current management time being devoted to it. Finally, in the case of loss makers, selling the subsidiary to its managers may be a cheaper alternative than putting it into liquidation, particularly when redundancy and other wind-up costs are considered.

(b)   The victim company could be an independent firm whose private shareholders wish to sell out. This could be due to liquidity and tax factors or the lack of a family successor to fill the owner-manager role.

Management buyouts are not a new phenomenon and their incidence grew quickly in the 1980s. However during the recession situation of the early 1990s, MBOs became few and far between.

2.3   Advantages of buy-outs

Advantages to the disposing company

- if the subsidiary is loss-making, sale to the management will often be better financially than liquidation and closure costs.

- there is a known buyer

- better publicity can be earned by preserving employee's jobs rather than closing the business down.

- it is better for the existing management to acquire the company rather than it possibly falling into enemy hands (eg, competitors).

Advantages to the acquiring management

- it preserves their jobs
- it offers them the prospect of significant equity participation in their company.
- it is quicker than starting a similar business from scratch.
- they can carry out their own strategies, no longer having to seek approval from head office.

2.4   Issues to be addressed when preparing a buy-out proposal

MBOs are not dissimilar to other acquisitions and many of the factors to be considered will be the same:

(a)   **Do the current owners wish to sell?**

The whole process will be much easier (and cheaper) if the current owners wish to sell. However, some MBOs have been concluded despite initial resistance from the current owners, or in situations of bids for the victim from other would-be purchasers.

(b)   **Potential of the business**

The management team engaged in the buyout will be making the switch from a relatively safe salaried position to a risky ownership position. They must, therefore, ensure that the victim business will be a long-run profit generator. This will involve analysing the performance of the business and drawing up a business plan (products, markets, required new investment, sources of finance, etc) for future operations. Research shows that MBOs are less likely to fail than other types of new ventures, but several have collapsed, and managers must appreciate the risks they are taking and attempt to reduce them as far as possible.

On the other hand, it is worthwhile noting that many loss-making firms have been returned to profitability via management buyouts. Managers of a subsidiary are in a unique position to appreciate the potential of a business and to know where cost savings can be made by cutting out 'slack'.

(c)   **Loss of head office support**

On becoming an independent firm many of the services that are taken for granted in a large organisation may be lost. The importance of these services varies from one industry to another but provision will have to be made for support in the areas of finance, computing, research and development, etc. Although head office fees might be saved after the buyout these support services can involve considerable expense when purchased in the outside market.

(d)   **Quality of the management team**

The success of any MBO will be greatly influenced by the quality of the management team. It is important to ensure that all functional areas (marketing, sales, production, finance) are represented and that all managers are prepared to take the required risks. A united approach is important in all negotiations and a clear responsibility structure should be established within the team.

(e)   **The price**

As in any takeover situation the price paid will be crucial in determining the long-term success of the acquisition. The usual valuation techniques may be employed, often with more confidence as managers are likely to have a clearer idea of the future prospects of the firm. Care must be taken to ensure that all relevant aspects of the business are included in the package. For example, trademarks and patents may be as important as the physical assets of the firm. In a similar way responsibilities for redundancy costs, etc, must be clearly defined.

Managers may be able to secure the buyout at a favourable price as they are known to the existing owners, and the final price paid will be a matter for negotiation. It must be remembered, however, that the current directors of the firm have a responsibility to shareholders to obtain the best deal possible. This can often result, particularly in a competitive bidding situation, in a full 'commercial' price being paid for the victim company.

2.5   Does an MBO offer a disposer good value?

This question can be answered by considering all the factors already described. A management buyout is likely to offer the best value for a disposer only if the following conditions hold.

- there are few, if any, other potential purchasers,

- the management have a proper plan to maximise the company's profitability and are therefore prepared to pay handsomely for the company. Other purchasers less intimately connected with the company would be unaware of the company's true potential,

- head office could continue to offer central support services for a price,

- there is no need to offer an artificially low price to help the management buy the company,

- the management had no trouble in putting together the financing for their purchase proposal.

2.6   Sources of finance for buy-outs

In an MBO, unlike a corporate-backed takeover, the acquiring group usually lack the financial resources to fund the acquisition. For small buyouts the price may be within the capabilities of the management team, but it is unlikely that many managers could raise the £100 million-plus figures involved in some buyouts.

Several institutions specialise in providing funds for MBOs. These include:

(a)   the clearing banks;
(b)   pension funds and insurance companies;
(c)   merchant banks;
(d)   specialist institutions such as the 3i group and Equity Capital for Industry; and
(e)   government agencies and local authorities (eg, Scottish Development Agency).

The types of finance and the conditions attached vary between the institutions. Points to be considered include:

(a)   **The form of finance**

Some institutions will provide equity funds. However, more commonly loan finance will be advanced. Equity funds will dilute the management team's ownership but on the other hand high gearing could put substantial strain on the firm's cash flow. Leveraged buyouts, with gearing levels up to 20 : 1, have been known.

(b)   **Duration of finance**

Some investors will require early redemption of loans and will provide funds in the form of redeemable loan stock or preference shares. Others may accept longer-term involvement and look to an eventual public flotation as an exit from the business.

(c)   **The involvement of the institution**

Some institutions may require board representation as a condition of providing funds.

(d)   **Ongoing support**

The management team should also consider the institution's willingness to provide funds for later expansion plans.   Some investors also offer other services such as management consultancy to their clients.

(e)   **Syndication**

In large buyouts it is possible that a syndicate of institutions may be required to provide the necessary funds.

All institutions will look for a 'significant' input of finance from the management team as a demonstration of their commitment. The term 'significant' relates to the size of the managers' personal wealth rather than the size of the MBO, and managers can expect to have to plough in their redundancy payments, take second mortgages on their homes and often provide personal guarantees on loans.

Institutional investors will also expect to see a well-prepared business plan and usually an investigating accountant and a technical advisor will be employed to investigate the proposal.

Finally, the management team can also look for other sources of finance to assist in the MBO. Hire purchase or leasing of specific assets may ease initial cash flow problems. Government grants might be available for certain firms, and the managers' and employees' pension scheme may be available to provide some of the required finance.

2.7   Mezzanine finance

Although gearing levels in management buyouts are often high, problems are sometimes encountered in that they cannot be pushed high enough to leave an affordable controlling equity interest for managers. If the required percentage of equity funds is too large it will become unaffordable to the management group and the buyout will fail.

One common solution to this problem is the use of mezzanine finance. Mezzanine finance is a layer of funding between senior debt and equity. It falls behind senior debt in terms of claim on income, and usually has little or no asset backing. To compensate investors for this higher risk it normally carries an enhanced coupon rate together with some participation in the equity of the business. The use of this 'quasi-debt' (or 'quasi-equity') allows the percentage of true equity in the total package to be smaller and control of the company can, therefore, be left in the hands of the management group.

The major characteristics of mezzanine finance are:

(a)   Floating interest rates, normally at a higher level than senior debt.

(b)   Equity participation, either by way of warrants or an initial subscription, to give a total return somewhere below that of straight equity but above that of straight debt.

(c)   Repayment terms of eight to ten years or more, normally falling due after the senior debt.

(d)   Security on the basis of second fixed and floating charges behind similar charges in favour of senior lenders.

2.8   Activity

The management buy-out industry has developed a range of colourful jargon terms over its period of existence. What do you think are the meanings of the following common MBO terms?

(i)   Bimbo
(ii)   Caps, floors and collars
(iii)   Junk bonds
(iv)   Lemons and plums
(v)   Living dead
(vi)   Ratchet arrangement.

2.9 Activity solution

(i) A deal involving both a buy-in by outside managers and a buy-out by current managers has been coined a bimbo by Investors in Industry (the 3i group) and unfortunately the name has stuck. Around 50% of recent deals take this form.

(ii) Caps, floors and collars are limits to which the interest rate charged in a leveraged buy-out can respectively rise, fall and range between.

(iii) Junk bonds are tradeable high yielding unsecured debt certificates issued by companies in US leveraged buy-outs. Their equivalent in the UK is mezzanine finance, though this is less easily traded than junk bonds since it is not usually issued in certificate form.

(iv) Lemons are deals that go wrong. Plums are successful deals.

(v) The living dead are companies which just earn enough cash to pay the interest on their borrowings, but no more. They can continue indefinitely, but are never expected to flourish.

(vi) A ratchet arrangement permits managers to be allocated a larger share of the company's equity if the venture performs well. It is intended as an incentive arrangement to encourage managers to be committed to the success of the company.

2.10 Assessing the viability of buy-outs

Both the management buy-out team and the financial backers will wish to be convinced that their proposed MBO is a 'plum' rather than a 'lemon' and that they avoid joining the 'living dead'.

They may wish to ask themselves the following questions

(i) Why do the current owners wish to sell? If the owners are trying to rid themselves of a loss-making subsidiary, are the new management being over-confident in believing that they can turn it round into profitability?

(ii) Does the proposed management team cover all key functions? If not, new appointments should be made as soon as possible.

(iii) Has a reliable business plan been drawn up, including cash flow projections, and examined by an investigating accountant?

(iv) Is the proposal purchase price too high?

(v) Is the financing method viable? The trend is now away from the highly geared buy-outs of the 1980s.

2.11 Management buy-ins

Definition A management buy-in occurs when a group of outside managers buys a controlling stake in a business.

Advantages

(i) Particularly effective when the existing management are weak and need to be replaced.
(ii) Efficient managers are able quickly to gain new responsibilities.

Disadvantages

(i) Employee resistance can be experienced when the new management try to impose new ways of running the business.

(ii) The new management might concentrate on short-term profitability at the expense of securing the company's long-term prosperity.

2.12   Conclusions on management buyouts

Management buyouts have been an important feature of the business scene. Before embarking upon the buyout road managers should consider the following points.

(a)   They are risky (approximately one in ten fail) and can involve managers losing their personal wealth as well as their jobs.

(b)   Problems will be encountered when the new company becomes independent. For example, head office support services will be lost, and existing customers may go elsewhere if they see the new firm being too risky.

However, they do bring advantages:

(a)   Although the risks are high so are the potential rewards. In the situation of leveraged buyouts, where the bulk of the equity is in the hands of the management team, the returns to shareholders once the loans have been covered can be very large.

(b)   They are usually considered to be less risky than starting a new business from scratch.

(c)   Firms that have been subject to MBOs tend to operate at a higher level of efficiency. The traditional divorce between ownership and control is effectively ended and managers (and shareholding employees) have great incentive to improve the efficiency of the firm.

2.13   Example question - Management buyout

(a)   The following information relates to the proposed financing scheme for a management buy-out of a manufacturing company.

	%	£'000
Share capital held by		
Management	40	100
Institutions	60	150
		250
10% redeemable preference shares		
(redeemable in ten years' time)		1,200
		1,450
Loans		700
Overdraft facilities		700
		2,850

Loans are repayable over the next five years in equal instalments. They are secured on various specific assets, including properties. Interest is 12% pa.

The manufacturing company to be acquired is at present part of a much larger organisation, which considers this segment to be no longer compatible with its main line of business. This is despite the fact that the company in question has been experiencing a turnover growth in excess of 10% per annum.

The assets to be acquired have a book value of £2,250,000, but the agreed price was £2,500,000.

You are required to write a report to the buy-out team, appraising the financing scheme.

(b)   What problems are likely to be encountered in assembling a financing package in a management buy-out of a service company as opposed to a manufacturing company?

Solution

(a)   **REPORT**

> **To:**   Buy-out team
> **From:**   Consulting accountant.
> **Date:**   X-X-19XX
> **Subject:**   **MBO Financing Scheme**

Overview

The financing scheme involves the purchase of assets with a net book value of £2,250,000 for an agreed price of £2,500,000. The finance that will be raised will provide funds of £2,850,000 in the form of:

	£'000
Equity	250
Preference shares	1,200
Loan	700
Overdraft	700
	2,850

Of the funds raised only £350,000 will be available to the business after the purchase price has been paid. This will be in the form of unused overdraft facilities.

Gearing

As is common to MBOs the gearing level will be very high. There is only £250,000 of equity compared to £2,250,000 of debt finance (including the preference shares and excluding the unused element of the overdraft). The gearing level will mean that the returns to equity will be risky, but the buyout team own 40% of a £2.5 million company for an investment of only £100,000. The rewards are potentially very high.

One consequence of the level of gearing is that it will be difficult to raise any additional finance. There are unlikely to be any assets that are not secured, and in any case the level of interest and loan repayments would probably prohibit further borrowing.

Cash commitments

The annual cash commitments from the financing structure are summarised below:

(i)   Loan repayments

Annual payments will have to be made in the repayment of capital and interest on the £700,000 loan. The annual amount will be:

$$\frac{£700,000}{3.605^*} = £194,000$$

*   The cumulative discount factor for 5 years at 12%

(ii)   Redeemable preference shares

The redeemable preference shares will be either cumulative or non-cumulative. Assuming that they are cumulative £120,000 will, on average, have to be paid every year. There is a little flexibility in that if the dividend cannot be met it can be postponed (but not avoided).

The redeemable preference shares will have to be repaid after 10 years. This can either be provided for over the 10 years, or an alternative source of finance found to replace the funds. Assuming that they will be required to be provided for according to the terms of the financing package this will require a commitment of £120,000 per annum.

(iii)   Overdraft

The element of the overdraft used to finance the purchase price is effectively a source of long term finance. The rate of interest is not known but if we make the (unrealistic) assumption that it is also at 12%, then the £350,000 drawn down will cost £42,000 per annum.

In total there will be a commitment to pay approximately £476,000 per annum. This will be the first priority of the new company. The management team will need to generate sufficient funds from the only available source, operations, in order to meet this commitment.

Other cash requirements

Apart from the need to generate cash to satisfy the requirements of the financing scheme the company will also need to generate funds to invest in working capital and fixed assets as required. At the moment these capital requirements are unknown. In the context of 10% annual growth in turnover, however, they might exceed the unused element of the overdraft facility.

Institutional involvement

By virtue of their stake in the company of 60% of the equity the financial institutions hold the controlling stake. This will be enhanced by their position as the providers of the remainder of the finance. Consequently the institutions will able to determine many aspects of the company's management, including the appointment of directors. The institutions are likely to have two overriding objectives:

(i)   The security of loan and interest repayments. Any breach of the loan arrangements might trigger the appointment of administrators or receivers, and the institutions' investment would almost certainly be lost.

(ii)   Realising their equity investment. The institutional investors will probably expect to realise their investment in a relatively short time frame. This is commonly set at between 5 and 7 years.

Profit growth

Apart from the requirement to generate cash as noted above the company must also generate steady profit growth. The institutional investors will require a history of profit growth in order to enable the sale of their stake through either flotation or a trade sale.

Conclusion

The financing scheme will place a heavy cash burden on the company, particularly in the early years. The involvement of the institutions will perhaps prove unwelcome, but the MBO would be impossible without accepting it.

(b)   There are three main problems particular to arranging a finance package for a service company.

(i)   The lack of tangible assets

Because MBOs normally have to be highly geared there is a requirement to provide security for the loans in a package. Service companies commonly have a very low level of tangible assets. It will therefore be difficult to attract much debt finance.

(ii)   'People' businesses

The success of service companies depends on their staff. Institutions tend to view such success with suspicion because people, unlike plant and machinery, can resign. Unless the people in question are tied into the company within the MBO financing package by, for example, insisting on their investing in equity there is little guarantee that they will stay with the company.

(iii)   Working capital

The nature of most service businesses is that they have unusually high working capital requirements. The main expense for a service company is staff costs. It is almost impossible to take extended credit from staff without losing their services. The supplies of service companies often involve a long period of work before customers can be billed. Consequently, a finance package would have to provide for the working capital, and working capital finance is particularly risky because it is difficult to secure and so may be equally difficult to raise.

3   CAPITAL RECONSTRUCTION SCHEMES

3.1   Introduction

Capital reconstruction schemes can be undertaken for a wide variety of purposes. It is useful to divide the types of transaction into two groups:

(a)   schemes for companies which are not in financial difficulties; and
(b)   schemes for companies which are in financial difficulties.

The boundary line is not clear cut however. Some provisions of company law can be used by both types of company. The capital reduction provisions of *s.135 CA 1985* for example can be used by a company to tidy up its balance sheet reserves or to write off debit balances arising from trading losses so that further finance can be obtained.

3.2   Solvent companies – commercial considerations

(a)   **Purpose of reorganisation**

Companies undertake restructuring to improve both their mix of different types of capital and the timing of availability of funds.

This can be done without altering the total capital requirement. The specific objects of the reorganisation may be one or more of the following:

(i)   To reduce net of tax cost of borrowing;

(ii)   To repay borrowing sooner or later;

(iii)   To improve security of finance;

(iv)   To make security in the company more attractive;

(v)   To improve the image of the company to third parties;

(vi)   To tidy up the balance sheet.

(b)   **Types of reorganisation**

We shall consider the following types of reorganisation:

(i)   Conversion of debt to equity or vice versa.

(ii)   Conversion of equity from one form to another.

(iii)   Conversion of debt from one form to another.

(c)   **Conversion of debt to equity**

The following are the most likely reasons for converting debt to equity:

(i)   Automatically by holders of convertible debentures exercising their rights.

(ii)   In order to improve the equity base of a company. This situation is particularly likely to arise when a company has financed expansion by short-term borrowings. Sooner or later, it will run into working capital problems, and if long-term loan funds are not available (because, for example, they would make the gearing excessively high) the only solution is to issue new shares, possibly by way of a rights issue.

(d)   **Conversion of equity to debt**

The most common reason for this taking place is the conversion of preference shares to some form of debenture. Although through the eyes of both companies and investors there is little to choose between securities bearing a fixed rate of return, be they debentures or preference shares, in the eyes of both tax and company law they are very different.

From the tax point of view, payments to preference shareholders are dividends, and are not, therefore, an allowable charge in computing taxable profits. Between the introduction of corporation tax in 1965 and the introduction of the imputation system in 1973 there was a steady trend to convert preference shares into debentures.

Since the introduction of the imputation system, the high effective cost of servicing preference shares compared to debentures has been reduced, and it is now therefore, not common to convert preference shares to debentures.

From the legal point of view, conversion of preference shares into debentures constitutes a reduction of capital. Company law provisions relating to redemption of shares must therefore be followed. In accounting terms the broad effect of these provisions is to reduce distributable profits by the nominal value of the preference shares redeemed (by transferring amounts from distributable profit to capital redemption reserve).

(e)   **Conversion of equity from one form to another**

This covers a number of different procedures, adopted for different reasons. They include, **inter alia:**

(i)   Simplifying the capital structure. It was once common to have a variety of types of share capital, designed to appeal to a variety of investors. This has now become less favoured, and the tendency is to have only one, or at most two, classes of share capital. Conversion of shares from one type to another can only be carried out in accordance with the procedures in the articles, normally approved by a prescribed majority of the class affected, subject to rights of appeal to the court.

(ii)   Making shares more attractive to investors, eg, by sub-division into smaller units, or conversion into stock.

(iii)   Eliminating reserves by issuing fully paid bonus shares. This is very much a tidying up operation, and may be especially useful to remove share premium accounts and capital redemption reserves. Additionally, in a period of inflation, it may be recognising the fact that a substantial part of the revenue reserves could never be paid out as dividends.

(f)   **Conversion of debt from one form to another**

This procedure might be undertaken to improve security, flexibility or cost of borrowing. For example:

(i)   **Security**

Consider the example of a company financing itself out of creditors and overdraft facilities, neither of which give any security. Rather than a rights issue, converting the creditors to long-term loans, eg, debentures, would be equally satisfactory in that it would give security as to the source of funds.

(ii)   **Flexibility**

Again, a company financing itself out of short-term borrowings has little room to manoeuvre. Flexibility could be improved by arranging more permanent financing.

Alternatively, a company already borrowing to the limits of its ability could reduce its borrowings and improve flexibility by using other sources of finance – leasing for example.

(iii)   **Cost**

Some loan finance is cheaper than others, eg, secured rather than unsecured, overdraft rather than HP. An opportunity may arise to shift from a relatively high cost to a relatively low cost source of funds.

3.3   Business failure and reconstruction

A company may 'fail' because:

(a)   profitable use has not been made of its resources; or
(b)   although profitable it has not managed its cash flow.

In either case, a company which realises it is on the brink of liquidation, may be able to return to profitability or a sound financial position if it can be kept alive by attracting fresh capital and/or persuading its creditors to accept some security in the company as settlement of its debts. In other words it would require a **capital reconstruction** which would allow the company to continue in business. Thus, a capital reconstruction scheme is a scheme whereby a company reorganises its capital structure.

3.4   Legal aspects of reconstructions

A number of provisions of company law allow the write off of debit balances on the profit and loss account against shareholders' capital and creditors' capital. A 'simple' capital reduction scheme under S135 CA 1985 does not allow creditors' rights to be prejudiced (therefore they cannot suffer a capital write off). A 'complex' scheme which can affect creditors' rights can be organised through the provisions of S425 CA 1985.

Under S425 CA 1985 the court can be asked to sanction a 'compromise' or 'arrangement' between a company and its creditors.

The procedure is as follows:

(a)   An application is made to the court, asking it to call a meeting between the company and its creditors or a class of creditor, eg, debenture holders.

(b)   The scheme of reconstruction is put to the meeting and a vote taken.

(c)   If there is 75% in value and including proxies vote in favour the court will be asked to sanction it.

(d)   If the court sanctions it, the scheme is then binding on all the creditors.

3.5   General principles in devising a scheme

In most cases the company is ailing: losses have been incurred with the result that capital and long-term liabilities are out of line with the current value of the company's assets and their earning potential. New capital is normally desperately required to regenerate the business, but this will not be forthcoming without a restructuring of the existing capital and liabilities.

The general procedure to follow would be:

(a)   Write off fictitious assets and the debit balance on profit and loss account. Revalue assets to determine their current value to the business.

(b)   Determine whether the company can continue to trade without further finance or, if further finance is required, determine the amount required, in what form (shares, loan stock) and from which persons it is obtainable (typically existing shareholders and financial institutions).

(c)   Given the size of the write-off required in (a) above and the amount of further finance required, determine a reasonable manner in spreading the write off (the capital loss) between the various parties that have financed the company (shareholders and creditors).

Note how the interests of the various suppliers of capital must be taken into account in a reconstruction situation:

(i)   The main burden of the losses should be borne primarily by the ordinary shareholders, as they are last in line in repayment of capital on a winding up. In many cases, the capital loss is so great that they would receive nothing upon a liquidation of the company. They must, however, be left with some remaining stake in the company if further finance is required from them.

(ii)   Preference shares normally, though not necessarily, give the holders a preferential right to repayment of capital on a winding up. Thus, the loss to be borne by them should be less than the loss borne by ordinary shareholders. They may agree to forgo arrears of preference dividends in anticipation that the scheme will lead to a resumption of their dividends. However, if they are expected to suffer some reduction in the nominal value of their capital, they may require an increase in the rate of their dividend or a share in the equity. The share in the equity will give them a stake in future profits if profits are made.

(iii)   Creditors, including debenture and loan stock holders, may agree to a reduction in their claims against the company if they anticipate that full repayment would not be received on a liquidation or they wish to protect (as far as trade creditors are concerned) a company which will continue to be a customer to them. Like preference shareholders, an incentive may be given in the form of a small stake in the equity of the company.

3.6   Case study – Wire Construction plc

Wire Construction plc has suffered from losses in the last three years.   Its balance sheet as at 31 December 19X1 shows:

	£	£
Fixed assets		
Land and buildings		193,246
Equipment		60,754
Investment		27,000
		281,000
Current assets		
Stock	120,247	
Debtors	70,692	
	190,939	
Creditors: Amounts falling due within 12 months		
Trade creditors	112,247	
Interest payable	12,800	
Overdraft	36,713	
	161,760	
Net current assets		29,179
Creditors: Amounts falling due beyond 12 months		
8% Debenture 19X4		(80,000)
		230,179
Ordinary shares – £1		200,000
5% Cumulative preference shares – £1		70,000
Profit and loss		(39,821)
		230,179

Sales have been particularly difficult to achieve in the current year and stock levels are very high. Interest has not been paid for two years. The debenture holders have demanded a scheme of reconstruction or the liquidation of the company.

During a meeting of shareholders and directors, it was decided to carry out a scheme of internal reconstruction. The following scheme has been agreed:

(1)   Each ordinary share is to be redesignated as a share of 25p.

(2)   The existing 70,000 preference shares are to be exchanged for a new issue of 35,000 8% cumulative preference shares of £1 each and 140,000 ordinary shares of 25p each.

(3)   The ordinary shareholders are to accept a reduction in the nominal value of their shares from £1 to 25p, and subscribe for a new issue on the basis of 1 for 1 at a price of 30p per share.

(4)   The debenture holders are to accept 20,000 ordinary shares of 25p each in lieu of the interest payable. It is agreed that the value of the interest liability is equivalent to the nominal value of the shares issued. The interest rate is to be increased to 9½% and the repayment date deferred for three years. A further £9,000 of this 9½% debenture is to be issued and taken up by the existing holders at £90 per £100.

(5)   The profit and loss account balance is to be written off.

(6)   The investment is to be sold at the current market price of £60,000.

(7)   The bank overdraft is to be repaid.

(8)   10% of the debtors are to be written off.

(9)   The remaining assets were professionally valued and should be included in the books and accounts as follows:

	£
Land	80,000
Building	80,000
Equipment	30,000
Stock and work-in-progress	50,000

(10)   It is expected that, due to the refinancing, operating profits will be earned at the rate of £50,000 pa after depreciation but before interest and tax.

(11)   Corporation tax is 21%.

Required:

(a)   Prepare the balance sheet of the company immediately after the reconstruction.

(b)   Advise the shareholders and debenture-holders as to whether they should support the reconstruction.

Solution

(Tutorial note: part (a) of this question is for demonstration purposes. Do *not* waste time producing a balance sheet unless it is specifically asked for by the examiner.)

(a)   **Wire Construction plc**
           Balance sheet at 1 January 19X2 (after reconstruction)

	£	£
Fixed assets		
Land at valuation		80,000
Building at valuation		80,000
Equipment at valuation		30,000
		190,000
Current assets		
Stock	50,000	
Debtors (70,692 × 90%)	63,623	
Cash (W1)	91,387	
	205,010	
Creditors: Amounts falling due within one year		
Trade creditors	112,247	
Net current assets		92,763
Total assets less current liabilities		282,763

Creditors:	Amounts falling due beyond one year	
	9½% Debenture 19X7	89,000
		193,763

Called up share capital		
	Issued ordinary shares of 25p each (W2)	140,000
	Issued 8% cumulative preference shares of £1 each (W2)	35,000
Share premium account (W2)		16,900
Capital reconstruction account		1,863
		193,763

WORKINGS

£

(W1)   Cash

	£
New share issue	
– Ords 200,000 × 30p	60,000
New debentures	
9,000 × 90%	8,100
Sale of investment	60,000
	128,100
Less: Overdraft	36,713
	91,387

(W2)   Shareholdings

	Ords. No.	Ords. £	Prefs No.	Prefs £	Share premium £
Per balance sheet	200,000	200,000	70,000	70,000	
Redesignation		50,000			
Exchange	140,000	35,000	(35,000)	(35,000)	
New issue	200,000	50,000			10,000
Debenture interest					
(12,800 – 5,000)	20,000	5,000			7,800
	560,000	140,000	35,000	35,000	17,800
Discount on					
debentures issued					
(10% × 9,000)					(900)
					16,900

(Tutorial note: as £12,800 of debenture interest is to be cancelled for £5,000 nominal of ordinary shares the excess is share premium (ie, the consideration for the shares is deemed to be the liability removed).)

Reconstruction account

Book value:	£	Revised values:	£
Fixed assets	281,000	Land and buildings	160,000
Stock	120,247	Equipment	30,000
		Investment	60,000
Debtors written off		Stock	50,000
10% × 70,692	7,069	Share capital reduced	
Profit and loss balance	39,821	200,000 × 75p	150,000
Balance –			
Capital reserve	1,863		
	450,000		450,000

(Tutorial note: the reconstruction account records the profit/losses arising during the reconstruction. The closing balance could have been arrived at by inserting a balancing figure in the balance sheet.)

(b)   **Advice to shareholders and debenture holders.**

Position of interested parties in a liquidation
(assuming assets can be sold at going concern value)

	£	£
Value of fixed assets		190,000
Stock		50,000
Debtors		63,623
Assets available		303,623
Secured debts		
Debentures		(80,000)
		223,623
Other creditors		
Overdraft	36,713	
Interest	12,800	
Trade creditors	112,247	
		161,760
Available to preference shareholders		61,863

The above statement of assets reflects the position of the three interested parties with no reconstruction scheme. The debenture holders would be sure of their capital repayment on a liquidation and most probably the arrears of interest. The preference shareholders would get part (how much depends on the difference between going concern and break up values of the assets). Ordinary shareholders would get nothing.

It follows that the scheme must be favourable to the debenture-holders if it is to have success. The holders are being offered an increased rate of interest but an extended repayment date.

The expected interest cover is reasonable:

	£
Expected profits	50,000

Interest

$$9.5\% \times 89{,}000 \qquad\qquad 8{,}455$$

Interest cover = 5.9

In financial terms it is a matter of comparing the prospective rate of interest with interest rates currently available elsewhere.

The preference shareholders are having half of their investment turned into equity. This is very reasonable as about half their capital would be lost on a liquidation. They will have $\dfrac{140{,}000}{560{,}000} \times 100 = 25\%$ of the ordinary share capital. In addition they will have an increased dividend rate and are not required to contribute any further capital.

The ordinary shareholders retain part of their stake in the company if they participate $\dfrac{200{,}000}{560{,}000}$ = 36% without any further cash investment. The further cash investment required of £50,000 leaves them with the majority holding.

The expected available earnings will be:

	£
Profit	50,000
Interest	(8,455)
	41,545
Tax at 21%	8,724
	32,821
Preference dividend 35,000 × 8%	2,800
Available to equity	30,021

$$\text{E.P.S.} \quad \frac{30{,}021}{560{,}000} \times 100 = \qquad 5.4\text{p}$$

However, as the shareholders would receive nothing on a liquidation, the additional expected return to them is twice 5.4p per share ie:

On old shareholding
    200,000 × 5.4p

On new shareholding
    200,000 × 5.4p

This therefore seems a reasonable proposition to the ordinary shareholders.

4   CHAPTER SUMMARY

For every buyer there must be a seller, so divestment strategy should be examined just as closely as investment strategy.

Management buy-outs and buy-ins are now a common feature of the business scene. Many have prospered despite the recession in the 1990s and have made significant money for the original equity investors.

Capital reconstructions can be carried out under either s.135 or s.425 of the Companies Act 1985. You must be able to devise a feasible scheme for a specific failing company in exam questions.

5   SELF TEST QUESTIONS

5.1   What is meant by the unbundling of a company's investments? (1.4)

5.2   When would a demerger be worthwhile? (1.4)

5.3   Define a management buy-out. (2.1)

5.4   Why might an existing parent company seek to dispose of a company through an MBO? (2.2)

5.5   Give examples of institutions specialising in providing funds for MBOs. (2.6)

5.6   What is mezzanine finance? (2.7)

5.7   State one advantage and one disadvantage of a management buy-in. (2.11)

5.8   Why might a company wish to convert debt to equity as part of a scheme of capital reconstruction? (3.1)

5.9   Distinguish between schemes under s.135 and s.425 of *CA 1985*. (3.4)

5.10   What form of capital should bear the main burden of the losses in a scheme of capital reconstruction? (3.5)

6   EXAMINATION TYPE QUESTION

6.1   Poorhopes plc

Poorhopes plc is a company which has suffered a significant reversal of fortune in recent years. The balance sheet of the company at 30 September 19X7 is set out below:

Fixed assets (at cost):

	Cost £	Dep'n £	£
Goodwill	30,000	10,000	20,000
Development expenditure	15,000		15,000
Land and buildings	40,000		40,000
Fixtures	3,855	1,225	2,630
Plant	36,315	19,284	17,031
Quoted investment	45,000		45,000
			139,661

Current assets:		
Stock	40,166	
Debtors	35,802	
	75,968	

Less:	Current liabilities:	
	Bank overdraft	15,209
	Trade creditors	63,420
	Directors' loans	10,000
	Accrued interest on debenture	4,200
		92,829

Net current liabilities		(16,861)
7% debentures		(30,000)
		92,800

Share capital:

	Authorised	Issued and fully paid
	£	£
Ordinary shares of £1 each	100,000	80,000
7% cumulative preference shares of £1 each	40,000	40,000
	140,000	120,000

Reserves:

Profit and loss account	(27,200)
	92,800

You are a management accountant with the company.

The directors of the company have sought your advice in drafting a scheme of reorganisation.

The following information is relevant:

(1)   the preference dividend is three years in arrears;

(2)   the debentures are secured on the freehold buildings, the entire debenture being held by the Lendem Bank plc. The bank has requested that the arrears of debenture interest be paid at once, but have intimated that they might be prepared to lend the company a further £10,000 in view of the increased value of the collateral, and if new shareholder funds are forthcoming;

(3)   the company banks with the Southern Bank plc. The bank has demanded that the overdraft be repaid immediately;

(4)   the directors have agreed to waive one half of the loans owed to them;

(5)   the land and buildings have been valued at £55,000, quoted investments at £50,000, stock at £24,000, and plant at £16,000;

(6)   the goodwill and deferred development expenditure are to be written off;

(7)   it is estimated that 10% of debtors may prove to be doubtful;

(8)   an investment of £40,000 in plant is needed. The working capital requires additional investment to maintain a satisfactory current ratio. The expected level of trade creditors is £50,000.

You are required to prepare a report to the board of directors of Poorhopes plc suggesting a scheme of reorganisation which you feel would be acceptable to all parties concerned. The report should contain a balance sheet of Poorhopes plc after the reorganisation.

Ignore any costs of reconstruction.   **(25 marks)**

7   ANSWER TO EXAMINATION TYPE QUESTION

7.1   Poorhopes plc

To: The Board of Directors
From: Management Accountant   4 November 19X7

Proposed capital reorganisation scheme

(a)   **Terms of reference**

This report deals with the proposed capital reorganisation scheme, prepared in such a manner as to be acceptable to all parties concerned in the reorganisation.

(b)   **Information**

This has been limited to the summarised balance sheet at 30 September 19X7 together with further information amplifying this balance sheet.

(c)   **General considerations**

The objects of the proposed scheme are as follows:

(i)   to bring the net assets of the company in line with current values; and

(ii)   to improve the fixed asset investment, liquidity and working capital of the company.

(d)   **Details of the proposed scheme**

Particulars of the proposed reorganisation scheme are as follows:

(i)   the ordinary shares are to be written down to 25p each;

(ii)   the preference shareholders are to waive their rights to the arrears of dividend, and in return they will not be asked to invest further funds;

(iii)   the Lendem Bank plc should be persuaded to take up a further £10,000 of the debentures in view of the increased value of the collateral and new shareholder funds;

(iv)   a 'one–for–one' rights issue at 75p is to be offered to ordinary shareholders;

(v)   it is noted that the directors have agreed to waive one half of the loans owed to them. It is suggested that the balance of these loans be met by the issue to them of ordinary shares of 25p;

(vi)   goodwill, deferred development expenditure and the balance on the profit and loss account are to be written off in full, whilst plant is to be revalued at £16,000;

(vii)   the land and buildings are to be revalued at £55,000 and the quoted investment is to be sold for £50,000;

(viii)   £16,166 is to be written off the stocks and a provision of 10% for doubtful debts is to be made.

(e)   **Effect of proposed scheme on the balance sheet of the company**

Assuming that the parties concerned accept the proposed scheme, the balance sheet of the company as at 30 September 19X7 would be as follows:

		£	£
Fixed assets:			
Tangible assets:			
Land and buildings, at valuation			55,000
Plant (16,000 + 40,000)			56,000
Fixtures and fittings, at cost		3,855	
Less: Depreciation		1,225	
			2,630
			113,630
Current assets:			
Stocks		24,000	
Debtors (35,802 – 3,580)		32,222	
Cash at bank and in hand (W6)		60,591	
		116,813	
Creditors: amounts falling due within one year:			
Trade creditors		63,420	
Net current assets			53,393
Total assets less current liabilities			167,023
Creditors: amounts falling due after more than one year:			
7% debenture loans (secured)			40,000
			127,023
Capital and reserves:			
Called up share capital (see note)			81,250
Share premium (W7)			43,750
Other reserves: Capital reserve arising under capital reorganisation (W5)			2,023
			127,023

Note to the accounts

Share capital

	Authorised £	Issued and fully paid £
Ordinary shares of 25p each (W7)	100,000	41,250
9% cumulative preference shares of £1 each	40,000	40,000
	140,000	81,250

WORKINGS

(W1)

<table>
<tr><td colspan="2" align="center">Capital reduction account</td></tr>
<tr><td></td><td>£</td><td></td><td>£</td></tr>
<tr><td>Amounts written off:</td><td></td><td>Revaluation – land</td><td>15,000</td></tr>
<tr><td> Goodwill</td><td>20,000</td><td>Profit on sale of investment</td><td>5,000</td></tr>
<tr><td> Plant</td><td>1,031</td><td>Loans waived</td><td>5,000</td></tr>
<tr><td> Stock</td><td>16,166</td><td>Balance c/d</td><td>57,977</td></tr>
<tr><td> Debtors</td><td>3,580</td><td></td><td></td></tr>
<tr><td> Development expenditure</td><td>15,000</td><td></td><td></td></tr>
<tr><td> P & L account</td><td>27,200</td><td></td><td></td></tr>
<tr><td></td><td>82,977</td><td></td><td>82,977</td></tr>
<tr><td>Balance b/d – amount
  required to be written off</td><td>57,977</td><td></td><td></td></tr>
</table>

(W2) **New funds required**

	£	£
Investment:		
Fixed assets	40,000	
Working capital (W3)	57,198	
Repayment of overdraft	15,209	
Arrears of debenture interest	4,200	
		116,607
Less: Sources of funds:		
Sale of quoted investment	50,000	
Additional debenture – maximum	10,000	
New share capital – minimum	56,607	
		116,607

(W3) **Working capital**

	£
After revaluations, write–offs and overdraft cleared:	
Stock	24,000
Debtors (35,802 – 3,580)	32,222
Creditors	(63,420)
	(7,198)

Assuming trade creditors are to be about £50,000 (lower than current figure which probably reflects extended credit taken), stock, debtors and cash will total £100,000 (giving a current ratio of 2).

	£
New net working capital	50,000
Existing	7,198
New finance	57,198

(Tutorial note: the question merely stated that an investment in working capital was required to maintain a 'satisfactory' current ratio. Clearly other current ratios than two may be satisfactory. The important point is that an answer must consider the issue of financing fixed assets and working capital.)

(W4)   **Write–offs and share issues**

(a)   Existing capital position

	£	£
Book value of net assets		92,800
Revaluations		
Write offs required	57,977	
Less: P & L Account balance	(27,200)	
Add: loan to be waived	5,000	
Net revaluation deficit		35,777
Going concern value of assets		57,023
Amount due to preference shareholders:		
Nominal value of shares	40,000	
Arrears of dividend		
$40,000 \times 7\% \times 3$	8,400	
		48,400
Amount due to ordinary shareholders		8,623

Thus on a going concern basis the preference shareholders' investment is fully covered, and the ordinary shareholders should bear most/all of the capital loss. However on a break up basis the preference shareholders' investment is not likely to be protected. It may therefore be reasonable for them to suffer some loss in the scheme.

(b)   **Allocation of write offs and share issues**

	Preference shares £	Ordinary shares £
Existing NV	40,000	80,000
Write–off required (W1) 60,000	-	60,000
	40,000	20,000
New share issue (W2) 60,000	-	60,000

No write–off of preference shares is required. It is reasonable that the ordinary shareholders should bear the full capital loss as the preference shareholders will be asked to forgo their arrears of dividend. For similar reasons the ordinary shareholders will be asked to finance the new investment.

(Tutorial note: there is no 'right' answer to working (4). What is important is to show certain principles:

(a)   brief justification of who suffers the write–off;

(b)   write off a round sum figure as the write–off has to be a reasonable figure per share. In this case, for example, the ordinary shareholders will receive one 25p ordinary share in place of one £1 share;

(c)   the share issue also needs to be a round sum which can easily be converted to a reasonable basis for a rights issue. In this case, for example, the rights issue could be a 'one–for–one' issue (resulting in 80,000 new 25p ordinary shares) at 75p per share ($\frac{60,000}{80,000}$).)

(W5)   **Balance on capital reduction account**

	£
Working 1: Amount to be written off	57,977
Working 4: Amount written off share capital	60,000
Capital reserve	2,023

(W6)   **Cash balance**

	£		£
Sale of investment	50,000	Balance b/d	15,209
Additional debenture	10,000	Arrears of debenture	
Rights issue	60,000	interest	4,200
		Plant expenditure	40,000
		Balance b/d	60,591
	120,000		120,000

(W7)   **Ordinary shares**

	NV	Share premium
	£	£
Old shares (W4)	20,000	
Rights	20,000	40,000
Directors in lieu of loan (deemed issue price at 75p)	1,250	3,750
	41,250	43,750

14 ECONOMIC INFLUENCES ON INTERNATIONAL FINANCIAL DECISIONS

INTRODUCTION & LEARNING OBJECTIVES

This chapter addresses many of the international questions facing today's financial manager. The powers of multinational companies are now so strong that MNCs can move their activities around the world to take advantage of global opportunities that arise. The arguments in favour of active international trade are stated, together with a summary of the most important international financial institutions.

When you have studied this chapter you should be able to do the following:

- Explain the role of multinational companies in the world economy
- Discuss whether free trade is preferable to protectionism
- Explain the main free trade areas in existence today
- Explain the role of GATT and the WTO , the IMF and the World Bank
- Appreciate the practical methods by which international transactions can be financed and insured against.

1 MULTINATIONAL COMPANIES

1.1 Introduction

 A multinational company (MNC) is defined as one which generates at least 25% of its sales from activities in countries other than its own. This rules out returns from portfolio investment and eliminates unit and investment trusts.

The United Nations describes what we have just defined as multinational companies as 'transnational companies' to illustrate more clearly their developing nature. There is some merit in this nomenclature and it may become the norm. Indeed one could go further and consider the concept of a 'global' company. It might take this form: capital in the billions is raised internationally, the head office is based in the most tax efficient and loosely regulated country, the operational headquarters is located in the most effective centre, subsidiaries are established worldwide and the personnel are international in character and multilingual. This brief snapshot describes the Bank of Credit and Commerce International (BCCI) now finally shut down by the Bank of England and subject to investigation in the UK and USA.

MNCs originated in the latter part of the 19th century, principally in Germany and the USA. They reached their present dominant position largely in the years after the second world war, following the great expansion in trade which they themselves did much to promote. The concept was not entirely unknown in previous times viz, the East India Company in the 18th century and possibly the Florentine bankers of the middle ages.

1.2 The importance of MNCs

The activities of MNCs are of major importance because of their size and the increasingly preponderant part they play in the world economy. The very largest have revenues greater than the GNP of all except the top 14 or so of national economies. Their significance is increasing all the time since they are growing (looking at the totality) at a rate of some 3 or 4 times the rate of the world economy. The size of the largest MNCs tends to put them in the limelight, but there are many small MNCs - about 10,000 in total.

The functions of MNCs in the lesser developed countries (LDCs) have received particular scrutiny. Their activities in these countries are often, though not exclusively, directed towards the extractive industries, oil and minerals, and agriculture, plantations, rubber and forestry. Many of the features of MNCs reviewed in this chapter are common to all of them and the special problems of the interaction of MNCs and LDCs are best treated separately when the question of LDCs is looked at as a whole.

1.3 Reasons for the development of MNCs

Much thought has been given to the reason why a company operating successfully in its own country should seek to extend its activities to other countries. It is an option which carries considerable risk and is far from uniformly successful. There is usually the alternative of exporting which, after all, has traditionally been and still is a principal way of increasing revenues.

Analysis has focused on those factors which need to be present if the transformation of a national company into a MNC is to be successful and these will be looked at in some depth later. But by themselves they still leave the basic question unanswered - why? Of course, from one point of view one could say that the MNC results from a natural progression - expansion from town to area, from area to country and from country to the world. The process has been immensely facilitated by the concurrent advances in communications, both physical and electronic and by the international mobility of capital. This sounds plausible but it should be noted that much of MNC expansion predated the current avionic and electronic marvels and it is far from clear that expanding from Birmingham to Frankfurt is of the same order of naturalness as expanding from Leeds to Birmingham.

1.4 Complementary competition and destructive competition

Perhaps we can get nearer to the answer if we consider more closely the nature of trade and competition. Although competition is an ever present factor in commercial activities the pattern of trade when it began to get under way in a significant sense in the 18th century was largely complementary in nature. Cotton goods would be exported in return for tea, for example, or later rails and locomotives would be sent abroad and wheat and cotton imported. At a later stage the makers of locomotives and rails would compete with one another as would the makers of machinery, electrical goods, chemicals and the whole plethora of modern industrial products. The age of competitive trade was born. Even so there was considerable demarcation of markets. Many British products would go to English speaking nations and many German ones to Eastern Europe and Russia. More so than today there were many unofficial 'understandings' which may account for Dr Johnson's remark that any two businessmen seen talking together is bound to represent a conspiracy against the public.

The world has moved on again. We are now in the era of destructive competition. As a result not merely companies but whole industries can be under threat. Rover, the last significant British owned car maker is now merely part of the MNC operations of a German company. The motor cycle industry, once the largest in the world, has vanished without trace. Midland Bank, itself once the largest bank in the world is the subsidiary of a Hong Kong bank, ironically as the result of an unsuccessful attempt to expand in California.

Peter Drucker, the world's leading management theorist, has pointed out that a hundred years ago the Germans learnt to operate local firms as national concerns to prevent competition from taking away their businesses and fifty years ago successful American companies had to think 'continental' for the same reason. Today this factor increasingly operates internationally. Competition never vanishes. It is always present, but the competition which increasingly restricts and sometimes eliminates is best dealt with by expansion. As a firm grows internationally it is still subject to attack but becomes increasingly difficult to topple.

1.5 Factors affecting the success of a MNC

Commentators believe that the existence of competitive advantage is not sufficient to guarantee foreign direct investment.

The factors which play a part in a MNC's operations and may affect its success can be conveniently divided into two classes: those that are internal to the firm and may be described as ownership specific and those that are external to the firm.

The theory of internalisation suggests that firm or ownership specific factors (see below) that can generate new information leads to foreign direct investment.

1.6   Ownership specific factors

(a)   **Process specialisation**

This is of two kinds. In the first place the move to standardisation of products both in terms of adhering to internationally accepted standards and in methods of production has made it possible and often desirable to locate stages of production in different countries - perhaps labour intensive activities in low wage areas and final assembly in the ultimate market. Secondly, it refers to the particular features of the firm which make it distinctive and confer on it a measure of competitive advantage, often referred to as 'know how' and embracing patents, trade marks and managerial skills.

(b)   **Product specialisation**

In spite of the move to standardisation mentioned above the vagaries of human taste are such that most markets exhibit different characteristics. Identifying these and matching products to them can be a potent factor in success, equally the failure to do so can be disastrous. In the simplest case consumers occasionally gain the impression (sometimes justified) that goods made for export are of a higher quality than those foisted onto the home market. But the process goes much further than that. For example, one well known beverage sold internationally is called the same everywhere and looks the same but is in fact produced in forty different varieties.

(c)   **Research and development**

The larger the part R and D plays in a company's activities the more sense it makes to spread the cost by operating internationally. Drugs companies are a good example. The largest have R & D budgets of more than half a billion pounds. Few, if any, national markets can support outlays of that kind. Logically there is no reason why R & D should not be regarded in the same light as process specialisation and after a hesitant start this is gradually becoming the case. It is becoming quite usual for R & D to be located wherever there is a natural affinity in terms of expertise, educational skills and university liaison to the desired activities.

(d)   **Vertical and horizontal integration**

Due to the large size of many MNCs the scope to integrate their activities often exists. Vertical integration occurs when a company gains control of its suppliers or raw materials (backward vertical integration) and/or its distribution networks (forward vertical integration). The classic example is an oil company which finds and controls the producing wells, refines the product and organises the distribution through its own outlets. A tobacco company, on the other hand tends to buy in its supplies, perhaps because of the complexity of blending, and cannot control the distribution because of the proliferation of brands. It therefore expands horizontally by setting up factories wherever deemed suitable.

(e)   **Transfer pricing**

This is an important technique which can offer major financial advantages to a MNC (although not always to any particular host country). It permits a MNC to minimise its tax liabilities by maximising profits as far as possible in the country with the most favourable tax regime. Essentially this is achieved by selling products between component parts of the group at artificial prices so that higher costs are incurred where taxes are high and lower costs where taxes are lower.   In the United States the state of California has attempted to deal with this problem by taxing MNCs in its jurisdiction on their world wide income in proportion to the ratio which the Californian activities have to the whole.   This attempt has recently been stalled by the US Supreme Court but in a way which leaves the issue still open.

(f)   **Exchange rate considerations**

There are two aspects to be considered.   The first is not strictly concerned with the rate of exchange but it is convenient to deal with it under this heading.   Further, although the restraints in question are externally imposed the structure of a MNC makes it expedient to regard them as ownership specific factors.

The first problem is that of **exchange control** and the restrictions on remitting profits and other monies.   There is a tendency for controls to be relaxed or abolished.   The move to floating rates makes this an easier option.   However, where they exist the structure of a MNC, as with transfer pricing, makes it simpler for them to be overcome.   The MNC can also finance its expansion by using local currencies and by raising loan finance on the local market.   Even more decisively, in the case of LDCs, the MNC may have been able to negotiate a way round the problem as a *quid pro quo* for going there in the first place.

Where **changes in the rate** are concerned a MNC is in a relatively strong position.   What it loses on its holdings in one country may be compensated by gains on its holdings in others.   In any case it is often the practice to set up a strong treasury function in the home country which controls cash holdings of the whole group very closely and by this means endeavours to minimise the risks.

1.7   Factors external to the MNC

These factors are listed below.   There is little point in describing them more fully since once mentioned the implications are self evident.   That is not to say that the detail is not formidable in some cases.   For example, in the case of 'Tax regime and incentives' the complexities in practice can be enormous, even esoteric, on which stout volumes can and have been written.   However, before coming to these factors there are some points worth mentioning.   First, there has been a swing away from expansion into LDCs and more emphasis placed on expansion into developed countries.   At first sight this is surprising for two reasons.   Political risk which is a strong deterrent has markedly lessened in recent years and, secondly, economic theory postulates that capital will flow to regions where it is scarce, as indeed it did on a large scale from Britain to the United States in the 19th century and as it has done from the United States to Latin America in the 20th.

There is no conclusive answer to this question but pointers can be gained by looking at a number of different aspects.   In the first place international trade has greatly expanded in the last half century and with it the rise of adversarial competition which has been described at length previously.   There is therefore an incentive for a company in the light of this new threat to meet its competitors head on in their own market place.   Next, the fast pace of technological change has created opportunities for new products to be introduced continually even in developed nations.   Further, the development of international capital markets has made it easier for MNCs to mobilise funds for their expansion.   Finally, some projects are now of such enormous cost that they are best undertaken by international co-operation and they are generally of such a nature that they can only be undertaken in the developed nations.

In the nature of things when discussing MNCs most attention is given to the great manufacturing and oil and mining companies, but it should be remembered that their success and impact on the world economy brings in train a parallel expansion in the cross border activities of service sector enterprises such as banks, insurance companies and brokers, financial service companies and accountants and law firms.

1.8   List of external factors affecting the success of a MNC

(a)   Location
(b)   Size of market
(c)   Competition
(d)   Tax regime and incentives
(e)   Political stability
(f)   Capital markets
(g)   Tariffs
(h)   Labour costs, skills, trade unions
(i)   Language.

*(**Tutorial note:** students should note that the examiner would expect more than one word bullet points in their answers. Explanations should consider the relevance of factors to the particular organisation's circumstances in the question.)*

1.9   Foreign direct investment motives

Motives for foreign direct investment can be categorised into strategic motives and economic motives.

(a)   **Strategic motives**

There are five principal strategic motives:

(i)   *Market seekers*

Such firms may be purely exporting to markets overseas or producing in foreign markets to meet local demand.   Overseas car manufacturers in the UK and communications firms in eastern Europe are examples.

(ii)   *Raw material seekers*

Oil extraction and overseas fishing rights are examples of firms taking raw materials from sources other than their home country.

(iii)   *Knowledge seekers*

This is a specific example of a raw material seeker. Firms may operate in overseas markets to gain access to operational or managerial expertise. For example Silicon Valley.

(iv)   *Production efficiency seekers*

A commonplace example here is the utilisation of low cost labour in the far east. Such relatively cheap resources result in higher profit margins for western firms.

(v)   *Political safety seekers*

Multinationals may seek countries in which there will be little political interference with foreign operations.

(b)   **Economic motives**

Competitive advantage can be achieved over local firms due to the economic strengths of the foreign investor. These strengths utilised by the investor fall into the following classifications:

(i)   technology - for example British Telecom moving into eastern Europe;

(ii)   economies of scale - through worldwide production and distribution networks;

(iii)   managerial/marketing capabilities - experience will outweigh that of local firms;

(iv)   financial strength - ability to undercut local firms and attract employees and suppliers;

(v)   defensive reasons - to relaunch products declining in other markets or establish international credibility in the eyes of customers and competitors.

The financing problems and risks associated with foreign direct investment are discussed later.

1.10 Regulation

Nothing so far has been said about control and regulation of MNCs. The fact is that they are largely unregulated, at least insofar as their operations as a whole are concerned. The UN has formulated a 'Code of Conduct of Transnational Corporations' but it is only that - a code of conduct. Individual countries have imposed their own restrictions from time to time by, for example, reserving certain shareholdings for their own nationals or by limiting the transference of profits or royalties. But even governments have to tread carefully lest the subject of their attentions abandons the market altogether.

1.11 Conclusion

In 'The Times' (June 1994) Mr David Davies, the chairman of Johnson Matthey - a hi-tech metals group said "It is no good patting yourself on the back and being top player in Britain. It is no good just being number one in Europe. You have to be the leader in your own business globally - and this is our aim". This, incidentally explains an apparent paradox, the sale by a successful company of a subsidiary itself successful, profitable and with an established market position. The point is that if the subsidiary does not fit in with the aims as outlined by Mr Davies above then it may be better to sacrifice it to further those aims.

Theories have been put forward to explain the phenomenon of MNCs and they are usefully descriptive of the features necessary for success. But to attribute the process to the existence of imperfect competition or the need to increase profits or simply to promote growth tends to miss the point. Certainly imperfect competition must exist - in a perfect world there would be no scope for improvement - and, true, any company would like to increase its profits, even the corner shop, and also growth is usually desirable. But if we look at the historical process and acknowledge the way in which relations between companies have moved from the complementary to the competitive to the destructive, we can see a more powerful imperative at work - the need to survive.

It is important, however, to preserve a balance. Not every company that spots opportunities abroad and becomes a MNC is necessarily motivated by the reasoning given above. Also, the human motivations of aggrandisement and doing what the others are doing play a part in this as in other spheres of activity. The case of Japanese MNCs is interesting. Due to the closed nature of the Japanese economy (a sore point with the Americans in particular) it is difficult for foreign companies to compete with them in Japan and the struggle takes place elsewhere. And, undoubtedly, a major consideration of Japanese companies expanding in Europe, car plants in Britain as an instance, is the need to escape the quota and tariff restrictions imposed by member states of the European Union.

2 INTERNATIONAL TRADE AND PROTECTIONISM

2.1 Introduction

Trading between nations has been a feature of human activity since pre-historic times. Development through the ages can be briefly summarised

- To mid 18th century - the theory of *mercantilism* was followed, whereby exports were promoted and imports denied, a policy that ensured the steady increase of a nation's precious metals reserves and thus (so it was thought) power. Policy makers were oblivious to the fact that it was also a grave impediment to commerce and a deterrent to increasing the world's wealth

- Later 18th century - Adam Smith, in his work 'The Wealth of Nations', pointed out that wealth was measured in terms of goods rather than gold; and that if each nation produced what they were best equipped for in terms of skills, natural resources etc, the interchange of such products would be to the benefit of all.

2.2   The ideas of David Ricardo

This still left open the situation which occurs when two countries are manifestly unequal in their capabilities in all respects. It seems that in these circumstances there would be little hope for successful trading since whatever country A produces country B can produce it better and cheaper. This problem was solved by David Ricardo in 'The Principles of Political Economy and Taxation' (1821). The principle involved is quite simple and in order to illustrate the underlying rationale quite easy examples are sufficient. Still, where something appears magically apparently out of nothing a mental block sometimes occurs and it will be useful to start with a simple example.

2.3   The theory of comparative advantage

A bright young man becomes a bookkeeper and takes to the subject extremely well. He masters the principles and after a time can produce a trial balance from an array of figures 'in a flash'. He progresses and becomes a highly paid consultant earning £000s per week. He recognises that the people working for him are not as effective in their roles as he was himself. He believes he can do their job in a fraction of the time they take. 'Even so' he also realises that it is better to earn £000s doing what he does best rather than saving £s per hour doing what they are doing. 'Even so' represents the theory of **comparative advantage** as enunciated by Ricardo.

We can now translate this principle into an arithmetical example involving trading between two nations. For equal inputs country A produces 20 cars and 180 motorcycles and country B produces 5 cars and 160 motorcycles. Prima facie, there is no reason to trade. If we make the simplifying assumption that resources are transferable at will between each avenue of production, so that in the case of A 1 car equals 9 motorcycles, we observe that B is much better at making motorcycles **compared** with cars, although still worse in an absolute sense.

Let us suppose that the two countries are open to new ideas and they mutually agree that A will produce only cars and B will produce only motorcycles. A can now make 29 cars and B 320 motorcycles (the original 160 plus 32 in respect of each car given up). There is an increase in value since cars are obviously worth more than motorcycles. A and B can now trade cars for motorcycles to their mutual advantage.

2.4   Comparative advantage in the real world

Of course the above examples were chosen merely to illustrate the principle and does not pretend to be a real life example. It will be instructive, therefore, to see what happens in the world as it is. The UK oil and gas industry is a high cost producer by world standards but the UK coal industry is even more so, except perhaps for the few remaining pits. Making the large assumption that it is possible to ignore the political dimension and with approximately correct guesses about future prices and costs it would have been possible to predict the final outcome as soon as the first well was successfully drilled - the rise of the oil industry and the decline of the coal industry. Note, however, that there is no direct transfer of resources. Capital is removed from one area and increased in the other.

2.5   Free trade and protectionism

Some important points concerning this subject are contained in the section dealing with Trade agreements below. Smith and Ricardo and their followers paved the way and this issue was finally settled in the 1850s when the UK opted for free trade. This situation persisted until 1915 when duties were once again imposed on a range of goods. This was not an abandonment of principle but a measure to free shipping space for the carrying of war supplies. Nevertheless, protectionism was reintroduced in 1921 in the difficult conditions following the end of the first world war in respect of key industries. Later a comprehensive range of duties on imported goods was imposed by the Import Duties Act in 1931.

Many reasons, not least self interest, can be advanced for protecting particular industries. Two main ones stand out. One, the need to preserve certain facilities at almost any cost if they are regarded as vital for defence. Two, the need to protect 'infant' industries to give them a change to grow to maturity. Little can be said about the first except to note that increasing interdependence makes it more and more difficult for all except the very largest countries to be self-sufficient. The problem with infant industries is that experience seems to indicate that they remain infantile indefinitely.

The inter-war period was one of protectionism on a world-wide basis with detrimental effects on international trade. The opportunity to remedy this situation was taken after the end of the second world war with the establishment of the General Agreement on Tariffs and Trade (GATT) which is described separately below.

2.6   Methods of protectionism

A country has many means of controlling the volume of imports entering the country, some direct, others indirect.

The main methods employed are summarised in the table below. The most commonly used are then discussed.

Direct methods:

Tariffs
Specific
Ad valorem

Quotas
Quantitative restriction
Price restriction
Voluntary export restraint

Fiscal
Export subsidy
Government procurement
Exchange controls

Indirect methods:

Fiscal
Regional subsidies
National industry subsidies

Administrative
Health and safety regulations
Environmental controls
Customs procedures

Tariffs are a straightforward levy on duty imposed on imports. It can be a fixed amount per unit (specific) or a percentage of the price (ad valorem). A tariff has the effect of raising the price of the imported goods and therefore reducing demand.

Quotas are a restriction on the number of physical units or the value of imports. For example, Japanese cars are restricted to 11% of the total number of cars sold in the UK each year. A quota therefore directly restricts the supply; this in turn may lead to a rise in price.

Where quotas have been used by the industrial world it has tended to be more recently in the form of voluntary restraints. These are employed by the exporting country but usually at the importing country's request (or even threat of more formal restraints). Such voluntary restraints may relate to quantity or price and have been employed in the trade of steel, automobiles, food, clothing and textiles and footwear.

For example, in 1981 Japan agreed to limit car exports to the US to 1.69 million units per annum for three years.

Due to the work of GATT in promoting free trade these direct methods are less commonly used. The emphasis has switched towards less obvious direct fiscal methods and indirect methods.

Direct fiscal methods include subsidies granted to domestic producers to ensure they are price competitive compared to imported substitutes and regulations (formal or informal) guiding government purchasing towards home produced goods and services.

Indirect methods include subsidies to geographical regions or nationalised industries, again improving competitive advantage vis à vis the imported products or services. Even less obvious are the examples of indirect **administrative** forms of protection.

Restrictive health and safety regulations, and environmental controls can at best prevent foreign companies from making sales in the home economy and at worst force high costs of compliance upon them. Complex and slow customs procedures can also act as an effective barrier slowing the rate at which imports can enter the economy.

2.7   Conclusion

The question of free trade and protectionism is one to which there are no easy answers. In a perfect world free trade would be the rule. In an imperfect world even the most committed of free traders has to face the fact that some countries and blocs, eg the European Union are more or less openly protectionist, for what seems to **them** perfectly valid reasons. There is therefore a strong temptation to reciprocate in kind. The establishment of GATT in 1947 has been of inestimable benefit in holding these pressures in check.

3   CUSTOMS UNION/COMMON MARKET

3.1   Introduction

 A customs union is established when two or more countries agree to remove trade barriers between themselves and to erect a common trade barrier against all other countries.

The most important example is the European Union (EU) (previously the EEC).

Economists in general are in favour of free trade as it is easy to demonstrate that the prosperity of the world as a whole would be increased under such a regime. There are, however, serious difficulties in translating the ideal into a reality. A customs union has therefore been regarded as a half way house, in the sense that free trade is at least permitted between the members of the union. Insofar as tariffs exist between the union and other countries this would appear to be no worse (and may be better from an administrative point of view) than the individual tariffs against other countries which existed before the union came into being.

3.2   Problems arising from customs unions

It has been recognised that there are some disadvantages in such an arrangement vis-à-vis other countries. It is acknowledged that there will be trade **creation** as the removal of trade restrictions between member countries will provide opportunities for more efficient specialisation, and high cost producers will be discouraged while low cost producers will be encouraged.

But there will also be a trade **diversion** effect. This occurs because trade will tend to flow to relatively high cost producers within the union who are protected from more efficient producers outside the union by the existence of a tariff wall.

This may be a worse position where international trade is concerned than the pre-existing situation as the common external tariff is likely to be set at a level to protect the highest cost producer within the union, whereas before the creation of the union that particular tariff may have protected the high cost producer in only one country.

When considering the pros and cons of a customs union the scale of the operation needs to be borne in mind. If two small countries with contiguous borders form such a union it is probably a convenience for both of them and not likely to be of any great consequence to anyone else (eg, the Benelux countries). But on a continental scale as with the EU quite different factors are involved and the two situations cannot be equated.

3.3   The need for a political dimension

Most economic phenomena can be quite usefully analysed from a theoretical standpoint. In the case we are considering it is necessary at once to admit to a complication. Both a free trade area and a customs union (and more especially where a customs union is concerned) involve quite drastic alterations to tariff arrangements that may have been in existence in some cases for centuries. This carries with it the need to integrate fiscal and monetary policies, as is explained later, and hence a serious political dimension is involved. For the moment, however, matters will be considered from a purely economic point of view.

3.4   Advantages arising from a customs union

The more important advantages claimed for a customs union are as follows:

(a)   A gain from the efficiency generated by the increase in specialisation mentioned above.

(b)   A greatly increased market permitting the benefits of large scale production to be achieved.

(c)   An increase in efficiency due to more competition from firms in the other member states.

(d)   Increased labour flexibility as barriers to working in one another's countries are removed.

(e)   A reduction in costs to the consumer following the abolition of duties on imported goods from other members.

Before analysing these claimed advantages further, it is important, and indeed vital, to remember that even if they prove to be unalloyed benefits, there is no reason why they should accrue to all members across the board. The hum of dynamic activity in North Rhine Westfalia may be only a faint murmur in the West Midlands. A very large customs union is in a similar position to the posited state of a free trade world. An overall benefit, perhaps, but not enjoyed equally by all. Some participants may be much worse off. It is therefore inevitable that these important concerns have to be viewed from a national standpoint. The 'Man from Mars' does not exist but the men from Manchester and Milan do.

3.5   Specialisation

Clearly, two countries, one strong in manufacturing and the other rich in agriculture can, prima facie, trade successfully with each other to their mutual advantage. Within the EU there will obviously be some scope for trade of this nature if only because no country is entirely self sufficient. Claims for the benefits flowing however, can easily be exaggerated. A large part of the UK trade with the continental countries is in goods which are close substitutes - cars, machinery, textiles and consumer durables. Of the remainder the common external tariff tends to redirect trade to high cost producers at the expense of more efficient producers elsewhere. It has been estimated that the existence of the common agricultural policy (CAP) costs each family in the UK an extra £1,000 per annum.

3.6   Large scale production

It is too easily assumed that the benefits gained from decreasing costs associated with large scale manufacturing (presumed necessary for a large market) are an unqualified good. Discrimination is required. Large scale manufacturing in the Soviet Union, of which there are some mighty examples, has done little for its people. On the other hand much smaller countries, eg Switzerland and Sweden have some of the highest standards of living in the world. The fall in cost per unit of output can just as easily, and more realistically, be attributed to increasing skill, experience, innovation and the substitution of cheaper raw materials.

3.7   Efficiency due to competition

It is necessary to be very careful about this. Competition often does bring about a general sharpening up all round. That is true. But it does not always result in increased efficiency. It can mean the wholesale destruction of the weaker industries, viz the television industry in the United States. An example closer at hand is the decimation of the soft fruits and vegetable growers in the Channel Islands. This provides a useful insight into the distinction between business efficiency and economic efficiency.

A business may be at the apex of efficiency in the way that it is run and yet be destroyed by economic factors. Thus producing tomatoes in heated greenhouses however well conducted is not likely to survive competition from tomatoes growing in the open in a warm climate.

3.8   Increased labour flexibility

All one can say here is that practice does not match up to theory. There is little evidence that the abolition of barriers to working as between members of the EU has increased labour flexibility. The fact is that most members of the EU have substantial and increasing levels of unemployment. This is not surprising for a number of reasons but one is certainly the rigidity built into labour relations. Hence the reluctance of the UK to take on the Social Chapter.

3.9   Reduction in prices to the consumer

At first sight there is an obvious reduction in prices due to the elimination of tariffs on goods imported from fellow members of the EU. To get at the reality the matter needs to be followed through. Duties may be imposed on imports for two reasons, one, as a straightforward protective measure, and, two, simply to raise revenue. But whatever the underlying purpose the result is a substantial contribution to Government revenue. If it is not substantial there is correspondingly not much benefit in abolition to the consumer.

If import duties are abolished the shortfall in revenue, given that the Government's pattern of income and expenditure is to remain unchanged, will have to be made good from another source, presumably general taxation.

To point the argument further, consider the situation where a country with high tariffs abolishes them unilaterally with the whole world. Assume also that the Government in question is running (unusually) a large budget surplus and has no need to replace the lost revenue with increased taxation. Even in this case the consumer is not likely to benefit nearly as much as might be expected.

The unilateral reduction in tariffs will certainly cause an increase in imports, and the higher the tariffs were in the first place the greater the increase. The increased imports will have to be paid for by an increase in exports. This is likely to require a devaluation of the currency to restore the trade balance. After the devaluation **all** imported goods (not merely those on which tariffs were levied) will cost more.

3.10   Political aspects of a European customs union

Politics enter into any discussion of the subject under review in two distinct ways. The first is ideological. The theme of a united Europe has fired the imagination of some and the EU is regarded as merely the essential foundation of a super state. This seems to be a matter of faith, involving a few super egos, and leaves little scope for rational argument. The second, however, is a necessary consequence of the working of a customs union. The need to harmonise external tariffs as well as the complications of abolishing duties on thousands of products between many nations must involve detailed practical political negotiations.

In addition the question of the relative values of currencies influences political thinking at the highest level, since decisions in this area have a major effect on the workings of the economies of the countries involved.

3.11   Need for a European Monetary System

The institution of the European Monetary System (EMS) in 1979 was considered (rightly) to be an essential element in the structure of the EU. The basic reason is that a freely floating currency or a 'managed float' can undo the benefits of the harmonisation and abolition of tariffs. The equality brought about by a zero tariff can be nullified if a country's currency is depreciated relative to the others.

The exchange rate mechanism (ERM) fixed each country's exchange rates within narrow bands against each other. The UK joined in 1990 but was compelled to leave in 1992. The EMS effectively foundered in 1993.

European politicians hope that the introduction of the Euro as a single currency throughout much of Europe with effect from January 1999 will have more success, though the first few months of trading have seen the Euro losing ground against other major currencies such as the US dollar and the pound sterling.

3.12   Conclusion

The conclusion seems to be that a customs union such as the EU may be too ambitious to be viable, as too many of its members have disparate rates of growth and are unequal in stages of development. This also leaves out of account matters of history and constitution which are highly relevant but not subject to economic analysis.

4   TRADE AGREEMENTS AND AREAS - GATT and the WTO , EFTA, etc

4.1   Introduction

Simple models of an economy portray relevant factors at work in a closed community, ie, one that is isolated from the complications of importing and exporting. When international trade is considered the benefits of specialisation and the idea of comparative advantage (considered elsewhere) are introduced. The picture then represented corresponds in a general sense with the common understanding of the matter. Countries tend naturally to export goods and services which they are proficient at producing, and to import goods to fill gaps in the home market. For example, oranges may be imported into the United Kingdom from the Middle East and the producing areas may in turn be insured against natural hazards in the London insurance market.

Often, however, trade flows do not naturally form such a neat pattern. Suppose that it is found that the UK is the largest importer of oranges from the area but that the insurance is placed in a country which is a small importer or one that is itself an orange producer, viz the United States. It might not be thought unreasonable for it to be suggested to the orange producer that it would be helpful if they reviewed their insurance arrangements, perhaps with the delicate hint that the UK might otherwise be tempted to look elsewhere for its oranges. This is a simplistic and hypothetical example but it does illustrate an important reality. The opportunities to improve trade flows by administrative action, to the advantage of some and the disadvantage of others, are so widespread that protectionism, with some exceptions noted later, has throughout history been the norm and not the exception. Protectionism is used here in the wide sense of embracing all those measures which have the object of altering trade flows artificially, eg, agreements, formal or informal, quotas, tariffs and over complex rules relating to health, safety or standards.

4.2   Definition of a free trade area

A free trade area is an association of countries which have eliminated or at least harmonised duties between themselves but where each member is free to negotiate its own arrangements with the rest of the world. A customs union, on the other hand, is similar but with the important difference that all members present a common tariff barrier to the outside world.

When considering the merits and demerits of such organisations it is necessary to keep in mind that these groupings are protectionist entities writ large. Words such as 'free trade', 'harmonisation' or 'union' may tend to obscure this fact.

4.3   Why are trade barriers not universally abolished?

It is indisputable, and no important economist thinks otherwise, that if trade barriers were universally abolished international trade would rapidly increase and the prosperity of the world would be greatly enhanced. This attractive prospect founders on one unfortunate fact. There is no guarantee that all parts of the world would benefit equally. Some parts might be considerably worse off even though the average level of prosperity has been raised. For this reason the search for the ultimate - a free trade world - is probably a chimera, at least in the foreseeable future. At the same time protectionism in any absolute form is self defeating if adopted by any one country because of the certainty of reprisals by its trading partners.

4.4   The Free trade v Protectionism debate

In the light of these facts the organisations described below can all be regarded as attempts to steer a middle way between the absolutes mentioned above - a synthesis between the possible and the practical. From a historical point of view they can also be looked at as the latest reflection of the great debate - Free trade v Protectionism which divided English politics at the turn of the century. The terms of this debate, the essential features of which are still alive today, have been distorted by two great historical events which may never be repeated.

One, England as the originator of the industrial revolution had a near monopoly of manufactured products for many decades. Hence she promoted free trade (why not?) and became the greatest importer and exporter in the world with beneficial effects all round. But when her position was eroded by the emergence of competitors, principally Germany and the United States, who it must be said achieved their prominence behind high tariff walls, doubts began to emerge and crystallised into the differences of opinion mentioned above.

Two, history curiously repeated itself for different reasons in the second half of the 20th century. In 1945 the United States emerged as the dominant economic power of the time with her competitors either shattered or exhausted by war. She in her turn became a protagonist of free trade (why not?), unlike the situation prevailing up until 1939, with beneficial results all round. Currently, however, her position has been eroded by the rehabilitation of the economies of Europe and Japan and the emergence of new competitors in the Far East. It should not be surprising, therefore, if a move to protectionism has begun to assert itself.

4.5   Free trade areas

(a)   **European Free Trade Association (EFTA)**

In 1947 a conference was held in Paris to formulate a plan to hasten the recovery of Western Europe from the ravages of the second world war. The participants (seventeen in all) formed the Organisation for European Economic Co-operation. Subsequently six of the members founded the EEC by the Treaty of Rome in 1957. Of the remainder, the UK, Norway, Sweden, Denmark, Austria, Portugal and Switzerland formed EFTA in 1959. Later Finland, Iceland and Liechtenstein were admitted as members.

In 1973 the UK and Denmark left EFTA and became members of the EEC, as did Portugal in 1986, and Austria, Finland and Sweden in 1995. The remaining members (Norway, Iceland, Switzerland and Liechtenstein) constitute the present EFTA which is a free trade area as previously defined.

The gathering strength of the EEC, now known simply as the European Union (EU) has persuaded the rest of the world to regard it as more and more of a unit. The protectionist tendencies which non EU countries detect in it have caused alarm and raised the prospect of their being shut out of 'Fortress Europe'.

Understandably, this concern is felt most by the EFTA countries (but also by the US and Japan) which are not only European themselves but in some cases have common borders with the EU. It is not surprising therefore that the remaining EFTA members are seriously considering applying for full membership of the EU.

(b)   **Latin American Free Trade Association (LAFTA)**

The formation of LAFTA paralleled in many ways that of EFTA. A group of countries comprising the major economies of South America formed a free trade area in 1960. Later Ecuador and Columbia joined in 1961 and Venezuela in 1966. Considerable success was achieved in reducing tariff barriers between themselves, but there was much less success in bringing about a common external tariff. The resultant entity remained a free trade area rather than developing into a customs union.

In 1981 LAFTA was replaced by three groups of countries in a new organisation known as the Latin American Integration Association. The attempt to follow a fixed timetable for tariff reduction was abandoned and negotiations subsequently have taken place on an industry by industry basis.

(c)   **North American Free Trade Agreement (NAFTA)**

The North American Free Trade Agreement was signed in 1992 by the leaders of the US, Canada and Mexico, with the objective of gradually eliminating tariffs and other trade barriers on products and services traded between their countries.

A spur to NAFTA's formation was the success of the European Union in eliminating tariffs in order to stimulate trade among its member countries. A US-Canadian free trade agreement had been signed in 1988, and NAFTA basically extended this agreement to Mexico.

The provisions of NAFTA came into effect on 1 January 1994. Some tariffs were removed immediately; others are being gradually reduced over periods of up to 15 years. The existence of NAFTA covering the three largest countries of North America should act as a balancing force to the power of the EU in Europe.

5   BALANCE OF PAYMENTS

5.1   Introduction

In the course of a year a country experiences a two way flow of goods, services and money across its borders. At the end of the year the summing up of these flows will indicate whether a surplus, a deficit or occasionally a rough balance with the rest of the world has been achieved. The current account of the balance of payments is defined as the measurement of all the items making up these flows with the exception of those deemed to be capital transfers. Capital items are loans, grants and investments made by both governments and private individuals.

The current account is conventionally divided into two parts - the visible and the invisible accounts. Visible refers to items such as raw materials, manufactures, semi-manufactures, food and commodities. Invisible refers to financial flows stemming from banking, insurance, shipping, aviation, tourism, interest and profits and dividends.

The investment account comprises flows representing fixed investment such as plant and machinery and the purchase and sale of portfolio assets represented by shares and bonds. The movement of government reserves is also included in this account.

5.2   What if the balance of payments does not balance?

It is unlikely that the balance of payments in any one year will in fact balance. There will almost certainly be a surplus or a deficit. Policy will normally be directed to achieving a rough balance taking one year with another over a period. Looking at the world as a whole there should be a balance since one country's surplus is another's deficit and vice versa. But delays and imperfections in recording usually record a gap, often known as a black hole.

Running a surplus on the balance of payments account is popularly regarded as a success and a sign of strength. In view of the necessary balance of the world as a whole a large country persistently running a heavy surplus on its account is bound to be a destabilising factor and in the end will have serious consequences for the world economy. But ignoring the international consequences of large surpluses it is true that the management of deficits is the problem that tends most to exercise the mind of government.

5.3   The UK balance of payments record

The UK has tended to have a deficit on its visible account counterbalanced by a surplus on the invisible account. A disturbing feature of the visible account is that the surplus on **manufactures** (remembering that the visible account as a whole consists of other categories than just manufactures) which had been positive since the beginning of the industrial revolution turned negative for the first time in the early eighties.

A balance of payments deficit is not necessarily a matter of concern. In certain circumstances it is almost inevitable if a country is industrialising or reindustrialising. The UK had a deficit for most of the period up until the beginning of the 20th century, as did Japan for many years after the second world war.

5.4   Action to remedy a balance of payments deficit

It remains true that a persistent balance of payments deficit usually requires some action to correct matters. There are a number of avenues open to a government faced with this situation.

(a)   **A change in the exchange rate**

In a system of fixed exchange rates a government may simply devalue the currency. This will make exports cheaper and imports more expensive and should after a time bring the account into balance or achieve a surplus. If the currency was overvalued in the first place because of external factors, say capital flooding into the country following the discovery of oil then nothing more needs to be said. But if the imbalance was due to inherent weaknesses in the economy because of lack of management know-how or a deficiency in skills or trade union obduracy then these faults will need to be corrected or the country concerned may correct its deficit but at the price of an indefinite lowering of its standard of living. If the currency is floating the movement of currencies across the exchanges (in the case of the UK represented by the surplus of £s being sold) will have the same effect.

(b)   **Monetary policy**

The government has the choice of restricting the money supply or raising interest rates. It cannot do both simultaneously, unless by the very happy accident that the interest rate set happens to coincide with what limiting the money supply would have brought about anyway. The position is analogous with a monopoly supplier who can produce to the maximum and accept what the market will pay or restrict production to the point where he gets the price he wants. Operating on the money supply has proved difficult and can cause unpredictable and excessive rises in the interest rate. Raising the interest rate will compensate holders of sterling balances for declines in the exchange rate and will tend to attract money into the money market from overseas and in this way offset the effect of the balance of payments deficit. It will also dampen activity and reduce the demand for imports.

(c)   **Fiscal policy**

Raising taxes will also dampen activity. Reduced consumer spending will tend to reduce imports and encourage producers to sell more abroad. Ideally this should be coupled with cuts in government expenditure both to reduce demand and to impress nervous holders of sterling with the government's resolution.

(d)   **Administrative action**

Tariffs, quotas and subsidies have been dealt with elsewhere. They can all be used to alter trade flows.

5.5   Consequences of such actions

All of these actions will impinge on the activities of companies, in some cases beneficially and in others adversely. The detailed consequences are manifold but some of the more obvious results are as follows:

(a)   Exchange rate: changes downwards will benefit exporters and hinder importers. This after all is what the policy is designed to do. But there will be variations in effect. Exporters with a high added value in their products will gain more than those heavily dependent on imported semi-manufactures, which will cost more. Clever forecasting and making use of 'leads and lags' in payments can benefit firms which are able to speed up or delay payments in and out.

(b)   Monetary policy: in general higher interest rates are a hindrance to business, but those firms which operate with large cash balances may well gain, just as holders of building society savings accounts will.

(c)   Fiscal policy: higher taxes are also disadvantageous but again it is sure that some will benefit. Money that might have gone into new housing, now perhaps deferred, will find other outlets if only betting shops or DIY.

(d)   Administrative action: these measures are likely to benefit all companies other than those with an interest in imports.

6   GENERAL AGREEMENT ON TARIFFS AND TRADE (GATT) AND THE WORLD TRADE ORGANISATION (WTO)

6.1   Introduction

GATT, now renamed the World Trade Organisation, is neither a customs union nor a free trade association. It is an international agreement with well over a hundred signatories set up in 1947 with the object, as its name indicates, of freeing international trade by the progressive removal of artificial barriers to such trade.

The difficult nature of this area of economic affairs can be gauged from the fact that originally there was to be a sister organisation to the International Monetary Fund (IMF) called the International Trade Organisation but agreement could not be reached and the attempt was abandoned. The genesis of GATT lies in the 'most favoured nation' principle. This is of long standing and played a useful part in promoting world trade even before the first world war.

6.2   The meaning of most favoured nation

It is worthwhile looking at the expression 'most favoured nation' carefully because as used in the context we are considering, it is an extremely clumsy one and leads to confusion. An analogy might be helpful.

If Alice says that Laura is her favourite friend there is no doubt as to what she means. If she says that Laura is her most favoured friend we can still understand her meaning. If she says that Laura is her most favoured friend and Susan is her most favoured friend too, this is precisely the semantic confusion that has to be overcome.

Bearing that example in mind we simply have to accept that there is no one favoured nation, there is an indefinite number. It will be useful if the phrase is replaced with the acronym MFN and the concept only is considered rather than what the initials stand for.

Now consider the case where country A has trade treaties with B, C and D and each treaty incorporates a MFN clause. A imports cameras from B and imposes a 25% tariff. They mutually agree to a reduced 15% tariff in future. The 15% tariff will now **automatically** apply to cameras imported from C and D because of the operation of the MFN clause in their treaties with A. This is the unconditional form of the MFN principle.

In the inter war period when protectionism became rampant an unconditional form of the most favoured nation clause tended to be replaced by a conditional one. This restricts the automatic extension of privileges only to those countries offering reciprocal concessions.

6.3   The GATT rounds

GATT commenced operating in 1948, a year after its founding in Geneva in 1947. Since then its sphere of operations has been progressively extended by seven further so-called rounds:

- Geneva 1947 (at the time of establishing GATT)
- Annecy, France 1949
- Torquay, England 1951
- Geneva 1956
- Geneva 1960–62
- Kennedy Round 1964–67
- Tokyo Round 1973–79
- Uruguay Round 1986–94

The Uruguay Round proved especially intractable, but finally adopted the most inclusive set of trade liberalisation agreements that the world had ever seen, widening the scope of GATT to include services for the first time, reducing agricultural subsidies, and continuing to reduce tariffs on industrial goods. By the end of the Uruguay Round, GATT had succeeded in reducing the average tariff on the world's industrial goods from around 40% of their market value in 1947 to around 5% in 1994.

The treaty at the end of the Uruguay Round created the World Trade Organisation (WTO) as a new international body to take up GATT's work in the future, and GATT went formally out of existence in April 1994.

6.4   The World Trade Organisation (WTO)

The World Trade Organisation started operations on 1 January 1995 with 104 countries as its founding members. The WTO exists to monitor member countries' adherence to all the prior GATT agreements that they had signed up to (including the Uruguay Round), and to negotiate new trade liberalisation agreements in the future. It is based in Geneva in Switzerland.

In early 1999, the US complained to the WTO that European countries were unfairly favouring banana imports from the Caribbean, while the EU complained that the US was exporting genetically modified crops which had been certified as GM-free. The WTO's role as a stronger organisation than GATT which monitors and resolves trade disputes (rather than just establishing agreements) is being continually tested.

7   SELF TEST QUESTIONS

7.1   What is the definition of a multinational company? (1.1)

7.2   What factors affect the success of a MNC? (1.5)

7.3   Are MNCs typically subject to tight controls? (1.9)

7.4   Explain the theory of comparative advantage. (2.3)

7.5   State three methods of protectionism seen in the real world. (2.6)

7.6   Distinguish between a customs union and a free trade area (3.1, 4.2)

7.7   Describe EFTA. (4.5)

7.8   What actions can be taken to remedy a balance of payments deficit? (5.4)

7.9   What is the role of GATT? (6.1)

7.10   What is the role of the WTO? (6.4)

15 THE INTERNATIONAL FINANCIAL SYSTEM

INTRODUCTION & LEARNING OBJECTIVES

When you have studied this chapter you should be able to do the following:

- Understand the role and functions of the major international financial institutions.
- Understand the institutions role, and functioning of international money markets.
- Understand the institutions role, and functioning of international capital markets.
- Understand the origins, nature, and significance of the international debt problem.

The following chart shows the relative importance of the international capital markets for financing.

1995 International capital markets financing activity

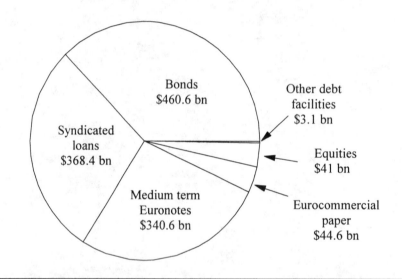

1 INTERNATIONAL FINANCIAL INSTITUTIONS

1.1 Introduction

The international financial institutions that are central to the operation of international trade and finance were, with one exception, created in the immediate post-war period. The most important of these are:

(a) The International Monetary Fund (IMF).

(b) The International Bank for Reconstruction and Development (IBRD) - more popularly known as the World Bank.

(c) General Agreement on Tariffs and Trade (GATT) - whose responsibilities have now been taken over by the World Trade Organisation (WTO).

(d) The Bank for International Settlements.

The design of these institutions was largely the result of negotiations between the USA and the UK and reflected two broad themes:

(a) A general belief in the value of an open system of free international trade and finance with a minimum of interference from governments. This was, in turn, a reflection of the general

It now acts as a clearing house and banker for central banks. It receives deposits from those central banks who are members of BIS. The principal functions of BIS are:

(a)   to encourage cooperation between central banks on matters associated with international payments;

(b)   to provide facilities for financial cooperation between central banks such as providing temporary credit for member banks;

(c)   providing bridging finance for members in the form of short term loans pending the securing of longer term finance for balance of payments deficits.

BIS loans are underwritten by member central banks but are essentially short term, temporary finance. BIS has not acquired the function of international lender of the last resort and therefore cannot really be regarded as the international equivalent of a central bank.

1.6   Activity

Consider the extent to which the international problems of the interwar period which gave rise to the establishment of the post-war international institutions have been replicated in recent years.

2   INTERNATIONAL BANKING

2.1   The nature of international banking

International banking consists of two broad types of banking activity:

(a)   Traditional foreign banking involving transactions in the domestic currency with non-resident business organisations, for example overseas business corporations borrowing or depositing sterling with UK based banks.

(b)   Eurocurrency banking involving transactions in currencies other than the domestic currency eg, UK banks accepting deposits or granting loans in currencies other than sterling.

2.2   Growth and development of international banking

The volume of international banking transactions has increased enormously in recent decades mainly centred on New York, London and Tokyo. The reasons for this growth in international banking include:

(a)   the growth of international trade and overseas investment increasing the demand for international funds;

(b)   the abolition of exchange controls encouraging the globalisation of international financial markets whereby national financial markets become integrated into a single international market;

(c)   deregulation of capital markets permitting securitisation of debt by which companies issue internationally traded debt instruments such as eurobonds and eurocommercial paper;

(d)   the development of multinational companies, including the major banks themselves, operating in a range of countries.

2.3   International money and capital markets

The primary function of banks is to act as financial intermediaries, that is to provide a link between net savers and net borrowers. In international banking the same function is fulfilled but across national boundaries. In addition international banks provide a range of banking services for their customers engaged in international business activity. These include:

(a)   the financing of foreign trade;

(b)   the financing of capital investment;

(c)   providing local banking services in a range of countries;

(d)   trading in foreign exchange markets;

(e)   provision of advice and information.

For their customers, the crucial services are those related to the international money and capital markets.

(a)   **International money markets** (or the 'international banking market') are markets for short and medium term funds. Business organisations with surplus funds can deposit these for periods ranging from overnight to five years. These funds are lent on to borrowers in these markets. The most important of the international money markets is the Eurocurrency market.

(b)   **International capital markets** are markets for long term funds. The instruments involved take a variety of forms including Eurobonds and Euro-equities.

The development of both international money markets and international capital markets have been closely linked to the development of the so called Euromarkets.

3   THE EUROMARKETS

3.1   The origins and growth of Euromarkets

> **Definition**   A Eurocurrency is a bank deposit denominated in a currency other than that of the bank's country (eg, dollar deposits in UK banks).

The Eurocurrency markets are international markets for bank deposits and loans. Thus banks accept deposits of foreign currencies; these can either be straight deposits or Certificates of Deposit (CDs). The latter are negotiable and there are secondary markets for these assets. The banks re-lend these deposits, often to other banks. Banks can also borrow Eurocurrencies from other banks, often on behalf of their international customers.

The original Eurocurrency markets were Eurodollar markets. These developed in the 1960s and had their origins in a variety of developments:

(a)   During the 1960s US capital markets were not integrated with the rest of the world.

    (i)   Restrictions on US interest rates encouraged holders of dollars to seek higher interest rates in Europe.

    (ii)   Foreign companies wishing to invest in the US could not raise dollar denominated capital on US capital markets.

    (iii) Restrictions on US companies wishing to invest abroad encouraged them to seek sources of funds abroad.

(b)   Large and persistent US balance of payments deficits led to a build up of holdings of dollars in other countries. Much of these balances were loaned to the Eurodollar markets.

(c)   The very large balance of payments surpluses of OPEC countries following the oil price rises of 1973 and 1979 produced large flows of dollars much of which were deposited with the Eurocurrency market.

The growth of the Eurocurrency markets continued even when these special factors lost their influence. This was a reflection of:

(a)   Continuing growth in world trade and capital flows creating a demand for foreign currencies and a supply as earners of foreign exchange deposited these with their 'local' banks.

(b)   As well as companies increasing their demands for funds, there has been a substantial increase in borrowing by countries. Countries with balance of payments deficits have often resorted to borrowing on the Eurocurrency markets rather than from the IMF, because the banks did not require the changes in economic policy normally required by the IMF.

(c)   The progressive reduction in capital and exchange controls has increased the ability of companies and banks to move funds internationally. This, combined with the fact that the Eurocurrency market is effectively unregulated, has encouraged the continued growth of these funds.

However, in the last ten years the Eurocurrency markets have experienced a significant slow down in the growth funds. This appears to be the consequence of:

(a)   the severe contraction in the balance of payments surpluses of oil producing countries as oil prices have fallen thus reducing the supply of Eurocurrencies;

(b)   a decrease in the demand for Eurocurrencies reflecting the reduction in many countries' large balance of payments deficits especially for oil importing countries,

(c)   the growth of disintermediation by which borrowers and lenders deal directly with each other without the intermediation role of banks;

(d)   the growing reluctance of banks to lend to developing countries after the experience of the international debt crisis.

3.2   Eurocurrency loans

[Definition]   A Eurocurrency loan is a loan by a bank to a company denominated in currency of a country other than that in which they are based.

Companies have a variety of financing needs. Multinational companies and large companies which are heavily engaged in international transactions may require funds in a foreign currency. Thus a UK company may require a loan in dollars which it can acquire from a UK bank operating in the Eurocurrency market. In effect the company has acquired a Eurodollar loan. Loans can take a variety of forms - straight loans, lines of credit, revolving loans. Borrowers must have first class credit ratings and wish to deal in large sums of money.

There are a variety of factors which will influence the decision whether to borrow in the domestic currency or in a foreign currency. The most important are:

(a)   The currency required is a major factor. Companies may have needs for foreign currency funds for either trading or financing purposes and the Eurocurrency market may be a more convenient or cheaper source of such funds than in the domestic market of the country whose currency is needed.

(b)   Cost and convenience. Eurocurrency loans may be:

  (i)   cheaper if interest rates are lower; even if interest rate differentials are small this may be significant for large loans;

  (ii)   quicker to arrange;

  (iii)   unsecured and large companies can rely on their credit ratings rather than the security that can offer.

(c)   The size of loans. The Eurocurrency markets hold very large funds and for companies wishing to obtain very large loans this may be a viable alternative to domestic banking sources.

Although the Eurocurrency markets have developed into very effective sources of funds for companies and countries, their operations have caused some difficulties. These arise mainly because such markets are unregulated and hence the monetary authorities, either national or international such as the IMF, have no real control over either the volume of lending or the conditions on which it takes place. Two problems in particular may arise:

(i)   excessive growth of lending increases international liquidity; to the extent that this raises world demand, it may have inflationary consequences;

(ii)   very large movements of funds from one currency to another (so called 'hot money flows') may lead to significant changes in exchange rates even when this is not indicated by the underlying competitiveness of the countries involved.

3.3   Other credit instruments

As well as a conventional Eurocurrency loans, the international money markets have developed alternative short term credit instruments:

(a)   Syndicated credits. This is a facility whereby a potential borrower can arrange to borrow funds when it requires but might not take up the full amount of the agreed facility. It therefore differs from a loan which involves a transaction for a particular sum of money over a specified period of time. Interest rates are relatively high (usually above the LIBOR rate). The common use of these facilities is in takeovers between companies:

(i)   a company may use the facility to fund a successful takeover bid;

(ii)   a company may use the facility to re-finance debts incurred in takeover if alternative funds are unavailable.

Much of these funds in the late 1980s were denominated in dollars as a result of the significant activity in the takeover of US companies by non-US (often UK) companies.

(b)   Multiple option facilities. This term covers a variety of financial instruments that have recently been developed. The common arrangement is for a panel of banks to provide a credit standby at a rate of interest linked to LIBOR and for another panel of banks to bid to provide loans when the borrower needs cash. The company can borrow from whichever panel of banks offers the cheapest funds. These funds can be in a variety of forms and denominated in a variety of currencies.

3.4   Euronotes

Euronotes are a form of eurocommercial paper issued by firms on the eurobond market. The firms issue promissory notes which promise to pay the holder a fixed sum of money on a specific date or range of dates in the future.

The eurobond market acts as both a primary and secondary market often underwritten by banks through revolving underwriting facilities. The notes are both short and medium term issued in single or multiple currencies. The medium term notes bridge the gap between the short term issues and the longer term eurobonds.

3.5   Activity

Identify the circumstances in which an organisation with which you are familiar would wish to resort to the Eurocurrency markets and the form this might take.

4   INTERNATIONAL CAPITAL MARKETS

4.1   International capital: Eurobonds

> **Definition**   A Eurobond is a bond issued in more than one country simultaneously, usually through a syndicate of international banks, denominated in a currency other than the national currency of the issuer.

In addition to short term credit, companies and government bodies may wish to raise long term capital. For this there is an international capital market corresponding to the international money market but dealing in longer term funding with a different range of financial instruments. The most important of these is the Eurobond.

Eurobonds are long term loans, usually between 3 and 20 years duration, issued and sold internationally and denominated in a single currency, often not that of the country of origin of the borrower. They may be fixed or floating interest rate bonds. The latter were introduced since inflation, especially if unpredictable, made fixed rate bonds less attractive to potential borrowers.

Eurobonds are suitable sources of finance for organisations which require:

(a)   large capital sums for long periods eg to finance major capital investment programmes;

(b)   borrowing not subject to domestic regulations especially exchange controls which may limit their ability to export capital sums.

However, Eurobonds involves the borrower in currency risk. If the capital investment generates revenue in a currency other than that in which the bond is denominated and exchange rates change the borrower will:

(a)   suffer losses if the currency in which the bond is denominated strengthens against the currency in which the revenues are denominated;

(b)   make gains if the currency in which the bond is denominated weakens against the currency in which the revenues are denominated.

4.2   The Euro-equity market

The Euro-equity market has not developed so extensively as the Eurobond market. In the mid-1960s some Eurobonds were issued with an option by which they could be converted into equity. More conventional share issues have also been made on the Euro-equity markets but with limited success. There have been numerous attempts to place the shares of US and Japanese companies on stock markets in Europe. These have had only limited success; the principal difficulty appears to be the absence of an effective secondary market in such shares thus reducing their liquidity for potential purchasers.

4.3   Activity

Identify the relative merits and drawbacks of Eurobonds relative to domestic borrowing for commercial organisations.

5   THE EUROCURRENCY MARKETS AND INTERNATIONAL DEBT

5.1   The role of international capital flows

> **Definition**   Sovereign debt is that debt which is owed to non-residents (notably banks) by governments or their agencies or is guaranteed by them.

Governments as well as companies have access to international borrowing via the Eurocurrency markets. A government may wish to borrow to finance domestic investment projects and, if domestic sources of funds are limited by a lack of savings, it may turn to international borrowing as an alternative. In addition, a country may face a deficit on the current account of the balance of payments. This will have to be financed by an inflow of capital on the capital account. An obvious source of such capital is international lending. The advantages of international borrowing of this sort are:

(a)   International borrowing enables a country to maintain a rate of domestic investment which is greater than the rate of domestic saving; the difference is made up by the international borrowing. This may be of particular importance to poor countries: they will be aiming at high investment rates in order to generate economic growth and yet, because of low income levels, be unable to maintain high domestic savings rates.

(b)   International borrowing provides a country with foreign exchange as well as capital. Thus it can be used to finance a deficit on the current account of the balance of payments. In the absence of such international financing it would be necessary to correct the deficit, probably by deflation. This would almost certainly involve a slowing down in the rate of economic growth.

Much of the flow of capital to developing countries prior to the mid-1970s was official aid flows:

(a)   bilateral grants and loans from developed economies;
(b)   multilateral loans from the World Bank and its associates.

Much of this flow of capital was on concessionary terms and hence did not imply too great a burden of repayment. The development of the Eurocurrency markets provided these countries with an additional source of international funds. These however would only be available on commercial terms and hence were not greatly used by developing countries until the impact of the oil crisis in 1974.

5.2   The origins of the global debt problem

In the 1970s the developing countries as a group experienced a very large deterioration in their balance of payments. This was the result of:

(a)   the rise in oil prices raising their import bills;

(b)   recession and slower growth in industrialised countries leading to slower growth of exports from developing countries;

(c)   growth of non-tariff barriers to imports in industrialised countries which began to restrict entry of goods from developing countries into these markets.

Developing countries had to choose between two broad approaches to their balance of payments problems.

(a)   Developing countries could correct their balance of payments deficits by deflationary policies. This would remove the need to finance the deficits but would imply a reduction in living standards and much reduced growth.

(b)   Developing countries could borrow to finance their balance of payments deficits and maintain their rates of economic growth.

Most developing countries chose the latter and turned to the Eurocurrency markets to provide the flow of international funds they required. The banks operating in international markets thus acted as international financial intermediaries on a very large scale. The current account deficits of the oil importing nations were matched by the current account surpluses of the oil exporting nations. The function of the international banking system was to channel the oil surpluses in an efficient manner to the deficit countries wishing to borrow. Thus developing countries became very large borrowers of international funds on the Eurocurrency markets. In doing so they accumulated very large international debts.

5.3 The nature of the global debt problem

> [Definition] Debt rescheduling is the renegotiation of debt repayment dates when a country is unable to repay its debts on time.

The accumulation of large international debts produced a financing problem for developing countries. The repayment of debt implies two burdens on the debtor country.

(a) Since there would to be a net outflow of capital, repayment requires that domestic savings rates need to exceed domestic investment rates, the difference providing the funds to repay debt.

(b) Since the debt must be repaid in foreign currency, the country must run a current account surplus to provide the foreign exchange to repay the debt.

The debt problem in the 1980s took on a particularly acute form. The principal difficulty for developing countries was one of ensuring a sufficient flow of foreign exchange to service debts. This problem was made worse in the 1980s by:

(a) limited growth in export earnings partly reflecting the fall in primary product prices;
(b) the high cost of servicing commercial debt especially when interest rates rose in the 1980s.

Thus many developing countries found the burden of debt repayment too great and there was the possibility of debt default. The following table show some examples of the debt burden.

Debt Service Ratios

Annual debt service as a % of export earnings	*1980*	*1992*
Tanzania	19.6	31.5
Uganda	17.4	40.2
Zimbabwe	3.8	32.0
India	9.3	25.3
Bangladesh	23.2	17.1
Brazil	63.1	23.1
Mexico	49.5	44.4
Argentina	37.3	34.4

Source: World Bank 'World Development Report' 1994

Latin American countries experienced some of the most difficult problems since they had been among the largest borrowers. The debt crisis was triggered in 1982 when Mexico experienced such serious financial difficulties that it was forced to reschedule its debts. Its external financial difficulties reappeared in an almost equally acute form in 1995.

5.4 The debt crisis and the international banking system

If a country reaches the point where it can no longer meet its debt service obligations it is faced with a clear choice.

(a) The country could unilaterally cancel its debt and, effectively, declare itself bankrupt. The disadvantage is that the country would be virtually unable to borrow ever again. Moreover a major cancellation of debts would threaten the viability of some western banks which had a significant proportion of their assets in loans to developing countries.

(b) The country could request rescheduling from its creditor banks. This would principally mean extending the loan period and agreeing a new schedule of debt repayment.

Since it was clearly not in the interest of either the debtor countries or the international banks that debt cancellation should take place, there was a considerable international effort in the 1980s to deal with the debt problem of developing countries and to arrange debt rescheduling packages. Since the IMF has insufficient funds to replace commercial debt and since many developing economies are reluctant to borrow from the IMF because of the lending conditions imposed, the IMF's role in the process has been one of encouragement and advice rather than as a major provider of funds.

During the 1980s two main sets of proposals for dealing with the global debt problem emerged.

(a)   The Baker Plan (1985). This plan was proposed by the US Treasury secretary, James Baker. Its immediate aim was to ease the debt repayment problems of the countries with the most serious debts by:

    (i)   increased commercial lending to these countries over a three year period to provide funds to meet current debt obligations;

    (ii)   economic reform by indebted countries along the lines advocated by the IMF in order to boost economic growth and improve their longer term capacity to service their debt.

The development of structural adjustment packages under the auspices of the World Bank can be seen as part of this development.

The weakness of the Baker Plan lay in the unwillingness of the major participants to co-operate.

    (i)   Debtor countries were not fully willing to adopt economic reforms on IMF lines;

    (ii)   Banks were unwilling to increase their lending to countries with debt repayment problems.

(b)   The Brady package (1989). This was a new US Treasury proposal to deal with the international debt problem. The main elements of this package were:

    (i)   a degree of debt cancellation by international banks either via new loans or by converting existing debt into bonds with a reduced face value (ie, discounted securitisation);

    (ii)   policy reform by debtor countries to improve economic performance.

By promising some reduction in countries' debt obligations and by encouraging the securitisation of debt, the Brady package has met with rather more success than the Baker plan.

Despite this welcome development, the international debt problem remains severe. Unless there is a marked increase in the flow of official lending via multilateral organisations such as the IMF and World Bank, developing countries will continue to experience debt repayment problems and debt rescheduling crises will continue to occur. This will hamper the economic progress of the developing countries and place a constraint on the further development of the international capital market.

5.5   Activity

Identify the principal variable which will determine the annual debt service repayments for an international commercial loan of a given size.

6   CHAPTER SUMMARY

This chapter has been concerned with the markets and institutions of the international financial system. The central issues considered are:

(a)   The development of the IMF and the World bank and their role in providing finance for countries with capital and balance of payments needs.

(b)   The development of Eurocurrency markets as the focus of international money markets and the services they provide for both commercial and sovereign borrowers.

(c)   The origins and nature of the global debt problem and the implications of this for both debtor nations and the creditor banks.

7   SELF TEST QUESTIONS

7.1   Outline the factors that influenced the design of international financial institutions in the post-war world. (1.1)

7.2   What are the principal functions of the IMF? (1.2)

7.3   Explain the factors that have limited the role of the IMF as a source of international finance. (1.3)

7.4   What is the role of the Bank for International Settlements? (1.5)

7.5   What have been the major factors behind the growth of international banking? (2.2)

7.6   Explain what is meant by Eurocurrencies and describe their origins. (3.1)

7.7   Explain the possible attractions of the Eurocurrency market as a source of funds for companies. (3.2)

7.8   Outline the origins of global debt and explain the nature of the international debt 'problem'. (5.2, 5.3)

16 FOREIGN TRADE

INTRODUCTION & LEARNING OBJECTIVES

When you have studied this chapter you should be able to do the following:

- Understand the means of conducting international trade and the risks involved.
- Understand the sources and nature of means of financing international trade.
- Be aware of the extent to which trade risks can be insured against.
- Be familiar with the nature and merits of countertrade.

1 THE RISKS OF INTERNATIONAL TRADE

1.1 Introduction

In principle, importing and exporting by companies is the same as any domestic commercial transaction. However, given the nature of external commercial transactions, especially exporting, international trade may entail some special problems for companies. Three main sets of problems exist.

(a) Export transactions are often more lengthy than domestic transactions. Thus the issue of trade credit is more likely to arise. The forms that this credit might take and the ways in which exporters can insure themselves against financial loss needs careful consideration by exporters.

(b) Because international trade involves the use of foreign exchange, there is an additional problem of currency risk. This arises if there are changes in the exchange rate between currencies.

(c) Political risks may exist in that commercial transactions in other countries may be affected either by instability in some countries or by unexpected changes in economic policy or commercial legislation.

1.2 Currency risk

Definition Currency risk is the possibility of financial loss arising out of unpredictable changes in exchange rates for currencies.

In a world of fixed exchange rates, there is minimal currency risk for companies engaged in international trade. In these circumstances the future exchange rate between two currencies is known and hence the determination of contract prices is straightforward and there is no risk of financial loss when payment is due. However if exchange rates are floating there is the possibility of financial loss when payment is made for:

(a) exporters if the contract is in the purchaser's currency and the domestic currency depreciates relative to it;

(b) importers if the contract is in the seller's currency and the domestic currency depreciates relative to it.

If there are significant short-term movements in exchange rates this may be enough to cause serious financial loss to trading companies. Moreover the knowledge of such shifts in exchange rates makes the determination of contract prices difficult and therefore, by creating uncertainty, discourages international trade.

Companies can limit their exposure to currency risk in a variety of ways. These are commonly related to hedging using forward as opposed to spot exchange rates. These are discussed in detail in the chapter on currency risk.

1.3 Political risk

Definition   Political risk is the possibility of financial loss arising from actions taken by the government or people of a country.

There is a wide range of types of risk which can be identified in this category. These are discussed in more detail in the chapter on International Operations but those most likely to affect companies involved in international trade are:

(a)   general political and social instability;

(b)   changes in exchange controls affecting the ability of companies to withdraw funds held in other countries;

(c)   changes in commercial laws/practices creating difficulties in ensuring prompt payment of debts.

2 EXPORT CREDIT AND FINANCE

2.1 Introduction

Given the lengthy nature of much of foreign trade, it is likely that customers will request credit from the exporting company. It is not uncommon for credit to be based on 30 or 60 day periods following the receipt of the goods, or, in some cases, of 90 days from the date of shipment of the goods. If credit is granted there are two sets of problems facing the exporting company.

(a)   The delay in payment will mean that the exporting company may build up a considerable investment in stocks of goods in transit and, effectively, in their debtors. These have to be financed and the economic cost of this financing is represented by the current rate of interest.

(b)   There is the possibility of debt default by the customer leaving the exporter with bad debts. Even if the probability of debt default is no greater than for domestic transactions, the exporter may face greater difficulty and cost in security payment since legal action would have to be taken in a foreign country.

There are broadly two approaches open to export companies to minimise these problems:

(a)   reduce the size of their investment in foreign debtors;

(b)   reduce the risks of acquiring bad debts, (export credit risk)

2.2 Reducing foreign debt investment

An exporting company can reduce the volume of investment tied up in customer debts when engaging in international trade by a variety of means:

(a)   Companies may insist on early payment for its goods. The difficulty is that international trade is very competitive and the granting of credit is an important element in the competitiveness of exporting companies.

(b)   Companies may use banks to provide the cash for payment of the goods in advance of their delivery to the customer. This can be done in several ways:

(i)   advances: the exporter's (seller's) bank may agree to advance cash against the instrument by which the payment is to be made by the customer. The instrument might be a cheque payment or a bill of exchange;

(ii)   letters of credit;

> **Definition**   A letter of credit is a document issued by a bank on behalf of a customer authorising a person to draw money to a specified amount from its branches or correspondents, usually in another country, when the conditions set out in the document have been met.

Provided all conditions are fulfilled within the time specified, letters of credit (LC) guarantee payment to the exporter and formally establish the payment period, which ranges from immediately upon presentation to the designated paying bank, to an unlimited period. However, a letter of credit is not simply a means of boosting the rights of the exporter: it also protects the customer against being pressed for payment before being presented with documentation, which conforms with the conditions originally set out with the exporter.

A letter of credit operates, in outline as follows:

- Buyer requests his bank to open a letter of credit in favour of the seller

- Seller/his bank is notified, and details are checked against original sales contract

- Seller delivers goods and supplies supporting documentation to the buyer's bank

- The seller is then paid under the terms of the letter of credit.

In normal circumstances, this procedure should guarantee payment. If the overseas bank fails, (which is unlikely), then it will not. A more likely reason for non-payment is that the importer (buyer) changes the terms of the letter of credit without informing the exporter (seller). This it can do if the letter of credit is revocable. Consequently, exporters seeking further security should refuse everything except an irrevocable letter of credit – the terms of which, by definition, cannot be changed once agreed except by prior consent of all concerned.

(iii)   bills of exchange. A bill of exchange represents written evidence of a debt. It has evolved through centuries of trade and is now covered by both statute and case law. The legal definition, under the *Bills of Exchange Act 1882*, is as follows.

> **Definition**   A bill of exchange is an unconditional order in writing, addressed by one person to another, signed by the person giving it, requiring the person to whom it is addressed to pay on demand or at a fixed or determinable future time a sum certain in money to, or to the order of, a specified person, or to bearer.

There are three main parties to a bill of exchange: the drawer (exporter), drawee (importer, or person to whom it is addressed), and payee (person the drawee must pay).

Under normal trade, the exporter makes out and signs the bill either at sight (cash on demand) or term (usance). If at term, the customer accepts it, by signing across its face, as payable at a fixed future date. Of course, the buyer could dishonour the bill by neither paying nor accepting.

As well as the drawer's and drawee's names and addresses, a bill of exchange will show the date drawn, the amount in both figures and words, terms (sight or usance) and the payee (or to order, or to bearer). It is more often payable to specified persons rather than bearer.

Bills of exchange are increasingly being used to obtain export finance. They can be discounted, negotiated and forfaited. Advances can be obtained against bills as well as acceptance credits.

It is advisable for the exporter to investigate the ways in which a bill of exchange can be turned into cash and how they compare to an overdraft or loan. The following is a short and simplified description of some of these financing mechanisms.

- **Negotiation:** bank buys ('negotiates') exporter's foreign bills when submitted for collection. The bank is repaid from the proceeds of the bill when they are received from the importer's bank. The bank has recourse to the exporter if the bill is not settled.

- **Advances against bills for collection:** exporter obtains from his bank a percentage advance against the bill of exchange's value. The bank retains recourse against the exporter. It is useful when only a limited amount of finance is required.

- **Acceptance credits:** a very popular form of finance. The bank accepts the bill of exchange drawn upon it by its customer, and then sells it into a secondary market at a discount, including an acceptance commission, passing the proceeds to its client. The bank then pays the bill at face value at maturity.

Acceptances have the advantage of enabling an exporter to give credit to an importer, while receiving cash up front. Also, by accepting a bill, the bank is adding its guarantee that it will be met in full at maturity and so the acceptance can then be sold at a rate which reflects the bank's credit rating. Acceptances are best timed for when borrowing rates are expected to rise, since they offer funds at a fixed interest rate for the term of the bill. A typical trading amount for a sterling acceptance credit would be a multiple of £100,000. The bank's commission represents its fee for undertaking credit risk on its customer, and is negotiable.

2.3 Activity

Consider how the prevailing rate of interest will affect the amount received by the exporting company relative to the face value of a bill of exchange issued on its behalf.

3 REDUCING EXPORT CREDIT RISK

3.1 Introduction

In addition to limiting the size of investment in overseas debtors, an exporting company can take appropriate steps to reduce the risk involved.

(a)   The company can act in a commercially prudent fashion in the light of the known risk of international trade. Companies should:

   (i)   avoid giving credit to customers whose creditworthiness is in doubt;

   (ii)   negotiate secure payment terms, procedures and mechanisms;

   (iii)   ensure that all documentation necessary for collection of payment under letters of credit are in order;

   (iv)   insist that payment is made in a convertible currency not subject to exchange controls.

(b)   The company can employ an intermediary to handle the financing problems of international trade on their behalf. Intermediaries provide a variety of means to reduce bad debt risks for both domestic and export transactions. The most important methods for doing so for bad debts arising out of foreign trade are:

(i)   export factoring;

(ii)   forfaiting;

(iii)   international credit unions;

(iv)   documentary credits (discussed in 2.2 above)

SWIFT is the Society of Worldwide Interbank Financial Telecommunications. It began operations in 1977 after European bankers wanted a more efficient method of sending payment instructions to correspondent banks than telex or mail. All major international banks are now members of the SWIFT communication system which offers an international network using common terminals and standard communication protocols. SWIFT is therefore not itself a cash transfer system; it is an instruction to transfer funds to a specified account at another bank. The actual transfer is made electronically, eg, by CHIPS (see below). However the SWIFT system is efficient, secure and cheap, available 24 hours a day every day.

3.2   Export factoring

Definition   Factoring is the process by which a company takes over the responsibility for collecting the debts of another.

Export factoring is, in essence, no different from the factoring of domestic trade debts. The service provided by the factor is effectively one of underwriting the client's debt; if the client's debtors fail to meet their debt obligations, the factor rather than the client bears the financial loss. In other words the factor has purchased the trade debts of the client and assumes the risk of non-payment. Factors will rarely advance sums against the whole value of the approved invoices representing the trade debt and the service is not costless:

(a)   administrative service charges of up to 3% may be payable;

(b)   finance charges will be levied at levels equivalent to the interest rate on commercial bank short term loans.

Nonetheless factoring is an effective and popular method of trade finance especially for small to medium sized firms engaged in international trade. This reflects its advantages.

(a)   Factoring eliminates much of the risk of non-payment of trade credit and relieves the exporting business of the cost of managing trade debt and pursuing non-payers.

(b)   Factoring minimises debt levels and hence is an important source of working capital for the company.

3.3   Forfaiting

Definition   Forfaiting is a medium term source of credit in which a bank discounts medium term promissory notes or bills of exchange.

Forfaiting is a source of medium term trade credit particularly suitable for the financing of transactions in which, because of the nature of the goods involved or the size of the transactions, payments are usually made over a period of years. It is a common means of trade finance in continental Europe.

In certain circumstances a buyer may require medium term credit. This may be the case with the purchase of capital goods since the income derived from them will take the form of a stream of receipts over the life of the capital goods. In order to secure the credit the buyer must be willing to:

(a)   pay some of the price of the goods on delivery;

(b)   arrange to pay the rest of the bill at regular intervals over a period of years.

In order to do so the buyer will arrange to:

(a)   issue promissory notes or bills involving regular payments and a final maturity date at the end of the desired credit period;

(b)   find a bank which will guarantee (avalise) the notes.

In turn the exporting bank must arrange for a domestic bank to act as the 'forfaiter'. This involves discounting the promissory note(s) thus effectively charging the exporter for the service provided. Once the exporter has received the guaranteed (avalised) notes or bills from the customer, it will sell them (at the agreed discount) to the forfaiting bank and thus secure payment for the goods.

Forfaiting is a complex means of securing trade credit and depending upon the current and expected level of interest rates, may be a relatively expensive method. Its popularity in some countries is a reflection of its advantages:

(a)   the importer receives the medium term credit required;

(b)   the exporter receives payment for the goods without significant delay;

(c)   the risks in trade credit of non-payment, currency risk etc are transferred to the bank acting as the forfaiter.

3.4   International credit unions

Definition   International credit unions are associations of financial institutions providing reciprocal arrangements for trade credit.

International credit unions (such as Credit Union and Eurocredit) are institutional arrangements by which export companies can initiate the process by which medium term credit can be made available to its overseas customer via a bank in that customer's country. Thus an exporter can approach a member of the credit union in its own country to arrange for credit finance for its customer. This bank will contact a member of the credit union in the customer's country which will arrange conventional credit for the customer. On completion the UK bank receives the payment for the goods from the credit granting bank in the customer's country and uses this to pay the exporter. The customer will repay the debt to the creditor bank on the agreed credit terms.

International credit unions have advantages especially for smaller companies:

(a)   the exporter receives full payment for the goods;

(b)   the importer receives medium term credit, repayable on conditions familiar to it;

(c)   risks of loss via currency movements, debt default are minimised.

3.5   Activity

Identify which method of credit risk reduction is most appropriate for your own business and give reasons for your choice.

4   EXPORT CREDIT INSURANCE

4.1   The Export Credit Guarantee Department (ECGD)

The Export Credit Guarantee Department (ECGD) is a department of the UK government. It was established in 1930 to provide an insurance service for exporters to recompense them in the event of non-payment by their overseas customers. The government clearly considered that the absence of such a provision would be likely to reduce the level of exports to a significant degree and hence regarded public provision as an appropriate step.

The ECGD was to achieve the objective of insuring exporters by:

(a)   selling credit insurance to exporters;

(b)   providing guarantees to banks on behalf of exporters in order to encourage the banks to grant credit to either the exporter or the exporter's customer.

The former function is now provided by a private company NCM UK which purchased the credit insurance division of the ECGD when it was privatised in 1991. The ECGD retained the function of providing guarantees to banks for exporting companies.

4.2   The need for credit insurance

It should be noted that the insurance service provided by NCM UK and previously the ECGD is an insurance against non-payment for the goods/service involved in the export transaction. It does not provide insurance for any other aspect of exporting eg, for the goods themselves when in transit. The charges for such credit insurance are relatively high whether provided by the ECGD or by the smaller private sector companies such as Trade Indemnity. Why then should exporting companies pay for such a service?

(a)   Exporting companies may pursue defaulting companies for non-payment via legal channels. However this may well be a lengthy and expensive process especially if it has to be conducted in the courts of the country of the defaulting customer rather than through domestic courts.

(b)   There is a variety of risks that may result in non-payment of debt by the customer (eg, political risks). Thus some forms of non-payment cannot be redeemed by legal action via the courts. The credit insurance provided by ECGD and its successor covers these risks as well as conventional non-payment.

4.3   The provision of credit insurance

The provision of credit insurance is now provided by NCM UK and takes the form of short term credit (up to maximum of 180 days) known as a short term guarantee. Like any insurance there are four issues to be considered with credit insurance:

(a)   what transactions are covered by the insurance?
(b)   what risks are covered by the insurance?
(c)   what level of cover is provided by the insurance?
(d)   what is the cost of the insurance?

The transactions covered by the credit insurance can vary from the whole of a company's export activity to selected transactions. The preference expressed by NCM UK is for comprehensive cover for all of a client's export business. This reduces administrative costs for both the insurer and the insured. Although this is the preferred approach, some limits are placed by NCM on which transactions are automatically covered without formal notification to the insurer. Above these credit limits, prior approval of NCM is required. The limits within which automatic insurance is given are:

(a)   orders up to £250 for new customers of the exporting company;

(b)   orders up to the specified limit in the insurance contract (usually up to £5k) for existing companies.

Credit limits above these levels must receive prior approval from NCM.

Short term guarantees from NCM do not cover all risks involved in international trade credit. Generally speaking the risks covered are in two broad groups: those arising from the creditworthiness or otherwise of the overseas customer, and those arising out of the economic and political features of the country to which the goods are exported. The former are called 'buyer risks' and the latter are called 'country risks'.

Examples of these include:

(a)   Buyer risks:

      (i)   the customer company becoming insolvent;

      (ii)   failure on the part of the customer to pay the bill within six months of the due date of payment;

      (iii)   non-acceptance of the goods by the customer.

(b)   Country risks:

      (i)   action by the government in the importing country which prevents payment, eg the imposition of exchange controls;

      (ii)   political, legal or administrative measures which prevent or seriously delay payment.

There are risks which are not covered by the credit insurance; many of these relate to the consequences of a failure on the part of the exporter to comply with legal and administrative requirements in either the exporting or importing country.

The extent of the cover provided by short term credit insurance will vary depending on the cause of the loss. The percentage cover is:

(a)   90% of the due payment for losses arising out of the poor creditworthiness of the customer (eg, insolvency);

(b)   90% of the due payment less 20% ('first loss') in cases of non-acceptance of goods;

(c)   95% of all other risks covered.

The cost of this service for exporting companies is composed of fixed annual premium and monthly premiums related to the volume of business covered by the insurance agreement.

4.4   Activity

Identify the sort of exporting activities that would most benefit from the service of the ECGD service provided by NCM UK.

5   COUNTERTRADE

5.1   Forms of countertrade

> **Definition**   Countertrade is a form of international trade in which the export of goods to a country is matched by a commitment to import goods from that country.

Countertrade occurs when a commercial transaction involves a commitment by the exporter to accept some imports from the company or country which is buying its products. This may merely represent an agreement to encourage mutual trade or it may represent a more direct exchange of goods in some form of barter.

Countertrade clearly implies a move away from the ideal of free multilateral trade in which all transactions are independent of each other and payment for each is made in the form of an internationally acceptable currency. Most countertrade occurs because some countries have limited access to internationally acceptable currencies ('hard' currencies). Examples of countertrade include oil/manufacturing goods exchanges in the 1980s and complex trade agreements seen in some UK defence industry exporting.

Countertrade can take a variety of forms:

(a)   **Barter.** This is the simplest form of countertrade in which a single contract involves the direct exchange of one set of goods for another. The contract may involve no monetary payments at all.

(b)   **Counterpurchase.** In counterpurchase the exporter agrees, as part of the export contract, to undertake the purchase of products from the customer country but with payment for the exported goods made in the normal fashion. The undertaking to purchase goods from the customer country may vary in detail: it may merely involve an agreement to purchase some volume of unspecified goods, or it may involve buying a specific set of commodities.

(c)   **Buyback.** This is most common where the export is of capital goods that will produce a stream of future output. The exporter may be willing to accept payment for all or part of these goods in the form of a specified share of the output produced by the capital equipment. Given the normal expected life of capital equipment, buyback deals are often of a long term nature thus adding to their complexity.

(d)   **Offset.** For countries which wish to reduce dependence on certain types of imports, it is possible to establish offset agreements designed to promote the development of indigenous industrial capacity. This can take several forms: the exporter may agree to:

    (i)   use some goods from the importing country in the manufacture of the export goods concerned;

    (ii)   establish local production capacity (eg, maintenance facilities in the aircraft industry);

    (iii)   provide technical assistance for local companies within the same industry.

(e)   **Switch trading.** This involves trading between three countries. If country A has a trade credit with country B this may be cleared by a third country (C) exporting to A and using payment to pay for imports from B. Thus country C has effectively acted as an intermediary between a creditor and debtor country.

(f)   **Evidence accounts.** A company may be required by a country to which it is selling a flow of exports to engage in counterpurchasing (ie, buying goods from that country) of an equal amount. Since matching every export with an equivalent import would be impracticable, the company would be required to provide accounting evidence of its counterpurchasing each year.

5.2   The sources of countertrade

Countertrade is clearly of a much more complex nature than conventional multilateral trade flows. Yet estimates suggest that over 10% of all international trade may be in one form of countertrade or another. It is quite common in western economies in defence contracting; however, countertrade is not evenly distributed among countries; the bulk of countertrade occurs in the trade of developing countries and the Eastern European countries which were part of the old COMECON trading group of economies. This concentration of countertrade suggests that the main reasons for countertrade may be found in the particular features of these economies.

(a)   Foreign exchange constraints. Some countries have serious limits on their ability to acquire the foreign exchange to pay directly for imported goods. This may be a reflection of:

    (i)   chronic balance of payments weakness eg, some developing economies and some ex-Soviet bloc economies of eastern Europe;

    (ii)   inability to secure credit because of poor international creditworthiness eg, for countries with large external debts.

(b) Industrial policy. In most developing countries the expansion of the industrial sector has been the main element of development strategy. Countertrade has been used to further this aim by tying imports of goods to the purchase of the products of the indigenous manufacturing sector.

(c) Absence of a free trade sector. For some countries, notably the Eastern European economies of the old Soviet bloc, there was no market mechanism and planning was the dominant means of resource allocation. For this reason trade was also planned and the planning of trade in terms of goods and services was the logical outcome of this. Hence countertrade was an extension of domestic economic policy.

5.3   Problems of countertrade

Countertrade may make sense for importing countries with payments difficulties or for those wishing to develop indigenous industry. However it can cause difficulties for the exporting business. These tend to fall into two groups: increased costs for the exporter and increased indirect risks.

(a) Increased costs:

   (i) increased transaction costs such as specialist consultancy fees, insurance costs, bank fees, disposal costs;

   (ii) reduced value of the countertrade goods: these often have to be sold at a discount.

(b) Increased trading risks:

   (i) risk of being unable to sell the goods accepted in part payment of the exports;

   (ii) unrealistic valuations: the customer may place unrealistically high valuations on the goods offered in exchange for the exports;

   (iii) increasing number of parties to a contract hence increasing the possibility of failure to comply with the contract.

The fundamental difficulty with countertrade and hence its limited popularity among exporters is the issue of liquidity. The exporter, instead of receiving payment in cash, receives goods with less than full liquidity. Most of the risks and costs involved in countertrade arise from this fact.

6   CHAPTER SUMMARY

This chapter has been concerned with risks to companies when engaged in exporting. The most important of these are:

(a) risks arising from unpredictable movements in exchange rates when operating under floating exchange rate regimes;

(b) risks arising from the trade credit given to overseas customers and the possibility of default or late payment.

The chapter has also considered ways in which such risks may be avoided or eliminated:

(a) the use of specialist businesses to minimise exposure to credit risks: the most important of these are factoring, forfaiting and international credit unions;

(b) using the services of the Export Credit Guarantee Department and its successor to insure against credit loss.

The chapter has also considered countertrade where some trade risks (eg, currency risk) are eliminated or reduced but involve other problems and risks.

7 SELF TEST QUESTIONS

7.1 Outline the three principal sources of risks for companies involved in exporting business. (1.1)

7.2 Explain how bills of exchange can be used to reduce exposure to credit risk for exporting companies. (2.2)

7.3 Explain what is meant by factoring and show its relevance to the problem of reducing exporting risks. (3.2)

7.4 Describe the circumstances under which forfaiting would be an appropriate procedure for an exporting company. (3.3)

7.5 What are the special advantages of international credit unions for small exporting companies? (3.4)

7.6 Outline and explain the role and functions of the Export Credit Guarantee Department and its successor. (4.1 to 4.3)

7.7 Distinguish between 'buyer risks' and 'country risks' for exporting companies. (4.3)

7.8 Explain the principal forms of countertrade. (5.1)

7.9 Why is countertrade of limited significance in world trade? (5.2)

8 EXAM TYPE QUESTION

8.1 Electronic equipment

A company manufacturing specialised electronic equipment has so far sold only inside the country where it is established. It has considerable surplus capacity and the chairman has asked you, as his finance director, to prepare a draft memorandum for the board on his proposal to open up export business to a number of countries.

You are required to draft this memorandum, setting out the main points that would need to be considered before arriving at a final decision, under the following headings:

(a) export pricing and profitability;
(b) credit terms and methods of obtaining payment;
(c) risks and methods of avoiding them;
(d) forms of representation or local organisation in export markets.

Where appropriate, indicate advantages, disadvantages or your own recommendations.

(20 marks)

9 ANSWER TO EXAMINATION TYPE QUESTION

9.1 Electronic equipment

COMPANY MEMORANDUM

19 November 19X5

From: Finance director

To: Chairman

Subject: Initiation of export trade

The following memorandum sets out the main points requiring consideration before a final decision is taken on whether or not to embark upon export trade.

(a)   **Export pricing and profitability**

    (i)   A starting point would be to consider the market situation for products of the sort we produce, in the various countries where we might consider initiating this export trade. Assuming that demand exists for this type of product, we must ascertain the current prices and quality of competing products in these countries. Provided that these foreign markets are effectively segmented from our existing home market (ie, our domestic customers cannot economically switch their purchases of our products to these new overseas markets), we may be able to set a lower price (as compared with our domestic price) for our output. Provided that the marginal costs of manufacture and sale are covered, the profits of the company would be increased as our surplus production capacity is available to meet the export demand. This may give us the ability to compete effectively on a price basis. Alternatively, we may be able to charge prices which exceed our domestic prices if local competition is such that this strategy would be successful. I suggest that potential markets be ranked in terms of their potential contribution to company profits (marginal revenue less incremental production and selling costs) and, assuming other factors to be similar, exploited in order of the size of their potential contribution to company profits.

    (ii)   A study should be made of the additional costs which might be necessary to achieve export sales in the potential overseas markets such as:

        (1)   transport, insurance and storage up to the point of sale;

        (2)   customs duties;

        (3)   additional documentation and certification of documents to satisfy import and possibly exchange control formalities;

        (4)   insurance against the special risks of export trade (see (c) below);

        (5)   new staff requirements for translation of correspondence, quotations, invoices and publicity materials;

        (6)   other advertising and promotion costs in the new market, especially on launching the product; and

        (7)   cost of establishing a physical presence in the new market such as agent's commission, warehousing and display facilities (see below).

(b)   **Credit terms and methods of obtaining payment**

    (i)   **Assessment of credit worthiness**

        (1)   Potential customers' accounting reports may be less informative for analytical purposes.

        (2)   Bank references may be available.

        (3)   Consular staff and the Export Credits Guarantee Department may be of assistance.

        (4)   Contacts with other United Kingdom companies who trade with our potential overseas customers may also provide useful information.

    (ii)   **Methods of payment**

        (1)   Collection of money may be facilitated by:

(A)   using and discounting bills of exchange; and

(B)   using letters of credit under which collection can be made from a bank in our country upon presentation of the shipping documents. We may wish the letters of credit to be made irrevocable and to ensure that they are 'confirmed' by a bank.

The costs of the above would have to be considered in our pricing policy.

(2)   Pre-payment or part-payment for our goods at the time of ordering may be possible if our products have clear advantages over those of our competitors.

(c)   Risks and methods of reducing such risks

(i)   The major risks of the export business include:

(1)   Insolvency of customer.

(2)   Customer's failure to pay within a reasonable time.

(3)   Customer's failure to take up goods ordered and sent to him.

The problems and cost of legal action in another country mean that the above three risks are increased in the export business.

(4)   Political and governmental influence or action (including war) preventing the completion of the contract.

(5)   Fluctuations in exchange rates, unless we can invoice in our own currency.

(ii)   **Avoiding risks**

(1)   We can obtain insurance to cover the risks mentioned in (1) to (3) above up to 90% and risks under (4) above up to 95%.

(2)   We shall also have to consider whether to insure our whole export turnover or to pay a higher pro-rata premium to cover selected markets.

(3)   The effects of fluctuating exchange rates could be reduced by:

(A)   undertaking forward exchange contracts; and

(B)   holding bank accounts in foreign currencies and repatriating balances when the exchange rate is relatively favourable.

(d)   Forms of organisation

(i)   For our type of product it would almost certainly be necessary to have local agents who would negotiate orders, ensure that they were adequately fulfilled, recover outstanding debts and provide an aftersales service.

(ii)   To reduce transit costs, it might be advantageous to establish local assembly facilities, either using local companies or setting up a subsidiary. The latter would ensure the quality but would mean a higher initial investment and might be prohibited by local law.

(iii)   Tax considerations may influence the form of organisation. We must investigate whether:

(1)   there is a double-taxation treaty with the country;

(2)   the foreign country uses the 'unitary' basis of tax, ie, whether it taxes a proportion of the company's world-wide profits; and

(3)   possibilities exist of framing transfer pricing policy to minimise the total tax payable.

17 EXCHANGE RATE SYSTEMS

INTRODUCTION & LEARNING OBJECTIVES

When you have studied this chapter you should be able to do the following:

- Explain the nature and working of the foreign exchange markets.
- Understand the relationship between exchange rates and the links between spot and forward rates.
- Understand the major factors involved in the determination of exchange rates.
- Outline the major changes in exchange rate systems and identify their advantages and disadvantages.

The following table highlights movements in major currencies over a recent five year period and UK current interest rates.

April 1999 UK interest rates (%)

3 month IBR	5.22
3 month TB	5.00
UK clearing bank base lending rate	5.25

Exchange rates (units $US)

Year	UK	Japan	France	Germany	Italy
1990	1.79	145	5.44	1.62	1,198
1992	1.77	127	5.29	1.56	1,231
1994	1.53	102	5.55	1.62	1,611
1998	1.67	129	6.08	1.81	1,787
1999	1.62	120	6.08	1.81	1,794

1 THE MARKET FOR FOREIGN EXCHANGE

1.1 The foreign exchange market

Definition The foreign exchange market is an international market in which national currencies are traded.

The foreign exchange (FOREX) market is an international market in national currencies in which the bulk of transactions are completed by telephone and telex links. The market is extremely large. The biggest centre is the London FOREX market with a daily gross turnover exceeding US $300 billion. The principal participants in the market are the banks; these operate on behalf of their customers including businesses and government but also on their own behalf. The latter now accounts for the bulk of the activity in the FOREX.

The existence of the FOREX market is rooted in the development of international trade since such trade requires the use of foreign currency. However as foreign currency has become a tradeable asset in its own right, most transactions are concerned with switching financial assets from one currency to another rather than purchasing currency for direct use in international trade.

The FOREX market is highly competitive:

(a) there are many buyers and sellers (over 350 banks deal on the London FOREX market);

(b) the commodity is homogeneous (one US$ is the same as any other US$);

(c) via computer systems there is near perfect information of prices charged.

The result is a highly competitive market in which the price of currencies (the exchange rate) is determined by supply and demand and virtually no differences exist between one FOREX market (eg, London) and another (eg, New York).

1.2   Exchange rates

Definition   An exchange rate is the price of a currency expressed in terms of another currency.

The demand for and supply of currencies in the FOREX determines the value of exchange rates. Since there are numerous currencies, this produces a whole series of prices for any single currency. In addition there are several exchange rates for each pair of currencies. For the exchange rate on a given day (the spot rate) there will be two prices:

(a)   a lower, 'offer' price which is the price a FOREX dealer is willing to pay for the currency;

(b)   a higher, 'bid' price which is the price at which a FOREX dealer is willing to sell the currency.

The difference between these two prices is known as the 'spread'; it represents the transactions costs and profits of the dealer in the currency. For small sums (eg, the sale/purchase of notes for small transactions such as personal tourism) the spread will be much larger than for wholesale dealing on the FOREX market. This is because of the fixed nature of some dealer costs and the more intense competition on the FOREX market. In April 1999 the spread for the £/US$ exchange rate as given in the *Financial Times* was $1.6162 – $1.6172: this is a spread of only 0.06%.

1.3   Spot and forward exchange rates

Definition   The **spot rate** is the current rate of exchange, the **forward rate** is the rate at which dealers will exchange currencies at some future specified date.

The spot rate for a currency is the current price. Thus the spot rate for sterling at some date could be:

$1.6690   – $1.6700
(Dealer sells)   (Dealer buys)

Above we referred to the 'lower' offer (buying) price and the 'higher' bid (selling) price - apparently contradicted here. But remember, the dealer's home currency in this case is the £, in which his costs and revenues will be denoted. The above spot rate spread could be translated into £/$:

£0.5992 - £0.5988

which now shows a lower offer price and higher bid price.

Thus if a UK company had received $30,000 in payment from a US customer it could exchange this immediately for £17,964. If it wished to purchase $30,000 immediately, it would cost the firm £17,975.

However, a company may wish to contract or sell foreign a currency at some future date. For this it can receive a future quote from a dealer: the rate quoted is called the **forward rate**. It is usual to quote for forward rates for one month, three months and twelve months ahead. Forward rates are given in two ways.

(a)   Outright quote

	$/£
Spot rate	1.6690 – 1.6700
1 month forward	1.6661 – 1.6675

At this rate a customer could agree to buy $ in one month's time at a price of 1.6661 or sell at 1.6675.

The increased spread for the forward quote reflects the increased risk faced by the dealer. There is no guarantee that dealers will predict the future spot rate with complete accuracy and hence they have the risk of financial loss if predictions are incorrect.

(b)   Premium quote

It is more usual for forward quotes to be expressed as a change from the spot rate. In the above example by buying forward a customer will get fewer $ for sterling than at the spot rate. From this we can conclude that sterling is weakening relative to the US$. In this situation the $ is at a premium. If it were weakening, there would be more $ per £ at the future date and thus the US$ would be at a discount. Thus the outright forward quote could be expressed as:

$/£ 1 month forward   29 cents – 25 cents premium

To determine the outright forward quote from the premium quote, simply add on the discount/take off the premium from the spot rate.

Spot rate   –   premium

1.6690   –   0.0029   =   1.6661
1.6700   –   0.0025   =   1.6675

Alternatively, the discount could be quoted as an annualised percentage. For example, the one month 29 cent premium is equivalent to $\dfrac{0.0029}{1.6690} \dfrac{12}{1} = 2.09\%$ per annum discount on the spot rate.

Thus a premium may be quoted as an amount followed by 'cpm' and a discount by an amount followed by 'dis'. Alternatively the percentage annual premium (+) or discount (-) can be given. This is the method now used by the *Financial Times*.

| Conclusion | To obtain the forward rate from the spot rate, it is necessary to

ADD   a discount
or   DEDUCT a premium.

1.4   Activity

Suppose that the spot rate for pounds was quoted at US$ 1.5815 – 1.5965 and one month dollars at 0.39 – 0.37 cpm. How much sterling would you receive in one month's time by selling forward $15,000?

1.5   Activity solution

Spot $ are quoted at $1.5965 to sell
One month $ are quoted at 0.37 cents premium
Deduct a premium

Therefore $15,000 will convert to $\dfrac{15,000}{1.5965 - 0.0037} = £9,417.38$

2   THE DETERMINATION OF EXCHANGE RATES

2.1   Changes in exchange rates

When forward exchange rates diverge from spot rates it is clear that dealers on the FOREX expect exchange rates to change over time. Measuring the size of changes in exchange rates is complicated however since there is no fixed standard ('numeraire') by which currencies can be measured. It is possible for a currency to appreciate relative to another currency while depreciating against others. In practice the exchange rate for sterling is normally measured against three measures:

(a)   US dollar. Most FOREX deals in sterling are in exchange for US$ and some international trade (eg, in oil) is conducted exclusively in US$. The £/$ rate is therefore of central importance.

(b)   Euro. The euro is the single currency throughout most of the European Union. It is described in more detail later.

(c)   A basket of other currencies. Here sterling's exchange rate against a series of currencies, weighted according to the pattern of UK trade will give a useful indicator of the 'average' exchange rate for sterling with other currencies as a whole. This clearly has to be shown as an index not as a rate and hence it shows changes in exchange rates not the rate itself.

Changes in exchange rates result from changes in the demand for and supply of the currency. These changes may occur for a variety of reasons:

(a)   Since currencies are required to finance international trade, changes in trade may lead to changes in exchange rates. In principles:

    (i)   demand for imports in the UK represents a demand for foreign currency or a supply of sterling;

    (ii)   overseas demand for UK exports represents a demand for sterling or a supply of the currency.

Thus a country with a current account deficit where imports exceed exports may expect to see its exchange rate depreciate since the supply of the currency (imports) will exceed the demand for the currency (exports). Thus any factors which are likely to alter the state of the current account of the balance of payments may ultimately affect the exchange rate.

(b)   There are also capital movements between economies. These transactions are effectively switching bank deposits from one currency to another. These flows are now more important than the volume of trade in goods and services. Thus supply/demand for a currency may reflect events on the capital account. Several factors may lead to inflows or outflows of capital:

    (i)   changes in interest rates: rising (falling) interest rates will attract a capital inflow (outflow) and a demand (supply) for the currency;

    (ii)   inflation: asset holders will not wish to hold financial assets in a currency whose value is falling because of inflation.

These forces which affect the demand and supply of currencies and hence exchange rates have been incorporated into a number of formal models.

2.2   Purchasing power parity theory

The main function of an exchange rate is to provide a means of translating prices expressed in one currency into another currency. The implication is that the exchange will be determined in some way by the relationship between these prices. This arises from the law of one price. The law of one price states that in a free market with no barriers to trade no transport or transactions costs, the competitive process will ensure that there will only be one price for any given good. If price differences occurred they would be removed by arbitrage; entrepreneurs would buy in the low market and resell in the high market. This would eradicate the price difference.

If this law is applied to international transactions, it suggests that exchange rates will always adjust to ensure that only one price exists between countries where there is relatively free trade. Thus if a typical set of goods cost $1,000 in the USA and the same set cost £500 in the UK, free trade would produce an exchange rate of £1 to $2. How does this result come about? Let us suppose that the rate of exchange was $1.5 to £1: the sequence of events would be:

(a)   US purchasers could buy UK goods more cheaply (£500 at $1.5 to £1 is $750);

(b)   there would be flow of UK exports to the US: this would represent demand for sterling;

(c)   the sterling exchange rate would rise;

(d)   when the exchange rate reached $2 to £1, there would be no extra US demand for UK exports since prices would have been equalised: purchasing power parity would have been established.

The clear prediction of the purchasing power parity model of exchange rate determination is that if a country experiences a faster rate of inflation than its trading partners, it will experience a depreciation in its exchange rate. It follows that if inflation rates can be predicted, so can movements in exchange rates.

The purchasing power parity model can be stated as

$$\frac{1+i_f}{1+i_n} = \frac{F}{S}$$

where i_f =   expected foreign inflation rate

i_n =   expected home inflation rate

F =   expected future spot rate

S =   current spot rate.

Example

The UK (home) inflation rate is expected to be 3% over the coming period, and the equivalent rate in Anyland is expected to be 6%. The current spot AL$/£ = 4.5. Estimate the spot rate at the end of the period

$$\frac{F}{4.5} = \frac{1+0.06}{1+0.03} = \frac{1.06}{1.03} \Rightarrow F = 4.5\left(\frac{1.06}{1.03}\right) = 4.63$$

The higher rate of inflation in Anyland has led to a weakening AL$ against the £.

In practice the purchasing power parity model has shown some weaknesses and is a poor predictor of short term changes in exchange rates:

(a)   it ignores the effects of capital movements on the exchange rate;

(b)   trade and therefore exchange rates will only reflect the prices of goods which enter into international trade and not the general price level since this includes non-tradeables (eg, inland transport);

(c)   governments may 'manage' exchange rates eg, by interest rate policy.

It is likely that the purchasing power parity model may be more useful for predicting long run changes in exchange rates since these are more likely to be determined by the underlying competitiveness of economies as measured by the model.

2.3   Interest rate models

Definition   The **Fisher effect** demonstrates the effect of inflation on nominal rates of interest.

The initial analysis of the relationship between exchange rates and interest rates was conducted by Irving Fisher. He postulated that nominal interest rates consist of two elements: the return required by the lender and a premium to cover expected inflation. If the real rate of return to lenders is the same in all countries because of free movement of capital and the operation of the law of one price, then any difference in nominal rates will reflect differences in inflation rates between countries. This is known as the **International Fisher Effect**.

The implication is that if there are differences in the real rate of return in countries because interest rates have not properly taken into account the rate of inflation, capital will move from one country to another in search of the highest real rate of return. Countries with high real rates of return will experience increased capital inflows and an appreciating exchange rate. Countries with low real rates of return will experience capital outflows and a depreciating exchange rate. This leads on to the **interest rate parity model**.

The interest rate parity model shows that it may be possible to predict exchange rate movements by referring to differences in nominal exchange rates. If the forward exchange rate for sterling against the dollar were no higher than the spot rate but US nominal interest rates were higher, the following would happen:

(a)   UK investors would shift funds to the US in order to secure the higher interest rates since they would suffer no exchange losses when they converted $ back into £;

(b)   the flow of capital from the UK to the US would raise UK interest rates and force up the spot rate for the US $;

(c)   the difference in nominal rates has thus predicted the change in exchange rates.

2.4   Forecasting exchange rates

In order to accurately predict movements of exchange rates forecasters would need to be able to do two things:

(a)   identify the factors that determined exchange rates;
(b)   predict future changes in those factors.

Since neither of these can be done with any certainty, exchange rate forecasting is unlikely to be entirely accurate. Nonetheless, various attempts are made to forecast exchange rate movements especially by banks since they must be able to do so in order to operate profitably in the FOREX market. Several models could be used:

(a)   The forward rates in the FOREX could be used by others to predict future exchange rate movements. Indeed if future spot rates diverge from the current forward rate for that day then dealers could clearly make a profit. If the quoted one month forward rate was $1.70 to the £ and it was expected that the spot rate on that day would actually be $1.65, one could contract at the forward rate to sell £'s at $1.70 but on the day buy at $1.65 thus making 5 cents profit on each pound. Since competition would remove this discrepancy, it might be argued that forward rates provide the best guide to exchange rate movements.

(b)   The major dealers on the FOREX market need to make predictions of exchange rate movements in order to guide their buying/selling policy for forward contracts. Banks have developed models in which a variety of factors are used to make such predictions:

      (i)   current and expected interest rate differentials as in the interest rate parity model;
      (ii)   current and expected inflation rates as in the purchasing power parity model;
      (iii)   current and prospective government policy changes, (that may affect inflation or stability of the economy).

These models are sophisticated and often accurate predictors of exchange rate movements. However such models are not entirely reliable; thus operating with forward exchange is, like any futures market, subject to a degree of uncertainty. Recent experience in futures trading by the merchant bank Barings has illustrated the difficulties and dangers involved.

| Conclusion | Although the main determinants of exchange rates have been identified forecasting exchange rates is imperfect because the future values of these determinants and their exact relationships cannot be perfectly known. |

2.5   Activity

Use the data given in the *Financial Times* on forward rates premiums and discounts for sterling to identify the market's predictions as to whether sterling is expected to appreciate or depreciate against other currencies.

3   EXCHANGE RATE SYSTEMS

3.1   Introduction

It is possible for countries to adopt a variety of exchange rate mechanisms. The two broad alternatives are:

(a)   fixed exchange rate systems;

(b)   floating exchange rate systems.

In practice there are unlikely to be either completely fixed exchange rate systems or entirely free floating exchange rate systems. The real issue is the degree of fixity in an exchange rate system and the degree to which governments are prepared to regard a particular exchange rate as an objective of economic policy.

The choice of exchange rate system is of importance because of its impact on three main economic issues:

(a)   the volume and growth of international trade;

(b)   the financing and correction of balance of payments disequilibrium;

(c)   the conduct of domestic economic policy.

These issues will be discussed in relation to fixed and floating exchange rate systems.

3.2   Fixed exchange rate systems

Definition   Under a fixed exchange rate system the government undertakes to maintain the exchange rate for its currency within a specific narrow band.

Under a fixed exchange rate system the government and the monetary authorities would have to operate in the foreign exchange market to ensure that the market rate of exchange was kept at (or very near) its fixed ('par') rate. However, within such systems, there are distinctions as to the form in which reserves are held and the degree of fixity in the exchange rate.

(a)   Reserves. A government (or more likely the central bank) would have to maintain official reserves. These would be required in order to:

    (i)   finance any current account deficit (fall in reserves) or surplus (rise in reserves) that occurred;

    (ii)   intervene in the foreign exchange market to maintain the par value of the currency: the currency would be bought with reserves if the exchange rate fell and sold in exchange for reserves when the exchange rate rose.

    The reserves may take different forms:

    (i)   gold as under the gold standard system that operated prior to 1914;

    (ii)   dollars as under the Bretton Woods System 1945-71;

    (iii)   a basket of major currencies as used since 1971.

(b)   No exchange rate system is truly fixed for all time. The issue is the degree of fixity:

    (i)   under the gold standard system it was held that, for all practical purposes the rates of exchange were fixed;

(ii) under the Bretton Woods System, exchange rates were fixed within narrow limits but with the possibility of occasional changes of the par value (an 'adjustment peg' system).

A fixed exchange rate system has a variety of advantages and disadvantages:

(a) because the system eliminates fluctuations in the exchange rate, it reduces currency risk faced by companies and hence encourages a higher level of international trade that would otherwise take place.

(b) the absence of flexibility in exchange rates means that balance of payments deficits on current account will not be automatically corrected. Since deficits cannot be financed for ever (reserves are limited), governments would have to use deflationary policies to depress the demand for imports. This is likely to cause unemployment and slow down the growth of output.

(c) fixed exchange rates place constraints on government policy: they must not allow the country's inflation rate to exceed that of its trading partners since this would cause current account deficits on the balance of payments and lead to downward pressure on the exchange rate. This constraint is known as policy discipline.

3.3 Floating exchange rate systems

Under a system of floating exchange rates the government has no obligation to maintain the rate of exchange at some declared level and leaves its determination to market forces. However there are degrees to which governments will allow market forces to determine the rate of exchange for their currency.

(a) **Free floating exchange rates.** Here governments would leave the determination of the exchange rate entirely to market forces. There would be no official intervention in foreign exchange markets and hence no need to keep any official reserves. In practice it is unlikely that governments would have no interest in the rate of exchange, for large changes in the rate have important domestic implications especially for economies with large trade ratios (trade to GDP ratio) such as the UK:

(i) currency appreciation reduces international competitiveness and has employment and output implications;

(ii) currency depreciation raises import prices and has implications for the rate of inflation.

Thus a system of managed floating is more likely to be adopted than one of genuine free floating.

(b) **Managed floating.** Under managed floating, governments allow markets to determine day to day movements in the exchange rates but may intervene to prevent very large changes. Two broad approaches to managed floating are possible:

(i) governments may allow the rate of exchange to fluctuate between very large bands (which are often not publicly stated) but intervene if the currency looks like moving outside of these bands;

(ii) governments may allow the market to determine the trend in the exchange rate but intervene to limit fluctuations around the trend ie, to engage in 'smoothing'.

The adoption of a floating exchange rates system has important implications.

(a)   Since there is greater movement of the exchange rate there is the possibility of currency risk. This might lead to a lower volume of international trade either because of the risk itself or because of the cost of minimising its consequences. The lower volume of trade implies a reduced level of economic welfare.

(b)   Under floating exchange rate systems balance of payments deficits/surpluses are, in principle, automatically corrected by movements in the exchange rate. For example a deficit leads to a fall in the exchange rate, this improves competitiveness and corrects the deficit. Thus there is no need for governments to hold foreign exchange reserves to finance payments disequilibria.

(c)   Since the balance of payments is self correcting, this removes constraints on government policy making. Governments can choose any combination of employment/inflation they choose because the balance of payments implication of their choice is automatically corrected. In effect floating exchange rates remove the policy discipline imposed by fixed rates.

3.4   Conclusion

Theories of fixed and floating exchange rates appear to produce radically different outcomes from each system for:

(a)   the volume/growth of trade;
(b)   the need to keep reserves and adopt active balance of payments policy;
(c)   the degree of freedom in the conduct of domestic economic policy.

The experience of both sorts of systems in the post-war economy has been that neither system operated exactly how the theory predicted.

4   THE BRETTON WOODS SYSTEM 1944-71

4.1   Features of the Bretton Woods System

At the Bretton Woods meeting in the USA in 1944, the main features of the post-war international financial and trading system were determined. Not all the elements of the system were adopted immediately, but by the 1950s there was an identifiable system of international financial payments. This was the Bretton Woods System.

The main features of the system were:

(a)   A system of fixed exchange rates on the adjustable peg system was established. Exchange rates were fixed against gold but since there was a fixed dollar price of gold ($35 per ounce) the fixed rates were expressed relative to the dollar. Between 1949 and 1967 sterling was pegged at $2.80 to the £. Governments were obliged to intervene in foreign exchange markets to keep the actual rate within 1% of the pegged rate.

(b)   Governments were permitted by IMF rules to alter the pegged rate - in effect to devalue or revalue the currency but only if the country was experiencing a balance of payments deficit/surplus of a 'fundamental' nature.

(c)   The dollar became the principal international reserve asset. Only the USA undertook to convert their currency into gold if required. In the 1950s the USA held the largest gold stocks in the world. Thus the dollar became 'as good as gold' and countries were willing to use the dollar as their principal reserve.

Initially the Bretton Woods System appeared to work well. World trade grew at record rates in the 1950s and 1960s and the world experienced what has since been described as the 'golden age of capitalism'. However in 1971 the system collapsed: clearly there were problems that had developed over the previous two decades.

4.2 The collapse of the Bretton Woods System

In 1971 the Bretton Woods System collapsed: the USA suspended the convertibility of dollars into gold and most countries moved to some system of floating exchange rates. What caused the demise of the system?

(a)   The system relied on periodic revaluations/devaluations to ensure that exchange rates did not move too far out of line with underlying competitiveness. However countries were reluctant to alter their pegged exchange rates:

    (i)   surplus countries were under no pressure to revalue since the accumulation of foreign exchange reserves posed no real economic problems;

    (ii)   deficit countries regarded devaluation as an indicator of the failure of economic policy. The UK resisted devaluation until 1967 - long after it had become clearly necessary.

    Thus the deficit countries were forced into deflationary policy to protect overvalued exchange rates. As inflation rates accelerated and diverged the problem became more serious and countries became less willing to accept the deflationary price of a fixed exchange rate system.

(b)   The system became vulnerable to speculation since speculation was a 'one way bet': a deficit country might devalue or not - it would never revalue. Thus pressures grew on deficit countries especially as capital flows increased with the development of the Eurocurrency markets. Once markets decided that a currency was overvalued, capital would flow out and it was almost impossible to maintain the pegged rate.

(c)   The system had an inherent flaw. The system had adopted the dollar as the principal reserve currency. As world trade expanded more dollars would be needed to provide sufficient internationally liquid assets to finance that trade. A steady supply of dollars to the world required that the USA ran a balance of payments deficit and financed it by exporting dollars. But eventually the world held more dollars than the value of the USA's holdings of gold: the ability to convert dollars into gold was called in doubt. Thus confidence in the dollar declined.

	US Gold Reserves	*Foreign Holdings of US$*
1949	$25 billion	$6 billion
1971	$12 billion	$60 billion

Thus the system eventually collapsed and countries moved to a system of floating exchange rates and the USA abandoned the convertibility of dollars into gold.

5 MANAGED FLOATING SYSTEMS

5.1 The move to floating exchange rates

With the collapse of Bretton Woods most countries moved to floating exchange rates of one sort or another. This was not so much a positive choice by governments as a recognition of the inability to maintain the previous system. Attempts were made to restore a fixed rate system but these failed.

It was soon recognised that a return to fixed exchange rates was not likely in the immediate future and steps were taken to formalise the new system, the most important outcome of which was an agreement that:

(a)   countries could fix currencies against any measure except gold;

(b)   floating exchange rates were accepted and IMF members were only required to maintain 'orderly exchange arrangements' and 'stable systems of exchange rates'.

However the experience of floating exchange rates clearly indicated problems. Exchange rates fluctuated a great deal and clear overvaluations/undervaluations persisted for long periods thus the fluctuations were not merely temporary. Such fluctuations were likely to damage long term competitiveness and discourage the growth of world trade and capital flows. Hence the major economies began to seek ways of 'managing' floating exchange rates.

5.2   The Plaza Agreement (1985) and the Louvre Accord (1987)

The governments of the five major industrial economies met in the USA in 1985 to consider the implications of what was considered to be the serious overvaluation of the US$. It was considered that such major misalignments of currencies were damaging to the growth of international trade. The result was an exercise in international policy co-ordination. All five countries agreed to undertake policies to engineer a steady fall in the exchange value of the dollar. This was broadly successful.

Given the apparent success of this co-operation the G7 group of countries (USA, Germany, Japan, France, UK, Canada and Italy) attempted to go further. Having considered that exchange rates were now 'about right', the G7 group agreed to maintain management of their exchange rates in order to generate stability in exchange rates. This involved:

(a)   Intervention in the foreign exchange markets to prevent serious short term fluctuations in the exchange rate. This was to be done on a large scale and in a co-ordinated fashion;

(b)   Co-ordinating overall fiscal and monetary policy in order to produce long term stability in exchange rates. The level of interest rates and the control of inflation would be central to this and to short term management of the exchange rate.

The details of the Louvre Accords were never made public. It was argued that managing markets would be made more difficult if the markets knew in advance when and how governments would intervene. This issue has since become a subject of considerable debate among economists.

The need for repeated public statements about the intention to co-ordinate policy to prevent exchange rate movements or to correct misalignments clearly indicates that managed floating has limited success. The steep decline of the dollar relative to the Yen in early 1995 is a further instance of the difficulty of maintaining exchange rate stability.

6   MONETARY CO-OPERATION IN EUROPE

6.1   The European monetary system

The members of the European Union decided long ago to move towards a system in which there was increasing stability between the currencies of members of the Union but that European currencies as a group may fluctuate relative to the currencies of non-member states. This objective was incorporated into the European Monetary System (EMS).

The EMS was established in 1979. Its objectives were:

(a)   **Exchange rate stability.** Members agreed to stabilise exchange rates within the narrow bands of the Exchange Rate Mechanism (ERM). The main features of the ERM were:

(i)   each country had a central rate in the system expressed in the European Currency Unit (ECU);

(ii)   currencies were only allowed to fluctuate within specified bands:

-       up to 2¼% to August 1993
-       up to 15% from August 1993

(iii)   within these there were narrower limits ('divergence thresholds'), measured in ecus, and acting as triggers for policy action by governments to limit further exchange rate movement.

(b)　　**To promote 'convergence'** in economic performance in member states especially in terms of inflation rates, interest rates and public borrowing. This was seen as a necessary step in the move to a single currency.

(c)　　A long term aim of achieving a **single European currency** as part of a wider economic and monetary union. The first stage was to establish the ecu. This was the central currency of the EMS and is a composite currency whose value is determined by a weighted basket of European currencies. Use of the ecu is largely restricted to official transactions.

The central feature of the EMS was the operation of the exchange rate mechanism and the experience of the UK illustrates the difficulties of achieving exchange rate stability within Europe.

6.2　　The UK and the Exchange Rate Mechanism

The UK delayed its entry into the ERM element of the European Monetary System until October 1990. The delay was the result of the way UK economic policy had been conducted prior to this date. Fiscal and especially monetary policy requires a target to operate on:

(a)　　prior to 1987 the target had been the money supply and the exchange rate was allowed to adjust accordingly;

(b)　　after 1987 the target shifted to an exchange rate target ('shadowing the Deutschmark') and monetary policy was directed to this rather than to the money supply.

The ultimate logic of this shift of policy was entry into the ERM. It was felt that this would provide an anchor for anti-inflation policy since it would prevent the rise in import prices associated with currency depreciation and companies which raised prices would find themselves becoming uncompetitive. The UK entered into the ERM with a wider band of 6% but with the intention of later moving to the narrow 2¼% band.

The UK's membership of the ERM ended in failure when sterling was suspended from membership in September 1992 and effectively devalued by 15%. There are several reasons for this failure:

(a)　　The rate chosen was too high (the central rate of DM 2.95 to the £). This made much of UK industry uncompetitive. The results of this were:

　　　(i)　　the recession in 1990-93 was made much more severe with higher unemployment than would otherwise have occurred;

　　　(ii)　　a very large trade deficit in 1990-92.

(b)　　The UK had to maintain very high interest rates despite the severity of the 1990-93 recession. High interest rates were necessary:

　　　(i)　　to attract capital inflows to finance the current account trade deficit and maintain the exchange rate;

　　　(ii)　　to match German interest rates since otherwise capital funds would flow from the UK to Germany.

The problem was made worse as German interest rates rose to contain the inflationary pressures caused by reunification with East Germany.

Thus the UK government was unable to conduct policy in order to meet the domestic problems of recession and was forced to conduct monetary policy in particular to protect the value of sterling within the ERM. In September 1992, despite spending over £10bn in foreign exchange reserves in buying sterling on the foreign exchange market and despite raising interest rates from 10% to 15% in one day, sterling was forced out of the ERM and devalued. Subsequently further currency disturbances occurred and the ERM was modified with much wider bands.

Following the devaluation of sterling, the UK economy recovered quite strongly from the recession. This recovery appears to have been export led and the current account of the balance of payments was approaching balance by 1995. This suggested that sterling had indeed been seriously overvalued within the ERM.

The ERM achieve some successes:

(a)   it achieved a degree of currency stability between the European currencies as a whole (as measured by the ecu);

(b)   some movement towards convergence of policy and performance in European economies.

Nonetheless the ERM showed up some serious problems:

(a)   the difficulty in maintaining stable exchange rates between economies operating independently;

(b)   the need for currency alignment and wider bands to keep the system as a whole viable.

6.3   Economic and Monetary Union (EMU)

The objective of EMU is to establish a single currency and a single monetary authority within all countries in the EU. The EMS and the ERM can be thought of as steps towards EMU, but it was not until the Maastricht Treaty of 1991 that all the members of the EU signed up to the principle of monetary union (though the UK and Denmark insisted on opt-outs to postpone their final consent).

The Maastricht Treaty envisaged a three-stage progress towards monetary union:

•   Stage 1 involved closer monetary co-operation between member states within the existing framework.

•   Stage 2 began on 1 January 1994 and set up the European Monetary Institute, as a prototype European Central Bank (ECB), though responsibility remained in national hands.

•   Stage 3 began on 1 January 1999 involving the irrevocable locking of exchange rates between participating countries. The ECB carries out the common monetary policy and manages the single currency.

A single currency would have some advantages for Europe:

(i)   it would remove exchange rate rates and hence encourage international trade within Europe
(ii)   it would remove transactions costs (eg, having to buy forward currency)
(iii) countries with traditionally high rates of inflation (such as Italy) see EMU as an effective way of reducing inflation by reducing inflationary expectations in the labour market.

However it would no longer be possible for countries to operate independent monetary policy: a single European monetary policy is the counterpart to a single European currency.

6.4   The euro

The EU's new single currency, the euro, was duly launched on 1 January 1999. 11 of the 15 EU countries agreed to participate. Three countries (Denmark, Sweden and the UK) opted out, while Greece failed to achieve the economic joining criteria.

The existing national currencies (such as the French franc) will continue in circulation until 1 January 2002, when they will be replaced by euro notes and coins. In the meantime the euro and the national currencies exist side-by-side for all countries in the euro-zone. Exchange rates for each national currency have been irrevocably locked in terms of euros.

The euro-zone is comparable in size to the US. The euro-zone contains approximately 300 million people with a GDP of about $6.5 trillion, compared to the 270 million people and $8 trillion GDP in the US. Some dreamers therefore believe that the euro could rival the US dollar as the world's favoured reserve currency. However the first months of the euro have seen it depreciate against both the pound and the dollar, partly due to disagreements over the role of the ECB.

6.5   The European Central Bank (ECB)

The ECB began operations in May 1998 as the single body with the power to issue currency, draft monetary policy, and set interest rates in the euro-zone. The Maastricht Treaty envisaged the ECB as an independent body free from day-to-day political interference, with a principal duty of price stability. But many political leaders, such as the leaders of the centre-left governments in France and Germany, believe that the bank should actively seek to reduce unemployment and pursue growth. Such policies would involve premature cuts in interest rates, and it is this prospect that has contributed to the euro's poor performance since its launch.

The ECB is based in Frankfurt, Germany, and comprises an executive board (members appointed on eight-year terms) and a governing council (the executive board plus the heads of the central banks of euro-zone countries). It will be some time before the board has convinced the international currency markets that it is genuinely independent.

6.6   Activity

Look up the exchange rate for the euro to the pound in a newspaper at the time that you are reading this. Determine whether the euro has continued to fall against the pound and the dollar, or whether it has recovered some of the value lost since its launch.

7   CHAPTER SUMMARY

This chapter has dealt with the issue of exchange rate systems. It has concentrated on:

(a)   the factors determining exchange rates especially relative prices (purchasing power parity), interest rates (interest rate parity) and government intervention;

(b)   the characteristics of exchange rate systems contrasting the advantages and disadvantages of floating and fixed systems;

(c)   the development of exchange rate systems since the Bretton Woods System and the effects on the way in which governments have attempted, with varying degrees of success, to manage exchange rates.

8   SELF TEST QUESTIONS

8.1   Distinguish between the bid and offer price for a currency and between spot and forward rates. (1.2, 1.3)

8.2   Explain the purchasing power parity theory of exchange rate determination. (2.2)

8.3   How do levels of interest rates influence exchange rates? (2.3)

8.4   Explain the main difficulties involved in forecasting exchange rates and show how they may be overcome. (2.4)

8.5   Compare the relative merits of fixed and floating exchange rate systems. (3.2, 3.3)

8.6   Outline the main features of the Bretton Woods System and account for its collapse. (4.1)

8.7   Why should governments wish to manage floating exchange rates and how might they attempt to do so? (5.2)

8.8   Explain the features and objectives of the EMS. (6.1)

8.9 Was entry of sterling into the ERM necessarily a mistake? (6.2)

8.10 What is the role of the European Central Bank? (6.5)

9 EXAMINATION TYPE QUESTIONS

9.1 Managed rates

(a) "There is no such thing as a floating exchange rate, as the price of a currency is managed by its central bank." How far is this statement true? **(10 marks)**

(b) Consider the case for and against a fixed system of exchange rates **(10 marks)**
(Total: 20 marks)

9.2 Establishment of exchange rates

(a) Explain how the exchange rate for a currency is established in a perfectly free foreign exchange market. **(6 marks)**

(b) Why might a government wish to see a rise in the exchange rate for its country's currency and how might it achieve this? **(14 marks)**
(Total: 20 marks)

10 ANSWERS TO EXAMINATION TYPE QUESTIONS

10.1 Managed rates

Answer Plan

(a) A definition of floating exchange rates, with a brief discussion of what factors affect them.

Central bank intervention in the foreign exchange market; reasons and methods.

(b) The advantages and disadvantages of fixed exchange rates.

(a) An exchange rate is the price of one currency in terms of another. The price of a currency is determined in a free market by the interaction of the demand for the currency and the supply of it, without this price being fixed by or interfered with by the government or the central bank of the country; this is what a floating exchange rate is. If the demand for the currency exceeds its supply, the price or exchange rate will rise; if supply exceeds demand, the exchange rate will fall. To understand changes in exchange rates under a floating system, we must consider what factors affect the demand and supply; we shall take as our example the exchange rate of the UK pound sterling (£).

The demand for £ arises: when people in other countries buy British exports of goods and services (as in order to pay they sell their currencies and buy £) when foreigners buy £ in order to save money in a £ account (when UK interest rates are high) when they make investments in the UK (e.g., lending money to British companies, or opening foreign subsidiaries in the UK) or when speculators buy £ (because they think its value will rise and they can later sell it for a profit). The supply of £ arises when the opposite's of all these things happen; ie, when the UK buys foreign imports, when people move balances to foreign currency accounts, when UK companies lend or invest abroad, and when speculators sell £ because they think its market value will fall.

A pure system of floating exchange rates would thus be affected by the above factors only. However, ever since the world's major currencies were allowed to float in the early 1970s, governments have always intervened in this free market, and the UK is no exception. The Bank of England, on behalf of the government, manages the exchange rate of sterling in accordance with general economic policy and so the price of the currency at any time is affected by this policy. The government may want the price of £ to be high in order to be able to import goods and services more cheaply and thus keep down inflation. Alternatively it may want the £ to depreciate in order to make exports cheaper and thus more competitive abroad, and to make imports dearer and thus less competitive at home, so that the balance of payments position will improve and at the same time to boost domestic employment.

The Bank of England can cause increases and decreases in the exchange rate of £ by two main methods. First, it deals directly in the foreign exchange market; if it wants £ to appreciate, it buys £ and sells some of its reserves of foreign currencies; if it wants £ to depreciate, it sells £ and buys foreign currencies. Second it alters the general level of interest rates; if it wants £ to appreciate it raises interest rates, thus attracting inflows of short-term foreign balances which are converted into £ bank deposits; this raises the demand for £ and the supply of other currencies; if it wants £ to depreciate, it encourages outflows of this 'hot' money from £ into other currencies.

Floating exchange rates are therefore managed by central banks. But it is not true to say that central bank intervention is the only factor which determines the price of a currency; this intervention happens on top of and in addition to what is already taking place in the free market and we can say that both factors are instrumental in causing exchange rate changes. It is certainly true that a central bank which intervenes regularly in the ways described above is not prepared to accept the price which the market gives; we often hear that during a day's trading, the pound fell but rallied by the close after Bank of England intervention. This is not the same thing, however, as having a system of fixed exchange rates where currencies' values are pre determined internationally and where central banks are obliged to intervene to keep them within certain agreed limits. Under a floating system, a central bank may intervene if it wishes, but is not obliged to and on many occasions it may be happy to allow the market to depreciate or appreciate the currency.

Fixed exchange rates existed under the Bretton Woods system between 1945 and 1971 and they have been readopted by the majority of the currencies of the European Community, with the exchange rates of 11 of the 15 EU members being fixed against the euro with effect from 1 January 1999.

(b)   The great advantage of fixed rates is stability. Firms which engage in international trade know within certain narrow limits how much they will be paying for their imports and receiving for their exports, and they are thus able to operate with much more certainty and to plan their budgets accordingly, without running the risk of losing if the exchange rate goes against them. Secondly, fixed exchange rates impose discipline on governments to take action when their currencies are consistently too high or too low; eg a currency with a low exchange rate probably reflects an unfavourable position on the country's balance of payments, which may in turn be caused by high inflation. The need to keep the currency's value from falling further will oblige the government not only to support the currency in the short run, but also to take more radical action to solve the underlying problem. Thirdly, under fixed exchange rate systems there is little room for speculation, which is an advantage as this only distorts currency values without representing trade in real goods and services.

The main disadvantages of fixed exchange rates are firstly that they can lead to currencies being kept unrealistically high or low before a revaluation or devaluation occurs. Secondly, they presuppose that central banks have enough foreign currency reserves to support their own currencies in the short run, and thirdly they take away from governments independence of economic policy-making and at the same time require them to give priority to balance of payments problems over domestic problems; eg, a central bank may be forced into raising interest rates to support its currency when the government may want to decrease them to combat unemployment.

10.2   Establishment of exchange rates

Answer Plan

(a)   (i)   Exchange rates determined by market forces. Demand and supply of currency on the foreign exchange market.

No intervention means a free float. Alternatives: government intervention - fixed exchange rate.

Demand and supply determined by desired trade. Diagram required. Demand curve downward sloping, supply curve upward sloping. Demand exceeds supply - £ will rise and vice versa. Shifts in curves changes equilibrium rate. Shifts due to:

- inflation;
- change in interest rates;
- changing expectations.

(b)   (i)   If rise in exchange rate of currency, imports fall in price, exports become more expensive - deflationary effect on the economy.

(ii)   Reasons for governments to desire this:

- If aggregate demand too high - inflationary pressure, increase in foreign exchange rate - lower demand for exports increases demand for cheaper imports.
- If economy has high propensity to import - these will fall in price - again reducing inflation.
- If country running a balance of payments surplus may wish to export capital - easier with higher exchange rate - to achieve an appreciation Government must intervene. Several ways:

    -    use gold and currency reserves to buy domestic currency on the foreign exchange markets therefore influencing price by increasing demand;

    -    raise interest rate - attract capital flows into country

---

(a)   Exchange rates are determined by market forces, modified to a greater or lesser extent by government intervention in the foreign exchange market. At the one extreme this means no intervention at all and free floating rates. At the other, it means government intervention to keep them fixed. The exchange rate system that falls in between is referred to as managed or 'dirty' floating ie, floating exchange rates but with intervention as appropriate.

In the absence of government intervention a currency's exchange rate is determined by the interaction between the demand for and the supply of the currency on the foreign exchange market. Demand and supply here are in turn determined by the desire to trade and transfer capital internationally. Diagram 1 below shows the demand curve for sterling, the supply curve, and the market determined price in terms of US dollars.

Diagram 1

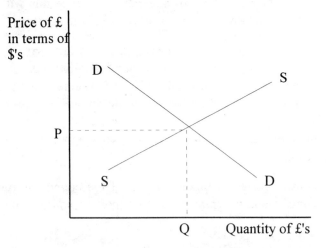

Price of £ in terms of $'s

Q   Quantity of £'s

The demand curve is drawn as DD because as the price of the sterling in terms of dollars falls it becomes cheaper for Americans to buy British goods. If their demand for these goods now rises then they will demand more £s to finance their purchases.

On the other hand, a fall in the £ makes US goods more expensive in Britain. This reduces the UK demand for American goods and the £s supplied to buy the $ finance for these. Hence the supply curve is upward sloping as SS. This analysis is oversimplified in that it neglects capital flows. However, other things being equal we might expect a lower £ to make capital flows to the UK (demand for £) more attractive (because the £ is less expensive to buy) and those from the UK to the US (supply of £) less attractive.

Given the demand and supply curves for £s are shaped as shown, the £/$ rate adjusts towards its equilibrium rate. If demand exceeds supply the £ will rise. If the reverse holds it will fall. Further, shifts in the demand and/or supply curve change the equilibrium rates and therefore themselves set up movements in the sterling exchange rate. Such shifts can arise from several sources. One is inflation: if the rate of inflation in the UK rises relative to rates of inflation abroad, our exports become more expensive and this may well shift the demand curve for £s to the left. At the same time imports into the UK become relatively cheaper and if this shifts the £ supply curve to the right the net result is a downward movement of the rate as in diagram 2. By a similar chain of reasoning a fall in interest rates in the UK would have the same effect on the £ through their impact on capital movements, and a rise in interest rates the reverse effect. There are many other things that can set up such shifts associated with capital flows and possibly 'expectations' is the best catchall term.

Diagram 2

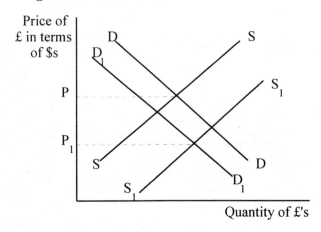

Price of £ in terms of $s

Quantity of £'s

(b)   If the exchange rate of a country's currency rises it has the joint effect of making imports cheaper in terms of home currency and exports more expensive to foreign buyers. In essence this will have a deflationary effect on the home economy which might be welcomed for the following reasons.

If aggregate demand in the economy is too high relative to supply this will lead to inflationary pressure. The firming of the exchange rate will lower the demand for domestically produced exports and increase the demand for imported substitutes for home produced and consumed goods, both of which should lead to a reduction in aggregate demand and hence reduce the inflationary pressure. If the country has a high marginal propensity to import in terms of raw materials, components and finished products, then the reduction in the domestic price due to the currency appreciation will also reduce costs and price levels in the home economy.

A further reason for a government to desire a currency appreciation is if the country is running a balance of payments surplus. In such circumstances it may wish to export capital and the firmer exchange rate should encourage this.

For a government to achieve a rise in the exchange rate of its currency it must enter the foreign exchange market. Such intervention can take several forms. Either it can enter the market directly by using its gold and currency reserves to buy its own currency, thus driving up the price of the currency by increasing demand. Alternatively the government can raise domestic interest rates encouraging capital flows into the country thereby raising demand for the domestic currency on the foreign exchange market, thus raising its price.

18 CURRENCY RISK

INTRODUCTION & LEARNING OBJECTIVES

Foreign currency risk has increased in importance to UK companies in recent years due to

- floating exchange rates. Despite initiatives such as the ERM and the euro, exchange rates have continued to prove highly volatile.
- the large growth in the volume of international trade and investment.

This chapter examines ways in which currency exposure risk can be minimised. The three categories of risk are identified and strategies suggested to deal with them.

When you have studied this chapter you should be able to do the following:

- Distinguish between transaction exposure, translation exposure and economic exposure.
- Suggest strategies for protecting against such exposure, including hedging with forward foreign exchange contracts.
- Discuss a range of internal methods of currency risk management.

1 TYPES OF CURRENCY RISK

1.1 Introduction

The foreign exchange risk exposure of companies is normally broken down into three categories:

(a) transaction exposure;
(b) translation (or accounting) exposure; and
(c) economic exposure.

We will deal with each in turn.

1.2 Transaction exposure

This relates to the gains or losses to be made when settlement takes place at some future date of a foreign currency denominated contract that has already been entered into. These contracts may include import or export of goods on credit terms, borrowing or investing funds denominated in a foreign currency, receipt of dividends from overseas, or unfulfilled foreign exchange contracts. Transaction exposure can be protected against by adopting a **hedged position** – ie, entering into a counterbalancing contract to offset the exposure. This is examined in more detail in the next section.

1.3 Translation exposure

This arises from the need to consolidate worldwide operations according to predetermined accounting rules. Assets, liabilities, revenues and expenses must be restated in home currency terms in order to be consolidated into group accounts. In the UK this is done in accordance with *SSAP 20* using the closing rate method and can result in considerable losses or gains on translation.

The most common means of protecting against translation exposure is balance sheet hedging. This involves attempting to equalise exposed assets and liabilities. For example, a company may try to reduce its foreign currency denominated assets if it fears a devaluation of the overseas currency, by running down cash balances, chasing debtors and reducing stock levels. At the same time it might increase its liabilities by borrowing in the local currency and slowing down payment to creditors. If it can equate its foreign currency assets and liabilities then it will have no exposure to changes in exchange rates.

1.4   Economic exposure

This relates to the possibility that the value of the company (the present value of all future cash flows) will change due to unexpected changes in future exchange rates. Its magnitude is difficult to measure as it considers unexpected changes in exchange rates and also because such changes can affect firms in many ways.

Consider the example of a British firm which operates a subsidiary in a country which unexpectedly devalues its currency. This could be 'bad news' in that every local currency unit of profit earned would now be worth less when repatriated to the UK. On the other hand it could be 'good news' as the subsidiary might now find it far easier to export to the rest of the world and hence significantly increase its contribution to parent company cash flow. The news could, alternatively, be neutral if the subsidiary intended to retain its profits to reinvest in the same country abroad.

Although economic exposure is difficult to measure it is of vital importance to firms as it concerns their long-run viability. The usual methods of protection are as follows:

(a)   **Diversification of production and supply.** If a firm manufactures all its products in one country and that country's exchange rate strengthens, then the firm will find it increasingly difficult to export to the rest of the world. Its future cash flows and therefore its present value would diminish. However, if it had established production plants worldwide and bought its components worldwide (a policy which is practised by many multinationals, eg, Ford) it is unlikely that the currencies of all its operations would revalue at the same time. It would therefore find that, although it was losing exports from some of its manufacturing locations, this would not be the case in all of them. Also if it had arranged to buy its raw materials worldwide it would find that a strengthening home currency would result in a fall in its input costs and this would compensate for lost sales.

(b)   **Diversification of financing.** When borrowing internationally firms must be aware of foreign exchange risk. When, for example, a firm borrows in Swiss francs it must pay back in the same currency. If the Swiss franc then strengthens against the home currency this can make interest and principal repayments far more expensive. However, if borrowing is spread across many currencies it is unlikely they will all strengthen at the same time and therefore risks can be reduced. Borrowing in foreign currency is only truly justified if returns will then be earned in that currency to finance repayment and interest.

International borrowing can also be used to hedge off the adverse economic effects of local currency devaluations. If a firm expects to lose from devaluations of the currencies in which its subsidiaries operate it can hedge off this exposure by arranging to borrow in the weakening currency. Any losses on operations will then be offset by cheaper financing costs.

1.5   Relative importance of different types of exposure to companies

Transaction and **economic** exposure both have cash flow consequences for the firm and they are therefore considered to be extremely important. Economic exposure is really the long-run equivalent of transaction exposure, and ignoring either of them could lead to reductions in the firm's future cash flows or an increase in the systematic risk of the firm, both resulting in a fall in shareholder wealth. Both of these exposures should therefore be protected against.

The importance of **translation** exposure to financial management is, however, often questioned. In financial management terms we must ask the question 'does a translation loss reduce shareholder wealth?' The answer is that it is unlikely to be of consequence to shareholders who should, in an efficient market, value shares on the basis of the firm's future cash flows, not on asset values in published accounts. Unless management feel that translation losses will greatly upset the shareholders there would seem little point in protecting against them.

2   PROTECTING AGAINST TRANSACTION EXPOSURE

2.1   Example 1 – Forex plc

Forex plc is expanding its operations into France and has ordered the construction of a factory near Nice. Final payment on the factory of 5,000,000 French francs is due in three months' time. Foreign exchange and money market rates are given below:

	French francs/£	
Spot	11.121 – 11.150	
Three months forward	10.948 – 10.976	

	Borrowing	*Lending*
Euro-franc	11%	9%
Euro-sterling	15.5%	12%

The value of the contract at the current spot rate $= \dfrac{\text{FF5m}}{11.121} = £449,600$

If Forex plc does nothing to hedge itself, and exchange rates fluctuate in the next three months, it exposes itself to risk - uncertainty about the final sterling cost of the factory. In particular, if the FF appreciates against the pound (as the forward rates imply), the cost will rise from the current value.

Some of the strategies that Forex could follow to protect itself are illustrated below.

(a)   **Hedge in the forward foreign exchange market**

Buy Ff5,000,000 forward to guarantee their cost. To obtain the required amount this will cost:
$\dfrac{5,000,000}{\text{Ff}10.948/£} = £456,704$ in three months' time (higher, but fixed).

(b)   **Make a lead payment**

> (Definition) Leading and lagging is a currency risk management technique in which the timings of payments in foreign currencies are adjusted
>
> **Leading** means making a payment before it is due.
> **Lagging** means delaying a payment after it is due.
> Both hope to take advantage of anticipated currency movements

As the Ff is strengthening it could be advisable for Forex to pay early, eg, buy Ff5,000,000 spot and pay the bill now. This would cost £449,599 now (as calculated above).

To convert this to an effective cost in three months' time (ie, to allow for the time value of money) we must assume the firm would have to borrow the funds for three months. This would then cost:

$$£449,599 \times (1 + \frac{0.155 \times 3 \text{ months}}{12 \text{ months}}) = £467,020 \text{ in three months' time.}$$

This appears a costly way of covering the exposure, but any discounts for early payment would also have to be taken into account. Note if the Ff had been weakening Forex would have attempted to pay late (a **lag payment**).

(c)   **Arrange to pay in sterling**

This would free Forex from foreign exchange transaction exposure but would load it onto the French supplier. Marketing considerations would need to be taken into account.

A more complex worked example follows.

2.2   A worked example using forward foreign exchange contracts

Example 2

An import-export merchant contracts on 1 January to buy 1,500 tonnes of product X from a supplier in Portugal at a price of Esc 11,820 per tonne. Shipment will be made direct to a customer in Germany to whom he has sold the product at DM 462 per tonne. Of the total quantity, 500 tonnes will be shipped now and the balance at the beginning of February. Payment to the suppliers is to be made immediately on shipment, whilst two month's credit from the date of shipment is allowed to the German customer.

The merchant arranges with his bank to cover these transactions in sterling on the forward exchange market, the exchange rates at 1 January being as given below:

	Escudos	*DM*
Spot	107.45 – 107.75	3.84 – 3.88
1 month forward	55 – 105 c dis	2.5 – 1.5 pf. premium
2 months forward	75 – 175 c dis	4 – 3 pf. premium
3 months forward	106 – 250 c dis	6.5 – 5.5 pf. premium

Exchange commission of 0.1% (maximum £10) is charged on each transaction.

You are required:

(a)   to calculate (to the nearest £1) the profit the merchant will make on the transaction;

(b)   to explain how calculations of further exchange profit or loss would be made if:

(i)   the February shipment were cancelled;

(ii)   the February shipment were delayed until April.

Solution

(a)   Purchase costs:

			Esc.	£
(i)	January	11,820 Esc.× 500 tonnes	5,910,000	
		Rate of conversion	107.45	
				55,002
(ii)	February	11,820 Esc. × 1,000 tonnes	11,820,000	
		Rate of conversion (107.45 + 0.55)* =108.00		
				109,444
		Purchase cost, in £		164,446

* add discount.

Sales value:

			DM	£
(i)	January	Sales (462 × 500)	231,000	
		Rate of conversion (3.88 – 0.03) **	3.85	
				60,000
(ii)	February	Sales (462 × 1,000)	462,000	
		Rate of conversion (3.88 – 0.055) **	3.825	
				120,784
		Sales revenue, in £		180,784

** subtract premium.

The commission of 0.1% on each of the four transactions would exceed £10 on each occasion, therefore the total commission is a ceiling amount of four times £10 or £40.

	£
Sales	180,784
Cost of sales	164,446
Profit on transaction	16,338
Commission	40
Net profit	16,298

(b)   (i)   If the February shipment were cancelled after the merchant has entered into his forward exchange contracts, the contracts would still have to be honoured. He would still have to buy 11,820,000 Escudos at a rate of 108.00, and would have to sell 462,000 Deutschmarks at a rate of 3.825. Without the February shipment, the merchant would be obliged to:

        (1)   sell off the Escudos he must buy, at the spot rate available at the time; and

        (2)   buy DM at the available spot rate on the foreign exchange market, to cover the forward DM sale contract made in January.

        In both (1) and (2) there could be a loss, because the respective sales of the foreign currencies might earn less (in £s) than it would have cost the merchant to buy them.

    (ii)   If the February shipment were delayed for two months until April, the contracts entered into at the start of January would still have to be honoured.

        The 11,820,000 Escudos would be obtained too early, and it is unlikely that the merchant would have sufficient funds in his business to hold on to them for two months. He would probably sell the Escudos he must buy in February, and then enter into another forward exchange contract to obtain 11,820,000 Escudos in April.

        The merchant must sell 462,000 DM in April, and will have to buy at the spot rate in order to cover the forward contract made in January.

        The merchant would probably decide to enter into another forward exchange contract to sell 462,000 DM two months later than originally expected, ie, in June.

        The effect of a delay in shipment is, therefore, likely to be the same as the effect of a cancellation, with the exception that the merchant would arrange two further foreign exchange contracts, one to buy more Escudos and another to sell forward more Deutschmarks. There is clearly the risk, in such circumstances, of making an exchange loss.

2.3   Currency overdrafts

If a company expects to receive numerous foreign currency receipts on uncertain dates, a better alternative to forward cover is to take out an overdraft in the foreign currency.

For example, if the receipts are going to be in dollars, a dollar overdraft should be taken out equal to the amount of the **dollar debtors plus the committed order book for dollar sales**.

The cash borrowed should then be converted to sterling and used to reduce sterling borrowings.

Each dollar receipt should be used to reduce the dollar overdraft, so that dollar receivables (+ orders) always match the dollar overdraft, and exchange risk is zero.

Periodically, the overdraft should be topped up to match debtors plus order book.

If the company expects to receive cash in many different currencies, it is not necessary to hold an overdraft in each of these currencies. Most currencies are fairly highly correlated with either the dollar, the euro, the yen or sterling; three currency overdrafts should be sufficient.

2.4   The currency of invoice decision

A company exporting goods or services has to decide whether to invoice in its own currency, the buyer's currency or another acceptable currency. As always with sales-related decisions, marketing and financing arguments must be balanced.

Invoicing in the home currency has the advantage of eliminating exchange differences, but the company is unlikely to compare well with a competitor who invoices in the buyer's currency. It is also necessary to revise prices frequently in response to currency movements, to ensure that the prices remain competitive.

Invoicing in the buyer's currency should promote sales and speed up payment, and currency movements can be hedged using forward cover. However, this is only available for major currencies.

A seller's ideal currency, in order of preference is:

(a)   Home currency.

(b)   Currency stable relative to home currency.

(c)   Market leader's currency.

(d)   Currency with a good forward market.

A seller may also have healthy interest in a foreign currency in which there is definitely, or likely, future expenditure.

A buyer's ideal currency is:

(a)   Own currency.

(b)   Currency stable relative to own currency.

(c)   Currency he has or earns.

(d)   Currency other suppliers sell in (for convenience and the ease of justifying a purchase).

2.5   Traditional (internal) methods of currency risk management

Methods of managing currency risk can be classified as external or internal. **External** methods involve taking out a contract with another business, usually a bank. Examples are forward contracts, futures, options and swaps. **Internal** methods simply reorganise the way that foreign transactions are dealt with inside the business, they are also called traditional methods. Examples include

- choosing the currency of invoicing as previously discussed
- leading and lagging
- netting
- matching
- internal asset and liability management.

Netting involves offsetting the group's debtors and creditors in the same currency and only covering the net position. For example there is no point in one subsidiary hedging a $1m receivable at the same time as another subsidiary is hedging a $1m payable. The parent company treasury department can assess the overall group position and only cover the group's net exposure.

Matching involves the use of receipts in a particular currency to meet payment obligations in the same currency. Successful matching depends on reliable forecasts of amounts and timing of future inflow and outflows of currencies. You will appreciate that matching is similar to netting; unfortunately some writers confuse the terms and use them interchangeably.

Internal asset and liability management involves choosing the different currencies in which the assets and liabilities of a company are denominated. Essentially assets should be in strong currencies and liabilities in weak currencies. Alternatively assets in foreign countries can be financed by loans denominated in that country's currency to reduce the group's exposure to movements in the exchange rate. This is an example of balance sheet hedging explained earlier.

3 CHAPTER SUMMARY

This chapter covers an area of the syllabus that is a particular favourite with examiners; the management of foreign currency risk is an important part of a company's financial strategy. After studying this chapter you should understand how risk can be hedged by forward foreign exchange contracts and by internal methods.

The next chapter covers another external method, the use of currency futures contracts.

4 SELF TEST QUESTIONS

4.1 State the three categories of foreign exchange risk exposure. (1.1)

4.2 Explain the meaning of economic exposure. (1.4)

4.3 What is leading and lagging? (2.1)

4.4 Are discounts added or subtracted to get a forward rate from a spot rate? (2.2)

4.5 Which currency would a seller prefer to invoice in? (2.4)

4.6 Which currency would a foreign purchaser prefer to pay in? (2.4)

4.7 Distinguish between netting and matching. (2.5)

4.8 Should liabilities ideally be denominated in a strong or a weak currency? (2.5)

5 EXAMINATION TYPE QUESTIONS

5.1 Runswick Ltd

(a) Explain what is meant by the terms foreign exchange translation exposure, transactions exposure and economic exposure.

What is the significance of these different types of exposure to the financial manager?

(8 marks)

(b) Runswick Ltd is an importer of clock mechanisms from Switzerland. The company has contracted to purchase 3,000 mechanisms at a unit price of eighteen Swiss francs. Three months credit is allowed before payment is due.

Runswick currently has no surplus cash, but can borrow short term at 2% above bank base rate or invest short term at 2% below bank base rate in either the United Kingdom or Switzerland.

Current exchange rates

	Swiss Franc/£
Spot	2.97–2.99
1 month forward	2½ – 1½ premium
3 months forward	4½ – 3½ premium

(The premium relates to the Swiss Franc)

Current bank base rates

Switzerland	6% per year
United Kingdom	10% per year

You are required:

(i)   To explain and illustrate three policies that Runswick Ltd might adopt with respect to the foreign exchange exposure of this transaction. Recommend which policy the company should adopt.

Calculations should be included wherever relevant.

Assume that interest rates will not change during the next three months.   **(9 marks)**

(ii)   If the Swiss supplier were to offer 2.5% discount on the purchase price for payment within one month evaluate whether you would alter your recommendation in (i) above.
(5 marks)

(c)   If annual inflation levels are currently at 2% in Switzerland and 6% in the United Kingdom, and the levels move during the next year to 3% in Switzerland and 9% in the United Kingdom, what effect are these changes in inflation likely to have on the relative value of the Swiss franc and the pound?
(3 marks)

(Total: 25 marks)

5.2   Leading and lagging

Certain organisational and policy adjustments may be made internally by a business for the purpose of minimising the effects of transactions in foreign currencies.

(a)   A group of companies controlled from the United Kingdom includes subsidiaries in Belgium, France and the USA. It is forecast that at the end of the current month, inter-company indebtedness will be as follows:

The Belgian subsidiary will be owed 144,381,000 Belgian francs by the French subsidiary and will owe the USA subsidiary $1,060,070.

The French subsidiary will be owed 14,438,000 French francs by the USA subsidiary and will owe it $800,000.

It is a function of the central treasury department to net off inter-company balances as far as possible and to issue instructions for settlement of the net balances. For this purpose the relevant exchange rates in terms of £1 are $1.415; French francs 10.215; Belgian francs 68.10.

You are required to calculate the net payments to be made in respect of the above balances and to state the possible advantages and disadvantages of such multilateral netting.
(10 marks)

(b)   You are required to explain the terms 'leading' and 'lagging' in relation to foreign currency settlements and state the circumstances under which this technique might be used.
(5 marks)

(c)   You are required to explain the procedures for matching foreign currency receipts and payments, having regard to the possibility that these might be on different time scales, and to state their possible advantages.
(5 marks)

This question is concerned with internal techniques and does not require reference to methods involving external bodies, such as forward contracts, options or swaps.   **(Total: 20 marks)**

6   ANSWERS TO EXAMINATION TYPE QUESTIONS

6.1   Runswick Ltd

(Tutorial note: this is a wide ranging question on foreign exchange exposure. In part (b) the answer provides five approaches to solving the problem although only three are required. For examination purposes you need to be familiar with all of them.*)*

(a) **Translation exposure** (Accounting exposure)

This arises from the need to consolidate the accounts of subsidiaries operating in differing currencies to the parent. Translation exposure relates to the possible gains or losses on consolidation of foreign denominated assets, liabilities, revenues and expenses.

Various translation methods exist; the one recommended for use in the UK, by *SSAP 20,* is a current rate (sometimes known as closing rate) approach.

Transaction exposure

This relates to the gains or losses to be made when settlement takes place of a foreign currency denominated contract that has already been entered into. These contracts may include import or export of goods on credit terms, borrowing or investing in a foreign currency or receipt of dividends from overseas.

Economic exposure

This relates to the possibility that the value of the company (measured in terms of the present value of all future cash flows) will change due to unexpected changes in foreign exchange rates. It is often considered as the long run equivalent of transaction exposure, including not only current but also future transactions.

The significance of the three types of exposure largely depends upon how they will be viewed by the stock market. Translation exposure does not involve cash flow (it is purely a book entry) and in an efficient market it should be ignored by shareholders. Therefore, if the financial manager considers the stock market to be efficient, translation exposure is of little relevance.

Transaction and economic exposure can both affect the future cash flows and the systematic risk of the business and therefore have direct implication for shareholder wealth. Both these exposures should therefore be protected against.

(b) Restatement of foreign exchange and interest rates.

	SF /£	
Spot	2.9700	2.9900
1 month forward	2.9450	2.9750
3 months forward	2.9250	2.9550

Note: premium indicates that the SF is strengthening. The premium figures refer to cents (ie, 0.01 of a franc).

	Current bank rates	
	Borrowing	*Deposit*
Switzerland	8%	4%
United Kingdom	12%	8%

(i) **Policies Runswick might adopt include:**

(1) **Hedge on the forward foreign exchange market**

Buy SF 54,000 3 months forward and make a certain payment in 3 months time of

$$\frac{\text{SF } 54,000}{2.925 \text{ SF} / \pounds} = \pounds\underline{18,462}$$

(2)   **Make a lead payment**

As the SF is strengthening it could make sense to pay early. For example if payment was made now it would cost

$$\frac{\text{SF } 54,000}{2.970} = £18,182$$

As this payment has to be made now we must consider the time value of money. Assuming the firm would have to borrow the funds this would have a cost in three months time of

$$£18,182 \times 1.03 = £18,727$$

Note this could be reduced if discounts for early settlement were negotiated.

(3)   **Use currency futures**

No details of the prices of currency futures are given but it could be possible to arrange cover similar to that given on the forward foreign exchange market by using Chicago IMM contracts. The main problem here would be the inflexible nature (in terms of size and duration) of these contracts.

(4)   **Do nothing**

This is effectively speculation on foreign exchange rates. Here the firm would take its chances on the SF spot rate in 3 months time. This is a risky proposition.

Conclusion

On the basis of information available covering on the forward foreign exchange market appears to be the best alternative.

(ii)   If the discount is taken Runswick will pay

SF 54,000 × 0.975 = SF 52,650 in one month's time.

Covering on the forward market

Cost in one month's time $= \dfrac{\text{SF } 52,650}{2.945} = £17,878$

To allow for the time value of money we will assume that this amount has to be borrowed for 2 months. Hence its cost in 3 months time is

$$£17,878 \times 1.02 = £18,235$$

Lead payment

Pay SF 52,650 now. This will cost

$$\frac{52,650}{2.970} = £17,727 \text{ now}$$

Allowing for borrowing this will have a cost of

$$17,727 \times 1.03 = £18,259 \text{ in 3 months time.}$$

Conclusion

The best alternative would be to take the discount and arrange forward market cover.

(c)   Using the relative version of purchasing power parity and assuming the exchange rates are currently in equilibrium

then $$\frac{(1 + i_f)}{(1 + i_h)} = \frac{F}{S}$$

where $E(1 + i_f)$ $= 1 +$ expected foreign inflation rate
         $E(1 + i_h)$ $= 1 +$ expected home inflation rate
         F $=$ expected future spot rate
         S $=$ current spot rate

Assuming the current spot rate SF/£ = 3.00 then the SF will strengthen to

$$\frac{1.03}{1.09} = \frac{F}{3}$$

$$F = 2.835 \text{ SF/£}$$

an increase in value of the SF of 5.82%.

6.2   Leading and lagging

(a)   Net payments. Advantages and disadvantages of multilateral netting.

(Tutorial note: set up a matrix in a common currency – £Sterling)

Conversion rates are £1 $= \$1.415$
                               $= \text{Ff}10.215$
                               $= \text{Bf}68.10$

	Belgium £	*France* £	*US* £
Belgian subsidiary owes			749,166
French subsidiary owes	2,120,132		565,371
US subsidiary owes		1,413,412	

Belgian subsidiary owes 749,166 and is owed 2,120,132

                                                    Net receipts   1,370,966

French subsidiary owes 2,685,503 and is owed 1,413,412

                                                    Net Payment   1,272,091

US subsidiary owes 1,413,412 and is owed 1,314,537

                                                    Net payment   98,875

The Central Treasury Department should issue instructions for the French subsidiary to pay the Belgian subsidiary £1,272,091 and the US subsidiary to pay the Belgian subsidiary £98,875.

Possible advantages:

Fewer transactions   – less administration
                          – lower transaction costs
Regular settlement   – less inter-subsidiary disagreement
                          – less exposure risk

Possible disadvantages:

Subsidiary loses flexibility over timing of payments and receipts. This will affect its cash flows and possibly its ability to choose advantageous exchange rates.

Central Treasury may not operate as efficiently as expected.

Inter-subsidiary transactions will be affected by changes in the exchange rate of the base currency.

Taxation may adversely affect the subsidiary.

(b)   **'Leading' and 'Lagging'**

'Leading' and 'Lagging' are terms relating to the speed of settlement of debts.

'Leading' refers to an immediate payment or the granting of very short term credit, whereas 'Lagging' refers to the granting (or taking) of long-term credit.

In relation to foreign currency settlements, additional benefits can be obtained by the use of these techniques when currency exchange rates are fluctuating (assuming one can forecast the changes).

If the settlement is in the payer's currency, then 'leading' would be beneficial to the payer if this currency were weakening against the payee's currency. 'Lagging' would be appropriate for the payer if the currency were strengthening.

If the settlement was to be made in the payee's currency, the position would be reversed.

In either case, the payee's view would be the opposite.

(c)   **Matching**

Matching of foreign currency receipts and payments is common in multi-national enterprises. Assuming a foreign subsidiary has both payments and receipts from a third country, then payments and settlements are made directly by the subsidiary.

Eg, a French subsidiary makes purchases from, and sales to Italy. It may open a currency account into which it receives lira, and from which it makes payments in lira, without converting into francs.

Possible advantages:

Transaction costs are virtually eliminated.

Transaction exposure is eliminated, except for any balancing figure.

Where the time-scale is significant, care must be exercised to ensure that large balances are not left idle, or unnecessary and expensive overdrafts incurred.

19 RISK MANAGEMENT

INTRODUCTION & LEARNING OBJECTIVES

Financial managers face risk arising from changes in interest rates and exchange rates ie, a lack of certainty about the amounts or timings of cash payments and receipts. Managers are normally risk-averse, so they will look for techniques to manage and reduce these risks.

The previous chapter examined internal methods of currency risk management and also hedging techniques using forward foreign exchange contracts. This chapter examines a further important possible means of managing both interest rate risk and exchange rate risk: the use of futures contracts.

The next chapter deals with two other risk management techniques, the use of options and swaps.

When you have studied this chapter you should be able to do the following:

- Explain the problems of interest rate risk and exchange rate risk.
- Describe the range of instruments available to manage such risk.
- Explain the nature of futures contracts and how futures markets operate in practice.
- Recommend how risky positions may be hedged using futures.
- Compare hedging using currency forward contracts with hedging using futures contracts.

1 THE VOLATILITY OF INTEREST RATES AND EXCHANGE RATES

1.1 Recent patterns of interest rates and exchange rates

The smoothed graphs below show how interest rates and exchange rates have moved over recent years.

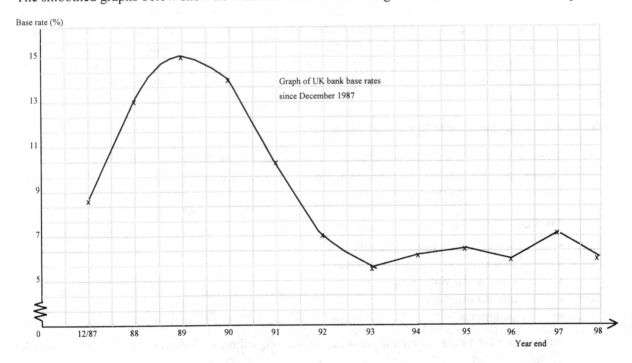

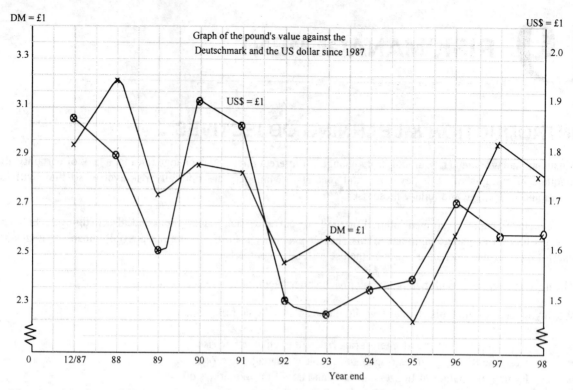

The graphs show that interest rates and exchange rates have fluctuated considerably over the period shown. Bank base rates peaked at 15% in 1989 in an effort to choke inflation out of the system and support sterling during ERM membership, but have since been lowered considerably. The pound's exchange rate was volatile even during ERM membership. After sterling left the ERM in September 1992 its value fell sharply though it has since recovered much of this fall.

1.2   Implications of rate volatility

Companies are exposed to risk if exchange rates and interest rates fluctuate when they are holding open positions eg, unhedged dollar receivables or floating rate overdraft balances. Managers are therefore unable to plan properly because they are unsure as to the actual amounts of sterling payments and receipts that their companies will be liable for in the future. A rational risk-averse management will seek to reduce the risk to which it is exposed as long as the expected benefits of risk reduction outweigh the expected costs of the reduction techniques.

1.3   Instruments available to manage such risks

There are a variety of different financial instruments which the modern financial manager can use to manage the risk arising from the volatility of interest rate and exchange rate. You must be totally familiar with the following methods.

Methods of managing interest rate risk

- interest rate futures contracts
- forward rate agreements (FRAs)
- interest rate options
- interest rate swaps
- swaptions

Futures and FRAs are covered in this chapter, the other three techniques in the following chapter.

Methods of managing exchange rate risk

- Internal methods (leading and lagging, netting, etc,)
- forward foreign exchange contracts
- currency futures contracts
- currency options
- currency swaps

Internal methods and forward contracts were dealt with in the previous chapter, futures are covered in this chapter, options and swaps in the following chapter.

2   THE NATURE OF FUTURES CONTRACTS

2.1   Introduction

The economic purpose of a commodity or financial futures market is to enable trading firms to fix in advance exchange prices whose variability might otherwise adversely affect them. It does this by effectively transferring the risk of price movements from these traders over to speculators, who are actively seeking the potential gains from taking high risks.

The financial futures market is a relatively recent addition to the financial manager's tool-kit for risk management, but it follows the same principles as the commodity futures markets which have been established for many years. The first financial futures market was started in Chicago in the mid-1970s; the London International Financial Futures Exchange (LIFFE - pronounced 'life') was started in 1982 and this has been followed by other similar exchanges around the world.

In March 1992 LIFFE merged with the London Traded Options Market (a division of the London Stock Exchange) to form the London International Financial Futures and Options Exchange. This is still described as LIFFE (not LIFFOE).

2.2   Meaning of financial futures

> **Definition**   A financial future is a standard contract between buyer and seller, in which the buyer has a binding obligation to buy a fixed amount (the contract size), at a fixed price (the futures price), on a fixed date (the delivery date), of some underlying security.

Using the above definition, if we bought a sterling future we would have a binding obligation to buy a fixed amount of sterling at a fixed price on a fixed date. Similarly the seller would have a binding obligation to deliver the sterling.

This is similar to a forward contract to buy sterling from a bank. However, certain important differences exist

(a)   Each currency future is traded in **units of a fixed size**. Fractions of contracts cannot be bought or sold.

(b)   Whereas forward contracts with banks can be drawn up for any date in the future, **delivery dates for futures exchanges occur on only four dates per year** (March, June, September and December). On first sight this appears a severe restriction but in practice most futures contracts are sold before they reach maturity. This process will be investigated later.

(c)   A financial futures exchange offers a **physical meeting place** for buyers and sellers. Dealing on the floor between member firms is by open outcry.

(d)   Transaction costs on futures exchanges are paid as a **% commission**.

(e)   Buyers and sellers of securities are required to deposit **margins** (see below) to ensure creditworthiness. Profits or losses on contracts are also received and paid throughout the life of a future. This process is further examined later.

2.3   Interest rate contracts

LIFFE offers futures contracts on both short-term and long-term interest rates and on interest rates in a variety of different currencies. The main contracts are summarised in the table below.

Contract	*Contract value*
Short-term interest rates	
3 month sterling	£500,000
3 month euribar	€ 1m
3 month euroyen	Y 100m
Long-term interest rates	
7% notional UK gilt	£100,000
6% notional Japanese Government Bond	Y 100m
6% notional German Bond	€ 100,000

2.4 Currency contracts

LIFFE has suspended trading of its currency futures contracts due to lack of demand; however such contracts can still be traded on other exchanges (notably in the USA) and they remain examinable.

Typical available contracts are as follows:

Contract	*Contract value*
US $/£	£62,500
US $/Swiss franc	SF 125,000
US $/yen	Yen 12.5m

2.5 Activity

Look at the relevant page in the 'Companies and Markets' section of the *Financial Times* to see what futures contracts are currently offered by LIFFE and by other exchanges.

2.6 Hedging with futures

It is possible to hedge currency and interest rate risks by buying and selling futures contracts. The objective is to set up a situation where the profit/loss on the underlying instrument (eg, on a holding of foreign currency) will be equal and opposite to the loss/profit on the futures contract so that all risk has been eliminated.

This would be a perfect hedge. In practice this is unlikely to be possible since futures contracts are only available in large round-sum quantities of each instrument. It is usual to over-hedge and round up the required number of contracts to the next whole number above.

The next section considers the use of currency futures to hedge exchange rate risk.

3   HEDGING EXCHANGE RATE RISK WITH FUTURES

3.1 Example

Problem: Assume that in September a UK company sold a machine tool to an American customer. The American customer has agreed to pay $1,216,250 in December. The current (September) spot rate is $1.40/£ and December sterling futures are trading at $1.39/£ on a contract size of £62,500.

The UK supplier is open to exchange risk on $1,216,250. If the £ weakens he will gain; if the £ strengthens he will lose.

Action: The UK supplier can establish a futures position to cancel out this risk. The purchase of a sterling future will yield profits as the £ strengthens: If one sterling future is purchased, this means the supplier has agreed to buy £62,500 for £62,500 × $1.39 = $86,875 in December. If the £ strengthens in the intervening period, the £62,500 should buy him more than $86,875 on the December spot market, yielding a profit.

At the futures price of $1.39 the dollar receipt is worth

$$\frac{\$1,216,250}{\$1.39/\pounds} = \pounds875,000$$

We therefore need to buy

$$\frac{\pounds875,000}{\pounds62,500/\text{contract}} = 14 \text{ sterling contracts}$$

(Note: This is very convenient as we can cover exactly. LIFFE does not deal in fractional contracts and sometimes we have to over cover slightly if the £ value of the trade position is not exactly divisible by the contract size.)

In December the trader will convert the $ receipt from the US customer on the spot market and take his profits on the future position (he doesn't actually have to physically deliver on the contracts).

Consider the profits or losses per single contract on the purchase of $1.39 December futures for different possible December spot rates.

December spot rate $1.50 (ie, £ strengthened)

	$
Future gives us right to buy sterling at $1.39/£: £62,500 × $1.39	86,875
On December spot market sterling will be bought at $1.50/£: £62,500 × $1.50	93,750
Profit (as expected)	6,875

December spot rate $1.30 (ie, £ weakened)

	$
Future gives us right to buy sterling at $1.39/£: £62,500 × $1.39	86,875
On December spot market sterling will be bought at $1.30/£: £62,500	81,250
Loss	5,625

If we combine these profits or losses on the futures contracts with the trader's cash market position, we obtain the following results.

December spot rate $/£	Receipt from trade item on cash spot market (£)	Futures profit/ (loss)(£) (14 contracts)	Net £
$1.30	$\frac{\$1,216,250}{\$1.30/\pounds} = \pounds935,577$	$\frac{\$5,625\times14}{\$1.30/\pounds} = (\pounds60,577)$	875,000
$1.39	$\frac{\$1,216,250}{\$1.39} = \pounds875,000$	-	875,000
$1.50	$\frac{\$1,216,250}{\$1.50/\pounds} = \pounds810,833$	$\frac{\$6,875\times14}{\$1.50/\pounds} = \pounds64,167$	875,000

It should be noted that whatever the December spot rate, profits on the future balance losses on the cash market, and vice versa, and the trader is in a hedged position.

3.2   Foreign exchange market analogy

The net result of this position can be obtained by 'pretending' that the contract is actually physically delivered. The purchase of 14 $1.39 sterling contracts means that in December we have agreed to exchange

$1,216,250 for £62,500 × 14 = £875,000

If we actually delivered on the contract we would exchange the receipt from the US customer for the £875,000, just as we would in the forward foreign exchange market. Note however that LIFFE contracts tend not to be delivered and the real situation is given above. The approach here can, however, be a useful short cut (at least in terms of forming a clear material view on the transactions).

3.3   Closing out a trade position

Problem: If the US customer in the example above paid the account in November the UK trader could be left in an exposed position. He would still be subject to profits or losses on the future but if he converted the dollar receipt into sterling in November he would have no counterbalancing cash market position.

Action: He needs to 'close off' his position in November. Assume that by November the pound spot had strengthened to $1.45/£ and we expected it to strengthen further to $1.50 by December. In the November futures market December contracts are now trading at $1.45.

In November the trader would convert the $ receipt of $1,216,250 to sterling and **sell** 14 futures contracts to close off his futures position - ie, to cancel out his purchase position; ie, it will 'lock in' a profit (or loss) on the futures contract in November, to be realised in December.

November

Convert \$ to £ $\dfrac{\$1,216,250}{\$1.45/£}$ = £838,793

Sell 14 sterling futures, now trading at $1.45/£.

December

Assume spot rate has risen to $1.50/£

Profit on purchase of 14 $1.39 sterling futures (see original example 3.1)

	$
14 × $6,875	96,250

Loss on sale of 14 $1.45 sterling futures

Future gives us right to sell sterling at $1.45/£: £62,500 × 14 × $1.45	1,268,750
On December spot market sterling is selling at $1.50/£: £62,500 × 14 × $1.50	1,312,500
Loss	43,750

Net futures gain

$96,250 – $43,750 = $52,500. At December spot $\dfrac{\$52,500}{\$1.50} = £35,000$

Total sterling receipt

£838,793 + £35,000 = £873,793

Once again we have virtually secured our receipt of £875,000. In reality the profit up to the November point could be taken at November, as it would have been received through the variation margin system (see 4.1).

By November the futures profit would amount to

14 contracts × £62,500 × $(1.45 – 1.39) = $52,500

and the total November receipt would be

$$\frac{\$52,500 + \$1,216,250}{\$1.45 / \pounds} = \pounds875,000$$

It should be noted that no matter the performance of the £ after closing off the position the profit would remain at £875,000. For example, if the £ were to weaken between November and December the profit on the futures sale would cancel out the loss on the futures purchase, leaving the net position unchanged.

3.4   Comparison of currency futures with forward contracts

The previous chapter showed how currency risks could be hedged using forward foreign exchange contracts. This chapter has explained how such risks can be hedged using currency futures contracts through a bank or taking a future position on a financial exchange.

	Banks	*Financial futures exchanges*
Credit risks	Users have to be wary of the creditworthiness of the other party in every deal.	Credit risk is virtually eliminated because the central body, the clearing house, guarantees deals through the margin system.
Credit lines	Credit lines with banks are used.	Credit lines with banks can be kept free.
Reversal	Deals have to be undone by going back to the original party and off-setting the deal. This can be a time consuming and expensive process.	Reversal is simple because there is a ready market in which those who have bought or sold can deal the other way and close their positions.
Size	A deal is for whatever size and date the parties agree.	Standard contracts are traded for fixed amounts and for delivery in a limited number of fixed months so a perfect hedge may not be possible.
Margin	No margin is generally required.	Users have to put up a margin.
Price	The price has to be checked with many different and physically separated participants (ie, offerors of forward contracts).	At any one moment in time there is the same market price for all financial futures contracts.

4   OTHER MATTERS ON FUTURES CONTRACTS

4.1   Margins on futures exchanges

Definition   'Margin' is the amount which you are required to advance as security against possible adverse price movements in your contract. It is made up of two components: 'initial margin' and 'variation margin'.

Initial margin is based on the volatility of the contract and varies between 0.1% and 3% of the contract value. Suppose that you are buying one £25,000 contract to buy dollars for sterling at a fixed rate of $1.39/£. Initial margin might be charged at 3% (£25,000 × 0.03 = £750). If the pound falls steadily against the dollar, you will not be asked for any further cash, as you are in a profit situation.

However, if the pound strengthened against the dollar, you would be in a potential loss-making situation and would have to pay over the full value of this loss on a day-to-day basis. This payment is called variation margin. For example, if on the first day following your purchase of a contract, the sterling contract price moved to $1.41, you would have to pay over £25,000 (1.41 − 1.39) = $500, and these payments would continue so long as the pound strengthened against the dollar.

Conversely, if the pound weakens, your variation margin becomes a cash gain, which will be paid over to you on a daily basis. Thus, you do not have to wait for the contract to mature before making your gain.

The following points should, therefore, be clear

(a)   The purpose of the initial margin is to guard against any adverse movement the following day. All adverse movements up to the end of the previous day's trading are covered by the variation margin.

(b)   The variation margin is simply the gain or loss you have made so far and is paid to or taken from you on a daily basis.

(c)   The situation of minimum outlay for a speculator is one where the exchange rate moves steadily in his favour. If there are large and rapid fluctuations, a final profit may have been made only after putting considerable sums at risk as variation margin.

(d)   Futures therefore have different cash flow characteristics from forward foreign exchange market agreements. Profit or losses on futures are realised throughout the life of the contract, whereas with forwards they occur only on delivery date.

4.2   Futures clearing houses

The buyer and seller of a futures contract meet on the floor of the exchange and agree their contract. However if there were no clearing house arrangement, each party to a contract would have to rely on the word of the counterparty to discharge their obligation under the contract, ie, they would be exposed to credit risk.

Each futures exchange therefore uses a clearing house to guarantee to each party that contracts entered into on the floor of the exchange will be honoured. Each party to a contract reports the details to the clearing house, and once matched and confirmed, the party is then obliged to the clearing house to carry out their side of the contract. Effectively the credit risk has been transferred from the parties to the clearing house.

Conclusion   The role of the clearing house is therefore twofold:

(i)   it registers and confirms all transactions in the market each day, providing an up-to-date record of all the positions taken by exchange members;

(ii)   it eliminates the risk of parties suffering from the default of their counterparty on a contract by substituting itself as the counterparty on each contract. Thus open outcry trading can operate without members having to assess the creditworthiness of potential other parties to their deals.

Clearing houses protect themselves from the risk of members' default by operating the system of margin requirements explained above. All margin payments are made to or received from the clearing house.

4.3   The recognition of price movements - Tick values

Each futures exchange specifies the minimum price movement permitted on each type of contract; this is called a tick. Price movements are then stated in numbers of ticks and the tick value is the change in value of a contract if the price moves by one tick.

Example

A typical 3-month Eurodollar future has a contract size of $1m and is priced at 100.00 minus the rate of interest (so that for example a December contract priced at 94.06 means that an interest rate of 5.94% has been fixed). The minimum price movement = 1 tick = 0.01%.

Tick value $= \frac{3}{12} \times 0.01\% \times \$1m = \$25$

If you own 20 contracts and the price of a contract rises from 94.06 to 94.66, each contract has risen in price by 60 ticks (ie, by 60 hundredths of a per cent).

Your total profit is 20 contracts $\times$ 60 ticks $\times$ $25/tick $= \$30,000$.

5   FORWARD RATE AGREEMENT

A forward rate agreement (FRA) for interest rates is analogous to the forward foreign exchange contract for exchange rates. FRAs offer companies the facility to fix future interest rates today on either borrowing or lending for a specific future period. For example, a company may wish to invest £10 million in six months' time at a guaranteed interest rate of 10% per year. The company might enter into an FRA with a bank at the agreed rate of 10% per year whereby if actual interest rates are lower than 10% the bank will pay the company the difference between 10% and the actual rate. If the interest rate is above 10% then the company will have to compensate the bank for the difference between the actual rate and 10%. No matter what level the market interest rate moves to, the yield to the company remains at 10%. FRAs do *not* involve any actual lending or investment of the principal sum. FRAs are usually for at least US $1 million (or equivalent in other major currencies) and can be arranged for up to two or three years in the future.

FRAs prices are quoted as interest rates for borrowing and lending, so that 7.40 – 7.25 means that borrowing could be fixed at 7.40% while lending could be fixed at 7.25%.

6   CHAPTER SUMMARY

This chapter has shown how futures contracts can be used to manage risks arising from movements in interest rates and exchange rates. You must be able to explain how futures contracts operate and to compare hedging strategies, say a currency future compared with a currency forward contract, or an interest rate future compared with an FRA.

7   SELF TEST QUESTIONS

7.1   Broadly how have UK interest rates moved over the past five years? (1.1)

7.2   Why did sterling's value fall sharply in September 1992? (1.1)

7.3   State three short-term interest rate futures contracts available on LIFFE. (2.3)

7.4   Why are most LIFFE hedges imperfect? (2.6)

7.5   State three differences between a hedge created with a currency futures contract and one created with a forward contract. (3.4)

7.6   Distinguish between initial margin and variation margin. (4.1)

7.7   What are the two main roles of a futures clearing house? (4.2)

7.8   How is a futures contract's tick value calculated? (4.3)

7.9   How are FRAs' prices quoted? (5)

8   EXAMINATION TYPE QUESTION

8.1   Plonk plc

(a)   On the 1 March 19X8 Plonk plc, a UK importer, purchased a consignment of wine from a Californian supplier for $5m, payable 3 months later. The spot rate at the 1 March was $1.50/£ and June Sterling futures (contract size £25,000) were trading at $1.60/£.

Required

(i)   Show the sterling cost of the purchase at 1 June, assuming no hedging, under the following spot rates:

$1.50/£
$1.60/£
$1.70/£

(ii)   Show how a futures market operation could hedge Plonk plc's transaction exposure.

(iii)   Describe the action Plonk plc would need to take if the bill fell due in May, rather than June, and it wished to avoid exposure.   **(10 marks)**

(b)   In November 19X8 the company's corporate treasurer realises that in mid December he will need to borrow $1m for 3 months. He is concerned that interest rates might rise in the intervening period. The following data is available in November:

November spot $ interest rate 10%
December 3 month Eurodollar futures 11%
The contract size for Eurodollar futures is $1m.

Required

Show how the treasurer might hedge his position using a futures market operation. Assume the funding requirements is on the last day of December futures trading. Illustrate your answer with reference to the following December spot rates:

9%
11%
13%   **(10 marks)**

9   ANSWER TO EXAMINATION TYPE QUESTION

9.1   Plonk plc

(a)   (i)   *June 1st*   *Sterling cost*
              Spot rate

$1.50/£ $\dfrac{\$5m}{\$1.50/£}$ =   £3.33m

$1.60/£ $\dfrac{\$5m}{\$1.60/£}$ =   £3.125m

$1.70/£ $\dfrac{\$5m}{\$1.70/£}$ =   £2.941m

It will be noted that the firm gains as the $ weakens.

(ii)   Plonk will suffer if the $ strengthens. If it sells £ futures it will earn profits as the $ strengthens and offset its losses on the trade position.

Hence they must sell

$\dfrac{\$5m \div \$1.6/£}{25,000}$ = 125 sterling contracts.

June spot rate	*Cash market cost*	*Futures profit (loss)*		*net*
	£m		£m	£m
1.50	3.333	$\dfrac{(1.5-1.6)\times 25,000\times 125}{1.50}$	= 0.208	3.125
1.60	3.125		0	3.125
1.70	2.941	$\dfrac{(1.7-1.6)\times 25,000\times 125}{1.70}$	= (0.183)	3.125

(iii)   If the $5m fell due in May Plonk plc would need to close out its futures position at that date. Otherwise it would be exposed to a weakening of the $. To do this it would need to buy 125 sterling futures contracts in May. Its net exposed position would then be zero once again.

(b)   If interest rates rise the prospective borrower will suffer. To hedge this position the treasurer must sell Eurodollar futures. This commits him to borrowing $ at 11% and he will profit if spot rates rise above this level. As the contract size is $1m this will involve the sale of 1 future.

The net position will then be:

December spot interest rate	Cost of borrowing $1m for 3 months in cash market	Profit/(loss) on future	Net cost
	$m	$	$
9%	22,500	$(9\% - 11\%) \times \$1m \times \frac{3}{12} = (5,000)$	27,500
11%	27,500	0	27,500
13%	32,500	$(13\% - 11\%) \times \$1m \times \frac{3}{12} = 5,000$	27,500

The net cost is secured at $27,500, ie, $\dfrac{\$27,500}{\$1,000,000} \times \dfrac{12}{3} = 11\%$ per annum.

20 OPTIONS AND SWAPS

INTRODUCTION & LEARNING OBJECTIVES

Options and swaps are further methods of risk management open to the modern corporate treasurer. Options give the purchaser the choice either to carry out a particular course of action (eg, to buy $1m at a rate of $1.50 = £1) or to do nothing (ie, let the option lapse). You will see that options enable a treasurer to avoid unfavourable price movements while still enabling him to profit from favourable price movements.

A swap is an agreement whose two parties agree to exchange cash flows over a particular period. There are both rate swaps and currency swaps and you will see how each can benefit a company.

Finally, more complex instruments such as swaptions are introduced.

When you have studied this chapter you should be able to do the following:

- Explain the terminology associated with options trading.
- Appreciate what factors determine the prices of options.
- Have an overview of the Black-Scholes pricing model without getting lost in its detail.
- Compare options with futures.
- Discuss the different types of interest rate options available.
- Explain swaps and their value to the corporate treasurer.
- Understand more exotic instruments such as swaptions and the other hybrids.

The following table shows the relative importance of risk management instruments:

Ernst and Young 1995 survey of 143 investment plan management complexes

31% of complexes surveyed used derivatives. The following data shows the percentage of these using the following derivatives:

Forex forwards	61%
Traded equity futures and options	56%
Traded options on interest rates	53%
OTC interest rate forward and options	36%
OTC Forex forwards and options	34%
Traded futures options	30%
OTC equity forwards and options	16%
Interest rate swaps	16%
Currency swaps	14%
Equity swaps	6%

1 THE MAIN FEATURES OF OPTION TRADING

1.1 Introduction

Definition An option is the right (but not the obligation) to buy or sell a specific quantity of a specific asset at a fixed price at or before a specified future date.

In practice options can be bought and sold over a bewildering variety of assets from coffee beans to pork bellies, but for this syllabus the underlying financial asset will either be an amount of currency, an interest bearing security or a company's shares.

We will look first at equity options to introduce some of the terminology necessary to be understood.

1.2   Equity options

There are two types of equity options which can be bought or sold:

(a)   **Traditional** options; and

(b)   **Traded** options.

Traditional options

Traditional options, also called over-the-counter options, have existed since the early days of the Stock Exchange. Each is tailor-made to the investor's particular requirements. The investor approaches a bank to explain what is required and the bank sets it up. There are three types which are described below:

(a)   **Put option**

An investor who buys a put option buys the right (but not the obligation) to **sell** shares at a given price (the **exercise price**) until the expiry date of the option. The two parties to the option are known as the **giver** and the **taker**; the giver buys the right to **'put'** the shares onto the taker who is usually an institution. The exercise price or **striking price** will be the market maker's bid price at the time the option was agreed.

(b)   **Call option**

Under this option, the giver would be able to 'call' on the taker to supply the shares; in other words, the giver would buy the right to **buy** shares at the exercise price. In this case, the exercise price would generally be the market maker's offer price in force at the time the option was agreed.

(c)   **Double option**

Under this option, the giver is buying the right to **either** put shares on the taker **or** call on the latter to supply. The exercise price for this option is a price mid-way between the bid and offer prices (the mid-market price).

Options are principally used as **hedges** to ensure that the investor loses only a minimum in any circumstances.

For example, an investor holding certain shares is undecided about whether or not to sell them, as he foresees a possible market rise. He has two solutions.

(a)   Sell the shares and buy a call option. Exercise the option if the price rises.

(b)   Buy a put option. If the price rises, allow the option to lapse ie, do not exercise it. If the price falls, the investor will be able to sell his own shares by exercising the option.

If the investor is reasonably confident about his predictions, his maximum loss will be the cost of the option.

Note that, if a price rise is anticipated, the first alternative would be preferable as it provides the investor with the use of his money between the decision point and the exercise date.

Traded options

Traded options started in the UK in 1978 and are now used more commonly than traditional options. They are however restricted, in the main, to the companies comprising the FTSE 100 index.

There are two types of option on each share, call and put options, which have the same meanings as in traditional options.

The differences from traditional options are as follows:

(a)   A range of option prices (**exercise** prices) is **quoted** and thus options can be bought and sold through brokers in a similar way to shares.

(b)   A range of **expiry** dates is available.

LIFFE traded options

Option		Calls			Puts		
	Jan	*Apr*	*July*		*Jan*	*Apr*	*July*
Courtaulds 300	36	47	53		9	13	18
(* 322) 330	19	29	35		21	26	32
360	8	19	-		42	45	-

Date 20 October 19X2

* Underlying security price

The notes will refer to Courtaulds but similar principles apply to the other securities in which options are traded.

The price of the underlying security is 322 pence, and it is possible to buy an option contract for exercise at a series of exercise prices. These are 300p, 330p or 360p. The exercise price is the price at which the shares will be taken up or delivered if the traded option is exercised.

The figures shown in the main body of the table are the option prices (premiums) - the amount that has to be paid to acquire the option itself. So a call option to buy a Courtaulds share at 330 pence in April will cost 29p.

Each contract is for 1,000 shares and it is possible to buy traded options up to nine months ahead. When the January series expires a new series will be introduced expiring in October 19X3.

1.3   Activity

Find the page in the Companies and Markets section of the **Financial Times** which relates to traded options. Select a company and write out a table for it equivalent to the one above.

1.4   In the money and out of the money

Definition   A call option (the right to buy) is **out of the money** if its exercise price is above its underlying security price. It is **in the money** if its exercise price is below the underlying security price.

A put option (the right to sell) is out of the money if its exercise price is below its underlying security price. It is in the money if its exercise price is above the underlying security price.

You can see that two of the exercise prices shown in the Courtaulds table are above the underlying security price and one is below. Thus the 360 and 330 **call** contracts are said to be 'out of the money' whereas the 300 contracts are 'in the money'.

A call contract to buy shares in January at 300, when the price of the shares is 322 today, is worth 22p on the basis that, if it were exercised and the shares sold, this would be the profit. This difference, 22p, is called the **intrinsic value of the option**. Since the option actually costs 36p the investor is incurring an extra cost. This extra cost is called **time value**. The investor is paying for the chance that, prior to the expiry of the option, the share price will rise sufficiently to give the investor a net profit overall.

The option price, therefore, has two components - intrinsic value (22p) and time value (14p). An examination of the April and July prices for the 300s shows that the time value increases over time. This is because there is a greater chance of the price of the underlying security rising over the longer period of time.

The prices of traded options are fixed by the forces of demand and supply, but the concepts of time value and intrinsic value are useful in understanding why the prices are as they are.

1.5   The uses of traded options

(a)   Traded options provide opportunities for speculation at low cost. If the value of Courtaulds shares rises by 10p, a rise of about 3%, then one would expect the price of the January 330 call to rise (from 19p). If it rose by 10p then the investor would show a gain of nearly 50% (10/19)! Similarly, of course, a small fall in the price of Courtaulds could wipe out the entire value of his option.

(b)   Traded options can be used as a form of insurance. Thus, an investor may decide to buy Courtaulds at 322, but consider that he wishes to limit his losses should the shares fall in value. He can buy a put option expiring in July at 300 for 18p and limit his loss to a maximum of 18p (the put price) plus 22p (322-300p minimum selling price).

(c)   If the investor considers that the market is going to rise, and expects to receive funds in, say, six months' time, it is possible to gain a foothold in the market now by buying traded options in the shares that he wishes to buy eventually.

(d)   Shareholders who expect a fall in market prices can liquidate their holdings and invest in short-dated gilts (government stock) or bank deposits. They can buy call options against the possibility that the market moves upwards so that they can return to the market when the danger is past.

(e)   Shareholders can sell call options ie, agree to provide the shares if called upon to do so. As many of the options will never be exercised, this is a useful way of adding to the income of a portfolio.

The main advantage of the traded option is that it can be sold during its life, a course of action not possible with traditional options.

1.6   Currency options

The terminology employed with currency options is very similar to that of equity options. The definition of a traded currency option is 'a standard contract which grants the buyer the right (but not the obligation) to buy or sell a fixed amount (the contract size) at a fixed price (the exercise price) on a fixed date (the exercise date) of some underlying currency'.

Buying a put option gives the right but not the obligation to **sell** the underlying currency.

Buying a call option gives the right but not the obligation to **buy** the underlying currency.

As with equity options, premiums will need to be paid to the option seller.

For example, suppose that in September 19X1 put and call options on Sterling for 1 December 19X1 at an exercise price of $1.60/£ had premiums of £500 and £600 respectively. Contract size is £25,000.

Buying a put option would cost £500 and give the right, but not the obligation, to *sell*:

a	fixed amount	(£25,000)
at a	fixed price	($1.60/£)
at a	fixed time	(1 December 19X1)

Buying a call option would cost £600 and give the right, but not the obligation, to *buy*:

a	fixed amount	(£25,000)
at a	fixed price	($1.60/£)
at a	fixed time	(1 December 19X1)

1.7   European and American options

The above examples are **European** options meaning that they can only be exercised on **one date**. If they were **American** options they could be exercised at **any date up to the exercise date**. In reality most futures exchanges trade American options.

Note that the description 'European' option and 'American' option is purely a description of when they can be exercised and has nothing to do with where geographically they are sold. LIFFE offers both European and American options, though as might be expected you pay more to buy an American call since you are buying rights over a longer period.

1.8   Hedging with options

Once again options can be used to hedge foreign exchange transaction exposure. The following example illustrates the approach.

Example

Keith plc has recently sold a packaging machine to a US customer for $160,000 payable on 1 December 19X1. The following traded options on sterling are available. Contract size is £25,000.

| 1 December 19X1 | $1.60 call options | – premium £600 per contract |
| 1 December 19X1 | $1.60 put options | – premium £500 per contract |

Requirement: show how Keith could hedge its foreign exchange exposure using currency options.

Keith needs to convert $ into £ on 1 December 19X1. It therefore needs to buy call options (keep in mind that Sterling is the underlying currency). As $160,000 will be received it needs to **buy**:

$$\frac{\$160,000 \div \$1.60 / £}{£25,000} = 4 \text{ call option contracts}$$

The result of this transaction will mean that Keith has the right, but not the obligation to **buy**:

a	fixed amount	(= £25,000 × 4 = £100,000)
at a	fixed price	($1.60/£)
at a	fixed time	(1 December 19X1)

It will therefore have secured a receipt of at least £100,000 (less premium payments) from its $160,000 sale and hedged its exposure. The cost of the premium will however have to be met.

Its exact payoff depends upon the spot rate prevailing on 1 December 19X1. The following table demonstrates possible payoffs.

Spot rate 1 December 19X1	Action	Receipt £	Premium (4 × £600) £	Net receipt £
$1.20/£	Abandon option (it is 'out of the money') and buy £ on spot market	$160,000 ÷ $1.20/£ = 133,333	(2,400)	130,933
$1.60	Exercise or abandon option (it is 'at the money')	$160,000 ÷ $1.60/£ = 100,000	(2,400)	97,600

$2.00/£   Exercise option $160,000 ÷ $1.60/£ = 100,000   (2,400)   97,600
             (it is 'in the money')

It will be noted that the options give Keith the opportunity to participate in the benefits of a strengthening Dollar but gives it protection from a weakening Dollar. The cost of this hedge is £2,400, the premium paid for 4 contracts.

In reality the dealing process for traded options is more complicated than the above analysis but this approach will suffice for our purposes.

1.9   OTC currency options

As with futures and equity options an over-the-counter (OTC) market exists for currency options. Authorised persons can make a market in currency options which are tailor-made or non-standardised. These options are mainly purchased from the banks, the advantage being that each is tailor made to suit the purchaser and/or seller's requirements. This market also provides a wider range of underlying assets than the traditional traded market.

1.10   Writing options

An alternative to buying options is to actually write the option for sale. A person writing a call option for instance is giving the right to the purchaser to buy the underlying asset at a fixed price from the writer. If the writer is 'naked' and does not actually own the underlying asset, the risk being faced depends upon the price of the asset when the purchaser exercises the option. If the underlying assets increase significantly in value, the writer will lose to the extent of the difference between the market price and option price when exercised.

1.11   Margins

Both the buyer and seller put up an initial margin based on the estimated sensitivity of the option price with respect to the price of the underlying asset. The actual payment or receipt of the option premium is effected when the position is closed, at the rate prevailing at that time. The difference between that and the option price at the outset is made up by daily payments of variation margin (as with futures).

2   THE DETERMINANTS OF OPTION PRICES

2.1   Introduction

In the preceding section we saw the use of options to hedge risk. The premiums required to purchase options were simply taken as given. In this section we will examine the determinants of option price or premiums.

2.2   Value of a call option

The major factors in determining the price of a call option are as follows

(a)   The price of the underlying instrument - the **higher** the price of the underlying instrument the more valuable the call option.

(b)   The exercise price, ie, the price at which the underlying instrument may be purchased. The **lower** the exercise price the more valuable the call option.

(c)   The time to go to expiry. The **longer** the period to expiry the greater the probability that the underlying instrument will rise in value. Remember that call options give protection against falls in value and, even though a move upward or downward may be equally likely, holders will benefit from increases in the value of the underlying instrument but will not suffer greatly from decreases.

(d)   The volatility of the underlying instrument.   Once again as we have protection against decreases in value, the **greater** the volatility of the price of the underlying instrument the greater the probability of the option yielding profits.

(e)   Interest rates. The seller of a call option will receive initially a premium and (if exercised) the exercise price at the exercise date. If interest rates rise the present value of the exercise price will diminish and he will therefore ask for a higher premium to compensate for his risk. Thus, as interest rates rise the price of call options tend to rise. Viewed from the buyer's view point, the cost of exercising the exercising price diminishes in present value terms as interest rates rise, thus the option becomes more valuable with **increasing** interest rates.

(f)   Whether a European option or an American option. We have already seen that American options are more expensive since you are buying more rights.

2.3   The Black-Scholes option pricing model

A model has been developed from the above points for use in the calculation of the value of a call option. Don't panic when you see the equation for the first time. You do not have to memorise it. It is unlikely that you will have to apply it in the exam. However you should be aware of the variables that are used as the inputs to the model, and how their movements affect the value, as discussed above.

Let P =   the price of the underlying instrument, eg, the current share price if modelling an equity option

$N(d_i)$ =   the probability that a normal distribution is less than d_i standard deviations above the mean

X =   the exercise price

r =   the risk free interest rate. (NB Quote this as an annual rate as a decimal number)

t =   the time to expiry (again quoted in years)

σ =   the standard deviation of the underlying instrument's returns

Then the basic form of the Black-Scholes model gives the value of a European call option as

Option price   = $PN(d_1) - Xe^{-rt}N(d_2)$

where d_1 = $\dfrac{\log_e\left(\frac{P}{X}\right) + (r + \frac{\sigma^2}{2})t}{\sigma\sqrt{t}}$

and d_2 = $d_1 - \sigma\sqrt{t}$

Example

The current share price of Moss plc is £2.90. Estimate the value of a European call option on the shares of the company, with an exercise price of £2.60, and has 6 months to run before it expires. The risk free rate of interest is 6% and the variance of the rate of return on the share has been 15%.

Solution

First we calculate d_1 and d_2.

$$d_1 \quad = \quad \frac{\log_e\left(\frac{2.90}{2.60}\right) + (0.06 + \frac{0.15}{2}) \times 0.5}{\sqrt{0.15} \times \sqrt{0.5}}$$

$$= \quad \frac{\log_e(1.1154) + (0.135 \times 0.5)}{0.3873 \times 0.7071}$$

$$= \quad \frac{0.1092 + 0.0675}{0.2739}$$

$$= \quad 0.6452. \qquad \text{Round this to } 0.65$$

$$d_2 \quad = \quad d_1 - \sigma\sqrt{t}$$

$$= \quad 0.6452 - (\sqrt{0.15} \times \sqrt{0.5})$$

$$= \quad 0.3713 \qquad \text{Round this to } 0.37$$

Option price $= 2.90N(0.65) - 2.60 \times e^{-0.06 \times 0.5} \times N(0.37)$

We need to refer to normal distribution tables to read off the $N(d_i)$ probabilities.

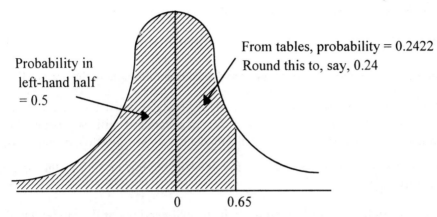

Probability in left-hand half = 0.5

From tables, probability = 0.2422
Round this to, say, 0.24

So $N(0.65) = 0.5 + 0.24 = 0.74$

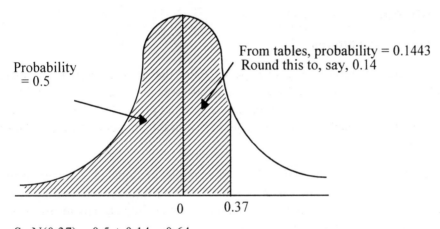

Probability = 0.5

From tables, probability = 0.1443
Round this to, say, 0.14

So $N(0.37) = 0.5 + 0.14 = 0.64$

$$\begin{aligned} \text{Option price} \quad &= \quad (2.90 \times 0.74) - (2.60 \times 0.97 \times 0.64) \\ &= \quad \pounds 0.53 \end{aligned}$$

The model suggests that a fair value for this call option is 53p. This seems reasonable, since the option has intrinsic value of 30p and so the time value is being valued at 23p.

2.4   Put-call parity

Once a value has been established for call options, the following equation can be used to establish the value of a put option:

Value of a put	+	Current value of underlying security	=	Value of a call	+	Present value of the exercise price

This relationship expresses what is known as put-call parity, ie, that put and call options must have the same time value when they are identical with respect to exercise price, expiry date and underlying security, otherwise arbitrage profits can be made. However, the proof of the formula is outside the scope of the syllabus.

2.5   Limitations of the Black-Scholes model

The basic form of the Black-Scholes model has been illustrated above. It is widely used by traders in option markets to give an estimate of option values, and more expensive scientific calculators include the model in their functions so that the calculations can be carried out very quickly.

However the model in its basic form does suffer from a number of limitations.

(i)   it assumes that no dividends are paid in the period of the option.

(ii)   it applies to European options only

(iii)   it assumes that the risk free interest rate is known and is constant throughout the options life

(iv)   the standard deviation of returns from the underlying security must be accurately estimated and has to be constant throughout the option's life. In practice σ will vary depending on the period over which it is calculated; unfortunately the model is very sensitive to the value of σ.

(v)   there are no transaction costs or tax effects involved in buying or selling the option or its underlying security.

Certain of these limitations can be removed by more sophisticated versions of the model, but the basic model is complicated enough for the purposes of this text.

3   OPTIONS VERSUS FUTURES

3.1   The choice between options and futures

The choice between options and futures largely depends upon the amount of risk the investor is prepared to take. Futures can guarantee the future cost of an asset (eg, a currency or a bond or an equity) but do not give any participation in favourable movements in price. Options on the other hand give downside protection but allow hedgers to participate in favourable movements; this is however at a price - the option premium.

Options offer traders the ability to fine tune their risks. For example, imagine a UK trader awaiting the receipt of US $486,500 in three months time. If three month sterling futures were trading at $1.39 he could lock into this price and guarantee his receipt by buying sterling futures. His receipt would then be £350,000 no matter the movement in the spot market.

Alternatively, he could go for a call option with an exercise price of $1.39, at a premium of £500 per contract of contract size £25,000. He would need £350,000/£25,000 = 14 option contracts.

If sterling weakened, however, say to £1.20/£, he would abandon the call option and receive

$$\frac{\$486,500}{\$1.20 / £} \text{ less } (£500 \times 14 \text{ contracts}) = £398,417$$

If he considered the price of the options too high he could go for a deep 'out of the money option' at an exercise price of $1.50 costing, say, £100 per contract. In this case the minimum guaranteed receipt would be smaller but the options would be far cheaper and allow more participation in weakening sterling. By judicious choice of exercise prices traders can select the amounts of upside and downside risk they wish to take.

Options are also useful when future obligations of the business are unsure. Imagine a UK firm making a takeover bid for a US company. It could lock into a $ price by selling sterling futures but if the deal fell through it would be left with an exposed position on the foreign exchange market. On the other hand if it had used a sterling put option and the takeover fell through it could walk away from the contract (if it was profitable to do so) and sacrifice only the premium.

4   TYPES OF OPTIONS AVAILABLE

4.1   Types of interest rate options

As with currency and share options, interest rate option contracts can be either exchange-traded (on a futures exchange such as LIFFE) or available OTC (over-the-counter, meaning that they are individually designed by a bank for a particular client's situation).

LIFFE offers option contracts as options on its futures contracts, eg, an option over one UK long gilt futures contract or an option over one 3-month sterling futures contract. Pricing of these contracts is best understood by looking at an example.

In April 19X4 the LIFFE long gilt option contract was priced as follows:

Long gilt futures options (LIFFE) £100,000 points of 100%

Strike price	CALLS		PUTS	
	Jun	Sep	Jun	Sep
106	1.51	2.38	1.25	3.06
107	1.19	2.11	1.57	3.43
108	0.58	1.51	2.32	4.19

The prices are quoted in hundredths of a percent of the underlying gilt par value, so that the tick value is

$$0.01\% \times £100,000 = £10$$

The price of a June call contract at a strike price of 106 would be:

$$1.51\% \times £100,000 = £1,510$$

Conclusion	An investor could pay £1,510 and buy one long gilt futures option, allowing him to buy a notional 7% UK gilt in June 19X4 at a price of £106 per £100 stock, an implied interest rate of $\frac{7}{106} \times 100 = 6.60\%$

4.2   Activity

Look at the table of April 19X4 long gilt option prices again. Interpret the 2.11 in the September call column.

4.3   Activity solution

Premium payable   = $2.11\% \times £100,000 = £2,110$

An investor could pay £2,110 and buy one option contract giving him the right to buy a 7% gilt in September 19X4 at a price of £107 per £100 stock, ie, an implied interest rate of $\frac{7}{107} = 6.54\%$.

4.4   Short-term interest rate options on LIFFE

The LIFFE long gilt futures option offers the chance to take a position on long-term interest rate movements. LIFFE also offers a short sterling options contract for investors interested in short-term interest rate movements. Each contract is to buy or sell one LIFFE 3-month sterling futures contract.

Consider the following pricing schedule from April 19X4.

Short sterling options (LIFFE) £500,000 points of 100%

Strike		CALLS			PUTS	
price	Jun	Sep	Dec	Jun	Sep	Dec
9475	0.11	0.13	0.10	0.11	0.39	0.79
9500	0.03	0.06	0.05	0.28	0.57	0.99
9525	0	0.03	0.02	0.50	0.79	1.21

The prices are again in points of 100%.

For example an investor could pay 0.11% × £500,000 = £550 to buy the right to buy a 3 month sterling futures contract in June 19X4 at a price of 94.75.

4.5   OTC interest rate options

Over the counter option contracts are designed specifically to a client's particular requirements; there is no need for standardisation of period, exercise price or underlying instrument.

Definition   A short-term OTC interest rate option contract (ie, for a period of up to one year) is called an interest rate guarantee (IRG).

Longer term contracts are referred to as caps, collars and floors and are described below.

Definition   A **cap** is an option to limit a price to a given maximum. For example, an interest rate cap can be used by a borrower to limit the interest rate payable to a given maximum. The cap would be purchased by the borrower for a fixed sum (the premium) and only exercised if interest rates on borrowings rise above the given rate. The borrower would, of course, still be able to take full advantage of any interest rate falls.

Definition   A **floor** is a similar option to limit a price to a given minimum, eg, a minimum interest rate for an investor.

Definition   A **collar** is the simultaneous use of a cap and a floor in order to set a maximum and a minimum price.

For example, a borrower could simultaneously buy a cap and sell a floor. This would fix the maximum and minimum borrowing rates. The disadvantage compared with simply buying a cap is that the floor would take away the gains that would have been made from a fall in interest rates.

However the advantage compared with buying a cap is that the premium cost is lower, being reduced by the sales proceeds of the floor.

Other terms also exist, eg, a **caption** is an option to buy a cap.

4.6   The nature of currency options

Currency options may also be exchange-traded or OTC. Although LIFFE no longer offers currency futures contracts, so cannot offer options on such contracts, several US exchanges (eg, Philadelphia) do offer option contracts on currency futures.

A typical pricing schedule for the £/$ currency option on the Philadelphia exchange is as follows

Strike		CALLS				PUTS		
price	Apr	May	Jun	Jul	Apr	May	Jun	Jul
1.475	3.12	4.11	4.42	4.94	0.06	1.25	2.15	2.66
1.500	0.91	2.67	2.99	3.51	0.27	2.34	3.16	3.85
1.525	0.08	1.43	2.04	2.48	1.89	3.70	4.61	5.31
1.550	-	0.75	1.27	1.74	4.25	5.44	6.30	6.94
1.575	-	0.36	0.76	1.26	6.82	7.47	8.15	8.92
1.600	-	0.14	0.43	0.73	9.31	9.80	10.34	10.90

The prices quoted are in cents per £, eg, a trader that wanted to buy an option to buy pounds in May at $1.500 would need to buy a May call option costing 2.67 cents per pound. These traded options on the Philadelphia exchange have a contract size of £31,250 each, so the trader must decide how many option contracts he wishes to buy.

The following examples illustrate the uses of currency option contracts.

Example

Problem: It is late September and the spot $/£ rate is $1.40/£1.

You are convinced the £ will weaken by Christmas to about $1.30/£. Sterling December put options, with an exercise price of $1.39, are trading at a premium of £500 per contract. The sterling contract size is £25,000, the same as in the futures market.

Action: Buy one $1.39 put option for £500.

You will appreciate that this gives you the right (but not the obligation) to sell £25,000 in December at $1.39/£ to yield $34,750. The profit depends upon the performance of the £ in the spot market

December spot rate $1.30/£ (the £ weakens)

The put option gives the right (but not the obligation) to sell sterling at $1.39

	$
£25,000 × $1.39	34,750

On the December spot market sterling is selling at $1.30

	$
£25,000 × $1.30	32,500
Profit in $	2,250

This is clearly a profitable position and would be referred to as 'in the money'. The net profit from the option would be the sterling value of this gain,

	£
$\frac{\$2,250}{\$1.30/£}$	1,730
Less: The option premium of £500	500
	1,230

December spot rate $1.50/£ (£ strengthens)

The put option gives the right (but not the obligation) to sell sterling at $1.39

	$
£25,000 × $1.39	34,750

On the December spot market it can be sold at $1.50

	$
£25,000 × $1.50	37,500
Loss	2,750

This is an unprofitable position and we would use our option to 'walk away' from the contract as it is 'out of the money'. Our loss would be confined to the initial premium of £500.

December spot rate $1.39/£

The put option gives the right but not the obligation to sell sterling at $1.39/£

	$
£25,000 × $1.39	34,750
On the spot market it can be sold at the same price	34,750
Profit and loss	0

Here the option is 'at the money', ie, at a break-even position before considering the premium. After the premium we would be facing a loss of £500.

Summary

December spot rate	Profit on $1.39 put option £
$1.30/£	1,230
$1.39/£	(500)
$1.50/£	(500)

From the above table we can see the major attraction of an option. If the £ strengthens we can walk away from the option and limit our losses to £500. This restricts our 'downside risk' (ie, the risk of losing money). On the other hand, if the £ weakens we can still earn a profit. Profits are less than on the futures market because of the premium paid for the option, but to compensate us for this the possible losses are much smaller.

Profit profile from buying a $1.39/£ put option

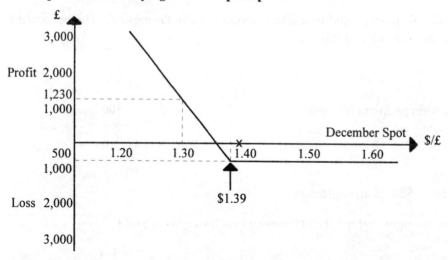

The above diagram shows the profit profile on a put option; it can clearly be seen that as the £ weakens profit are unlimited, but as the £ strengthens our losses are restricted to £500.

4.7   More on speculation

Problem: Assume the same situation as above but we now suspect the £ will strengthen.

Action: To profit from a strengthening £ we buy a December call option on sterling with an exercise price of $1.39 for £500 (the current premium). This gives us the right but not the obligation to buy sterling at $1.39.

Once again the profit depends upon the performance of the £ in the spot market. We will examine three possible spot rates.

December spot rate $1.30/£ (the £ weakens)

The call option gives us the right (but not the obligation) to buy sterling at $1.39

	$
£25,000 × $1.39/£	34,750
On the December spot market it could be bought for: £25,000 × $1.30	32,500
Loss	2,250

The call option is 'out of the money' and we would therefore choose not to exercise. Our loss would thus be restricted to the £500 premium.

December spot rate $1.39/£

The call option gives us the right (but not the obligation) to buy sterling at $1.39

	$
£25,000 × $1.39	34,750
On the December spot market it could be bought at the same price	34,750
	0

The option is 'at the money' and the loss will be restricted to the premium of £500.

December spot rate $1.50/£ (£ strengthens)

The call option gives us the right (but not the obligation) to buy sterling at $1.39

	$
£25,000 × $1.39	34,750
On the December spot market it can be bought at $1.50: £25,000 × $1.50	37,500
Profit	2,750

The option is 'in the money' and should be exercised. This gives a sterling profit of $\left(\dfrac{\$2,750}{\$1.50} \right) - £500$

$= £1,333$

Summary

December spot rate	Profit on a $1.39 call option £
$1.30/£	(500)
$1.39/£	(500)
$1.50/£	1,333

In this case the option gives participation in a strengthening £, but limits losses when the £ weakens, as illustrated in the following diagram.

Profit profile on a $1.39 sterling call contract

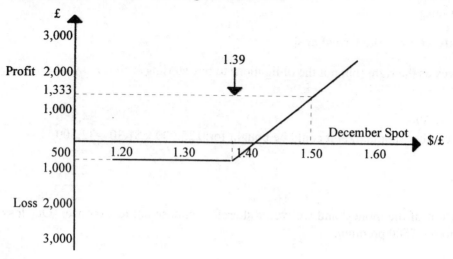

Here we can see that the call moves into profit as sterling strengthens.

4.8   Straddles

Unlike futures, options can be used to give profits if the trader feels that prices are likely to be volatile but is uncertain whether they will go up or down.

Example

Problem: Once again it is September and we feel that the $/£ exchange rate is going to change considerably before Christmas, but we are unsure as to which way it will go.

Action: Buy a December $1.39 sterling **call** for a premium of £500. Buy a December $1.39 sterling **put** for a premium of £500. Such a combination is referred to as a **straddle**.

The profitability of this strategy will depend upon future spot rates. We have already calculated the profitability of individual put and call contracts in the previous example. All we need to do here is add them together.

	£
December spot rate $1.30/£	
Profit on put	1,230
Loss on call	500
	———
Profit	730
	———
December spot rate $1.39/£	
Loss on put	500
Loss on call	500
	———
Loss	1,000
	———
December spot rate $1.50/£	
Loss on put	500
Profit on call	1,333
	———
Profit	833
	———

Graphically [which is derived simply by adding together the two individual put and call diagrams)

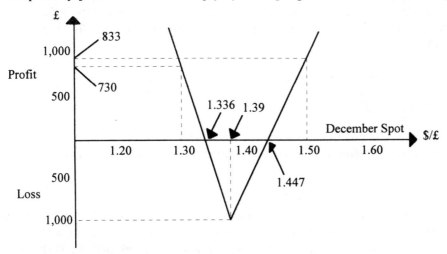

It is possible to calculate the points where the graph cuts the axis (break-even), as shown. Thus profit is earned if the £ moves out of the $1.336 - $1.447/£ range.

4.9   Low cost and zero cost options

The straddle strategy above involved the purchase of two options, one call and one put, so that two premiums were payable.

> **Definition**   Low cost option strategies involve the simultaneous purchase and sale of two separate option contracts, so that the premium receivable on the sale tends to offset the premium payable on the purchase.

You will appreciate that it can be possible for the premium receivable on the sale entirely to eliminate the premium payable on the option purchased, in which case a zero cost option strategy has been established.

An example of a low cost option is a cylinder, in which options are bought and sold on the same quantity of the underlying instrument but at different exercise prices. A company might buy one July 600 call option at 20p and sell one July 560 put option at 8p. Some protection against adverse movements can be achieved at lower cost than a single option strategy.

5   EVALUATION OF HEDGING SCENARIOS

You must be able to assess the merits of particular hedging scenarios using interest rate and currency options. Numerous examples have been provided throughout this chapter and you are recommended to return to them and rework the figures if you are still unsure as to how hedgers can use options to reduce risk.

6   SWAPS

6.1   Introduction

Swaps are one of the fastest growing sectors of the international credit market.

> **Definition**   A swap is an agreement between two (or more) parties to exchange cash flows related to specific underlying obligations.

Two types of swap may be identified:

(a)   interest rate swaps; and

(b)   currency swaps.

Interest rate swaps are now far more important than currency swaps but both represent a large volume of transactions. The notional principal involved in interest rate swaps is about US $1,500 billion with the US dollar market accounting for about two thirds. The notional principal involved in currency swaps is about US $500 billion.

The mechanics of these swaps and some of their applications are discussed below.

6.2   Interest rate swaps - the principle

Here parties agree to make interest payments to each other based upon the other's underlying obligation (notional or actual). Interest rate swaps are conducted in a single currency.

Consider the following example:

(a)   A plc wishes to raise fixed interest debt capital. Because of a currently poor credit rating it considers a debenture issue to be out of the question and the best fixed interest rate loan it can obtain is at 12.5% pa. A plc can, however, borrow at a variable rate of LIBOR (London Inter-Bank Offered Rate) + 0.5%.

(b)   B plc (the other party to the swap) can issue fixed rate debentures at 11% or alternatively borrow at a variable rate equivalent to LIBOR. B plc want a floating rate (variable rate) loan.

Iff A and B arrange to swap, the following steps must be taken (assume each firm requires £1 million of funds):

(i)   A borrows £1 million at the variable rate of LIBOR + 0.5%;

(ii)   B borrows £1 million at the fixed rate of 11%; and

(iii)   In the swap agreement A agrees to pay B interest of $11\frac{3}{4}$% (fixed) on the £1 million, while B agrees to pay A an interest rate of LIBOR (variable) on the same sum.

The net cost of financing to each party is then:

A plc

Interest payable on variable rate loan	LIBOR + 0.5%
Less: Received from B	LIBOR
	0.5%
Add: Interest payment to B	$11\frac{3}{4}$%
Net cost	$12\frac{1}{4}$% (fixed)

B plc

Interest payable on fixed rate debenture	11%
Less: Received from A	$11\frac{3}{4}$%
	($\frac{3}{4}$%)
Add: Interest payment to A	LIBOR
Net cost	LIBOR – $\frac{3}{4}$% (variable)

Overall both parties have received the type of financing they require and each has made a saving, A paying $\frac{1}{4}$% less for fixed interest funds and B paying $\frac{3}{4}$% less for variable rate funds.

Note that this is simply an example of the working of 'comparative advantage' (a term with which you should be familiar from your study of economics – it is normally discussed in the context of a justification for foreign trade). B can borrow cheaper than A at both fixed and variable rate – but there is a differential of 1.5% on their fixed rate borrowings but only 0.5% on their variable rate borrowings. ie,

	A	B	Difference
Fixed rate	12½%	11%	1½%
Variable rate	LIBOR + ½%	LIBOR	½%
Saving that can be achieved via a swap			1%

(This is before taking account of arrangement fees.)

Under the above swap agreement this saving is split:

A	¼%
B	¾%
	1%

It is possible to arrive at an agreement whereby the saving of 1% is, for example, shared differently or equally between the two companies [the latter will result from a fixed rate paid by A to B of 11½% **or** a variable rate of LIBOR + ¼% paid by B to A - try it for yourself].

6.3   Interest rate swaps - the risks

A feature of swaps which should be considered is the risk involved.

This is particularly relevant if, for example, a company has fixed interest debt and is considering swapping into floating rate debt (most typically because the company expects interest rates to fall).

If company B above had issued the 11% debentures and **subsequently** considered entering a swap agreement with A, it would gain by paying interest below what it would otherwise pay for a floating rate loan but would bear the risk of a loss if interest rates increased. Consider the detail already given for A and B, and an agreement under which A agrees to pay B interest of 11½% (fixed) on the £1m while B agrees to pay A an interest rate of LIBOR.

We can evaluate the effects on A and B of a LIBOR of:

(a)   8%;

(b)   17%.

Effects on B

	(a)	*(b)*
Cost of fixed rate debenture	11%	11%
Interest received from A	(11½%)	(11½)
Interest paid to A	8%	17%
Net cost to B	7½%	16½%

ie, if interest rates increase B would naturally lose by swapping into floating rates.

Effects on A

	(a)	(b)
Interest on variable rate loan	8 + ½% = 8½%	17 + ½ % = 17½%
Interest paid to B	11½%	11½%
Interest received from B	(8%)	(17%)
Net cost to A	12%	12%

By swapping into fixed interest A has eliminated exposure to changes in interest rates.

6.4   Currency swaps

These are similar to interest rate swaps, but the underlying obligations are in different currencies.

Consider the example of an American company wishing to borrow French francs to finance an investment project in France. If the American firm were unknown in France it could well have to pay higher interest rates than French companies on the French money markets. To arrange a swap the American company would have to locate a French company facing similar problems over borrowing US dollars. The two parties could then arrange the following swap:

(a)   The US company borrows US dollars and the French firm borrows an equivalent amount of French francs. The two parties then swap funds at the current spot rate.

(b)   The US company agrees to pay the French company the annual cost of the interest on the French franc loan. In return the French company pays the dollar interest cost of the US loan to the US company.

(c)   At the end of the period the two parties then swap back the principal amounts. This could be at prevailing spot rates or at a predetermined rate in order to reduce foreign exchange transaction exposure.

By following the above procedure each party has taken advantage of the other's credit standing in their respective capital markets and therefore reduced their financing costs. Note that if the US company could not locate a suitable French company the transaction could have been arranged with a French bank. In the long term each participant can benefit due to forex and hedging effects. As each party is taking out a loan in its own currency and can choose when to close down the deal, exchange rate movements can be minimised.

Market participants are not restricted to swapping new liabilities. In a similar way to interest rate swaps, parties can also swap existing liabilities to obtain preferred repayment currencies. Another variant on the currency swap is where parties agree to exchange currencies at some future date at a given exchange rate. These may be used to cover foreign exchange transaction exposure in much the same way as with a forward foreign exchange contract.

6.5   The value of swaps to the corporate treasurer

Swaps offer the following benefits to a corporate treasurer.

(i)   Access to capital markets which it is unable to approach directly, eg, low cost fixed interest funds are only available to large companies with good ratings.

(ii)   Favourable interest rates on borrowings; this was demonstrated in the examples above.

(iii)   Change the structure of a company's loans obligations without having to redeem the loans. For example a treasurer with fixed rate loans who believed that interest rates were going to fall should swap into floating rate loans.

(iv)   Foreign currency loans are often cheaper if raised by an institution in the relevant foreign country. A currency swap enables a company to raise funds in its own country and then swap this obligation with a foreign bank into the required foreign currency.

(v)   **Flexibility**

Swaps can be arranged for any sum (typically $5m – $50m) over varying time periods, and may be reversed by re-swapping with other counter-parties.

(vi)   **Low transaction costs**

These are limited to the legal fees in agreeing the documentation and arrangement fees.

(vii)   **Off balance sheet transactions**

Swap arrangements are forward contingent commitments and are accounted for off balance sheet.

6.6   The role of banks in swap activity

The major participants in the currency swap market to date have been US corporations and banks. The World Bank has been particularly active in converting $ loans into currencies with lower interest rates. Leading British companies are likely to became more involved in the future.

As swaps need to be tailor-made to customer requirements, certain banks have come to prominence as intermediaries in matching the needs of customers and counter-parties. At the moment these are mainly American banks, but certain of the British merchant banks are heavily involved.

6.7   Types of risk associated with swaps

Credit risk. This is the risk that the counterparty to the swap will default before the end of the swap and fail to carry out their agreed obligations. Such risk is reduced if a reputable bank is used as an intermediary to the deal.

Market risk. This is the risk that interest rates or exchange rates will move unfavourably against the company after it has committed itself into a swap. For example a company may have swapped out of fixed rate debt into floating rate debt when anticipating a reduction in general interest rates, but such rates may actually rise. Market risk is less, the shorter the term of the swap since there is less time for things to go wrong.

Sovereign risk. This is the risk associated with the country in whose currency a swap is being considered. Sovereign risk covers political instability or the possibility of exchange controls being introduced. Sovereign risk may lend to credit risk in a currency swap.

Banks arranging swaps may be exposed to further types of risk, eg, mismatch risk, the risk that a bank will not be able to lay off with another client the position that it takes with a party to a swap.

7   HYBRID FINANCIAL INSTRUMENTS

7.1   The value of financial engineering

[Definition]   **Financial engineering** is the process of combining together two or more different financial instruments to produce a new financial instrument.

Examples are

- swaptions
- low cost and zero cost options
- synthetics

> **Definition**   A **swaption** is an option contract on an interest rate swap. The purchaser buys the right to enter into the swap on or before a fixed date.

Swaptions are arranged on an OTC basis with a bank, so that the exact requirements of the client can be specified in each swaption contract made. They may be on a European or an American basis, depending on the client's wishes.

Low cost options have already been considered earlier in this chapter.

Synthetic securities can be created by combining together appropriate combination of options. This area can become complex, but the broad idea is to hold a combination of options whose risk/reward characteristics simulate the holding of a security, at a lower initial outlay than if the underlying security itself had been bought.

8   HEDGING SCENARIOS USING SWAPS AND SWAPTIONS

8.1   Hedging with swaps

Since swaps enable floating rate debt obligations to be converted into fixed rate obligations, and cashflows in a foreign currency to be converted into sterling, it is clear that swaps offer a yet further means of reducing risk exposure.

8.2   Hedging with swaptions

Once a swap has been entered into, it can be difficult to get out of early. Perhaps it can be terminated early on payment of a penalty, or perhaps an equal and opposite swap can be arranged. Either method can be problematical and expensive.

A swaption gives the treasurer more flexibility in the arranging of the company's affairs.

Example

Atherton plc is planning to take out a three year sterling loan in six months time. The company is unable to access sources of cheap fixed rate funds so is planning to take out a three year floating rate loan and swap it into fixed rate. The treasurer of the company believes that interest rates will soon increase so he decides to buy a six months floating to fixed rate swaption for a three year period starting in six months time with the fixed rate set at 9%.

What fixed interest rate will the company have to pay over the three year period of the loan if the market rate of interest in six months time is

(i)   8%
(ii)   10%?

Solution

(i)   Atherton plc will allow the swaption to lapse and take out a three year loan at the market rate of 8%.

(ii)   Atherton plc will exercise the swaption and pay the swap's fixed rate of 9%.

9   CHAPTER SUMMARY

Options and swaps offer today's corporate treasurers further ways of managing exchange rate and interest rate risk exposure. The temptation might be to take one look at the Black-Scholes formula and give up for the rest of the chapter. This is not justified since the examiner has stated that no detailed questions will be set on the mechanics of the formula.

It is more important that you can appraise prospective hedging strategies using options and swaps, and compare these with other strategies using, say, futures and forwards. One key point is the way in which options enable a company to enjoy favourable rate movements while being protected against adverse movements. Of course such protection has to be paid for.

This chapter ends the section of the syllabus dealing with risk and techniques of risk management.

10   SELF TEST QUESTIONS

10.1   Distinguish between a call option and a put option. (1.2)

10.2   When is a put option said to be in the money? (1.4)

10.3   What is the time value of an option? (1.4)

10.4   Distinguish between a European and an American option. (1.7)

10.5   What are the main determinants of the price of an option? (2.2)

10.6   State five limitations of the basic Black-Scholes model. (2.5)

10.7   What is an interest rate guarantee? (4.5)

10.8   What is a low cost option strategy? (4.9)

10.9   Define a swap contract. (6.1)

10.10   What types of risk are associated with swaps? (6.7)

11   EXAMINATION TYPE QUESTIONS

11.1   Hessey International plc

Hessey International plc has recently purchased a consignment of cleaning fluid from a United States supplier for $300,000 payable in three months' time. Recently the company has experienced foreign exchange losses on similar deals and the financial director has decided that henceforth all transaction exposure will be covered. After discussions with the bank the following data have been made available.

Foreign exchange market

	$/£		
Spot rate	1.5000	–	1.5050
Three month forward premium	1.00	–	0.80 cents

Money market

Base rates are 18% per annum in both the UK and USA.

Hessey can borrow at 2% above and deposit at 2% below the relevant base rate in either country.

Options

The bank has offered a call option on $300,000 at an exercise price of $1.49/£ at a cost of £3,000, payable in arrears.

The financial director is also aware that transaction exposure may be hedged by the use of financial futures exchanges but is uncertain of the advantages they offer as opposed to services offered by banks.

You are required:

(a)   To calculate the net cost of the transaction assuming it was covered in:

   (i)   the forward foreign exchange market; and
   (ii)   the money market.   **(3 marks)**

(b)   To explain to the financial director the nature of the foreign exchange risk cover provided by the call option and calculate the exact future spot rate at which the option would start to give a cheaper cost than the forward contract.

(4 marks)

(c)   To discuss the advantages and disadvantages of forward contracts and currency options offered by banks as opposed to currency futures and options available from financial futures exchanges.

(4 marks)

(Total: 11 marks)

11.2   Manling plc

(a)   Explain and illustrate what is meant by disintermediation and securitisation. How can disintermediation and securitisation help the financial manager?

(8 marks)

(b)   Manling plc has £14 million of fixed rate loans at an interest rate of 12% per year which are due to mature in one year. The company's treasurer believes that interest rates are going to fall, but does not wish to redeem the loans because large penalties exist for early redemption. Manling's bank has offered to arrange an interest rate swap for one year with a company that has obtained floating rate finance at London Interbank Offered Rate (LIBOR) plus $1\frac{1}{8}$%. The bank will charge each of the companies an arrangement fee of £20,000 and the proposed terms of the swap are that Manling will pay LIBOR plus $1\frac{1}{2}$% to the other company and receive from the company $11\frac{5}{8}$%.

Corporate tax is at 35% per year and the arrangement fee is a tax allowable expense. Manling could issue floating rate debt at LIBOR plus 2% and the other company could issue fixed rate debt at $11\frac{3}{4}$%. Assume that any tax relief is immediately available.

You are required:

(i)   to evaluate whether Manling plc would benefit from the interest rate swap:

(1)   if LIBOR remains at 10% for the whole year;

(2)   if LIBOR falls to 9% after six months.   **(6 marks)**

(ii)   If LIBOR remains at 10% evaluate whether both companies could benefit from the interest rate swap if the terms of the swap were altered. Any benefit would be equally shared.   **(6 marks)**

(c)   Manling expects to have £1 million surplus funds for three months prior to making a tax payment.

Discuss possible short-term investments for these funds.   **(5 marks)**

(Total: 25 marks)

11.3   Interest rate futures

It is late November. On LIFFE the three-month time-deposit interest rate futures contracts are priced as follows:

	Dec	*March*
£	93.57	92.77
US $	94.00	93.51
Swiss Franc (SF)	94.84	94.63
Euro (€)	93.99	93.62

All contract sizes are for one million units of the currency except £ where the contract size is £500,000. The tick size is 0.01%.

(a)   A company can currently borrow on the money markets at 10% per annum. It has a need for a £3.8m, 5-month loan from mid-February.

Hedge the company's exposure to interest rate risk and compute the hedge efficiency if, by mid-February, market interest rates have moved to 11%.   **(8 marks)**

(b)   Another company will have SF 11.7m surplus for one month from 1st January. Current short term money market SF deposit rates are 5% per year. Set up the hedge and compute the hedge efficiency if, by 1st January, SF deposit rates have risen by 0.5% and March Euro SF contracts are priced at 94.03.   **(6 marks)**

(c)   A third company has a floating rate € 50m loan with a three month roll over at LIBOR + 0.5%. The next roll is due on 1st January, and the company fears that LIBOR will rise over the next few months. Show how the company can hedge the next **two** roll overs. (No calculations are required).   **(4 marks)**

(Total: 18 marks)

12   ANSWERS TO EXAMINATION TYPE QUESTIONS

12.1   Hessey International plc

(a)   **Net cost of the transaction**

(i)   **Covering in the forward market**

	$/£
Spot rates	1.5000 – 1.5050
3 months forward	1.4900 – 1.4970
	(take off premiums)

Net cost $\dfrac{\$300,000}{\$1.49/£} = £201,342$ in three months' time

(ii)   **Covering on money market**

Borrow in the UK £192,308
Convert to $ (£192,308 × $1.5000/£)   = $288,462
Invest for 3 months to mature at ($288,462 × 1.04)   = $300,000
Repay UK loan   £192,308 × 1.05   =   £201,923

Net cost £201,923 in three months' time

(b)   **Nature of cover provided by call option**

Call options give the right but not the obligation to buy the underlying instrument ($US) and give protection from downside risk whilst securing participation in favourable currency increments. By using the option the firm could secure a maximum cost for the consignment of

$$\frac{\$300,000}{\$1.49/£} + £3,000 = £204,342$$

However, if the $ were to weaken the option could be abandoned and the necessary currency purchased on the spot market. For example if the $ weakens to $1.60/£ then the cost would be

$$\frac{\$300,000}{\$1.60/£} + £3,000 = £190,500$$

If the $ does strengthen the forward contract would give the best protection as no premium is payable. However, if the $ weakens to a level where the benefits of participation in the weak currency outweigh the premium then the call option would be preferable.

This point would occur when x (the critical future spot rate) was:

$$\frac{\$300,000}{x} + £3,000 = £201,342 \text{ (the cost of covering forward)}$$

$$x = \$300,000 \div £198,342 \equiv \$1.5125/£$$

Conclusion: if the $ is likely to weaken further than $1.5125/£ then the call option would be attractive.

(c) **Use of financial futures exchanges**

Financial futures exchanges offer standard contracts which are traded for fixed amounts at fixed delivery times during the year. The standardised nature of contracts can cause some initial problems in that the amounts or timing of delivery may not fit in with individual user requirements. These problems are, however, quite small for regular participants who can choose slightly to under or over cover and can close out positions early by simultaneously buying and selling contracts.

Financial futures exchanges operate a margin system where deposit and variation margins need to be paid during the life of the contract. This can cause some cash flow problems to users as opposed to bank contracts where funds are exchanged at the end of the contract. Note, however, that option premiums are usually payable in advance on bank options but on exercise with financial futures exchange options.

Surprisingly the credit risk of financial futures exchanges is normally considered to be less than that of banks. This is due to margin payments being held by the clearing house which effectively guarantees all users against default, whereas with banks users have to be wary of the creditworthiness of the institution in question. This point is unlikely to become crucial unless dealing with fringe banks.

Use of financial futures exchanges removes the need to ring several banks to obtain quotes for forward market transactions and also leaves bank lines of credit free. Reversal of positions is also more straightforward and can be obtained simply by reselling the particular contract that has been purchased. When dealing with banks reversal is a process of negotiation and can be time consuming and costly.

In conclusion, there is often little to choose between the alternatives and rates quoted will usually be very close. The two factors that need to be most carefully balanced by users are the extra flexibility offered by financial futures exchanges as opposed to the cash flow implications of the margin system.

Note: LIFFE has ceased to trade in currency futures with effect from 1990. However, Sterling currency futures are still traded on other financial futures exchanges and therefore remain relevant.

12.2 Manling plc

(Tutorial note: it is always important to check that all parts of a question can be attempted before choosing to answer a particular examination question. This question includes three topics - designed to catch out students who try to 'question spot'.)

(a) Disintermediation refers to removal of intermediaries or 'cutting out the middle man'. It occurs in the case of large public limited companies which wish to raise finance or to lend funds. Rather than dealing with a bank which serves the function of matching funds from depositors with loans required by companies, the companies deal directly between themselves ie, they avoid using the bank, or other financial intermediaries.

Securitisation refers to the process of creating new financial instruments (or 'paper') which is tradeable and issued to support fresh corporate debt. Bonds, floating rate notes (FRNs) and debentures are all examples of securitised paper.

A good example of increasing disintermediation and securisation is seen in the development of the sterling commercial paper market in the UK. This market has grown within the confines of the international money markets, which were traditionally short-term unsecured funding markets dominated by the banks, financial institutions, and a few of the highest quality non-financial corporates. Disintermediation has in large part been caused by the declining financial performance, standing, and credit ratings of the banks, resulting in more non-financial corporates appearing in the money markets to directly trade with each other. Many securitise their borrowings with commercial paper - short-term promissory notes that are issued to the lender and are tradeable - ie, capable of being sold on to realise cash.

Disintermediation and securitisation can help the financial manager in the following ways:

(i)   Disintermediation makes it possible to raise funds more cheaply than by borrowing from the bank - this assumes that the company has a suitable credit rating to be able to participate in borrowing from other non-financial corporates.

(ii)   Certain types of bank loan have conditions attached to them eg, provision of security. These conditions may be avoided by borrowing from others.

(iii)   Securitisation offers more flexibility in terms of the type of borrowing obtained; for example, financial managers can tailor the maturity date to the exact financing needs of the company.

(iv)   Securitisation raises the profile of corporate issuers, whose names are seen more prominently in the financial markets.

(v)   Securitisation makes debt easily marketable, producing finer interest rates for the borrowers and flexibility for lenders.

(vi)   It avoids the queuing system which exists for some debt issues.

(vii)   Alternative sources of finance and ways of investing surplus funds are made available to financial managers.

(b)   **(*Tutorial note:* there are two ways in which to evaluate the effect of a swap:**

(1)   Assess the effect on the overall interest rate incurred - not taking account of whether that rate is fixed or floating.

(2)   Evaluate the effect on the ability of the company to raise funds with interest rates of a particular type.

Part (i) of the question focuses on the first effect, part (ii) on the second effect.)

(i)   **Evaluation of whether interest rate swap is beneficial**

(1)   **LIBOR remains at 10% for whole year**

Existing commitment

Fixed rate of   12%

Commitment after the swap

(A)   Cost of fixed rate loan   12%

(B)   Floating rate paid to the other company
          10 + 1½   11½%

(C)   Rate received from the other company   (11⅝%)

Net rate incurred   11⅞%

	£
Saving in interest £14m × (12% - 11⅞%)	17,500
Arrangement fee	(20,000)
Increase in cost	2,500

Therefore, swap would not be beneficial, although the final cost, after tax, is mitigated to £2,500 (1 - t) = £2,500 (1 - 0.35) = £1,625

(2)   **LIBOR falls to 9% after six months**

Commitment after the swap

	First six months	Second six months
(A) Cost of fixed rate loan	12%	12%
(B) Floating rate paid to other company		
10 + 1½	11½%	
9 + 1½		10½%
(C) Rate received from other company	(11⅝%)	(11⅝%)
Net rate incurred	11.875%	10.875%

Saving in interest: £

First six months £14m × (0.12 - 0.11875) × 6/12   8,750

Second six months £14m × (0.12 - 0.10875) × 6/12   78,750

	87,500
Arrangement fee	(20,000)
Net benefit	67,500

Therefore, swap is beneficial. After tax, the benefit of the swap over the year will equal £67,500 (1 - 0.35) - £43,875

(Note: there is a timing difference which should be taken into account ie, the arrangement fee is presumably payable now whereas the interest savings will accrue in one year.)

(ii)   **Evaluation of whether both companies can benefit - given LIBOR remains at 10%**

(Tutorial note: in this example part (i) asks for a calculation of the final outcome which will depend on what happens to the floating rate. If LIBOR falls to 9% Manling will benefit from the swap. In (i) the other effect of the swap is for Manling to obtain funds at LIBOR + $1\frac{7}{8}$ from the other company ie, a saving of (LIBOR + 2) - (LIBOR + $1\frac{7}{8}$) = $\frac{1}{8}$% on the rate at which it can otherwise obtain floating rate debt.

It is this other effect that has to be considered from the viewpoint of both companies in (b)(ii).)

Cost to the other company

(1)	Cost of floating rate finance 10 + $1\frac{1}{8}$	$11\frac{1}{8}$%
(2)	Fixed rate interest to Manling	$11\frac{5}{8}$%
(3)	Amount received from Manling floating rate of 10 + $1\frac{1}{2}$ ($11\frac{1}{2}$%)	

Net cost of fixed rate finance $11\frac{1}{4}$%

The other company would otherwise pay $11\frac{3}{4}$% for fixed rate finance, and is thus saving $11\frac{3}{4}$% - $11\frac{1}{4}$% = $\frac{1}{2}$% under the swap.

Therefore, under the present swap agreement, with LIBOR = 10%, the savings being achieved are:

(1)	Manling	$\frac{1}{8}$%
(2)	Other company	$\frac{1}{2}$%

Total saving $\frac{5}{8}$%

It is this saving which needs to be shared equally between the two firms.

Shared equally = $\frac{5}{8}$ ÷ 2 = $\frac{5}{16}$% to each company

At the moment, the other company obtains a $\frac{1}{2}$% saving compared to the $\frac{5}{16}$% it would obtain if savings were shared equally. It must therefore give, by way of the interest rates applied to the swap, $\frac{3}{16}$% ($\frac{1}{2}$% - $\frac{5}{16}$%) of additional benefit to Manling plc. This would give Manling an equal $\frac{1}{8}$% + $\frac{3}{16}$% = $\frac{5}{16}$% benefit in comparison to the finance it would otherwise obtain.

Thus, the other company should either pay $\frac{3}{16}$% more as a fixed interest charge to Manling (making that charge $11\frac{5}{8}$% + $\frac{3}{16}$% = $11\frac{13}{16}$%, or receive an interest charge of $\frac{3}{16}$% less from Manling by way of floating rate charge - ie, commit Manling to paying LIBOR + $1\frac{1}{2}$% less $\frac{3}{16}$% - ie, LIBOR + $1\frac{5}{16}$% ($11\frac{5}{16}$% if LIBOR = 10%). In summary the overall finance costs for both companies under both options become either:

	Manling	*Other company*
Fixed rate	12%	
Floating rate		$11\frac{1}{8}$%
Floating rate swap	$11\frac{1}{2}$%	($11\frac{1}{2}$%)
Fixed rate swap	($11\frac{13}{16}$%)	$11\frac{13}{16}$% (bal fig)
Overall cost:	$11\frac{11}{16}$%	$11\frac{7}{16}$%

or:

	Manling	*Other company*
Fixed rate	12%	
Floating rate		$11\frac{1}{8}\%$
Fixed rate swap	$(11\frac{5}{8}\%)$	$11\frac{5}{8}\%$
Floating rate swap (bal fig)	$11\frac{5}{16}\%$	$(11\frac{5}{16}\%)$
Overall cost	$11\frac{11}{16}\%$	$11\frac{7}{16}\%$

Thus, the benefit to each company is:

	£
$14m \times \frac{5}{16}\%$	43,750
Less: Arrangement fee	20,000
Net benefit before tax	23,750

Net benefit after tax $23,750 \times (1 - 0.35) =$ £15,437

Each company could thus benefit by $\frac{5}{16}\%$ compared to its alternative finance options.

(c) The following short-term investments are available:

(i) Short-term bank deposit in domestic or foreign currency.

(ii) Treasury Bills - issued by the government and risk-free.

(iii) Local authority debt - carrying slightly higher interest than Treasury Bills to reflect higher risk.

(iv) Certificates of deposit issued by British or foreign banks.

(v) Bills of exchange and trade bills issued by companies.

(vi) Deposits with building societies.

(vii) Purchase of equity shares. This is likely to be undesirable because of the risk of capital loss and transaction costs.

(viii) Placement in the money markets. Such placements are unsecured, but generally very low risk as borrowing counter parties will be prime organisations.

(ix) Purchase of commercial paper - ie, promissory notes issued by prime borrowers. Such investment is highly flexible - commercial paper being easily sold when needed to realise cash.

(x) Working capital. The company could look to see whether sales could be boosted to advantage by investing more in debtors or inventory.

The company could also consider discount availability on early settlement of creditor balances.

The factors to take into account when comparing these alternatives are yield, risk of default and marketability. The yield will normally be higher as the risk increases.

12.3   Interest rate futures

(a)   Target: £3.8m × (5/12) × 0.10 = £158,333

Hedge: £3.8m/£0.5m = 7.6

Given the maturity mis-match between the loan's term and the future's life, there is a requirement for:

7.6 × (5/3) = 12.7 contracts,

which needs to be rounded up to 13.

As the company wishes to hedge a loan, it needs to sell £ March futures, therefore the company will sell 13 £ March contracts at 92.77.

By mid-February, given that money market rates have increased by 1%, we will assume that the price of March £ futures has fallen by 1 point to 91.77.

The company borrows £3.8m for 5 months at 11%/year interest, incurring an interest charge of:

£3.8m × (5/12) × 0.11	=	£174,167
Target interest charge	=	£158,333
'Loss' on target	=	£15,834

The company buys 13 £ March futures at 91.77 in order to close out its futures position, yielding a profit of:

Value of one tick: £500,000 × (3/12) × 0.0001 = £12.50

Futures bought at	:	91.77
Futures sold at	:	92.77
Profit per contract	:	1% = 100 ticks

Total profit: Number of contracts × ticks/contract × value/tick.

Total profit: 13 × 100 × £12.50 = £16,250

Hedge efficiency: $\dfrac{\text{Profit}}{\text{Loss}} = \dfrac{£16,250}{£15,834} = 102.6\%$.

(b)   Target: SF 11.7m × (1/12) × 0.05 = SF 48,750

Hedge:

No of contracts: SF 11.7m/SF 1m = 11.7

Given the maturity mis-match, the number of contracts required for the hedge is:

11.7 × (1/3) = 3.9 round up to 4

Given the company wishes to hedge a deposit against a fall in interest rates, the company needs to buy 4 March futures at 94.63.

When the cash is deposited on 1st January, the company will receive:

SF 11.7m × (1/12) × 0.055	=	SF 53,625
Target interest	=	SF 48,750

Profit on target	=	SF 4,875

Closing out its futures position, it sells 4 March futures at 94.03, resulting in the following loss:

Value of one tick: SF 1m × (3/12) × 0.0001 = SF 25

Futures bought at	:	94.63
Futures sold at	:	94.03

Loss on futures	:	0.6% = 60 ticks

Total loss: 4 × 60 × SF 25 = SF 6,000

$$\text{Hedge efficiency} = \frac{\text{SF } 4,875}{\text{SF } 6,000} = 81.25\%$$

(c)   As they are 3 month futures and there is a 3 month roll-over period, there is no maturity mismatch. The number of contracts required to hedge will be:

€ 50m/€ 1m = 50

Therefore the company sells 50 March contracts (to hedge the 1st January roll-over) and also sells 50 June contracts (to hedge the 1st April roll-over).

On the 1st January, it will close out its position on the March contracts and will make a profit or loss depending upon whether LIBOR has fallen or risen.

Similarly, on the 1st April, the company will close out its June position.

21 TRANSFER PRICING

INTRODUCTION & LEARNING OBJECTIVES

Many modern business organisations are established as an international group with separate individual companies in each country, whose results are all consolidated into one set of group accounts.

The question arises as to the best price to set for intra-group sales when one group company sells goods or services to another group company. You will see that there are tax, motivational and legal influences on the price decision.

The chapter concludes by examining methods of measuring the performance of overseas operations. Although conventional ratio analysis can be used, there are specific problems that need to be borne in mind.

When you have studied this chapter you should be able to do the following:

- State the criteria for a good transfer pricing system.
- Discuss bases on which transfer prices can be established.
- Appreciate the advantage of using tax havens.
- Compare the return on capital employed and the residual income as methods of performance measurement.
- Discuss the particular problems in evaluating the performance of international companies.

1 TRANSFER PRICES AND MULTINATIONAL COMPANIES

1.1 Introduction

[Definition] The transfer price is the price charged by one part of an organisation when supplying goods or services to another part of the same organisation.

Large diversified groups will be split into numerous smaller profit centres, each preparing accounts for its own sphere of activities and paying tax on its profits. Multinational groups are likely to own individual companies established in different countries throughout the world; transfer pricing is the process of deciding on appropriate prices for the goods and services sold intra-group.

This chapter begins by examining the theory of transfer pricing in a one-country context, then expands to consider the setting of transfer prices between parts of a group located in different countries. You can appreciate that international transfer pricing requires a consideration of multiple currency effects and multiple tax regimes.

1.2 Criteria for judging transfer pricing systems

The general rules for the operation of most systems apply also to transfer pricing. A transfer pricing system should be reasonably easy to operate and to understand, as well as being flexible in terms of a changing organisation structure. In addition, there are three specific criteria which a good transfer pricing system should meet:

(a) it should allow divisional autonomy to be maintained, since continued autonomy should motivate divisional managers to give their best performance;

(b) it should allow divisional performance to be assessed objectively;

(c) it should ensure that divisional managers make decisions that are in the best interests both of the divisions and of the whole company.

There are broadly three types of transfer prices:

(a) market-based prices;
(b) cost-related prices;
(c) negotiated prices and dual prices.

1.3 Market-based transfer prices

Where the product (or service) that is subject to internal transfer could be sold to other outside organisations by the supplying division and, similarly, where the product could be purchased from other outside organisations by the receiving division, a competitive market exists and a market price will have been established under normal supply and demand conditions. Such a market price would be a very suitable basis on which to make inter-divisional transfers.

It would allow each division to remain autonomous, so that the profit of the division would not be affected by any decision to buy/sell externally or to trade internally. The resultant profits would be determined in an objective way. In most situations the use of a market price as a transfer price will not lead to any divergence between divisional and company goals as the true cost to the overall company of an internal transfer is the opportunity cost of the lost external sales price; thus divisions will be making decisions on a price relevant to the company overall. However, there is a particular problem when there is spare capacity; this is dealt with in the next section.

Market prices are sometimes adjusted downwards for use as transfer prices, to recognise the benefits or savings from internal trading. Such a reduction might relate to lower packaging and advertising costs for goods transferred internally in comparison with outside sales. An adjusted market price should encourage internal trading because it should lead to higher divisional profits than buying or selling in the open market.

1.4 Problems with market-based transfer prices

In a situation where there is spare capacity in the supplying division, the use of a market-based transfer price will not ensure that the divisional managers will be motivated individually to take independent action which is in the best interests of the whole company. This is because the manager of a receiving division may see his divisional profits fall as a result of a move to utilise spare capacity, even though it would benefit the overall profits of the company. A comprehensive example follows to illustrate this situation, and it will be referred to again in a later section.

Example

Kwaree Ltd, producing a range of minerals, is organised into two trading groups – one group handles wholesale business and the other deals with sales to retailers.

One of its products is a moulding clay. The wholesale group extracts the clay and sells it to external wholesale customers as well as to the retail group. The production capacity is 2,000 tonnes per month, but at present sales are limited to 1,000 tonnes wholesale and 600 tonnes retail.

The transfer price agreed is £180 per tonne, in line with the existing external wholesale trade price.

The retail group produces 100 bags of refined clay from each tonne of moulding clay which it sells at £4 per bag. It would sell a further 40,000 bags if the retail trade price were reduced to £3.20 per bag.

Other data relevant to the operation are:

	Wholesale group	Retail group
Variable cost per tonne	£70	£60
Fixed cost per month	£100,000	£40,000

You are required to prepare estimated profit statements for the current month for each group and for Kwaree Ltd as a whole when producing at:

(a)   80% capacity; and

(b)   100% capacity, utilising the extra sales to supply the retail trade.

Solution

(a)   **Estimated profit statement for the current month**

Transfer price: £180 per tonne

Wholesale group operating at 80% capacity.

	Wholesale group £'000	Retail group £'000	Kwaree Ltd £'000
Sales outside the company:			
1,000 tonnes @ £180/tonne	180		180
60,000 bags @ £4/bag		240	240
Internal transfer of 600 tonnes	108	(108)	Nil
Less: Costs:			
Variable:			
1,600 tonnes @ £70/tonne	(112)		(112)
600 tonnes @ £60/tonne		(36)	(36)
Fixed	(100)	(40)	(140)
Profit	76	56	132

(b)   **Estimated profit statement for the current month**

Transfer price: £180 per tonne

Wholesale group operating at 100% capacity.

	Wholesale group £'000	Retail group £'000	Kwaree Ltd £'000
Sales outside the company:			
1,000 tonnes @ £180/tonne	180		180
100,000 bags @ £3.20/bag		320	320
Internal transfer of 1,000 tonnes	180	(180)	Nil
Less: Costs:			
Variable:			
2,000 tonnes @ £70/tonne	(140)		(140)
1,000 tonnes @ £60/tonne		(60)	(60)
Fixed	(100)	(40)	(140)
Profit	120	40	160

If it is assumed that the group (divisional) managers of Kwaree Ltd are being measured in terms of the profitability of their divisions, then the effect on divisional profits of utilising the spare capacity in the wholesale group can be summarised as follows:

	Profits in Wholesale group £'000	Profits in Retail group £'000	Profits in Kwaree Ltd £'000
80% capacity	76	56	132
100% capacity	120	40	160
Increase/(decrease)	44	(16)	28

As a result of utilising spare capacity the profits of Kwaree would increase by £28,000. However, the wholesale group profits would increase by £44,000, whereas the manager of the retail group would see his division's profits fall by £16,000.

This fall is caused by the reduction in the selling price per bag of the moulding clay, affecting all the sales of the retail group and not only the additional sales. The manager of the retail group, acting independently, is unlikely to accept a decision to increase his production and sales if, as a result, the profit on which he is assessed is likely to decline. The action which he sees to be most beneficial for the retail group, for which he is responsible, is not the action which is in the best interests of the whole company. This is an example of **sub-optimisation**. Ideally the transfer price should be such that the profits of wholesale and retail groups and the company would all increase as a result of moving from the 80% to 100% capacity. Transfer price bases which would give rise to this situation are identified in a later section (as they are cost-related).

Where the goods produced by the supplying division are only transferred internally to the receiving division, so that there is no existing market price, it may be possible to establish the identity of a substitute product which is freely available and does have a market price which could be used as the basis for the transfer price. The problems are associated with determining whether the other product is a valid substitute and, if so, what is the appropriate market price.

1.5   Cost-related transfer prices

The following cost-related transfer prices will be considered in this section:

(a)   total cost;
(b)   variable cost;
(c)   fixed charge plus a variable charge per unit;
(d)   apportionment of contribution.

In all cases the use of standard rather than actual cost ensures that the cost of inefficiency is reflected in the producing division's results, rather than being passed on via the transfer price to the receiving division.

(a)   **Total cost**

This approach involves the determination of the total cost per unit for the supplying division. This cost would include both fixed and variable elements. Such a total cost per unit would then be used to price **each** unit of product internally transferred.

There is a fundamental problem with a transfer price based on an absorbed total cost, in that its use in a decision-making context by the manager of the receiving division can lead to action which is not optimal in terms of profit for the company. The reason for this is that, although the total cost is made up of fixed and variable cost elements relating to the supplying division, the one transfer price per unit is regarded by the receiving division manager as variable. This is understandable because the manager in the receiving division is always charged an amount equal to:

Number of units of product × Same transfer price per unit

In other words, the receiving division manager recognises the cost behaviour of the transfer price he is charged as having the exact qualities of a truly variable cost ie, varying directly with the quantity (of units transferred).

The receiving division manager, making decisions for his own area of responsibility and thinking primarily of optimising the profits of his own division, is likely to treat the transfer price as a variable item in the analysis. The danger is that in situations where the receiving division has spare production capacity, the manager may make the decision not to accept business at a lower selling price than usual, because it would apparently not make a profit or even a contribution for that division. However, for the company as a whole the special price does exceed the variable costs and in the short term it would be worthwhile to accept the business.

The following example illustrates this situation.

Example

A company has two divisions – P and Q. Division P manufactures a product which it transfers to Division Q at a transfer price equal to the total cost of manufacture in Division P. Division Q incorporates each unit transferred from Division P into a product which it manufactures and sells. Divisions P and Q currently have spare production capacity. Cost and selling price data are as follows:

	Division P £/unit	Division Q £/unit
Variable cost	3	
Fixed cost	2	
Total cost (= Transfer price)	5	5
Variable cost		6
Fixed cost		3
Total cost		14
Profit		1
Selling price		15

If an opportunity arose for Division Q to sell the same product for £12 per unit, without affecting its normal existing business and its selling price of £15 per unit on that business, the manager of Division Q would reject it, as the divisional profit would fall. The total cost per unit of £14 would exceed the selling price of £12. However, the manager may apply a contribution approach and argue that the additional business, to utilise separate capacity in the short term, is worthwhile because it would still make a divisional contribution. His calculations would be based on:

	£/unit	£/unit
Selling price		12
Less: 'Variable' costs to the division:		
Transfer price	5	
Variable cost	6	
		11
Contribution to the division		1

Using the same set of data, but now assuming that the additional units could only be sold at a price of £10 each, the manager of Division Q would reject the business on both grounds ie, a reduction of divisional profit and the fact that the business apparently does not even produce a contribution for the division. However, it would be in the best interests of the overall company, in terms of short-term profit, if the additional business were accepted, even at a selling price of £10 per unit, as the following demonstrates:

	£/unit	£/unit
Selling price		10
Less: Variable costs in:		
Division P	3	
Division Q	6	
	—	9
Overall company contribution		1

The foregoing illustrations are based on the following major assumptions:

(i)   the variable cost per unit and the total fixed costs of both divisions remain unchanged at all levels of activity under consideration;

(ii)   the additional business at the special selling price in no way affects existing business at the existing selling price;

(iii)   the manager of the receiving division regards the total cost transfer price as a variable cost as far as his autonomous decision-making process is concerned;

(iv)   divisional managers are being assessed in terms of the profitability of their areas of responsibility.

As far as the making of optimal decisions is concerned, **a transfer price based on total cost is to be avoided**. In addition, if transfers are made on this basis, the manager of the producing division will not be making a profit on goods traded internally (but neither will he be making a loss), so it will be difficult for profitability to provide an objective measure of the performance of the producing division and its manager.

(b)   **Variable cost**

If the producing division transfers units at a price equal to its own variable cost of manufacture, there is no way that the producing division manager will show a profit on or even a contribution from that business. Again, an objective measure of performance based on profitability would not be achieved. Such a basis would not be motivational as far as the producing division manager is concerned.

The use of variable cost as a basis for setting the transfer price would mean that the receiving division manager would be provided with the most meaningful cost information as far as decision-making in his division is concerned. There should be no sub-optimisation, so that decisions made should be in the best interest of the division **and** the overall company.

(c)   **Fixed charge plus a variable charge per unit**

In effect this represents a two-part transfer price – a fixed amount per period, which is charged irrespective of the number of units transferred, plus an amount which represents a fixed rate per unit. This concept is similar to the way in which domestic consumers are charged for electricity, gas and the use of the telephone. An element of profit could be included in the two-part tariff to give the producing division manager the necessary motivation.

The advantage of this type of transfer pricing structure is that it will generally encourage the receiving division to accept more units from the producing division as long as the extra revenue is greater than the extra cost involved. It would be logical to base the fixed element in the charge on the fixed costs arising in the producing division, and to restrict it to any limit on the availability of capacity to supply the receiving division. The variable element would then approximate to the variable or marginal cost of manufacture (possibly plus a profit mark-up).

The application of this type of transfer price would also avoid the problem that arose in the example above (Kwaree Ltd).

If in Kwaree Ltd the transfer price were set as follows:

£50,000 fixed charge **plus** £96.66 per tonne transferred,

then the resultant profits for each division and the company as a whole when the wholesale group is working at:

(i)   80% capacity; and

(ii)   100% capacity

could be summarised as follows:

		Profit in Wholesale group £'000	Profit in Retail group £'000	Profit in Kwaree Ltd £'000
Wholesale group working at:				
(i)	80% capacity	76	56	132
(ii)	100% capacity	86.66	73.34	160

The following points should be observed:

(i)   The resultant profits for each group and the overall company are exactly the same, when working at 80% capacity, as those when the market price was applied in the original example. Therefore, the divisional managers would be indifferent, in terms of resultant profit, between the application of the market price or the two-part transfer price.

(ii)   The fixed charge of £50,000 per period represents 50% of the total fixed costs of the wholesale group, on the argument that up to 50% of its capacity could be used to produce moulding clay for the wholesale group.

(iii)   The profits on both the wholesale **and** the retail group, as well as those for the company as a whole, would increase if the divisional managers decided to utilise the spare capacity and work at 100% capacity. They would be motivated to move to the optimal production levels automatically. It should be recalled that in the original application of the market price as a transfer price, moving from 80% to 100% capacity would have resulted in a fall in the profits of the retail group.

(d)   **Apportionment of contribution**

Another suggestion for establishing transfer prices is based on working out the total contribution made by the company on goods subject to internal transfer, and then applying some logical but arbitrary method of apportionment of this contribution between the two divisions involved. For example, it might be agreed that each division was to make the same contribution margin ratio on the goods subject to internal transfer.

1.6   Negotiated prices and dual prices

In any practical application of transfer pricing there is usually going to be some element of negotiation between the two divisional managers involved. Such negotiation may be loosely based on a market price or on costs, because it is difficult to negotiate in a complete vacuum. Empirical evidence has suggested that, where divisional managers are left to negotiate freely, market prices and costs do figure in the exercise. However, in addition the strengths and weaknesses of individual managers in a bargaining situation will play a role.

The problem with negotiated prices is when the two divisional managers cannot agree: they then have to seek a decision from higher central management on what transfer price to charge. This conflicts with one of the main criteria set out for transfer prices ie, that the divisions should remain as autonomous decision-making units. Management theory suggests that decisions should always be made at the lowest appropriate level in an organisation structure.

Another approach to transfer pricing is the use of dual prices ie, one price for crediting the supplying division and another (usually lower) price for debiting the receiving division. The inter-divisional profit would have to be removed when combining the results of the two divisions. This is intended to represent a motivational approach to transfer pricing but the problem is that both divisions would appear favourably, in terms of profit, from the application of this approach. One then questions the objectivity of profit as a measure of performance in these circumstances.

1.7   A general rule for transfer pricing

The following general rule has been put forward for setting transfer prices.

Transfer price per unit   =   Standard variable cost in the producing division **plus** the opportunity cost to the company as a whole of supplying the unit internally

The opportunity cost will be either the contribution forgone by selling one unit internally rather than externally, or the contribution forgone by not using the same facilities in the producing division for their next best alternative use.

The application of this general rule means that the transfer price equals:

(a)   the standard variable cost of the producing division, if there is no outside market for the units manufactured and no alternative use for the facilities in that division;

(b)   the market price, if there is an outside market for the units manufactured in the producing division and no alternative more profitable use for the facilities in that division.

1.8   Motivational effects of transfer pricing

These have been described throughout the above analysis. A well set transfer price will motivate managers:

(i)   to work hard

(ii)   to act in accordance with group objectives.

If transfer prices are imposed by the parent company managers, even for the best possible intentions, divisional autonomy will have been compromised and divisional managers will be less committed to overexerting themselves.

1.9   International transfer pricing

The additional factors that need to be considered are

- currency risk management
- cash funds management
- tax management

Currency risk management has already been studied in a previous chapter. The following decisions should be made:

(i)   In which currency should the transfers be denominated? Possibilities include the supplier's currency, the receiver's currency or the parent company's currency.

(ii)   In which currency should the supplier's invoice be settled, ie, which currency should be used for the intragroup transfer?

Cash funds management refers to the decision as to where and in which currency should cash balances be held. Some governments place restrictions on dividend payments by subsidiaries to foreign parents.

It would be tempting in such a situation to sell goods intragroup to such a subsidiary at an artificially high transfer price to shift the subsidiary's cash to the parent without a dividend being paid. Such a tactic is not possible where foreign governments require transfer prices to be set on an arm's length basis.

The use of tax havens as part of the tax management of transfer pricing is looked at in the next section.

2   LEGAL REGULATIONS AND TAX ASPECTS AFFECTING TRANSFER PRICING

2.1   Transfer pricing and tax authorities

One common approach to setting international transfer prices adopted by multinational companies is to seek to minimise the group's overall total tax liability. The objective is to set transfer prices in order to report low profits in countries with high tax rates and high profits in countries with low tax rates.

This objective is frustrated in many countries whose governments require that transfer prices are set on an arm's length basis, ie, using the prevailing market price. The principle is still useful however as a broad objective and particularly valuable when transferring goods for which no external market price exists or when operating in countries without an arm's length transfer price requirement.

If transfer prices are set on the basis of minimising tax, this can have consequences for the whole company. Remember the three principles identified earlier for a good transfer pricing system:

- maintain divisional autonomy
- assess divisional performance objectively
- ensure goal congruence.

Clearly autonomy will be compromised if the parent company fixes transfer prices throughout the group to minimise total tax. This can have adverse motivational consequences. In extreme cases the diminished autonomy can even have adverse tax consequences, since the division could be taxed as a foreign branch rather than a subsidiary. So the objectives of reducing a group's total tax bill can even result in the group paying a higher tax bill than if the group was left alone!

2.2   The use of tax havens

Definition   A tax haven is a country which imposes low rates of tax.

Usually a country is offering low tax rates in an effort to attract foreign investment to create jobs for its workforce. A tax haven will be most attractive with the following criteria:

- low rate of corporation tax
- low withholding tax on dividends paid to overseas holding companies
- comprehensive tax treaties with other countries
- stable economy with low political risk
- lack of exchange controls
- good communications with the rest of the world
- developed legal framework so that rights can be safeguarded.

3   PERFORMANCE MEASUREMENT

3.1   Introduction

We start this section by revising the key methods of measuring the performance of business entities that you will already have met in your previous studies. Then the discussion broadens to consider the implications of certain of the divisions being in different countries of the world.

The most important measures of business performance are either the **return on capital employed (ROCE)** or the **residual income (RI)**.

3.2   ROCE used to measure divisional performance

ROCE can only be used to measure divisional performance if each division is a profit centre and if an investment base can be ascertained for each division. Some assets will quite clearly belong to one division rather than to another, but there is the question of whether to apportion the value of shared assets. It is perhaps better not to apportion if the method of doing so would be purely arbitrary. The shared assets are then ignored for all divisions. Besides this problem there is the problem of how to treat leased as opposed to owned assets. A divisional manager might be tempted to lease rather than purchase an asset if this improved the ROCE of his division. However, this is not the best criterion on which to base such a decision (discounted cash flow methods are preferable).

ROCE is sometimes referred to as **return on investment.**

3.3   Residual income

An alternative means of comparing divisions is to calculate not a percentage figure (ROCE) but an absolute figure of **residual income**, which is calculated as profit minus a notional figure of interest on capital employed, calculated at the company's cost of capital or target rate of return. This method is probably less well understood than ROCE and suffers from some of the same difficulties, but it has the advantage that it avoids the problem of managers optimising their own division's performance at the expense of the whole organisation – the so-called danger of 'sub-optimisation' or 'lack of goal congruence'. An example comparing ROCE and residual income follows:

Example 1

XYZ Ltd's target rate of return is 12%. Division X is currently making a 20% return on capital employed of £1m. A new project becomes available to Division X which would yield a return of 14% on total investment of £250,000.

Should the project be undertaken?

From the company's point of view, the project should be undertaken because it earns a return above the target rate.

However, if it undertook the new project, Division X's result would deteriorate in terms of ROCE:

	Capital employed £m	ROCE %	Profit £'000
Existing	1.00	20.0	200
Proposed	0.25	14.0	35
Overall	1.25	18.8	235

Division X's manager would be more likely to take the 'right' decision if performance was evaluated on the residual income basis:

	Profit £'000	Notional interest @ 12% £'000	Residual income £'000
Existing	200	120	80
Proposed	35	30	5
Overall	235	150	85

The division's residual income is increased by accepting the project. Therefore, the divisional manager is likely to interpret the situation correctly by wishing to accept the project, as it will increase the reported income for his division, and also such action is in the best interests of the overall company.

3.4   Activity

Division Z has the following financial performance:

Operating profit	£40,000
Operating assets	£150,000
Cost of borrowing	10%

Would the division wish to accept a new possible investment costing £10,000 which would earn profit of £2,000 pa if the evaluation was on the basis of

(i)   ROCE;

(ii)   Residual income?

3.5   Activity solution

(i)   Current ROCE $= \dfrac{40,000}{150,000} = 26.7\%$

If the investment is accepted, revised ROCE

$= \dfrac{42,000}{160,000} = 26.3\%$ ie, REJECT the project

(ii)   Current RI $= 40,000 - (10\% \times 150,000) = £25,000$
Revised RI $= 42,000 - (10\% \times 160,000) = £26,000$
ie, ACCEPT the project

3.6   Defining divisional 'profit'

Whether ROCE or residual income is used, there is the question of how to define the profit of a division. In particular, should non-controllable costs be assigned to a division or not?

There are four basic levels at which divisional 'profit' can be assessed:

(a)   divisional contribution (divisional sales less divisional variable costs);

(b)   divisional contribution less direct divisional fixed costs;

(c)   divisional contribution less divisional fixed costs less an apportionment of company/headquarters costs (this is equivalent to divisional net profit before tax); and

(d)   divisional net profit after tax.

The level of profit will depend upon the purpose of the divisional assessment. It is important to distinguish between:

(a)   the assessment of the divisional **manager's** own performance; and

(b)   the assessment of the division itself.

In assessing the **individual manager's** performance, it is usual to apply a responsibility accounting basis and only include those **items which he can control or influence**. This would suggest an assessment based on level (a) or (b) profit. In most cases the divisional manager should control all the elements in the divisional contribution, but in addition there are some direct divisional fixed costs which he controls and which are deducted at the level (b) profit. On the other hand, there are other divisional fixed costs which can be traced directly, but which are outside the control of the divisional manager in the short term (divisional rates, rent and depreciation, for example, will usually depend on earlier decisions). Neither profit level (a) or (b) is perfect, and a decision on which to use is necessarily a subjective decision; but once decided upon it should be applied consistently.

When the **division** itself is being assessed, top management is considering the total investment in the division and the return it is making. All costs **caused by the existence of the division**, whether or not controllable by its manager, should be taken into account. This should be the basis when top management are assessing whether to increase the investment (or a disinvestment) in a particular division.

3.7   Defining divisional capital employed

The problems associated with the determination of divisional capital employed are similar in nature to those identified in the previous section on divisional profit. These can be listed as:

(a)   Is the capital employed to be used in a ROCE calculation to assess the division's or the manager's performance?

(b)   Which assets should be included and which excluded?

(c)   For those included, how are they to be valued?

If the whole division's performance is being assessed, then the net current assets employed in the division should be used. On the other hand, the criterion should be one of controllability when the divisional manager's performance is being measured. The responsibility for some assets (eg, cash) is often assumed by the central management function of the organisation and for other assets the responsibility changes over time. For example, the credit sales and creation of debtors, under the usual terms of trade for the business, are the responsibility of the division. However, if the organisation operates a central credit control function for all divisions, then if there is any delay in the collection of amounts outstanding from debtors, should the division be penalised (by still carrying the debtors in its capital employed)?

Arguments can arise also about where the true responsibility lies for the medium and large investment decisions concerning fixed assets in divisions. Despite the possible contention that these are central management decisions, and therefore not controllable within the division, it is most common in practice to find that fixed assets (on a replacement cost basis), together with net current assets, are included in the divisional capital employed.

3.8   Assessing managerial performance

When assessing the performance of someone as senior as a divisional manager, it must be remembered that his job is not only to run his division efficiently, but to co-operate with the managers of other divisions to promote the interests of the company as a whole. Performance assessment must take into account this need for integration – and it might be necessary to examine such factors as the record of a division in supplying components needs by another division at the time required.

Furthermore, the performance of a division can often be assessed in purely financial terms, whereas assessment of the manager's performance must take into account his record, for instance, on industrial relations and employee development.

3.9   Guidelines for reports from overseas operations

When overseas divisions are to be appraised on the basis of regular financial reports received at head office, it is worthwhile considering appropriate guidelines that should be used in drawing up the reports.

Divisional reports will be useful for the following purposes

(i)   Interpretation of financial accounts.   The usual ratio analysis can be applied to assess profitability, liquidity, gearing, etc.

(ii)   Early warnings if actual results are failing to meet budgets. Is something going wrong or were the budgets unrealistic?

(iii)   Evaluation of managers' performance.

(iv)   Deciding on the allocation of group resources in future.   Scarce investment funds can be channelled to divisions experiencing rapid growth with good prospects for high future profitability.

A combination of financial and non-financial measures should be used to draw up the report. The most suitable financial measures will be

- comparison of actual profit against budgeted profit.
- comparison of actual sales against budgeted sales.
- return on capital employed.
- residual income.

Suitable non-financial measures might be:

- market share achieved.
- quality measures, eg, number of customer complaints, proportion of output scrapped, etc.
- employee turnover.

3.10   Evaluating the performance of international companies

Certain specific problems arise in using ratio and other traditional forms of analysis to evaluate the performance of international groups of companies. These are considered below.

Which currency?

Should analysis be carried out in the group reporting currency or the individual company's own domestic currency? Since the objective of the whole group is assumed to be to increase the wealth of the holding company's shareholders, and these people receive their dividends in the parent company's currency, it is normally considered best to carry out all analysis in the parent currency. This begs the next question.

Which exchange rate?

Should a subsidiary's results be translated at the budgeted rate, the year-end rate or at an average for the year? SSAP 20 lays down how historical accounts should be drawn up, but there is no guarantee that this method is also appropriate for evaluation purposes. This is a complex discussion area, but one possible answer is to assess the degree to which the subsidary's managers are able to manage the exchange risk arising from their company. If they have no expertise or training in this area, then they cannot be held responsible for exchange rate differences that arise, ie, their results should be translated at the rate used when their budget was drawn up at the start of the year. However, if the subsidiary's managers are trained to manage their exchange risk, closing actual rates can be applied to their results and the exchange gain or loss highlighted in the financial report from the company.

Effect of transfer prices

Where transfer prices have been set artificially to reduce the group's overall total tax bill, profits reported by each division will be distorted and will need to be adjusted before analysis is carried out.

4 CHAPTER SUMMARY

This chapter began by revising the definition of transfer price and the discussion of why transfer pricing is important. Three possible bases of devising a transfer price were looked at: market-based, cost-based and negotiated. The additional problems encountered in setting transfer prices within an international group were then addressed.

Managements may not be free to set their own group transfer prices. Many governments insist that companies in their countries adopt an arm's length policy to set transfer prices.

Conventional ratio analysis can be used to evaluate the performance of international companies and groups, but you must be able to discuss the additional factors that must be taken into account.

5 SELF TEST QUESTIONS

5.1 Define a transfer price. (1.1)

5.2 State three criteria that a good system of transfer pricing should meet. (1.2)

5.3 What are the disadvantages of setting a market-based transfer price? (1.4)

5.4 State the general rule for setting a correct transfer price. (1.7)

5.5 What is a tax haven? (2.2)

5.6 What features would an attractive tax haven display? (2.2)

5.7 What is the advantage of residual income over return on capital employed? (3.3)

5.8 State three suitable financial measures for assessing an overseas company's performance. (3.9)

5.9 State three suitable non-financial measures for assessing an overseas company's performance. (3.9)

5.10 In which currency should a foreign subsidiary's results be analysed? (3.10)

6 EXAMINATION TYPE QUESTION

6.1 Goal incongruence

(a) 'Because of the possibility of goal incongruence, an optimal plan can only be achieved if divisional budgets are constructed by a central planning department, but this means that divisional independence is a pseudo-independence.'

Discuss the problems of establishing divisional budgets in the light of this quotation.

(9 marks)

(b) 'Head office' will require a division to submit regular reports of its performance.

Describe, discuss and compare three measures of divisional operating performance that might feature in such reports. **(8 marks)**
(Total: 17 marks)

7 ANSWER TO EXAMINATION TYPE QUESTION

7.1 Goal incongruence

Notes:

(1) There is a common link between the two parts of this question - divisional organisation. Be sure not to include too much detail in part (a) concerning divisional performance appraisal, otherwise you may find yourself struggling for an answer to part (b).

(2) Read the questions carefully: they are more specific than they may appear at first reading.

(3)   In part (a) concentrate on budgets for planning: ensure that an answer covers goal congruence, optimal planning and divisional independence.   Remember that the question asks for a discussion on problems; do not spend too much effort on stating advantages.

(4)   Remember to describe, discuss and compare three performance measures; ensure that you have three measures in mind before starting. It may be best to describe and discuss the three measures separately and attempt a comparison as a final paragraph.

(5)   When answering part (b) concentrate on control.

(a)   In a divisionalised organisation the master budget is the head office budget plus the divisional budgets.   Thus, if the master budget is to constitute the optimal plan for the company as a whole, it is essential that the divisional budgets are the optimal plans from the company's point of view, not from that of the divisions.   However, there is the possibility that the divisional budgets will reflect the optimal plan for the divisions which may not reflect the goals of the whole company.   This is where goal incongruence is said to arise.

One method to avoid this goal incongruence is to plan centrally, which should ensure that the sum of the divisional budgets is the optimal plan for the company.   However, this will result in the loss of divisional independence which could mean a loss of local management motivation. The plan may well be 'company optimal' but, with reduced motivation, will it be achieved? There must have been a reason (or reasons) why the company organised itself on a divisional basis, one of which will have been the improved management decision-making that can result from decentralisation.   Decentralisation and divisionalisation are not the same thing but they tend to go 'hand in hand': the benefits originally sought may be lost with lost motivation.

There is a special problem with divisional units in that they trade with each other - transfer prices.   The transfer pricing problem is a difficult one to solve and there are several methods of establishing transfer prices.   Which is the optimal will vary from one organisation to another. Centrally-imposed transfer prices are not always the best, especially from a motivational perspective.

The answer may well be to let the divisions construct their own budgets, with certain constraints imposed by central management, and the budgets must be centrally approved.   This may lead to the optimal plan of the company, as a divisionalised organisation.   This will minimise the cost of goal incongruence, which will probably be far outweighed by the benefits of decentralised decision-making.

(b)   When central management have decided that decentralisation should take place and operating divisions are established, some system of control or performance appraisal becomes necessary. Three possible measures of divisional operating performance are:

(i)   controllable divisional profit;
(ii)   return on divisional investment (ROI);
(iii)   residual income (RI).

(i)   **Controllable divisional profit**

This performance measure is defined as revenues less costs controllable at the divisional level.   Thus this measure would only be applicable to profit centres where the revenues and costs incurred at the division can clearly be seen and where only controllable head office costs can be calculated.   The major problem with this measure is how are costs to be analysed into controllable/non-controllable, and who is to do the analysis - head office or the division.

(ii)   **ROI**

This is calculated using the formula:

$$\frac{\text{Net income}}{\text{Invested capital}}$$

This is a very useful measure when the division is run virtually as a business on its own, the divisional manager being responsible for all decisions relating to the division, including stock control, credit control and project appraisal. However, there are again problems relating to controllability at divisional level, trying to decide what constitutes net income and valuing the invested capital. ROI is usually expressed as a percentage.

(iii)   **RI**

This is the net income of a division less 'imputed' interest on the invested capital used by the division. Again, like ROI, this is a measure which can only be used by what is often referred to as an 'investment centre'. The RI, however, is expressed in monetary terms, not as a percentage. One specific problem with RI is the 'imputed' interest - the percentage is often centrally determined, thereby undermining the independence of a division.

When comparing the three measures it is obvious that the applicability of controllable divisional profit is limited to profit centres only. This makes ROI and RI appear to be superior. However, they are not: the profit measure cannot be used for investment centres but that does not mean that it is less useful.

The comparison of the two investment centre performance measures is more meaningful. Here it is the distinction between using a percentage in ROI and a monetary value in RI which is important. If the 'imputed' interest is correctly calculated, then the use of RI will reduce the level of dysfunctional behaviour that can result from the use of a divisional organisation structure. If divisional operating performance reports are based on RI, local management will probably make decisions which are optimal to the company as a whole. However, if the reports emphasise maximisation of divisional ROI percentage, then divisional management may well reject projects which, while reducing the division's ROI percentage, may result in an increase in company-wide profits.

22 THE INTERNATIONAL TREASURY FUNCTION

INTRODUCTION & LEARNING OBJECTIVES

The treasury function plays an increasingly important role in modern international companies, often established as a centralised profit centre expected to generate profits for the group rather than acting as simply a support agency.

This chapter explains the role of a treasurer in an international group and discusses the advantages and disadvantages of centralisation of the treasury activities and of the profit centre approach.

The chapter concludes by describing the main forms of international cash transfer mechanisms and the main short term investment opportunities open to the treasurer in the modern business world.

When you have studied this chapter you should be able to do the following:

- Describe the role of the corporate treasurer.
- Explain how a treasury can generate profits on its own.
- Discuss whether a treasury should be set up as a cost centre or as a profit centre.
- Discuss whether the treasury function should be centralised or decentralised throughout the group.
- Describe the variety of available international cash transfer mechanisms.
- Describe the variety of available international short term investment opportunities.

1 THE TREASURY FUNCTION

1.1 Introduction

The term 'treasurer', and therefore 'treasurership department', is an old one that has been resurrected in a modern context. This modern term is an import from the USA and essentially covers the following activities:

(a) banking and exchange;
(b) cash and currency management;
(c) investment;
(d) risk and insurance; and
(e) raising finance.

These roles have always existed, but the modern concept is to bring them all together and combine them under a corporate treasurer. All the areas above are concerned with managing the liquidity of a business. A business must maintain an inflow of cash in order to survive and a further inflow of funds if it is to expand. Cash should be regarded as just as important as profits. Certainly the business must be profitable in its existing and prospective activities, but the profitability objectives can only be achieved within the constraints imposed by funding requirements.

1.2 Reasons for the development of the treasurership department

As indicated above, the functions carried out by the corporate treasurer have always existed, but were previously absorbed within other finance functions. A number of reasons may be identified for the development of a separate treasurership department.

(a) Size and internationalisation of companies. These add to both the scale and the complexity of the treasury functions.

(b)   Size and internationalisation of currency, debt and security markets.   These make the operations of raising finance, handling transactions in multiple currencies and investing much more complex. They also present opportunities for greater gains.

(c)   Sophistication of business practice. This process has been aided by modern communications, and as a result the treasurer is expected to take advantage of opportunities for making profits or minimising costs which did not exist a few years ago.

For these reasons, most large international corporations have moved towards setting up a separate treasurership department.

1.3   The role of the treasurer

The treasurer therefore reports to the finance director, with a specific emphasis on borrowing, investment, cash and currency management.

In addition, although the major responsibility is held by the finance director, the treasurer will have a direct input into the former's management of debt capacity, debt and equity structure, resource allocation, equity strategy and currency strategy.

Finally, often in common with the financial and management accountant, the treasurer will be involved in the investment appraisal process; and the finance director will often consult the treasurer in matters relating to the review of acquisitions and divestments, dividend policy and defence from takeover.

In summary, the treasurer works closely with the finance director in key aspects of the latter's specific responsibilities, and with important decision-making responsibilities of his own. These responsibilities will vary slightly from group to group, but the underlying themes of borrowing, investment, cash and currency management will remain the same.

1.4   Establishing a treasurership department

Traditionally in the UK the corporate treasurer, in common with other senior finance personnel, has been drawn from the ranks of qualified accountants. This contrasts with the USA, where only a minority of treasurers and finance directors are qualified accountants. However, even in the UK the position is changing against the accounting profession, and more corporate treasurers are drawn from other sources eg, MBA and the corporate treasury department of a multinational.

Treasurer departments are not large, since they are not involved in the detailed recording of transactions. They tend to rely heavily on new technology for information.

1.5   Should the treasury be a cost centre or a profit centre?

As a cost centre the aggregate treasury function costs would simply be charged throughout the group on a fair basis. If no such fair basis can be agreed, the costs can remain as central head office unallocated costs in any group segmental analysis.

However it is also possible to identify revenues arising from treasury departments and thus to establish the treasury as a profit centre. Revenues could be realised as follows

(i)   Each division can be charged the market value for the services provided by the treasury. The total value charged throughout the group should exceed the treasury's costs enabling it to report a profit.

(ii)   By deciding not to hedge all currency and interest rate risks. Experts in the treasury could decide which risks not to hedge, hoping to profit from unhedged favourable exchange rate and interest rate movements.

(iii)   Hedging using currency and interest rate options leaves an upside potential which could be realised if the rate moves in the company's favour.

(iv)   Taking on additional exchange rate or other risks purely as a speculative activity eg, writing options on currencies or on shares held.

The trend in recent years has been for large companies to turn their treasuries from cost centres into profit centres and to expect the treasury to pay its way and generate regular profits each year. However the following points should be noted:

(i)   A treasury engaged in speculation must be properly **controlled** by the company's board of directors. Millions of pounds can be committed in one telephone call by a treasurer, so it is crucial that limits are set on traders' risk exposures and that these limits are monitored scrupulously. The temptation has been for directors to let treasurers 'get on with whatever they do' as long as regular profits are being earned. Such a policy is no longer acceptable; the finance director in particular must control the treasury on a day-to-day basis.

(ii)   Treasury staff must be well trained (eg, members of the Association of Corporate Treasurers) and probably well paid, so that staff of the right calibre are secured.

(iii)   The low volume of foreign currency transactions undertaken by a small company would probably make a profit centre approach unviable. A regular flow of large foreign transactions is needed before the cost centre approach is abandoned.

Recent high-profile disasters in treasury departments have underlined the importance of control.

(i)   Allied Lyons' treasury took a speculative high-risk position on the level of volatility of the $/£ exchange rate in 1990. Unfortunately they got it wrong and the company was forced to report £150 million of losses on treasury activities in their 1990/91 accounts.

(ii)   In 1993 the German oils and metals company Metallgesellschaft managed to lose $1 billion after becoming over-exposed to oil derivative contracts.

(iii)   In 1994 the US consumer products group Procter and Gamble reported an after-tax charge of $102m in the first quarter's results arising from two leveraged swap contracts allowing the company to swap fixed rate loans into floating rate, believing that US and German interest rates would stay low. Unfortunately both interest rates rose sharply after the US authorities raised rates in February 1994, and it appears that some of the company's officers did not fully appreciate the implications of a rise in rates.

Conclusion   Large companies can generate significant profits by establishing their treasury functions as a profit centre rather than a cost centre. However profit centre treasuries must be supervised closely by trained senior management to ensure that risk exposure limits are not exceeded.

2   THE INTERNATIONAL TREASURY FUNCTION

2.1   Introduction

The corporate treasurer in an international group of companies will be faced with problems relating specifically to the international spread of investments.

(i)   He may be able to set transfer prices to reduce the overall tax bill as described in the previous chapter.

(ii)   He will be heavily involved in currency exposure policies and procedures, using both internal and external methods.

(iii)   He will be responsible for transfers of cash across international borders; such transfer mechanisms are examined below.

(iv)   He will be expected to devise investment strategies for short-term funds from the range of international money markets and international marketable securities. These areas are also examined below in this chapter.

2.2   The centralisation of treasury activities

The question arises in a large international group of whether treasury activities should be centralised or decentralised. If centralised, then each operating company holds only the minimum cash balance required for day to day operations, remitting the surplus to the centre for overall management. This process is sometimes known as **cash pooling**, the pool usually being held in a major financial centre or a tax haven country. If decentralised, each operating company must appoint an officer responsible for that company's own treasury operations.

Advantages of centralisation

(i)   No need for treasury skills to be duplicated throughout the group. One highly trained central department can assemble a highly skilled team, offering skills that could not be available if every company had their own treasury.

(ii)   Necessary borrowings can be arranged in bulk, at keener interest rates than for smaller amounts. Similarly bulk deposits of surplus funds will attract higher rates of interest than smaller amounts.

(iii)   The group's foreign currency risk can be managed much more effectively from a centralised treasury since only they can appreciate the total exposure situation. A total hedging policy is more efficiently carried out by head office rather than each company doing their own hedging.

(iv)   One company does not borrow at high rates while another has idle cash.

(v)   Bank charges should be lower since a situation of carrying both balances and overdraft in the same currency should be eliminated.

(vi)   A centralised treasury can be run as a profit centre as described earlier to raise additional profits for the group.

(vii)   Transfer prices can be established to minimise the overall group tax bill.

(viii) Funds can be quickly returned to companies requiring cash via direct transfers.

Advantages of decentralisation

(i)   Greater autonomy leads to greater motivation. Individual companies will manage their cash balances more attentively if they are responsible for them rather than simply remitting them up to head office.

(ii)   Local operating units should have a better feel for local conditions than head office and can respond more quickly to local developments.

2.3   Multilateral netting

Multilateral netting is a process which minimises misdirected funds (those funds which are unnecessarily converted from one currency to another). Multilateral netting is an extension of bilateral netting where two companies in different countries each owe the other money and a single transfer of the net amount owed is made rather than two separate transfers.

Multilateral netting involves a matrix of several companies, with the minimum number of net payments being made.

3   INTERNATIONAL CASH TRANSFER MECHANISMS

3.1   Introduction

The international treasurer must choose the best method for transferring amounts of cash between group companies and between companies and the outside world. A centralised treasury will be expected to use more sophisticated transfer mechanisms than decentralised treasury officers in different countries.

The choice of transfer mechanism will depend on

- cost
- currencies involved
- legal restrictions imposed on certain currency transfers
- tax rules imposed.

Cost does not simply refer to the direct cost charged for each transaction. The company should also look at the indirect costs, ie, overheads involved in running a sophisticated centralised treasury, and the cost of float time.

> **Definition**   Float time refers to the period between initiation of payment by the payer and the time when the funds become available for use by the recipient.

For example, if a payer sends a cheque in the post to a creditor, the float time will consist of

(i)   the time the cheque is in the post; plus

(ii)   the delay between receiving the cheque and banking it; plus

(iii)   the time needed by the bank to clear the cheque.

These delays are called, respectively, transmission delay, lodgement delay and clearance delay.

3.2   Possible transfer mechanisms

The following cash transfer mechanisms are available to the international treasurer:

- payment by cheque
- CHAPS and CHIPS
- EFT
- EDI
- Letter of credit (see Chapter 16, section 2.2)
- Bill of exchange (see Chapter 16, section 2.2)

Payment by cheque is still a common method of settling bills in Europe, despite the delays and bank charges that may be involved. One way of speeding up settlement by cheque, common in the USA, is the use of a lock box.

> **Definition**   A lock box is a post box at a local bank to which a company instructs its customers to send payments. The box is emptied and the payments processed several times a day by the bank.

Large American banks offer lock box processing as a cash payment service to their corporate customers, though lock boxes have now expanded throughout Europe. The advantage is clearly the avoidance of lodgement delay. A Spanish debtor can be instructed to send his cheque to a lock box in a Spanish bank; this cheque is cleared like any other Spanish cheque and the funds are sent electronically to the treasury bank account.

SWIFT is the Society of Worldwide Interbank Financial Telecommunications. It began operations in 1977 after European bankers wanted a more efficient method of sending payment instructions to correspondent banks than telex or mail. All major international banks are now members of the SWIFT communication system which offers an international network using common terminals and standard communication protocols. SWIFT is therefore not itself a cash transfer system; it is an instruction to transfer funds to a specified account at another bank. The actual transfer is made electronically, eg, by CHIPS (see below). However the SWIFT system is efficient, secure and cheap, available 24 hours a day every day.

CHAPS is the Clearing House Automated Payments System, a banking system used to make computerised same-day sterling transfers between banks in the UK. A member bank of CHAPS allows its corporate customers to make immediate transfers of funds through the system. CHAPS' New York cousin is CHIPS, the Clearing House Interbank Payment System, which operates a similar computerised transfer systems for international dollar payments.

Electronic Data Interchange is the electronic communication of business transactions between computers of different organisations. For example a standard format for purchase orders and invoices can be established and sent via EDI to replace paper documents used in manual systems. EDI and Electronic Funds Transfer (EFT) systems can be integrated so that the whole business cycle becomes computerised, from requisitioning a purchase order to payment of the final invoice. In practice some customers or suppliers will lack the necessary computer skills to be able to participate within an EDI system so that a manual system is usually run in parallel with the EDI.

4   INTERNATIONAL SHORT-TERM INVESTMENT OPPORTUNITIES

4.1   Introduction

When deciding where to place short-term funds, the corporate treasurer must weigh the usual factors of risk, reward and liquidity. Risk includes default risk, interest rate risk and currency risk. Reward may be fixed for the period of the investment or may be floating. Liquidity measures how quickly the investment can be sold for a reasonable price. Illiquid short-term investments should generally be avoided, for example a speculative short-term investment in the shares of an unquoted company.

4.2   Short-term investments available

The treasurer can choose from the following list of possible short-term international investment opportunities

- short-term bank deposits. These can be repayable on demand or with a short notice period (up to one year). The longer the notice period, the better the interest rate that is available. Bank deposits are unsecured advances so it is best to choose a bank with a good reputation and credit rating.

- Eurocurrency deposits. These are unsecured deposits in banks outside the country in whose currency the deposit is denominated.

- Certificates of Deposit (CDs). These are receipts issued by commercial banks for time deposits issued for a stated time period and normally paying a fixed rate of interest. They are usually issued in negotiable form and can be easily traded. Maturities may be as short as seven days or as long as seven years or more.

- Treasury Bills are issued by several governments (eg, the UK) at a discount to nominal value and redeemed at par. They are guaranteed by the relevant government and therefore carry very little risk. They are highly liquid and traded on an active market.

- Trade bills and bank bills are issued respectively by a company or bank as a form of short-term IOU. The discount rate offered depends on the credit rating of the issuer; normal bank bills are sold on a lower discount since they provide better security than an ordinary trade bill. They may have maturities up to one year and are also traded on an active market.

- Commercial paper is a form of trade bill issued by large companies with a good credit rating. Interest rates offered would typically be higher than Treasury Bills but lower than less secure trade bills. Maturity is usually up to one year but may extend further up to, say, five years.

- UK local authority bills and deposits. These are usually non-negotiable with a maturity of up to two years.

- Federal funds are unsecured advances to US banks. Most 'fed funds' are sold on an overnight basis, though longer terms are also possible. Fed funds involve large amounts of money, with a minimum advance of $1m usually.

5   CHAPTER SUMMARY

The treasury is responsible for obtaining a group's necessary finance on a worldwide basis and for controlling the uses of that finance. As long as risk exposures are controlled by management, creating the treasury function as a profit centre can bring substantial rewards.

There are advantages associated with both the centralisation and decentralisation of treasury activities.

The chapter ended by examining the cash transfer mechanisms and short-term investment opportunities open to the modern corporate treasurer.

6   SELF TEST QUESTIONS

6.1   What are the responsibilities of the modern corporate treasurer? (1.1)

6.2   Why have treasury departments become more important in recent years? (1.2)

6.3   Name three ways a treasury can generate income of its own. (1.5)

6.4   What is the name of the professional body for treasury employees? (1.5)

6.5   State two advantages of centralising treasury activities. (2.2)

6.6   State two disadvantages of centralising treasury activities. (2.2)

6.7   What is float time? (3.1)

6.8   Distinguish between CHAPS and CHIPS. (3.2)

6.9   What is a lock box? (3.2)

6.10   What is commercial paper? (4.2)

23 INTERNATIONAL OPERATIONS

INTRODUCTION & LEARNING OBJECTIVES

As the volume of international trade continues to grow, it is increasingly likely that a company will wish to trade in markets beyond its own domestic market. Should the company just export its goods, or should it establish an overseas manufacturing base where raw materials and labour might be cheaper? Should the overseas operation be structured as a branch or a subsidiary?

This chapter starts by addressing such questions. Broader issues relating to foreign direct investments are then dealt with, such as the appropriate method of financing the investment, the implications of political risk and the impact of blocked funds.

When you have studied this chapter you should be able to do the following:

- Describe the various forms of entity that are available for carrying on international operations and the advantages and disadvantages of each.
- Discuss the impact of political risk on the investment decision.
- Suggest methods of solving the problem of blocked funds and restrictions on the remittance of funds to the parent company.

1 FORMS OF ENTITY FOR INTERNATIONAL OPERATIONS

1.1 Strategic objectives

In drawing up its strategic plan, a company may identify **direct foreign investment** as a means of fulfilling its strategic objectives. Possible reasons may be:

- Financial. An NPV analysis might suggest a positive net present value for such an investment, increasing the wealth of the parent company shareholders. However the selection of an appropriate discount rate may be difficult; NPV analysis of international projects is covered in more detail in the next chapter.

- Production efficiency. Raw materials or labour might be cheaper in the overseas market than at home.

- Demand-led. A manufacturing base could be established to satisfy the overseas market's demand for the company's products.

- To avoid tariffs. If tariff barriers have been established by an overseas country to frustrate imports into that market, a base set up in the country will not be subject to the tariffs.

A company wishing to sell its products beyond its domestic market is faced with the choice of legal entity by which its expansion is structured. The discussion of multinational companies in previous chapters has assumed that the structure is one of separate companies operating in each country. This chapter examines whether that structure is always the best possibility and appraises other legal forms.

1.2 Different forms of entity

Export from the home country

A company may decide not to establish any permanent set-up in the foreign country, but instead to export its goods directly from the home country. Such a policy is cheap and low risk; no significant capital expenditure need be incurred in the foreign country.

Advantages

- Low risk.
- Immediate returns.
- Low capital needs and start-up costs.
- High learning possibilities.

Disadvantages

- Little knowledge of local market gained.

- Slow response to market changes.

- Locals may perceive little commitment from an importer.

- The salesforce will find it hard to gain a detailed feel for the market since they will only visit from time to time. Their travelling expenses will also be high.

- It is difficult for customers to contact the company.

- Sales could be frustrated by the imposition of tariff barriers on imports by the overseas country. One key way of avoiding tariff barriers is to set up a manufacturing plant in the overseas market (eg, Japanese car manufacturers setting up in the UK).

Set up an overseas branch

The quickest way to establish an overseas presence is to set up a branch in the overseas country. This can be as simple as one person with an office and a telephone, but normally includes a distribution warehouse from where the country's demand is met. A branch is cheap to run and solves some of the limitations identified above. However the company might be accused of lack of commitment to the foreign economy if the branch is just a skeleton operation. There are also tax consequences of running a branch; it is likely that the profits of the branch would be treated as profits of the parent company, which might be inconvenient.

Set up an overseas subsidiary

This demonstrates a longer-term commitment to operations in the foreign country. There may be tax advantages since home country taxation will not be incurred until profits are remitted home, and there may be opportunities to set transfer prices to reduce worldwide tax liabilities. However there will be legal costs associated with setting up the company and ongoing costs in resourcing it.

See later sections in this chapter.

Joint venture

 A joint venture is an undertaking by which its participants expect to achieve some common purpose or benefit. It is controlled jointly by two or more venturers.

The Companies Act 1989 introduced the term 'joint venture' into company law for the first time and lays down how such ventures should be consolidated into group accounts. A common example of a joint venture is where a UK company wishing to expand into the former Soviet Union identifies a local company and agrees to undertake a project jointly while carrying on with their other main activities at the same time.

The advantages of joint ventures are that the existing management should have a detailed knowledge of the overseas market, and the overseas government should treat the venture more favourably than if it was all overseas owned and so grants or other incentives may be available. They also enable venturers to pool their expertise and are less risky than starting operations from scratch. Establishing a joint venture with a local company will also help when obtaining local loans, government approval and tax incentives.   Use can be made of established distribution networks, trained labour, raw materials suppliers in existence and local management.

The disadvantages of joint ventures are mainly practical.   They can take up large amounts of management time with few profits to show from the effort, disagreements can break out between the venturers as to the future course of action to take and they are difficult to value in annual accounts.   The disagreements may be caused by numerous factors such as dividend policy, transfer pricing, transfer of technology, marketing strategy, management personnel and remuneration.

Licensing agreements

> [Definition]   A licensing agreement permits a foreign firm to manufacture the company's products in return for royalty payments.

Such agreements are a cheap low-risk way of rapidly expanding into foreign markets.   However the quality of goods produced may not be as good as are produced at home, potentially damaging the value of brand names.   Once the licensing period is over, there is also the possibility that the foreign company will use the knowledge it has learnt to compete against the home company.   The cash flow from licensing is also often very low when compared with exporting.

Economic Interest Groups

Economic Interest Groups (EIGs) are legal entities set up to encourage co-operation between firms based in different countries.   They help small and medium-sized companies enter into arrangements which they would avoid entering under a joint venture agreement because they might feel at a disadvantage.

The main example of EIGs is European Economic Interest Groups (EEIGs).   Since July 1989 EEIGs have been allowed to be formed and operated under EC law.   All the parties to the Group therefore know that the Group's activities are governed by a law common throughout the EC; no party can gain an advantage by use of their domestic law.   EEIGs are available for groupings employing up to 500 employees; in this way large companies are excluded.

An example EEIG is a grouping of seven small and medium-sized distributors of pharmaceuticals, each from a different EC state, which have together formed an EEIG called ORPHE.   The aim of ORPHE is to give its members a better position in the European pharmaceuticals market, which is currently dominated by a few very large companies.   This should improve competition and result in a better deal for consumers.

The disadvantage of EIGs is the time and cost involved in their setting up.

2   FOREIGN DIRECT INVESTMENT - POLITICAL AND OTHER RISKS

2.1   Political risk

> [Definition]   Political risk is the possibility of loss arising to a firm from actions taken by the government or people of a country.

Examples of political risk are explained below.

2.2   Confiscation political risk

This is the risk of loss of control over the foreign entity through intervention of the local government or other force.

A subsidiary in a stable industrialised country may seem free from this risk, but as a parent company reviews the list beginning with countries vulnerable to changes of regime, eg, Chile, or invasion by powerful neighbours, eg, Lebanon, passing on to countries in which a transition to local ownership is already law, eg, India, then to countries in which confiscation is a very real possibility, it must be prepared for principled or unprincipled expropriation, nationalisation, or mere interference with its control and management or its ability to operate, and with anything from full to zero compensation.

The parent company can respond to this risk in part by the way it finances the subsidiary, and sometimes by confiscation insurance. In the UK the Export Credits Guarantee Department (ECGD) operates a confiscation cover scheme for new overseas investments only, and Lloyds offers such a cover for existing and new investments in comprehensive (non-selective) form.

The financing tactics which minimise this risk consist of

(a)   high gearing,

(b)   minimising intra-group sources of finance,

(c)   maximising finance from local sources,

(d)   subject to the above, to avoid parent group guarantees,

(e)   in suitable cases to have the subsidiary partly owned by local shareholders.

The literature lays much stress on the need to value the risk. What is sometimes overlooked is the commercial consequences of confiscation: it may deprive the group of access to a significant share of the world market. The critical issue may be which competitor will gain that share.

2.3   Commercial political risk

This is a large area of risk. The Portuguese revolution of 1974 was followed by several years of left-wing military rule in which wages were compulsorily raised and prices controlled at unrealistic falling real levels. Subsidiaries of foreign parents found their margins squeezed and little sympathy from the authorities. Those which happened to be suppliers to the government were hit hardest and also had to face serious attempts by the unions to take control of the management. Many such subsidiaries were either abandoned by their shareholders or sold at knockdown prices to local interests. What drove their parents out was not confiscation but interference with the commercial processes of supply and demand.

There are other forms of commercial discrimination against foreign-controlled companies. Protectionist authorities can starve them of orders, give commercial or financial advantages to locally-owned competitors, restrict import licences for imported materials or products, or refuse work permits to expatriate staff.

The financing responses to these risks are much the same as to expropriation above. The selling of equity to local shareholders, by creating a national lobby, may be the most effective way to make the authorities sensitive to the needs of the local foreign investment.

2.4   Financial political risk

This risk takes many forms:

(a)   Restricted access to local borrowings. This is sometimes discriminatory against foreign-owned enterprises. Access is often barred or restricted particularly to the cheapest forms of finance from local banks and development funds. Some countries ration all access for foreign investments to local sources of funds, so as to force the company to import foreign exchange into the country.

(b)   Restrictions on repatriating capital, dividends or other remittances. These can take the form of prohibition or penal taxation.

(c)   Financial penalties on imports from the rest of the group such as heavy interest-free import deposits.

Financing policies to deal with these risks are often difficult. If access is merely barred to the cheaper local funds, the economics of using the more expensive sources of local money must be analysed against the economics and risks of using non-local funds. Where it is not possible to remit dividends, the parent must appraise how fundamental dividends are to its objectives in investing in the company.

2.5   Measurement of political risk

(a)   'Old hands'

Experts on the country such as existing businessmen or journalists may provide advice upon the risk of investment in a specific country.

(b)   'Grand tours'

The home firm may send a selection of employees to the potential investment country to act as an inspection team. However this technique is generally considered inferior to the use of advice from well established experts as outlined above.

(c)   Surveys

Commercially produced country political risk indices are available. These are produced by experts via the ranking of key risk variables.

(d)   Quantitative measures

Measures such as GNP and ethnic fractionalisation are combined to give countries an overall score. Again commercially produced indices are available such as the Business Environment Risk Index (BERI). This index gives each country a score out of 100, anything below 41 indicating unacceptable business conditions.

2.6   Management of political risk

(a)   Prior to investment

(i)   *Planned local ownership*

Target dates can be set on which proportions of company ownership will pass to the local nationals. These should be spread into the long term so that local authorities can see the eventual benefits that will be gained through allowing successful foreign investments.

(ii)   *Pre-trading agreements*

Prior to making the investments agreements should be secured with local authorities regarding rights, responsibilities, remittance of funds and local equity investments.

(b)   During investment

Political risk can be managed on a continuous basis through consideration of the following areas:

(i)   *Distribution control*

Control and development of such items as pipelines and shipping facilities will deter expropriation of assets.

(ii)   *Market control*

Securing markets through copywriting, patents and trademarks deters political intervention as the local markets come to depend on 'protected' goods.

(iii)   *Location*

Oil companies frequently mine oil in a politically unstable area but refine it in western Europe. Expropriation of assets would not therefore benefit the less stable countries.

(iv)   *Supplies*

By using local materials and labour it becomes in the interest of the country for the company to succeed. However following success the locals may then have the knowledge to continue operations alone.

(v)   *Local finance*

As the foreign investment grows, further finance can be raised locally to maintain the authorities' interest in the success of the business. Also the wealthier locals who provide this finance often have considerable power. As a result there is less likelihood of others expropriating the assets.

2.7   Exchange control risk

This risk is not necessarily different from the others, and some specific exchange controls have already been referred to in the above forms of risk. The purest form of exchange control risk is that the group may accumulate surplus cash in the country where the subsidiary operates, either as profits or as amounts owed for imports to the subsidiary, which cannot be remitted out of the country. A good example is the French regulation under which intra-group trade debts of a French subsidiary to its associated companies, if not made within 12 months of import, become unremittable as 'capital invested in the subsidiary'. Often the French subsidiary delays payment by more than 12 months because of a shortage of cash created by other French official actions or policies.

A similar case is where goods are shipped to Nigeria for a price in naira, the local currency. As the currency is unconvertible, the funds become blocked in Nigeria. There have been many such problems in other countries, eg, India.

Most of the remedies in this field have less to do with financing than with the commercial precautions taken when contracting with such countries. The rule must be to ship no goods without full prior clearance of the exchange control and licensing regulations. This is irrespective of whether an overseas subsidiary is involved.

However, in financing investments in such countries, it may well pay to have as much local debt as possible, which can often be repaid from such blocked funds if they arise. A low equity also makes it easier to accept restrictions on remittances of capital or profits.

2.8   Currency risk

The issues to remember with special care here are:

(a)   Currency risk needs to be managed

(i)   for the group as a whole, and
(ii)   for the investment in its own right.

(b)   The best defensive policy (for a risk-averse group) is to match assets with liabilities in the same currency both for the group and in the subsidiary. This means that if the Malaysian subsidiary has a DM liability and the German subsidiary DM assets, then the Malaysian subsidiary may still need to cover that liability forward, thus turning it effectively into a ringgit liability both for the subsidiary and for the group, and consciously aggravating the net surplus of DM assets in the group.

2.9   The group vs the subsidiary

Conflicts of interest may appear even between a wholly-owned overseas subsidiary (ovsub) and the group as a whole. This apparent lack of identity between the ovsub and its parent may at first sound odd, but the subsidiary and its parent may have to pursue the following purely local objectives:

(a)   **Solvency**

If a currency position is balanced for the group as a whole, but open for the ovsub (and therefore matched by an equal and opposite position elsewhere in the group), then if the exchange rate moves so as to cause a loss in the ovsub, that ovsub may become legally insolvent. If that happens, under most systems of law it may have to cease trading and the group as a whole may lose its market in that country. In this potentially serious matter the group must look specifically at the ovsub and its separate financial health.

(b)   **Local regulations**

The ovsub must evidently comply with local regulations. The ovsub may be forced to borrow a foreign currency. It must in that case cover the repayment forward, but if local regulations deny access to such a market, then the ovsub must comply and accept the currency risk. In that case the parent may be able to balance the risk at least for the group as a whole by borrowing the local currency offshore.

(c)   **Good corporate citizenship**

Most multinational groups recognise that they cannot expect to promote their corporate objectives in any country in which they operate unless they are 'good corporate citizens' in that country, and seen to work in harmony with the economic and social interests of that country. Where a country has a controversial or undemocratic regime (say Nigeria, Ghana, Iran), there may be some doubt as to what those interests are: for example, if there was a coup tomorrow! But very few companies have prospered by ignoring this need for good corporate citizenship.

3   FUNDING OVERSEAS INVESTMENT

3.1   The general financing problem

The four issues in financing any business, even if owned within the domestic country, are:

(a)   Can the financing be improved by economies in the net operating assets themselves? For example by better inventory control or by giving less or taking more trade credit?

(b)   The maturity structure: what blend of longer- and shorter-term finance?

(c)   How much gearing (debt in proportion to equity)?

(d)   Just what is being financed? If this is mainly large integral contracts, the most effective policy is to arrange finance for each individual contract, with maturities suited to the cash flow profile of that contract.

3.2   Cost of funds: currency and interest factors

Here there are two very important perceptions.

(a)   **The interest rate trap**

If euros cost 6.5% pa to borrow and Greek drachmas 18%, and the market believes that the drachma will over the next year fall against the euro to 106.5/118 of its present exchange value, then before tax they are equally dear. In that case the interest saving on borrowing euros will be exactly balanced by the currency loss on the principal. The borrower should therefore, in the view of the market, be indifferent between borrowing drachmas or euros for the next 12 months at these rates. All this is before tax. After tax the outcome depends on the tax system under which the borrower is liable to pay tax on his income. Under most tax systems the interest is taxable or (in the case of the payer) tax deductible, but any loss on the principal is not deductible. Unless they are tax deductible, it is safer and cheaper to pay the higher rate of interest, which is tax deductible, than to face the strong chance of an unrelieved loss on the principal.

It should be noted that this rule applies to business taxation, not to the taxation of individuals, that it depends on the particular tax system under which a particular company operates, and that it accepts the market view of the relative strength of various currencies.

(b)   **The case of hyper-inflation**

This is best illustrated in terms of countries such as Brazil. The Brazilian rate of inflation has recently been about 210-220% per annum. As US inflation was about 3%, this means that the rate of devaluation of the cruzeiro against the dollar should be of the order of at least 207-217% in order to maintain the dollar purchasing power of the cruzeiro. In a case like this it is inconceivable that the rate of devaluation should deviate very substantially from this level. It is also very improbable that the cost of local 'investment market' funds deviates markedly from some level like 200 – 230%. Therefore what matters is that the cruzeiro rate of return on capital employed in the Brazilian subsidiary should be greater than the higher of:

(i)   the rate of inflation,
(ii)   the rate of currency devaluation, and
(iii)   the cost of investment market funds

by say 10%, measured in cruzeiros.

If this is the case, the subsidiary is viable. Otherwise it is not. There is no substitute for adequate profitability in local currency terms.

3.3   Intra-group sources of funds

This is perhaps the largest difference between financing an overseas subsidiary (ovsub) and financing a single independent company.

We have so far found a host of reasons for keeping the wholly-owned subsidiary highly geared, as far as possible financed by debt from local sources and in local currency, and without guarantees from group sources.

This ideal is hard to attain in many countries. If nevertheless the financing of an ovsub could be arranged with only 1% parent capital, 99% local debt and no parent guarantees, then the subsidiary would clearly be vulnerable to unforeseen setbacks to its profits or cash flow. To guard against this possibility it might be possible to arrange more standby borrowing facilities; but if not, then the parent must be ready to act as emergency provider of funds. In what form?

Once again, the obvious weapons are capital subscriptions or loans from the parent. However, if there are exchange control or fiscal obstacles in the country of the ovsub, such loans can be impractical at short notice or undesirable. Parent finance by way of capital or loans should always be considered, but better alternatives are usually available.

There is a widely held view that intercompany pricing or other forms of profit transfers are a common way of redeploying cash within an international group. These devices include getting the ovsub to pay or not pay for internal services, or waiving internal interest or other charges. However their key characteristic in the present context of redeploying cash is that in the short term they are usually slow to shift cash, and that in the longer term the cash effect tends to be substantially reduced by the effect of taxation.

By far the most effective, flexible, and most easily reversible weapon open to a group is to vary the terms of intercompany credit, allowing one subsidiary to pay intra-group trade payables more slowly, and requiring another to pay its internal payables faster. This process is called 'leading and lagging' in the context of currency risk management. Its usefulness is of course restricted to ovsubs which have important intercompany purchases or sales, and whose local exchange control restrictions permit some latitude in payment terms.

3.4 Restrictions on the remittance of funds

The primary objective of parent companies in making foreign direct investments is to increase the wealth of the group's shareholders. This can only tangibly be achieved if the overseas company can pay amounts of cash (dividends and payments of supplies) to the parent company. However many countries impose restrictions on such remittance of funds.

Definition Blocked funds are balances in overseas bank accounts subject to exchange controls, such that restrictions are placed on remitting the funds out of the country.

A number of ways have been devised to try and avoid such restrictions. They mainly aim to circumvent restrictions on dividends payments out of the account by reclassifying the payment as something else.

Royalties

The parent company can charge royalties to the ovsub for use for patents, trade names or knowhow. Royalty fees may be paid as a fixed amount per year or varying with the volume of output. A cash payment is therefore due from the ovsub to the parent.

Management charges

Similarly, the parent company can impose a charge on its subsidiary for the general management services provided each year. The fee would normally be based on the number of management hours committed by the parent on that subsidiary's activities.

Transfer pricing

The parent can charge artificially high transfer prices for goods/services supplied to the subsidiary as a means of drawing cash out. However it has already been noted that such methods are often prohibited by foreign tax authorities.

Leading and lagging

The subsidiary can pay early for goods supplied from the parent, while the parent pays late for goods supplied from the subsidiary. Again such a strategy might be prohibited by the authorities.

3.5 The partly owned subsidiary

Whether to have a subsidiary partly owned, is probably the most critical decision about financing an overseas operation.

The case against shared ownership is

(a)   It often makes single-minded management impossible. Yet profits are seldom made by any other kind of management.

(b)   It imposes a need to manage the subsidiary by an extreme and punctilious application of the arm's length principle, so extreme that it may actually cost extra to monitor. The alternative is constant friction with the other shareholders who may believe that the subsidiary's profits are being syphoned off by the majority shareholder's group. This problem gets even worse when a majority or minority shareholder provides any local facilities for the subsidiary, eg, if it is a tenant on such a shareholder's industrial estate.

(c)   The two sets of shareholders may have very different policies for dividends. After all, the dividend may be the only tangible reward for the minority, who may also suffer far less taxation on it.

(d)   Minority shareholders may be reluctant to bear their proper share of the burdens of keeping the subsidiary financed or of guaranteeing its obligations. This can effectively rule out certain sources of finance. It would be unfair to the parent's shareholders to give them a disproportionate share of these burdens.

The case for having local minority shareholders is:

(a)   In some countries it is required by law.

(b)   In others it is a political necessity.

(c)   In many countries influential local shareholders open vital doors to customers and authorities, and protect the company against political discrimination.

(d)   In many cases there are sound commercial reasons for genuine joint ventures.

Where there are outside shareholders, the most important consequences are:

(a)   Corporate objectives may differ from the wholly-owned case, eg, in the matter of currency risk – local minority shareholders are not interested in the group's exposure;

(b)   On the whole such companies are nearly always very low-geared because it is so difficult to agree with the minority on

    (i)   profit retentions,
    (ii)   extra capital or other finance from shareholders,
    (iii)   guarantees from shareholders.

Guarantees are altogether impracticable from a minority held by the public.

It should not be forgotten that some such partly owned subsidiaries are public quoted companies: this reinforces some of the points already set out. The public physically cannot give guarantees to such a company, and it is at least costly and time-consuming to raise additional capital from such shareholders. Moreover, where the local shareholders must hold a legal minimum percentage of the capital, the parent company does not even have the option of just subscribing more capital itself. All these problems favour a generous initial capitalisation and perhaps high retentions of profit.

4   CHAPTER SUMMARY

When a company wishes to trade overseas it has a choice of available forms of entity for its international operations. The 'branch versus subsidiary' argument is the traditional exam question, but make sure that you appreciate the advantages and disadvantages of each of the possible entities.

The political risk of international operations should be appraised before they are set up, including confiscation risk, commercial risk and financial risk.

Remittance of funds to the parent company may be prohibited or may be subject to penal rates of taxation. Note the various methods that can be tried to circumvent such restrictions. If funds are blocked, this is another reason to gear up the investment and use the funds to pay the interest charge.

5   SELF TEST QUESTIONS

5.1   What are the disadvantages of servicing overseas demand by exports only? (1.2)

5.2   What are the advantages of setting up an overseas branch? (1.2)

5.3   What is a joint venture? (1.2)

5.4   What are the disadvantages of licensing agreements? (1.2)

5.5   Are EIGs intended to help small companies or large companies? (1.2)

5.6   What is political risk? (2.1)

5.7   How can political risk be reduced by appropriate financing tactics? (2.2)

5.8   What are blocked funds? (2.12)

5.9   How can management charges be used to solve the problem of blocked funds? (3.4)

5.10   What are the advantages of having minority local shareholders in a foreign direct investment? (3.5)

6   EXAMINATION TYPE QUESTION

6.1   Electronic equipment

A company manufacturing specialised electronic equipment has so far sold only inside the country where it is established. It has considerable surplus capacity and the chairman has asked you, as his finance director, to prepare a draft memorandum for the board on his proposal to open up export business to a number of countries.

You are required to draft this memorandum, setting out the main points that would need to be considered before arriving at a final decision, under the following headings:

(a)   export pricing and profitability;

(b)   credit terms and methods of obtaining payment;

(c)   risks and methods of avoiding them;

(d)   forms of representation or local organisation in export markets.

Where appropriate, indicate advantages, disadvantages or your own recommendations.

(20 marks)

7   ANSWER TO EXAMINATION TYPE QUESTION

7.1   Electronic equipment

COMPANY MEMORANDUM

19 November 19X5

From: Finance director

To: Chairman

Subject: Initiation of export trade

The following memorandum sets out the main points requiring consideration before a final decision is taken on whether or not to embark upon export trade.

(a)   **Export pricing and profitability**

         (i)   A starting point would be to consider the market situation for products of the sort we produce, in the various countries where we might consider initiating this export trade. Assuming that demand exists for this type of product, we must ascertain the current prices and quality of competing products in these countries. Provided that these foreign markets are effectively segmented from our existing home market (ie, our domestic customers cannot economically switch their purchases of our products to these new overseas markets), we may be able to set a lower price (as compared with our domestic price) for our output. Provided that the marginal costs of manufacture and sale are covered, the profits of the company would be increased as our surplus production capacity is available to meet the export demand. This may give us the ability to compete effectively on a price basis. Alternatively, we may be able to charge prices which exceed our domestic prices if local competition is such that this strategy would be successful. I suggest that potential markets be ranked in terms of their potential contribution to company profits (marginal revenue less incremental production and selling costs) and, assuming other factors to be similar, exploited in order of the size of their potential contribution to company profits.

(ii)   A study should be made of the additional costs which might be necessary to achieve export sales in the potential overseas markets such as:

(1)   transport, insurance and storage up to the point of sale;

(2)   customs duties;

(3)   additional documentation and certification of documents to satisfy import and possibly exchange control formalities;

(4)   insurance against the special risks of export trade (see (c) below);

(5)   new staff requirements for translation of correspondence, quotations, invoices and publicity materials;

(6)   other advertising and promotion costs in the new market, especially on launching the product; and

(7)   cost of establishing a physical presence in the new market such as agent's commission, warehousing and display facilities (see below).

(b)   **Credit terms and methods of obtaining payment**

(i)   **Assessment of credit worthiness**

(1)   Potential customers' accounting reports may be less informative for analytical purposes.

(2)   Bank references may be available.

(3)   Consular staff and the Export Credits Guarantee Department may be of assistance.

(4)   Contacts with other United Kingdom companies who trade with our potential overseas customers may also provide useful information.

(ii)   **Methods of payment**

(1)   Collection of money may be facilitated by:

(A)   using and discounting bills of exchange; and

(B)   using letters of credit under which collection can be made from a bank in our country upon presentation of the shipping documents. We may wish the letters of credit to be made irrevocable and to ensure that they are 'confirmed' by a bank.

The costs of the above would have to be considered in our pricing policy.

(2)   Pre-payment or part-payment for our goods at the time of ordering may be possible if our products have clear advantages over those of our competitors.

(c)   **Risks and methods of reducing such risks**

(i)   The major risks of the export business include:

(1)   Insolvency of customer.

(2)   Customer's failure to pay within a reasonable time.

(3)   Customer's failure to take up goods ordered and sent to him.

The problems and cost of legal action in another country mean that the above three risks are increased in the export business.

(4)   Political and governmental influence or action (including war) preventing the completion of the contract.

(5)   Fluctuations in exchange rates, unless we can invoice in our own currency.

(ii)   **Avoiding risks**

(1)   Insurance cover is available for the risks mentioned in (1) to (3) above up to 90% and risks under (4) above up to 95%.

(2)   We shall also have to consider whether to insure our whole export turnover or to pay a higher pro-rata premium to cover selected markets.

(3)   The effects of fluctuating exchange rates could be reduced by:

(A)   undertaking forward exchange contracts; and

(B)   holding bank accounts in foreign currencies and repatriating balances when the exchange rate is relatively favourable.

(d)   **Forms of organisation**

(i)   For our type of product it would almost certainly be necessary to have local agents who would negotiate orders, ensure that they were adequately fulfilled, recover outstanding debts and provide an aftersales service.

(ii)   To reduce transit costs, it might be advantageous to establish local assembly facilities, either using local companies or setting up a subsidiary. The latter would ensure the quality but would mean a higher initial investment and might be prohibited by local law.

(iii)   Tax considerations may influence the form of organisation. We must investigate whether:

(1)   there is a double-taxation treaty with the country;

(2)   the foreign country uses the 'unitary' basis of tax, ie, whether it taxes a proportion of the company's world-wide profits; and

(3)   possibilities exist of framing transfer pricing policy to minimise the total tax payable.

24 INTERNATIONAL INVESTMENT DECISIONS

INTRODUCTION & LEARNING OBJECTIVES

The NPV/APV/CAPM analysis so far carried out in this book has all been in a domestic context, ie, without the additional risks and rewards of overseas investment possibilities. This chapter completes the picture, looking at international CAPM, international APV and the extra difficulties posed by fluctuating exchange rates, multiple tax regimes and varying political risks. Some of these topics have been examined already in the previous chapter.

The chapter concludes by further discussion of the international capital structure decision - what are the advantages and disadvantages of low and high gearing in the holding company and to fund subsidiaries, and in what currencies should financing be denominated?

When you have studied this chapter you should be able to do the following:

- Extend your knowledge of CAPM to the international context.
- Appraise international investment possibilities by the adjusted present value (APV) method.
- Explain the effects of taxation on international investments, especially the impact of double taxation.
- Discuss the advantages and disadvantages of international portfolio diversification.
- Discuss the factors influencing the type of finance used in international operations.

1 THE INTERNATIONAL COST OF CAPITAL

1.1 Introduction

An earlier chapter in this text introduced the Capital Asset Pricing Model and showed how it can be used to derive an appropriate discount rate for appraising prospective investment opportunities. In the domestic context you should recall that

$$R_s = R_f + \beta(R_m - R_f)$$

where R_s is the expected return from a security
R_f is the risk-free rate of return
R_m is the expected return from the whole market
β is a measure of the systematic risk of the security

The return from the whole market could be estimated in the UK from looking at domestic stock market indexes such as the FT - SE Actuaries All-Share index, which covers more than 900 of the top shares listed in the UK.

We now want to turn to the international choice of investment opportunities and estimate the international cost of capital of sources of finance. This is done by looking at the international CAPM.

1.2 International CAPM

A company involved in international operations will be exposed to currency risk and political risk on top of the usual risks associated with domestic operations. Currency and political risks are mainly unsystematic and can be diversified away by holding an international diversified portfolio.

A fully diversified UK investor can achieve further risk reduction by investing in other countries, so that part of the systematic risk of the UK market is in fact unsystematic risk from an international viewpoint.

<u>Conclusion</u>   Much of the UK systematic risk can be eliminated by investing in an internationally diversified portfolio.

The international CAPM equation will then read:

$$R_s = R_f + \beta_w (R_w - R_f)$$

where R_s is the expected return from a security
R_f is the risk-free rate of return
R_w is the expected return from the whole world portfolio
β_w is a measure of world systematic risk, ie, how returns on the security correlate with returns on the world market

An investor should choose the combination of risk-free investments and investment in the whole world portfolio which maximises his utility; this is exactly comparable to selecting the point on the capital market line studied earlier.

In practice it is impossible to hold a share of the whole world portfolio, but significant international diversification can be achieved by

- direct holdings in overseas companies
- holdings in unit trusts specialising in overseas companies
- investing in multinational companies.

You should appreciate that in principle risk reduction can be achieved either by investing directly in an international portfolio of shares or investing in local companies with significant overseas activities.

2   THE APV METHOD OF APPRAISING INTERNATIONAL INVESTMENTS

2.1   The adjusted present value method

The APV method of investment appraisal was introduced in a previous chapter in the context of domestic investments. There are essentially three steps to the technique:

<u>Step 1</u>   Estimate the base case NPV assuming that the project is financed entirely by equity.

<u>Step 2</u>   Estimate the financial effect of the actual method of financing.

<u>Step 3</u>   Add the values from steps 1 and 2 to give the APV.

If the APV is positive, accept the project.

We now examine the applicability of the method in appraising international investments. The normal procedure of determining the relevant cash flows and discounting at a rate of return commensurate with the project's risk should be followed as before, but several specific problems may be encountered which are examined below.

2.2   Parent or project viewpoint

Any overseas capital project can be assessed from the point of view of the parent company or the local subsidiary. Relevant cash flows may vary between the two viewpoints due to the following factors

(a)   timing of the receipt of funds

(b)   impact of exchange rate changes on the value of the funds

(c)   impact of local and home country tax on the value of funds received

(d)   effects on other parts of the organisation (eg, sales by the subsidiary reducing the parent's export market sales).

As the objective of financial management is to maximise shareholder wealth, and the vast majority of the shareholders are likely to be located in the parent country, it is essential that projects are evaluated from a **parent currency viewpoint**. After all, only sterling receipts can be used to pay sterling dividends. Accordingly, the following three-step procedure is recommended for calculating project cash flows

(a)   Compute local currency cash flows from a subsidiary viewpoint as if it were an independent firm.

(b)   Calculate the amount and timing of transfers to the parent company in sterling terms.

(c)   Allow for the indirect costs and benefits of the project in sterling terms (eg, the cost of lost sales elsewhere in the group if the project is adopted).

You will find an example of this type of problem in the questions at the end of the chapter.

2.3   Remission of funds

Certain costs to the subsidiary may turn out to be revenues to the parent company. For example, royalties, supervisory fees and purchases of components from the parent company are costs to the project but result in revenues to the parent. Care should be exercised in identifying exactly how and when funds are repatriated. The normal methods of returning funds to the parent company are

(a)   dividends
(b)   royalties
(c)   transfer prices and
(d)   loan interest and principal.

It is also important to note that some of these items may be local tax-deductible for the subsidiary, but taxable for the parent.

2.4   Exchange risk

Changes in exchange rates can cause considerable variation in the amount of funds received by the parent company. In theory this risk could be taken into account in calculating the project's NPV, either by altering the discount rate or by altering the cash flows in line with forecast exchange rates. Virtually all authorities recommend the latter course, as no reliable method is available for adjusting discount rates to allow for exchange risk.

2.5   Political risk

This relates to the possibility that the NPV of the project may be affected by host country government actions. These actions can include

(a)   expropriation of assets (with or without compensation)

(b)   blockage of the repatriation of profits

(c)   suspension of local currency convertibility

(d)   requirements to employ minimum levels of local workers or gradually to pass ownership to local investors.

The impacts of these actions are almost impossible to quantify in NPV terms, but their possible occurrence must be considered when evaluating new investments. High levels of political risk will usually discourage investment altogether, but in the past certain multinational firms have used various techniques, such as those discussed in the previous chapter, to limit their risk exposure and proceeded to invest.

2.6   Project discount rates

In the same way as for domestic capital budgeting project cash flows should be discounted at a rate that reflects their systematic risk. Many firms assume that overseas investment must carry more risk than comparable domestic investment and therefore increase discount rates accordingly.

This assumption, however, is not necessarily valid. Although the total risk of an overseas investment may be high, in the context of a well-diversified parent country portfolio much of the risk may be non-systematic. Because of the lack of correlation between the performance of some national economies the systematic risk of overseas investment projects may in fact be lower than that of comparable domestic projects.

Overall a reliable estimate of the beta factor for a foreign project is almost impossible to obtain, the international application of CAPM being at a very early stage. However, it must be realised that the automatic addition of a risk premium simply because a project is located overseas does not always make sense, and any discount rates used for foreign projects should be viewed with caution.

2.7   The interaction of inflation rates and exchange rates

We have discussed the purchasing power parity theory earlier in this text. If our overseas investment is in a country with a very high rate of inflation (eg, South America, Russian Federation, some of Eastern Europe) we would predict that any cost increases resulting from the inflation in the overseas country will be countered by the depreciation of the overseas currency against the pound.

One notable point is the effect of taxation charges arising in the foreign country. These will be lower in real terms to the UK holding company because there will be a time delay between the period on which the profits are calculated and the payment of the tax (eg, on year). The tax liability will be converted at a more favourable exchange rate to the holding company.

2.8   Mechanics of the international APV method

> **Step 1**   The base case NPV assumes that the project is financed entirely by equity, so the discount rate must be the cost of equity allowing for the project risk but excluding financial risk - using the international CAPM equation with an ungeared 'world' β.

> **Step 2**   Adjustments should be made for

> - tax relief on debt interest and issue costs
> - subsidies from overseas governments
> - projects financed by loans raised locally
> - restriction on remittances

> **Step 3**   Add the values from steps 1 and 2 to give the APV.

This is basically the same approach as for domestic appraisal, with a little more care needed in identifying the appropriate appraisal rates and adjustments.

3   THE EFFECT OF TAXATION ON INTERNATIONAL INVESTMENT

3.1   Double tax relief

Where a parent company owns an overseas subsidiary, there are two tax authorities involved, both of whom will want their share of the profits. The examiner will specify the rules to be applied in each situation, but commonly relief will be given against double taxation.

> **Definition**   Double taxation arises where the same profits are liable to tax in more than one country.

Double tax relief is given either under the terms of a treaty between the two countries or unilaterally by the UK authorities. In either case a credit is usually given against UK tax for the lower of the overseas tax liability and the UK tax liability.

Example

X plc receives a £60,000 gross dividend from its overseas subsidiary, from which a 50% withholding tax has been deducted, in a year in which the corporation tax rate is 30%.

X plc's corporation tax payable can be calculated as

	£
30% × (profits chargeable to corporation tax including £60,000 overseas dividend)	X
Less: Double tax relief (lower of 50% × £60,000 and 30% × £60,000)	(18,000)
Corporation tax payable	X

4 INTERNATIONAL PORTFOLIO DIVERSIFICATION

Advantages

(i) International diversification reduces systematic risk. We have already seen how domestic systematic risk turns out to be unsystematic (and therefore capable of elimination through diversification) from an international viewpoint. The less positive correlation there is between countries, the better the risk reduction possible. In practice different countries will always be at different stages in the economic cycle and will offer different economic specialisations, so it is not surprising that low correlation does exist between countries' returns on securities.

(ii) Fluctuations in exchange rates are just as important as domestic market indexes in assessing international returns. If the pound falls against the yen, then even a flat Tokyo stock exchange performance still offers a positive return in sterling terms.

(iii) The international CAPM presents a structural argument for how to obtain the best return for any agreed level of risk.

Disadvantages

(i) Total risk may be increased in an international portfolio, when both currency and political risks are taken into account. However CAPM argues that total risk is less important than aggregate systematic risk.

(ii) The argument that international diversification can be achieved by investing in multinationals does not work in practice. The share price of a multinational, eg, Hanson, reflects the performance of the UK stock market rather than any notional world market. International diversification is best achieved by direct holdings in overseas companies, which can be expensive and for which limited advice is available domestically.

(iii) The tax implications of investing in overseas companies are complex, and expensive mistakes may be made unless expensive specialist advice is sought.

5 THE INTERNATIONAL CAPITAL STRUCTURE DECISION

5.1 Introduction

This section deals with the question of the optimal capital structure of international investments, covering

- the financing of the holding company; and
- the financing of overseas branches/subsidiaries.

The overriding aim of the group is still assumed to be the maximisation of shareholder wealth; in this context the following questions should be asked:

- What gearing levels should be employed?
- In which currency should borrowings be denominated?
- What split of short-term and long-term finance should be adopted?

These questions have already been examined earlier in this text but they are brought together here in the international context.

5.2   Factors influencing the type of finance used

(i)   **Availability of sources of finance**. There is no point in recommending high overseas gearing if loans cannot be raised in that particular currency, and no point in recommending 100% equity ownership of a subsidiary in a country where minority local shareholders are mandatory. Financing recommendations must be tempered by what is practical.

(ii)   **Cost of each type of finance**.

(iii)   **Availability of tax relief**. In many tax regimes debt interest payments are allowable against tax while dividends are not. Gearing up may therefore increase post-tax profits, especially in a regime with high rates of tax.

(iv)   **Risk**. Each source of finance has its own risk and return characteristics. Gearing up may increase the risk suffered by shareholders, since interest must be paid before any dividends are paid.

(v)   **Volatility of the earnings stream**. Companies with volatile earnings are generally better financed by equity rather than debt so that an already risky situation is financed by risk finance and the situation is not made worse by introducing further risk into the equation with debt finance.

5.3   The strategic implications of international financing

These have already been considered in the previous chapter. A large equity investment in an overseas subsidiary implies a long-term commitment to the business; a minority holding, or small equity investment combined with large amounts of debt raised locally, suggests a short-term investment horizon.

The currency chosen for each source of funds to be denominated in will depend principally on the overall hedging strategy adopted by the group. The holding company can hedge its currency risk exposure on a foreign investment either by raising foreign loans in its own books or by requiring subsidiaries to match their own exposures as much as possible.

5.4   Appraisal of international capital investment proposals

A favourite exam question combines basic NPV or APV analysis with fluctuating exchange rates and you must be prepared for such a question. See the questions at the end of this chapter for practice in this area.

When calculating the NPV regarding an international capital investment, it is important to identify the relevant incremental cashflows.

As previously discussed, one of the most important factors is to recognise on whose behalf the appraisal is being performed. When appraising on behalf of the managers of the foreign company itself, such flows as management charges to head office and interest paid on head office loans will be relevant costs. The NPV of the company will be after deduction of all such costs to head office and after any receipts therefrom. The project flows will then be discounted using a rate reflecting the risk of the environment in which the foreign company is operating, if available. (If not available the rate reflecting the risk of the group may be used).

However, if the company is being appraised on behalf of the head office in the UK, then the relevant flows will be those being transferred to and from the subsidiary. Such flows would therefore include initial capital investments, royalties, management fees, dividends received and eventual sale proceeds of the subsidiary if applicable. These flows into head office would be after any foreign taxation and double taxation relief available. Again a discount rate to reflect the risk of the flows transferred would be used.

In the latter case where the company is being evaluated for head office, the flows would have to be converted into the home currency at the rate ruling at the time of transfer, prior to discounting. If forward markets are utilised these rates would be incorporated.

6   CHAPTER SUMMARY

Both CAPM and the APV technique can be expanded to the international context. International diversification offers the chance to reduce systematic risk, since some UK systematic risk can be diversified away when UK securities are combined with an international portfolio.

The main capital structure decision is whether a foreign subsidiary should be financed by equity, or by a combination of equity and local debt. Interest payments may be tax-allowable and free from restrictions on remittances, while dividends are generally not tax-allowable and may be blocked. Gearing increases financial risk but may hedge currency risk. There are no immediate answers, but a series of advantages and disadvantages for you to discuss.

7   SELF TEST QUESTIONS

7.1   Are overseas political risks generally systematic or unsystematic? (1.2)

7.2   Explain the international CAPM equation. (1.2)

7.3   What are the three steps involved in the APV method? (2.1)

7.4   Should project cash flows be assessed from the viewpoint of the parent company or the local subsidiary? (2.2)

7.5   What is wrong with the argument that an amount should be added to the domestic discount rate when appraising overseas investments, since overseas investments are more risky? (2.6)

7.6   How is double tax relief given? (3.1)

7.7   State two advantages of international portfolio diversification. (4)

7.8   State two disadvantages of international portfolio diversification. (4)

7.9   Is gearing up more profitable in a high or low tax regime? (5.2)

7.10   Does a highly geared overseas subsidiary suggest that the investment is for the long-term? (5.3)

8   EXAMINATION TYPE QUESTIONS

8.1   Stoppall plc

Stoppall plc specialises in the construction of dams. The company has an excellent reputation and has been contacted by the representatives of a water authority in Scotland and a developing country, Bargonia, as each wishes to have a large new dam constructed. Stoppall has a full order book, but with the use of sub-contractors, could undertake one further project only. Both the Scottish and the Bargonian projects would take five years to complete.

The estimated cash outflows associated with the two projects are presented below:

Scottish project

Year	0 £m	1 £m	2 £m	3 £m	4 £m	5 £m
Plant and machinery	20	5	3	1		
Vehicles	5	5	3	1		
Materials		25	24	26	28	14
Labour		12	14	15	16	17
Other expenses		11	10	12	14	16
Interest payments		35	42	42	42	42

Bargonian project

Year	0 £m	1 £m	2 £m	3 £m	4 £m	5 £m
Plant and machinery	10	7	4	1		
Vehicles	5	3	4	2		
Materials		28	26	29	23	25
Labour		17	16	18	22	26
Other expenses		16	17	16	16	14
Interest payments		38	49	50	50	50

All expenses are payable in pounds sterling at the end of the year concerned, with the exception of the initial outlays which are payable at the commencement of the projects.

Payment would be received in stages for both projects. The Scottish water authority would make an initial payment of 15% of the total price of £420 million, with a further 20% payable at both the start of year 2 and year 3, 25% at the end of year 4 and the remainder on completion of the project.

The Bargonian government has offered to make payment in either the local currency, the Dowl, or in $US.

Stoppall has indicated that, because of uncertainty about the future strength and convertibility of the Dowl, a 50% initial payment would be required with a further 20% at the end of year 2 and the balance on completion. The total price of the Bargonian project is 140,250 million Dowl or $US 900 million.

Payment in $US would require a 20% initial payment, with the remainder in equal annual instalments, the last being on completion of the project.

UK taxation, at the rate of 35% on worldwide net operating receipts, is payable one year in arrears. Tax allowable depreciation exists on all fixed assets at 20% per year on a straight-line basis. The fixed assets are expected to have a negligible value at the end of the five year projects. Stoppall has other taxable income besides these proposed projects. No foreign taxation would be payable in connection with the Bargonian project.

Stoppall bases its estimates of future foreign exchange rates on projections of inflation.

Projected annual inflation levels

Year	UK	USA	Bargonia
1	5%	5%	20%
2	5%	5%	30%
3	5%	7%	30%
4	5%	7%	30%
5	5%	7%	30%
6	5%	7%	30%

The systematic risk of the Scottish project is estimated to be 1.5 and the Bargonian project 1.625. The risk free rate is 7% per year and market return is 15% per year.

Cash flow estimates already include the effects of projected inflation.

Current exchange rates are:

$/£	Dowl/£
1.60	250.0

Required

(a)   Evaluate whether Stoppall should construct the dam in Scotland or in Bargonia. If Stoppall selected Bargonia should it request payment in Dowl or $US?

State clearly any assumptions that you make.   **(20 marks)**

(b)   What other factors might be important to Stoppall when considering which project to select?
(5 marks)
(Total: 25 marks)

8.2   Axmine plc

(a)   The managers of Axmine plc, a major international copper processor are considering a joint venture with Traces, a company owning significant copper reserves in a South American country. If the joint venture were not to proceed Axmine would still need to import copper from the South American country. Axmine's managing director is concerned that the government of the South American country might impose some form of barriers to free trade which puts Axmine at a competitive disadvantage in importing copper. A further director considers that this is unlikely due to the existence of the WTO.

You are required to briefly discuss possible forms of non-tariff barrier that might affect Axmine's ability to import copper, and how the existence of the WTO might influence such barriers.   **(8 marks)**

(b)   The proposed joint venture with Traces would be for an initial period of four years. Copper would be mined using a new technique developed by Axmine. Axmine would supply machinery at an immediate cost of 800 million pesos and 10 supervisors at an annual salary of £40,000 each at current prices. Additionally Axmine would pay half of the 1,000 million pesos per year (at current prices) local labour costs and other expenses in the South American country. The supervisors' salaries and local labour and other expenses will be increased in line with inflation in the United Kingdom and the South American country respectively.

Inflation in the South American country is currently 100% per year, and in the UK it is expected to remain stable at around 8% per year. The government of the South American country is attempting to control inflation, and hopes to reduce it each year by 20% of the previous year's rate.

The joint venture would give Axmine a 50% share of Traces's copper production, with current market prices at £1,500 per 1,000 kilograms. Traces's production is expected to be 10 million kilograms per year, and copper prices are expected to rise by 10% per year (in pounds sterling) for the foreseeable future. At the end of four years Axmine would be given the choice to pull out of the venture or to negotiate another four year joint venture, on different terms.

The current exchange rate is 140 pesos/£. Future exchange rates may be estimated using the purchasing power parity theory.

Axmine has no foreign operations. The cost of capital of the company's UK mining operations is 16% per year. As this joint venture involves diversifying into foreign operations the company considers that a 2% reduction in the cost of capital would be appropriate for this project.

Corporate tax is at the rate of 20% per year in the South American country and 35% per year in the UK. A tax treaty exists between the two countries and all foreign tax paid is allowable against any UK tax liability. Taxation is payable one year in arrears and a 25% straight-line writing-down allowance is available on the machinery in both countries.

Cash flows may be assumed to occur at the year end, except for the immediate cost of machinery. The machinery is expected to have negligible terminal value at the end of four years.

You are required to prepare a report discussing whether Axmine plc should agree to the proposed joint venture. Relevant calculations must form part of your report or an appendix to it.

State clearly any assumptions that you make.   **(18 marks)**

(c)   If the South American government were to fail to control inflation, and inflation were to increase rapidly during the period of the joint venture, discuss the likely effect of very high inflation on the joint venture.   **(4 marks)**

(Total: 30 marks)

9   ANSWERS TO EXAMINATION TYPE QUESTIONS

9.1   Stoppall plc

(a)   **Scottish project**

Calculation of tax payable

Year	1	2	3	4	5
	£m	£m	£m	£m	£m
Revenue (Note 1)	63	84	84	105	84
Less:					
Costs:					
Materials	25	24	26	28	14
Labour	12	14	15	16	17
Other expenses	11	10	12	14	16
Capital allowances	5	7	8	9	14
Total	53	55	61	67	61
Taxable profits	10	29	23	38	23
Tax payable	4	10	8	13	8

Cash flows

Year	0	1	2	3	4	5	6
Revenue	63	84	84	-	105	84	-
Less:							
Plant & machinery	20	5	3	1	0	0	0
Vehicles	5	5	3	1			
Materials		25	24	26	28	14	
Labour		12	14	15	16	17	
Other expenses	11	10	12	14	16		
Taxation			4	10	8	13	8
Total	25	58	58	65	66	60	8

Net cash flows	38	26	26	(65)	39	24	(8)
Discount @ 19% (Note 2)	1.0	0.840	0.706	0.593	0.499	0.419	0.352
Present Value	38	21.8	18.4	(38.5)	19.5	10.1	(2.8)

$$NPV = £66.5m$$

Note 1:

This solution assumes that payment at time 0 falls in the same tax year as expenses at time 1. Other assumptions are possible but this is the simplest approach.

Note 2:

Using CAPM $E_r = R_f + (R_m - R_f)\beta = 7\% + (15\% - 7\%)1.5 = 7\% + 12\% = 19\%$

Bargonian project

(i)   Payment in Dowl

Dowl exchange rate using purchasing power parity theory $\left(F = S \times \dfrac{1+iF}{1+ih} \right)$

Year	1	250	×	[1.2/1.05]	=	285.7
	2	285.7	×	[1.3/1.05]	=	353.7
	3	353.7	×	[1.3/1.05]	=	438.0
	4	438.0	×	[1.2380952]	=	542.0
	5	542.2	×	[1.2380952]	=	671.3

Calculation of tax payable

Year	1	2	3	4	5
	Dm	Dm	Dm	Dm	Dm
Revenue	70,125	28,050			42,075
	£m	£m	£m	£m	£m
Less: Costs:					
Materials	28	26	29	23	25
Labour	17	16	18	22	26
Other expenses	16	17	16	16	14
Capital allowance	3	5	7	8	15
Total costs	64	64	70	69	80
Taxable profits	216	15	(70)	(69)	(17)
Tax payable	76	5	(25)	(24)	(6)

Cash flows

Year	0	1	2	3	4	5	6
	£m	£m	£m	£m	£m	£m	£m
Revenues	280		79				63
Less:							
Plant & machinery	10	7	6	1			
Vehicles	5	3	4	2			
Materials		28	26	29	24	25	
Labour		17	16	18	22	26	
Other expenses		16	17	16	16	14	
Tax payable			76	5	(25)	(24)	(6)
Total	15	71	145	71	36	41	(6)
Net cash flows	265	(71)	(66)	(71)	(36)	22	6
Discount @ 20%	1.0	0.833	0.694	0.579	0.482	0.402	0.335
Present Value	265	(59.1)	(45.8)	(41.1)	(17.4)	8.8	2.0

$$NPV = £112.4m$$

Note 3:

Using CAPM 7% + (15% − 7%)1.625 = 7% + 13% = 20%

Bargonian project

(ii)   **Payment in $**

$ exchange rate: Years	1&2				1.60
	3	1.60 ×	(1.07/1.05)	=	1.6305
	4	1.6305 ×	(1.07/1.05)	=	1.6615
	5	1.6615 ×	(1.07/1.05)	=	1.6932

Calculation of tax payable

Year	1	2	3	4	5
	$m	$m	$m	$m	$m
Revenue	324	144	144	144	144
	£m	£m	£m	£m	£m
	202	90	88	87	85
Less:					
Costs as above	64	64	70	69	80
Taxable profit	138	26	18	18	5
Tax payable	48	9	5	5	2

Cash flows

Year	0	1	2	3	4	5	6
	$m	$m	$m	$m	$m	$m	$m
Revenues	180	144	144	144	144	144	
	£m	£m	£m	£m	£m	£m	£m
Less:							
Plant & machinery	10	7	6	1			
Vehicles	5	3	4	2			
Materials		28	26	29	24	25	
Labour		17	16	18	22	26	
Other expenses		16	17	16	16	14	
Tax payable			48	9	6	6	2
	—	—	—	—	—	—	—
Total	15	71	117	75	67	71	2
Net cash flows	97	19	(27)	13	20	14	(2)
Discount @ 20%	1.0	0.833	0.694	0.579	0.482	0.402	0.335
Present Value	97	15.8	(18.7)	7.5	9.6	5.6	(0.7)

NPV = £116.1m

Conclusion

Stoppall should construct the dam in Bargonia, and should request payment in $.

(b)   *(**Tutorial note:** Try to take a practical viewpoint, ask yourself 'what points would I raise if I wished to persuade the firm not to accept the project'.)*

Other important factors include:

1	Political risk	- government stability - risks of even greater inflation - devaluation of currency - remission of funds
2	Accuracy of data	- cash flows - inflation levels - exchange rates - cost of capital - systematic risk
3	Other problems in Bargonia	- labour - material suppliers - work permits for expatriates
4	Could both projects be undertaken?	- sub-contracting - joint ventures
5	Is the company anxious to work?	- in Scotland - in Bargonia

9.2   Axmine plc

(a)   Axmine's ability to import copper from the South American country might be affected by the following forms of non-tariff barrier:

(i)   deliberately obstructive customs procedures. The authorities might require time-consuming documentation to be filled out before exports of copper are permitted, or might carry out detailed quality assurance inspections. Such inspections would be justified in the name of safety or quality control, but in reality the purpose is to reduce the volume of exports.

(ii)   export quotas. The country might set maximum limits of copper that it is prepared to export each quarter, say. The purpose would be to reduce supply and therefore hope to increase the price of copper provided.

(iii)   artificial exchange rates. The country might insist that an artificially high exchange rate is used to pay for goods exported. Perhaps a range of different rates could be set by the country for different forms of exports (copper, electrical goods, timber etc) so that control can be exercised over each category.

(iv)   selective embargo. The country might totally refuse to permit exports to a certain country, either on human rights grounds or to retaliate against alleged unfair trading practices from that other country. Essentially this is a special case of export quotas, with the quota to particular countries set at zero.

(v)   withdrawal of government assistance. Governments commonly offer their exporters a range of export credit guarantees to encourage foreign trade, taking on the risk of other countries not honouring their debts. Where these guarantees are reduced or withdrawn altogether, exports will be discouraged. Similar points apply to other forms of government assistance eg, grants or soft loans.

The World Trade Organisation (WTO) has now taken over the work of the General Agreement on Tariffs and Trade (GATT), which was signed in 1947 by 23 countries in an attempt to encourage world-wide trade after the second world war. The aims of GATT were to reduce existing barriers to free trade, to reduce discrimination in world-wide trade and to prevent protectionism by encouraging member countries to consult with others before taking protectionist measures.

The WTO is committed to enforcing previous GATT agreements.

The implications of the WTO and GATT on Axmine plc depend on a number of factors:

(i)   if the South American country is not a signatory to GATT and the WTO, then they are irrelevant.

(ii)   GATT was generally successful in driving tariff barriers out of the world trade scene, but was much less successful in non-tariff barriers. Many countries continue to impose non-tariff barriers, especially against imports rather than exports, since they see doing this as in their domestic best interests.

(iii)   GATT contained a number of facilities to favour less developed countries at the expense of developed countries, so the South American country might not contravene GATT terms by its actions of imposing barriers.

(b)   **REPORT**

To: the management, Axmine plc

From: the chief accountant

Date: X-X-19XX

Subject: Proposed joint venture with Traces

Introduction

Axmine plc is considering entering into a joint venture with Traces in order to import copper from XX country in South America. The cash flows arising from the project have been appraised in present value terms.

The discounting exercise reveals that the projected cash flows have a positive net present value of £4.71m. It is therefore concluded that the joint venture should be proceeded with in the absence of any more lucrative proposals.

The large magnitude of the NPV suggests that the decision is probably insensitive to any of the input parameters. However it is recommended that a formal sensitivity analysis exercise should be carried out to prove this contention.

Assumptions which have been used include the following:

(i)   the price of copper grows by 10% pa in sterling terms. Metals prices are notoriously volatile, and the implications of this assumption should be investigated.

(ii)   Traces will honour its obligations under the joint venture.

(iii)   14% is an appropriate discount rate, reflecting the systematic risk of the project. The 16% minus 2% justification is unreliable.

(iv)   Axmine has the management, financial and other resources to be able to control and complete the project.

Appendix

First we must use the purchasing power parity theory to estimate future exchange rates for the peso against sterling.

Year	Forecast South American inflation %	Forecast UK inflation %	Forecast exchange rate (pesos/£)		
1	80	8	$140 \times \dfrac{1.80}{1.08}$	=	233.3
2	64	8	$233.3 \times \dfrac{1.64}{1.08}$	=	354.3
3	51.2	8	$354.3 \times \dfrac{1.512}{1.08}$	=	496.0
4	41	8	$496.0 \times \dfrac{1.41}{1.08}$	=	647.6
5	32.8	8	$647.6 \times \dfrac{1.328}{1.08}$	=	796.3

Further workings are necessary for the annual supervisors costs and the 50% share of the local labour costs.

Year	Supervisors' costs £'000	Exchange rate (pesos/£)	Forecast cost (million pesos)
1	400 × 1.08 = 432	233.3	101
2	432 × 1.08 = 466.6	354.3	165
3	466.6 × 1.08 = 503.9	496.0	250
4	503.9 × 1.08 = 544.2	647.6	352

Year	Local labour (million pesos)		
1	½ × 1,000 × 1.8	=	900
2	900 × 1.64	=	1,476
3	1,476 × 1.512	=	2,232
4	2,232 × 1.41	=	3,147

Tax computation (pesos millions)

Year	1	2	3	4
Sales (W1)	1,925	3,215	4,951	7,111
Payments				
Labour	900	1,476	2,232	3,147
Supervisors	101	165	250	352
WDA	200	200	200	200
	1,201	1,841	2,682	3,699
Taxable profits	724	1,374	2,269	3,412
Tax at 20%	145	275	454	682

WORKINGS

Year 1: $50\% \times £1,500 \times 1.1 \times \dfrac{10 \text{ million}}{1,000} \times 233.3$ = 1,925 million pesos

Year 2: $50\% \times £1,500 \times 1.1^2 \times \dfrac{10 \text{ million}}{1,000} \times 354.3$ = 3,215 million pesos

Year 3: $50\% \times £1,500 \times 1.1^3 \times \dfrac{10 \text{ million}}{1,000} \times 496.0$ = 4,951 million pesos

Year 4: $50\% \times £1,500 \times 1.1^4 \times \dfrac{10 \text{ million}}{1,000} \times 647.6$ = 7,111 million pesos

The cash flow in pesos millions can now be established.

Year	0	1	2	3	4	5
Machinery	(800)					
Profits		724	1,374	2,269	3,412	
Tax			(145)	(275)	(454)	(682)
Add back WDA		200	200	200	200	
	(800)	924	1,429	2,194	3,158	(682)
Exchange rate	140	233.3	354.3	496.0	647.6	796.3
Cash flow (£m)	(5.71)	3.96	4.03	4.42	4.88	(0.86)
UK tax (W)			(0.47)	(0.58)	(0.69)	(0.79)
Net cash flow	(5.71)	3.96	3.56	3.84	4.19	(1.65)

Discount factor at 14%	1	0.877	0.769	0.675	0.592	0.519
Present values	(5.71)	3.47	2.74	2.59	2.48	(0.86)

Net present value   £4.71m

WORKINGS

Tax has been paid in South America at only 20%. A further 15% is therefore payable in the UK.

Year 2: $\dfrac{724\text{m}}{233.3} \times 15\%$ =   £0.47m

Year 3: $\dfrac{1,374\text{m}}{354.3} \times 15\%$ =   £0.58m

Year 4: $\dfrac{2,269\text{m}}{496.0} \times 15\%$ =   £0.69m

Year 5: $\dfrac{3,412\text{m}}{647.6} \times 15\%$ =   £0.79m

(c)   If the purchasing power parity theory of exchange rates holds true, then rapidly increasing inflation during the period of the joint venture is likely to lead to a higher net present value for the project.

The sales, labour costs and supervisory costs all increase at a constant rate per annum, so it is immaterial in NPV terms whether the national inflation is low or high.

The favourable effect comes from the tax effects. The writing down allowance is calculated on the original cost of the machinery, so there is some benefit lost as inflation rises. However this disbenefit will be more than compensated for by the one year delay in payments of taxation. The higher that inflation is, the lower the tax payment becomes in real terms, so that the expected NPV of the project will rise as the inflation level rises.

This is another factor which should be considered in the decision as to whether the joint venture should be entered into. If the government's previous attempts at controlling inflation have failed, it is likely that so will the current inflation reduction programme, leading to a more attractive expected NPV prospect.

HOTLINES

Telephone: 00 44 (0) 20 8844 0667
Enquiries: 00 44 (0) 20 8831 9990
Fax: 00 44 (0) 20 8831 9991

AT FOULKS LYNCH LTD

Number 4, The Griffin Centre
Staines Road, Feltham
Middlesex TW14 0HS

Examination Date:
☐ December 2000
☐ June 2001

	Publications				Distance Learning	Open Learning
	Textbooks	Revision Series	Lynchpins	Tracks	Include helpline & marking (except for overseas Open Learning)	

Module A – Foundation Stage

	Textbooks	Revision Series	Lynchpins	Tracks	Distance Learning	Open Learning
1 Accounting Framework	£18.95 UK IAS	£10.95 UK IAS	£5.95 UK IAS	£10.95	£85 UK IAS	£89
2 Legal Framework	£18.95	£10.95	£5.95	£10.95	£85	£89

Module B

3 Management Information	£18.95	£10.95	£5.95	£10.95	£85	£89
4 Organisational Framework	£18.95	£10.95	£5.95	£10.95	£85	£89

Module C – Certificate Stage

5 Information Analysis	£18.95	£10.95	£5.95	£10.95	£85	£89
6 Audit Framework	£18.95 UK IAS	£10.95 UK IAS	£5.95 UK IAS	£10.95	£85 UK IAS	£89

Module D

7 Tax Framework FA99 - D00	£18.95	£10.95	£5.95	£10.95	£85	£89
FA00 - J01	£18.95	£10.95	£5.95		£85	£89
8 Managerial Finance	£18.95	£10.95	£5.95	£10.95	£85	£89

Module E – Professional Stage

9 ICDM	£18.95	£10.95	£5.95	£10.95	£85	£89
10 Accounting & Audit Practice	£22.95 UK IAS	£10.95 UK IAS	£5.95 UK IAS	£10.95	£85 UK IAS	£89
10 Accounting & Audit Practice (IAS)	£23.95 IAS					
11 Tax Planning FA99 - D00	£18.95	£10.95	£5.95	£10.95	£85	£89
FA00 - J01	£18.95	£10.95	£5.95		£85	£89

Module F

12 Management & Strategy	£18.95	£10.95	£5.95	£10.95	£85	£89
13 Financial Rep Environment	£20.95 UK IAS	£10.95 UK IAS	£5.95 UK IAS	£10.95	£85 UK IAS	£89
14 Financial Strategy	£19.95	£10.95	£5.95	£10.95	£85	£89

P & P + Delivery	Textbooks	Revision Series	Lynchpins	Tracks	Distance Learning	Open Learning
UK Mainland	£2.00/book	£1.00/book	£1.00/book	£1.00/tape	£5.00/subject	£5.00/subject
NI, ROI & EU Countries	£5.00/book	£3.00/book	£3.00/book	£1.00/tape	£15.00/subject	£15.00/subject
Rest of world standard air service	£10.00/book	£8.00/book	£8.00/book	£2.00/tape	£25.00/subject	£25.00/subject
Rest of world courier service †	£22.00/book	£20.00/book	Not applicable	Not applicable	£47.00/subject	£47.00/subject

SINGLE ITEM SUPPLEMENT FOR TEXTBOOKS AND REVISION SERIES:
If you only order 1 item, INCREASE postage costs by £2.50 for UK, NI & EU Countries or by £15.00 for Rest of World Services

TOTAL
Sub Total £ _____
Post & Packing £ _____
Total £ _____

†*Telephone number essential for this service*   *Payments in Sterling in London*   Order Total £ _____

DELIVERY DETAILS

☐ Mr ☐ Miss ☐ Mrs ☐ Ms Other

Initials _____ Surname _____

Address _____
_____
_____

Postcode _____

Telephone _____   Deliver to home ☐

Company name _____
Address _____
_____

Postcode _____

Telephone _____   Fax _____
Monthly report to go to employer ☐   Deliver to work ☐

PAYMENT

1 I enclose Cheque/PO/Bankers Draft for £_____
   Please make cheques payable to AT Foulks Lynch Ltd.

2 Charge Mastercard/Visa/Switch A/C No:

   |_|_|_|_|_|_|_|_|_|_|_|_|_|_|_|_|_|_|_|

   Valid from: |_|_|_| Expiry Date: |_|_|_|
   Issue No: (Switch only) |_|_|

   Signature _____   Date _____

DECLARATION

I agree to pay as indicated on this form and understand that AT Foulks Lynch Terms and Conditions apply (available on request). I understand that AT Foulks Lynch Ltd are not liable for non-delivery if the rest of world standard air service is used.

Signature _____   Date _____

Please Allow:	UK mainland	- 5-10 w/days
	NI, ROI & EU Countries	- 1-3 weeks
	Rest of world standard air service	- 6 weeks
	Rest of world courier service	- 10 w/days

Notes: All delivery times subject to stock availability. Signature required on receipt (except rest of world standard air service). Please give both addresses for Distance Learning students where possible.

Form effective June 00   *All details correct at time of printing*   *Source: ACCATXJ00*